HARVARD ECONOMIC STUDIES

VOLUME CXIII

Awarded the David A. Wells Prize for the year 1949–50 and published from the income of the David A. Wells Fund.

A & P

A Study in
Price-Cost Behavior
and Public Policy

M. A. ADELMAN

HARVARD UNIVERSITY PRESS

Cambridge, Massachusetts

1 9 5 9

N1056

TO THE MEMORY OF
MY MOTHER

ACKNOWLEDGMENTS

This study originated as a paper presented to the seminar in industrial organization at Harvard University. Most of the research was conducted during the academic year 1947–48 under a fellowship with the Social Science Research Council, to whom I am indebted for the opportunity to follow the trail of knowledge wherever it led. As a doctoral thesis the study was filed in the Widener Library in 1948. The extensive revision presented here was undertaken with the aid of occasional grants from the Council's Committee on Economic History and the Merrill Foundation for the Advancement of Financial Knowledge. Some of the work has appeared previously as brief portions of "The A & P Case: A Study in Applied Economic Theory," *Quarterly Journal of Economics*, May 1949; "The Great A & P Muddle," *Fortune*, December 1949; "The Consistency of the Robinson-Patman Act," *Stanford Law Review*, December 1953; "Price Discrimination as Treated in the Attorney General's Report," *University of Pennsylvania Law Review*, November 1955; "The 'Product' and 'Price' in Distribution," *Papers and Proceedings of the American Economic Association*, May 1957.

The basic material was the Transcript of Record and some 5,200 exhibits in the case of *U.S. v. The New York Great Atlantic and Pacific Tea Co.*, mercifully abbreviated to A & P. Access to the Transcript was afforded by Holmes Baldridge, formerly Assistant Attorney General of the United States; access to the exhibits, by James V. Hayes of the New York bar. It has been impossible to agree with both of these gentlemen on the issues in the trial, and I have often managed to agree with neither, but I am grateful to them both. At a later date, access to the record was by courtesy of Lawrence J. McKay of the New York bar.

This study has been a principal research interest for a decade, but the pressure of other tasks has repeatedly thrust it aside, often for extended periods. The delay has not been a total loss.

For some acquaintance with the substance and procedure of the antitrust laws I am greatly indebted to Robert R. Bowie; to my year as lecturer at the Harvard Law School, where my students and my colleague Kingman Brewster, Jr. strove mightily to educate me; and to service with the Attorney-General's Committee to Study the Antitrust Laws. I was also able to speak informally with a number of businessmen in the food industry. So much of what they said was unverifiable or off the record, and so many were unwilling to be identified, that it has seemed best not to name any. Yet what I learned from them, combined with some knowledge of the law which conditioned their acts, caused me to review carefully the documentary evidence underlying Part II of this study and in the end to rewrite it completely. I think most of them would largely disapprove of both the original and the revision. But I am no less thankful to them. A & P, unfortunately, cannot be included in this acknowledgment, since they did not grant my request for information.

Part of the manuscript was read by Arthur H. Cole, Edwin B. George, Margaret Hall, Richard B. Heflebower, and George J. Stigler, who were all as ruthless as they were friendly. Drafts were typed and retyped with stoic patience by Inez J. Crandall and by Beatrice A. Rogers, who also prepared the index.

My greatest debt is to Edward S. Mason, but for whom this book would never have been started or finished, and who is the main source of whatever merits it has. The shortcomings are my own.

M. A. ADELMAN

Newton, Massachusetts
September 3, 1958

CONTENTS

PART III

ECONOMIC THEORY AND PUBLIC POLICY

APPENDIXES

TABLES, CHARTS, AND FIGURES

TEXT TABLES

APPENDIX TABLES

CHARTS AND FIGURES

NOTE ON REFERENCES
AND TERMINOLOGY

Most of the references in this work are to documents and testimony at the trial of the A & P Company. Testimony is indicated by the name of the individual testifying and the page of the transcript where his testimony is found, thus "Hartford, Tr. 20,452." Every document was either a Government Exhibit (GX) or a Defendants' Exhibit (DX). Letters are indicated by the name of writer and addressee, date, and exhibit number, thus "Smith to Black, December 28, 1939, GX 2841." Meetings at A & P headquarters are indicated by "DPM" for Divisional Presidents' Meeting, or by the name of the specialized group, e.g., "Merchandising Committee," together with date and exhibit number. Divisional meetings, whether of the executive board or of a specialized group, are indicated only by the division, date of meeting, and exhibit number. The government briefs in the Federal District Court and Appeals Court are designated as GB (DC) and GB (AC), respectively; the corresponding defense briefs are DB (DC) and DB (AC).

The term *expense rate* means the total of all expenses (other than the costs of goods) divided by the sales. For a grouping less than the whole company, for example, a division or one of its units, this includes both the actual outlays and an allocation of expense incurred at higher levels.

The term *gross profit rate* or *gross margin* means the difference between the cost of goods purchased and the receipts from the sale of those goods. When used without any qualifying word or phrase, *gross profit rate* means the rate as finally determined at the close of the fiscal year. It is strictly comparable with the *expense rate*, and the difference between the two is the *net profit rate*. However, there will be frequent reference to the "operating gross profit rate," which is an interim figure. It differs from the final *gross margin* or *gross profit rate* in that it does not include discounts on goods purchased through headquarters, the profits of manufacturing subsidiaries, etc., which are allocated on the basis of sales, partly at the end of the quarter and wholly at the end of the year (see Appendix Table 17). Since *expense rate* includes headquarters expense, but "operating gross profit" excludes headquarters deductions from cost (or addition to income), the two are obviously noncomparable, and the difference between them is not equal to the *net profit rate*. Whether the headquarters "distribution" constitute a reduction of the cost of goods or an allocation of profits, and whether they may lawfully be made, is a matter of considerable legal dispute (see Part III).

The term "markup" is the difference between receipts and cost of the goods, expressed as a percentage of the cost. It is used only in a general sense in this study, as loosely synonymous with *gross margin* or *gross profit rate*.

A & P

A Study in
Price-Cost Behavior
and Public Policy

INTRODUCTION

> The social process is really one indivisible whole. Out of its great stream the classifying hand of the investigator artificially extracts economic facts. The designation of a fact as economic already involves an abstraction, the first of many. . . . A fact is never exclusively or purely economic; other — and often more important — aspects always exist.[1]

THE opening words of Joseph Schumpeter's great survey of the whole economic process apply equally well to this microscopic study of a single business concern. Out of a basic source comprising perhaps 50,000 pages has been constructed a book about one per cent of that length. But even were this study to be as long as the court record, it would still be highly selective. As many as 100,000 persons have been employed by A & P at a given time; the record involves a few score of them. There is practically nothing in it about the relationship of employer to employed, the cardinal social fact of our era. The administration of a vast enterprise, the techniques of handling goods, people, and pieces of paper, have received little more attention. Yet this is what most business activity consists of.

It is best to explain at the outset how special and specific are the goals of our inquiry. Much of this study is historical in form; but it is not a business history, comparable, say, to the admirable history of Sears, Roebuck & Company,[2] although it might fit into the developing field of entrepreneurial history. Nor is this a rounded study of the food distribution industry, though one may hope that it is a contribution. Primarily we have aimed at knowledge in two areas. One of them is cost-price policy in a large corporation. The other is the judicial process in an antitrust case: the ascertainment of facts as related to the formation of legal doctrine. Ours is and should be a system of justice administered by

---

[1] Joseph A. Schumpeter, *The Theory of Economic Development* (Cambridge, 1934), p. 3.

[2] Boris Emmet and John E. Jeuck, *Catalogues and Counters* (Chicago, 1950).

laymen, into whose language, as Judge Learned Hand once put it, the essential conclusions of unfamiliar disciplines — including economics — must somehow be translated.[3] We have tried to make this work intelligible to noneconomists.

Even aside from this language problem, it is an old and a good tradition to have important cases written up as narrative and analytical studies. A recent and highly interesting such work begins with a quotation from an eminent writer on evidence, Edmund M. Morgan: "The trial . . . is not an investigative but a demonstrative proceeding." And Mr. Packer adds: "It is up to the parties to supply the information on which a verdict rests. What comes out depends on what goes in."[4] And the purpose of such works, aside from the sheer interest of writing and reading them, is to have an appraisal of how efficient a trial is in finally establishing "the facts."

One need be neither lawyer nor economist to realize that facts come in layers or hierarchies. In any given layer, a fact is not a physical object, but rather that hypothesis which best agrees with the facts in the adjoining lower layers. If we regard it as a fact that a certain car skidded on a certain road at a certain time, this is simply the conclusion which is least in conflict with the statements of those who saw the event, or at least saw the condition of the road, the marks on tires and fence, etc. And the finding of this fact of the car skidding may call for considerable special knowledge, not to mention deductive skill. Every fact of any importance embodies a theory, and if the theory is wrong, the fact has no support.

A principal object of this study, then, is to re-examine a set of primary or ultimate facts — largely the A & P trial record — to find out *what actually happened*. This, it seems to me, is by far the greater part of whatever contribution economics can make to public policy. An economist may have his views on standards for policy, the right to urge those views, and, occasionally, a chance to be heard. But standards for antitrust policy are quite a minor part of this work and can be omitted altogether. The

---

[3] See George H. Dession, "The Trial of Economic and Technological Issues of Fact," *Yale Law Journal*, 58: 1019–1049; 1242–1271 (1948–49).

[4] Herbert L. Packer, "A Tale of Two Typewriters," *Stanford Law Review*, 10:409 (1958).

important conclusion is that what the judicial process ground out from the A & P record were not facts but "unfacts," a set of conclusions which contradict both documentary and testamentary materials in the light of economic analysis.

Such a conclusion leads to no ringing call for action to save the Republic or its institutions. Yet it may be easier today than it was a decade ago to get a hearing for the argument that the most important defect of antitrust law is simply its awkward and inept handling of data, whereby records of frequently intolerable size yield a negligible fact content, and whereby the findings of tribunals are at complete variance with ascertainable facts. Nor can it be said that other areas of government regulation — notably the public utility field — are in essentially better condition.

Part I of this study is concerned exclusively with economic research: price policy and innovation as seen through the eyes of top management in a large business concern. These are the groups which receive and interpret the signals from the outside world, decide what responses shall be made to those signals, and see that those responses actually are made. The theory of the firm in economics is a theory of what these people do. The first four chapters analyze the impact of the forces of demand and cost, and of changes in these variables, on top management; and the way in which its response was conditioned by the nature of the organization, the difficulties of communication, the force of inertia and the clash of opinions as to what the signals really meant. It is a case study, sprawling over the boundary between business organization and economic theory, of interaction between objective realities and their imperfect reflection in the minds of men. Between their endless jar the economic process resides. But the facts of supply and demand are primary to their reflection. This is a study of *why* certain decisions were made, insofar as we can understand them, not a study of "how they do it," or an attempt to escape from the many difficulties of explanation into the appearance of "realism," as if the minutiae of price-making added up to understanding.

Part II covers a larger part of the social process. It is still primarily an economic study: the buying methods of A & P; the relation of suppliers to a large buyer which itself manufactured a substantial portion of its requirements. At this point, however, the noneconomic aspects of our inquiry begin to intrude. Our purpose is still to explain economic behavior. But we cannot understand or explain our economic data until we introduce facts of a noneconomic kind. The best way to explain this is by example.

To the analytical economist a very important question raised in Part II is that of price discrimination by the suppliers of A & P. In establishing the nature and extent of discrimination, the first step is to inquire into the kinds of markets where A & P purchased. The data in the record suggest three general types — which of course merge into each other. The first class is of "trading items" sold in markets composed of many small sellers of products which are either homogeneous or else can be classified into well-defined grades, such as U. S. No. 1 in produce. Each seller has so small a portion of his market that he can sell all his output at the market price, and can have no effect on that price. The second broad type is of oligopoly — relatively few sellers of a relatively standard product in a national or a local market. The third type is of products differentiated by branding and advertising; and the degree of differentiation varies from nearly zero — at the borders of pure competition — to a very high degree such that consumers will not accept substitutes but will go elsewhere to get the "one and only." Differentiation may be practiced by many or few, so that it may and often does overlap with oligopoly.

According to accepted economic theory, price discrimination is possible under differentiated competition and/or oligopoly, where sellers have some substantial degree of market influence. A seller or group of sellers may increase profits or reduce losses if they are able to divide the market into submarkets and get a higher net revenue from some customers than from others. In fact, we do find examples of price discrimination in favor of A & P and are led to propound the hypothesis that discrimination will be at a maximum where the sellers have a wide trading margin between prices and marginal or average cost of *production*, but are saddled with heavy fixed distribution costs. Hence, a sale at a discriminatory price lower than market price is a large addition to profit.

But it also appears that when differentiation is so successful that all buyers can be induced to pay the higher price, discrimination in favor of A & P becomes less likely, and quasi-political considerations enter which make it practically impossible. Thus the relation between market control or monopoly power (in the purely economic sense) on the one hand, and discrimination on the other, is not a one-way relation, but reversible — up to a point the two correlate positively; after this point, negatively or not at all.

So far, so good; but one thing we find difficult to explain is the feeling of many A & P buying personnel that they were being discriminated *against*. Like everyone else, businessmen like to complain of ill treatment; yet these were internal opinions, with no public to impress. According to economic theory, the lowest prices would be charged to the buyer possessing the greater alternative sources of supply (i.e., whose demand was most elastic), and surely this was the case with A & P. But if alleged discrimination against them is a little puzzling, so is the language used in these grumbles. Rarely do we see the word "discrimination"; we read that others have an "advantage" over A & P, or own their goods at a lower cost, etc. These people have discrimination in mind, yet they do not use the word: a linguistic puzzle within a puzzle.

So much for markets under oligopoly or differentiation. Sellers of "trading items," without market control, have neither the motive nor the opportunity to discriminate; for in this kind of market they can sell as much as they have at the going price. It may be a very unsatisfactory price. But they cannot charge a higher-than-market price to any buyers who can go elsewhere. Nor need they charge a lower-than-market price to anybody; for they can sell everything to others at the market price. Hence, in these markets, which encompass "trading items" in manufactured foods, and practically all produce, there could have been no discrimination, in favor of A & P or against it.

But this is startling. For the A & P data are the by-product of a lawsuit where the prosecution insisted, and the courts (and public opinion) agreed, that the many sellers under (very roughly speaking) pure competition are weak, lack any "bargaining power," and hence are easily exploited by large buyers who have much "bargaining power" and can obtain discriminatory concessions. This is almost universally believed. But what does it mean? "Bargaining power" is nowhere explained. The economist may search as he will, and try to improve upon Shakespeare:

> Tell me, where is power bred,
> Or in the heart, or in the head?
> How begot, how nourished?
> Reply, reply.

But there is no reply. The idea that price discrimination is caused by buyers' monopoly (monopsony) has no logical foundation; moreover, there are almost no examples of A & P's being a monopsonist of any product. The constant talk in and out of the A & P record about "coercion" reveals much — but only about those who use such language. The competitive market is a system of coercion. Let the seller try to charge more than the price set by that unfeeling tyrant, the Market, and his wares are left to rot on his hands. The costs the seller has incurred, his heavy labors and risks, his just deserts, his upright behavior, his place in the community as a businessman — these all-important facts are less than sounding brass and a tinkling cymbal: meet the price, or you sell nothing. And it is of the greatest importance that economists interested in public policy never forget the deep human resentment which any competitive market arouses in those whom it whips and goads to stay in line and keep moving. In any event, "force" and "threats" and "compulsion" tell us nothing about discrimination.

We therefore turn to the detailed evidence, hoping to construct a meaningful explanation of bargaining power. There is little direct price information in the record, and a vast amount of irrelevancy. In Appendix IV (an appendix to Chapter X) are compiled the dealings of A & P with every supplier for which there existed any substantial evidence in testimony or documents. We have 142 agreements with 46 suppliers, some evidence on groups of buyers as groups, and a number of individual transactions or negotiations.

Upon close examination, much of the alleged discrimination

under pure competition simply vanishes. Alleged "trading items" turn out to be nationally advertised products; lower prices paid by A & P turn out to be merely the lower price granted to someone performing the investment and the function of a wholesaler, which the company did; and so on. But many transactions in undifferentiated products, particularly in fresh fruits and vegetables, are not thus explained. For example, there is a so-called cash buying system, with A & P often, though not always, getting allowances apparently in excess of any savings incident to receiving cash. There is another impressive fact. The District and Appeals Courts said that many buying personnel of A & P were engaged in a large-scale evasion of the Robinson-Patman Act, a statute which declares that it is "unlawful to discriminate in price." The writer must agree with this judgment. Correspondence, arrangements made with sellers to provide various subterfuges, etc., leave no other conclusion possible. The area in which this is most obviously true is the one most nearly approaching pure competition — fresh fruits and vegetables — but there is evidence of the same condition in processed foods.

This presents a dilemma. According to economic theory, there could not have been any discrimination under pure competition; but this appears to fly in the face of evidence that there was discrimination. Yet to accept the conclusion that there was discrimination is to rack one's brains for an explanation of why any seller should have discriminated. Why should any seller accept a lower net return from a buyer who represented less than one tenth of the market, when he had the other nine tenths to sell to at the market price? The courts, as we shall see much later, never could reach this common-sense question because they had no access to economic analysis, and lacking it they were snowed under a mass of data with which they could not begin to cope. But no economist worth his salt could at this point accept either conclusion: that A & P received discriminatory concessions, or that it did not.

This is not, however, an unfamiliar situation in any science: theory and facts do not seem to jibe, and either or both must give way.[5]

---

[5] "Let us suppose we wish to discover whether our 'space' is Euclidean, that

We consider Cohen and Nagel's last hint first: that the theory may be correct but not applicable to these particular facts. Upon re-examination, it appears that, although competition in certain markets was pure, it was very imperfect. Temporary gluts and scarcities were always occurring, so that a buyer or seller who represented only a small part of the market in the course of a whole month or quarter might represent a very large part of total supply or total demand for an hour, a day, or a week. This fact is important in itself, explains certain economies of A & P operation, and explains some but not much price discrimination.

We turn therefore to the first possibility: errors of observation. Do these documents, authentic as they appear on re-examination, imply what they seem to imply? What was the nature of the acts which these people realized they were committing? Consciousness of guilt is impressive evidence, but we know from bitter experience what it can lead to if mishandled. One of the worst miscarriages of justice in American history occurred when two defendants' consciousness of the "guilt" of being aliens and anarchists was used to convict them of murder.[6]

We turn therefore to examine the statute which these people knew they were avoiding or evading. This is the *raison d'être* of Chapter VIII, on the Robinson-Patman Act. There we discover

is, whether the angle sum of a physical triangle is equal to two right angles. We select as vertices of such a triangle three fixed stars, and as its sides the paths of rays traveling from vertex to vertex. By making a series of measurements we can calculate the magnitude of the angles of this triangle and so obtain the angle sum. Suppose the sum is less than two right angles. *Must* we conclude that Euclidean geometry is not true? Not at all! There are at least three alternatives open to us:

1. We may explain the discrepancy between the theoretical and 'observed' values of the angle sum on the hypothesis of errors in measurement.

2. We may conclude that Euclidean geometry is not physically true.

3. We may conclude that the 'lines' joining the vertices of the triangle with each other and with our measuring instruments are not 'really' straight lines; that is, Euclidean geometry is physically true, but light does not travel in Euclidean straight lines in stellar space."

Morris R. Cohen and Ernest Nagel, *An Introduction to Logic and Scientific Method* (New York, 1934), p. 220.

[6] Felix Frankfurter, *The Sacco-Vanzetti Case* (Boston, 1927), ch. 3; and G. Louis Joughin and Edmund M. Morgan, *The Legacy of Sacco and Vanzetti* (New York, 1948), pp. 9, 11, 68–72, 81–82.

that the conduct forbidden by this law is not price discrimination (in the economic sense) at all. The Act requires price *uniformity*, and "price uniformity in the face of cost diversity is price discrimination." [7] And this is most obviously and most strongly true in just the area where our dilemma is the greatest — the selling of fruits and vegetables. It is perfectly clear that where A & P was a lower-cost buyer, the Act required A & P to pay as much as or more than other buyers; *it required the seller to take a larger net return from A & P than from others.*

Once this is understood, the dilemma vanishes, and the facts fall neatly into place. Since A & P was required by law to pay a higher net price than was paid by other buyers, sales to A & P were more profitable than sales to other buyers. Where sellers were few and able to follow a common policy — which the law made easy for them to do and difficult not to do — A & P paid higher prices and that was all. To them that had the most, the law gave the most.

But where sellers were many and independent of each other, they were often willing to compete for this attractive business; which means that each was willing to bid for it by offering terms a little better than his neighbor's. It cannot be said that A & P waited very long for this willingness to come to fruition! On the contrary, it went aggressively in search of buyers whom it could persuade to lower prices part way toward a nondiscriminatory level, to the refrain of — If you don't, I know who will. Here is a complete explanation — the only one to date — for its "power" and "bargaining power" and "coercive power" and "oppressive power" and all the rest of it. But the limit to A & P's efforts — the farthest north it could go — was to achieve nondiscrimination. For if it demanded more than the extra profits which the law granted the seller, he no longer had any incentive to meet its terms.

The minor riddle also disappears now: the A & P complaints of being discriminated against, which are now seen to be well founded. And its peculiar avoidance of the word "discrimination" fits neatly into the semantic pattern. For to A & P personnel, as to businessmen and lawyers generally, price "discrimination"

[7] Fritz Machlup, *The Basing-Point System* (Philadelphia, 1949), p. 175.

meant price differentials or, in particular, violation of the Robinson-Patman Act. Discrimination as economists understand it, i.e., differences in price *net* of differences in cost, rarely was considered under that name.

Following our ground-clearing operation, we attempt to locate and measure discrimination in the economic sense — i.e., the extent to which price differentials were not fully reflected in cost differentials. This is purely a question of measurement and analysis, and at this point we raise no questions about any good or bad aspects of discrimination or nondiscrimination.

Our method of measurement in Chapters X and XI must, because of data limitations, be a peculiar and special one. At every point where we could not attempt an estimate of the most probable figure, we used the maximum. Thus, the estimate that in 1941 discrimination in favor of A & P amounted to a maximum of 0.24 (twenty-four hundredths) of one per cent of total purchases of processed foods means that it could have been no higher, and must have been considerably lower; unfortunately, we cannot say how much lower. All would agree that there must have been some cost savings on selling to A & P. Also, there was substantial discrimination against A & P on some products, which needs to be offset against discrimination in its favor, and so on. Since we are unable to put any numerical values on these offsetting amounts, we simply reckon them at zero but warn the reader that they are there.

Whether there was on balance *any* net discrimination at all in favor of A & P for the period 1936–1943 will probably never be known. The passionate belief that there was substantial net discrimination in its favor is only an important psychological and political fact. There has of course been discrimination against A & P since 1946. Only for the period before 1936 may discrimination have been large enough to have any perceptible influence. Assuming that it did, in order to have license to explore the consequences, the most probable though far from certain conclusion is a rather surprising one — that the effects were to raise the general level of A & P prices, and therefore to help competitors take markets from the company.

But whatever the merits of this particular conclusion, something of first-rate importance is involved. Any reasoned judgment, however approximate, about the impact upon the food trade of A & P buying must take into account the actual facts on price discrimination. It is easy to slide from price differentials to price discrimination; thence to substantial discrimination; thence to a decisive effect upon competition. It is all such obvious common sense that one is not even aware of the journey. And so, instead of a doubtful maximum of one fourth of a per cent, discrimination becomes 5 per cent or whatever is convenient, and one is deep in the pointless debate of whether "great power" has been "benevolently" or "properly" used.

Not only is it good to avoid irrelevant conflict on policy grounds; it should be carefully distinguished from pursuit of the facts. It is a fact that A & P was discriminated against by being forced to pay phantom brokerage, etc. The discrimination was largely but not wholly required by law. It did not "entitle" A & P to get offsetting discrimination in its favor. Like Mount Everest, the discrimination against A & P was simply there, and it had foreseeable consequences which the facts bear out. Whether any of this was good or bad has nothing to do with finding out when and how discrimination started and how much it amounted to, in order to see what the results were or might have been. The prosecution, the courts, and some others assumed everything and investigated nothing.

In Part III, Chapters XVI and XVII, the A & P prosecution briefs and court opinions are examined in search of two things. First, we wish to discover the general theory of the case, the "vision," as Schumpeter called it, of what was happening. (This has been partly anticipated by the inquiry into price discrimination.) The second object of this inquiry is to discover the public policy underlying the statements of the prosecution and the courts.

So much time spent analyzing the doctrines and ideas of "judge and company" may seem excessive. Indeed, the reader interested in a case study of business cost-price behavior will have little interest in these chapters. Yet economics is the traditional handmaiden of public policy, and must supply not only basic data but also tools of analysis. The need is easiest to miss precisely where it is greatest — under a common-law system, where the growth of the law takes place by small movements and small changes of course whose ultimate direction is not immediately clear, and where changing purposes come to life inarticulate and almost unrecognized. Hence our two inquiries might be expressed in two types of questions. How well equipped were the prosecution and courts to discover the economic facts? What kinds of legal rules were implicit in what they decided?

Unfortunately, the two questions are interrelated in a subtle fashion. Again, we can best explain by example. The prosecution charged A & P with predatory or cutthroat warfare, the "elimination of competition by sales in selected areas below [the] cost of doing business." This seems clear: A & P allegedly cut prices and incurred losses in order to inflict them upon rival stores, which were forced to close down, leaving the company with a set of local monopolies which it could exploit by raising prices. Now, such a campaign would have been foolish and useless. No reasonable and prudent A & P management would have incurred losses to drive out competition because it would have been impossible to claim the pay-off. Entry into the food trade was so cheap and easy that any attempt to raise prices would immediately have resurrected competition. Over and above this, predatory warfare would have been political and legal insanity. In view of the political power of the retailers, evidenced in chain-store taxes, sales-below-cost laws, the Robinson-Patman Act, and the Miller-Tydings Act, A & P management would have needed to be altogether mad to embark on a predatory campaign.

In order to overbear these considerations, therefore, one might expect powerful and impressive evidence of "elimination of competition" on a large scale. True, even long lists of competitors who had gone out of business would in itself mean little or nothing in a trade with so high a rate of turnover.[8] But in fact the government does not offer a single example of an eliminated

---

[8] Edmund D. McGarry, "The Mortality Rate of Independent Grocery Stores in Buffalo and Pittsburgh, 1919–1941," *Journal of Marketing*, xi (1947).

competitor. Yet even in sham battles like army maneuvers there are at least a few casualties. And just as army maneuvers are full of sound and fury, so also is the government's case full of phrases extracted from correspondence, like "turn on the heat," "crack down," "hit them with meat and produce," etc., every one of which is singled out and lovingly dwelt upon. Atmosphere is built up in lieu of fact.

Then there is the recital of "red-ink stores," as they were called in company records, and the display of red ink is indeed impressive — as the reader will have seen in Part I. One almost forgets (and the courts forgot) to ask for some connection between red-ink stores and eliminated competitors; for a few thousand — or hundred — or dozen — or at least *one* example of the sequence: a formerly profitable store or unit first cutting prices in order to run losses, then eliminating local competitors, and then raising prices. The facts were entirely to the contrary: the red-ink stores swiftly disappeared when and as top management was successful in getting prices *reduced.*

But one's attention is already distracted by a different species of "loss" (and this constant distraction is the secret of persuasion). A & P had an elaborate wholesaling, supervising, purchasing, and advertising organization whose expense of operation was allocated to the stores as a percentage of their respective sales. Apparently the prosecution considered these expenses as bona fide retail expenses and did not object to their allocation. But the savings secured through the supervising and purchasing organization must not be allocated in the same way — they were "nonretail profits." Similarly, the profits of A & P's manufacturing subsidiaries were wholly "nonretail profits," even though those profits could never exist if there were no retail stores, to which goods could be transferred cheaply. Under this method of accounting, plus a little chicanery, many stores could be portrayed as losing money. Since losing money means "selling below cost," and since "selling below cost" can *only* be practiced for "elimination of competition," there we are!

Towering above it all was the grand design whereby A & P prices were set not by applying a conventional markup to the invoice price but by lowering the gross profit rate and keeping it down *permanently* in order to increase the volume and lower the expense rate to the point of maximum profit. An "honest retailer" would attempt to "price his merchandise in the traditional American way [!], that is, cost, plus expenses, plus a profit." Any departure from this "orthodox" method is "selling below cost" regardless of whether it is temporary or permanent, profitable or unprofitable.

What are we to say of all this, and of a great deal more? The logical implications are all too clear: a broadside attack on price competition and on integration of manufacturing with wholesaling and retailing. Competition and integration are treated as illegal per se — that is, even when no ill consequences, or the probability of such results, have been demonstrated. Far from attempting to show that the nature of the industry would cause the defendant's policies to have certain consequences, the prosecution was fairly successful in keeping others from showing that it would not. It is beside the point to quote pious (and probably sincere) declarations that the prosecution is "really" in favor of price competition, and that integration is "of course" not illegal, etc., etc. Self-serving declarations deserve no more respect from plaintiffs than from defendants. Anyone who asks for six has also asked for half-a-dozen.

There is an alternative and more obvious explanation: that the government lawyers, although competent in their profession, were so sadly illiterate in economic facts and economic analysis that they simply did not realize what they were saying.

There is considerable truth in both explanations; but the best one may lie somewhere between the two extremes of a deliberate attack on competition on the one side and sheer economic incompetence on the other. The antitrust laws are par excellence a common-law system, growing and changing by the gradual and almost unperceived assimilation of new ideas. Rules of law do not spring into existence as finished creatures. They come to birth in an implicit and unstated form. Somehow new kinds of evidence are admitted, and old kinds are barred or little attention is paid them; what were formerly minor qualifications now become major premises; the cases wear a different aspect and are now differently decided. After a time, as the pattern is pricked out by case after case, the new rule is visible to all and is bluntly cited as such.

Considered from this viewpoint, the A & P case is best understood as an attempt, successful at least in the one instance, to infuse the Robinson-Patman Act into the Sherman Act. In the field of distribution, Robinson-Patman standards and ideology were (and are) as familiar as the air one breathed. The hostility to price competition, the yearning for secure entrepreneurial status, the envy and hate of the small businessman for big business were long ago embodied in a set of standard myths. Great gobs of misunderstood evidence were forced into these molds to produce the case for the prosecution.

Whether this infusion of Robinson-Patman into Sherman has became permanent is something else again. The very knowledge of what is happening may provoke a sufficient reaction against it, and so prevent it from happening at all. No important element of the prosecution's case was rejected by the courts, but not all were explicitly adopted. The case has thus far not been the important precedent it was designed to be. It has not even had the melancholy honor of being most frequently distinguished: it has largely been ignored. Furthermore, it is a striking fact that a civil suit, where the issue of liability was already foreclosed, i.e., decided in advance against A & P because of the previous criminal conviction, collapsed after years of preparation.

Even this bare sketch of the prosecution case has run to several pages; its actual dismemberment will consume many more. But if one is interested in the legal fact-finding process and in the organic growth of the law, there is no alternative to taking apart the government thesis, piece by piece, to see what each part means before putting it back to examine the whole. Anyone who conscientiously attempts to go through the A & P case is reminded of an earlier traveler:

The shop seemed to be full of all manner of curious things — but . . . whenever [Alice] looked hard at any shelf, to make out *exactly* what it had on it, that particular shelf was always quite empty.

Unfortunately, there are a great many shelves. Let the reader consider the following passage of English history:

My, you ought to seen old Henry the Eight when he was in bloom. He *was* a blossom. He used to marry a new wife every day and chop off her head next morning. . . And he made every one of them tell him a tale every night, and he kept that up till he had hogged a thousand and one tales that way, and then he put them all in a book and called it Domesday Book — which was a good name and stated the case. . . Well, Henry he takes a notion he wants to get up some trouble with this country. How does he go at it — give notice? — give the country a show? No. All of a sudden he heaves all the tea in Boston Harbor overboard and whacks out a declaration of independence and dares them to come on. That was *his* style — he never give anybody a chance.

All things considered, the proportion of fact to fiction in this passage is about as high as in the "vision" of the A & P prosecution. But let the reader now imagine that he must explain the scholarly limitations of Huckleberry Finn to some intelligent but uninformed listener. Certainly this passage has much truth in it. There was a King Henry VIII. He did have an unusually large number of wives, and he did behead an unusually large proportion of them. A king of England was directly responsible for the tea's being dumped into Boston Harbor. Let the reader imagine how he would need to explain that these were two *other* kings of England, seven hundred years apart; that the thousand and one tales were told to a king, but it was a different sort of king. Besides, it was not Henry, or even the other kings, who actually issued a declaration of independence. Let the reader now imagine the wealth of detail, the citations of authority he would need; above all, he must realize that his explanation would be several times as long as Huck's original narrative.

One curious feature may be mentioned of this inquiry into the economic and legal reasoning of "judge and company." The analysis presented here is not new. It is now nearly ten years since Donald F. Turner and I published articles on the A & P cases almost simultaneously.[9] Our conclusions, as already explained,

[9] Turner, "Trouble Begins in the New Sherman Act," *Yale Law Journal*, 58: 969 (1949); Adelman, "The A & P Case," *Quarterly Journal of Economics*, 63: 283 (1949); "Integration and Antitrust Policy," *Harvard Law Review*, 63:53 (1949).

were that either the courts and their counsel were unspeakably confused, or they had made "a direct attack on the competitive process." [10] The quickest (though not the surest) way of confirming Professor Turner's analysis and mine is to read what has been written in opposition to it. It has been said that the courts and counsel "really" did not mean what they plainly said; or that they simply could not have meant it; or that anyway the operations of A & P were not in the public interest, etc. But no writer has cared to take up systematically the argument of the briefs and decisions, analyze them step by step, and show that conclusions other than ours were indicated. The prosecution and courts are right, and the critics wrong, but the better part of demonstration is simply repeated assertion. Their lady is beautiful, but we are not to see her face.

If the doctrine of the A & P prosecution, and to a lesser extent of the courts, was to thwart competition by writing the Robinson-Patman Act into the Sherman Act, this doctrine is not necessarily "wrong." Perhaps there are good reasons of social policy for blocking competition. The legislatures of the civilized world have never had any difficulty in discerning such reasons.

But even if one accepts my preference for more competition, it does not follow from any refutation of errors that the operations of A & P contributed to more competitive markets, or that they should not have been convicted, or that the company should not have been dismembered. True, the reasons offered on behalf of these policies were unsound or amounted to an attack on competition. But this does not prove that sound ones could not exist. A good cause is not refuted merely because bad arguments have been offered on its behalf, or because it has been grievously misstated. A man might so mumble and mutter the Ten Commandments that they sounded like gibberish or worse. Yet they would be no less our fundamental moral law.

Chapters XVI and XVII in Part III can then be viewed as simply a groundclearing operation. In the last chapter we attempt a general appraisal of the evidence to discover where A & P opera-

---

[10] Turner, p. 977.

tions promoted competition and where they reduced it; for, as one would expect, both effects were present.

We close with a brief discussion of the legal significance of the case. First, it is still much the most complete "depth" story of the corporation which was the outstanding target of the Robinson-Patman Act, and that Act has not shrunk in importance. Second, chain stores are by their nature extreme examples of "diversified" or "conglomerate" firms, whose over-all profitability is nearly independent of earnings in any one place; and such firms draw considerable attention nowadays. Third, the Anti-Merger Amendment to the Clayton Act is beginning to acquire a meaning, and strenuous attempts are being made and will be made to give it the meaning intended by the A & P prosecution.

The writer wishes his subject were less contemporary; but what he likes or dislikes has little enough to do with the state of the cosmos.

PART I

SALES AND PRICE POLICY

I

BEFORE 1929

Introductory, 1859–1925

I~N~ 1859, one George F. Gilman began selling tea in New York City at less than the current dollar a pound, and pushed it with premiums and flamboyant advertising.[1] Whether these ideas originated with Gilman or with George Huntington Hartford, his ex-clerk and junior partner, is not known. But in 1878, Gilman retired[2] from active participation in the business, and Hartford was left as active partner in a firm selling annually approximately a million dollars worth of tea and coffee through about a hundred stores, most of them in metropolitan New York. During the 1880's and 1890's, the firm gradually branched out into a full line of dry groceries and relied on peddler wagons as well as stores.

Progress was not spectacular. By 1901, when the firm incorporated, it operated about two hundred stores. Sales for the preceding year had been $5.6 million, and profits during the preceding three years had averaged $125 thousand on an investment of $936 thousand — a 13.4 per cent rate of return.

During the early years of the century, the company expanded along the established lines, and with very fair success. In 1907, total assets (disregarding "good will") were $1.7 million, appar-

---

[1] The following brief account of A & P's colorful beginnings is based on two articles, "The Early History of the Great A & P Tea Company" and "The History of the A & P Tea Company Since 1878," by Roy J. Bullock in the *Harvard Business Review*, April and October 1933; "Biggest Family Business," *Fortune*, February 1933; and, as cited, the financial manuals and the testimony of Mr. John A. Hartford.

[2] Because of illness, according to Hartford, Tr. 20,434; according to *Fortune*, "in order to cut a frightfully nouveau dash . . . in a fancy tallyho upholstered with gala ladies."

ently a sizable relative increase since 1900.[3] Henceforth, dividends were paid on the common stock,[4] which had originally represented little more than a means of control and a wish for profit. By 1912, the company operated about four hundred stores. But the A & P of even five years later represents a very different type of retailing business. Apart from the red fronts on the stores, the two do not have much in common.

Exhaustive research would doubtless show that some unsung genius conceived, perhaps even started up somewhere, the innovation of what A & P called "the economy store."[5] However that may be, the honor for its introduction on a large scale unquestionably belongs to John A. Hartford, the younger son of the founder. We do not know how he hit upon the idea. But the wisdom of hindsight makes the economy store appear as a very obvious and logical step, both because of current retailing practice and because of the hardships experienced by many low-income families in American cities.

Since the turn of the century, the cost of living had risen steeply. Retail food prices were up 35 per cent between 1900 and 1912.[6] The increase had started in 1896, and on the eve of World War I it appeared to represent a permanent shift in the terms of trade between the farm and nonfarm population of the Western world.[7] Wage earners in manufacturing and public utilities received wage increases just about sufficient to maintain their real income; clerical, salaried, and professional employees were less

[3] If the $936 thousand given for 1900 was net of good will, as seems most likely but not certain, the 1900–1907 increase would be 82 per cent. See *Moody's Industrial Manual* (hereafter referred to as *Moody's*), 1907, p. 2051.

[4] *Moody's*, 1915, p. 3834.

[5] According to Hartford, Tr. 20,432, this change was forced by competitors opening cash-and-carry stores that took a great deal of A & P's business away. But the *Fortune* article, which was based on personal interviews with the Hartfords, mentions no such tendency. Surely Mr. Hartford was somewhat more modest than accurate.

[6] Paul H. Douglas, *Real Wages in the United States* (Boston and New York, 1930), p. 36.

[7] The "parity" legislation of the New Deal took as a base the 1909–1913 "golden age" of American agriculture. Urban wages were relatively low then. See John D. Black, "Measures for the Improvement of American Agriculture," *Papers and Proceedings of the 53rd Annual Meeting of the American Economic Association (1940)*, pp. 166–167. See also J. M. Keynes, *Economic Consequences of the Peace* (London, 1920), pp. 24–25.

fortunate; and government employees lost about one fifth of their real incomes during this period.[8] In 1911 the federal government and in 1912 the State of New York held investigations on the high cost of living, and it was a campaign issue in the election of 1912. Doubtless the pinch of rising food prices had contributed to the prosperity of A & P and other chains. Some of their stores were cash, some were carry, and some were both. One observer, surveying the city of Philadelphia in 1913, ascribed the chains' success (he did not mention A & P) to cash sales, the absence of bad debt losses, quantity purchasing, the use of motor trucks in centralized distribution, and more efficient management generally.[9] But the drift to such economical methods was little more than a drift. Costs and prices were blurred by the heavy reliance on premiums and trading stamps. (In 1900, A & P had given away premiums valued at half its investment in the business, and more than three and one half times the annual profits.) Grocery distribution was carried on largely though not exclusively by a vast network of minuscule monopolists,[10] each one effectively protected by the distance between him and his neighbor. The customer saw little point in going out of her way to save a small fraction of a small purchase. Convenience, credit, delivery, or special favors were of far greater importance. Price competition had to be injected into the system by a series of positive acts before retail food prices could conform a little more closely to the norms of the economic theorist.[11] In a word, the urban public had been sen-

[8] Douglas, *Real Wages in the United States*, pp. 230–231, 340, 353, 364, 376, 386, 392. Bituminous coal miners improved their position, but they are not part of the urban population.

[9] C. L. King, "Can the Cost of Distributing Food Products be Reduced?", *The Annals* (of the American Academy of Political and Social Science), 48:199–224 (July 1913).

[10] "The nearest thing to a retail monopoly we ever had in this country was the village grocery store." Geoffrey S. Shepherd, *Marketing Farm Products* (Ames, 1946), p. 393. But Professor John D. Black has pointed out that the most competitive of retail food stores were also in country towns: those where customers drove in from the surrounding areas and thought nothing of extending their trip by a few blocks. These mobile consumers were a prototype of the automobile public which made the supermarkets in the 1930's.

[11] Cf. Alfred Marshall, *Principles of Economics* (1920 ed.), pp. 328–329; 616n. Knut Wicksell, *Lectures on Political Economy* (1934) I, 86–88, discusses retail pricing as an example of "imperfect competition" through joint supply of goods and retailers' services, and through the spatial monopoly of the shop-

sitized to the price appeal, but something more was needed to complete their education and to change their buying habits.

Early in 1913, after a successful trial [12] in Jersey City the year before, the company began to open economy stores throughout the East. John Hartford, 32 years later, described the type: "It was a cash and carry store, no deliveries, no credits, no advertising, no telephone. Generally located in a small neighborhood location, a small investment, managed by one man and a helper, and in those days, we closed the store from twelve to one, so that the manager could go to lunch." [13] There were no premiums, trading

TABLE 1. A & P Growth, 1878–1921

Year	Sales		Profits before taxes, (millions of dollars)	Number of stores (approximate)
	In millions of dollars	In physical volume (1914 = 100)		
1878	1.0	..	..	100
1901	5.6	24	0.125	200
1907	15.0	52	..	370
1914	31.3	100	..	650
1915	44.4	143	1.8	1,500
1916	76.4	220	..	3,250
1921	202.4	417	8.4	5,200

Sources. For 1901, Bullock, "The History of the A & P Tea Company Since 1878"; for 1907, a rough estimate based on *Moody's*; for 1914–1916, *Moody's*; for 1921, see Appendix Table 5. The estimate of physical volume is based on the food cost indexes in Douglas, *Real Wages in the United States*.

keeper. Wicksell formulates in words something very much like E. H. Chamberlin's tangency solution. See the latter, *Theory of Monopolistic Competition* (1939), p. 76, and Appendix A, where he discusses Hotelling's well-known example which is, again, from the retail trade. The glaring discrepancy between the purely competitive model and this branch of industry — a discrepancy with which one is so often impressed in daily life — is surely responsible for much of the thinking which produced the modern theory of monopolistic and imperfect competition. But it may also have given that theory a distorted emphasis. Joseph A. Schumpeter, *Capitalism, Socialism, and Democracy* (New York, 1947), p. 85.

[12] The experimental store was opened around the corner from one of the A & P's most successful conventional stores, which was quickly forced out of business. Hartford, Tr. 20,437.

[13] Hartford, Tr. 20,436.

stamps, or other inducements. In the next three years, with the somewhat bewildered approval of George Huntington Hartford, his sons opened 7500 such stores — and closed down more than half of them. The pattern was set: preliminary experiment, quick action, and willingness to cut away deadwood (Table 1 summarizes the results).

Such stores had to be small. John Hartford's formula was one thousand dollars each for equipment, the opening stock of goods, and cash. Leases were as short as possible. Not only were all store fronts painted red, but the arrangement of goods inside was made as uniform as possible. The very skimpiness of the new stores, and their standardized appearance, must have been a highly effective advertisement for the cheapness of their wares. Customers were not the only ones to be impressed. Some supplying manufacturers were indignant because their goods were sold at cut prices; Cream of Wheat refused to sell A & P any more of its product, and successfully defended its right of resale price maintenance, through refusal to deal, against an A & P suit.[14] The best judgment on the economy stores was furnished by A & P's competitors — who rushed to imitate them.

The expansion was financed entirely from retained profits up to 1916. When the corporation was reorganized in that year, $5 million was borrowed from banks, and $5.1 million raised by selling notes, later converted into preferred stock.[15] This was the first and last time that the company ever had recourse to the long-term capital market. By 1920, although some of the old type of stores were still being operated, the economy line *was* the A & P, and the next five years would see the harvest.

Appendix Table 3 reveals, far better than any verbal description, the swift growth of the company from 1920 to 1925. Appendix Table 9, on sources and uses of its funds, shows how reinvested profits furnished the means for a second revolution.

In the early days there had been only one warehouse for all the stores.[16] But it is obvious from the minutes of meetings held in 1925 that the company not only was acting as its own wholesaler,

[14] Great A & P Tea Co. v. Cream of Wheat Co., 227 Fed. 46 (1915).
[15] *Moody's,* 1917, p. 2354–5; 1921, p. 1535.
[16] Hartford, Tr. 20,436.

but also was manufacturing groceries and baking bread on a fairly substantial scale. As the business grew in width and depth, its organizational seams threatened to burst. "We handled all operations from headquarters in Jersey City," John Hartford said later. "All departments. All divisions. Everything." [17] There was some reluctance to change, but in 1926 a corporate reorganization was matched by a thoroughgoing decentralization of functions.

Six geographical divisions (which became seven in 1938) [18] were set up like separate corporations, each headed by a president who had a fairly elaborate staff organization of his own, with men in charge of engineering, operations, sales, purchases, and personnel.[19] The directors of each division were drawn from the staff and met four times a year; there were also frequent meetings of key personnel with more specialized interests. Design of the stores was standard within each division, but not all store leases had to be approved by the president; however, leases running over five years had to be referred to headquarters.[20]

Each metropolitan area was organized into a unit, centered around the warehouse which served the individual stores. The unit president had his own staff, consisting of a buyer, a sales manager, and an operations director who was concerned largely with running the warehouse. There were a number of supervisors, one supervisor to about eight stores but sometimes to as many as twenty-three, to visit the stores and provide a two-way contact with unit headquarters.

The store manager needed divisional approval to stock a new product; thus he was supposed to benefit by experience elsewhere within the organization. Other than that he bought at his own discretion and could order "anything or nothing" from the local

---

[17] Hartford, Tr. 20,436.

[18] The divisions and their headquarter cities were as follows: New England — Boston; Eastern — New York; Atlantic — Philadelphia (1938); Southern — Philadelphia; Central — Pittsburgh; Central Western — Detroit; Middle Western — Chicago. There were also some small units in Los Angeles and Seattle, attached to the Eastern Division.

[19] This description is based largely on the testimony of Mr. John M. Toolin, president of the Central Western Division, who has been with the company since 1908. Tr. 1624–1674.

[20] "It is more or less of a safety valve, that is all. Some of those rents go up pretty high, you know." Toolin, Tr. 1647.

warehouse. Prices were set by the unit sales manager but, as might be expected, the store manager had discretion in perishable items like produce, which might have to be quickly moved by price cuts in order to avoid spoilage.

But this extreme degree of local discretion was only a limiting case; it held at some times for some products or some methods. Headquarters never intended to delegate any class of decisions permanently. Local matters were to be handled by local people only up to that point where decisions could better be made by the higher echelons. Moreover — and probably more important — the system permitted decisions to be made sometimes locally, sometimes centrally, as conditions changed. This sort of flexibility was and is the most striking feature of all A & P operations. Like all good things, it had its price. The heavy fixed cost of this elaborate system was easily carried in good times; but not when the company ceased to grow rapidly.[21]

Although functions within the company were widely delegated, ultimate responsibility was tightly concentrated at the top. The corporate structure, while complex, need not be given in detail; [22] the Hartford brothers, through a voting trust, held practically all of the voting stock and most of the preferred, and could hire or fire all A & P officers and employees.[23] Policy was set at headquarters, at the quarterly meetings of the divisional presidents. The headquarters group was a larger-scale division center, composed of specialists. There were none but the Hartford brothers and perhaps two or three other persons to take a broad view of the company as a whole.[24]

[21] See DPM, June 25, 1925, GX 103: "The responsibility of the sales of the different products should be left to the division, not only [because] . . . they were better able to meet local conditions, but [because] it allowed them to build up the organization, which is so necessary with the rapid development that we are doing. . . . We must have men to take over the more responsible positions," and it seemed clear to headquarters that they were best developed within the system. For the other side of the coin, see DPM, March 8, 1934, GX 207.

[22] Charles W. Parr, who had been with the company since 1919 and in charge of all field buying offices since 1929, testified (Tr. 195): "I know nothing of the corporate structure at all. To me, it is all the A & P Tea Company."

[23] See the stipulation, GX 1, Exhibit A; and Hartford's testimony, especially 20,442ff.

[24] Cf. Parr, Tr. 214: "Q. . . . Who in the Headquarters organization, Mr. Parr,

The Crisis of 1925–1926

The first meeting of the divisional presidents was held in Jersey City on June 25, 1925.[25] The problems they faced were those of rapid expansion of both stores and other facilities, and the most attractive possibilities for future growth. John Hartford explained the "capital tie-up in stores, warehouses, bakeries, factories, etc., and the effect which the outside activities had on the return on investment." The consensus was that there should be no more building unless unavoidable: capital used in opening new stores promised both greater return and greater safety and liquidity. But the decision was not clear-cut: the normal profit on a factory investment was 30 to 35 per cent; the final decision was that bakeries, at least, should be built wherever possible because they made it easier to undersell competition.

The second important issue was expansion from straight grocery into combination stores selling meat as well. A recent experiment in Detroit seemed to indicate that meat sales were not only profitable in themselves, but drew more customers into the grocery department. All relevant experiences would be discussed at the next meeting.

The next meeting was held in October.[26] Hartford's optimism was echoed in almost identical language by the presidents. A score of tables and some charts were displayed (inaugurating an important practice at such meetings), showing not only growth of the company but its increasing share of the available business. Hartford emphasized that success was measured not by profit on sales but by return on investment; the goal was 25 per cent, which had been surpassed in most years of the company's existence. There was agreement, again unanimous, that the right policy for the immediate future was to push sales as aggressively as possible. But

---

would have the most knowledge of the operations of the A & P generally? . . . A. I don't know of anybody else there outside of Mr. Bofinger or Mr. Hartford who would have an over-all knowledge of all branches of the special activities." F. W. Wheeler acted as business secretary to the president (John Hartford) until his death in 1941, and R. W. Burger as his assistant (Tr. 1609, 198). There is no indication of their influence. Mr. Burger succeeded John Hartford to the presidency upon the latter's death in 1952.

[25] GX 103. The company directors were present at these meetings.

[26] DPM, October 27, 1925, GX 104.

there was also agreement that during the past four months expansion had been pushed too hard; since most of the new stores were losing money, it would therefore be better to follow a more conservative policy. Hartford's lecture on return on investment was probably intended to discredit the rate of profit on sales. The atmosphere of the meeting seems confused and the agreement all too unanimous. Davidson of the New England Division, of whom more will be heard, struck a discordant note by saying: "The increase in the expense rate since 1921 stands out clearly, which necessitates us raising our retail in order to get a satisfactory return on our investment."

The reasons for disquiet became abundantly clear by the beginning of February 1926.[27] Hartford was openly troubled by the sales and development policy. The immediate symptom, he explained, was an increase in the 1925 [28] profit of only half a million dollars despite an increase of ten million in the investment. The return of 5 per cent on the additional investment was "nothing to be proud of" and "chiefly due to mistaken sales and development policies."

Salvation lay in volume. The figures here were encouraging but misleading. Since the company was growing, total sales were also up. A slight rise in food prices contributed to the same trend. But the position of the company in its established market was best gauged by tonnage sold per store, and this had been declining. Hartford pointed out that, without intending to, the company had changed its policy for the worse: "I think that we are steering the boat wrong . . . a low volume and a high expense rate [are] driving us out of the Economy business."

The divisional presidents responded with more sound than sense. One of them described how, at the last meeting, he had realized that Hartford "was losing a great many nights' sleep. When he went back to his territory and informed the men of Mr. Hartford's worry the tide started to change." Hartford listened as long as he could, and then requested "a definite statement . . . with

27 DPM, February 3 and 4, 1926, GX 105.
28 This refers to the fiscal year ending February 28, 1926. The last quarter results are estimated; this in fact has been standard operating procedure to the present day.

regard to a policy." The divisional president's response was to assure Hartford that he was supporting him, but without saying in what way. The organization should have started sooner, but they were already "making a little headway." The others indicated their agreement. Hartford asked them to be frank with him. Receiving no specific answer, he proposed a goal of $200 (about 15 per cent) additional sales per store per week. But when he mentioned that losing stores had absorbed $4.6 million in 1925, the meeting found its tongue, and most voices were in favor of a more "conservative" policy, and slower openings of new stores. Hartford then proposed that only one thousand new stores be opened the following year, but that the sales policies become more aggressive than ever. In particular, this meant "reducing the gross profit in order to increase the volume and revamping the equipment and generally dressing up." [29]

Hartford kept after the directors.[30] The year 1926 was a highly profitable one, and the meeting at the end of January 1927 was completely different in tone. When the congratulations subsided, Hartford pointed out a chart which indicated "pretty consistently . . . a one point cut in the expense rate for each dollar increase in average sales" per store per week, and this despite falling prices. Furthermore, the divisional system had proved itself to the extent where divisional key men should be given full authority to enable "the presidents at their meetings to give . . . consideration to only the major problems of the business." [31]

The way was open for some longer range planning, which could profit by the experience of the crisis of 1925. Two developments constituted a vicious circle. A high markup repelled customers and cut down the volume. Low volume increased the burden of fixed costs per dollar of sales, hence the expense rate; but then it seemed all too natural to raise the gross margin.[32] Neither cost nor price is primary: John Hartford was undoubtedly right in

---

[29] DPM, January 27–28, 1927, GX 108; this is an account after the fact.

[30] DPM, June 30, 1926, bound in with DX 486. Hartford said he lived with statistical tables, and reiterated that "the rate of return on the invested dollar in the business was the test of our efficiency."

[31] DPM, June 30, 1926, bound in with DX 486. See also DPM, November 10, 1927, GX 111.

[32] The following nomenclature is conventional: *Gross profit* is the difference

linking them together as the elements of a bad sales policy. But why should the physical volume of sales per store have remained stagnant, and the gross profit have risen, from 1920 to 1925? It is common knowledge that by the mid-1920's the old type of economy store, as Hartford described it, had passed out of the food retailing picture.[33] For the first time there was evidenced a curious regressive tendency about competition in food retailing. The A & P method could be and was easily imitated. Presently all the economy-type competitors found themselves doing business at roughly the same level of costs, making more or less satisfactory profits, but with more capacity than was fully utilized. Greater volume promised lower costs and higher profits. The obvious means was to lower prices; but A & P's experience suggests that this course, so natural to the economist, is one which businessmen follow with some reluctance and dread. It seemed wiser, instead, to offer services which cost "only a little" more, were much more noticeable to prospective patrons than was a small price cut, and hence promised bigger increases in sales per dollar of outlay (or per dollar of sacrificed revenue). Therefore, credit, delivery, inclusion of slow-moving items in order to widen the selection, local advertising, and all-day operations were slowly reintroduced as competitor followed competitor. Slowly the cost structure rose as part of the benefits of the innovation were competed away. Some customers wanted these additions to the product, but others had no desire to pay for them.[34]

In the A & P stores, the expense rate rose steadily after 1919.[35]

---

between the cost of goods delivered to the place of business and the selling price of the goods. *Markup* is the gross profit divided by the delivered cost. *Margin* or *gross margin* is the gross profit divided by the selling price.

[33] See W. S. Hayward, "Chain Stores and Distribution," *The Annals*, 59: 220–225 (September 1924); "H. C. Bohack — This Chain System Finds That Price is Losing Its Appeal," *Printers Ink*, 144: 25–26 (July 19, 1928); A. M. Michener, "Chain Stores in the Grocery Field," *Commerce Monthly*, 10: 3–12 (December 1928).

[34] Professor Malcolm P. McNair has called this phenomenon "trading up." See his "Expenses and Profits in the Chain Grocery Business in 1929," Bulletin No. 84 (Bureau of Business Research, Harvard University, June 1931), pp. 13–21, especially the last paragraph. This discussion owes much to him and to Professor John D. Black.

[35] The growing importance of produce after 1919 and the very slow introduction of meat after 1923 were secondary factors.

Unit sales managers were busy men, responsible for a profitable showing with no time to measure elasticities of demand; conventional markups were increased a little here and there to cover the larger expenses, and gross margins rose along with expense rates. The process was one of infinitely small local gradations, false moves, competitive reprisals, and so on, but the end results are obvious. Insistence on lower prices as a means of attracting business was essentially a long-run idea; perhaps only from the top of the company structure could there be such a general view.

Renewed Expansion and Leveling Off, 1926–1929

A three-year plan incorporating the idea of lower prices was drawn up at the end of January 1927. Under four alternative assumptions, of which only the two extremes are shown in Table 2, sales were to reach $1 billion in 1929. The net profit rate (after tax) was to be 2 per cent, which would mean total profit after taxes of $20 million, or 25 per cent on the planned investment of $80 million.[36]

TABLE 2. A & P Sales Projection, 1926–1929

Year	Assumptions A and D on part of company	Number of stores at end of year (thousands)	Average weekly sales per store (dollars)	Total sales (millions of dollars)
1926	(actual)	14.8	762	574
1927	(A)	17.1	827	686
1927	(D)	16.3	847	686
1928	(A)	18.7	892	830
1928	(D)	18.0	930	830
1929	(A)	21.5	957	1,000
1929	(D)	20.0	1,011	1,000

Source. Adapted from Report No. 1, meeting of divisional sales directors, March 30, 1927, GX 109. Assumptions A and D are the most and least optimistic assumption, respectively.

By the first quarter of 1927, sales were already ahead of the program.[37] By November of that year, Hartford was hoping for

[36] DPM, January 27, 1927, GX 108.
[37] See Appendix Table 3.

weekly sales of $1,200 per store in the not too distant future, or roughly $1.2 billion in total annual sales.[38] Even as early as the spring of the year, it was reported that since the start of the campaign of advertising-cum-price cutting, many competitors were attempting to sidetrack well-known brands of merchandise and to push private-label goods on which they could not be undersold, in order to avoid following A & P price cuts.[39] The few jarring notes sounded at divisional presidents' meetings in 1927 and 1928 largely concern the angry reactions of manufacturers who resented price cuts on their goods.[40] In February of 1928, the billion-dollar goal was aimed at for that very year,[41] and was actually missed by only 4 per cent. Whereupon, in February 1929, the expansion program for the year was set at 23 per cent.[42] Like all men who make a practice of studying charts, the A & P high command knew how to extrapolate, and the sales line pointed into the blue.

But the first quarter of 1929 showed a decline in sales from the last quarter of 1928, quite contrary to the normal seasonal movement.[43] After the normal decline in the second quarter, sales again moved up in the third and fourth, but only moderately so; the year as a whole showed only an 8 per cent gain over 1928. And well before the year was over, at the end of June,[44] "the rise in almost every item of expense, and the increase in our gross profit rates . . . retarding our sales expansion, was considered alarming." Again a strong sales campaign was resolved upon. But by the end of October it was obviously not succeeding, and a divisional presidents' meeting found it "distinctly disappointing" that the upward trend in sales was halted for the first time since 1925.

Four reasons were given. (1) The organization had become too conservative, as evidenced by too high a net profit — that is, gross margins had been lowered too slowly when expenses were falling

[38] DPM, November 10, 1927, GX 111.

[39] Meeting of divisional purchasing directors, April 6, 1927, GX 404.

[40] See GX 107–112.

[41] Special presidents' meeting, February 2, 1928, GX 113.

[42] DPM, February 20, 1929, GX 116.

[43] In 1920–1921, during a rapid price decline, sales were steady; in every other year, there was an increase. The reference is to fiscal quarters, beginning respectively in March, June, September, and December. See Appendix Table 3.

[44] DPM, June 27, 1929, GX 118.

and raised too quickly when they were rising. The excessive profit was linked to a less aggressive attitude — it was considered a slack and careless way of doing business. (2) Competitors, "both chains and voluntary chains," had grown more efficient. (3) The store selection and development program had not been carried out. (4) Many stores had shown actual decreases in sales, indicating poor supervision,[45] a recurrent complaint.[46]

[45] DPM, October 24, 1929, GX 117.

[46] See DPM, January 27, 1927, DX 487: "The turnover rates for Managers and Office Employees were considered alarming." But by the latter part of the year, the rates were much lower. DPM, November 10, 1927, GX 111.

II

DECLINE, 1929-1936

"A policy of making too much money," 1929–1932

THE four years following the turn in A & P's sales curve are difficult to understand and harder to describe. The company was slowly drowning in its own good fortune.

There can be no doubt of the fortune. Profits climbed steadily to new peaks in 1929 and 1931–1932. Financial health was never better. In fact, it was much too good. As Appendix Tables 8–10 show, cash[1] piled up in unprecedented amounts. In 1929, liquid assets were barely in excess of our calculated "normal" amount; three years later, cash necessary for company business was, in round figures, $28 million, while total cash was practically 100 million — nearly four times as great. Appendix Table 9 shows clearly that this condition resulted from the combination of large profits with no expansion — even a slight contraction of operations.

Such stagnation was not planned. The onset of the 1929 depression offered A & P an opportunity to expand into areas newly sensitized to price competition, and this was clearly seen at the time. The divisional presidents' meeting of March 1930[2] was shown charts of wholesale price movements. "The softness of the food market since the stock market upset in October and the probable trend of prices for a long period of years following other great wars was thoroughly discussed. . . . All were of the opinion

---

[1] Includes a very small amount of marketable securities, mostly government bonds.

[2] DPM, March 18, 1930, GX 120.

that by promptly passing market declines on to our customers we can again procure a healthy increase in our volume of business."

But it did not happen. Sales slowly fell off after the last quarter of 1929, and the expense and gross profit rates rose. True, the dollar volume did not fall as rapidly for A & P as it did for the food trade in general. But in part this is explained by the ominous fact that A & P prices did not fall as quickly as urban food prices in general. In the three years following fiscal 1929, the Bureau of Labor Statistics food price index was successively 92, 76, and 63 per cent of the 1929 level; while the corresponding figures for the A & P retail price index were 94, 83, and 73.[3] In a word, the top management called for price reductions, the company was in excellent shape to cut faster than its competitors; nevertheless, the relative price of company goods was on the *increase*. The inability to enforce a price policy led to a reorganization of the divisional sales departments, but apparently with no visible effects.[4]

The year 1931 offers a strange contrast between the income statement of the company and its state of mind. For example, a Central Division meeting early in January almost disregarded profits, but noted that the expense rate was climbing with "alarming" speed.[5] A Central Western meeting held the same day [6] held a brief wake over 1930 and resolved to do better. At the divisional presidents' meeting in March,[7] "agreement was unanimous that too large a profit was made in the third and fourth quarter of 1930." As they had done five years previously, the meeting agreed that a low net profit rate and a high turnover were the correct policy, and that return on investment rather than margin on sales was the right criterion of success. They warned that "the rates of return on the investment decided upon [for the several divisions] are not to be exceeded."

John Hartford had never neglected the divisional meetings, and there was more reason than ever to pay attention to them. The end of the month found him in Chicago, conferring with the Mid-

[3] See Appendix Table 6.
[4] DPM, September 25, 1930, GX 426.
[5] January 7, 1931, GX 120.
[6] January 7, 1931, GX 121.
[7] DPM, March 5, 1931, GX 122.

dle Western group.[8] Since the 1929 turn, he explained, the fall in sales per store, the rise in the expense rate, and the even bigger rise in the gross profit were due to "getting away from the low price feature and . . . from our policy of selling only quality merchandise." He pointed out that the 71.5 per cent of all stores whose sales had *decreased* between the third quarters of 1929 and 1930 had earned a net profit of precisely 25 per cent *more*. The process had been as follows: the desired profit was (correctly) determined by multiplying the desired rate of return by the investment. Desired profit was then divided by expected sales to arrive at the net profit rate. This figure was in turn multiplied by the ratio of gross to net profit to obtain the gross. The root of the evil was not the procedure, but the fact that when sales had begun to fall off, the ratio of gross to net profit had been raised not only to compensate (which was wrong) but actually to overcompensate. Therefore both the rate and the amount of net profit were likewise too high.[9]

So far we have given the company's view — perhaps it would be both more generous and more accurate to call it Hartford's view — by direct quotation and paraphrase. It may also be put in the more familiar jargon. Because the retail food trade was only imperfectly competitive, it was possible for A & P to have a short-run price policy, and to raise or lower its prices relative to those of comparable retailers as its interests seemed to dictate. In this case, a combination of habit, inertia, and factors at which we can only conjecture had resulted in raising relative prices in such a way as greatly to increase net profits. Thus an unwilled result was exactly the one which would have been attained by a firm intent on maximizing its short-run gains — the usual textbook case. And it was exactly this type of success which made Hartford issue his alarums, and made the rest of the organization at least somewhat uneasy.

Attempts at better price control

But precisely in what sense did Hartford consider profits excessive? And furthermore, to what extent did he communicate his

[8] March 31, 1931, GX 124. The rest of the paragraph merely summarizes his remarks.

[9] See also DPM, June 25, 1931, GX 131.

fear or his reasons to the rest of the system? We can find only fragmentary evidence in this respect. Even so relatively articulate a group as A & P seem to play mostly by ear, and most of the essential assumptions and reasons are never stated. Perhaps some of them are never considered.

In June of 1931, Hartford complained not only that profits had been too high in 1930 but that the earnings planned for 1931 were being exceeded. Since these excessive profits resulted from lower volume, and resulted in still lower volume, they encouraged competitors.[10] Prices had been ordered cut and were not. Therefore, a new technique was necessary for controlling price policy to the necessary degree of closeness. The markup system was not abandoned. But it was made clear that to estimate the particular cost of each of thousands of items was an arbitrary procedure. By mid-1931 it was reasonably apparent that the joint-cost and common-cost problem could be solved on a higher level. If one considered the stores to be selling not groceries but grocery service, the payment for that service was obviously the spread, or gross margin, between total invoice costs and total selling prices in any given period. The margin ought to be the object of policy; individual prices could, as a matter of routine, be left to unit sales managers.

This realization was not in itself new: we have already seen that gross margin was in the forefront of the company's thinking even in 1926. Its re-emphasis during and after 1931 grew out of the need for better control of retail prices. The usual competitive practice was to make deep, even spectacular, cuts on conspicuous items, often selling them below full cost (including expenses) or even below invoice cost, and trying to make up the losses by raising prices on other items. But this was self-defeating. In effect, loss leaders are premiums or advertising — nonprice competition. Price-conscious consumers were aware of the higher prices on the other items, and did not buy them. It was easy for local people, pressed from above for aggressive sales action, to forget that A & P had grown great by introducing price competition, and to attempt

[10] DPM, June 25, 1931, GX 131. As an experiment, the Central Western Division profit was planned for only 11.32 per cent in order to regain volume. March 24, 1932, GX 140.

to outdo their neighbors at the latters' own game. Hence the continual year-in year-out resolutions at the headquarters and divisional levels, that "wholesaling," or selling below invoice cost plus three per cent, was to be discontinued immediately.[11]

But the 1931 thinking was more constructive. Not only were the unsystematic reductions to cease: the policy should henceforth be to maintain consistently low prices throughout the week, without attempting any weekend specials. In a word, it was a wager on the rationality of the consumer.

However, it is not at all clear to what extent this was disseminated throughout the organization. John Hartford visited the Central Western Division twice in May 1931. He explained that special drives were only temporary helps — peaks followed by valleys. Steady consistent gains were wanted, and these could be had only by consistently, not sporadically, offering cheaper goods, as well as by "revamping, remodeling, seeking better locations," etc. An experiment had already been carried out in Rochester, where the "organization has been completely sold on the new policy of discontinuing . . . sales on specially priced merchandise. . . . The entire line has been reduced," and apparently with very good results. Doubters were told not to worry about competition selling below cost; it could not be maintained. The effective countermove was to sell the whole line of goods cheaply.[12] A meeting of Central sales managers, held the next day, received the same doctrine, which, it was made plain, came from Hartford himself. Cuts were to be made even on commodities whose cost had not declined: the variations in gross margins on particular items were too large and too erratic, and should be evened out.[13]

Hartford was apparently keeping a close eye on this division, for by the end of June 1931 he attended a special meeting, exhorted

[11] This sounds very controversial but is not. The charge by the prosecution was that A & P sold below the sum of invoice cost plus retail expenses. See GB(DC) 636–7. This is entirely compatible with selling at invoice cost plus three per cent; few stores have ever had an expense rate of even six or nine per cent. For evidence of resolutions against "wholesaling," see the *Brief of Appellants* (AC), Appendix A, vol. 1, pp. 140–144.

[12] Meetings of May 11 and June 2, 1931, GX's 128 and 129.

[13] Meeting of June 3, 1931, GX 130.

it to greater performance, and emphasized that headquarters policy meant little if it were not carried out. A little plaintively he quoted, "Sometimes the body gets so large that the pulsations fail to reach its extremities." [14]

But the program ran into difficulties from the start. By the end of July, a meeting in Hartford's absence noted that "the present policy of certain drastic cut prices, leveling out the irregular lines, and maintaining consistently low prices all week without the need of additional weekend stimulants calls for the very best merchandising." [15] It called for some courage as well. By the end of August, it was evident that competitors were responding by drastic cuts on staples (such as butter, sugar, bread, etc.), which were lavishly advertised. The executive committee was plainly doubtful of its future course. [16]

There is no further mention of the program, either in the Central Western or any other division. Moreover, the records of the New England and Southern Divisions reveal that, if anything, the contrary policy was being followed; [17] in both divisions, the declared policy to feature individual specials turns up in 1932 and 1934. [18]

At any rate, during 1931 the relative price of A & P goods continued to increase, along with the expense rate and the gross profit rate. These three quantities are so interrelated that it would be illogical to call any of them the primary factor: if any one of them went up, the others did likewise. It was precisely this baffling circularity which made the discussions among A & P officers so fruitless. The New England Division, for example, could observe that it was burdened by too much expensive equipment, too many warehouses and meat storage plants, too elaborate a delivery service, too many stock takers. [19] "Our expense rate *seems to be*

[14] June 27, 1931, GX 134.

[15] July 29, 1931, GX 133.

[16] August 26, 1931, GX 163.

[17] New England Division: executive committee meetings of March 31, May 26, and October 7, 1931, GX's 125, 126, and 2627. Southern Division: meetings of March 13, 1931, GX 127, and August 13, 1931, DX 434.

[18] New England: meetings of December 30, 1932, and February 20, 1934, GX's 2635 and 2641. Southern: meetings of March 15 and April 25, 1934, GX's 9787 and 9789.

[19] Meeting of March 31, 1931, GX 125.

growing continually despite the fact that the volume is holding reasonably well" [20] (it was not holding up well at all). The same feeling of having lost control of the situation is reflected in the Central Division: the expense rate kept going up, and the gross profit up to offset it, "almost perpendicular. . . . Dangerous. . . . The trends pointed in the same direction as in 1925." [21] But the discussion of causes went no further than "lack of sales promotion."

In a word, the company was no longer setting its price policies: they were being set for the company. It was one thing to feel intuitively that the vicious circle must be broken, quiet another to see and point out that the mistake lay in passively meeting a situation instead of creating one. Perhaps Hartford could not inspire the organization to follow his policies (which were in themselves correct enough) because he was unable to explain precisely where the fault lay. The impending results were clearly foreshadowed in the Southern Division by August 1931. After expressing "keen disappointment" over the loss of sales and even of net profits, the low-margin policy was discarded: "It was felt that we would be justified in taking any extra profit that our sales might yield at this time when business apparently cannot be forced by the offering of low priced specials." [22] Thus all-week low prices were not even to be given a trial, and gross margin was to be raised because net profit was declining — although it was an excessive gross margin which was the original cause of the lower net.

Attempts at reform in 1932–1934

The year 1932 opened with a display of good intentions. Minutes of divisional meetings,[23] sometimes attended by John Hartford, record that all present resolved to be more aggressive, to banish "wholesaling" (selling at or below invoice cost plus three per cent), and to keep the gross profit down. But on this crucial last point,

---

[20] Meeting of October 7, 1931, GX 2627 (italics added).
[21] October 14, 1931, GX 136.
[22] Meeting of August 13, 1931, DX 434.
[23] GX's 137–142.

the will was plainly lacking. Thus, the Southern Division again showed that their concept of low gross margin was "attractive specials" instead of low prices throughout, and after all their good resolutions, they thought it was

still a question for debate as to whether it is not better business at this time to work on a somewhat higher gross profit than last year to combat an increased expense rate since it is granted that limited household budgets will not permit the laying in of large food supplies. . . .[24]

A month later, they recognized that "our trend of lower sales, higher expenses and higher gross profit rate is not in the right direction and not a healthy condition." But net profits had revived, and it was more comfortable to doubt, as they did, that the higher gross had actually sacrificed sales.[25]

A meeting of the New England Division in May 1932 was of the opinion that A & P prices seemed "right," but that

it seems that people have very little money with which to trade and it is very difficult to show an increase.

The feeling of the committee was that we *should discontinue talking about gross profit or expense rate* . . . and devote our entire time to concentrating on volume and enthusing the organization and in getting them into the right frame of mind.[26]

A better example of decadence could hardly be imagined. The old pattern of estimating expense and adding on a few points for net had been easy and successful. When difficulties arose, it was carried on by force of habit. But when a thought-out method of business — the calculation of income and outlay — continued to bring unsatisfactory results, the remedy selected was not better thinking but no thinking. Incantations would raise volume and "enthuse" the company back to success. One can hardly escape the likeness to the rat in the experimenter's maze. His accustomed path to food or water disrupted, he tries another and another; finally, unable to find the right path, he hurls himself blindly at the nearest obstacle, receiving for his pains a thorough self-inflicted beating.

It is possible that Hartford had caught wind of such thinking

[24] Meeting of June 1, 1932, DX 439.
[25] Meeting of July 20, 1932, DX 440.
[26] May 2, 1932, GX 2629 (italics added).

in New England; at any rate, he paid a visit there a month later,[27] and explained his position at length. "The Company as a whole operated on a policy of making too much money during the past two years which [he forebore to say I told you so] enabled competition, both chain and voluntary chain, to develop their own business." Perhaps most important and most ominous was the decline in tonnage sales. "He felt pleased at the recent change in policy to operating at a low gross profit. . . . The customer of today is the shopper of tomorrow . . . all customers are out to get as much as possible for their money."

His statement was almost a point-by-point refutation of the division's. And he made it clear that the company's liquid assets were unusually large, ample for the financing of the low-profit, high-volume program.

The other divisions were not as openly heretical, but their performance was not much better. At a Central Western meeting in January 1933, Hartford offered to let the division operate with no operating profit whatever for a limited time if they would lower prices and regain lost volume. The minutes break into capital letters at this point: LOWER EXPENSE RATE   INCREASED TONNAGE   INCREASE IN CUSTOMERS. Perhaps a corps of cheer leaders would have been more effective than Hartford and the president of the division:

Mr. Hartford and Mr. Toolin urged that we take hold of this proposition sincerely and honestly [since] . . . the policy that has been outlined cannot result in anything but what we are seeking. Experience over the years [has] always shown that an aggressive sales policy, with a steady increase in the volume of business, without fail, turns the expense rate line in the right direction.[28]

It is obvious from the context that the policy, or rather the philosophy of price making as active rather than passive, seemed like a novelty, and possibly a dangerous one. The Southern Division, during 1933, seemed more concerned with the need for immediate retail price increases as soon as wholesale prices went up.[29]

[27] June 16, 1932, GX 143.
[28] Central Western Division, January 13, 1933, GX 146.
[29] June 1, 1933, DX 443; September 19, 1933, DX 445.

There is no evidence that anything ever came of the plan suggested to Central Western; certainly the data on relative prices, sales, and expense and gross profit rates, all point the other way.[30] *Business Week* summed up for the executives of all food chains: "They are now being converted to the theory that it is better to do less volume at a profit." [31]

During the slow revival of 1933–1934, A & P sales actually declined, even in dollar terms. This should have been clear warning of a deteriorating position, but only in the relatively successful Middle Western Division was there some wonderment as to why sales and profits were not increasing and this

led to a discussion of the basis for predicting the gross. . . Having determined the expense rate, a certain number of points is added for net, and this determines what the gross profit prediction will be. *The basis for gross profit predictions should be entirely a separate thing from the expense.* It has to do with the fixing of retail prices through the entire line with due consideration given to competitors' prices, etc. . . .[32]

The theory was for once correct, but the action did not follow.

Attempts to close losing stores

We have seen that the policies of all-week low prices and of lower gross profit to induce volume both fell into the void of habitual practices and expired quietly there. The last major error of the pre-NRA days lay in not closing the low-volume stores.

The problem was of long standing. Chart I shows that below a certain sales volume, a grocery or combination store could not hope to be profitable. Considering the fact that 1927, 1929, 1934, and 1935 are so widely different, the stability of the pattern is all the more striking. Although the A & P executives never made any such graphical analysis, they were well aware of this relationship. It was understood in January 1927,[33] and a generally accepted truism in 1928, that the unprofitable stores were the very small

---

[30] See Appendix Table 3.

[31] "Chains' Heads Watch Sales Drop: Turn From Volume To Profit," *Business Week*, June 1, 1932, p. 9.

[32] September 5, 1934, GX 3456 (italics added).

[33] DPM, January 27, 1927, DX 487, and see DPM, November 27, 1927, DX 488.

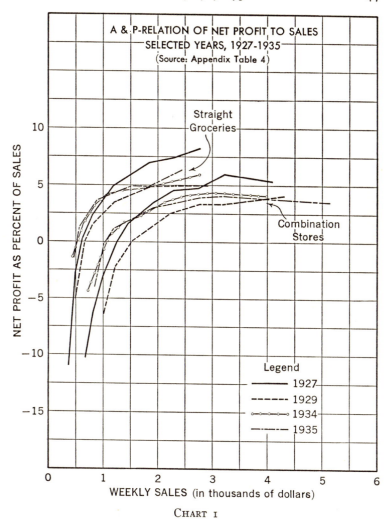

A & P-RELATION OF NET PROFIT TO SALES
SELECTED YEARS, 1927-1935
(Source: Appendix Table 4)

Straight Groceries

Combination Stores

Legend
———— 1927
------ 1929
○—○—○—○ 1934
—·——·— 1935

NET PROFIT AS PERCENT OF SALES

WEEKLY SALES (in thousands of dollars)

CHART I

ones, and that either sales ought somehow to be increased or these stores closed.[34] Instead, the drain grew steadily larger. As Appendix Table 12 shows, stores losing money went from 13.4 per cent of all stores in 1929 to 25.8 per cent in 1934, and their combined losses

[34] Special meeting of divisional presidents, February 9, 1928, GX 113.

rose from 7.2 to 19.5 per cent of total profits. But more revealing of the company's morale is the fact that the percentage of losing stores which the company closed fell from 21.1 to 6.6 per cent. The worse the performance of A & P, the more it needed to get rid of the incubus, the less it tried.

Why was it impossible to take such an obvious and obviously beneficial step? The answer is suggested by discussions in September 1929 at a meeting of divisional sales directors.[35] Since volume had not increased much that year, the suggestion was made that additional small stores be opened to absorb the overhead of the warehouses. Thus, even though they lost money on a full-cost basis, if they returned something over out-of-pocket costs, they would be a net benefit. This sort of textbook reasoning on marginal revenue and marginal cost was entirely sound, but within very narrow limits. The meeting recognized them: the small stores might be worth while *if the gross profit remained high enough* to allow some surplus over expenses; but if the gross profit were to be lowered, the stores would be a dead loss. Again, as with the price policy, an action correct in the short run was very ill-advised in the long. Once established, the small stores became a positive barrier to lowering the gross profit rate. Thus they reinforced the inertia which was creeping over the organization and freezing it into existing molds.[36]

For example, the Central Division noted in January 1931 [37] that red-ink stores were 28 per cent of the total during the preceding quarter. They were recognized as a serious drag on the division. Many were "undoubtedly" past revival, and "often" it would be better to close them. Then a highly revealing sentence: "Courage is needed in dealing with red-ink stores." At a June meeting, "this was considered one of our most difficult problems. . . . The stores were gone over in detail and . . . the sales managers indicated that plans had already been formed to take care of them." [38] Later

[35] September 25, 1929, GX 119.
[36] For a different explanation, see *Fortune*, "A & P Goes to the Wars," April 1938, p. 97. The delay is blamed there on "paternalism." The writer, however, has seen only one reference (in 1937) to the personnel of closed stores; see below, Chapter III.
[37] Advisory board meeting, January 7, 1931, GX 123.
[38] June 3, 1931, GX 130.

that month, at a special meeting to discuss chain store taxes, "the talks centered on the small stores. . . . It was believed that the little store would gradually disappear from the picture especially in the cities."[39] Significantly, the two other references to red-ink stores made that year are progressively weaker and more "inspirational" in tone.[40]

A Middle Western meeting in March 1931 was attended by John Hartford. In explaining the dangers of a high gross profit rate, he pointed out that not only was it undesirable in itself, but it encouraged "an unhealthy development" — the opening of stores doing between seven and eight hundred dollars of sales per week. He added that they might pay in the short run, but that the lower gross profit, at which the organization must aim, would make it necessary to close them.[41]

But the dangers of such action seemed too great. A Central Western meeting in April 1932 [42] solemnly resolved "to remove all hopeless red figure stores." But units were warned to investigate them carefully, "for it must be kept in mind that closing these ruthlessly may automatically throw a further group of stores which are now profitable, into this same classification." This was a somewhat different way of noting that closing the stores would impose a greater burden of overhead. And if nothing were involved but the red-ink stores, then it would of course have been folly to close them and sacrifice an incremental revenue larger than the corresponding incremental cost. What seems obvious, however, is that such closing was a part of a larger campaign to decrease gross margin first and bring expense rates down in its wake. The original sin was in assuming a passive and rigid policy; the consequences drawn were entirely logical.

The same Central Western Division, meeting nine months later,[43] was obviously no nearer a solution. The final decision was as timid as ever: "Those that were in the red during our best years of 1928 and 1929 should certainly be closed." This comment is worth more than a good many statistics. For data on losing stores

---

[39] June 28, 1931, GX 134.
[40] October 14, 1931, GX 136; December 28, 1931, GX 131.
[41] March 31, 1931, GX 124.
[42] April 15, 1932, GX 170.
[43] January 11, 1933, GX 148.

as a class do not indicate whether the losers have been consistently so, or whether stores keep crossing and recrossing the margin of profitability from year to year. But as this one remark makes perfectly clear, the problem was one of stores which had lost money even during the best years, and had then stayed in the red for five or six years.

Thereafter, the problem was virtually ignored.[44] Red-ink stores were, indeed, mentioned from time to time in the minutes of the various divisions; at an Eastern meeting they were characterized as a "drag to the stores with the better volume"; and Hartford, who attended the meeting, "expressed himself as being very much alarmed regarding the number of stores losing money consistently for four years." [45] It is not necessary to annotate the many other meetings of a similar tone; in not a single one were definite plans made for correcting the losing stores. A Central meeting in May 1933 was back on the old theme: "It was not thought advisable to close these small stores as long as they were able to carry their share of the general overhead and break even." [46]

Political burdens, 1933–1936: NRA, Robinson-Patman, chain-store taxes

We have seen that following the turn in early 1929, the company drifted along for about four years; in retrospect it is easy to see how its position was deteriorating. Presently the respite was over. It seems to be the rule that once the tide of business fortune begins to ebb, there are always currents which "happen to be" flowing in the same direction. In the case of A & P, we certainly cannot blame the NRA, the chain-store taxes, the Robinson-Patman Act, and similar troubles, on defective management. But our thesis is that they would have been mere irritants for a healthy growing concern. The real threat — the supermarket — is a story in itself, to be told later.

---

[44] The New England Division occasionally resolved that the unprofitable low-volume stores ought to be closed. See the meetings of November 3, 1933; February 20, 1934; January 3, 1936 — after the divisional president had resigned. GX's 9438, 9452, 9497. There was also occasional mention in the Central Division and the Eastern.

[45] May 17, 1932, DX 504.

[46] May 23, 1933, GX 149.

This is not the place for any but the sketchiest discussion of the retail grocery code of the NRA. In September 1933, Hartford was rather apprehensive of its effects: "it will undoubtedly place certain restrictions and burdens upon our operation." Nevertheless, particularly if competitors also obeyed the rules "the industry as a whole" might benefit, he thought. At any rate, no predictions or plans were made for the fourth quarter of the year, when the code was scheduled to go into effect.[47]

The company was unfavorably affected in four ways. First, although wage and hour provisions had very little direct effect in raising labor costs,[48] as Table 3 shows, there were frequent complaints that competitors, especially independent retailers, were not obeying the code.[49]

TABLE 3. A & P Labor Force and Wages Under NRA

Week ending —	No. of part-time clerks	No. of full-time clerks	Wages, part-time	Wages, full-time	Wages, total
(1) July 29, 1933	26,579	56,285	$137,361	$1,621,142	$1,758,503
(2) Aug. 19, 1933 [a]	31,265	63,935	167,468	1,801,161	1,968,629
(3) Increase over (1)	4,686	7,650	30,107	180,019	210,126
(4) Feb. 23, 1935	30,503	57,807	165,894	1,666,894	1,832,347
(5) Increase over (1)	3,924	1,522	32,533	45,752	73,844

[a] Highest week since NRA began.

Second, although the code did not actually fix any prices, it set certain standards by which retailers had to abide. For example, transportation charges had to be added to invoice cost, instead of being absorbed by the warehouse. Moreover, minimum markups prevented the company from offering merchandise at lower prices. "No longer are the prices of our staples attractive to the con-

[47] Central Western Division, September 20, 1933, DX 177.

[48] *Annual Binder*, 1935, DX 495. (The *Annual Binder* was prepared every year for A & P management, and contained many important statistical series.) Hereafter referred to as *Annual Binder*.

[49] Southern Division, October 16, 1934, GX 2737. Central Division, July 16, 1934, GX 157. New England Division, May 9, 1934, GX 443. These are only examples; there are a good many others, but it is impossible to separate fact from rumor.

sumer. With the markup and transportation charges added, we lose the advantage over the independent merchant."[50] In fact the independent, less fearful of the law, now undercut both the code and A & P, and it must have humiliated company officers to run to code authorities as their only recourse.[51] In August 1934, a Southern board meeting put it perhaps a little too strongly:

We have little if any advantage over the independent or cooperative groups. . . . We cannot emphasize retail price advantage because generally speaking we haven't got it. But there still are a few advantages which we do have, and they are: higher average quality and more efficient and courteous service, besides cleaner and more inviting stores in which to shop.[52]

So far did A & P seem to have drifted from its original supremacy, based upon the introduction of price competition. However, this was somewhat exaggerated. A survey by the Central Division, carried on at about the same time, "showed our retail prices on a great majority of the items lower than our principal chain store competitors."[53] As will be shown later, the most important competition was from the independents rather than from the other corporate chains.

Third, in a number of codes covering the manufacture and sale of foods at wholesale, it was made illegal for a purchasing office to collect brokerage on sales for its parent organization. It is not clear, however, how great a burden this actually was. As Appendix Table 22 shows, the company's brokerage income actually increased from 1932 to 1933, although it declined the next year; the income from its produce purchasing agency (the Atlantic Commission Company) increased throughout. Doubtless brokerage income would have been larger but for the NRA; but the loss was very hard to measure, and probably not very large in relation to the total company income.[54]

[50] J. J. Byrnes to the Central Division, May 22, 1934, GX 154.
[51] Central Division, meeting of sales managers, October 2, 1934, GX 160. Central Western Division, November 6, 1933, DX 179.
[52] August 22, 1934, GX 159. See also October 16, GX 2737.
[53] October 2, 1934, GX 160.
[54] When the Millers Code had just been signed, the Central Division meeting of June 18, 1934, estimated that their brokerage loss on flour would run to about $600,000 per annum (GX 155). But we have not seen any further mention of such losses.

Fourth, the food-processing codes also attempted to equalize discounts and allowances which manufacturers granted for cash payment, advertising services real or fictitious, etc.[55] Unquestionably these provisions had some effect. Income from this source, which had been $8.48 million in 1932, fell to $7.72 and $6.58 million during the next two years. Since it recovered to $7.9 million in 1935, it appears a fair inference that the reduction was due to the NRA rather than to the general deterioration of A & P sales and buying power.[56]

By mid-May 1935, administration of the codes was collapsing in the wake of the Supreme Court decision, and the status quo ante was being very quickly restored.[57] But the respite was very short. In 1936, the Robinson-Patman Act re-enacted the NRA grocery codes. The steam behind the new law was much greater, it was aimed directly at chain stores,[58] the Federal Trade Commission was designated to enforce it, and the effect was felt almost at once. "Advertising allowances" for 1936 fell to $4.74 million, and then to $3.01 million in 1937. There was a nice coincidence of the political and economic drift. Many a supplier found his markets reviving simultaneously with his conscience. He realized with modest horror that he had been living in sin with A & P and hastened to break off the alliance.[59]

Last on the list of irritants was the chain-store tax. It was not a new one: there had been discussions as far back as 1927,[60] and in that year four states enacted them. By the end of 1936, forty-eight such laws had been passed, and despite many invalidations, eleven were still in effect. Nor was the campaign over: by mid-1941, there would be twenty-one more such laws passed, with nine

---

[55] See the testimony of Paul S. Willis, president of the Grocery Manufacturers of America, Tr. 153.

[56] See Appendix Table 22. *Fortune*, April 1938, page 134, mentions "the rather amazing total of $6,105,000 for the year 1934," which was revealed to a Congressional investigating committee the following year.

[57] C. W. Parr to J. V. Beckmann, May 16, 1935. It is cited in the record at Tr. 280, but is not a separate exhibit.

[58] See Mr. Patman's remark on the morrow of the bill's passage: "There is no place for chain stores in the American system."

[59] This will be discussed at length in the chapters on purchasing of processed foods.

[60] DPM, November 10, 1927, GX 111.

remaining effective.[61] The effect on the company is shown in Table 4.[62]

TABLE 4. Taxes on A & P, 1932–1938 (millions of dollars)

Year	Social security	Sales & chain store	Other	Total operating	Income taxes	Total
1932	0	.65	2.9	3.5	3.8	7.3
1935	0	2.2	4.0	6.2	2.6	8.8
1936	1.0	2.1	5.1	8.3	4.1	12.4
1937	3.0	2.4	4.8	10.2	2.0	12.2
1938	4.1	2.1	3.9	10.1	3.6	13.7
Increase, 1932–1938	4.1	1.5	1.0	6.6	− .2	6.4
Increase in per cent	. .	227	36	187	−7	87

Source. *Annual Binder*, 1939, DX 499.

Two things are apparent: first that the chain-store taxes were by no means the heaviest tax burden the company was carrying; secondly, that Hartford's nonchalance in 1928 ("The public . . . would not countenance radical legislation that would penalize efficient distribution") was mistaken.[63] But sweet may be the uses of penalty taxation: they were a spur to the establishment of fewer and larger stores.[64] In the writer's judgment, the chain-store taxes were a blessing to A & P.

Deterioration, 1933–1937

Table 5 is a convenient summary of the years we have just described. Looking at it as an officer of the company might have done in 1936, we can find much justification for complacence. The physical volume of sales was below the 1933 peak, but higher

[61] The regional distribution is interesting. Four out of five border states, and eight out of eleven southern states passed and sustained chain-store taxes. Of the other eight, four were in the Rocky Mountain area, and four in the midwest. Roy G. Blakey and Gladys O. Blakey, "Chain Store Taxation, Part 1," in *Taxes* (October 1941), pp. 595–6.

[62] *Annual Binder*, vol. 14, 1939, DX 499.

[63] DPM, August 16, 1928, GX 114.

[64] Blakey and Blakey, "Chain Store Taxation, Part 2," in *Taxes* (November 1941), p. 672.

than the last prosperity year. The company's share of its most relevant market was down only one percentage point, although this had been done by raising relative prices. The embarrassingly high profits of 1930–1932 had disappeared, and the return on investment, most important figure of all, was far down. But it was still very much higher than that of most corporations in the mid-

TABLE 5. A & P Sales, Market Share, and Profits, 1929–1936

	Sales index numbers		A & P sales as per cent of sales of			Profits, before tax (millions of dollars)	Per cent rate of return
Year	Dollars	Tons	All food stores	All grocery and combination stores	All chain G. & C. stores		
1929	100	100	9.5	14.1	36.7	29.5	26.6
1933	78	106	11.9	16.1	27.7	23.9	15.0
1935	83	100	10.3	13.6	34.9	19.2	11.9
1936	86	105	9.9	13.0	34.2	20.4	12.7

Sources. Appendix Tables 2, 5, 6, 7.

1930's. It seemed as though the business had settled into a very comfortable maturity. The fact that a recovery in dollar sales of 11 per cent from 1933 to 1936 was accompanied by a decline in profits of 15 per cent could doubtless have been argued away. In fact, anxiety about the company's future could only have been based on rather vague projections of recent history.[65] The gradual loss of supremacy and of extremely high profits were pretty well understood and, we will conjecture, accepted. The threat of swift extinction by the supermarket was harder to imagine. Let us explore each in turn.

"We have been educating the independent grocer to become more efficient." In these words the president of the Middle Western Division summed up the common impression of A & P management.[66] Late in 1935, the Central Western Division discussed

[65] Vague, perhaps, but meaningful. See Carl N. Schmalz, "Expenses and Profits of Food Chains in 1934," Bulletin No. 99, Bureau of Business Research, Harvard University (April 1936), pp. 9–10. Prof. Schmalz expected that "in the future chain food companies . . . will find themselves increasingly vulnerable to competition from new types of low-cost distributors." A & P would have been well advised to be alert to see the new types.

[66] At a special board meeting of the division, September 13, 1933. See also the Central Western meeting, July 29, 1931, GX 133.

a questionnaire among housewives in Cleveland, in the neighboring Central Division. "The survey indicates quite clearly that our competition is largely with the independents, [who] are more efficient today and are operating on a low expense rate." Moreover, this was considered to hold true throughout both the divisions.[67] An earlier survey in the Central Division "showed our retail prices on a great majority of the items lower than our principal chain store competitors." [68]

The voluntary chains — federations of independent retailers or wholesalers — were nothing new; one is known to have flourished in Philadelphia in 1892.[69] They imitated the chains by pooling their purchases; on the selling side, they relied on standardized store fronts, common advertising in and out of newspapers, and the lower prices their joint operation permitted. We have no data with which to compare their warehousing operations with that of A & P, but there seems to be no reason why they should have been any less efficient. In fact, we would generally suppose the latecomer to know about as many tricks of the trade, and be burdened with less physical, financial, and intellectual overhead. Data compiled by the Federal Trade Commission seem to confirm the superiority of the voluntary chains to independents and corporate chains, on the average.[70]

By the middle of 1932, John Hartford considered the voluntaries to be "making great strides." [71] Four and one half years later, a Central Division meeting found itself dismayed at "the inroads made into the food business by the voluntary chains. . . . Apparently we are holding our own with the corporate chain and the small independent." [72]

[67] Meeting of November 25, 1935, GX 170.
[68] Meeting of October 2, 1934, GX 160.
[69] C. L. King, "Can the Cost of Distributing Food Products be Reduced?" *The Annals*, 48:199–224 (July 1913).
[70] Federal Trade Commission, *Report on Distribution Methods and Costs*, Part I (1944), pp. 206–215. Unfortunately this material refers to 1939, and contains some obvious incomparabilities. But see the testimony of Paul S. Willis, Tr. 154–180. In 1945, there were about 1,000 chains in existence, and about 20,000 retailer-owned wholesale warehouses.
[71] Eastern Division, May 17, 1932, GX 504.
[72] Meeting of December 3, 1936, GX 186, which continues: "The company is aware of this trend and seems determined to take steps to get a better share of the new deal [*sic*] prosperity."

What was to be done about this new competition? Broadly speaking, there were two possibilities: either the company could make some drastic change in its own methods, or else it could leave the system basically unchanged, but slough off any imperfections it might have gathered in the course of time. We have seen that John Hartford and those around him thought in terms of the second type of possibility, which was not carried into effect. The thinking of the lower echelons, up to the middle of 1935, seems almost completely barren. But there is some ground for believing that it was now the top which was less receptive to new ideas.

For example, there was the possibility of moving stores to better but more expensive locations. When, in 1931, the Central Western Division was assigned an especially low profit to earn, they resolved to take better locations.[73] And doubtless there was no objection to the expense. But many sites could only be had on long-term leases, and George L. Hartford was implacably opposed (in 1933, 94 per cent of all store leases ran for only one year).[74] The financial conservatism of the older brother may have served the company well. His care that the company's $47 millions of government securities all be in maturities of less than one year, because the federal budget was not balanced,[75] probably cost the company something near half a million dollars a year in interest foregone. The natural conjecture that George Hartford might have been as conservative in operation as in finance will be borne out later.

The Central Division meeting which resolved on "the necessity of doing something spectacular and unusual [in large combination stores] in order that they may enjoy the volume of business necessary to offset their high cost of operation" [76] was making a prognosis perhaps more accurate than it realized. It was not difficult to draw up estimates showing how much increased business would

[73] May 11, 1931, GX 138. The New England Division complained that the First National chain was able to take better locations since they were willing to sign leases for 15 or 20 years. Meeting of February 20, 1934, GX 2641. Of course, the report may have been exaggerated. But it is a far cry from a one-year lease.

[74] *Fortune*, March 1933, p. 129.

[75] *Fortune*, March 1933, p. 129.

[76] Meeting of September 1, 1932, DX 172.

lower the expense rates, thereby permitting both lower gross and larger net profit. But there was no definite idea of just what the "spectacular and unusual" action was to be.

There was some tightening-up of buying procedures early in 1934, with headquarters taking more direct charge; [77] as might be expected, the divisions greeted this with little enthusiasm, although there were no audible complaints.[78] But the 1934 reform program was timid, almost trivial. Five-year leases were permitted, but none might run over five thousand dollars; in fact, no contracts of any kind could be made which obligated the company for more, except when merchandise was regularly ordered in such amounts. Company brands were to be promoted more actively. There was to be better control of petty cash in the stores, because there had been "some peculation," and auditing was to be generally tightened up. Statistical reports were to be more carefully prepared. More economy was needed in all kinds of operations. That was all; one seeks in vain for a general view of the progress and needs of the business.[79]

In April of 1935, there was a National Meat Meeting at headquarters. R. L. Pierce of the Central Division spoke for the whole group when he observed that the reason for low volume and consequent losses in meat departments was not poor quality, "but the fact that our markets were equipped to do two to three times the business they were now enjoying, which adversely [affected] their expense rate." [80] Here and there it had been possible to reduce gross profit rates, build volume, lower expense, and thus earn a profit. But there was no discussion of how this might be done generally.

In fact, there seems to have been something of a retrogression in company thinking during 1934 and 1935. A Central Western meeting in June 1934 heard John Hartford say that his chief concern was the shrinkage in physical volume, "which now, as in the past, always leads to a higher cost of doing business *with the*

[77] Divisional purchasing directors, meeting of March 27, 1934, GX 434.
[78] New England meeting, March 13, 1934, GX 433. Central Division meeting, April 9, 1934, GX 442. The decision had been made by a divisional presidents' meeting which is not in the record.
[79] GX 257.
[80] April 30, 1936, GX 164.

necessity of increasing our gross profit to take care of it." [81] He seemed to have forgotten that price might determine demand as well as vice versa. Even the old rule of not selling below cost was relaxed late in 1935, the divisional president now being given discretion.[82]

However, as usually happens, deterioration and regeneration were proceeding at the same time, and 1936–1937 would see the issue resolved. By that time, all discussion centered around the supermarket.

The supermarket

Fortune once described the supermarket as "a very big self-service store surrounded by a certain amount of ballyhoo." [83] Today, the ballyhoo is largely gone, the size and self-service are too familiar to elaborate. As usual, nobody knows where and how they started.[84] Their development on a large scale seems to have taken place first in Southern California, as might be expected of an area so automobile-minded. But if large parking spaces made it possible to attract the driving public, lower costs and prices actually drew them.

The Great Depression, as A & P had realized so helplessly, offered price competition its greatest opportunity. But it is significant that supermarkets did not begin to open at a rapid pace until the latter half of 1932; apparently it took at least the abortive upturn of those months to thaw out a little of the spirit of enterprise. As usually happens, the inherent advantages of this new type of store were both accentuated and disguised by some of the transitory ones. Abandoned factories on the outskirts of metropolitan areas were especially favored as locations, partly because of the very low rentals at which they could often be had, partly because there was usually a second floor which could be used as a warehouse. One of the earliest stores (in Jamaica, New

---

[81] June 12, 1934, GX 156 (italics added).
[82] Middle Western Division, October 2, 1935, GX 180. Since John Hartford was present at the meeting, the report may be called authoritative.
[83] April 1938, p. 138.
[84] The following paragraphs are based on Charles F. Phillips, "The Supermarket," *Harvard Business Review*, 16.2.188–200 (Winter 1938).

York) used empty boxes and cases for its fixtures. Like the chain stores, the supermarkets could buy in large amounts; self-warehoused, they could often lay down goods in their stores at a lower cost than an A & P store; self-served, they could sell at prices lower than competitors' and yet make very large profits. The proprietors of one of the best-known opened it late in 1932, in an abandoned automobile factory in Elizabeth, New Jersey. They invested $10,000; sales the first year were over $2.0 million, and the net profit was $167 thousand, or over 16 times the investment. As with the early A & P economy stores, these were typical profits of innovation.

It seems impossible to draw any accurate picture of the cost-price structure of the early supermarkets: Professor Phillips was able to offer only the most fragmentary indications.[85] As the next best thing, it is possible to compare the operations of all A & P stores in 1937 with those of A & P supermarkets in the Central Western Division in 1938. This comparison in Table 6 has at least the advantage that the accounting classifications are homogeneous; and that, in general, the method of conducting the business is the

TABLE 6. Analysis of A & P's Expense Rates — All Stores, 1937,
and Central Western Supermarkets, 1938
(in per cent of sales)

Item	All A & P stores, 1937	All supermarkets, Central Western Division, 1938, average sales per store per week (thousands of dollars)				
		4.1	6.1	8.4	12.4	17.5
Clerks' salaries	3.76	3.52	3.41	3.55	3.53	3.44
General branch	2.70	2.13	1.72	1.53	1.57	1.84
Advertising	0.60	1.04	0.80	0.85	0.70	0.80
Handling and delivery	2.51	1.16	1.16	1.01	0.98	0.96
Rent and write-off	1.39	2.44	1.78	1.55	1.23	1.10
Managers' salaries	4.75	2.53	1.75	1.32	1.10	0.74
Supervision and administration	1.94	1.58	1.01	0.72	0.49	0.34
Total	17.65	14.40	11.63	10.53	9.60	9.22

Source. For 1937, computed from *Annual Binder*, vol. 15, DX 500; for 1938, computed from *Annual Binder*, vol. 14, DX 499.

[85] *Harvard Business Review*, 16.2:191, 198.

same, save only for the one critical feature of regular store versus supermarket operation.

As Table 6 shows, the great saving of the supermarket operation (as distinct from savings in purchasing) was in supervisory labor and in the traditional items of overhead — rent, depreciation, taxes, and the losses incurred in opening new stores.[86]

To a certain extent, the declining expense rate reflects increasing economy as a given plant is more fully utilized. But this is largely eclipsed by the influence of varying the plant itself. In short, the table represents the long-run cost curve. There is no doubt that it was so regarded by the A & P management.[87]

It seems very likely (see also Chartz, p. 79) that the $17- to $20-thousand class was the minimum point. There are no signs of any yielding on the part of the constant ratios (i.e., the variable costs), and there is little or no room for further reduction in the decreasing ratios (i.e., the costs of indivisible factors). But this is not to say that the many independent supermarkets with sales higher than $20,000 were past the scale of minimum cost: the proprietors probably did not know, and we certainly do not. The point is simply that if we set aside, as does the chart, all the accidental advantages of opening in the depths of a depression, the supermarket could profitably sell goods at prices which would be ruinous to a conventional store.

It was this simple fact which A & P would not recognize. Their blindness is astounding, because as far back as 1927, at a divisional presidents' meeting, the chairman of the Southern Division reported that "they had adopted the Self-Service Method in some

---

[86] The last-named item was around 0.3 per cent.

[87] See the Middle Western meeting, August 26, 1940, GX 293: "Our expense rates by volume groups show interesting possibilities. The curve indicates that a rate of 12 per cent is accomplished at a volume level somewhere between $6,000 and $6,500. From this point the line goes down fairly rapidly, to 11 per cent at a volume between $7,500 and $8,000. Then from this point on, progress is comparatively slow, and at the $10,000 sales level the rate is approximately .1035. We still think Headquarter's belief in a 10 per cent expense rate at $10,000 volume is possible. . . . Current expense rates are influenced strongly by the comparatively heavy store closing program of the second quarter." See also the Southern Division meeting of August 1, 1938, GX 466 (where John Hartford referred to "the $10,000 Supermarket type store as the epitome of the program"); and the Atlantic Division, February 16, 1940, GX 3192. Also see Chapter IV.

stores in Texas and it has proved very successful." [88] And in 1928, several divisions had experimented with large self-service stores. The conclusions drawn were, in the light of hindsight, entirely correct: that large economies were possible, but that size and location had to be carefully selected and controlled; and that there ought to be such experimenting in all divisions.[89] Nothing more was heard of these early trials.

Surely it is a revealing fact that when A & P was at the height of its success in carrying on with the old methods, the minds of its personnel were not closed to new ideas; they could recall that innovation was the father of their company. Yet at the first adverse blast, the attitude became defensive rather than inquiring, in search of arguments against the new, rather than facts about it. How else can we explain the failure to try any more such experiments at a time when everyone in the company professed to be worried about falling sales, when the Hartfords were willing to allow a whole division to work with no operating profit, and when liquid funds were so ample and profits so large as to be embarrassing?

"We did not take it very seriously at first," said John Hartford in 1945.[90] This attitude was general among chain stores.[91] But perhaps the reactions at the divisional level are more important. The earliest one known to the writer was at the Central Western meeting of March 18, 1932,[92] where it was felt, correctly enough, "that some serious consideration should be given to this new method of retailing as undoubtedly they are securing a very large amount of business." A month later, *Business Week*, referring to them as "warehouse stores," reported that "A & P stores [in Detroit] have fought fire with fire, conducted a 'Gigantic Food Sale' using much the same advertising tactics. . . ."[93] But there was no hint of similar *sales* tactics. Early in 1933, *Business Week*,

[88] DPM, November 10, 1927, DX 488.
[89] Meeting of divisional sales directors, January 23, 1929, GX 115. According to verbal information, the self-service stores in the Chicago area were very successful.
[90] Testimony, Tr. 20,438.
[91] Testimony of Professor Malcolm P. McNair, Tr. 17,183.
[92] Central Western meeting, March 18, 1932, DX 169.
[93] "Now Come Warehouse Stores to Threaten the Food Chains in Detroit," *Business Week*, April 20, 1932, p. 9.

although it referred to them rather scornfully as "cheap-jack," pointed to intrinsic economies and considered that "their price-wrecking activities can be fatal even to chain stores." [94] Three months later, the journal noted that "Super Markets Breed Fast," and ascribed this to operating economies.[95] A little earlier, another business journal had estimated the sale of the average "Big Bear" at a hundred times those of the average A & P store.[96] This was probably a gross exaggeration; but it was essentially correct, and a sufficient explanation for the low operating costs. And as early as September 1934, the supermarkets had traveled so far from the old days of crates for counters and old warehouses for stores that the *Architectural Record* ran a discussion of the layout of a super-market.[97]

These scattered items indicate only that to the general public and the business public, these stores had established themselves and would continue to grow. But one looks in vain for any recognition of this fact by A & P management during those years. The NRA furnished an opportunity for explaining away the super-markets' success on the ground that they did not abide by the labor or price provisions, and, as we would expect, it was the New England Division which resorted to it.[98] Again, in September of 1934, the meeting was told that if supermarket prices were met in A & P stores immediately adjoining, *"it has been found* that the supermarkets gradually either readjust their prices on to a reasonable price basis, or else curtail their operations, or go out of business." [99] Two months later, in John Hartford's presence, the head of the division resigned.[100]

In July of the same year, an aggressive supermarket operator had opened a price war in Cincinnati, Kroger had met it, "and the price structure will probably be demoralized as a result."

[94] "Cheaping Thrives, Cheap-Jack Cash and Carry Depots," *Business Week*, February 8, 1933, pp. 11–12.
[95] "Super Markets Breed Fast," *Business Week*, June 10, 1933, p. 9.
[96] O. F. Rust, "Super Market X-Ray," *Advertising and Selling*, 20:17–18 (April 13, 1933).
[97] "Big Bear Shopping Center," *Architectural Record*, 76:204–205 (September 1934).
[98] Meeting of May 9, 1934, GX 443.
[99] Meeting of September 6, 1934, GX 444 (italics added).
[100] Meeting of November 12, 1934, GX 2643.

A & P was of course ready to match the prices, but there is no recorded enthusiasm at the prospect.[101] Apparently the fears of the meeting were premature and the price war quickly faded; but by the end of August it again loomed on the scene, this time precipitated by Pay-N-Tak-It.[102]

As late as November of 1935, the supermarkets were still being exorcised by incantation — or perhaps by that time some company officials could see nothing else to do: "Our only hope of combating such [supermarket] competition is to continually extend our efforts to decrease the expense rate." There are no suggestions on how this is to be done. "All units should keep divisional headquarters advised currently regarding this kind of competition." [103] Doubtless they were glad to adjourn.

This is as far as we need go in describing the policy of drift. By 1936 and 1937, as we shall see, the current was a little quicker and its direction more definite. But in the meantime, a reverse movement was already in process.

[101] Central Western meeting of August 3, 1934, DX 184.
[102] Central Western meeting of August 31, 1934, DX 185.
[103] Southern meeting of November 5, 1935, GX 171.

III

CRISIS, 1936-1938

Progress in the divisions, 1935–1936

In 1934, the State of Kentucky imposed a chain-store tax. It was immediately contested in the courts, but in the meantime the Central Western Division accumulated funds for its payment. In March of 1935, the tax was declared unconstitutional. The $67,000 of funds could now have been assigned to surplus; instead, they were kept in a special account, and allocated, $52,000 to the Louisville Unit and $15,000 to Cincinnati, for those units to "plough back into their business . . . in the way of lower prices."[1]

Some time in the late spring of 1935, after discussions which had lasted nine months,[2] the division set up a new store within the Louisville unit in Paducah, "in an attempt," as divisional president John M. Toolin put it, "to justify our belief that future development may be along the lines that are being so successfully operated by some of our competitors." The target was an expense rate of 12 per cent, and a gross margin of 13 per cent, of which the 1 per cent operating profit would be matched by "other refinements, such as advertising allowances, subsidiary earnings, etc." for the desired 2 per cent net profit on sales. The first few weeks were quite disappointing. Only in early June did the expense rate come down to 16.78, far short of the goal of 12.[3] But during the next month, the expense rate went down to 13.26, and Toolin

---

[1] Central Western meeting, March 14, 1935, GX 188.

[2] It is not clear whether these discussions were within the Central Western board, or with headquarters.

[3] It was an ambitious goal, for the company's 1934 and 1935 expense rates had been, respectively, 18.73 and 17.56 per cent. Toolin's statement is from the Central Western meeting of June 12, 1935, GX 166.

received headquarters permission to conduct experiments with whole units.[4] The Louisville unit was directed to try "nothing more or less than what we should have had the courage to follow a long time ago, namely a definite gross profit rate for each unit," forcing the responsibility for local inefficiencies back to the sources in the units, warehouses, and stores.[5]

The city of Nashville, with fourteen stores, was selected for a special sales campaign, which would consist of price reductions on the entire line, without resorting to weekend specials. It was, in short, nothing more nor less than John Hartford's idea, which had fizzled so dismally in 1931. But by the end of August 1935, success was apparent, and with the permission of headquarters,[6] the trial was not only continued in Nashville during the third quarter of 1935, but also applied to two other towns, and conducted in the Cincinnati unit as well.

The urge to continue was doubtless helped by some success in reducing the expense rate throughout the division.[7] But it took some doing. The increase in sales had been encouraging, but the division had made even less profit than anticipated. Still, "with the public now acquainted with our price structure, plus the advent of cooler weather," they hoped for still larger sales and more satisfactory profits.[8] During the third quarter, sales in the Louisville unit were 30 per cent higher than in 1934, and much more was hoped for because of the momentum gained; for the second and last time, the tax accruals were plowed back.[9] By December 1935, the returns were in: "the constant low price policy with the practical elimination of specials, has resulted in a splendid increase in business, as well as a satisfactory profit." John Hartford, on a visit to Detroit, could see the results charted, and pronounced them successful.[10] Two months later, other units were being urged to try the all-week low-price plan, and they were

[4] Central Western meeting, July 23, 1935, GX 167.
[5] Central Western meeting, July 23, 1935, GX 167.
[6] Central Western meeting, August 21, 1935, GX 168.
[7] Central Western meeting, August 21, 1935, GX 168.
[8] Central Western meeting, September 10, 1935, GX 169.
[9] It would be more correct to say that they were risked for the second time, since they had not been lost on the first trial. The relative niggardliness of this policy is worth noting.
[10] Central Western meeting, December 11, 1935, GX 174.

ordered to conduct no more than four large sales drives per year — there had been too many in the past.[11] By July 1936, four of the six Central Western units were operating exclusively on that basis.[12]

In the meantime, the Central Division had also been active. Their first attempt, late in 1934, was timid and abortive. Probably nothing else was to be expected, for in proposing it the divisional president put the cart squarely before the horse. He had "a plan that would, if carefully followed, enable us to reduce expenses thereby offering an opportunity to sell groceries cheaper. This in turn is bound to result in higher volume." [13]

The Cleveland unit did make an effort to lower prices, and for just two weeks late in 1934, their operating gross profit was down to 15.04 per cent. Then the supply of risk-taking was exhausted: "The low gross profit rate of .1504 *has failed* to bring the desired reaction. Possibly if we could afford to carry the low gross profit rate of .1504 for a period of six months or a year, sales would increase but it was felt that such a policy was not advisable and steps have already been taken to gradually bring the operations to a more satisfactory level." [14] These "steps" were duly taken, and gross profit was soon up to 17.15.[15]

Early in September 1935, however, R. R. King, head of the Pittsburgh unit, designated over 100 stores as "Baby Bears," and they were given "special treatment" in order to promote much lower prices in them.[16] They selected items on which there was direct delivery from carlot purchases, or which were carried in nearby warehouses, and on which A & P costs were therefore lowest. These items were featured at lower prices. But they "eliminated heavy special reduction" — the price cuts were to considered permanent and the "BB" stores received no special credits for them. In short, prices were cut in stores where costs were lower, and this inevitably focused attention on variations among stores. The result was to "curtail the competitors' programs and practi-

[11] Central Western meeting, February 7, 1936, GX 177.
[12] Central Western meeting, July 23, 1936, GX 182.
[13] Central meeting, November 26, 1934, DX 249.
[14] Central meeting, December 17, 1934, DX 251 (italics added).
[15] Central meeting, January 28, 1935, DX 250.
[16] Central meeting, November 25, 1935, GX 170.

cally eliminate the need for special credits to meet any of their prices." [17]

But an even more important step was to group the reduced-price items into a self-service department in every Baby Bear. Signs, circulars, and inside public-address systems were used to call attention to them — comments would be made through the microphone when the other sections of the store became crowded.[18] Moreover, the stores which were not included in the program promoted the BB's, through large store signs, as having the lowest prices in town. To the astonishment of the Central Division, these stores even increased their own sales while so doing.[19]

The great merit of the Pittsburgh Baby Bear program was that instead of trying to improve piecemeal on current practices, it boldly set the goal at "12 per cent gross and 10 per cent expense," [20] as John Hartford had apparently wished all along. It then became clear that in few stores could such rates be attained. The stores had to be carefully selected. Location was important in a double sense — proximity to warehouses and good buying markets, and also location at a good shopping point so that the public might be aware of the lower prices. New patterns had to be set — restocking had to be scheduled for off-peak periods, and, in general, it was both possible and necessary to analyze expenditures carefully and to be on a specially low expense rate. The chief saving was in labor: the "clerk hire rate" of the self-service department was only one third of the rate for the whole BB store, and therefore even less than one third of its service department.[21] But obviously it was not merely less labor per sales dollar, but a different type of labor to perform different tasks.

Like the supermarkets, therefore, if not to the same extent, the Baby Bears were a new method of food retailing quite distinct from the regular stores, and not merely an improvement upon them. The expense rates are evidence enough. Many BB's attained

[17] DPM, January 21, 1936, GX 176.
[18] DPM, January 21, 1936, GX 176.
[19] Central Western meeting, January 24, 1936, GX 175, which contains a report of its neighbor division experience.
[20] Central Western meeting, January 24, 1936, GX 175.
[21] DPM, January 21, 1936, GX 176.

rates of 10 and 11 per cent, with "tremendous" increases in sales.[22] The group as a whole raised their sales by 25.5 per cent in nine weeks.[23] Many of the stores lost money at first, but of these, most were expected to show a profit by the second quarter of 1936. "Possibly in some cases cuts in the gross profit were too drastic, however it proved the point that if prices are sufficiently low the public is responsive."[24] Even before the year was out, King had decided to have nothing but BB stores in the Pittsburgh unit and considered a 12 per cent gross profit rate perfectly feasible for the whole division.[25] He was invited to the divisional presidents' meeting which met in New York in January 1936, "gave a most interesting talk" and some elaborate reports, which we have already cited, and which were ordered circulated throughout the company.[26]

Slow action at headquarters

The case might seem to have been proved, and we might expect headquarters either to change over to supermarkets forthwith, or, at the very least, to experiment with them in various locations, sizes, etc. But nothing of the sort was done. The year 1936 saw a general business revival. A & P sales rose by less than 4 per cent, and the company lost ground to every other type of food store, but profits improved a little. The Central Western and Central Divisions continued with their new policies, apparently as successfully as in the past year: "The every-day low price policy now in effect [in four cities] has met with wonderful response,"[27] and at the end of the year, the subject of the first trial, the Paducah store, was selling almost seven times as much as the average A & P store, with an expense rate of only 10.50 — and this despite the distance from the Louisville warehouse, which accounted for 1.13. The division thought that future company development would "unquestionably" be along two lines: the small self-service store doing $4,000 to $6,000 of weekly sales (the company average for

[22] Central meeting, June 4, 1936, GX 172.
[23] Central meeting, June 4, 1936, GX 172.
[24] Central meeting, June 4, 1936, GX 172.
[25] Central meeting, November 25, 1935, GX 170.
[26] DPM, January 21, 1936, GX 176.
[27] Central Western meeting of July 23, 1936, GX 180.

the year was not quite $1,660), and the supermarket doing about $10,000.[28] In the light of later developments, this was a rather conservative forecast.

As for the Central Division, the Pittsburgh unit was brought down to an expense rate of 12.79 for the year, a notable achievement.[29] But in both divisions, the good showing was confined to the experimental areas: elsewhere business was being steadily lost to the voluntary chains and the supermarkets. Here and there, whole units were showing losses. One of them was Detroit, where sales had fallen more than fifty per cent since the peak year. In Cincinnati, a supermarket operator, who had threatened to "demoralize" the market in 1935, now had eight stores and 9.5 per cent of the city's business. A & P had 56 stores, and only 7.7 per cent.

But no signal came from headquarters. In May 1936, a divisional presidents' meeting came no closer to the problem than to review tables which showed that low-volume stores had gone even further downhill. No action was taken.[30]

Why could the company do nothing? John Hartford hinted obliquely at it, nine years later. There was, he said, "no fundamental opposition. Some were more sold on it than others. Of course, it takes courage to reduce the gross profit when your volume is dropping."[31] Although he did not say so at the trial, there seems no doubt that he knew the company was going quickly downhill, and knew the remedy. In October of 1936, he told a Central Western meeting[32] that his major worry was the inability to show a reasonable current profit (a far cry from 1931). Apparently he did not regard labor costs as excessive, for he remarked on the need for better working conditions, shorter hours, higher pay, and some liberality in vacations and sickness benefits. The overweening fact was that A & P had been losing ground, above all to the supermarkets. "The future development of our own business must certainly be along these lines."

---

[28] Meeting of December 12, 1936, DX 192.
[29] Meeting of December 3, 1936, GX 186.
[30] DPM, May 7, 1936, GX 181.
[31] Testimony, Tr. 20,432.
[32] October 22, 1936, GX 185.

The initial barrier to that development was George L. Hartford. This elderly gentleman, leading an incredibly secluded life, far from his subordinates in the company and from the business at large,[33] must simply have forgotten what it looked like. His world had become bounded by the company records. Few knew A & P finances half as well as "Mr. George"; apparently few knew less about the immediate needs of the business. And as the senior brother, with at least an equal voice, he could block any constructive action.

In October 1936, the divisional presidents' meeting saw the closest approach to an open clash. George Hartford made one of his rare speeches. "In the past . . . *too much emphasis had been placed on the procuring of a large volume* at the expense of sufficient attention to the determination and promotion of profitable commodities." Thereupon, he reviewed the past few years, expressing no concern about new competition, and announced the next year's program which embodied higher gross profit rates. "Mr. John expressed his surprise at the ready acceptance of the program by the presidents. He said *it would not be accomplished by increasing the gross profit and losing volume*. . . . We have not progressed nor adapted our business in pace with the changing times, . . . with the result that we have lost ground." He stressed the supermarket invasion. The reader of the minutes can only guess at the embarrassed tension that hung over the meeting. But no action was taken.[34]

During the next month, John Hartford confided his worries in a letter: "The development of the large type of market by our Company [is] now at a very critical stage. As you will no doubt recall very vividly, Mr. George's opposition to such a development has been based on the contention that it would not be successful except by resorting to below cost selling in large volume as a bait. I have tried to convince him." [35] Obviously Mr. George did not recognize the supermarket for the lower-cost mechanism it was. Only the loud carnival noises had filtered through the curtains.

[33] George L. Hartford was the only defendant who did not appear at the trial (Tr. 5). The description of his seclusion and his functions in the company are based on the article in *Fortune*, March 1933. The judgment is my own.
[34] DPM, October 6, 1936, GX 184 (italics added).
[35] John A. Hartford to C. A. Brooks, January 27, 1937, DX 1017.

In March,[36] the same issue was again thrashed out. With sales barely above the previous year despite the 1936–1937 boomlet, and profits unmistakably down, John Hartford was moved to declare that the company would either adopt supermarkets or go under. "Mr. George Hartford said that although he is not as pessimistic about the outlook for the Company, he is strongly in favor, nevertheless, of going ahead with a conservative development of supermarkets." The plan adopted was to open 100 such markets, "of the $10,000 average sales [per week] type." Since this meant roughly $50 millions of sales out of a total of $900 million, it seems rather exaggerated to call it even a conservative development. It was rather a modest experiment, which should of course have been undertaken three to four years earlier.[37] But John Hartford, realizing that the first step was the hardest, was pleased: "This is the most constructive move the Company has made in a long time."

But constructive or not, this action was promise only. The performance was still that of the regular stores, and in the second quarter, when higher money and real incomes might have been expected to offset the normal seasonal decline, sales instead fell off, and were some eight per cent lower than in the second quarter of 1936. By the end of June, John Hartford had decided on a company-wide development. Some 2650 losing stores were finally to be closed, and replaced by 190 supermarkets doing about the same volume of sales. In addition, 76 supermarkets would be opened as the first move toward sales expansion since 1929.[38]

The divisional presidents' meeting of August 31, 1937 [39] was doubtless the gloomiest ever held. Not only had sales fallen by 10 per cent since the previous quarter, but the expense rate was up since the second quarter of 1936, from 17.24 to 18.44 per cent. Net

---

[36] DPM, March 24, 1937, GX 188.

[37] Assuming sales of $52 million, at a loss rate of 3 per cent (which was as bad as the worst A & P stores in 1937), the company would have been out about $1.5 million on the experiment. This was so small an investment that we can only marvel why it had not been made. As it turned out, during the second quarter of 1937, the company ran 50 supermarkets, at a loss of about $18,000. Thereafter, the supermarkets paid their way.

[38] Central Western meeting, June 30, 1937, GX 187.

[39] GX 189.

profits [40] before taxes were down by two thirds; the Eastern and Southern Divisions were running at a loss, and the New England Division and the company as a whole was nearing the break-even point. The unthinking use of the markup system had once acted as a subtle drain on the company's vitality; now it was a galloping disease. As John Hartford said: "The condition of the business is even worse than the figures indicate because of the continuous marking up of shelf goods during the past several quarters." Obviously the overpricing of many items would result in short-run profits all right, which would be maintained just as long as customers did not notice them. "Unless we can regain the volume that has been lost, there is no possibility of profitable operation." George L. Hartford said he "had hoped . . . that the Company could continue earning dividends during these uncertain times without running the risks of an aggressive sales promotion program, but the past quarter had convinced him."

Instead of general exhortations, John Hartford proposed an interesting plan. This was to cut the price of grocery items by not more than $100 per store per week, and gross profits not more than 0.0100, and feature the reduced items (although not by any formal advertising). It was hoped that sales would be thereby increased by $100 to $150 per store.[41] Lower gross profit rates, varying from 19.85 per cent for the Eastern Division to 16.31 for the Middle Western, were set for the third and fourth quarters. The supermarket campaign, of course, was ordered speeded up.

Insofar as an outsider can judge, the program was well executed, at least at the top divisional levels. Two divisions may serve as examples. The Central Western called a special board meeting in early September.[42] The president explained the program in lucid fashion and added: "Headquarters are willing to consider this . . . in the light of an investment during the third quarter, which it is expected will produce permanent results from then on." Thus, the fear of incurring a bad record by cutting prices was allayed. Then a significant warning: "At the presidents' meeting some very

[40] These include all elements of profit, as well as retail "operating" profit.

[41] It is possible to calculate the elasticity of demand implied in this plan, both with respect to grocery prices and grocery service. See Appendix II, "Two Calculations of Implied Elasticity of Demand."

[42] September 9, 1937, GX 191.

definite sales and operating policies were adopted that must be made standard for supermarkets. *Positively no credit or delivery.*" The emphasis is ours, on the most tantalizing clue in the record. How far had the A & P stores gone in granting these services? It must have been a widespread practice if it was discussed at a divisional presidents' meeting. Were there only statistics on the subject, they would serve as an important inverse index of the company's morale. Even more important, their importance as a distribution cost might be measured. Unfortunately, these are vain surmises.

The Southern Division called two special meetings of all unit heads and sales managers.[43] Copies of the divisional presidents' minutes had been furnished beforehand, and it was explained in detail. The $100 out was not to be at random, but

on those shelf items which from the individual unit's experience are known to have been priced at a gross which presently retards the sales thereof. Also, merchandise often featured by competitors. . . . It would be the means of re-establishing A & P Food Stores in the minds of the people as leaders in value giving . . . the most forward step the Company had taken in many years. . . . In addition to the favorable impression it will make on the public, it will also stimulate the morale of every manager.

Pleasure was also expressed at the carefully qualified permission to take 5-year leases, especially on supermarkets.

Letters were also sent out to the sales directors, emphasizing that price policy ought to be guided by the competition of the newer and bolder stores. The Central Division sales director passed one such letter on to one of his sales managers, with the comment: "It bears out our contention right along — your eyes are too much fixed on the local chains who are in the same boat with us. This is the same story we get from all the salesmen. You are in line with chains, but what we should be is in line or lower [sic] with all competition. . . . This must be a gradual process but not too gradual."[44]

Despite all this activity, total sales in the latter half of 1937 were below 1936; but sales per store increased and net profits revived, although they were less than half of the corresponding 1936

[43] September 7 and 13, 1937, GX 190.
[44] October 26, 1937, GX 193.

period. Whether this was in consequence or in spite of the pro-grammed cut in gross margin cannot be stated with any assur-ance.[45]

By the end of the year, the program of store closings and super-market openings had been approximately fulfilled. But looking at the matter in somewhat longer perspective, as did John Hart-ford, there seemed little room for encouragement. The campaign would be continued; so far it had not reversed the fall in sales and profits. With all possible speed, the losing low-volume stores (and one third of all stores lost money that year) had to be re-placed by supermarkets. "He mentioned that the wholesale store closings will involve many heartaches," but "we can do nothing else." The dissension of December 1936 had been erased by De-cember 1937. George Hartford said he was "in thorough accord. . . . He has become completely convinced that Mr. John's plan is the only salvation." There was the usual expression of unani-mous delight, and "Mr. John" pressed home the point by display-ing a chart based on indexes of the U.S. Department of Com-merce.[46] From February 1936 through November 1937, the sales of all chains were approximately unchanged, while those of the company had declined about $7\frac{1}{2}$ per cent. Appendix Table 2 shows that the company's position vis-à-vis nonchain competitors had deteriorated even more rapidly. But the die was now cast.[47]

[45] My opinion, for what it may be worth, is that the cut in gross profit paid off even before the year was out. From 18.58 per cent in the second quarter, the margin was cut to 18.03 in the third, and rose to 18.25 in the fourth. Sales per store increased steadily from $1104 to $1173 to $1226; the expense rate fell from 18.40 per cent to 17.76 to 17.23. Hence the margin of net profit rose from 0.18 to 0.27 to 1.22 per cent. These data are at least consistent with the hypothesis that the price cut (supermarket openings were still of negligible im-portance) was profitable, i.e., that demand was sufficiently elastic.

[46] This should not give the impression that the use of such data was a novelty. The A & P statistical department were using Bureau of the Census data through-out, and it might be an interesting task to trace the expanding informational activities of the Department of Commerce as reflected in A & P statistics.

[47] DPM, December 7, 1937, GX 194.

IV

REVIVAL, 1938-1941 AND AFTER

Survival in 1938–1939

THE year 1938 was undoubtedly the decisive one. As Appendix Table 12 shows, the losing stores closed down during the year actually exceeded the number left open at the end of the fourth quarter (this continued in 1939, 1940, and 1941). Rent paid on closed stores, which had gone lower than $11,000 in the third quarter of 1936, was over $85,000 in the second quarter of 1938. The tree was finally being pruned.

Over five hundred supermarkets were opened, although not all stayed open. Too many small supermarkets were started, with too high expense and gross profit rates, as the divisions pushed to convert from regular stores. Hartford advised the presidents to shut down the small ones and if need be to assign special men to hunt locations: he wanted to open a round thousand by March of 1939.[1] This was not quite achieved. Nevertheless, as early as the end of May 1938, the supermarkets constituted 5 per cent of all stores, did 23 per cent of all sales, and earned nearly half the profits. The regular stores, despite the fact that the closing of small unprofitable ones tended to cut the average expense rate and raise the average net profit, were running at an even higher expense rate, and their profits fell by 42 per cent from the second quarter of 1937 to the second quarter of 1938.[2] Later quarters were better, for the second was always the year's low. But it was painfully apparent that the company's decision had not been made

[1] DPM, March 8, 1938, GX 196.
[2] DPM, September 21, 1938, GX 199. See tables presented at the meeting, GX 200.

a moment too soon: the ground seemed to be slipping from under the regular stores. Perhaps it was this realization that the world could come to an end which accounts for the urgent, even anxious, tone of the divisional presidents' meetings during that year; and for John Hartford's constant adjurations to speed things up.

Despite the craving for sales volume, and the temptation to run specials, the policy of all-week low prices was reiterated and maintained.[3] Another key policy was to concentrate on the large supermarket. "The $10,000 average [weekly] sales type" is mentioned at every divisional presidents' meeting in 1938,[4] and at innumerable divisional meetings. To keep down the gross profit, units had to be controlled more effectively from divisional headquarters.[5] The reason was fairly clear. As he explained to the Atlantic and Middle Western divisions, Hartford doubted that there could be lasting success if the supermarket operating gross profit rates were over 12 or 12½ per cent. He feared that where volume had initially been lower than expected, the gross profit rates were sometimes raised to cover operating costs higher than budgeted. "He felt this was unhealthy, because if we are to get our predicted volume, we certainly must have the courage to maintain our low gross profit rate."[6] The warning, and the advice that "we must have the courage to reduce the gross profit rates in stores which have not produced the predicted volume" were underlined by the divisional president the next month.[7]

In October 1938, probably irritated by the relatively poor showing of the Atlantic Division, Hartford went further than an insistence on a gross profit figure which, if adhered to, would eventually return the desired profit: "In the opening of all Super Markets in the future our entire line of merchandise shall not exceed a gross profit of 10 per cent . . . until we feel that their security has been definitely fixed."[8] Assuming, as is always the case in A & P correspondence, 1½ per cent in allowances, this would indicate a plan to maintain gross margins at 11½ per cent, or

[3] DPM, June 8, 1938, GX 198.
[4] GX's 196, 198, 199; DX 208.
[5] Atlantic meeting, October 18, 1938, GX 265.
[6] Middle Western meeting, October 18, 1938, GX 266.
[7] Middle Western meeting, November 15, 1938, GX 267.
[8] Atlantic meeting, October 18, 1938, GX 265.

below the target of 12 per cent gross profit, until it was possible to raise prices and restore the 12 per cent. This was different from maintaining the same gross profit throughout, and it was not mentioned again.

The difficulties of the buying department, hobbled by the Robinson-Patman Act, were considerable: allowances from suppliers for the year were down to less than $2.9 million.[9] Yet despite this loss of revenue, not only sales but also profits for 1938 were back at practically the 1936 level. Considering the loss of discounts and the expensive character of any transition period when mistakes and lessons must be paid for, and also the 1938 recession, this seems like a surprisingly good showing. To be sure, there were mistakes. Many store leases were too hastily signed; headquarters was reluctant to approve five-year leases, and choice locations were thereby lost.[10] Chart 2 indicates that a source of large savings through supermarket operations was in managers' salaries. But as might be expected, a good regular store manager might or might not do as well in a supermarket, and many were tried and found wanting — a process expensive to the company and unpleasant to both parties. For example, the Central Western Division was undoubtedly one of the more efficient. Yet during the 12 months ending May 28, 1938, the rate of turnover among supermarket managers was 35 per cent, and in meat departments it was 43 per cent. The units were warned to be very careful in selecting men for these posts.[11]

During 1939, the corner was definitely turned. One can hardly help but be impressed by the gradual return of confidence in the company's survival.[12] By the end of June, the divisional presidents' meeting could almost take a wry satisfaction in noting

[9] It will be recalled that these were $7.9 million in 1935, and $4.7 million in 1936. See Appendix Tables 20 and 21.

[10] An unsigned letter, obviously from someone high in the company (the writer guesses at John M. Toolin) to R. W. Burger, John Hartford's assistant, July 24, 1940, GX 225.

[11] Meeting of July 26, 1938, GX 199.

[12] Thus, a letter from R. M. Smith of the Southern Division to M. A. Hogewood, December 12, 1939, GX 2764: "It is quite encouraging for me when businessmen call at my office and state how well they think we are doing as compared with our competitors. Not more than a year ago, the story was entirely different."

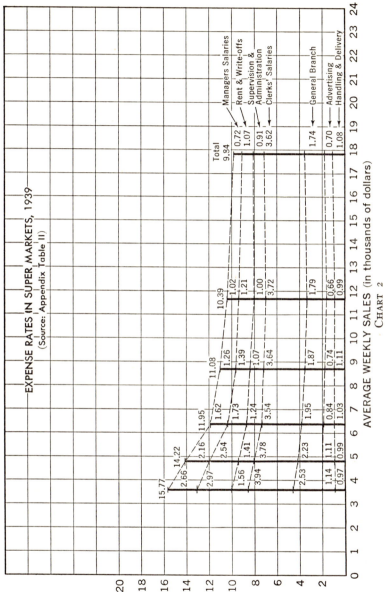

EXPENSE RATES IN SUPER MARKETS, 1939
(Source: Appendix Table II)

CHART 2

AVERAGE WEEKLY SALES (in thousands of dollars)

EXPENSE RATE (Percent of Sales)

	Managers Salaries	Rent & Write-offs	Supervision & Administration	Clerks' Salaries	General Branch	Advertising	Handling & Delivery
Total 9.84		0.72	1.07	0.91	3.62	1.74	0.70	1.08
10.39		1.02	1.21	1.00	3.72	1.79	0.66	0.99
11.08		1.26	1.39	1.07	3.64	1.87	0.74	1.11
11.95		1.62	1.73	1.24	3.54	1.95	0.84	1.03
14.22	2.16		2.54	1.41	3.78	2.23	1.11	0.99
15.77	2.66		2.97	1.56	3.94	2.53	1.14	0.97

that the National Association of Retail Grocers had petitioned for an investigation of A & P. It was referred to Carl Byoir, who was now operating an elaborately casual publicity program for them.[13]

But earlier, at the end of March, Hartford was pointing with alarm, as he had been doing at every meeting, to the rising gross margins, and he "urged the divisional presidents to return to a price policy appropriate to supermarket operations," since anything else would slow down the transition, help competitors, and injure the volume. But his plan for the new fiscal year reflected both a newly found assurance and the experience of 1929–1933.

Although Hartford now dared to look to the regaining of the peak years, he urged that the billion dollars of sales be so planned that net profit be not more than two per cent of sales. Then "the Company could earn its former dividend rate of seven dollars which is considered adequate and all we should attempt to make in profits." [14] Hartford reiterated the policy in a letter he sent out a week later to all divisional presidents,[15] in which he enclosed the detailed tables (see Table 7) of the 1939–1940 plan. The backward Atlantic and New England divisions were to maintain a 12 per cent gross margin in the stores to get themselves into line, despite the expectation that this would result in an interim operating loss — the divisional closing figure for the year would of course show a profit. Hartford concluded the letter by pointing out just how a more aggressive program would operate: "Supermarket development made possible by lower supermarket gross profit . . . [leads to] progressively lower gross profit and expense rates and should place our business on a most firm foundation where we won't have to fear competition taking it away from us."

The 1939 plan was fulfilled to the extent of a little over 98 per cent. In every quarter, 1939 sales were higher than for any year since 1931, and profits were up by $3.6 millions.[16] But although

[13] DPM, June 27, 1939, GX 210.
[14] DPM, March 28, 1939, GX 203. The plan presented in Table 7 was prepared and sent out to the divisions a few days later. See the next footnote.
[15] Letter, John A. Hartford to William M. Byrnes, president, Eastern Division, April 4, 1939, enclosing various tables from which my own has been drawn. GX 205.
[16] Compare Table 7 with Appendix Table 7.

there was reason for satisfaction, there was none for complacency. A letter [17] to John Hartford, presumably from John Toolin, shows

TABLE 7. Sales and Profit Program, A & P, 1939

(dollar amounts in thousands, rates in per cent)

Division	Peak sales Year	Peak sales Amt.	Sales 1938	1939, Planned sales	Profit rate, 1938	1939, Planned profit rates Total [a]	1939, Planned profit rates Operating Interim	1939, Planned profit rates Operating Final
New England	1930	176	111	123	1.0	0.87	−0.64	1.51
Eastern	1930	188	153	185	2.64	2.38	0.77	1.61
Atlantic	1930	144	109	123	1.18	1.19	−0.46	1.75
Southern	1930	93	87	99	2.41	2.15	0.49	1.66
Central	1929	171	166	182	2.65	2.39	0.73	1.66
Middle Western	1930	149	128	156	2.72	2.46	0.67	1.79
Central Western	1929	132	101	122	2.49	2.23	0.55	1.68
Total		1,053	866	1,000	2.21	2.00	0.36	1.64

Source. Various tables enclosed in letter, J. A. Hartford to W. M. Byrnes, April 4, 1939, GX 205.
[a] Includes distribution of manufacturing profits, etc.

that the regressive tendency toward "trading-up" and offering of services was now fully understood:

At the moment, the Company is doing a splendid job in the operation of these markets because our prices are attractive, and our stores are neat and clean in appearance without the luxury of expensive equipment and fixtures.

Until some worthy competitor finds how to operate [super] markets below 10 per cent [expense rate], we need have no fear of losing our position. It is easy to build up a complicated and expensive structure, but very difficult to adjust and reduce it to the demands of time and conditions.

The pressure for servicing certain departments is rapidly growing. The Atlantic Commission Company talk of service in the produce department — the Bakery Division is strong for 100 per cent service — the Dairy Department must be serviced — the Coffee Corporation advocates service, and the Quaker Maid [the A & P manufacturing subsidiary]. . . . They may all be correct, . . . but we would like to move slowly.

[17] December 19, 1939, GX 213.

Judging by the trend of expense rates after 1939, A & P took these words to heart. The tendency of the markup system to make prices follow costs rather than vice versa was not allowed to operate in 1940 and 1941. A company-wide policy was adopted of 12 per cent gross and 10 per cent expense rates for supermarkets, and divisions and units which exceeded them were called upon to explain. The following instructions to the New England Division are revealing:

If we sometimes run into profit difficulties, we should not let this swerve us from our course. We must hold to the scheme [12 and 10]. . . . We must set our course and stick to it. . . . There must be one policy in connection with gross profit in the operation of our supermarkets and nothing must make us deviate from that course.[18]

During 1939–1941, the Hartfords watched individual units and even stores, and promptly called excessive gross or net profit figures to the attention of the divisional officials concerned. The lesson had been learned of how difficult it is to enforce a limitation of profits in a retail enterprise. They were determined that this time the pulsations would reach the extremities.

The Southern Division as the reluctant dragon

The best place to watch headquarters' program carried out is probably in the Southern Division, for there it was most difficult to enforce and generated the richest body of discussion and explanation. In August 1938, John Hartford attended a board meeting, pointed out that the division had lost heavily in volume of sales; had barely broken even in 1937, and was losing sales in 1938; unless volume was regained, some units would have to be shut down altogether. "It is my feeling to some little extent," continued Mr. Hartford, "that everyone is not entirely sold on the development of the $10,000 Super Market type of store. . . . I would like to ask each of you gentlemen to reassure me that you are wholeheartedly in accord with your Company's future plans." All were of course in agreement.[19]

[18] New England meeting, May 7, 1940, GX 2656.
[19] Southern meeting, August 2, 1938, GX 466.

But although the first supermarkets opened in the division during 1937 had operated at a margin of 12.8 per cent, this had risen steadily to 15.7 per cent in the last quarter of 1938.[20] In February 1939, therefore, Oliver C. Adams, chairman of the combined board of the Atlantic and Southern Divisions, was urging R. M. Smith, the Southern president, to get the supermarket gross profit down: "Let's start off for a total figure on all supermarkets not to exceed 14 per cent and gradually get it even lower. We will have to take less profit, but I do want to get away from the criticism that we are constantly receiving." After all, the other divisions could do it.[21] An abnormally low gross profit, say 10 per cent or even as low as 8 or 9 per cent, was permissible, for the volume thus attracted "is usually held, and the gross can be worked up after a short period of several weeks." [22] That this represented Hartford's thinking is evident in a letter to Adams written at almost the same time, stressing the importance of "the first impression on the public." [23] And Hartford went on to warn Smith that his gross profit rate was too high, and would presently lead to loss of business. The divisional sales director wrote a unit sales manager that 14 per cent was a ceiling for every individual supermarket, not merely a unit average,[24] and on the same day a telegram to the head of the Dallas unit made the same point.[25]

The reaction in Dallas was unfavorable, almost angry: Safeway would meet the lower prices anyway, the warm weather was coming, and the gross profit ought not to be reduced.[26] The Dallas sales manager referred to the lower gross as "the desired (?) effect." [27] The division sales manager replied, noting the question mark: "Does that mean that you are not entirely in accord with the program?" The least that could be expected of everyone, he noted, was to give the national and divisional plans a fair trial.[28]

[20] Tables presented at Southern meeting, September 2, 1940, GX 2746.
[21] Adams to Smith, February 28, 1939, GX 2795.
[22] Adams to Smith, February 28, 1939, GX 2795.
[23] Hartford to Smith, March 2, 1939, GX 313.
[24] Carlton to Clanton, March 2, 1939, DX 460.
[25] Telegram, Smith to Crocker, March 2, 1939, GX 3095.
[26] Hunnewell to Carlton, March 2, 1939, GX 3096; Crocker to Smith, March 3, 1939, GX 3097.
[27] Hunnewell to Carlton, March 8, 1939, GX 2798.
[28] Carlton to Hunnewell, March 16, 1939, GX 2799.

By April 1939, definite progress was reported in getting gross down to 14 per cent in a number of supermarkets, and in most such instances, "the sales have reached . . . new high peaks. This would seem to indicate that the program is sound. . . ." [29] The next month, this conclusion seemed even more strongly indicated, despite some supermarkets which were losing money under the rule of 14 per cent maximum.[30] Later in the month, however, progress was considered too slow, since there were still a dozen supermarkets (outside of the difficult Dallas area) above that mark, and the units were behind the program on both sales and net profits.[31] Just a week later, Hartford prodded Smith by reminding him that of all the company's supermarkets with gross profit over 14 per cent, half of them were in the South.[32] At the June meeting, the losing supermarkets were told in effect to stop complaining about gross being too low but to do something about expense being too high — the low gross was company policy, and would not be changed.[33]

In August, Crocker, the superintendent of the Dallas unit, was discharged. The Southern president testified at the trial that Crocker had never willfully violated instructions, yet neither had he carried them out fully.[34] Crocker testified that he was fired because he was not "ruthless" enough; [35] Smith denied using the word.[36]

The new superintendent was O. I. Black, who was brought in from Birmingham. Black was certainly more "ruthless" in closing down losing stores — he withdrew completely from Fort Worth — and also more aggressive in opening new supermarkets.[37] The main competitor in the Dallas unit was Safeway and, as volume expanded, Smith was hopeful that they "and many other com-

---

[29] Meeting of April 11, 1939, GX 1042.
[30] Meeting of May 30, 1939, GX 2739.
[31] Meeting of May 30, 1939, GX 2740.
[32] Hartford to Smith, June 5, 1939, GX 2822.
[33] Meeting of June 6, 1939, GX 2741.
[34] Smith, Tr. 16,875.
[35] Tr. 10,791–2.
[36] Tr. 16,879–82.
[37] Black to Smith, September 9, 1939, DX 429; October 4, 1939, GX 2826; October 17, 1939, GX 2829; October 30, 1939, GX 2833; December 20, 1939, GX 2839.

petitors will begin to feel the effects of the heat once it is turned on." [38]

But the men of the Southern Division, as Hartford said at the trial, "were pretty hard people to convince." [39] Later in the year, at Hartford's personal urging, Smith sent a circular telegram to all units ordering them to comply with the low-gross policy.[40] Apparently Hartford was dissatisfied with this action,[41] and Smith sent a lengthy circular letter explaining the policy in detail: "Regardless of circumstances I want all supermarket gross rates to be held down [i.e., below 14 per cent]. Mr. Hartford is quite disturbed. . . . Do not permit any local conditions to influence your judgment about these rates. They have definite ideas about keeping the rates low and we must go along." [42] It was obedience rather than agreement, for Adams wrote to Smith: "I am not inclined to agree with Mr. Hartford's views on this, nor do I think you are. . . ." [43]

The resistance in the lower ranks was not quite inarticulate, and there is one interesting example of the difference in viewpoint according to the height of position in the company. Smith wrote to the head of the Charlotte unit:

I appreciate just how anxious you are to make a good showing in the way of profits; however, it is highly important that your supermarket rates be controlled and no store allowed to go over 14 per cent except Hendersonville. We must do this in order to avoid criticism from Mr. Hartford. He is quite confident that we have regained our business and are doing so well today by reason of the fact that we have opened large stores and are selling food to the public at prices as low as, or lower than, our competitors.[44]

Smith had reason for his satisfaction: from 1937 to 1939, the gross profit rate in the Southern Division had been lowered from 19.11 to 18.54 per cent, the expense rate from 18.39 to 15.96 per cent, and total profits had risen from $1.36 to $2.51 millions. But

[38] Smith to Black, December 28, 1939, GX 2841.
[39] Tr. 20,452.
[40] Dated October 3, 1939, GX 2759.
[41] Adams to Smith, October 6, 1939, GX 2760.
[42] Dated October 6, 1939, GX 2762.
[43] GX 2760.
[44] R. M. Smith to Hogewood, December 12, 1939, GX 2764.

when Smith submitted to Adams "a conservative program" for the
1940 fiscal year [45] it drew no applause. Adams had conferred with
Hartford, and

> I want to give you an idea of how Mr. John's mind is working. . . . There
> is one thing that I think you should watch more than any other — and that
> is not let the gross profit run up too high in these stores. If we can get a
> 50-point [i.e. 0.5 per cent] operating profit, with the overage [46] and 1½ per
> cent coming back from subsidiary and Headquarters allowance, we will
> still have an actual 2 per cent net. For example, your accumulated [sic]
> for the supermarkets up to the end of December 30, 1939, was [1.17] net,
> which actually shows a [2.67] final profit.

Hartford had repeated the goal of limitation of profits and said
that he had no criticism of subordinates who were not earning
enough. Hartford then explained the 10 and 12 formula; for the
time being, the Southern Division could go as high as 12¾, but
12½ was certainly better.[47]

For the third quarter of 1939, there were only 72 supermarkets
in the Division, only 6 per cent of the total number of stores. Yet
they accounted for about a quarter of the sales and the profits.[48]
One reason for the slower supermarket development in the South
was that there were relatively few large towns or cities.[49] But
many of the difficulties in accelerating the program were subjective rather than objective, and they are best illustrated by re-
turning to Black and the Dallas unit. In January of 1940, he
asked that gross profit rate inside the city of Dallas (not the
whole Dallas unit) he increased to 16 per cent since expenses
had increased, and he did not think it possible to make a profit
on a 14 per cent gross. The lower gross would not attract more
business, for he was "convinced that competition will follow us
on any price changes that we make, whether they are up or
down." Almost wistfully he added: "I have never had an unprofitable operation for the Company, even when I ran an 'Old-

---

[45] Smith to Adams, January 3, 1940, GX 2766.

[46] Overage means the difference between estimated current store profit and
final actual current store profit. Adams, Tr. 16,243. One might call it a semi-
hidden allowance for contingencies.

[47] Adams to Smith, January 10, 1941, GX 2767.

[48] GX 2767.

[49] Southern meeting, February 20, 1940, GX 2743.

Line' store, and I am most anxious to protect that record and believe that it can be done if we are allowed to operate this business here as we feel it should be." [50] Smith replied that while gross might possibly be increased in regular stores, Hartford simply would not compromise on supermarkets, and Smith could only offer his sympathy.[51]

Black was out of step, but not because he lacked nerve. When Safeway began a price war on coffee early in 1940, he was anxious to stay with them, and now it was headquarters which held back and would not authorize a lower wholesale price to let Dallas meet competition on their leader commodity.[52] Again, Black was not scared off by initial losses in the new stores he had opened,[53] where Safeway (which had its largest West Texas store near one of them) and some independents were competing very aggressively.[54] It is even possible, although this cannot be ascertained, that these losses might have been even larger than the $1\frac{1}{2}$ per cent profit allocation, and the stores may have shown a final and not merely an interim loss. Yet Black was clearly out of step with headquarters. They were relatively indifferent to price competition on a particular commodity — even, of all things, on coffee, a pillar of A & P consumer attraction. And they insisted on lower supermarket gross profits throughout, and not merely in some localities. Black was aggressive enough in meeting competition as he found it, but he had not yet understood the need for making the situation rather than merely adapting to it.

In mid-July, Smith again had to write Black to pass on headquarters criticism. He knew how Black felt, but "I am reasonably sure that I will hear further from Mr. Hartford if these rates are not reduced in the supermarket stores in the City of Dallas" and he asked Black to "please give the Dallas supermarket gross profit rate your immediate attention." [55] He had no

[50] Black to Smith, January 5, 1940, GX 2843.

[51] Smith to Black, January 10, 1940, GX 2844.

[52] See the correspondence, GX's 2851 and 2856, and DX 470.

[53] Black to Smith, May 13, 1940, GX 2859.

[54] At Greenville, a town for which Black had high hopes, "Safeway is giving us a battle at this point." Black to Smith, December 20, 1939, GX 2839. The largest Safeway was at Wichita Falls.

[55] Smith to Black, July 15, 1940, GX 2864.

objection to raising the gross profit in Shreveport, which had no supermarkets, provided that this resulted in no loss of sales. This implies that the Shreveport gross might have been lower than it needed to be in view of the relative prices of A & P and competitors, and that profits were simply being sacrificed by selling under the market. Moreover, Smith noted, store reports on regular stores were made quarterly rather than weekly, apparently hinting that they were not paid nearly as much attention.

Six weeks later, Adams reported to Smith on a personal conference with the Hartfords. Apparently George Hartford had been fully converted to his brother's point of view:

Mr. John continually hammered on our high gross profits in the [supermarkets] throughout the Southern Division. . . . Mr. John and Mr. George both expressed themselves as feeling that if we got our gross profit down where it should be we would get some business.

The tyranny of routine figures was still a barrier to understanding, as it had been earlier in the year (above, note 45). There was insufficient planning of gross profit rates, insufficient realization of the difference between operating profit and final profit, and too much localism:

You should outline to each Unit the gross profit that you desire them to operate on beginning very soon so that our gross profit in supermarkets will wind up the quarter at a certain figure. . . . Of course, they [the Hartfords] look at, we will say, Dallas figures with a [14.40] gross in the supermarkets, to which they add 1½%, and that means we are operating the supermarkets at a [15.90] gross. I realize there should be some difference probably in Dallas, but I could not sell that idea to Mr. John or Mr. George. . . . They would not care how much money we lost as long as we got our prices down where they felt they should be for this type of operation [supermarket] . . . as long as we kept our gross profit down. They think we are making a terrible mistake throughout the Southern Division.[56]

Adams was aware of the regressive tendency to "trade up," and increase the expense rate. He wondered whether Southern stores were not giving too much service, "and whether they haven't gotten into the habit of carrying a lot of packages to the cars because some of our competitors do. I believe if you will get after the boys that an improvement can be made."

[56] Adams to Smith, August 30, 1940, GX 2873.

Black was "very much impressed" with the Hartfords' views as relayed to him, gave them "careful thought, and we are in accord with their ideas. In other words, we are ready to crack down." And he was able to translate this into the action needed in his local situation: keep about 29 of the 42 Dallas stores, lower their prices, particularly on produce and meats, and gradually eliminate the other thirteen.[57] It was a perfect microcosm of the whole process. The gross profit in supermarkets was to be kept at the definite low figure, and one must willy-nilly put out of mind any hope of raising it. Lower gross was generally profitable in itself, and it also spotlighted the variations in expense rates. Stores where the expense rate could not come down would be in the red and must be eliminated and if possible replaced. Three years had passed since the crucial meeting of August 1937, and a year since Black's arrival in Dallas, but he had only now realized the implications of the program he had been called to administer; price reductions in every store, and then the elimination of one third of them.

In preparing to crack down, Black found encouragement in a slackening of Safeway's aggressiveness, and in what he felt was an unnecessarily expensive building program, with too elaborately furnished stores, which would make it difficult for Safeway to meet a low-price program.[58]

The limitation on net profit announced early in 1939 was reiterated in 1940 and 1941.[59] In November 1940, Smith could write Black that headquarters was pleased with his showing. But there was no resting on past accomplishments, for it had been decided that the company as a whole should operate on a gross profit rate of 0.5 per cent less than its rate for the first six months of fiscal 1940. Since the Southern Division had operated at a rate of 14.45, this meant a program of 13.95, and after deducting 1.38 for the adjustments, an operating rate of 12.57. The weekly supermarket report to New York, therefore, was not to exceed that figure as an average, and Smith strongly recommended that no individual store, even a regular store, be permitted to go over 13.50.[60]

[57] Black to Smith, September 17, 1940, GX 2876.
[58] GX 2876.
[59] DPM, March 27, 1940 and April 8, 1941; GX's 218 and 93.
[60] Smith to Black, November 27, 1940, GX 2877.

Scarcely a month later, another divisional presidents' meeting decided to get the Southern operating gross down to 11.42 for the last quarter. When profits ran ahead of estimates in 1940, and the desired earnings were reached by the end of the third quarter, all divisions were ordered to cut gross even further, in order to obviate the making of any significant store profit during the remainder of the year.[61] Smith sent Black the minutes of the meeting. "The Company has good and sufficient reasons for holding the profit down for the remainder of this year." Not that there needed to be a uniform gross reduction in all units: some could be left untouched "provided it is felt that a lower rate can be used more advantageously in another unit." [62]

The average gross profit "is an absolute program and must be accomplished." But the details were left entirely to unit discretion. For example, a letter to the Atlanta unit suggested that supermarkets be divided into three price "zones," on the basis of respective competitive conditions. Reductions had to be selected according to areas and to items. For example, Miami would see no drastic reductions, since "our prices there now are well under competition, except on those below cost items which we cannot meet under any circumstances, and our sales are entirely satisfactory." As for particular commodities, "there is no need reducing items which have little or no sales qualifications. . . . There are many points where meat and produce [reductions] will yield more business than a lot of grocery reductions." [63]

By 1940, Mr. John and Mr. George were apparently successful in bringing Southern supermarket operations close to those of the other divisions.[64]

There is no evidence of any such prolonged struggles in any other division. Apparently they fell into line more easily. Thus, in the Middle Western Division, Hartford had informally set a

[61] DPM, December 17, 1940, GX 38.

[62] Smith to Black, December 26, 1940, GX 230.

[63] "W.A.C." [Carlton, division sales director] to Clanton.

[64] For the twelve months ending March 1, 1941, the expense rates of Southern supermarkets were below those of the company in the small markets, and only slightly higher in the large ones. In the four largest sizes, A & P and Southern expense rates were (per cent of sales): 11.21 and 11.19; 10.91 and 10.62; 10.84 and 10.25; 10.28 and 9.75. The largest difference is 6 per cent. See tables ("charts") 185–192 in the *Annual Binder*, vol. 16, DX 501.

gross profit rate of 12.00 or 12.50 as early as October 1938,[65] and the divisional president reiterated this a month later.[66] In warning units not to increase gross profit "to cover the cost of operation," both Hartford and Hoadley remarked that it took "courage" not to do so. Apparently both of them knew the tropismatic impulse of the small merchant to tack every cost increase onto the sales price, and they were concerned to teach the doctrine of elasticity of demand. Significantly enough, there seem to have been few complaints about the Middle Western performance. However, there were letters such as one to Hoadley in July 1940,[67] where the complaint was of too high a net profit in the Milwaukee unit during the latest two weeks. The failure to cut prices quickly enough in the wake of expense reductions, even in effect only two weeks, and even in a well-managed division, called for an explanation.

The company's new position, 1941

By the end of 1941, the conversion was far from complete. But about 68 per cent of the stores had been eliminated, and replaced by supermarkets doing a much larger aggregate volume of business.

In four years A & P had nearly regained the 1929 share of its market and made up most of the loss of profits. The money cost of handling a given physical quantity of goods had fallen by precisely one-third, and this during a period of generally rising prices (see Appendix Table 6). By any standard, it was a very impressive achievement.

There were still plenty of regular stores to close down and supermarkets to open [68] and many of the operating supermarkets were poorly located or managed. But the attitude toward losing stores is strikingly different from that of years earlier. In one division, the unsatisfactory stores had been designated (there

---

[65] October 25, 1938, GX 266.

[66] Meeting of November 21, 1938, GX 267.

[67] Hartford to Hoadley, July 29, 1940, GX 4137.

[68] Central Western meeting, April 23, 1940, GX 220; Central meeting, May 7, 1940, GX 221; DPM, June 25, 1940, GX 223.

were 49), and they would be either mended or ended within six months.[69]

The concept of gross margin as the price of grocery service had largely ousted that of individual prices of specific commodities.[70] There is an interesting example, dating from the first half of 1939, of how Atlantic divisional and unit management became aware of this. The head of the Scranton unit kept complaining that various competitors were selling leaders below cost.[71] At first he was merely offered sympathy. Early in March, Hodgson, the divisional sales director, told him of an experience in Philadelphia where Food Fair and Giant Market were selling items below cost "for weeks on end." Since it was impossible (apparently because of company policy) to meet such prices, as a second choice they made general reductions in meat and produce. "For some reason" business actually improved.[72] Three months later, he wrote again in a very different and very assured tone:

There isn't a thing we can do to combat [a] . . . competitor who sells his merchandise below our cost. . . . According to your gross profit on meats you have ample room to cause competitors quite a little concern if you really make up your mind to do so, but you will have to stay with such a program for quite some time before it starts to bring about the results you desire.

Here in Philadelphia the Food Fair and the Giant Markets used the same merchandising practices as are now being used by the Giant and Acme in your territory which we ignored completely. We made up our minds to have our own program and run our own business and you know what the results have been. . . . They are through as leaders and we intend to keep them in the background. . . . [A] duplication of [these results] is entirely possible in Scranton or any other Unit in the Division.[73]

A year later, in similar circumstances, Toolin wrote to one of his subordinates:

[69] Central Western meeting, September 1941, GX 240.
[70] Variations in markup for any given item are very wide among food stores. In part, this reflects constant adjustment to changing supply and demand; in part, it is sheer rote without reason. See Paul D. Converse, Warren Z. Cordell, and Paul A. Baumgart, *A Report [on] the Pre-Korean Food Margin Survey . . . by the Office of Price Stabilization* (Chicago: A. C. Neilsen Co., 1953).
[71] V. G. Perrin to H. F. Hodgson, March 4, 1939, GX 4204; March 29, 1939, GX 3302; telegram, May 15, 1939, GX 4089; May 24, 1939, GX 4009.
[72] Hodgson to Perrin, March 7, 1939, GX 4205.
[73] Hodgson to Perrin, June 1, 1939, GX 3819.

If the appeal is based on price alone, we should enjoy all the cash and carry business in both Paducah and Jackson. Both you and I know there is no one in the retail food business in either of these cities . . . anywhere near a gross profit like ours.

It would be futile to expect us to under-sell everybody on everything. . . . Find some way of impress[ing] upon the public that in the long run they will be money ahead if they spend all their food dollars in our super-markets.[74]

If the "commodity" could be transformed from a particular food item, which was a negligible part of the consumer's income, to the total food bill, which was a very large fraction, consumers would be that much more sensitive to A & P's appeal. "All-week low prices" had arrived to stay. The wasteful, haphazard, uncontrollable cutting of prices on individual items was to be abolished. But the 1941 plans went even further — they contemplated the standardization of gross margins and even of retail prices, thus abandoning the price zones or competitive areas through which prices had previously been set at levels corresponding to competition — subject, of course, to general company policy.[75] But this practice of meeting competition involved guessing the state of the market in every unit and even its subdivisions, never-ending readjustment to changes, correction of mistakes, etc. It was no longer necessary to pay such a price. If the company was under-selling practically every competitor in practically every territory, why bother to make many fine variations in the degree of that underselling?

The task of standardization was not easy, and had scarcely more than begun by the end of 1941, although much attention had been paid to it. A letter of July 23, 1941,[76] stressed that the standardization of retail prices on both A & P's brands and on nationally advertised products had made considerable progress, and that "it is our intention to carry this still further as soon as the very violent market situation has eased up somewhat." The reasons given for the policy are interesting:

[74] Toolin to Dejarnett, August 5, 1940, GX 226.
[75] For a good summary of the "zone" system, see Tr. 11,049–11,050.
[76] From "Director fo Sales" to C. W. Staufenberg of the Middle Western Division, GX 236.

In arriving at this decision, we concluded that competition, as it was known in the old days, does not exactly exist today. By that we mean there isn't anyone in the industry selling food at a markup as low as ours and at the same time we find fairly generally, an inclination on the part of all competition to follow our lead on prices of any important merchandise. Then, too, we are able to exercise much closer control which we feel is necessary today in view of the agitation and investigations with reference to price control.

Two months later, the national Merchandising Committee [77] agreed that price variations were too large, not only from one division to another, but even within divisions. This made it "difficult to justify our position," especially when there were large differences in closely adjoining stores. It was also decided that gross margins had often been cut too much: often as low as 4.5 per cent on fresh produce. Ten per cent was felt to be a good round figure at which to aim, both for house brands and purchased goods. But the problem was recognized as a difficult one by the resolution to make it part of the regular order of business at every monthly meeting.

The divisional president's meeting, at the end of the year,[78] pushed matters further by setting 10.5 per cent as the operating gross margin for all supermarkets. It should be neither exceeded nor reduced. Moreover, "all prices in the same type of stores are to be absolutely uniform in the same competitive area." This of course left a good deal of room for divisional discretion in setting up competitive areas. The fact was recognized at a merchandising committee meeting held a week later:[79] the divisions were admitted to be the best judges of such matters, but were urged to standardize as much and as quickly as possible.

Moreover, the essentially arbitrary nature of costs and therefore profits on particular lines was becoming much better recognized. An important report made in March 1940 pointed out that departmental expense rates in the stores were useless because common costs made allocation inaccurate or simply meaningless. Furthermore:

The great majority of Divisional executives agreed that departmental ex-

[77] Meeting of September 16, 1941, GX 241.
[78] DPM, December 9, 1941, GX 244.
[79] Meeting of September 16, 1941, GX 241.

pense rates were seldom the basis of determining the retail price policy on
the separate commodities. . . . They would be satisfied to study only the
expense rate of the total store — provided that detailed figures were available on certain controllable items of departmental expense, such as salaries,
warehouse supplies, etc.[80]

Accordingly, the calculation of these rates was discontinued.[81]
Furthermore, there was some discussion of the allocations of subsidiary profits and other headquarters' sources of income which is
interesting as illustrating the extent to which people become serv-
ants or remain masters of their accounting devices. As noted
earlier, the practice was for the units to reckon only "operating"
profit until the quarterly or annual "distributions" of manufacturing profits, etc., which would indicate the final total profit. The
New England president, at the beginning of 1939, when the supermarket development program was in full swing, complained as
follows. The goal was a 15 per cent final gross profit rate. The
unit managements should have known that, in order to reach
this, their operating profit needed to be under this by at least one
percentage point. Yet they obviously were not keeping this in
mind "because at the end of the quarter when certain adjustments
are made to the grosses, some of them go up extremely high." [82]
Not long afterward, a Central Western official complained to headquarters that under the existing system "at the end of the 12th
week, the unit is apparently in the red . . . while at the end of
the 13th week the unit is in black. . . . When conditions such
as this occur, *it is impossible to fairly pass judgment on the
operations of the unit.* At the end of the 12th we might be tempted
to suspend the entire unit organization while at the end of the
13th week we might feel like promoting them all. Isn't there
something we can do to correct this situation?" [83] The McCarthy-
Thomas report recommended that the headquarters' profit distribution be made more regularly and less frequently, because as
they stood they were distorted and . . . useless for comparison." [84]

[80] "Report of Survey — Office Policies and Procedures," by D. J. McCarthy
and R. D. Thomas, p. 19, March 1, 1940, GX 319.
[81] "Report of Survey . . . ," p. 23, March 1, 1940, GX 319.
[82] Byrnes to all unit heads, January 24, 1939, DX 385.
[83] Dole to Wheeler, March 3, 1939, GX 3521 (italics added).
[84] But the "distorted and . . . useless" figures were a treasure-trove for the
Department of Justice. See below, Chapter XVI.

They noted (probably with approval) that two divisions favored discontinuing them altogether.[85] But the Atlantic sales director wrote the Baltimore sales manager later in the year: "I like to bear in mind as I look at each week's figures that we do have an 'ace in the hole' when the final reckoning is done." [86]

That the system should have acquired greater importance is a reflection of the company's new competitive position. A year before John Toolin of Central Western had written headquarters:

We have no competition from a price point of view. . . . No supermarket operator, either a corporate chain or so-called independent, operating stores in this part of the country, has a retail price structure that will come within 2 per cent of the 12 per cent we are striving for in our supermarkets; therefore, while we recognize them all as competitors, we do not take them into serious consideration as a factor in determining where we shall locate our own markets.[87]

Toolin was if anything too conservative. The company expense rate for fiscal 1941 (which included January and February 1942 and was therefore biased upward) was 11.78 per cent. Appendix Table 19 shows that this was more than five percentage points lower than three other chains in the largest size group, and from five to eight percentage points below chains in other size groups.

This dovetails perfectly with headquarters' anxiety to keep gross profit down. If the A & P price level was distinctly lower than its competitors', this means that it was at any given moment below the market level, less than what the traffic would bear. Gross profit could at any moment be increased with only a trifling loss of business, and of course with a considerable increase in net profit. In 1941, the net profit rate was somewhat less than 2 per cent. If Toolin was right in thinking that no competitor was within two per cent of the A & P price level, then the company could have approximately doubled its net profit any time it chose, simply by raising prices to the point where it was just meeting competition. With such constant upward pressure impinging on every one of six thousand stores, a firm repressive hand needed to be applied at all times in order to keep gross mar-

---

[85] GX 319, p. 21.
[86] Hodgson to Kelly, December 16, 1940, GX 398.
[87] Toolin to R. W. Burger, July 24, 1940, GX 225.

gins and net profit from rising to the market level. The sacrificed profits were in effect to be continuously invested in a peculiar type of advertising — which appealed to the consumer's rationality by benefiting his pocketbook. At any given moment it was possible to cash in on this investment by letting prices go to competitive levels, or above them, as had been done after 1929. The great concern of headquarters was to see that it did not happen again.

Competitors could of course match any particular A & P price they chose, but few of them could match the price level because few could lay goods down on the counter as cheaply. Their most formidable chain competitor, Safeway, was now lagging far behind them, just as A & P had once lagged behind Safeway. According to some A & P correspondence in 1941, the scale of Safeway operations was much smaller than A & P's: instead of concentrating on stores which would do $10,000 weekly, as A & P was strenuously attempting to do, Safeway stores were planned to do between $2500 and $3500.[88] If Appendix Table 19 is any guide, their expense rate must have been some 4 per cent higher than A & P's, and in fact A & P believed their gross to be about 16 per cent as compared with A & P's gross of $12\frac{1}{2}$ to $13\frac{1}{2}$ per cent.[89] Safeway matched A & P prices on groceries as a matter of principle, but did not match on meats and produce. Safeway practice differed from A & P also in that they charged and advertised the same prices in small and in large stores, regardless of the difference in expense rate, unlike A & P's separation of supermarkets from old regular stores for pricing purposes.

As of 1941, Safeway and other important competitors were slow to develop the supermarket, and A & P was making hay in consequence. This was a temporary advantage, as the latter knew perfectly well,[90] but could be used to entrench more permanently.

[88] Hodgson to Bieber, July 7, 1941, GX 3291. See also Hoadley (Middle Western president) to Reilly (headquarters), October 8, 1941, DX 89.

[89] The A & P operating gross would only be comparable with another operating gross calculated in the same manner. From the letter it appears that the comparison was explicitly being made, which indicates that the A & P and Safeway data are calculated in similar fashion. However, the difference is so wide that even an error of $1\frac{1}{2}$ per cent, for A & P "distribution," would not invalidate the picture of a much higher Safeway gross margin and price level.

[90] See, e.g., Toolin to Burger, July 24, 1940, GX 225.

Hoadley, the Middle Western president, said in October 1941, that A & P

had the advantage of being pretty much alone in the field of supermarket operation. . . . As our competitors follow our lead . . . we must seek out other advantages of operation, management and merchandising. . . . Experiment with labor saving equipment, and study of store operation, will result in greater efficiency and a lower expense rate. We have a wage scale that is second to none, and we should be satisfied with nothing less than the best personnel in the grocery field.[91]

Appendix Table 19 confirms that the company was much more efficient in the day-to-day business of warehousing and retail operation. The A & P expense rate (see Chart 3) for 1941 was actually one-third lower than the average for three other chains with annual sales over $100 million, and the advantage over smaller chains was even greater. The statistics do not show any significant association between size and efficiency; they do show A & P to be ahead of the crowd.

Efficiency, however, is not only a matter of moving goods, but also of understanding the market and being able to cope with it. The realization that prices could determine sales and therefore costs had permeated not only top management but the organization as well. The company had perfected the means whereby it could fix its prices and margins in thousands of local markets so as to approximate with a fair degree of precision the set of prices which best suited the company's long-run advantage.

The immediate goal was now 25 per cent of all food sales in all localities where the company had located its stores. It is difficult, however, to separate political from economic considerations. The cash-and-carry market was probably much larger than 25 per cent in most cities; yet it seems only sensible to keep well short of a limit which can, without notice, contract as well as expand. In any event, as Appendix Tables 15 and 16 show, the 25 per cent goal was sufficiently far off to allow plenty of time for revisions as it was approached. But the fear of hostile public opinion was possibly decisive. In mid-1940, John Hartford had gone even fur-

---

[91] Middle Western meeting, October 20, 1941, DX 143.

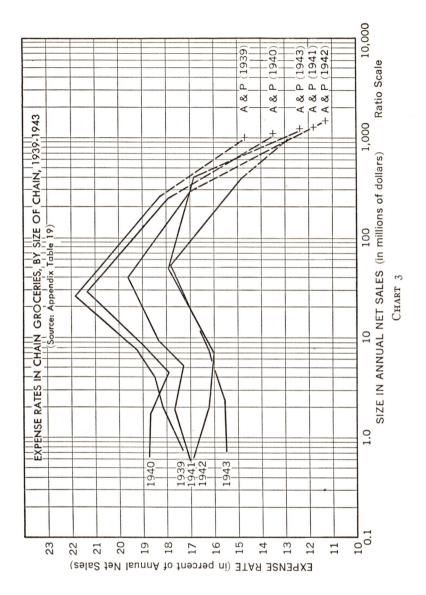

EXPENSE RATES IN CHAIN GROCERIES, BY SIZE OF CHAIN, 1939-1943
(Source: Appendix Table 19)

CHART 3

ther, and questioned whether A & P "should have over 10 per cent of the business in any given city because . . . if we get too much business we will make ourselves better targets for the sharp-shooters." [92] Apparently this extreme conservatism was overcome by the next year; perhaps it was nothing more than an off-hand, pessimistic remark, but two seasoned executives agreed with it.

War and postwar, 1941–1957

We have neither the materials nor the need for a detailed account of later years. The peacetime boom year of 1941 ended on December 7, when the conversion of the American economy to "all-out defense," which had seemed beyond the powers of the United States government, was quickly accomplished by the Imperial Japanese Navy. A & P, along with other chains and independent supermarkets, found themselves hampered by gasoline and manpower shortages. Moreover, when price control and rationing were introduced, "there was a tendency for some consumers to shift to independent food stores where an established personal relationship enabled them to obtain certain scarce items with a greater degree of regularity." [93] In less inhibited language we may say that the politically vulnerable chain stores were unable to charge, or, therefore, to pay, black-market prices. Hence they lost supplies and therefore customers.

The year 1946 saw the end of OPA and an upward leap in A & P sales relative to all other food stores. By the end of 1957, A & P had recovered its wartime losses; as Appendix Table 2 shows, its share of the national food market was comparable to 1941. However, A & P has almost no representation on the Pacific Coast, the area which grew most quickly in population and trade from 1940 to 1950. Hence they probably fared better in their local markets than this table indicates, and were it possible to bring

[92] Adams to Smith, July 10, 1940, GX 217–A. Adams agreed with Hartford, and Smith answered soon thereafter, in an even more gloomy tone, GX 217–B.

[93] Reba L. Osborne, "Sales of Chain Grocery and Combination and Variety Stores by Regions, 1944," *Survey of Current Business*, October 1945, p. 16. See also, Clement Wilson and Reba L. Osborne, "The Pattern of Chain Store Sales in Retail Distribution," *Survey of Current Business*, June 1947.

Appendix Table 15 down to date, the picture would be more favorable.

There was certainly expansion. The total number of A & P stores declined from just under six thousand at the end of 1943 to 4.2 thousand at the end of 1957; but at the former date, only 1.7 stores were supermarkets (see Appendix Table 5). It is a safe guess that A & P had over twice as many supermarkets in 1957 as in 1943. There was also an increase in employment — from a 1941 peak of 75.1 thousand to about 97.0 thousand in 1957. The latter figure is only a guess, however. Another indication of growth during recent years is the increase in fixed assets, which were $30.7 million in 1941, $22.9 million in 1945, and $151.3 million in 1950 (Appendix Table 8). If we assume that book depreciation is about equal to physical deterioration, and that postwar costs were roughly double the average of interwar costs, it required about 15.6 million postwar dollars to restore the 1941 assets. Actual expansion of fixed assets was $128.4 million in excess of this, or $64.2 in interwar dollars. Thus one can say very roughly that the A & P net physical plant nearly tripled between 1941 and 1957. Like the change in the number of stores, however, this is a residual of two opposite tendencies — writing off the old stores and setting up the new.

The restoration of profits is impressive. That dollar earnings were at an all-time peak is not particularly meaningful because of the general price rise. But the rate of return on net worth averaged 26.2 per cent, and even in 1948–1950 — when there was little distortion of reported profits by inventory gains — it averaged 23.7 per cent. In part, this figure is inflated because of the under-depreciation of fixed assets carried on the books at prewar valuations; in part, it is understated because a period of rapid expansion always involves nonrecurrent costs which are in the nature of capital investment rather than current expense. The company is obviously in sound condition, but lacking access to its internal records, we can say nothing about its market strategy, or how successfully it has pursued its policy of profit limitation. The death of John A. Hartford in August, 1951, may have brought a decisive change in the company's operations, but I see no reason to suppose so.

Conclusions

A firm which had accomplished two major innovations in two decades failed to probe its third and greatest opportunity. When others did so, this onetime leader was unable even to follow. Moreover, it could not even carry on its familiar activities in a satisfactory way. Within seven years of its greatest successes, it faced disaster. The story has been told as briefly as seemed possible, and there remains the problem of why A & P as entrepreneur first stumbled and then recovered.

The same problem, as we have tried to make clear, was faced in 1925, 1929, and 1937. It concerned the relation of cost to price in a firm composed of many small retailing units. Most firms of small or moderate size, which sell in a market where buyers are either unable or unwilling to switch quickly from seller to seller in search of the best price, tend to set price according to some kind of "full cost" principle. That is, cost as some particular level of output is taken as a datum, and some conventional percentage is added on for profit. Of course, the firm would do better by considering output as a variable; it would probably be more profitable to charge a higher price for a smaller sales volume, or a lower price for a larger volume. For only by very unlikely chance would the conventional markup be the most profitable one which could be chosen. However, and this is easy to overlook, many a firm will start out with a full-cost price and be induced, by an actively competitive market, to raise or lower it. They may even expect and welcome this: bargaining must start somewhere.

But even when the "full-cost" principle is actually followed through, it is not necessarily irrational. For the effort of estimating elasticities of demand and cost may be so great, and results so uncertain, that on strictly rational principles, it will not be worth while to make it. This is particularly true for the small retail establishment which sells a variety of goods. The reaction of sales volume to a price increase or decrease is not only uncertain: in the great majority of cases it cannot be traced at all. No more ludicrous spectacle could be imagined than that of a shopkeeper trying to calculate the demand elasticities and cross-elasticities of the hundreds of items on his shelves.

It follows that reactions to changes in demand are very different from those in response to changes in cost of goods. The latter are as palpable as changes in the weather. A price move will follow, and practically always in the same amount. But although the retailer may have a notion, at best hazy, that price changes on one or more items or lines could profitably be raised or lowered disproportionately to changes in the cost of goods, this is so uncertain and risky a proposition that it is usually unwise to consider it. Hence the retailer is bound to be out of touch with demand, and the lag between change and his awareness of it is bound to be great.

There is of course one saving factor. The retailer is highly volume-conscious. Increased purchases do not raise the unit price he pays.[94] The "expenses" of labor, rent, etc., vary but little with sales, and there is normally some excess capacity in the short run. A larger volume is therefore viewed as the infallible road to higher profits, and is sought by every available device of salesmanship and advertising within the reach of the firm.

If, therefore, some god from the machine were to promise a retailer larger sales in return, the retailer would cheerfully promise lower prices. But the relation does not hold both ways. To cut price by a given per cent is, for the instant present, to cut revenues by a very much larger per cent. To pursue a lower price policy is to gamble on a probability. The odds may be in the gambler's favor, but his bank roll must be sufficient to support a long enough run for those odds to work themselves out. A small firm (or sometimes a large one) is not necessarily held in its cost-plus routine only by lack of intelligence or aggressiveness; cost-plus pricing may actually be the best course to follow, for it affords a better chance of survival and profits. In many situations it is only big business which can use the law of large numbers and take the gamble.[95] The numbers are large in one or two

[94] This assumes that the retailer is not so large a proportion of the market that changes in his demand have an influence on price. Later discussion will support this conclusion (see Part II).

[95] See Lancelot Hogben, *Mathematics for the Million* (New York, 1936) pp. 573–574, 589–590. When this eminent scholar discusses economists and economics, he generally displays more wit than substance. But his intuition has served him well in this instance.

dimensions: in space, i.e., in many outlets or customers; and in time, i.e., in enough weeks, months, or years for the policy to have a fair trial. It may be one of the most important economies of scale for the firm.

But if the great advantage of size is that it permits this kind of gamble, the process is not automatic or easy. It is necessary to see the probability, to devise means for exploiting it, and then put them into effect. But this is in itself a peculiar problem of the scale of the firm, for as circumstances grow more complex and the organization larger (there is no nice proportionality between these two), the departments of the corporate staff and line replace the compartments of an individual entrepreneur's mind, and their coordination becomes a task in itself.

A & P as an entrepreneurial mechanism was peculiar in that it was a big business composed of thousands of small retailing units. At the very highest level, the corporate entrepreneur did well throughout. The use of "expense" and "gross margins" gave "cost" and "price" a precise and operational meaning. John Hartford and others at headquarters and in the divisions knew that the consumer could be induced to look at "price" in the same way, and would respond to the promise of a lower food bill, of being "money ahead," as Toolin said. But there was a missing link. The Hartfords and their colleagues were unable to enforce their price policies in the stores. The cost-plus habits of the small retailing unit were in full contradiction to the policies of top management and would not change. One might as well describe the color red to a blind man as describe elasticity of demand to a local employee. These unit and store managers were not stupid or complacent. Their habits were well adapted for survival in small retailing; but they were out of joint with the larger scheme at headquarters. The unit or store manager wanted a record of profitable operation in order to keep his job and advance in the company, and he was not responsive to a policy which might indeed produce larger company profits, but wipe out his own. Even a trusted unit head like Black found it hard to believe that if he followed instructions he would not be held responsible for low profits or losses. Nor were unit or divisional executives too anxious to keep gross profit down everywhere, throwing some stores hopelessly into the red, for that would mean closing those stores, and higher overhead costs per unit until the losses in sales could be made up. "Courage" was needed, and it was hard to muster without a clear idea of the reasons for running risks. Here head-quarters was certainly at fault in that they did not clearly explain to the lower ranks just what they were about. Perhaps they did not realize it clearly enough themselves. They were snatched back from the brink of disaster by the heavily disguised good fortune of the supermarket. But for eight or nine years, top management pointed one way and the company went another. They could not teach their employees the concept of elasticity of demand, or the possibility that prices may determine costs.

Everything seems so simple, all the kinds of knowledge required seem so plain, all the combinations so insignificant. . . .

Everything is very simple in war, but the simplest thing is difficult. These difficulties accumulate and produce a friction of which no one can form a correct idea who has not seen war.[96]

As in war, so in business or in any undertaking which requires men to be organized into large groups.

Yet the seemingly insuperable difficulties tumbled one after the other in 1938–1941. A low gross margin, all-week low prices, and closing of the red-ink stores were quickly carried into effect, despite the company's being in the throes of the supermarket revolution, with relatively little time to spare for reforms. But to say "despite" the change is of course misleading: we ought really to say because of it. For, once the crust of inertia was broken, and the A & P personnel began to move, the tasks of improvement became relatively easy to accomplish. Why did it happen? To speak of a sense of urgency as the new element means little. Such a sense conduces more to panic than to purposeful action unless there is a sound organization waiting to be sparked by it.

It was easier to set up a new method of business than to perfect an old one: more precisely, the old problems were simply swallowed up and solved as part of the new one. Perhaps in many industries there is little of the adaptation along existing production functions with which economists are so concerned. Rather do

[96] Karl von Clausewitz, *On War* (New York: Modern Library, 1943), p. 53.

the firms in the industry become frozen within their respective places until a major innovation, like a spring flood, sweeps the whole structure away.

The A & P crisis thus underlines both the uses and the limitations of economic analysis. It is clear to any economist who reads the record that John Hartford's was the right way to increase profits, and "to increase [company] profits," as one of the headquarters group wrote in another connection, "is our one aim." [97] But to get others to put a few basic ideas into practice concerns not economic science but executive art, and the futility that dogs all human effort.

In a sense, the best analysis of the A & P crisis, like that of untold organization crises before and since, is written in a famous bit of history. In August 1864, hope of preserving the federal Union was at an all-time low after a Confederate army had again opened the back door to Washington through the Shenandoah Valley, and nearly captured the town. General Grant designated a force to be sent after the Confederate column to destroy it. Nobody in Washington liked the plan except Mr. Lincoln, who wrote Grant: "This, I think, is exactly right as to how our forces should move, but please look over the despatches you may have received from here, ever since you made that order, and discover if you can that there is any idea in the head of any one here of . . . [following it]. I repeat to you, it will neither be done nor attempted, unless you watch it every day and hour and force it." For three years Mr. Lincoln had been tried beyond human endurance because he had seen that this was the only way to handle the menace; for all his clear vision as to what was needed, and his power as commander-in-chief of the armed forces, he had for three years been unable to get anybody to do as he wished, until Grant, with some coaching, began to see it. All we need do is change the x's and y's; the equations are the same.

[97] See below, Chapter 12.

PART II

PROCUREMENT OF GOODS

V

THE DEVELOPMENT OF THE
BUYING SYSTEM FOR
PROCESSED FOODS

The market in processed foods is really an infinite number of markets held together by a network so complex and so constantly in flux that it nearly defies generalization. The degree of concentration in the manufacturing group "food and kindred products" does not differ greatly from that of manufacturing at large: in 1954 the median concentration ratio among food products was 40; for all manufactured products it was 34.[1] More decisive than concentration, perhaps — or what comes to the same thing, greatly lowering the effective concentration over time — are generally low entry barriers, both in respect to capital and to access to raw material. The balance of professional opinion appears to consider food manufacturing as one of the more competitive sectors of the economy.[2] But this is an issue that we need not probe deeply. There will be general agreement that almost any degree of competition and monopoly is represented. Even where competition is very keen, it may be very imperfect. The rivalry of sellers leads both to price adjustments in the classic pattern

[1] *Concentration in American Industry*, Report of the Subcommittee on Antitrust and Monopoly to the Committee on the Judiciary, U. S. Senate, 85 Cong., 1 sess. (Washington, 1957), table 5.

[2] See the following TNEC Monographs: No. 1, Saul Nelson and Walter Keim, *Price Behavior and Business Policy* (Washington, 1940); No. 21, Clair Wilcox, *Competition and Monopoly in American Industry* (Washington, 1941), especially pp. 52–53; No. 35, A. C. Hoffman, *Large-Scale Organization in the Food Industry* (Washington, 1940), Chapter IX. See also William H. Nicholls, "Imperfect Competition in Agricultural Processing and Distributing Industries," *Canadian Journal of Economic and Political Science*, 10:150–164 (1944).

and to product differentiation. Elements of monopoly are always appearing; they may be local or national, temporary or permanent. If they do last, it is not because those on the other side of the market have not tried to circumvent them.

The A & P buying system reflects these market structures, and to some extent it has reacted back upon some of them. The whole process is a seamless web of cause and effect, so that no matter where one cuts into it some difficulties are met. To describe the buying system is a good introduction to the markets in which it operates, yet some of the conditions for A & P buying will not be fully apparent until the markets are explicitly rather than implicitly covered.

The headquarters organization

The A & P buying system took permanent shape around 1925–1926 and has not changed greatly since. At its center until his death in 1950 stood David T. Bofinger, an A & P employee since 1899,[3] who was perhaps the most important man in the whole company, after John A. Hartford. Assisting him in the New York office were ten to twelve specialists. F. W. Gundrey, in charge of national buying arrangements, and Charles W. Parr, head of all the field buying offices, were apparently the most important of them; and both had been with the company for over thirty years. The other assistants were each given national control over a single type of product. They were all old-timers, with no particular rank or precedence.[4]

Responsible to the headquarters group are the purchasing directors of the several divisions, who in turn control the unit or warehouse buyers within the division. There are few rigid rules as to who approves or buys any particular lot of goods. A manufacturer wishing to sell in more than one division "should go to one of the field buying offices if it is an item in their line, or we like for him to come into headquarters," although this desirable procedure is not actually necessary.[5] It goes without saying that the higher echelons can always overrule the lower, but the system

---

[3] Tr. 20,332.
[4] Parr, Tr. 206–207, 213; Gundrey, Tr. 1618.
[5] Parr, Tr. 207, 210, 1610.

is flexible enough to keep the top management from wasting its time on local matters. As has been seen, and will be further detailed, the flexibility has a high cost. The thirty-eight warehouses (at the time of the trial) bought on requisition through the nearest field office, but were also able to make local purchases where the product was highly perishable.[6]

There was hardly any coherent purchasing system until the reorganization of 1925. The decentralization at that time of all possible duties to the divisions was precisely what made possible greater centralization of buying policy. In June of 1925 it was decided that all large buying arrangements were to be made by headquarters; divisional buyers were required to work closely with Bofinger, and unit buyers were required to exchange price and supplier lists, and generally profit by pooling experience.[7]

The other important development was that of the field buying offices. Some had been opened in fairly haphazard fashion in large canning centers, acting as brokers both to A & P and to the trade, and collecting the usual fees.[8] In October 1925, a suggestion was made to open a buying office in Baltimore because it was a great vegetable canning center. John Hartford thought the idea "very constructive" and it was voted to look into the matter.[9] How little time was wasted may be judged by the fact that only three months later Bofinger regarded as a success both the Baltimore office and the one started in Milwaukee just a little later. He mentioned the avoidance of anticipatory price increases and a saving on brokerage. Moreover, there was an added advantage in the superior information furnished the company by its own man "rather than [depending] on rumors and various incorrect reports." It was easier to get better and more uniform quality.[10]

By the end of 1926 the Baltimore office was sufficiently mature to serve as a model for the rest. J. M. Zoller, its director, read what John Hartford called "a very fine report" to the divisional purchasing directors; [11] and it is worth examining at length be-

---

[6] Parr, Tr. 207, 209, 424.
[7] DPM, June 25, 1925, GX 103; Bofinger, Tr. 20,389.
[8] Parr, Tr. 208.
[9] DPM, October 27, 1925, GX 104.
[10] DPM, February 3, 1926, GX 105.
[11] Divisional purchasing directors, December 29, 1926, GX 438.

cause it shows A & P adaptation to markets where supply arrived in discontinuous packages, and prices fluctuated sharply.

First, the policy was "always bearish," and purchases and turnover were kept as small as possible. But this must not be taken too literally. In response to Hartford's questions, some of the buying men explained that "there is a difference between investment and speculation. . . . Their policy was to buy a little heavy when the market was right."

Second, there were no temporary stampedes on rumors of short crops, etc., with panic spreading among branches (units' warehouses) which then tried to outbid one another for the supposedly short supply.

Third, the company was able to buy strictly according to its requirements "and yet secure advantage of its combined requirements buying." For example, a large distress lot of canned corn (80,000 cases) had been available at a very low price. A joint bid was made through the Baltimore field buying office by twelve warehouses. They did not need the whole lot, but were confident that they could dispose of the excess, and they did. The saving on this one transaction was sixteen thousand dollars. In the one year of its life the Baltimore office had been able to absorb "thousands of bargain offerings" of this type, although of course not this size.

Developments since 1925

By 1929 there were field buying offices in San Francisco, Baltimore, Milwaukee, Rochester, Seattle, New Orleans, and Minneapolis. In 1930 the national meat department was established in Chicago to operate, in effect, as a field buying office confined to meats.

The writer knows of no important changes in buying policy since that time. But the attempt to aggregate purchases so as always to be buying in the largest possible amounts has been a perennial problem, as in the nature of the organization it had to be. Thus, late in 1929 it was recorded that:

Instances have been brought to the surface where a commodity had been stocked in more than one Division for a considerable length of time before it was referred to Headquarters for the purpose of effecting a satisfactory relationship between the manufacturer and ourselves.[12]

The same problem was discussed at the meeting of two months later, but it does not seem to have been regarded as acute.[13] In 1931 there were complaints that the national meat department was not functioning as intended, and accounted for only about 10 per cent of A & P meat purchases. Buying should be funneled through the Chicago office

not only from the standpoint of the savings to be effected due to pooling quantity orders, but to . . . [raise] standards of quality and [maintain] more uniform grades throughout the organization. Furthermore, with our fresh meat business expanding, it is becoming more and more important that the present competitive buying among our own units be reduced to a minimum.[14]

The reader will note how this parallels the discussion five years earlier.

In 1934 buying procedures were tightened somewhat. A divisional presidents' meeting early in the year [15] decided to "give Headquarters the advantage of the Company's buying power" not only on price but on the quality and standardization of the product.[16] No unit head was permitted to sign buying contracts, although he could still make spot purchases. Only the purchasing department of the divisions was permitted to sign advertising contracts.[17] Apparently persons outside of the departments were not trusted to sign advantageous ones; moreover, and this was considered worse, they had been signing buying contracts.

The divisional purchasing directors, meeting late in March, voted an immediate end to buying by persons outside of the purchasing department, e.g., by "field supervision and unit sales departments." It was the old conflict between staff and line, and the staff was reasserting itself with the approval of the top management. The purchasing directors urged that unit buyers try to

[12] Divisional purchasing directors, October 16, 1929.
[13] Divisional purchasing directors, February 19, 1930, GX 425.
[14] Divisional purchasing directors, April 23, 1931, GX 431.
[15] Probably at the beginning of March. The writer is unable to locate this document, but it is extensively paraphrased in the next three references.
[16] Central Division meeting, April 9, 1934, GX 442.
[17] New England meeting, March 13, 1934, GX 433.

channel the maximum of buying through headquarters; moreover, divisional purchasing directors should supervise them closely to see that this was actually done. Decisions on which products were to be stocked rested with headquarters. Finally, brokers were to be dispensed with as much as possible and replaced by the field buying offices, which did the same job.[18]

Four years later, when the company was in the throes of conversion to supermarkets and badly hampered by the Robinson-Patman Act, Bofinger addressed a meeting which he said had been called

to bring out the need for strong, concerted, and uniform action by the key buyers in each division to protect our purchasing position. . . . It seemed necessary to stem the trend toward practices . . . that penalize our buying powers and retact unfavorably upon our competitive retailing position.

These practices were essentially the making of local agreements with suppliers, particularly with those who had refused to make deals with headquarters, citing the Robinson-Patman Act as their real or ostensible reason.[19] As we shall see later, that Act imposed a system whereby the company often paid higher net prices than did others, i.e., the same price to the supplier while performing and incurring the cost of such functions as contact (brokerage), wholesaling, etc. Nevertheless, no important changes in policy resulted from this meeting.

The situation in 1939 is well defined in a letter from Parr to Zoller, urging that a certain deal had to be completed quickly or not at all:

We cannot commit the company for any definite quantity nor should we book any firm orders in order to obtain a quantity price.[20]

We cannot put the whole company's selling efforts behind any product which is sold on the basis of flat list price to everybody. At the same time, we cannot prevent warehouses from placing orders for such a product.

[The deal should be closed in time.] Otherwise, as you know, they [the

[18] Divisional purchasing directors, March 27, 1934, GX 434.

[19] Divisional purchasing directors, April 22, 1938, GX 315.

[20] In the context, it is clear that Parr is using the term "quantity" to mean "volume," i.e., the total amount bought over some extended period of time, not an amount bought in one delivery unit, such as a carload. This ambiguity is very widespread in the grocery trade, and it generates much confusion.

warehouses] would likely go ahead and place orders on the basis of the full list price. Furthermore, it is always more difficult to negotiate for a price if the shipper knows warehouses are going to order the goods anyhow.[21]

Imperfect control of local personnel cropped up that same year in meat. New England was the worst offender:

Boston's buying plan played directly into the hands of the big packers and has encouraged the latter in the belief that if they are successful in making local hook-ups with the various A & P units, they will be able to circumvent the centralized buying control exercised by our Chicago Office, which, admittedly, had diverted a big percentage of our purchases to independent packers at considerable savings to the Company. . . . Boston's buying through local jobbers [is] entirely contrary to the Company's policy.[22]

Headquarters would sometimes be concerned about the susceptibility of its local personnel to the blandishments of manufacturers and brokers. This problem was a hardy perennial which would never, in the nature of a large organization, be altogether solved. The Chicago unit, in 1940, prepared a manual on "Control of Direct-Delivery Vendors." [23] The main emphasis was on keeping manufacturers' representatives away from display shelves or any other shelves. "Let's be clear on this — no one is to visit your store to check merchandise, display merchandise or handle it in any way except as specified by this office."

In February 1941, Mylott wrote to a subordinate that he disliked the influence of salesmen from Crosse & Blackwell upon store managers, since they were able to foist a lot of slow-moving items on them.[24] There was no displeasure when Crosse & Blackwell discontinued store servicing (visits by representatives) early in 1941; quite the contrary, for Crosse & Blackwell calculated that it was saving 5.14 per cent this way, and allowed it to A & P as a reduction from list price.[25]

There are occasional passing references to the problem, which is difficult to solve because the responsibility is divided between

[21] Parr to Zoller, April 3, 1939, GX 930.
[22] Connors to Parr, June 21, 1939, GX 618.
[23] Dated May 12, 1940, DX 45.
[24] Mylott to Meehan, February 24, 1941, GX 779.
[25] Testimony of Sidney H. Thornton, vice-president and general sales manager, Tr. 2690.

buying personnel and store management. Space allocation is one of the most important variables determining profits, and a study of eleven successful supermarkets in 1953 showed a none too satisfactory situation: 30 per cent of the grocery items studied had average sales of one unit per week or less.[26] Small wonder that the problem never ceased to be discussed by A & P executives.

I would sum up buying procedures and policies in three words: centralization, flexibility, and preferences (which might or might not be discriminatory). They have never changed to any significant degree. There was a continuous tendency for local personnel, under continuous pressure by sellers' agents, to forget company policy, but the failure does not seem to have been of any serious extent, and whatever effects it may have had were swamped by those of the Robinson-Patman Act.[27]

[26] U. S. Department of Agriculture, Marketing Research Report No. 80, *Space Allocation for Grocery Items in Food Stores* (Washington, February 1955).

[27] See the circular of the purchasing director, Atlantic Division, May 22, 1940, GX 1094.

VI

PRODUCT TYPES
AND MARKET STRUCTURES

A SYSTEM of prices and price differentials can only be understood with two basic facts in mind. The first is the existence of many steps or functions between the manufacturer and the consumer: making contact, assembling, transportation, breaking bulk, storage, etc. Every such function requires an investment and a working force, and commands a market price. It may be performed either by a separate firm or as part of an integrated firm. As goods pass down the line, their prices reflect the accretion of services. Price comparisons can be made only if the commodities are not only similar physically but carry with them the same package of services. Whether one source of supply or another is more advantageous to a business management can be ascertained only if both are put on the same basis: whether f.o.b., or laid down cost at destination, or some other. It is idle to call any particular combination of goods-plus-services "the" price or cost, or the "true" price or cost. It is only necessary to be consistent when making comparisons.

The second principle is that both buyers and sellers are constantly trying to protect their respective positions by acquiring some kind of limited monopoly or monopsony power.[1] But no sooner is the position established than the other side of the mar-

---

[1] "Monopoly" as we use it here has no necessarily good or bad meaning. A processor who improves the quality of the product, or its freshness after days on the shelf, etc., acquires a "monopoly" for so long as he is not successfully imitated. A clever advertising campaign, based on no facts whatsoever, but serving to persuade customers that the product is unique, may also confer a degree of monopoly. And it may even confer greater "utility" on the consumer.

ket tries to undermine it. Temporary successes and failures are always occurring; one needs to watch the main drift to judge any group's tactics.

Trading items

It must be more than a coincidence that the rise of the food chain stores in the 1920's was paralleled by the swift growth of brands and labels for processed foods and by the growth of advertising to build up those brands.[2] A brand is a species of monopoly, and there is no more fundamental dichotomy in the minds of A & P buyers than that between "trading items," which are bulk merchandise and packaged goods lacking the nationally known label, and "list price" items or "branded goods," which do have this symbol of merchandise aristocracy. The testimony of Charles W. Parr, who distinguished them in this manner, is worth quoting at some length. He states that trading items consist of

bulk merchandise and any other merchandise, even though it is in packages, which does not bear some nationally known or semi-nationally known brand, and which is sold on an open trading basis, or "horse-trading" basis, rather than on a list price basis.

List price basis, he says,

means the so-called nationally advertised grocery items, such as Ivory soap, Crisco, Del Monte goods. . . . On dealing with trading items, we want a buyer — a real buyer — a fellow who is shrewd — a fellow who can hold his own in dealing with the shipper. On a list price item, all they need is an order clerk. . . . Take a trading item — like flour, for instance. The price of flour is based on the wheat market, and might change twenty times a day.

Q. What about the list price [items]? A. Some of them never change. . .[3]

In 1929 the estimated weight of these various types was approximately as shown in the tabulation,[4] and it probably did not change much over the years. Products may of course cross the

---

[2] See the testimony of Paul S. Willis, president of the Grocery Manufacturers' Association, Tr. 153.

[3] Parr, Tr. 407–408. See also note 4, below.

[4] DPM, March 18, 1930, GX 120. The average price decline since July 20, 1929, had been: trading items, 16 per cent; advertised brands, less than one per cent; meats, 3.5 per cent; perishables, up 2.5 per cent.

Type	Per cent of total
Trading items	40.5
Advertised (list price) items	33.8
Meats	12.0
Perishables	13.7
Total	100.0

line, at least temporarily. Meat is not easily classified. Fresh meats are sold on a basis of negotiated prices by telephone and personal consultation, on the basis of daily current livestock receipts and prices, competing offers, etc., with the price changing hourly. Even in the case of canned meats:

While canned meat packers, like other food processors, issue price lists, they do not adhere to them as closely as some grocery manufacturers. This is due perhaps to the frequent fluctuations in their raw material market. We know that concessions are frequently obtained on large orders. It is also true that occasionally a packer's local branch will cut prices on a small lot without authority from the main office.[5]

Obviously, trading items (and perishables) are sold in highly competitive markets. But even though many of them verge on the purely competitive, it is obvious from the record that they are *imperfectly* competitive, although the degree of perfection may vary greatly in a very short time. The products are often seasonal, sometimes highly so. Products can never be fully standardized:

Price of trading goods constantly varies. We have known [canned] tomatoes to be sold at three different prices in the same day when the market was active. Also quality is quite a consideration as regards to price of trading goods. This, of course, is not true of specialties [list price items].[6]

Furthermore, large amounts are often needed on short notice, or come into the market suddenly. Zoller's example of the distress lot of canned corn was probably only a tiny fraction of all canned corn of that grade sold in Baltimore during the year, but it must have been a large part of what was available during that particular week. A & P's asset, on which it realized so handsomely, was its continuous contact with a much wider market than could be found in Baltimore overnight. In such markets the asking price

[5] Fraser (national meat department) to all directors of purchases, February 5, 1940, GX 859.
[6] Zoller to Parr, September 26, 1939, GX 1450.

and the offering price depend on a judgment of how quickly another such lot can be made available; of the cost of taking a less
suitable lot now, or an equally good lot a week hence, versus the
slight premium the lot fetches today. The situation is very similar
to the organized commodity and security exchanges. These markets are purely competitive. Yet increments of goods which are
small relative to the total amount traded during the year will
send prices sharply up or down for the moment. The mechanics
of trade call for experienced specialists; and large fortunes are
made or lost by buying or selling a few days or even hours before
or after the crowd. The markets in trading items are not as extreme a type as the exchanges. But "a real buyer, a fellow who is
shrewd," who knows when to come in and stay out of such markets, and who can dispose of large amounts that others cannot
touch, is obviously going to acquire goods at a lower average cost
over a month or a year than the market at large. This does not
necessarily mean that the A & P warehouse acquires these goods
at a lower cost; for one must include in their total acquisition
cost the maintenance of the field buying office, salaries of skilled
personnel, etc.

The functions just described are the linkage of manufacturer
with wholesaler, and could also be performed by a broker, or by
a manufacturer's agent, or by the salaried sales force of the manufacturer. Why did its own buying offices appear like such a gift
from heaven to A & P? The essential advantage seems to be in
its vertical integration of the wholesale function with the middleman or "contactual" function.[7] Because of the large size of the
A & P market, the law of large numbers comes into play. Buyers
are able to take goods on the most advantageous terms because
they do not need to wait to ascertain requirements; they can
forecast requirements accurately because the sample is large. Furthermore, and partly implied already, they are able to turn an
arbitrage profit by exploiting any small temporary geographical
differences in price and availability.

We just [illegible] and shipped some of Feeser's High Extra-Standard
Whole Kernel Bantam to Buffalo and Rochester. Immediately, Mr. McAu-

[7] Edmund D. McGarry, "The Contactual Function in Marketing," *Journal
of Business of the University of Chicago*, 24:96–113 (April 1951).

liffe's canners [McAuliffe was field buying man in Rochester], who had been very bullish as you can see by the market letter, have now become weak.[8]

In such markets the field buying offices are in their element. Price differences in time and space can be exploited by systematically finding and paying the lowest. When a buyer of canned salmon proposed a contract which provided for the "general market price" at Seattle for nonadvertised brands of similar quality,[9] Parr maintained (although we do not know whether successfully or not) that the price should be "the lowest price named by any reputable packer of equal quality.[10] He later explained that average price was to be avoided in a contract because there were nearly always some sellers who would undercut the prevailing figure; so long as such an offer was made anywhere, A & P was to have the benefit of it.[11] Precisely the same principle held good in the buying of canned vegetables.[12] Wide market fluctuations in the same type of product — even when there was only one price in the market at any given moment — offered a very satisfactory opportunity for more favorable prices.[13]

The advantage to A & P here, and the asset which smaller buyers lack, is that of size and money. It can look at the whole range of the market, take the best of the many alternatives open to it, anticipate opportunities and await them without having its hand forced. Smaller buyers with a narrower range do not have such alternatives. The traditional economies of scale — "bulk transactions, massed reserves, and the principle of multiples" [14] — operate here to take advantage of imperfections in the market, and reduce or eliminate them. In fact, the gross gain to A & P (from

[8] Zoller to Parr, March 1, 1940, GX 1685.
[9] H. B. Friele (not to be confused with B. Friele) to Parr, April 22, 1940, GX 461.
[10] Parr to H. B. Friele, May 7, 1940, GX 462.
[11] See the correspondence, Friele to Parr, May 13, 1940, GX 463, and Parr to Friele, May 15, 1940, GX 464.
[12] Zoller to Parr, January 3, 1939, GX 854.
[13] Vogt to Gundrey, August 31, 1936, GX 533.
[14] P. Sargant Florence, *The Logic of Industrial Organization* (London, 1933), pp. 16–20. The "principle of multiples" relies heavily on the full utilization of skilled personnel. This is borne out by the testimony of Malcolm P. McNair, Tr. 17,168–72.

which expenses must be deducted) is essentially for elimination of market imperfections. But this is no recipe for popularity in the trade. The canners of corn who went from bullish to bearish because of A & P arbitrage, or the salmon packers who received a lower price because somebody in the market was quoting one, can scarcely be expected to listen with any patience to discussions of the logic of industrial organization. The task and opportunity of A & P buyers is to promote knowledge. But "he who increaseth knowledge increaseth sorrow."

Brokerage on trading items

When the field buying offices were set up, as was noted earlier, one purpose was the saving of payments which would otherwise be made to food brokers who dealt in the undifferentiated trading items. It must not be supposed that brokers (or the field buying offices) confine themselves to such items; both are often active in handling list price items also. But at this point we confine ourselves to the logic of brokerage on trading items only.

By 1931 the system was working to the satisfaction of A & P and also to that of at least some manufacturers.[15] Since our authority for this statement is an internal letter extant long before the Robinson-Patman Act appeared on the horizon, there is no reason to doubt its correctness. But it aroused great dissatisfaction on the part of others, and a review of the controversy with the meat-packing industry will illustrate the nature of the conflict.

The eastern office of the meat department, during 1930 or 1931, had bought meat from various East Coast packers, paying the same prices and buying on the same terms as brokers, including a brokerage allowance. But early in January 1932, Swift & Company notified the Chicago office of the meat department that "since the first of the year their eastern plants were owned outright by Swift" (apparently Swift had bought out some previously independent packers). Henceforth they would, like the Chicago packers, allow no brokerage. Connors, the A & P representative in Chicago, argued that A & P buyers did a broker's work, and

---

[15] Parr to Bofinger, November 11, 1931, GX 482.

more, and hence deserved at least a broker's fee, "especially as he was not only acting as a broker [and selling to the trade] but as exclusive buying agent for [A & P], . . . and afforded their subsidiaries an outlet . . . [and] an opportunity for business that they never previously enjoyed." [16] No decision was reached. But a scant month later the Institute of American Meat Packers issued a bulletin to its members condemning the payment of brokerage to the agent of a customer,[17] and circularized the offending Eastern meat packers. Brokerage payments to A & P were considered discriminatory and "secret." The bulletin explained that "publicity . . . does not prevent its being a secret concession if it is actually not a brokerage but a rebate on the price." In other words, "secret" is simply another spelling of "discriminatory," which is defined as follows:

The real test of whether a special allowance is in fact a brokerage or is a disguised form of rebate and concession to the buyer depends upon the fact of whether the payment is retained by an independent broker or directly or indirectly reaches the buyer himself.[18]

This "real test" disregards whether the direct buyer performs the same services for the seller and realizes (to him) a net price which is at least no lower than the price available through a broker. Nor does the opinion give any weight to a seller's having two alternative means of distribution which are competing to give him the larger net return. Were brokers not used in the meat industry, one might of course suspect that brokerage was a mere camouflage for discrimination. But the opinion is fairly clear on the point of competing outlets:

The question whether the seller may be accustomed to paying a true brokerage to an actual broker in connection with other sales is of course immaterial so far as the allowance to this buyer is concerned.

Connors of A & P was not discouraged. He believed that "the Eastern packers have continually resented the control of the Institute by the so-called Big Four," of which Swift was the most aggressive in opposing brokerage, and he suggested strong steps,

[16] T. A. Connors to C. J. Noell, January 26, 1932, GX 81.
[17] The bulletin is in the record as GX 83.
[18] GX 83, para. 3.

such as stopping purchases from them, and concentrating on buying from smaller packers.[19] But after an interview with President Woods of the Institute, Connors advised delay. Woods was conciliatory but firm. Brokerage payments to an A & P buying office offended the Institute code, and in his opinion were illegal. But he had no objection to A & P's simply paying a price lower by the amount of brokerage: "The brokerage should be reflected in the price where [A & P] dealt direct with the independent rather than through a broker." Connors remarked that "this undoubtedly would be a compromise if it was practical." [20]

The same emphasis on cost differences and functional differences was noted in a letter written the same day, where A & P's East Coast meat buyer paraphrased his approach to meat packers:

We would give them a much greater outlet for their merchandise and render them a service that no one broker could possibly do, and in order to do so this office is put to an expense which naturally reduces their selling expense and therefore earns the commission being paid. . . . Everyone that we have contacted has treated this office as they would any broker's office and [we] believe that everything will continue to go smoothly unless the Institute [is] able to make them change their method of doing business.[21]

A few days later the Institute reaffirmed its stand, as did A & P.[22] Clearly, the two parties were talking at cross purposes. The Institute was not concerned with price discrimination as economists understand it. For, had it been a fact or even a plausible argument that A & P was buying at lower *net prices*, or that packers were realizing a lower *net return* by selling to A & P, the Institute would certainly have said so. But it never did. This could not have been a mere oversight, for the contrary argument was explicitly made, and it was never answered. "Discrimination" was merely the Institute's name for a trade practice it disliked — the integration of the brokerage function with the wholesaling function. In fact, we are able to pinpoint its objection even more precisely. So far as sales for the use of A & P were concerned,

[19] Connors to Parr, February 15, 1932, GX 84.
[20] Connors to Parr, February 19, 1932, GX 88.
[21] Telegram, Connors to Parr, February 25, 1932, GX 90, and telegram, Parr to Connors, February 25, 1932, GX 91.
[22] Trunz Pork Stores, Inc., v. Wallace, 70 F.2d 688 (2d Cir. 1934).

it did not object to allowing A & P a brokerage equivalent in the form of a lower price; as Connors put it, this would have been "a compromise if practical." There remains only one cause of conflict. About 75 per cent of the meat purchased by the A & P offices passed into company warehouses, and about 25 per cent was resold to the trade. The company's buying offices were large enough to find out the lowest prices at any given moment, and to take advantage of them, whether the company actually needed the cheap wares or not. In this way they could spread lower prices throughout the system much more quickly. This would of course be objectionable to the meat packers; for the average level of realized prices would thus be lowered. In other words, they needed no special instruction, either in economics or in the Bible, to understand how appropriate was our earlier quotation from Ecclesiastes.

A & P continued to operate its buying offices. The next year Secretary of Agriculture Wallace acted under the Packers and Stockyards Act to issue a cease and desist order against a meat packer's selling to A & P, and the order was upheld on appeal.[23]

Payment of brokerage to an agency was considered by the court discriminatory. "By the payment of the commission, the . . . Company received an advantage over competitors. . . ." The A & P buyer "performed no service. . . . He did not search for a buyer . . . as an independent broker might be obliged to do. . . . It is difficult to say that there was any real service performed. . . . The evils involved were that not only did . . . [A & P] receive its purchases at lower prices than competitors but it shared in the commissions on products sold by competitors."[24]

The reasoning of the court is the same as the Institute's. The question is never asked whether the seller did not realize just as high a net return on sales to A & P as to others. For if that question had been asked and answered affirmatively, as it had to be, there would have been no escape from the conclusion that, if there was any net "advantage" to A & P above the costs of operating its office, that net advantage could have one and only one possible explanation — the economies of integration. It is impor-

---

[23] Trunz Pork Stores, Inc., v. Wallace, 70 F.2d 688 (2d Cir. 1934).
[24] Trunz Pork Stores, Inc., v. Wallace, 70 F.2d, 689 (2d Cir. 1934).

tant to note that no monopsony elements were alleged. It was never claimed that the meat packers were not free to choose the selling method more advantageous to them. The only restraint, of course, was the code of the Institute!

The argument of the Institute and of the court that the A & P buyer did not search for a buyer, and hence "performed no service," neatly begs the question as to just what constituted service. If the service consisted of insuring to the seller the highest net realization possible, then obviously brokerage and direct buying are two alternative and competing means of rendering the service, and the seller will follow his own interests and choose the better method — provided he is free to choose. By arbitrarily defining the service as brokerage — not as obtaining a net return to the seller — the conclusion follows smoothly that there was no service rendered. But the verbal arbitrariness reflects a policy — the blocking of competition in the offering of service.

We need only note in passing the additional "evil" that the buying office was also making profits on products sold to A & P competitors. This ancient fallacy will be discussed later.

List-price items

Here we enter a set of markets where sellers are often large and almost by definition few. Extensive branding and advertising exist only to differentiate the product and render all other products imperfect substitutes for it. Hence, the discussion of trading items has only a secondary relevance here. Each producer of list-price items can, within limits, raise or lower his prices without losing all his business. He must pay attention to his rivals' reactions to any move of his. If he wants more volume, he has the alternatives of cutting prices or of spending more on selling and advertising. Choosing the wrong tactic will mean lower profits than he might have earned, or unsold inventories that he might have moved. Here we encounter the kinds of price structures typical of oligopoly. The effort never ceases to create a consumer demand which will force distributors to take his goods on his terms.

Food processors much prefer to sell under their own label than under the chain's, and their mark becomes their most prized possession.[25] For the same reasons A & P tries to encourage its suppliers to leave their goods unlabeled.[26] When difficulties arose with Stokely Brothers in 1936, and Parr suggested to his Milwaukee buyer that they be put on the "unsatisfactory list," the reply was: "This is OK on trading items where you can shift from one account to another, but how about that other group?" [27] As for Libby and California Packing Company, nothing at all could be done with them, because only branded goods were in question.[28] No such doubts bothered Vogt a few months later when he cancelled a contract with Van Camp:

We are not averse to telling you the principal reasons, the first one being your company's cancellation of all arrangements. Secondly, other firms have not done this and on top of it in recent weeks there have been some unusually attractive offerings of pretty good quality soup.[29]

Building product differentiation

How does a manufacturer take his product across that line, or zone, which separates the gray mass of trading items from the brightly colored brands? H. A. Carpenter testified that the potato sticks he sold were no novelty. "What we really had to sell was the packaging, which kept it fresh over a long period of time." [30] Of course, it also took extensive advertising, in several media, to bring it to consumers' attention.[31] After it had become very popular, A & P had cooperated on advertising it. But Carpenter had no very high opinion of the value of this advertising; he called in

[25] See the testimony of the following witnesses: W. F. Redfield of Hills Brothers, Tr. 4641; Fred W. Catterall, Jr., of Walkers Austex Chile Company, Tr. 3040; Ward H. Patton of Minnesota Valley Canning Company, Tr. 3996; E. B. DeSurville of Sylmar Packing Corporation, Tr. 5096 (a very nervous and evasive witness, however); H. A. Carpenter of Olney & Carpenter, Tr. 5321. But the existence and importance of advertising allowances (see Chapter VII) constitute the most important evidence.

[26] See, for example, Parr to A. W. Vogt, March 24, 1939, GX 828.

[27] Vogt to Parr, September 4, 1936, GX 569.

[28] Vogt to Parr, September 4, 1936, GX 569; but see Appendix IV for the special deals.

[29] Vogt to Van Camp, December 30, 1936, GX 577. This was prior to the Stokely–Van Camp merger.

[30] Tr. 5321.

[31] Tr. 5322–5324.

a consulting firm and paid the company only what the firm told him it was worth.[32] This arm's-length position toward the company could be maintained despite the fact that he had about thirty-eight competitors.[33]

A much better example of how bargaining power is built up is that of V-8 vegetable juice, manufactured by Loudon Packing Company.[34] Stewart Rose, Jr., of that firm described how it took over V-8 in lieu of an unpaid debt. All the products it was making at that time (around 1937) were sold to wholesalers and chain stores for private labels.[35] Loudon's hoped to get national consumer acceptance by means of heavy advertising and promotion. But it feared retaliation by its existing customers, and felt that the promotion of V-8 must be consummated quickly or not at all. Paradoxically enough, its concern for speed made it keep its product *out* of areas where it was unable to wage a full-scale promotional campaign. Apparently it feared a lukewarm acceptance as a sort of antitoxin against a very hearty one.[36]

The campaign was launched in 1938. Loudon's sold through distributors, who paid 20 per cent less than the suggested retail price, and sold retailers at 15 per cent under it. (There was also a carload discount of 2.5 per cent and a cash discount of 1.5 per cent.) A & P received only the standard 15 per cent; to add insult to injury, Loudon's distributors made store-door delivery, which all chains, including A & P, were opposing at that time.[37] Hence the attitude of A & P headquarters was unfriendly. For a time they stopped all distribution in the Atlantic Division, but relaxed somewhat as V-8 gained in popularity. Rose was permitted to visit division headquarters on promotional trips, but his representatives were excluded from company warehouses.[38] Vogt, the head of the Milwaukee field buying office, wrote to Rose:

We certainly cannot consistently recommend our organization stock or

---

[32] Tr. 5325.
[33] Tr. 5328.
[34] Absorbed by Standard Brands in 1943. See Tr. 4672.
[35] This was either inaccurate or a change since 1935, when Loudon had been selling "Doggie Dinner," a branded dog food. See GX 11.
[36] Rose, Tr. 4729–4733.
[37] Rose, Tr. 4673–4679.
[38] Rose, Tr. 4687–4696.

push the item when the policy you pursue in effecting sales is inconsistent with our company's position.[39]

Neither side was disposed to yield. Late in 1940, Rose spoke confidently to Vogt about the "primary introductory campaign" being finished by the end of the year, and an even closer control of resale prices and sales methods.[40] Vogt completely misjudged the situation, and wrote headquarters that Rose was "disturbed . . . [and] beginning to feel the pinch of competitive products." [41] Parr agreed, still resentful at having to pay "the same price that any little independent retailer would pay. . . ." With a competitive product, which Parr considered "not only a similar product, but a better product, at a more attractive price and without the restricted retail, we see no reason why any warehouse should continue with V-8." [42] Perhaps Rose's polite manner was deceptive, but a very courteous letter from him was also quite firm on price maintenance as "vitally necessary to the success of our plan for department store and key store demonstration and promotion, which in turn is vitally necessary to the success of our entire merchandising program." He thought A & P was much too rigid in objecting to a kind of price maintenance which was quite different from that on "well-established merchandise." [43] A few months later Loudon's felt that V-8 was well established, and hence applied retail price maintenance more firmly than ever, announcing that distributors must conform "strictly" to the suggested price.[44] Very shortly afterward, distribution was given exclusively to Kraft's, which continued the retail price maintenance, but offered a scale of quantity discounts a little more attractive to large buyers.[45] It is doubtful that A & P was much mollified by such small concessions. A form letter circulated to divisional purchasing directors suggested the more important considerations: "We were astonished when we learned the extent of Loudon's national busi-

[39] Vogt to Rose, May 27, 1939, GX 1317.
[40] Rose, Tr. 4707.
[41] Vogt to Parr, November 18, 1940, GX 1330.
[42] Parr to Vogt, November 20, 1940, GX 1333.
[43] Rose to Vogt, undated, but probably written shortly after November 18, 1940, GX 1331.
[44] Rose, Tr. 4722.
[45] Rose, Tr. 4725.

ness. . . . In many of the large markets where it has . . . between 75 per cent and 82 per cent, our warehouses are not handling this product at all." [46] By 1945 A & P was one of Loudon's largest customers, having "worked out" their differences in some unspecified manner.[47]

Resale price maintenance

The experience of Loudon's suggests that resale price maintenance is both a means of attaining preference for one's goods, and one of the benefits of that position once attained. This hardly seems obvious. Demands for resale price maintenance do seem to come more from the retailers' ranks; the Miller-Tydings and McGuire Acts and the host of state "fair trade" acts are the fruit of their efforts.

In the food trade this sort of price control seems to arise from an incomplete and precarious sort of dominance on the part of the manufacturer. His product is distinctive enough so that its withdrawal would do *some* damage to the retailer. But it is not in such great demand that the producer can dictate to retailers as a class. Drastic price-cutting by a few retailers may cause the rest of the trade to discourage consumers from buying it at all. Unless it is so much in demand that price cuts simply must be met because consumers will invariably go elsewhere to get it, the item will suffer an informal but effective retailers' boycott. As one canner put it: "If a fellow can't make a profit, he goes out of business, so if he has an item which is footballed too much, he will hide it under the counter — won't display it, feature it." [48] This canner was quite aware that a lower price tended, other things being equal, to stimulate demand; in correspondence with an A & P field buyer, he had remarked that his canned peas were more popular because they sold at a lower markup.[49] But the letters between him and one of his chief salesmen about the sinful price-cutting by chains and independents alike show what con-

[46] Undated, GX 1334.
[47] Tr. 4735–4736.
[48] Ward H. Patton, vice-president of Minnesota Valley Canning Company, Tr. 3999.
[49] Patton to Vogt, August 1, 1938, GX 1146.

siderations were uppermost in their minds. As important as the content, perhaps, is the violent and sometimes abusive (and sometimes unintentionally funny) tone of the letters. However, the meaning is clear: "We just cannot have the merchandise footballed around and expect to retain the good will of the trade. [Selling at] cost is bad enough, but below cost is the nuts." [50]

The great battles over resale price maintenance, so far as the company was concerned, came in the late 1920's. Late in 1926 Clicquot Club ginger ale was carrying on an intensive promotional campaign when the Central Western Division began advertising three bottles for 31¢. This amounted to $2.93 per case when the wholesale price to the trade was $3.35. Promptly the salesmen of Clicquot's competitors armed themselves with sheaves of copies of the advertisements, pointed out to wholesalers and retailers that A & P showed no such brutality in treating *their* product, and intimated that A & P really owned Clicquot anyway. Clicquot saw "no reason why we should be slaughtered this way" and demanded that the campaign cease. [51]

The final outcome is not definitely known, but A & P probably backed down; a meeting of divisional sales directors [52] held soon afterward considered both Clicquot and Palmolive soap, which had been aroused by spectacular A & P price cuts, and threatened to stop the allowances they were paying the company. Hershey chocolate had moved more drastically: upon hearing that its bars were being sold at three for ten cents in Louisville, it had stopped all shipments there.

Bofinger pointed out that many other manufacturers felt the same way, and that it was dangerous to ignore them. Most of their sales were of course to independents, and naturally there was a mutual sympathy between the two groups, he said. A & P had always refused price maintenance agreements, and would continue to do so. But a general rule would have to apply: price must not be cut below cost to the individual dealer.

It must be recalled that the problem was of special seriousness

[50] Patton to Henry Latourelle, July 15, 1940, GX 1156.

[51] Letter from the vice-president of Clicquot Club to purchasing director of the Central Western Division, November 4, 1926. Incorporated in the minutes of the meeting cited in the next footnote.

[52] December 27, 1926, GX 107.

because A & P was growing rapidly by means of lower prices and because the consideration overriding everything else was to continue that growth. This was the viewpoint clearly expressed at a meeting held three months later.[53] Bofinger was not acutely concerned, because only a small minority of manufacturers were insisting on price maintenance. But when he mentioned that Canada Dry had just cut off sales to the Indianapolis unit, John Hartford broke in to say that some drastic action was needed soon. With 15,000 stores, the company was too big to be dictated to by anybody. He suggested that perhaps one of the company's own products ought to be sold to outside distributors, including competitive independents and chains. Perhaps this "demonstration" would bring about a radical change of attitude on the part of processors intent on price maintenance.

A week later [54] Hartford's thinking had crystallized. If retail price maintenance were to be enforced, the savings of the A & P methods of operation would all go for naught, because they would be unable to undersell the individual grocer, and hence unable to expand. He stressed this last point. To fight with private brands was ineffective; the large manufacturers were not worried by them. Why not do the same with manufactured goods as was being so successfully done with produce? The company's subsidiary for buying fresh fruits and vegetables always bought more than the A & P retail stores needed, and sold the excess at a profit. Why not manufacture more than the company needed, and sell to outside sources at low prices, eliminating all middlemen? "This would be a very radical step." The meeting agreed that such a demonstration would put manufacturers into a much more reasonable frame of mind. Nothing more was heard about manufacturing for resale, however, and such disputes disappear from the record for about ten years.

[53] Meeting of divisional sales directors, March 30, 1927, GX 109.
[54] Meeting of divisional purchasing directors, April 6, 1927, GX 404.

VII

PRODUCT TYPES
AND MARKET STRUCTURES
(continued)

In the last chapter we saw that there were (and are) two broad classes of processed foods purchased by A & P: trading items which approximate pure competition, and differentiated list price goods that often give rise to very complex market relationships, where relative advantage is often unstable and shifting. Now to be explored are the particular forms of discounts and allowances on list price goods, and some aspects of bargaining tactics.

As was indicated in the last chapter, many list price items are sold through brokers and wholesalers, while many are sold through the manufacturer's own sales force. The service rendered is essentially the same as for trading items: making contact and arranging shipment. But we need to explore more thoroughly the types of allowances which are more peculiar to list price items. In order of importance, so far as A & P was concerned, were (1) advertising allowances, (2) quantity discounts, (3) local feature services, (4) cost savings agreements, (5) floor space rental agreements, (6) sign space rental agreements, and (7) special newspaper supplement sales. Numbers (3), (5), (6), and (7) are local, and number (4) only came into existence with the Robinson-Patman Act. They are merely variants of the first two.

Advertising and related allowances

Advertising allowances can be paid only in connection with branded products; in fact, they began to be known only in the

1920's, when brands became of wide importance.[1] But from the first, advertising was only one of the things to be paid for. Early in 1927 the terms "rebate" and "confidential allowance" were officially dropped, since "advertising allowance" covered the situation well.

Every precaution should be taken, so far as advertising allowances were concerned, to keep this information from becoming general knowledge in order to protect the manufacturers.[2]

And in February 1928, John Hartford added:

Our success in the future in our relations with large manufacturers depends largely on our ability to keep whatever arrangements we are able to make on a strictly confidential basis.[3]

And at a meeting of divisional sales directors held later that month,[4] there was much discussion of an obviously difficult problem: how could divisions and units participate wholeheartedly in pushing items when it was impossible to tell them why those goods were so well worth promoting?

But it must not be supposed that advertising allowances were a mere screen for rebates. The matter is far more complex. In the first place, we have a semantic reminder. That deals were kept secret does not necessarily mean that they were discriminatory in the economic sense. It does not mean that the manufacturer realized less per unit of product sold, over the cost of that product, than on sales to others. On the contrary, charging a retailer a price which gave the manufacturer the same net return as selling to a wholesaler was widely regarded in the trade as an unclean and unethical innovation. J. M. Clark, writing in the early 1920's, noted the existence of conventional price structures whereby a retailing firm which had absorbed the wholesale functions was still being charged the same price as other retailers who did no wholesaling, and he expressed the hope that this form of implicit discrimination would disappear.[5] But A & P, which tried to hasten

---

[1] Testimony of Paul S. Willis, Tr. 152.
[2] Meeting of divisional purchasing directors, April 6, 1927, GX 404.
[3] Special DPM, February 9, 1928, GX 113.
[4] February 29, 1928, GX 948.
[5] J. M. Clark, *The Economics of Overhead Costs* (Chicago, 1923), pp. 425–426.

the process, was not concerned merely to avoid discrimination against itself. It was just as happy to obtain discrimination against others. Undoubtedly it obtained both. Unfortunately we cannot say how important was one relative to the other. But either was a sufficient cause of secrecy in the 1920's, when the discriminatory price structure was maintained by a trade custom; or after 1936, when it was reinstituted by law.[6] At any rate, evidence of furtive behavior proves only the consciousness of such behavior. It tells us nothing about the economic substance of the behavior, which we may now consider.

The seller of any advertised product has at least some elements of a monopoly position; as a group, the sellers of such products have immeasurably more bargaining power than the sellers of trading items. Hence the bargains over allowances run the whole range from A & P dominance to agreements where the company got into line with everybody else.

Contracts for allowances fall into three broad groups, defined at headquarters in 1937 as follows:

"(1) Those setting forth a specific and definite service to be rendered;

"(2) Those requiring definite proof of service rendered before payment of allowance by advertisers;

"(3) Those drawn on our standard Company advertising form naming flexible stipulations of performance." [7]

Very similar language was used a year later, at the very important meeting of divisional purchasing directors already mentioned.[8]

The advantages of the third type were stressed. The emphasis on flexibility meant simply that the company would, wherever possible, collect definite amounts for indefinite services. The standard company form is almost evidence enough.[9] Gundrey's comment on it is conclusive:

[6] This will be discussed at length in Chapters VIII and IX on the Robinson-Patman Act.

[7] Gundrey to C. Neumann, April 1, 1937, GX 1083.

[8] April 22, 1938, GX 315.

[9] It is in the record as GX 771, and reads as follows: "The Distributor

The whole idea of the procedure was a method to satisfy the writer in accepting checks that some service had been given in justification of the acceptance . . . [in accordance with] the standard flexible advertising contract of our Company.[10]

Contracts of the first type were regarded with anything but enthusiasm. For one thing, A & P received no comparative advantage; an Armour & Company contract was "offered to our chain competitors" and therefore submitted to the organization without recommendation for adoption.[11] But the most disliked were the contracts with the soap companies. Lever Brothers gave everyone the same contract; [12] and it required two feature sales each quarter, with newspaper advertising or store display; partial service received partial payment. As for mere mention in a larger display, that merited nothing.[13] The company made no secret of its disgust with such arrangements,[14] and on more than one occasion Bofinger suggested to Lever's that they drop their advertising allowances, since he preferred to feature other brands; but apparently he felt that he could not afford to pass up the Lever contracts.[15]

At the other extreme was a small mayonnaise producer whose practice was to offer large chains a 5 per cent allowance, unless they bought through brokers, in which case the broker took 2 per cent and the chain took 3.[16] This was an obvious subterfuge.

But the great mass of advertising allowances were far more

obliges itself to render certain Special Advertising and Special Distribution service, supplementing the National, Sectional, and Local Advertising of the Advertiser, which special service includes periodic newspaper advertising, handbill advertising, periodic store displays with Advertiser's merchandise in a prominent position readily accessible to consumers, and periodic notifications to branches of support to be rendered Advertiser's products at point of sale, for which the Advertiser agrees to pay the following advertising allowance for such service between the period commencing on — — —, 19. ., and expiring on — — —, 19 . .."

[10] Gundrey to Fraser, November 22, 1940, GX 1085.
[11] Memorandum, national meat department, February 18, 1941, GX 1287.
[12] Tr. 9171.
[13] Lever Bros. to H. B. George, April 18, 1941, GX 2564.
[14] See, for example, the Southern meeting of April 11, 1939, GX 1042.
[15] Testimony of Arthur F. Bernhard, vice-president of Lever Bros., Tr. 18677. The defense unconvincingly tried to infer from this that "A & P was opposed to advertising allowances." DB(DC), p, 211.
[16] Statement of Richard Wheatley, GX 1030.

complex and interesting. They were a mixture of net price reductions and reimbursement for services rendered. The peculiarity is that the service, the act of advertising, is a joint cost and a joint benefit.

A given amount of advertising, at a given cost, can be much more effective, produce a greater return, and have a much higher value to the firm paying for it if it is run by a retailer. As one manufacturer put it:

Well, you take, for instance, an ad of a column inch, fourteen lines; you could not say much in it; . . . incorporate it in the space of any distributor, it focuses the attention of the housewife on where she can go and buy it . . . and it has the advantage of what prestige the retailer has.[17]

Since it is impossible to calculate who gets how much of the benefit, there is no automatic apportioning of the saving; it depends on the opportunity cost of both parties, and this varies from one situation to another.

Let us consider two kinds of advertising activity by A & P: the normal, or routine, and the special advertisements for which it is specially paid. Under the standard advertising contract "it is not intended that this should be an extra or exceptional [advertising] activity but ought merely to constitute what is usually done in the ordinary course of business. . . ." [18] This is largely a fixed cost; a certain minimum amount of advertising must always be done if the business is to remain in operation. But A & P does not simply advertise itself; it names specific kinds of merchandise. Its suppliers are not at all indifferent as to whether their goods or some others are named. Thus the service which constitutes an overhead cost to A & P can create additional sales value to the suppliers, who can be made to pay for some of it. The overhead cost to A & P becomes the incremental expense to the supplier.[19]

The matter is a little different when A & P carries on a special advertising campaign. In the first place, it may indicate a stronger

[17] Testimony of Ward R. Patton, vice-president in charge of sales and advertising, Minnesota Valley Canning Co., Tr. 3976.

[18] Gundrey to W. A. Carlton (sales director, Southern Division), April 28, 1939, GX 1074.

[19] Meeting of divisional sales directors, October 26, 1929, GX 119.

bargaining position on the part of suppliers who can compel the special activities. Secondly, the expenses are incremental for both the company and the suppliers. But the joint value is, again, greater than the cost, and the excess is shared between the two parties.

It is interesting to see how the doctrine of joint advertising expenses developed with the company. Back in 1929, it was decided not to use any manufacturers' signs in A & P retail stores unless the manufacturer paid for them. Early in 1939, the divisions reported on their policy in charging for space in store circulars. Most of them attempted to cover costs and have something left over. Only one division said that the charge "is determined by the advertisers' capacity and willingness to pay." [20]

The matter was confused in the minds of many because cost to the advertising retailer and value to the supplier were even further separated by a universal newspaper practice. National advertisers usually pay over twice as high a rate as local merchants. Therefore, quite aside from the greater consumer appeal of the retailer's advertisement, the manufacturer has a strong incentive to place his advertising through the retailer. He may not be prepared to pay twice as much as the local rate, but he will almost certainly be prepared to pay sufficiently over it to assure a substantial profit to the retailer with whom he has a joint advertising agreement.

The merchandising committee sought a way of retaining the profit, while avoiding the difficulties — of an essentially political nature — to which they gave rise.

Purchasing space from newspapers at local rates, and in turn, selling to manufacturers at national rates and pocketing the difference, could be said to find us competing with the newspapers insofar as their national accounts were concerned, and sooner or later they would take exception to this scheme. . . . There was a growing tendency on the part of national advertisers to purchase liberal space in sections and lift their regular copy from run of paper including it in A & P supplements without changes, thereby eliminating the need for purchasing space in the usual pages of the paper. Naturally, the newspapers lose revenue by such steps. . . .

A procedure is recommended . . . . To the cost of any given amount of

[20] Paris & Peart (A & P advertising agency) to S. S. Shea; undated, but written after April 28, 1939, GX 1076.

space at the A & P local contract rates, should be added an amount not less than 100 per cent of that figure to compensate us for collateral store merchandising.

An example was offered: if a given space cost $18.35, twice that would be $36.70; the charge to the manufacturer should be $40.00.[21]

When agreements were made at the national level, the surplus over cost to A & P was credited to the "702 Account," and appeared in the final figures of profit. The divisions followed similar procedure. They were instructed in 1938 that "there exists a nice distinction between the cost of service rendered and the value of service rendered." [22] But the concept was not clear at all even two years later. For example, we have a letter from J. P. Wallace of headquarters to the Southern Division, in which he indicated that headquarters was approving three contracts calling for specific performance:

under protest, however, because . . . these suppliers require entirely too much newspaper support for the money they are paying. . . . Contracts such as these should be on the basis of the *value of the advertising we give to the supplier and not of the value to us.*[23]

Whereupon Hodgson, a Southern official, penciled on the side:

I wonder what the hell Wallace thinks we run these big promotions for if we don't feel they are of value to us. The guy's off his base.

However, not Wallace but Hodgson was off base. Wallace knew that the maximum which manufacturers would pay was what it would cost to obtain the same amount of advertising service in some other way. This would actually be higher than the national rate, since the advertiser was obtaining not merely undifferentiated newspaper space, but space in an A & P ad, that is, space whose "pulling power" was much greater than the equivalent amount of space by itself. This set the upper limit. But the manufacturer knew that anything over and above the cost of the advertising effort to A & P was a gain to the company, so that cost was

---

[21] Merchandising Committee meeting, February 27, 1939, GX 119.
[22] Circular letter to all purchasing directors, July 14, 1938, quoted in GX 1108.
[23] Wallace to Churchill, October 17, 1940, GX 1089 (italics added).

the minimum they would conceivably take. The two parties were sufficiently bilateral monopolists that there was no particular intermediate rate which was uniquely determined and stable.[24] Hence the incessant bargaining.

Nevertheless, this was far from being pure bilateral monopoly. For both parties did have alternatives. The manufacturer could and did advertise elsewhere, and the higher the cost to him of A & P space, the more he would shift to other methods. This, in fact, defined his demand curve for A & P service. The supply curve of that service is not so easily determined; for there was no cost function, or set of functions, on which to base it. However, we need not pursue the matter any further because the solution was not set by economic but by public-relations factors. That is, A & P might have earned more profit by charging less and attracting more advertising. But this would have been the last straw to the newspapers, whose local monopoly position exploited through discriminatory advertising schedules was thus being undermined by the resale of the product — the nemesis of all discrimination.

To the extent that A & P made a profit from the sale of advertising space, it meant that manufacturers' competition via advertising had really turned into its opposite: competition by price cuts. That is, the sacrifice of net revenue to the advertiser did not increase the amount of advertising done, but merely lowered the net disbursement by A & P for its goods. This conclusion is strictly true of the third type of advertising contract, which was the most important; it is largely true even of the other two types, for even on the special campaign the increment to A & P's revenue was usually much larger than the increment to its advertising outlay.[25]

Quantity discounts, volume discounts, and discrimination

We must distinguish at the outset between quantity discounts strictly speaking and volume discounts. The resemblance between

[24] William H. Nicholls, *Imperfect Competition within Agricultural Industries* (Ames, 1941), pp. 168–172.

[25] See Appendix IV, entry on Colgate-Palmolive-Peet.

the two is superficial at best, yet in ordinary trade speech they usually are known by the one name.

Quantity discounts are for large shipments or for large orders placed, or for both. The rationale is that the amount of expense which the seller undertakes in order to assemble and prepare a shipment increases less than proportionately with the size of the shipment. Thus the cost per unit of the product is less. A quantity discount schedule may be set up to reflect this saving in cost, and it may be passed on to the manufacturer. The saving is simply the expression of less labor and capital expended per unit of the product.

The volume discount, usually miscalled a quantity discount, is quite another matter. It refers to the total amount bought over some time period, most often a quarter or a year. Obviously, there is no necessary connection between large volume and large quantities, although in practice there is usually a correlation. At any rate, large volume in and of itself does not insure the economies of large quantities. It may, however, permit other economies. The manufacturer may be able to buy and plan ahead; there may be a saving in selling expenses; he may be able to set up long production runs and save the expense of stopping for small product variations. Economies of this type may in any given instance be quite important, but they are less obvious and perhaps less important than quantity discounts. However, the two types of economies are in practice often so intermingled that it is difficult to say where one stops and the other begins. So far as A & P was concerned, they could not have been of first-rate importance because the company seldom undertook any firm commitments. Nevertheless, a supplier might have a good gambling chance of continued orders. If so, he might make considerable savings.

Quantity discounts and the types of volume discounts just mentioned are simply allowances for services foregone by the buyer. Other volume discounts stand on an altogether different footing because they involve price discrimination, which the preceding types do not. The rationale (or rationalization) is well expressed in the one cost study of a manufacturer's costs which was introduced into the A & P record.

Olney & Carpenter sponsored two analyses of their accounts by an independent certified public accountant, who was familiar with canning and packing accounts.[26] The first analysis related to March 1940, the second to August 1942; [27] and it is apparent that manufacturing costs had not changed significantly in the interim. The procedure is interesting because it shows the mixture of discriminatory and nondiscriminatory elements in a single business bargain.

A & P orders were assumed to carry no selling expenses, since "with respect to customers who buy an a volume discount basis, you had a negligible amount of selling and travelling expense." Savings per case on this score were 15.53 cents per case, which amounted to a little over 10 per cent of the selling price. By mid-1942 there had been "a substantial decrease in the selling and traveling expenses treated as a segregated saving." That is, there had been a decline of nearly 45 per cent in selling outlay per case and hence the *relative* economy in selling to A & P was correspondingly much less. (In the extreme case of no selling expense to any account, the economy in selling to A & P would of course have disappeared.)

The discount schedule in selling to A & P had been a sliding scale, with larger discounts on successive increments: 5 per cent on 25,000 to 34,999 cases, and so on up to a maximum of 10 per cent off on 60,000 cases or over.[28] If the calculations of the accountant were correct, the discounts schedule did not reflect the full savings in cost attendant on selling to A & P, since all its purchase was free of selling and traveling cost, at a 10 per cent saving; but only a portion received this allowance.

But in addition to these cost savings, there was another set of calculations. Overhead costs were estimated for the plant as a whole, including products other than potato sticks. It was then assumed that the only sales of this product were the 140,000 cases not subject to volume discounts; a share of the overhead was distributed to potato sticks according to the ratio of this 140,000 cases to the value of sales of all products of the plant. The overhead so assigned came to 28.05 cents per case. A schedule was

[26] See Carpenter's testimony, Tr. 5333.
[27] They are, respectively, GX 1514 and GX 1515.
[28] Quantity discount agreement, GX 1513.

then drawn up to show how, as additional cases were manufactured and sold, the overhead cost per case would gradually fall; until at 85,000 additional cases, it was only 17.45 cents per case.

In brief, average total cost fell, at a decreasing rate, throughout what was regarded as the normal range of output and was always higher than marginal cost. Since the lower price on the additional business did not affect the price received on the rest, the order was well worth taking even at the lower price. Of course, the 140,000 sales to others were more "responsible" for these economies than the 85,000 to A & P; it was arbitrary to put A & P in the position of the marginal buyer and discriminatory to make it the beneficiary of low marginal cost at high volume. The discriminatory "saving" of 10.6 cents was a little more than 7 per cent of the total selling price.

In short, savings to A & P were somewhat over 10 per cent, and the discount to the company was about 14 per cent, so that there was a net discrimination of 4 per cent.

In addition to savings on sales expense, some manufacturing and buying economies were expected because of "more economical use of direct labor in manufacturing, including less labor turnover. Economy through purchase of larger quantities of raw materials." [29] Carpenter himself confirmed very emphatically the savings on raw materials. He called the figures:

ultra-conservative, and I might say very conservative. . . . We have several times made as much as sixty cents a bushel by being able to buy potatoes in the fall, which would show a saving of twenty cents a case . . . on potato sticks.[30]

Figure 1 illustrates the discriminatory aspect of this type of calculation. On the original volume of business AD, the price is D and the profit is $ABCD$. On the marginal block, the price has been assumed as barely equal to average cost I of the total output. But the average cost is so far above the marginal that the marginal profit is $HEJI$. In the Olney & Carpenter case (disregarding the genuine savings of selling and other costs), the price to A & P was somewhat above average cost, and marginal profit

[29] The cost analysis, GX 1514.
[30] Tr. 5385. Some of this should be discounted. Carpenter considered it a defense to a charge of price discrimination.

all the larger. But, as the diagram shows, the marginal business could be taken even at less than cost, and still add to total profit. The area $HEJI$ is positive so long as I is greater than J — so long as average cost is above marginal.

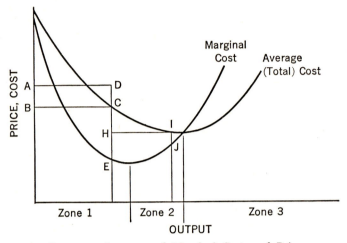

FIGURE 1. Average and Marginal Cost, and Price

Note: Zone 1, falling marginal cost; Zone 2, rising marginal cost; Zone 3, marginal exceeds average cost.

A letter from Bofinger in 1941 is instructive:

The question of the company entering the Doughnut Flour manufacturing field [is] a matter with which we are thoroughly familiar. . . . We are buying Doughnut Flour from 25 cents to 75 cents per cwt. under what we, ourselves, could actually produce the flour.

You might ask: why is it that the Company cannot do as good a job as an outside organization? Our answer is just this, manufacturers . . . are willing to take tonnage business at an attractive price, thereby reducing overhead, and secure a margin of profit on the remainder of the business done with smaller accounts at a much higher price. This practice holds true of many other commodities we purchase on the outside. If I were in the manufacturing business, I would consider it good principle to take a large attractive volume at cost, thereby reducing my overhead which is virtually a profit, and depend on the remainder of the accounts for the profit on my investment. . .[31]

[31] Bofinger to Toolin, August 27, 1941, GX 1370.

One might wish that Bofinger had indicated not only "many" but "how many" other commodities were involved. Since list price items, subject to price discrimination, composed 34 per cent of A & P purchases, the number could have been very large.

Price discrimination of the type Bofinger discussed is a symptom of excess capacity, as commonly defined in economics (marginal cost below average), and cannot exist in its absence. Clearly, excess capacity would be unusual among manufacturers selling trading items. For they would have little difficulty in selling their whole output at whatever price they could realize, aside from the short-run gluts and scarcities which afflict them. They would take the price as given, and tailor their operations toward the best profit position. Whether they tried to sell a great deal more or a great deal less, it would still be so small a part of the total supply on the market that it could not affect the price. The one exception — it is important, and will be discussed later — is the trading item with few buyers and sellers.

But the highly advertised and expensively "sold" product, like the product sold by one or a few sellers, is vulnerable. The manufacturer may have so misjudged his market that his price is out of line, and some of his goods remain unsold or the volume of orders is disappointing. Several choices are open to him. He may reduce prices all around; but this is a step which he is naturally reluctant to take. Or the manufacturer may spend still more on advertising and sales effort in an attempt to lift his demand curve high enough to take off capacity or near-capacity production without cutting prices. This is the most usual reaction, and it may be successful. But everyone may have been increasing selling and advertising expenditures, all merely offsetting each other, so that nobody has benefited except the advertising agencies.

The effectiveness of advertising-selling expenditures is limited partly by consumer resistance and partly by other sellers' expenditures. For each seller, the expense of merely holding his market may steadily increase; and the "cost" structure of the whole industry may thus rise. The attractiveness of sales involving no such expenses must correspondingly increase. But at this point we must distinguish between advertising and selling costs.

The consumer buying an advertised product really buys a joint product — the physical commodity plus "glamour." The production cost of glamour is the expense of advertising. One cannot argue that sales to A & P or another such buyer involve no advertising expense because A & P does not care about or need advertising. For the value to A & P is derived from the price it can realize in selling the commodity-plus-glamour to the public, and the combination presumably fetches a higher price than the commodity alone. Therefore, when a lower price is made to A & P supposedly because no advertising expense is incurred, this is merely a subterfuge and a rationalization for price discrimination. Advertising is not part of short-run supply price; but it is part of long-run supply price, since the glamour component of the product cannot exist without it.

Things are otherwise with the services of a sales force. In the short run, they constitute a fixed expense. A sale to A & P which involves no "traveling or selling expense," as with Olney & Carpenter, may involve no real saving in the very short run, since the seller will not discharge salesmen merely because of this one sale. But even over so short a period as a quarter or a year, reductions in force are possible; and, where there is a continuing relationship, "selling" is a cost which can be and is economized by selling to a firm like A & P.

So far we have found two courses of action for the firm which is operating at excess capacity and is not hopeful of making any net gain from further advertising or selling effort. It may discriminate in price by selling the commodity-plus-glamour to a large buyer at a price which makes no allowance or only partial allowance for the cost of producing glamour. Or it may make a change in its channels of distribution by selling to direct buyers without salesmen and allowing them some of the savings made thereby. It is doubtful that they would allow them all of the savings. A third course of action is to dispense with glamour on some of the output and sell the commodity alone, for the private label of the buyer. In this case, neither advertising nor selling cost is incurred.

Given a state of deadlock, therefore, the next step may be on the initiative of either seller or buyer. Advertising and sales effort may be by-passed and their expense may be saved by finding a market which does not require any. Instead of making higher outlays, the seller accepts a lower price; and, if the cost saving is greater than the price cut, the seller is better off. Thus the wheel comes full circle; under the pressure of heavy advertising expenses and strong buyers, we are back to price cuts as a method of attracting business. The markets in list-price goods thus are characterized both by price competition and by its avoidance. Both of them are due to the desire for greater volume.

For analytical purposes, it is necessary to separate out these various kinds of solutions. But it goes without saying that any given manufacturer may do all three things, or enter into some arrangement which is a mixture of all three. He may with some justification see a choice not of three or more but of only two alternatives: more advertising-cum-selling, or less.

Given the need for volume arising from excess capacity and marginal cost below price or from the pressure of heavy selling costs, the situation is obviously unstable, and there is room for a great deal of bargaining and an infinite variety of solutions. Deals may be made which are ostensibly discriminatory and actually not, or the reverse, or they may be a mixture of several kinds of considerations; and the names they are given may not have much relation with the economic realities. An advertising allowance may really be partly advertising, partly a volume discount, which in turn may be partly a reflection of costs saved through larger quantity shipments, partly a reflection of selling costs saved, partly a discriminatory price cut. With costs so heavily overhead in composition, it would be impossible to segregate them with any great accuracy. Furthermore, one manufacturer's cost saving translated into a lower price may become a competitive offer to other manufacturers, who thereupon cut price simply to retain business, without asking whether the cut is discriminatory or not. In fact, it may be either.

But the need for additional volume or for lower selling costs is itself unstable. It does not affect the seller of trading items in the strict sense, nor does it apply at the other extreme — the firm selling under a trademark so much in demand that it does not need to make any kind of discount to anybody. It is in the intermediate ranges that we have the confusing tangle of discounts and differentials. Obviously, every seller would like to get through this "sonic barrier" into the range of undisturbed high demand; and, if lucky or skillful enough, large firms like the soap manufacturers, or small ones like Loudon and Olney & Carpenter, may be able to do so. Furthermore, a dramatic increase in per capita national income, such as happened after 1939, may do it for many others; and price structures broken down during depressed years may be restored in prosperous times.

The problem, however, is a permanent one because it is inseparable from product differentiation and large selling and advertising costs. When selling and advertising expenses reach the size indicated in Tables 8 and 9, it is clear that the problem of

TABLE 8. Distribution Costs of Manufacturers as Per Cent of Sales, 1931

Group	No. of industries	No. of reports [a]	Direct selling expenses	Advertising and promotional	Combined selling plus advertising [b]
Grocery products	1	9	11.08	6.21	17.29
Consumer goods industries: median	19	163	11.47	5.98	17.29
Producers' goods industries: median	10	158	10.12	2.21	11.88

Source. *An Analysis of the Distribution Costs of 312 Manufacturers*, a study conducted by the Association of National Advertisers, with the cooperation of the National Association of Cost Accountants (New York: A.N.A., 1933), pp. 64–65, 106–107.

Note. Since there were no dollar figures, it was impossible to compute any weighted averages. They would probably be misleading anyway.

[a] The number of reports exceeds the number of companies (321 as against 312) because several manufacturers submitted separate reports for more than one plant.

[b] The figures do not represent the sum of medians, but the median of sums for all industries in the two groups. Grocery products happened to be a little below one median and a little above the other; but their combined expenses were the median for all combined expenses among consumer goods.

price structures is a major one. Thus, in the extreme case of bread and bakery products, a cut of only 20 per cent in selling-advertising expense would suffice to double the net profit. So long as manufacturers continue to have a wide trading margin above *marginal* cost or *average* cost of manufacture, the price structure will be under *short-run* or *long-run* pressure to sag through discriminatory cuts, *or* through reductions which make a belated recognition of cost savings and remove existing discrimination.

TABLE 9. Advertising and Selling Costs, Eight Food Groups, 1940

Commodity	No. of compa- nies	Sales (millions of dollars)		Expense per dollar of net sales:			Net profit per dollar of net sales
		Total	Per com- pany	Adver- tising	Selling	Total	
Bread and bakery products	82	329.8	4.0	2.63	24.24	26.87	5.30
Cereal preparations	14	129.3	9.2	13.08	5.77	18.85	12.37
Biscuits and crackers	7	167.6	23.9	13.56	2.60	16.16	11.47
Fruit and vegetable canning	49	384.5	7.9	4.49	6.87	11.36	10.01
Flour milling	22	362.9	16.5	3.05	6.22	9.27	3.21
Beet sugar refining	11	129.3	11.8	0.17	1.57	1.74	11.51
Cane sugar refining	17	376.5	22.2	0.20	1.21	1.41	1.83
Dairy products	129	1,125.9	8.7	1.10	n.a.	..	3.68

Source. Federal Trade Commission, respective *Industrial Corporation Reports*.

VIII

THE ROBINSON-PATMAN ACT

In works of this kind, it is customary to present economic description and analysis before turning to issues of public policy and law. However, a chapter on the law is needed at this point.

The Robinson-Patman Act was part of the environment within which A & P buyers functioned; so important a part, and so ever-present in their minds, that we cannot understand their actions unless we understand what conditioned them at every step. Another reason is one of semantics. Economists have written a good deal about price discrimination; the Robinson-Patman Act deals with "price discrimination"; and it is therefore taken for granted that the law and the economists — not to mention the general public — are talking about the same thing. Nothing could be more incorrect. Not always, but more often than not, the two concepts are literally contradictory, in that Robinson-Patman "discrimination" rigorously proves the existence of nondiscrimination, and vice versa. Since the speech patterns of A & P management are those of Robinson-Patman, it is necessary to translate in order to understand what they were saying and doing.

One caution is necessary. We are not trying to "contrast" an economists' definition with a legal definition. There can be no contrast or conflict because the two exist in different universes. The economists have worked out a consistent scheme for classifying *facts*; the economist can divide all groups of transactions into two classes, discriminatory and nondiscriminatory. The law states a system of *rights and duties*; and the lawyer can also divide into two classes: legal and illegal. It follows that any group of transactions must belong in one and only one of the four categories:

(1) Discriminatory — legal
(2) Nondiscriminatory — illegal
(3) Discriminatory — illegal
(4) Nondiscriminatory — legal

What we shall attempt to prove is simply that under the Robinson-Patman Act many and perhaps most transactions must fall into classes (1) and (2). From this are deduced certain economic and legal consequences.

The legislative background

The Robinson-Patman Act is generally considered to be directed against price "discrimination" by sellers coerced or influenced by the "power" or "bargaining power" or "coercive power," or something, of large buyers. If "power" means monopoly power or market control in the economic sense, it must be said at once that there is no logical foundation for this. There is simply no way discovered by economic analysis to make any connection between *monopoly power on the buying side* to *price discrimination on the selling side*. A monopoly buyer, or monopsonist, might indeed pay a single very low price; or he might discriminate in the prices he paid, making separate bargains with his suppliers, and paying some of them more than others. But he could not get sellers to discriminate in price unless the sellers themselves had some monopoly power. A seller with zero monopoly power (pure competition) would never have the motive or the power to discriminate in price. A seller who was only a small part of the market would not charge a lower price to the big buyer; he would sell all he could to the better paying buyers. If all sellers did this, the final result would be to equalize the price paid by the large semimonopolist buyer with the prices paid by others. This less than competitive price might of course be as objectionable as a higher than competitive price, but it would not be discriminatory.

Monopoly power of *buyers* (monopsony) leading to price discrimination by *sellers* is therefore like the Emperor's new clothes: one's professional duty is to say that there is no such thing. Sellers with some appreciable market control may be able to charge higher prices to smaller buyers, who cannot shop around, than to

large buyers, who can. In other words, the monopoly power of
certain sellers is limited by buyers who do enjoy an economy of
larger *absolute size* — the ability to maintain a buying organization. Monopsony power is an irrelevancy.

There is a widespread impression that the Chain Store Investigation of the Federal Trade Commission disclosed much price
discrimination in favor of large buyers. The Investigation established no such thing. It estimated that roughly 85 per cent of the
differences in selling price between chain and nonchain stores was
accounted for by lower operating expenses.[1] Even this was a gross
underestimate because the Commission made no attempt to find
out whether and to what extent quantity discounts corresponded
to cost savings; they considered as "preferential" the granting of
the wholesaler's discount to a chain store, even though the latter's
warehouse was physically and economically indistinguishable
from a wholesaler's warehouse, and sales to it netted the seller no
less and probably more. Again, the equivalent of brokerage allowed
the buyer was counted as "preferential," even though there was
no reason given for supposing that the seller netted any less in
allowing the brokerage equivalent to a buyer rather than to a
broker.

As a matter of fact, the economist in charge of the Investigation
wrote elsewhere that quantity and related discounts usually failed
to make full allowance for cost savings — which means that even
before Robinson-Patman there was some discrimination, in the
economic sense, *against* the "preferred" buyers.[2] Another FTC
study showed that in 1936 the net return to the sellers of fresh
fruit and vegetables was *greatest* on sales to the chain stores[3]
(the latter study was barred from the A & P record, on the objection of government counsel).

It is perfectly clear that the FTC was investigating not price
discrimination, in the economic sense, but price differentials. To
be sure, there was occasional recognition that differentials might

[1] FTC, *Final Report on the Chain Store Investigation* (Washington, 1934),
p. 55.

[2] W. H. S. Stevens, "An Interpretation of the Robinson-Patman Act," *Journal of Marketing*, 2:44 (1937).

[3] FTC, *Report on Distribution Methods and Costs* (Washington, 1944),
pp. 140–41.

do no more than reflect differences in cost, but this was never carried into practice.

What is true of the FTC report is even more obvious in the congressional hearings on the Robinson-Patman Act.[4] (As for the floor debates, the less said the better.) The fact that Congress plainly was not directing its legislation against price discrimination in the economic sense does not necessarily mean that it was legislating badly. There may have been the best of reasons why Congress should legislate against price differentials rather than price discrimination. But there is no evidence whatever that Congress was ever made aware of the distinction, or realized the consequences of its act. There is no way of telling whether they thought they were legislating against price discrimination, or whether they were trying to require discrimination against lower-cost buyers by prescribing price uniformity. Doubtless some knew what they were doing; obviously most did not.

This is rather curious. No brief or opinion in a Robinson-Patman case is complete without great argument about the act and about "the legislative intent" behind it. Any self-respecting law firm has reams of memoranda on the subject. Yet if ever there was a perfect example of the legislature not knowing the consequences of its actions, and not knowing what it intended, this was it.

> When a Legislature has had a real intention, one way or another, on a point, it is not one in a hundred times that any doubt arises as to what its intention was. . . . The fact is that the difficulties of so-called interpretation arise when the Legislature has had no meaning at all; when the question which is raised on the statute never occurred to it.[5]

The economics of price discrimination

Price discrimination, in the economic sense, exists when price differentials do not correspond altogether with cost [6] differentials.

[4] *Hearings Before the Special Committee of the House on Investigation of the American Retail Federation*, 74 Cong., 1 sess. (1936); *Hearings Before the Committee on the Judiciary of the House to Amend the Clayton Act*, 74 Cong., 1 sess. (1936).

[5] John Chipman Gray, *The Nature and Sources of the Law* (Boston, 1909), pp. 172–173.

[6] Cost in the strictest sense means long-run marginal cost. But if it be defined as average cost, the conclusions of this chapter are not seriously affected. See Technical Note at end of chapter.

Discrimination may exist without any price differences when two or more buyers are charged the same price although it costs less to serve one than another. A buyer paying a lower price is actually discriminated against if the lower price does not fully reflect a lower cost of serving him. The "lower costs" may arise from the omission of certain manufacturing processes, or distributive services, or for many other reasons; and, since price less cost equals profit, it follows that price discrimination, in the economic sense, is rigorously defined as a difference in the profit earned from one customer as against another.[7]

This condition is of course very widespread in the business world. Most of these profit differentials, which we will henceforth call discriminations, are transitory and fortuitous. If there were established a condition of perfect nondiscrimination this morning, by nightfall there would be plenty of discrimination, if for no other reason than unforeseen changes in supply and demand. Those changes make some customers, some products, some localities, some channels of supply, more remunerative than others, and an alert business management will always be on the lookout for these more profitable opportunities and exploit them as best it can.

But this process must under active competition destroy the discriminations which initiated the process. As business concerns devote their labor and capital to these more profitable sales, and *pro tanto* withdraw from less profitable ones, they increase supply in the one market and decrease it in the other. So long as there is any profit differential — any discrimination — there remains an incentive to continue the process until the discrimination has been

---

[7] More precisely, it is the profit rate on the current value of the necessary investment, converted to a per-unit basis. A minor ambiguity is whether, under nondiscrimination, all price differentials are *equal* or are *proportional* to all cost differentials. Under pure competition prices are equal to marginal cost, so that discrimination cannot exist. Under nonpure competition, if prices to various customers are proportional to the respective marginal costs, there is no discrimination. Cost in economic discourse always includes a normal or minimum profit. This has become a practical question in antitrust law. See FTC, Re Investigation of Plate Glass Pricing: Memorandum Submitted on Behalf of Pittsburgh Plate Glass Co., September 17, 1952; and FTC, Thompson Products Co., Docket No. 5872, Initial Decision, March 20, 1958, which clearly rejects any return on investment as an element of "cost" under the Robinson-Patman Act. It is discussed below.

completely removed; but in the meantime, other changes in market conditions have created new differentials. Thus, under competition, discriminations are always being created and always being destroyed. To block either the creative or the destructive part of the process is to block competition.

Under active competition, there cannot be any stable and permanent price discrimination on any given product. Price differentials net of cost differentials, i.e., variations in profit per unit as between two or more buyers, cannot be maintained permanently. For sellers will try to switch from the low-margin to the high-margin buyers until all the margins are equalized and there is no more discrimination. The only genuine exceptions to this rule arise from irremovable differences in efficiency and from the ignorance or inertia of buyers or sellers about better alternatives. All other "exceptions" are spurious and, upon examination, turn out to involve cost differentials which merely cannot be precisely measured or which may be random or irregular fluctuations in margins.

It cannot be emphasized too much that cost differentials in economic language do not mean "cost justification" under the Robinson-Patman Act. That is an altogether different subject — a statutory command, not an economic category. We are concerned with cost-price differentials which exist as business facts and which at least a minority of buyers or sellers know to exist,[8] whether or not they have a precise idea of just how much they amount to. Profit-and-loss statements are "mere estimates," with wide margins of error, and yet they are used as guides to business policy. The reader should be disabused once and for all of the notion that cost differences in the economic sense refer to cost accounting records — still less to that tiny minority of cost accounting records which would pass FTC scrutiny. Capitalist enterprise and profit incentives existed long before cost accounting records; and relatively few business decisions are based merely on cost accounting records, useful as these may be. Our experience with price control taught us that much.

If, therefore, stable discrimination on any given product is im-

[8] The reason why only a minority need know of the cost difference is explained below.

possible under active competition, its presence indicates some block somewhere to the competitive process. To take an extreme case: a monopolist will increase his profits if he is able to divide his customers and get from each of them the highest price each is willing to pay. The current price of refined copper is around 30 cents per pound; but there are customers who if need be could be made to pay ten or a hundred times that much. A monopolist of copper would try to sell to them at the high price if he could prevent those who bought at the lower price from reselling. What is perhaps not so readily apparent is why our fictitious copper monopolist accepts the lower price from these other customers. He does so because if he tried to divert copper from the lower-paying to the higher-paying customers, some of it would remain unsold, because these customers would take no more at the higher price. So we arrive at a general rule: a seller who accepts lower net prices (lower profit per unit) from some buyers than from others does so because he is better off selling some output at the lower margin than if he tried to push it into the higher-margin market; for he could not sell it in the higher-margin market except by lowering the price so far as to reduce his total profits.

Of rather different but perhaps greater significance is stable discrimination practiced by a group of sellers. It can only exist if they have some agreement or understanding to get higher margins from some buyers than from others. The essence of such an understanding is that nobody will undercut the agreed-on price schedule and offer better terms to the higher-margin buyer, even though the lower price may much exceed cost. If some of the sellers do this, they will begin to attract away this higher-margin trade, and others will jump on the band wagon. Starting perhaps with offers to pass on a fraction of the higher margin, the competitive process would in time erode away all of it. Hence its persistence over time cannot be explained except as resulting from some kind of understanding to inhibit competition. (This is, of course, no necessary proof of illegal behavior. See below, pp. 157–158.)

The tie between discrimination and monopoly power is often hard for lawyers steeped in Robinson-Patman to accept because discrimination seems to them to be found mostly among small, powerless concerns. This impression is largely derived from price "discrimination" in the Robinson-Patman sense, not in the economic sense. A firm with a one-price policy is often really discriminating by getting more from some customers than from others. Conversely, the "discriminating" firm may be a nondiscriminator, doing no more than bid for the wider-margin business by offering some or all of the margin to gain additional trade — to the disgust of its fellows.

This deserves a moment of attention. Let the reader consider the very small firm with an infinitesimal share of its market — for example, the grain farmer. On anybody's definition, such a firm has no power or "bargaining power" whatsoever. Yet nobody ever heard of it discriminating in price. A reasonable farmer has no need to shade the price to anyone, since he can sell all he desires to sell at the current price. Nor can he hope to get more than this price from anyone, since a customer has plenty of other suppliers from whom to buy. He cannot, therefore, discriminate in price; any differential he grants is and must be merely an allowance for lower quality, or for freight or other service performed.

As we get farther away from these markets, the possibility of discrimination by small sellers with little market power does arise — for a rather special, but often important, reason. A small seller, let us suppose, is practicing genuine price discrimination — taking larger net returns from some customers than from others. Obviously, he must be better off doing it than by trying to sell everything at the higher price. A monopolist, as already seen, knows that he has sold all that the higher-margin market will absorb at the existing price and that he is better off dumping the excess at the lower price than bringing down the price in the other markets. If the small seller does not attempt to sell everything at the higher price, it follows that there is some inhibition on his freedom of action. If he passes up the apparent chance to take a higher profit, it is because he is convinced that the sellers as a group are better off trying to get the higher price on smaller sales and disposing of the excess to some more favored customers.

When a seller thinks and acts in terms of sellers as a group, of industry welfare as a whole, he is of course thinking and acting precisely as would a monopolist, who *is* the industry as a whole. Hence the small seller who follows a consistent and stable pattern of price discrimination in the economic sense, not in the sense of Robinson-Patman "discrimination," is adhering to an industry-wide understanding — which need not be an agreement or conspiracy in the legal sense. It may be a time-honored custom, followed by all because it increases profit; or it may result from informal pressure by others.

So far it looks as though discrimination, except when unintended or "passive" discrimination,[9] is always evidence of monopoly behavior. However, this is not so. For when a noncompetitive price is being maintained at a higher than current level, and a seller wants more volume, the temptation is great to reduce the price to some buyers for the sake of the additional sales volume and larger total profits. Under these circumstances, discriminatory selling may be evidence not of a functioning monopoly but of an ineffective or disintegrating one.

This leads us to a paradox which is of great practical importance. Let us imagine a group of sellers who charge discriminatory prices to several classes of buyers. One seller wants to shade prices for more volume, and he therefore offers a better deal to some buyers. It is quite likely that his offer is simply the recognition of lower costs of serving those buyers, i.e., the recognition of higher margins per unit. His price cut may be discriminatory in either or both of two senses: he is not lowering his prices to all buyers; and the new lower prices may not be offered to all of the lower-cost (wider-margin) buyers. But his new price structure is yet *less discriminatory* than the old price structure, in that some of the discrimination has been eroded away through the constant tendency to seek out the wider-margin business. A discriminatory method leads to a less discriminatory result.

Thus, general or theoretical reasoning would lead us to expect just the sort of complex situations we meet in real life, where discrimination and nondiscrimination are mingled; where some discriminations may indicate control of the market and others, the breakdown of control; where a given price change may in part be discriminatory and in part nondiscriminatory. It is perhaps disorderly, but that is the kind of economic system we have.

---

[9] For this useful term, I am indebted to my former student, Benjamin H. Stevens.

Thus far, we have dealt with price discrimination only as an indicator of price competition failing to operate — or sometimes, operating after a lag in time. This is perhaps its most important aspect, to flag situations which require explanation. When business concerns accept permanently lower returns from some customers than from others, it is a case of water flowing up hill. The situation may be trivial or actually desirable, or it may indicate an overdue corrective action, or it may indicate control of the market; and even when it signals control, that may not be violation of law. But signal something it does.

Why, however, should there be any objection to discrimination as such? To the extent that economics has developed a science of welfare, there is no disagreement that passive discrimination, resulting from nothing more than pursuit of opportunities as they arise, is positively beneficial; and that corrective discrimination, which serves to break down a noncompetitive price system which may itself be discriminatory, is at least useful. Why should there be any objection to stable and permanent discrimination, however? So far as discrimination among ultimate consumers is concerned, the answer is by no means clear. Discrimination makes the distribution of real income different from what it would be under competition; but it is difficult to prove that this latter distribution is "optimal" in any rigorous sense. Perhaps we need nothing so refined, but merely a sense of injustice that some people are getting more than others despite their rendering no additional service, either of their own efforts or their own property, that anyone can see. In any case, the problem is of no legal importance.

Discrimination among business concerns, however, is more clearly objectionable if, and only if, competition is needed as the great selective agent of our economy. If we desire the competitive process to insure that only the most efficient processes and producers survive, then discrimination serves to distort the system of rewards and punishments of a profit-and-loss system: it means that the survivors will not necessarily be the most efficient. For those to whom competition means some more lofty goal than efficiency — say the social and political benefits, so well exemplified in contemporary France, of keeping as many small businessmen in existence as possible — there is no such basic objection to discrimination. Those to whom competition means "many happy competitors" must support discrimination in favor of their protégés and against others, and in fact they do. Witness the Robinson-Patman Act as currently interpreted, to which we now turn.

The unifying principle

The legal profession has a rather low opinion of the Act as a piece of craftsmanship, quite aside from its policy, and their comments have become (in the words of the Dean of the University of Chicago Law School) "a contest of witticisms to relieve an otherwise dreary picture." [10] But, contrary to a common impression,[11] the various provisions of the Act are strikingly consistent. Substance and procedure are well integrated with one another and with the economics of distribution. The Act has a single unifying principle: *to enforce discrimination against the lower-cost buyer or the lower-cost method of distribution.* The lower-cost buyer may be such because he orders in large quantities which permits the saving of certain costs. Or he may have integrated backward and do some things for himself which other buyers need to have the seller do for them — storage, transport, assembly, breaking bulk, making contact, etc. Whatever the reason, the Act prescribes discrimination against such customers.

It sounds unpleasant to say that the Act prescribes and requires price discrimination, while advertising itself as a law against discrimination. Indeed, Dean Levi has spoken of "the disease of duplicity with which the Act is infected." [12] Yet he probably did not mean, and we certainly do not mean, that the sponsors of the Act were hypocrites. There is little or no point in discussing what they had in mind. In actual fact, the statute requires price uniformity.[13] But "price uniformity in the face of cost diversity

---

[10] Edward H. Levi, "The Robinson-Patman Act — Is It in the Public Interest?" American Bar Association, Section of Antitrust Law, *Proceedings of the Annual Meeting* (Chicago, 1952), p. 60.

[11] See Automatic Canteen Co. v. FTC, 346 U.S. 61, 65 (1953).

[12] Levi, *Proceedings of the Annual Meeting*, p. 69.

[13] Cyrus Austin, *Price Discrimination and Related Problems under the Robinson-Patman Act* (American Law Institute–American Bar Association, Philadel-

is price discrimination." [14] It logically follows that the statute requires price discrimination.

Special provisions

Certain provisions of the Robinson-Patman Act explicitly disregard cost variations to maintain uniform prices.

First of all, Section 2 (c) of the Act unconditionally forbids a particular type of cost differential — brokerage — from being passed on to buyers. Some buyers, by integrating backwards, are able to serve as their own middlemen. In dealing with such buyers the seller is able to save whatever he would otherwise have to pay a broker. Yet costs saved or services rendered are irrelevant: "The prohibition of the statute . . . is absolute." [15] Anyone who buys on his own account, whether he is a wholesaler,[16] a co-operative,[17] a chain store,[18] a buying agent,[19] or anything else, is forbidden to receive a price reduction even though the seller may realize more by selling to him and allowing the brokerage than by selling through a broker.

The discrimination inherent in Section 2 (c) lies in the fact that the integrated buyer, who has eliminated the brokerage expense from the seller's cost, must pay the same price as the buyer who cannot perform this function. For example, if the price of an article is one dollar and the customary brokerage fee is 3 per cent, the seller collects 97 cents when he sells through a broker, but

phia, 1950), pp. 25–38. It will be noted that Mr. Austin rightly contrasts the concept of discrimination in the delivered-price cases with all other Robinson-Patman cases. We are concerned only with the latter. The delivered-price cases could have been brought and decided no differently had there been no Robinson-Patman Act.

[14] Fritz Machlup, *The Basing-Point System* (Philadelphia, 1949), p. 173.

[15] Great A & P Tea Co. v. FTC, 106 F.2d 667, 674 (3d Cir. 1939), *cert. denied*, 308 U.S. 625 (1940).

[16] Southgate Brokerage Co. v. FTC, 150 F.2d 607 (4th Cir. 1945).

[17] Independent Grocers Alliance Distributing Co. v. FTC, 203 F.2d 941 (7th Cir. 1953); Modern Marketing Service, Inc. v. FTC, 149 F.2d 970 (7th Cir. 1945).

[18] Great A & P Tea Co. v. FTC, 106 F.2d 667 (3d Cir. 1939), *cert. denied*, 308 U.S. 625 (1940).

[19] Oliver Bros., Inc., v. FTC, 102 F.2d 763 (4th Cir. 1939); Biddle Purchasing Co. v. FTC, 96 F.2d 687 (2d Cir. 1938).

receives a full dollar from the direct or integrated buyer — a price which includes 3 cents for "phantom" brokerage, i.e., brokerage never paid for by the seller. A buyer is clearly discriminated against when he must pay a price of one dollar which includes a fee for brokerage, though the buyer himself is performing this function and incurring its expense.

Of course, if a seller made price adjustments for brokerage which was fictitious, or in excess of the actual cost, this would bring a lower net return to the seller and would be discriminatory in fact as well as under the provisions of the Act. Nondiscrimination would exist only where price differentials in fact reflected cost differentials due to a saving of brokerage. The important thing about Section 2 (c) is that it forbids any investigation of facts. This obvious bad conscience has earned a nearly universal contempt among writers on the Act.

The second provision of the Robinson-Patman Act which openly disregards cost differentials is the quantity-limits provision included in Section 2 (a). Even if price reductions to quantity buyers can be "justified" by showing lower costs — and we shall see that "justification" is seldom possible — even then the Federal Trade Commission is authorized to designate the markets in which quantity discounts may be "unjustly discriminatory and promotive of monopoly" and to set limits upon discounts there. Thus, discounts may be declared "unjustly discriminatory" without any reference to underlying cost differentials. This section was not invoked until 1951, when the Commission issued an order restricting quantity discounts in the sale of automobile tires for replacement purposes. The purpose of the quantity-limits proviso was stated clearly: to prevent the "economies" of large orders "from being reflected in price." [20] The contempt for cost differentials shown in this action is startling even to those acquainted with Robinson-Patman administration. Any and all price differences are considered "discriminatory," with no attention paid to varying quantities, channels of distribution, etc., which are responsible for obvious and very large cost differences. The ostensible purpose of the order is to prevent monopoly, but the economic basis of the alleged monopoly approaches the frivolous.

[20] FTC Quantity-Limit Rule, 310.1, 17 Fed. Reg. 113 (1952).

Since "only" 63 buyers, who constituted 29 per cent of the market, were able to purchase in carload quantities, discounts in respect of amounts greater than one carload were held to promote "bilateral oligopoly." The order was blocked by procedural litigation. Our only interest in it is as an example of the basic theme of Robinson-Patman: uniform prices despite nonuniform costs.

The third provision of the Act which disregards cost is Section 2(e), which forbids the furnishing of services except to all buyers "on proportionally equal terms," whatever that means. In a recent case, a seller tried to prove that the different services furnished only corresponded to the "differences in [his] costs in dealing with the two classes of customers." But the Supreme Court held that "neither 'cost-justification' nor an absence of competitive injury" could excuse the service differential.[21]

"Cost justification"

The provisions which officially disregard cost deal with special cases — brokerage, quantity limits, and services. Elsewhere, cost differentials have apparently been taken into account, since the Act provides that cost differences may be offered as a "justification" for price differences. The use of the word "justification" is significant. A price differential which reflects a cost differential and nets the seller the same amount is not considered in the Act as nondiscriminatory. It is rather a "discrimination" permissible only because of special exculpatory circumstances.[22] The supposed inconsistency is that cost is considered in some situations but disregarded in others. However, this inconsistency is more apparent than real.

When and if a cost differential is recognized by the Federal Trade Commission, a seller may still charge prices which make no allowance at all, or a partial allowance, or a full allowance for

[21] Federal Trade Commission v. Simplicity Pattern Co., 360 U.S. 55, 58, 70 (1959).

[22] "Proof that a differential makes 'only due allowance' for differences in cost has been treated as a *justification* for a *discrimination* in price otherwise prohibited, not as taking such differentials out of the category of discriminations." Austin, *Price Discrimination*, p. 58 (italics in original).

the differential. Only a full allowance would be nondiscriminatory. Therefore, even when a cost differential is legally established, nondiscrimination is not legally required. *Nondiscrimination is simply the extreme limiting case of what the law permits.* Short of this limit, the Act permits price discrimination against the buyer who is served at lower cost. It is immediately apparent that taking all transactions together, there must on the average be discrimination against lower-cost buyers.

But in practice, as will now be seen, the Act not only permits but in fact requires such discrimination. This is a more important reason why the Act is actually consistent though apparently contradictory.

The interaction of substance and procedure [23]

If all of the Act were the same as its special provisions, if there were a uniform and explicit rule that cost differentials could not be considered, then it would be obvious that the Act itself instituted discrimination and did this consistently. Such is not the case. Except for its special provisions, the substance of the Act permits a "justification" of differentials. This substance, however, is consumed by procedure, and discrimination is accomplished indirectly.

To understand how this happens one must examine the economic context in which "justification" might be attempted, where an attempt is feasible at all. The price-cost structure of any seller involves large elements of overhead and common costs (even in the absence of true joint costs), and this results in large areas of imprecise information.[24] The burden of proof of a cost differ-

[23] This section draws on an excellent seminar paper by my former student at the Harvard Law School, now Professor of Law there. See Donald T. Trautman, *"Due Allowance" of Cost Differences under the Robinson-Patman Act* (1951). Both of us are indebted to Messrs. James W. Cassedy, Hammond E. Chaffetz, Roswell L. Gilpatric, Murray W. McEniry, and Thomas E. Sunderland, who afforded access to the records and briefs of the *Indiana* and *Minneapolis-Honeywell* cases.

[24] FTC, *Case Studies in Distribution Cost Accounting*, p. 12 (1941); *Accountants' Handbook* (3d ed. 1943), pp. 299–300, 336–338; Mark A. Massel, "Cost Factors under Section 2 (a)" in *Chicago Bar Association Symposium on Robinson-Patman Act* (1947); Corwin D. Edwards, in *CCH Robinson-Patman Act*

ential is on the seller; any cost differential is presumed to be "unjustified" unless and until the Commission finds to the contrary. The procedural requirements are such that a cost differential must be disregarded unless it is certain and precise. But, since cost differentials are inherently uncertain and imprecise, most of them cannot exist in the contemplation of law.

Prohibitive cost of assembling data. To begin with, there is the burden of coming forth with the evidence. This in itself would be a powerful deterrent to attempting cost justification, since the expense of assembling data is heavy.[25] Therefore, in many instances when a differential exists and could be proved to the Commission's satisfaction, it is a losing game for the seller to establish it. Consequently, he must act as though no cost differential existed, and must charge uniform prices discriminating against lower-cost buyers.

The burden of proof. Over and above the financial burden of coming forward with the detailed evidence is the legal burden: demonstration or proof. Every component of a cost differential which is less than completely precise must be treated as though it did not exist. The doubt must always be resolved in one direction. Therefore, many genuine cost differentials are rejected — or are not brought forward at all. Again, the result is price discrimination via uniform prices.

The relevant cases clearly illustrate this principle. The last important case under the old Clayton Act was *Goodyear Tire &*

Symposium 60 (1947); Warmack in *CCH Robinson-Patman Act of 1936,* 46, 105–107; John T. Haslett, "Price Discriminations and Their Justification under the Robinson-Patman Act of 1936," *Michigan Law Review,* 46: 450, 472 (1943). The large areas of imprecise information are not due to the time needed to adapt to the law; few business firms have changed their methods to reflect the improvements which the Act was supposed to bring about. See Donald W. Longman, *Distribution Cost Analysis* (1941); pp. 247–250; FTC, *supra,* pp. 21–22; Haslett, *supra;* p. 472. Otto F. Taylor, "How to Cost Justify," *CCH 1957 Antitrust Law Symposium,* p. 116; FTC, *Report of the Advisory Committee on Cost Justification* (1956).

[25] See the testimony of William J. Warmack, *Transcript of Record on Petition for Review,* p. 1639, Minneapolis-Honeywell Regulator Co. v. FTC, 191 F.2d 786 (7th Cir. 1951): "I certainly do not advocate making an extensive cost survey too often because these things cost a lot of money." Yet he could not suggest validity for even five years, even with supplementary interim studies.

Rubber Co. v. FTC.[26] Here the respondent urged various savings
in selling to Sears Roebuck, e.g., stability of manufacturing operations, the assumption by the buyer of credit risks and of losses
arising from a drop in raw-material prices. Nobody would seriously urge that these savings were fictitious.[27] Reasonable men
might well differ as to the amounts actually saved, and the Commission accountant, if called upon to estimate them, might well
have come out with a lower figure than did the respondent.[28] But
this approach was never contemplated. The FTC held the savings
"too remote and speculative" to estimate, and therefore totally
disallowed. This procedural rule had a factual result: in effect,
savings were officially found to equal zero. This in turn had a
substantive result: to forbid savings from being reflected in
price.

The first important case under the new law was *Standard
Brands*.[29] The respondent estimated its total distribution costs for
the item bakers' yeast at 23 per cent of sales receipts. Standard
Brands then applied this percentage to the receipts from the various channels of distribution to determine how much of the total
distribution expense went out by each channel. The higher the
basic percentage, obviously, the higher would be the absolute
difference in cents between any two channels. It was a fair question whether the estimate of 23 per cent might not be too high.
Had the true figure been, not 23 per cent, but 22 or 21 per cent,
the error would have been negligible and would have justified
Standard's differentials. If the figure had been as low as 12 per
cent, it would have served to "justify" differentials half as great.
But the Commission made no such estimates. They simply rejected the cost justification as a whole, thus declaring cost savings to be effectively zero, and not permitted to be reflected in
price.

Standard Brands is revealing if read in conjunction with an

[26] 101 F.2d 620 (6th Cir. 1939). The Robinson-Patman Act apparently did
not introduce this rule of law. It only made it of first-rate importance.

[27] Nor were they subject to the marginal-cost fallacy discussed in the Technical Note at the end of the Chapter.

[28] They might also come out with a higher figure, for Goodyear in dealing
with Sears would not have tried to exaggerate.

[29] FTC 121(1939).

earlier case, *Kraft-Phenix Cheese Corp.*[30] The Commission accepted a price differential of $2.50 as "justified" by a cost differential of $3.62, half again as great. The moral is obvious. Sellers must allow large safety factors, which is another way of saying: only at their peril may sellers pass on to the lower-cost buyer nearly as much as he actually saves them. The effect is reinforced by the many Commission decisions without opinion, and by its failure to lay down, in or out of its opinions, what accounting methods are acceptable.[31] The greater the uncertainty, the larger must be the safety factor, and the larger the elements of discrimination through uniform prices and diverse costs.

The more recent *Minneapolis-Honeywell* case [32] strikingly illustrates this principle because it is one of those rare cases where a cost justification was actually approved — in part, at least. The respondent retained a well-known firm of certified public accountants, whose elaborate study [33] impressed the FTC and cost the company a very large sum directly, and even more indirectly, in consuming the expensive time of corporate officials. Annual manufacturing costs of the product in question were $1,205,000; its annual distribution costs were $600,000. Yet all that the auditors tried to analyze was $165,000 of distribution costs — one fourth of total distribution costs, and less than one tenth of total costs. Only that one tenth contained some cost savings so clearly provable that they could be shown to the FTC. Common sense suggests that the discarded nine tenths probably contained a larger amount of cost savings than did the retained one tenth. Not only were all manufacturing costs excluded, but many others which could not be apportioned in an uncontroversial way.[34] Obviously, a prohibition of controversy amounts to settling the controversy in advance, always in favor of the negative.

But even within this saving remnant, assurance needed to be doubly or triply sure. Thus:

[30] 25 FTC 537 (1937).
[31] See below, note 48.
[32] FTC v. Minneapolis-Honeywell Regulator Co., 344 U.S. 206 (1952).
[33] Respondent's Exhibits 170, 186.
[34] Transcript of Record on Petition for Review, pp. 1260–61, FTC v. Minneapolis-Honeywell Regulator Co., 344 U.S. 206 (1952).

Brackets compared	Actual difference in cost	Difference in price
First and second	$7.10	$2.90
Second and third	2.32	.90
Third and fourth	.89	.55
Fourth and fifth	.53	.55

Disregard of capital costs. Even in the most primitive of economies there has always been a cost of capital, i.e., of even the simplest artifacts needed for useful tasks. In a developed economy of private enterprise, the cost of capital consists of the return which must be paid to the owner of capital in order to secure its services.

In order to see whether there is a cost differential between two or more buyers, one must inquire whether the amount and quality — that is, the cost — of any productive factor used to serve one, is greater than what is used to serve another. It follows that one should ask, among other questions, whether it takes more capital to serve one rather than another.

But in the spirit of Section 2(c), this question is not permitted to be asked under 2(a). Or, what comes to the same thing, the cost of capital is officially to be reckoned at zero.

This issue was squarely presented for the first time in a recent case, *Thompson Products*.[35] Here the respondent stated without contradiction that to distribute their products to certain kinds of customers involved an additional investment in distribution facilities of some nine million dollars. An appropriate cost of capital was stated to be the return this company earned upon its whole investment. This particular rate seems appropriate, since it states the opportunity cost of furnishing the facilities rather than doing something else with the money. Perhaps, however, the appropriate rate should be set in some more refined fashion. But that issue is not to be reached because the cost of capital is not to be considered at all. The return on the money used to provide certain customers with additional services is to be officially reckoned at zero. This, according to the Commission, is the mandate of the Act, which permits the reckoning only of "actual" cost dif-

[35] Docket No. 5872, *Initial Decision*, March 20, 1958 (mimeographed), pp. 17–20; and *Final Order*, February 19, 1959 (mimeographed), pp. 10–11.

ferences, not "allocated" or "imputed" ones.[36] There is the usual semantic maneuver — who wants to consider costs which are not "actual" costs?

The importance of the *Thompson Products* case is that only after 22 years did a respondent even try to have the cost of capital included in Robinson-Patman "cost." Their failure shows that in this as in other respects, cost "justification" is a contrivance to prevent the consideration of facts on cost.

Necessity of proving all cost elements. Cost elements doubtful in amount may not only be disallowed, but they may so taint the rest of the presentation that it will be disallowed *in toto*. The best example was the *Standard Oil of Indiana* case,[37] where the respondent was required to prove (!) that it cost less to serve a wholesale customer who took large amounts and stored the gasoline until needed, than to serve a retail customer who took small amounts and did no storage. A few hours of library research among independent documentary materials would have indicated probability of a cost differential of about that claimed by the respondent. But the ritual of cost "justification" interposed. The schedule presented by the respondent contained various elements which of course were not all of equal validity. The Commission singled out those they considered the weakest. One wholesaler had sometimes taken delivery from a tank truck making several deliveries, rather than invariably taking a whole truckload. It would be surprising — or suspicious — to find anything else. The Commission did not ask whether there had been enough multiple deliveries to affect the computation to any significant degree; they simply disallowed.[38]

In this case, controversy concerned four wholesalers as a group. Justification of a lower price to them was attempted by using

---

[36] Docket No. 5872, *Initial Decision*, March 20, 1958 (mimeographed), pp. 19–20; and *Final Order*, February 19, 1959, p. 10.

[37] 41 FTC 263 (1945), *affirmed*, 173 F.2d 210 (7th Cir. 1949), *reversed, on other grounds*, 340 U.S. 231 (1951), *reissued with new findings*, 49 FTC 923 (1953); *set aside*, 233 F.2d 649 (7th Cir. 1956); *affirmed*, Jan. 27, 1958 (U.S. Law Week, 4111). See Adelman, "Integration and Antitrust Policy," *Harvard Law Review*, 62:60 (1949), for a detailed factual account; and John S. McGee, "Price Discrimination and Competitive Effects," *University of Chicago Law Review*, 23:398 (1956).

[38] Finding of Fact 9 (b).

delivery cost data from another state. If there was any bias in this study, it was probably unfavorable to the respondent; but the Commission made no attempt to estimate bias, simply finding "no probative value."[39] Respondent then made a study of the area in question. The total discount to be justified was 1½ cents. On the basis of the new data, the trial examiner thought an allowable discount would be less than one cent, but did not explain how he arrived at this estimate. In fact, on appeal to the Commission, the respondent claimed without refutation that it was impossible as a matter of arithmetic to take the accounts mentioned by the trial examiner and reach his conclusion.[40] An FTC accountant testified that he was unable to say what the actual cost saving was.[41] The most important objection to the new cost study was that it included a larger area than was concerned in the litigation. No records existed for the smaller area; but one of the Commission accountants had agreed that comparative cost figures for these two areas would only differ by two one-hundredths of one cent.[42]

Another disputed point involved employee-welfare payments for the services previously rendered. Whether or not one included them would make a difference of six one-hundredths.[43] This is still a long way from the 150 one-hundredths sought to be justified. But since these and still smaller elements were in doubt, the Commission rejected the *whole* cost schedule. Cost differentials were officially found to be zero; storage and distribution must be free gifts of nature, requiring no investment of capital and no service of labor.

The Attorney-General's Committee to Study the Antitrust Laws stated that "the cost defense has proved largely illusory in practice."[44] Few commentators have been of the contrary opin-

---

[39] Finding of Fact 10.

[40] Respondent's Exceptions to Trial Examiner's Report, Transcript of Record on Appeal, p. 5147, Standard Oil Co. v. FTC, 340 U.S. 231 (1951).

[41] At p. 3767.

[42] At p. 4514.

[43] At p. 4617.

[44] *Report of the Attorney-General's National Committee to Study the Antitrust Laws* (Washington: Government Printing Office, 1955), p. 171. Chapter IV, on antitrust policy in distribution, is generally considered one of the most successful parts of the Report. (See Edward S. Mason, *Economic Concentration*

ion. The Committee disregarded, as being obviously irrelevant, the fact that some complaints had been answered with allegations of cost justification, together with other defenses; and that the complaints had subsequently been dismissed without opinion, or settled by consent. Nothing is easier than to *assert* a defense. A case dismissed without stating which of the several possible grounds (including cost justification) upon which it might have been based, is no proof that cost justification was even feebly effective in that instance. The decided cases set the standards for those which are not contested, and the decided cases show clearly that "cost justification" is a process of official nonnotice of facts on cost differentials.

Arbitrary classification of sellers

Now that we have seen how powerful an instrument is the presumption that cost differentials are zero until proved otherwise, we can better appreciate another aspect of the *Standard Oil of Indiana* case. The customers who had bought at jobbers' prices were integrated jobber-retailers. The Commission never claimed that they did not do the work of jobbers, saying only: "Although selling a substantial portion of [their] gasoline direct to the consuming public [they] were nevertheless arbitrarily classified by the respondent as jobbers." [45] To classify on the basis of functions actually performed, labor and capital actually expended, is "arbitrary." Not whether one reduces a seller's cost by performing the wholesale function, but whether or not one is also a retailer determines the price one may legally pay. Whatever one thinks of this rule, it is the only one consistent with the Act's recurring theme of uniform prices despite diverse costs.

This rule is simply a legal penalty on integration. [46] It appears

---

and the *Monopoly Problem*, Cambridge, 1957, p. 390.) This chapter has probably inspired more defamatory attacks on the Report and its authors than all the others combined.

[45] 41 FTC 263, 274 (1945).

[46] It is therefore an incentive for even more complete integration, avoiding or encompassing the market where the buyer knows he will be discriminated against.

most clearly when a given customer resells through more than one channel or by more than one method.[47] Suppose that a customer resells 60 per cent of his taking at retail, and 40 per cent at wholesale. To remain within the law, the supplier must charge him the wholesalers' price on 40 per cent of his purchases, and the retailers' price on 60 per cent. The buyer may (and almost invariably does) take all his purchases in precisely the same way, incurring the same costs both to himself and his supplier, but if he has extended operations into retailing, he must pay a proportionately higher price. Furthermore, the supplier is warned by able counsel that "it would be prudent for him to reserve and exercise the right to have an independent auditor come in and inspect the customer's records for the purpose of verifying that the price he has paid is in accordance with the functions actually performed."[48] Since the supplier and his integrated customers are probably in competition, no comment is necessary on this requirement. Were it not shielded by the Robinson-Patman Act, it would be a per se violation of the Sherman Act or the Federal Trade Commission Act.

To summarize: The higher the standard of proof, and the greater the number of cost differentials which must be ignored, the greater is the aggregate discrimination against the lower-cost buyers. Requirements of proof have in fact been so high, so rigid, and — as in the *Indiana* case — so perverse, that very few cost justifications have been attempted, and fewer accepted.

To say that the cost-justification section of the Act might just as well not be there would be only a negligible exaggeration. It follows that taking all transactions as a group, the lower-cost buyers must under the Act be discriminated against, in that the sum of price differentials in their favor must fall very far short of the sum of cost differentials. The cost "justification," brokerage and quantity-limit provisions — far from being contradictory — are unified and complementary.

---

[47] See FTC v. Ruberoid Co., 343 U.S. 470 (1952); Standard Oil Co. v. FTC, 340 U.S. 231 (1951).
[48] Cyrus V. Anderson, *Antitrust Compliance in Pricing Matters* (Legal Aspects of Marketing, Practising Law Institute, 1953), p. 24.

The competitive process

If the Robinson-Patman Act is inherently a legal device to maintain price discrimination, then its provisions dealing with cost differentials are well calculated to achieve that result. These provisions are reinforced by the manner in which the Act handles "competition." Here again economic analysis reveals a basic consistency.

Economic background. If sellers are compelled by law, or collusive agreement, or trade custom, to take consistently wider profit margins from certain buyers, sales to these buyers become especially attractive. For example, where profit margins are relatively narrow, an extra 3 per cent phantom brokerage may mean that sales to direct buyers are twice as profitable as sales to others. If a supplier happens not to be making such profitable sales, the temptation is very great to secure this kind of business by offering to give up some of the extra profit in order to secure the rest — to allow, say, one per cent off the price in order to get the additional 2 per cent profit. But others can play the same game, and offer 2 per cent off in order to get an additional one per cent. It can go even lower, since any net return over 97 per cent of the list price is pure gain to the seller. Hence suppliers may often be eager to get and keep this business, and willing to give up some of the extra profits if necessary to be sure of the rest. The entire food trade knows perfectly well what at least one of its members has said openly:

Section 2c is violated continuously. A buyer phones a canner, sees him at the convention knows him from years of business dealings; he asks him his price on 1,000 cases of his product. The canner says his price is $1.25 doz. The buyer offers $1.20 — says the canner is too high. This is a direct deal, no broker. The canner realizes this, calculates the brokerage saved, so finally says "o.k." and the deal is closed.[49]

This paragraph is a good brief summary of much buying under the Robinson-Patman Act, since the brokerage section is only slightly more stringent than the rest of the Act. (One could sub-

[49] *Wholesale Grocer News*, February 1950, p. 32.

stitute the word "cost" for "brokerage," and the paragraph would be just as accurate.)

A moment's reflection will show how complex a market situation is imposed here. Some supplier, somewhere, on some item, grants a lower price to a lower-cost buyer. He may not be violating the law even in the strictest sense, because he may be selling his entire output of that particular product to one or to a few low-cost buyers, all of whom pay the same price. But each of these buyers now has an offer which he can show to other suppliers. There is a competitive price which he may ask them to meet. Even with no such offer, the presumption is that one could be made. What are the other suppliers to make of it? If they refuse the deal, and turn from the lower-cost buyer to the rest of the market, they sacrifice some of the extra margin. Hence they will often be responsive to such an offer — or threat, if you like — and meet the competitive price.

But this is not a necessary result. First, the seller may have so strong a market position that buyers must purchase his product anyway. Second, large suppliers may fear exposure and prosecution. Third, for reasons to become apparent soon, the seller may feel that lower-cost buyers really do not have the many alternative sources of supply they claim to have. All three deterrents to cutting price are affected by market conditions, and all are the subject of bargaining, bluffing, etc.

The legal doctrine. As just seen, the wider margins set up by the Act would, under competition, tend to disappear because of the rivalry of sellers, each offering better terms. The end result of this process would be nondiscrimination, and this would conflict with the purposes of the Act. Hence the competitive process must be blocked. Once we understand this necessity, we can readily understand the special meanings of the key phrases "injury to competition" and "meeting of competition in good faith."

It is axiomatic that active competition, as the term is used outside of Robinson-Patman land, must discomfit some of the competitors. If even one of them — "any person" — is "injured," that suffices to violate the law. One may still ask, however, what "injury" to the individual competitor means. In other words, at what point will the law take cognizance of the harm done to him? It is not necessary to show that he has been ruined, or has suffered a dollar of losses. In the *Standard of Indiana* case, the following sufficed: First, certain retailers had lost customers — at least they said they had lost them.[50] Second, a large oil company's sales manager complained that the practice attacked by the FTC "creates a very difficult competitive situation and usually leads to retail price cutting." A dire prospect! The FTC's action in his opinion "should improve the competitive situation." [51] In the *Minneapolis-Honeywell* case it sufficed, as the FTC saw it, that lowering prices had prevented Honeywell's competitors from taking business away from Honeywell — and certainly this was an injury to Honeywell's rivals. The Court of Appeals did not agree,[52] and was upheld in the Supreme Court, but on purely procedural grounds.[53] The dissenting opinion said that on the merits the "Court of Appeals decree . . . is so clearly wrong that it could well be reversed without argument," [54] because the Supreme Court had held in the *Morton Salt* case that once a price differential was proved, "the Commission found what would appear to be obvious, that the competitive opportunities of certain merchants were injured." [55] That sufficed.

The *meeting of competition in good faith* has been a prominently litigated issue. No definitive statement of it is possible, and perhaps never will be. But as matters stand today a price change to a particular customer or group of customers can only be made to meet the equally low price of a competitor — no more and no less. It is settled that one may not undercut a competitive offer.[56] It is not yet settled in the courts but is forcefully urged by the Federal Trade Commission that a seller may not go part way toward meeting a competitive offer. It is all or nothing. Further-

[50] Brief for the Commission, p. 24, Standard Oil Co. v. FTC, 173 F.2d 210 (7th Cir. 1949).

[51] At pp. 22–24.

[52] Minneapolis-Honeywell Regulator Co. v. FTC, 191 F.2d 786 (7th Cir. 1951).

[53] FTC v. Minneapolis-Honeywell Regulator Co., 344 U.S. 206 (1952).

[54] At p. 213.

[55] FTC v. Morton Salt Co., 334 U.S. 37, 46 (1948).

[56] Samuel H. Moss, Inc. v. FTC, 148 F.2d 378 (2d Cir. 1945), *cert. denied*, 326 U.S. 734 (1945).

more, the competitive offer cannot be said to exist because of the responses of buyers or other market conditions:

A multitudinous network of apperceptions suggests to the man in the trade whether the buying or selling blade of the shears is being sharpened. To mention a few: salesmen's reports about willingness of customers to buy at the prices asked and the condition of their stocks, the number of telephone calls that materials buyers receive from their suppliers, how suppliers or customers react to the opening moves of a purchase or sale, shop talk around the luncheon table about what competitors are doing, changes in prices of raw materials, the volume of trading done, which buyers are in and out of the market, and whether . . . operating margins lie within an acceptable range.[57]

These "multitudinous apperceptions" are of competition at work. But one does not meet "competition" — this is the phrase discarded from the Clayton Act by the Robinson-Patman amendment. One meets "the equally low price of a competitor," which only exists when a seller is offered unmistakable proof of a definite offer at a definite price by an identified competitor.[58] Furthermore, the competitive offer must itself be lawful, and known to the buyer as lawful, although it is not settled just how far the buyer's responsibility extends in knowing it to be lawful.[59]

All this has a familiar sound. The rule that nobody is to reduce prices until and unless somebody else cuts them first means that we may wait quite a long time before anybody cuts them at all. The rule that they must be matched *exactly* is of course reminiscent of complaints against basing-point and similar pricing systems. (That the Federal Trade Commission has taken drastic action against particular systems may perhaps be cited as an instance of bureaucratic monopolization — no open-price arrangements except by authority of the FTC!)

Also invoking familiar sights is the *Indiana* order before it was

---

[57] Ruth P. Mack, "The Process of Capital Formation in Inventories and the Vertical Propagation of Business Cycles," *Review of Economics & Statistics*, 35:181, 194 (1953).

[58] Brief for the Commission, pp. 48, 67, Minneapolis-Honeywell Regulator Co. v. FTC, 191 F.2d 786 (7th Cir. 1951).

[59] Automatic Canteen Co. of America v. FTC, 346 U.S. 61 (1953); Standard Oil Co. v. Brown, 238 F.2d 54 (5th Cir. 1956); C. E. Niehoff & Co. v. FTC, 240 F.2d 238 (7th Cir. 1957).

upset by the Supreme Court, for it prescribed resale price maintenance of the gasoline resold by the buyer.[60]

But all these legal sanctions only exist to protect a natural aversion to price reduction, and therein lies their real strength. Let us return to the market, where the suppliers are drawing higher net returns from some buyers. If each individual seller acted independently and without collusion, he would know that he and every other seller would be asked to shade his price. He would be willing to cut price in order to get or keep the specially profitable business. Over a period of time, the extra profits would gradually erode away, and would approach nondiscrimination. But under the Act the seller is aware that every other seller finds it difficult or impossible to "cost-justify" a lower price. It is expensive in itself and even more in the litigation which vigilant rivals will persuade upon the FTC, or in private treble-damage suits. Attempts to lower prices without cost "justification" are risky and usually illegal. The chances of other sellers shading their prices are therefore small. Indeed, they are much smaller than if the sellers entered into a collusive agreement. For the maintenance of uniform prices is not enforced through *sub rosa* collusion but by an agency of government. The seller, his hand thus greatly strengthened, can often or usually run the risk of refusal to cut prices. But the degree of his assurance varies greatly among markets and from one time period to another. Sometimes it can only be verified by trial and error.

Conclusion

Our analysis has revealed that the Robinson-Patman Act requires price discrimination against lower-cost buyers and an open-price arrangement of the NRA type for any group of sellers who can take advantage of it. No other conclusion was to be expected. The Robinson-Patman Act was hardly any more than a re-enactment of the relevant NRA codes; and the general enabling act of NRA, it will be remembered, suspended the antitrust laws to

[60] Standard Oil Co. v. FTC, 173 F.2d 210 (7th Cir. 1949), *reversed on other grounds*, 340 U.S. 231 (1951). Resale price maintenance did not need discussion in order to dispose of the case.

the extent that they conflicted with any codes. The Retail Food and Grocery Trade Code and the Wholesale Food and Grocery Trade Code both prohibited "discrimination," in general terms and in the shape of advertising allowances.[61] The Code for the Wholesale Fresh Fruit and Vegetable Distributive Industry contained the brokerage clause.[62] Others, including the notorious Sugar Institute Code, also contained provisions for implicit price discrimination by prescribing uniform prices; and they too had a brokerage clause.[63] The reaction of A & P divisional presidents is not without interest:

> The newly formed Sugar Institute came in for quite a bit of thought; and while no preventive measures were adopted, the feeling was that the formation of a practical Trust in any large industry would not work to our advantage, and that everything possible should be done to break down the present set-up.

> The feeling was that if the Sugar Institute was successful, it would be only a question of time when other industries would follow the same line of thought.[64]

They could scarcely have foreseen that eight years later the Sugar Institute would have been destroyed by the Supreme Court, while the Congress was passing enabling legislation to let other industries "follow the same line of thought"; appropriately enough, the Act was sponsored by, and written by the attorney for, parties who had been held in criminal contempt of a Sherman Act decree against price fixing.[65]

That Section 2(c) is nothing but the reincarnation of NRA has been clearly stated by Corwin Edwards.[66] Yet, as we saw earlier, Section 2(a) accomplishes by indirection and procedural

[61] NRA Codes of Fair Competition, vol. IV, p. 457; vol. V, pp. 1, 10; Prentice-Hall *Trade and Industry Service*, 15,041.25 4(1), 15,061.29, 1(c)(1934).
[62] *Hearings Before the House Committee on the Judiciary on H.R. 8442*, 74 Cong., 1 sess. (1935), p. 77.
[63] Sugar Institute, Inc., v. United States, 297 U.S. 553 (1936); James L. Fly, "Observations on the Anti-Trust Laws, Economic Theory, and the Sugar Institute Decisions," *Yale Law Journal*, 45:1339 (1936).
[64] DPM, May 2, 1928, DX 488.
[65] See below, Chapter X.
[66] Corwin D. Edwards, "The Bearing of the Robinson-Patman Act upon the Policy of the Sherman Act" (Legal Aspects of Marketing, Practising Law Institute, 1952), p. 2.

requirements what 2(c) does directly. If so, the whole Act is nothing but an adaptation of NRA, and one which avoids the latter's infirmities. It is enabling legislation for price maintenance, useful and used only when the economic structure of the market permits it. As a price-maintenance device, therefore, the Act is highly flexible, does not attempt too much, is largely self-administered, yet it can invoke the sanctions of the Federal Trade Commission.

TECHNICAL NOTE: AVERAGE AND INCREMENTAL (MARGINAL) COST

The cost of any good is the sacrifice of the resources which are absorbed in making it: what would be saved, other things being equal, by not making the good. The cost of any particular *amount* of product is the increment which must be added to total cost in order to obtain it. Cost is therefore defined as long-run incremental (marginal) cost. But the Robinson-Patman Act, as is well known, disregards incremental cost and refers only to average or full cost. The economist's reaction has usually been to shrug off the work of benighted politicians as unworthy of his analysis. Yet we submit that if our object is to frame a public policy, the two definitions are for most practical purposes interchangeable.

One reason for this opinion may be indicated by dismissing a common objection to incremental cost. Suppose that a manufacturer produces one million items; that his total fixed costs are $500,000 and his total variable costs (materials, labor, etc.) are also $500,000. Hence the cost of any item is fifty cents fixed cost and fifty cents variable cost, total one dollar. Suppose that this manufacturer wishes for some reason to discriminate and grant a lower price to some buyer, and rationalizes his policy as follows: To fill this order involves no increase in fixed costs; the only incremental expense is in the fifty cents' worth of labor and materials per unit, and therefore there is a cost differential of fifty cents between this buyer and all others.

We need not stop to ask whether the discriminatory action is in any sense good or bad, competitive or noncompetitive, legal or illegal, etc. Our only concern is with the plainly fallacious reasoning as to cost. In the example just given (as in the many refined variations) there was no difference *either in the marginal cost or the average cost* of serving this buyer as against all other buyers, for it was an altogether arbitrary act to classify him as "the" marginal buyer. He might, with equal logic, have been considered the "first" buyer and have the whole overhead loaded onto him, as to be called "marginal" buyer and have none of it imputed to him. There was no saving attributable to his order which was not equally attributable to other orders. One might as well say that the first game of the baseball season is vastly more important than the last, since the proportion of games won at the end of the first day is either 1.000 or .000, while the proportion is altered only in the third decimal place by the result of the last game. Actually, every game has an equal weight in the final standing. Similarly with the "first" and "marginal" orders. Hence, although we might never know either the marginal costs or the average cost of serving the various buyers, we would know that either average or incremental cost was equal if the product and the associated services were equal. Consequently, any price differential would express an equal price discrimination. Whichever definition of cost we chose — average or marginal — it would not affect the result.

The second reason for regarding average and incremental cost as interchangeable for our purpose is that our interest is in long-run rather than short-run incremental cost. Our public policy is concerned not with individual transactions but with persisting relationships: discount schedules, customary allowances and the like. But long-run incremental cost includes all those elements which, once in existence, become fixed or overhead and hence excluded from short-run incremental cost. This is another way of saying that short-run average cost is a fair working approximation to long-run incremental cost. Indeed, unless there are economies of larger scale (not higher volume) involved, average cost is identical with long-run incremental cost.

Not all situations would be thus indifferent to the definition. In the previous chapter, we had to pay some attention to true joint costs, where the average cost of one product does not exist,

and only incremental cost has any meaning; and the problem
will recur in Chapter XI. But to the extent that situations exist
where some buyers would receive a lower price on the basis of relative incremental cost than on the basis of relative average cost,
they remain as a fortiori reinforcements to the main argument.
Hence this chapter has been written in terms of average cost.

I X

ADAPTATION TO THE ROBINSON-PATMAN ACT

Brokerage and allowances in general

THE brokerage offices were notified "in an informal sort of way" that hereafter they would remain in operation but they would not be known as brokerage offices.[1] Brokerage was no longer collected, and it disappeared from the accounting records. Instead, A & P bought on a "net" basis which meant simply the price reduced by a brokerage equivalent.[2] Early in 1937 Attorney Ewing was highly concerned over the use of "brokerage office expenses" and similar terminology, and wanted the accountants to eliminate them forthwith.[3]

The New Orleans buyer reported that "many of the canners are of the opinion that they cannot quote us a price taking into consideration the brokerage." But many others apparently thought they could. In dealing with the former, "we will just have to pay the market [inclusive of phantom brokerage] until such time as we can get around this phase of the bill." [4] A month later the Milwaukee buyer wrote that "we are issuing contracts . . . at the list price less the trade discount and then less 5 per cent without saying what it is, although seller, buyer, and ourselves know it is the former brokerage." [5] Later the same day he gave

[1] Testimony of Charles W. Parr, Tr. 270.
[2] Parr to Vogt, July 3, 1936, GX 515.
[3] Ewing to Bofinger, February 2, 1937, GX 590. The following two GX's, 591 and 592, show that this was done.
[4] Wilson to Parr, July 13, 1936.
[5] Vogt to Gundrey, August 21, 1936, GX 528.

more details. The wide price fluctuations in trading items might make it easier — or more difficult — to allow disguised brokerage. It depended on the burden of proof. On the one hand, a seller might despair of proving that the particular lot he sold to A & P was at the same price that would have been made to anybody else at that time of day. Others felt that

if ever they are called upon to substantiate their position they will have no trouble in doing it by using the excuse of market fluctuations and difference in quality and on both these points quite sure you will concur with us it is going to take half the population of the United States to police anything of this kind.[6]

It is not easy to say how successful they were, in the aggregate, in retaining the old payments under the new name. The first impression, apparently, was that "in practically all cases, especially on trading lines . . . the seller is willing to reflect [the] amount of brokerage in the price."[7] But it was clear by October that many suppliers objected strenuously.[8]

The reaction of some large sellers was particularly marked. Stokely Brothers terminated advertising allowances, brokerage, and everything else.[9] A & P buyers were angry, but could do nothing. They were in a stronger position vis-à-vis Van Camp's, and cancelled an order; [10] there was a drawn battle with Phillips Packing Company, with a compromise outcome.[11] California Packing Company (Del Monte) announced that it would henceforth sell at the list price to everyone. The A & P reaction was to stress private labels and possible manufacturing. As Parr wrote to Vogt:

Taking the announcement at its face value, we have immediately started negotiations toward restocking a full line of A & P canned fruits for the first time in about fifteen years, and, as you know, we are making a general survey toward further expansion of our own manufacturing activities.[12]

[6] Vogt to Gundrey, August 21, 1936, GX 533.
[7] Circular letter, Parr to all divisional presidents, purchasing directors, sales directors, and field buying offices, July 7, 1936, GX 12.
[8] Gundrey to R. U. Wilson, October 30, 1936, GX 532.
[9] Stokely Brothers to Wilson, August 21, 1936, GX 560.
[10] Vogt to Van Camp's, Inc., December 30, 1936, GX 577.
[11] Zoller to Parr, August 14, 1936, GX 548.
[12] July 3, 1936, GX 515.

Two months later Stokely Brothers issued a circular letter like Del Monte's, adding that they reserved the right to raise prices on future orders.[13] Parr considered this "a rather arbitrary attitude" and a "selfish interpretation." Canners showing so little cooperation "we feel should be placed on the Unsatisfactory List." [14] There followed negotiations with Stokely, but little progress; as previously noted above, they could be cut off on trading items with little loss, but not on branded goods. Furthermore, Libby and California Packing had gone so far as to announce that they would sell only on a "net" basis "when our [A & P's] net price from other canners meets their view." [15] They felt themselves strong enough to defy the pressure of competitive offers; and one wonders what advice Libby and CalPack gave canners who did not "meet their view." Ten days later Parr and his assistants were discussing "how far we should go in putting the heat on [Del Monte] . . . It is not our desire to penalize the business in the slightest degree by discontinuing any Del Monte items for which there is a demand." [16]

By the third week of September, opinion had hardened at headquarters. Another letter by Parr stated their reasoning very clearly:

Tendency here at Headquarters to favor expansion of our manufacturing facilities. . . . This is not a threat and we are not letting out a lot of publicity about it.

The fact remains that if some of the concerns whom you mentioned are unwilling to reflect in the sales price to us the savings which are definite and which can be easily substantiated, there is going to be little else for us to do than to put up private label merchandise similar to their own.

We have already done this in the case of canned fruits.[17]

Private label merchandise was thus to be substituted as much as possible for items on which A & P was discriminated against; manufacturing at home was only one means of providing it.

[13] See the "Dear Ray" and "Dear Tony" correspondence beginning June 15, 1936, with GX 553, between Vogt of A & P and Culp of Stokely's. Stokely's had themselves "lost preferential arrangements in supplies" because of the Robinson-Patman Act, and this "increases our costs materially."

[14] Parr to Vogt, September 2, 1936, GX 566.

[15] Parr to Vogt, September 4, 1936, GX 569.

[16] H. B. George to J. V. Beckmann, September 15, 1936, GX 578.

[17] Parr to Vogt, September 21, 1936, GX 534.

Parr's apprehensions were correct. Negotiations with Stokely practically collapsed four days later, most of the remaining business was cancelled late in December,[18] and there were almost no sales during the next three years.[19] Nor is there any evidence of a later *rapprochement*.

The story seems much the same with Del Monte. By mid-October Bofinger had decided to retaliate by stopping divisions or units from sending their estimated future requirements to California Packing, in order that the latter might plan production. Moreover, headquarters insisted upon passing upon all firm bookings before they were made; it was expected that in the near future, all Del Monte products would be ordered on a strictly hand-to-mouth basis.[20] A week later Bofinger himself wrote the San Francisco buying office, promising to inform the divisions "how shabbily we have been treated and what an advantage the Independent has over us in buying the merchandise from now on." [21] In December Bofinger wrote California Packing Company, complaining that "since the corporation's action in withdrawing all promotional allowances on the Del Monte line, our business is, and will continue to be, treated no different than any jobbers or retailers buying direct." [22] (It is not clear why this confers an "advantage" to independents as against A & P, unless "jobbers" refers to those buying in smaller amounts than wholesalers.) But there is no evidence that Del Monte ever budged.

A & P success with other sellers was short-lived. "Net buying" and similar devices to get brokerage equivalent were of a fairly transparent sort, and early in 1938 the Federal Trade Commission issued a cease and desist order against them. Anticipating the possibility of an adverse decision in the courts, the decision was made to seek quantity discounts wherever possible; [23] moves had already been made in that direction.

[18] Culp (of Stokely's) to Vogt, September 25, 1936, GX 574. See also the letter from Vogt, December 30, 1936, GX 577, cited above.

[19] Kittelle to Bofinger, January 27, 1940, GX 1623.

[20] Parr to Beckmann, October 21, 1936, GX 579.

[21] Bofinger to Beckmann, October 28, 1936, GX 580.

[22] Bofinger to Del Monte, undated, but written previous to December 10, 1936. Attached to GX 580.

[23] Remarks of Bofinger at the meeting of divisional purchasing directors, April 22, 1938, GX 315.

On January 2, 1940, came the Supreme Court decision denying certiorari and thereby upholding the Circuit Court decision in support of the FTC.[24] On January 25 the company issued a press release [25] stating that henceforth it would not purchase from suppliers who sold to *any* customers through brokers. Since a seller who used no brokers could not be accused of paying disguised brokerage to one customer as the equivalent of open brokerage to another, there could be no question of A & P's wrongfully collecting brokerage. "By avoiding purchases from a manufacturer who currently pays brokerage, no inference can be drawn that a permissible discount represents in whole or in part brokerage so currently being paid."

The policy was soon abandoned as a rigid rule. Perhaps the threats of brokers in Baltimore to bring triple damage suits under the Sherman Act had some effect. In reporting the threats to Parr, Zoller remarked: "These brokers are dying hard." [26] Parr commented: "This is pure intimidation, as we know of no law which prevents any seller from selecting his own customers." [27] The January interviews with the midwestern suppliers (tabulated in Appendix III) were probably more decisive. In mid-February Parr wrote:

It is impossible from a practical standpoint for the Company to take the arbitrary position that it will not under any circumstances deal with shippers who employ brokers; but . . . it will endeavor, so far as possible, to deal with exclusively direct shippers. . . . We have no doubt that there will be many transactions with concerns who do employ brokers, but that still will not prevent our trying to carry out the announced intentions to throw all the business possible to the direct shippers.[28]

A & P took pains to let the trade know what its new policy was: meetings of its own buying personnel, contacts with suppliers at conventions and individually, etc.[29] It is difficult to say how successful this campaign was because it was a matter of individual

---

[24] Great A & P Tea Company v. Federal Trade Commission, 106 F.2d 667 (3d Cir. 1939), *cert. den.*, 303 U.S. 625 (1940).

[25] DX 1008.

[26] Zoller to Parr, February 3, 1940, GX 1656.

[27] Parr to Zoller, February 6, 1940, GX 1657.

[28] Parr to Zoller, February 14, 1940, GX 1666.

[29] See the testimony at Tr. 315, 318, 3326; also GX 2392.

dealings and contacts with suppliers of all types and sizes. The buying staff understood the general situation quite well. An intra-company memorandum or draft dated a day after the Supreme Court decision, but whose length and clarity suggest a leisurely composition, explained:

> Eventually all manufacturers will unquestionably line up into three distinct groups — (a) exclusively direct sellers; (b) exclusively indirect sellers; and (c) a few large manufacturers of nationally advertised goods who may sell both directly and indirectly. The last-named group will, of course, be unable to make any allowance for brokerage savings in their sales to direct buyers. Direct buyers will find it necessary to buy from such sources chiefly because of public demand for these sellers' goods engendered by consumer advertising.[30]

In September 1939, Zoller had written Parr that it would take longer for larger canners to go exclusively direct, "as the larger canners are more in the specialties or sell their products on a brand. Also [they] use brokers to a large extent where there are pool car distributions." [31] Large orders — "pool car distributions" — were precisely the service which the A & P field buying offices performed but could not collect for under the Act.

The question arose early of a manufacturer who sold branded and unbranded goods. There were some legal-economic puzzles:

> If a concern sells a nationally advertised brand article under their own label and also packs a similar item for private label distributors, he can sell his own nationally advertised brand through brokers and sell the private label merchandise exclusively direct at a lower price. However, it is our understanding that in this case the manufacturer's brand must actually be a nationally advertised article, one on which money has been spent in developing a consumer demand by brand. . . . This would not hold true in the case of a brand of canned goods which might be considered merely a "packer's brand" sold on a trading basis approximately in line with the prevailing market of similar products under private brands. Just where a line can be drawn between what constitutes a nationally advertised brand and mere packer's label would be hard to define.[32]

At some point or other, they expected, the division would take place, however, and "two price levels will develop of which the

[30] Unsigned memorandum, January 3, 1940, GX 1622.

[31] Zoller to Parr, September 26, 1939, GX 1450.

[32] Parr to Zoller, July 10, 1940, GX 770.

direct will average lower." [33] Furthermore, "the difference between the two will be considerably more than the brokerage rate itself, because the direct sellers are going to save and be able to pass on to their customers a great deal more than mere brokerage. . . . [because] exclusively direct sellers will have for their customers only large concerns who buy in quantity lots, pay promptly, and immediately put the merchandise into consumption." [34] These were three separate kinds of cost savings over and above brokerage. Zoller estimated that "the spread we discovered will vary but eventually it will average about 5 per cent. . . . The direct sellers will get the cream of the business carrying with it the volume they will build up and will be in a position to materially undersell indirect sellers." [35] The implication seems clear that the exclusively direct sellers who dealt with a few large buyers would have lower unit costs, and competition among these sellers would pass on a "material" part of the savings as lower prices.

The reaction of manufacturers had some relation to their size. In 1936, when Zoller was trying to convert brokerage into net buying, he had written:

It is a surprise to see some of these large concerns try to jump away from their deals. In fact the very small proportion of our business that we have not been able to turn over to a net basis has been from the largest sellers. These parties are influenced very much by their brokerage connections, through whom they claim to sell the bulk of their products.

The writer is not making any brief for this class of defaulters on contract, as he feels very strongly in the matter, but we must cite that some of them are obviously frightened. [36]

The letter has been worth quoting at length because it shows the intricacies of the large seller's market position. These "defaulters" defied A & P because they were large and brand-powerful; and also because their power was limited, they needed the good will of the brokers. Furthermore, as large firms, they felt much more vulnerable to Robinson-Patman prosecution. Since

[33] Zoller to Parr, February 8, 1940, GX 1662.
[34] Parr to Zoller, February 10, 1940, GX 1663.
[35] Zoller to Parr, February 17, 1940, GX 1664.
[36] Zoller to Parr, September 25, 1936, GX 545.

their fright was propelling them in a rather pleasing direction, perhaps they did not resist it too hard.

It is probable that in some areas, but not all, enough sellers came in exclusively direct to supply the great bulk of A & P needs. As early as February 17, 1940, Zoller wrote Parr that "as reported before, we really have more direct sellers in some lines than we want right now." [37] By March 1 he could write:

We are glad to report that we are able to buy about 90 per cent of our products from exclusively direct sellers including some of the largest and best canners of this section and the entire country.

It is not an easy problem for some of these canners to decide to give up as high as fifty brokers selling quite a proportion of their products, but they did so decide.[38]

Similarly, the New Orleans buying office was able to report that "this office has almost completely lined up all producers which we purchase from onto a direct buying basis." [39]

In dairy products it was impossible to go exclusively direct. Here it was the big companies which were the direct sellers; A & P did not want to buy from them alone, "and I am sure the big fellows would not want to sell all their make to us." There followed another of those clever remarks which prosecuting attorneys in the Antitrust Division justly cherish:

Butter . . . is a fast trading product and during the course of a day there is a variance in market conditions of as much as $\frac{1}{4}\cent$ per pound either way and at times more.

Does this not satisfactorily answer your letter? Please advise.[40]

The cheese buyer was less optimistic. The great bulk of the cheese business was done by five companies. In the course of the year they were bound to use some brokers, and therefore if the company was not going to buy from sellers also using brokers, "it's going to be just too bad." They would be without cheese.[41]

[37] Zoller to Parr, February 17, 1940, GX 1664.
[38] Zoller to Parr, March 1, 1940,, GX 1682.
[39] Wilson to Parr, April 4, 1940, GX 52. This may have been exaggerated. See note 45 and text below.
[40] G. W. Diehl, head of the National Butter Department, to Parr, February 21, 1940, GX 1673.
[41] E. G. Harris, head of the National Cheese Department, to Parr, March 1, 1940, GX 1677.

In general it seems clear that firms with strong brand positions were most aided by the Robinson-Patman Act; as seen earlier, the strong brand position was more important than size.[42] As Bofinger pointed out in 1938:

because of such recent legislation as the Robinson-Patman Act, costs to us on advertised brands were the same or, very often, higher than to others, amounting to discrimination against us, which is a vastly different picture than that of ten years ago.[43]

It is in interesting contrast with a discussion among the purchasing directors in 1929. The company seemed rather pleased at that time by the formation of Standard Brands, Inc. They might, of course, integrate forward to the retail store door. However,

the so-called Morrow and Morgan interests are much more friendly and in line with our ideas. We look rather favorably upon the recent consolidations such as Standard Brands, Inc., insofar as their activities offer competition to the General Foods Company, Inc., because of their elastic policies and the possibility of their methods inducing the latter concern to change the present . . . policy.[44]

Of course, the situation was not comfortably settled in 1940, and never could be; six months later Wilson of New Orleans reported with great satisfaction that he had recently lined up some large Texas packers.[45]

As for Milwaukee, we have another quotable letter from Vogt to Parr.[46]

Have had so many discussions I'm screwy. However, from them I am sure Headquarters will figure out a way for us to continue to collect brokerage either as we have in the past or some other form.

Don't kid yourself about A & P not having any friends amongst these sellers. I am really surprised the way they come in and offer suggestions to permit us to get the brokerage or its equivalent.

[42] See also the letter of Zoller to Ewing, February 8, 1940, GX 1661; product differentiation seems to be considered more important than size in making suppliers hard to handle.
[43] Joint meeting of merchandising committee and divisional sales directors, November 7, 1938, GX 317.
[44] Divisional purchasing directors, October 16, 1929, GX 401.
[45] Wilson to Parr, October 28, 1940, GX 2403.
[46] GX 79, undated. The government contended, and Judge Lindley agreed, that it was probably written early in 1940.

A substantial part of A & P requirements still continued to be filled by sellers who used brokers.[47] Nevertheless, the campaign to assure direct supplies must be considered a success, especially in view of the cooperative attitude of a few of the larger packers.

The larger the "exclusively direct" market, the better chances of inducing sellers to join it. A & P was disappointed by the failure of the voluntary chains to adopt the same strategy, but counted on them eventually:

When the voluntary groups . . . come around to A & P's way of thinking (which they will do when the FTC gets through with them) [a manufacturer] may find that there are enough direct sellers to provide him an ample market.[48]

This was fairly good prophecy, but the effects were slow in coming. The Red & White group did not finally lose out in the courts until 1945; the Independent Grocers Alliance (IGA), not until 1953.[49] Other buying groups may have gone direct at an earlier date; others continue to thrive to this day by flouting or evading the law. Brokerage-clause suits are the most frequent of FTC suits, and are almost always successful.

How successful was A & P in maintaining brokerage equivalent? We cannot tell. The picture would in any case be distorted by the rising income and price levels during 1940 and the later years. There is little doubt that the company did expect substantial differentials. We have already seen how Zoller and Parr agreed that "two price levels" would come into existence, one set by direct sales and the higher by brokerage sales.[50] Of course, A & P could not hope to recover the full brokerage equivalent and achieve complete nondiscrimination. For then the seller would have no inducement to go exclusively direct, and lose much freedom of action.[51] There is at least one instance where a supplier set up a

[47] Parr to Vogt, August 5, 1941, GX 76.
[48] Kittelle to Bofinger, January 27, 1940, GX 1023.
[49] Modern Marketing Service v. FTC, 149 F.2d 970 (7th Cir. 1945); Independent Grocers Alliance v. FTC, 203 F.2d 941 (7th Cir. 1953).
[50] See above.
[51] See the intracompany memorandum, GX 1622: "Manufacturers who decide to adopt the direct-selling method should be careful that they do so fully and without reservation. Some of them may feel that if they sell the great bulk of their goods direct, or through their own salesmen, it will do no harm for them

subsidiary through which it sold through brokers, while the parent sold exclusively direct.[52] But this only spotlights the effect, which must always take place when a seller's (or, for that matter, a buyer's) range of alternatives is narrowed.

So much for the economic effects. Let us now imagine that the company entered into an agreement with every supplier that the latter would under no circumstances make a sale through a broker. This seems like obvious restraint of the trade of the suppliers, the brokers, and other retailers. Such agreements would be illegal under the Sherman Act, though (or because) they were the natural result of the Robinson-Patman Act. Let us now suppose the contrary: that the decision to buy only from exclusively direct firms was kept a complete secret. Then A & P would simply hunt through the market places, ask its question, and make its purchases. Very soon everybody in the trade would draw the moral. Firms hoping for A & P patronage would go exclusively direct and so notify the company. The effect would be about the same in both cases. If, as a judge once said, "the Anti-Trust Act aims at substance," [53] A & P needed no contracts with suppliers, no press releases, to back squarely into the Sherman Act while trying to avoid the Robinson-Patman Act. But suppose the company had given up the struggle, and had bought through its offices at the same prices charged those who bought through brokers. Then the net return to the sellers would have been greater on A & P sales than on brokerage sales, obvious price discrimination against A & P. In fact, both situations exist today, A & P having in effect obtained a license to go exclusively direct without making agreements.[54]

Interestingly enough, the brokers counter-attacked with infiltration tactics. Vogt of Milwaukee suggested to Parr in March, 1941, that warehouse buyers might be spending entirely too much

---

to make an *occasional* sale through a broker. As a matter of fact, this would make the entire method illegal, unless the seller increased the price charged direct buyers by the amount of brokerage, which would defeat the whole purpose of the arrangement" (italics added).

[52] U.S. Products Corporation. See GX 848 and GX 851.

[53] Chief Justice Hughes, in Appalachian Coals, Inc., v. United States, 288 U.S. 344 (1932), p. 377.

[54] See below, Chapter XVII.

time with brokers, and that headquarters take the situation in hand. "On the few accounts the broker handles he uses them as a pretext to get in to see the buyer, probably spending . . . 90 per cent [of the time] on other commodities.[55]

Quantity discounts

Parr testified that few quantity discounts existed before the Robinson-Patman Act.[56] Of the 362 products in the list he submitted to the Congressional Committee in 1935,[57] only forty-two were covered by quantity discounts. But after the passage of the Act, there was a shakeup of price and discount lists, which

had to be evaluated in the light of any savings . . . and some manufacturers did revise their quantity discounts to conform. . . . Since the Robinson-Patman Act . . . the manufacturers by legal advice have tailored their quantity discounts to fit the Robinson-Patman requirements.[58]

Wherever possible A & P tried to have its brokerage contracts changed to quantity discounts. Apparently it was not very successful. A few such conversions were made, but the predominant note seems to be of suppliers' fear of the law, and the largest suppliers were the most difficult.[59] They might agree that the brokerage allowance had been worth while, but "they could not . . . see where any saving in sales or manufacturing expense would warrant it." [60] A good example of this situation is in the correspondence with Cranberry Canners in Appendix IV. But the most important evidence consists of some of the discussions within the A & P high command. In September 1939, George J. Feldman and Sumner S. Kittelle, attorneys to the company, submitted a memorandum to Bofinger.[61] They feared that the usual quantity

[55] Memorandum, "Buying Policies," Vogt to Parr, March 10, 1941, GX 792. See also above, Chapter V, note 21.

[56] Tr. 222.

[57] See below, Chapter X.

[58] Paul S. Willis, Tr. 158, 172–73.

[59] Wilson to Gundrey, August 14, 1936, GX 919; Wilson to Parr, September 15, 1936, GX 543; Vogt to Gundrey, August 21, 1936, GX 533; Zoller to Parr, September 25, 1936, GX 545.

[60] GX 919, preceding note.

[61] In the record as GX 620.

discount form would prove treacherous because savings on quantity purchases could not in fact be substantiated for A & P. "Savings in handling, billing and shipping costs depend on the quantity of the individual shipment, not the total yearly or monthly purchases. A large volume ordered out in small shipments rarely involves any savings in and of itself." They went on to suggest the genuine economies, demonstrated in the FTC brokerage proceedings,[62] as follows:

The use of field men located in producing centers saved the manufacturers substantial amounts of money otherwise expended in the form of salesmen's salaries and commissions, travel expenses, communication expenses, cost of rejections, and the like.

Moreover, the Company's habit of paying its bills on time and of otherwise accommodating manufacturers produced additional savings.

and in a subsequent letter to a New England official, they added:

Market information, advice on packing.[63]

The first suggestion is probably the most important, but in our opinion it is little different from brokerage — the "contactual" function, in Professor McGarry's phrase. Feldman and Kittelle went on to suggest that the company hire a small cost accounting staff to visit suppliers and ferret out economies of the above sort so that A & P "could be more bold in demanding discounts."[64] It is significant that nothing more was heard of this proposal.

The other suggestion made by Feldman and Kittelle was to substitute "cost savings agreements" for the existing quantity discounts. The new form would recite the economies named in the memorandum, justifying any special concessions made to the company. The cost savings form would have been a stronger barrier to legal action; there can be no doubt that A & P tried hard to have it adopted as widely as possible. After the Supreme Court had upheld the Federal Trade Commission suit in January, 1940, and following a conference with FTC lawyers, the company issued a manual on the Robinson-Patman Act late the following

[62] See above, note 24.
[63] Feldman to Douglas C. MacKeachie, October 20, 1939, GX 648.
[64] Feldman and Kittelle to Bofinger, September 13, 1939, GX 620.

May.[65] Cost savings agreements were emphasized, while the usual quantity discounts were hardly mentioned. In part this may be due to the fact that the manual would have public circulation. In part, the emphasis on cost savings agreements was addressed to company buying personnel, to induce as many such agreements as possible. As Parr wrote:

> They would like to have as many of these arrangements as possible on the cost savings form. While the advertising and quantity discount arrangements are all right . . . the cost savings agreement is the best; . . . any manufacturer can justify savings in his cost, manufacture, sale of, or delivery on, our business.[66]

It is therefore significant that the company failed to get any appreciable number of such contracts. More than six months after receiving the letter from Parr, Vogt had been unable to obtain even a single one; [67] and Bofinger testified in 1945 that there were only about seventeen such contracts in force.[68]

Premium deals

The winter of 1940–1941 saw a good many special campaigns by manufacturers who featured premiums, to which A & P had always been opposed. Especially annoying was General Foods and its Wheaties. Headquarters informed General Foods that it would have nothing to do with the deal, and divisions were instructed to register their disapproval with local representatives. The merchandising committee spent some of its meeting of March 18 discussing the problems, and decided to make representations to other manufacturers as well.[69] The committee claimed to have made some progress, but there is no definite evidence of this.[70]

One reason for its annoyance comes out clearly in a letter from a unit sales manager to his divisional superior:

[65] Issued May 29, 1940, DX 1.
[66] Parr to Vogt, January 17, 1941, GX 66.
[67] Vogt to Parr, July 30, 1941, GX 78.
[68] Bofinger, Tr. 20,404.
[69] Daily Bulletin (presumably of Quaker Maid), March 10, 1941, GX 1425. See also GX 1425–GX 1440.
[70] GX 1436 is a letter to a unit sales manager, saying, "Headquarters feels very strongly about this premium business. . . . They have been able to make some very substantial headway with the manufacturers."

Since the announcement of the Wheaties Camp-Lamp deal, the boys in the stores have been under extreme pressure from the customers . . . [which] is greater in the case of the children who insist that their mothers buy Wheaties after seeing the announcement . . . or hearing of it on the radio.

Frankly, this is one of the most difficult things which we have to overcome. . . . Several customers . . . accuse the store personnel of misappropriating the premiums.[71]

It was precisely this kind of devotion to a manufacturers' product which A & P always wished to undermine.

Store-door delivery

As an important problem in supplier relations, drop shipments or store-door delivery were an unmistakable product of the Robinson-Patman Act. The first mention of large-scale store-door delivery is a letter to Bofinger from the Middle Western purchasing director, H. B. George, dated October 15, 1937.[72] He remarked that the trend was growing rapidly: manufacturers would sell exclusively through distributors, who in nearly every case received a larger discount than A & P, and who delivered store-door to retailers. A list of such distributors was enclosed: their advantage over A & P ranged from 7 per cent to 21 per cent. George disliked the idea of store-door for A & P: "Keep the numerous manufacturers' salesmen out of our store, which we would certainly like to do."[73]

In February, 1938, headquarters was sufficiently concerned to send out a circular letter to all purchasing directors.[74] A practice has "developed during the past year" whereby store-door delivery was being made at carload rates, regardless of the quantity actually delivered. "The retailer has the merchandise delivered direct to his store at the carload price and the jobber [who received his margin nonetheless] is saved the expense entailed in warehousing

[71] R. B. Rinehart to W. A. Carlton, March 7, 1941, GX 1435.

[72] H. B. George to Bofinger, October 15, 1937, GX 2609.

[73] See also above, Chapter V, note 27.

[74] Dated February 16, 1938. The writer has been unable to find it in the record, but there is a detailed paraphrase of it which was sent out the next day by Leach of the Southern Division to his subordinates, GX 2610.

and trucking the merchandise." There was naturally "a tremendous saving to retailers." (This form of freight absorption was an obvious price discrimination, in the economic sense, against A & P.) The large corporations were the worst offenders, especially Babbitt and Lever Brothers. "They justify this practice by blaming competitive conditions and, while they all agree that it is a bad practice, none of them do anything about abolishing it." Headquarters feared that they had been caught napping, and demanded that all local personnel check to find out how long the practice had been going on, and to forward the reports to headquarters. Store-door at carload prices was "a direct menace to our business and must be stamped out as rapidly as possible. There should be no compromising with any manufacturer."

Headquarters' fear that they had been asleep was well founded. George wrote Mylott from Chicago late in March; he had just learned that some large companies, including Kellogg, Babbitt, Brillo, Lever Brothers, and Jergens-Woodbury, had been doing this for over a year. The one hopeful note was that Babbitt had just stopped the practice in Chicago and Milwaukee.[75]

The matter was exhaustively discussed at the very important meeting of divisional purchasing directors, already mentioned, held April 22, 1938.[76] First, the operating problems of store-door delivery were considered, and possible economies to be got by using it. The practice was not altogether new; it had been used on staples such as flour, feeds, and canned milk.[77] Obviously, the smaller (larger) the retail store, the greater (less) the trouble and expense of store-door delivery. Therefore, since the company was going over to supermarkets, many items which had been more economically distributed through the warehouses could now be handled directly.

The Purchasing Directors intimated that a great deal of study was being carried on in their units by the local buyers, and traffic men, to establish where and how such operating economies could be effected, and it was

[75] George to Mylott, March 31, 1938, GX 2611.
[76] GX 315.
[77] In 1929 there had been a small experiment with store-door delivery in the Pittsburgh area; the appraisal was a mixed one. See the divisional purchasing directors' meeting, October 16, 1929, GX 401.

assured that greater results on this will be forthcoming as the supermarket program expands.

At this point Bofinger took the floor. Drop shipments had "been rapidly developing since the Robinson-Patman Act." Furthermore, as a result of "conferences and discussions . . . with many sellers," he had concluded that prices of carload lots were not as far below LCL as they ought to be, in the light of operating costs. Therefore "it was the duty, aims and objectives of the purchasing staff . . . to constantly strive to get these and all manufacturers to widen the spread when there was a justification for doing so." If merchandise was to go "through the normal and legitimate channels," A & P's advantage in buying would be retained and increased, "as contrasted with the many instances prevailing to-day where the independent owns his merchandise at or below our present cost."

But the program to widen the CL-LCL spread was vitiated in the next breath. Unfortunately, "some manufacturers . . . as they become sufficiently large and strong, extend their operations to the point of taking in retail customers and selling them direct. . . . We must suit our activities to their conditions," and therefore take direct shipments if they were cheaper. Certainly the supermarkets were a more promising vehicle for direct delivery than the old regular stores, he concluded; "comprehensive study" was needed, especially of the "warehouse type" of supermarket. H. B. George spoke up to express his doubts: warehouses were a cheaper method of handling most types of goods if for no other reason than that warehouse property was so much cheaper than retail store property.

There can be no doubt that A & P was discriminated against. The meeting cited the case of the Babbitt Company, which allowed jobbers 20¢ a case, of which 10¢ went to the retailer. Yet A & P received only 10¢ off on its warehouse deliveries. Sometimes the manufacturer would deliver direct to the retailer out of the stocks of the jobber, yet at 20¢ off. "Many instances were reviewed of this identical nature."

The company went ahead experimenting with store-door to the rapidly developing supermarkets. A year and a half later George wrote Gundrey that direct delivery had increased. But in approaching "nationally known manufacturers, we are not wholly consistent in that for the past few years we have attempted to have them widen the spread between direct delivery and warehouse delivery. . . . A number of manufacturers, of course, were prevailed upon to widen the spread." [78] There is no hint of the size of the "number," nor is there any other record of any success in this direction.

Gundrey replied that "there is, to our way of thinking, no serious [conflict] between these two principles." Naturally, they preferred to see the differentials widened. But if the sellers refused to do so, A & P took store-door. This was of course an additional burden and expense on the sellers, "who we are inclined to believe did not anticipate having to sell us in that manner." [79]

We catch a glimpse, through some Central Division correspondence, of a more or less stabilized situation in the first quarter of 1941. Canned meats were being delivered in the stores at a delivered price equal to the ordinary warehouse price.[80] But early in 1941 headquarters recommended that store-door delivery on canned meats be discontinued. Direct money costs were not the whole story. Where orders were taken by salesmen, there was a tendency to load the stores with slow-moving items, many of which merely duplicated items handled through the warehouse on other brands. Store-door tended to build up canned meat tonnage through Armour branch houses; and this benefited competitors more than it did A & P. Hence the recent refusal to handle Armour canned meats through direct delivery, although independent brands could be so taken. Since that decision, many competitors of A & P had asked Armour to prevail upon A & P to resume.[81]

Enough has been said to show that there are two distinct problems involved in A & P policy on store-door. The legal problem arises from the attempts to influence manufacturers, and it had best be left with the courts. The economic problem is in our province.

In shipping some particular kinds of items to some particular

[78] George to Gundrey, December 12, 1939, GX 2613.
[79] Gundrey to George, December 28, 1939, GX 2614.
[80] "W.F.E." to A. G. Schinke, March 4, 1941, GX 2616.
[81] Fraser to Meehan, March 12, 1941, GX 2617, citing the decision of the merchandising committee meeting of February 18.

kinds of stores, direct delivery was more economical; elsewhere it was not. The discussion at the April 1938 meeting, which contemplated an item-by-item approach to the problem, was the only correct one. The company records also show that economy was not only a matter of savings on cartage and handling of goods. As George pointed out, it also involved the best use of real estate, and the keeping of inventories down to the minimum. To let salesmen into the warehouses, where they could influence local buying personnel, was unnecessarily to increase the company's investment in merchandise.[82] One might also ask whether it did not unnecessarily increase the suppliers' investment in salesmen.

It was the larger manufacturers who took the initiative in setting up store-door. It was an expensive procedure, for they absorbed the extra cost of LCL deliveries when they took payment at CL rates. In part, this was simply a disguised price reduction to certain retailers. A customer who received goods *plus* LCL store-door delivery was receiving much more than one who bought the goods plus CL warehouse delivery. The manufacturers were discriminating against the chain stores in order to weaken their market position. To the writer it seems one of the obvious restraints of trade via price discrimination in the A & P record; much though not all of it is an obvious economic waste; and it followed as a logical consequence of the Robinson-Patman Act.

[82] See above, note 55.

X

THE INCIDENCE OF PRICE
DISCRIMINATION IN
PROCESSED FOODS

Differentials related to functions

W E have seen that A & P bought in many kinds of markets,
and that discrimination in its favor was possible, under oligopoly
and product differentiation, where sellers had some monopoly
power. The Robinson-Patman Act was designed to produce discrimination against A & P, and other low-cost buyers, by imposing
uniform prices. The latter tendency cannot be measured; hence,
it is not possible to estimate the net effect of these two countervailing forces.

Appendix IV is an analysis of the agreements with all 46 suppliers of whom there is a detailed record. This chapter is essentially a commentary on it. The summary tables in Appendix
IV (Appendix Tables 23 and 24) estimate what proportion of
each allowance, discount, or other price concessions to A & P was
a net differential in the sense that it was not received by all other
customers purchasing under the same conditions. However, the
estimates of net differentials, for each case and in the aggregate,
are not the best or most probable estimates of price discrimination.
They are a substantial overestimate, for the following reasons:

1. The sample is biased upward. It was selected by the prosecution to prove discrimination.

2. For the sake of consistency, we have used only such evidence as the prosecution would accept. Thus, in the instance of
Ball Brothers, we have disregarded tabulations to which the

prosecution objected, although the court accepted them. Had we accepted them, the ratio of net to gross differentials would have been smaller.

3. We have made no allowance in any instance for saving in the cost of manufacture, sales, or delivery, no matter how definite and substantial the record showed them to be. Savings are arbitrarily equated to zero by our rule, in order to get a maximum estimate, and in order to maintain comparability with FTC data to be examined in a later chapter.

4. Where there were several differentials, we have compared A & P's, not with the average of all other customers but with the smallest. We departed from this rule only when there was actual evidence that purchasers receiving smaller differentials had bought under conditions not comparable to A & P.

5. Discrimination *against* A & P has not been offset against discrimination in its favor, but arbitrarily counted as zero. This last element, consisting of phantom brokerage and higher prices buttressed by the Robinson-Patman Act, must have been substantial, as a look through Appendix IV shows; of the suppliers, at least twelve, or roughly one fourth, were clearly discriminating against A & P during most of 1936–42.[1] But we are unable to make any estimate of this bias.

Trade function or trade status?

In one respect, however, we have departed from the prosecution scheme in estimating net and gross differentials. It is fundamental: we have treated A & P as an integrated concern, and have compared its buying price with those of *buyers who perform the same buying functions*. A & P as buyer is a wholesaler, and its prices must be compared with those of other wholesalers in order to determine whether and to what extent any gross or net differentials exist.

[1] Albany, Cal Pack (aside from the sporadic pro-A & P discrimination noted in Appendix IV), Capital City, Colgate-Palmolive-Peet, Lever Brothers, Procter & Gamble, Consolidated Biscuit, Hills Bros., Loudon, Minnesota Consolidated Canneries, Minnesota Valley, R. J. Peacock, Sylmar. This classification is *not* on the basis of the summary tables (Appendix Tables 23 and 24), where arbitrary procedures must be followed, but on the basis of all the evidence in Appendix IV.

The prosecution did at times stress that A & P acted as a wholesaler integrated with retailing:

By virtue of their operation of a network of warehouses, [A & P] were in a position to take direct warehouse deliveries from suppliers, thus avoiding the necessity for purchase through wholesalers . . . . These direct deliveries resulted in substantial savings . . . [whereas retailers] ordinarily purchase through wholesalers . . . at prices higher than direct sale price, since they include compensation for the performance of the middleman's function.[2]

This is not unreasonable, although it is exaggerated by a factor of at least ten. When A & P buys under wholesale conditions and pays the price charged to wholesalers, it does not necessarily make "substantial savings" or any savings at all over retailers who pay others to perform the wholesale function. A & P's warehouses involve an investment, a risk of loss, and a cost of operation which is around nine tenths of the wholesale gross margin. The net saving must always be a small percentage of the price differential and it may well be zero or negative. An unsuccessful warehouse operation is more expensive than buying as a retailer.

But in considering specific examples, the prosecution made no concession to reason at all. "It seems a strained and tortuous justification of A & P's discriminatory buying prices as a *retailer* to point . . . to the fact that two *wholesalers*" received greater discounts [3] (the italics are in the original). Nothing so aroused the honest indignation of the prosecution as the "retailer" A & P daring to buy at wholesalers' prices. The student will search in vain for the slightest acknowledgment that under competition the A & P warehouse would pay the same price as a wholesale warehouse — especially since it usually bought in larger amounts — since there would be the same net return to the sellers. But no such recognition was to be expected. In the world of Robinson-Patman, a wholesaler who is integrated with retailing *should* pay the retailers' price, and the prosecution theory was Robinson-Patman theory.

The same principle is involved in our treatment of brokerage. As the reader is aware, the receipt of brokerage is forbidden to an integrated (direct) buyer under the Robinson-Patman Act; such

[2] GB(AC), pp. 49–50.
[3] See GB(AC), Appendix IV, Sylmar Packing Corporation.

buyers are forced to pay phantom brokerage and hence suffer discrimination. The prosecution found a number of instances where A & P had evaded the brokerage clause, and had paid to sellers *the same net amount as that paid by others.* This was evasion — and it was also nondiscrimination.

We make no attempt to answer the meaningless question whether or when A & P "deserved" brokerage. The very use of such a word shows hopeless confusion between the analysis of fact and the rule of law. Our interest is in comparing the net return to the buyer from various customers, and in finding out when sales to A & P netted the seller an amount larger, smaller, or equal to that received from other customers. Zoller's classic memorandum showed that A & P field buying offices were organized to take large amounts off the market at short notice. No broker can do any more for a seller. The zeal of the brokers in having Section 2(c) passed is conclusive proof that they agreed with this principle.

However, for the sake of consistency with our rule of using the maximum estimate, we have made it a rebuttable presumption that brokerage *is* fictitious. *Only* when a seller used brokers to a large extent, *and* also treated A & P as a broker prior to the Robinson-Patman Act, *and* there is no evidence that the brokerage was fictitious or a cover for discrimination, have we treated A & P as a broker and subtracted the customary fee for the commodity from the gross differential. Where, however, it has been impracticable to assign a definite value to the brokerage, it has been disregarded, equated to zero, even though its nondiscriminatory character was obvious; hence there is a further upward bias.

The economist and the world of Robinson-Patman — An example

The difference between our method and the prosecution's is startling when we come to evaluate specific transactions. Thus, we may consider the instance which is alphabetically first on the list — Albany Packing Company. The prosecution devotes six pages to this supplier in its presentation to the Circuit Court;[4]

---

[4] Appendix to GB(AC), pp. 42–48.

they obviously consider it one of their strongest cases to show "how particular suppliers, under the impact of A & P patronage withdrawals, gradually lose their economic freedom and ultimately reach a stage of such subservience that they grant any and all concessions made by A & P." A drab tale is enlivened by colorful language — "Albany's sentence was commuted" (page 43); "Albany issued "a declaration of independence" (page 47). There is lengthy quotation and paraphrase from the correspondence of negotiation. But what is the economic substance? Albany allowed wholesale customers three cents per pound off its list price to retailers. Around 1931–1933, after six or seven years of business dealing and pressure, A & P finally achieved equal treatment with other wholesale customers. And this is the very head and front of the offending: "This three cents per pound preference was given A & P, though no other Albany customer received it *with the exception of a few wholesalers* who bought for resale to A & P's competitors and *did not themselves compete with A & P"* (pages 43–44, italics added). The "few wholesalers" must have comprised all wholesalers; for there was never an assertion that other wholesalers had been overcharged. But the wholesalers resold to the trade, not to the general public, and therefore "did not themselves compete with A & P"! There is not the slightest recognition that A & P competed with other wholesalers as a buyer, a warehouser, and a distributor; the fact that A & P is integrated into retailing puts it out of the wholesale class and makes it not entitled to the same price. A & P's attempt to pay the same net price arouses the honest indignation of the prosecution, just as much as it aroused the ire of Albany, of wholesalers, and of unintegrated retailers.

To the economist, A & P's investment and function made it a wholesaler, the only relevant difference being that it generally bought in much larger volume than the average wholesaler. The Albany experience can then be summarized briefly: for a time A & P paid a price no higher than that paid by other wholesalers. At all other times it was discriminated *against*.

The whole picture looks so different under the rules of Robinson-Patman! A & P sells to the public, therefore it is a retailer. Therefore, if it pays a price lower than that charged "other retailers," this is "price discrimination," and illegal unless it can be "justified." To base a sales policy upon one's chances of "justifying" a set of differentials is about as prudent as basing one's standard of living upon one's chances of winning steadily at the race track. Let us disregard this fact. The information on distribution expenses can be obtained only at a high money cost. Let us disregard this too. There remains the fact that the company called Albany — its true name is legion — *does not want to allow or "justify" any differential.* It did so for a time only because somebody else would have allowed some part of the cost savings enjoyed in selling to A & P. But the Robinson-Patman Act made the great difference: Albany now could act secure in the knowledge that every other competitor would have precisely the same obstacles as it did in trying to extend a price differential; it knew that the possibility of competitive offers to A & P was reduced or wholly eliminated. The essence of any price-fixing agreement is the assurance that the parties agreeing will not undercut. The Robinson-Patman Act provides this assurance, by first forbidding price cuts unless "cost-justified" and then making it impossible to cost-justify.

Therefore, after the passage of the Act, we see Albany and the other Albanys issuing "declarations of independence" and charging higher net prices to A & P, confident that all others were doing the same. But this assurance was not complete; it diminished at the periphery of the differential. Albany might be certain that nobody would give a chain warehouse equal treatment with a wholesale warehouse and allow both of them the same three cents off list. But, might some allow them two cents, or one cent? Hence there was a disposition to give away some of the velvet in order to be sure of the rest, and of this disposition A & P knew how to make good use by citing competitive offers. There is no doubt that it constantly and successfully hammered away at the edges, and received price concessions which were nondiscriminatory but illegal.

This result was just what one expects under a cartel which sets up a discriminatory price scale. Sellers get larger net returns from some buyers than from others. There is an inducement to get more of the wide-margin business. The cartelists nibble at the agreement by offering slight concessions under the agreed-on price. Food manufacturers were willing to compete away *some* of the required super-profit on A & P sales. A & P was persistent and skillful in promoting this illegal injection of competition into the market.

Finally, we must recognize the curious way in which the Robin-son-Patman Act gave A & P a queer kind of "monopsony" power it would not otherwise have had. Absent the Act, A & P was too small a part of the food market, nationally or regionally, to influence the price level of the goods it bought. But the Act had segregated buyers, roughly coterminous with the chain stores and voluntary groups, into an extra-profit market. Here A & P was not one tenth of the total outlet, but over a third. And this share is really an average of all the products it bought. On some, A & P's share of the extra-profit market must have been much less, and on others much more. In these markets of few buyers we need no vaporings about "power"; the monopsony conferred by the law is a sufficient explanation. And where there were also few sellers, the condition was bilateral monopoly.

Thus we can appreciate the voluminous record of bargaining; of A & P's trying to obtain what it was not legally entitled to get. But once we accept this conclusion and try to analyze *what* it was that it got, most of the apparent discrimination vanishes.

Market structures and discrimination

It is not accidental that much of the discussion of A & P buying is couched in terms of "buying power" or "bargaining power." For these phrases are so vague that they are nearly invulnerable to any analysis. And to make assurance doubly sure, "power" is a resounding word that evokes a picture of the giant A & P leaning across the table at a cowering little man, pounding the table and laying down the conditions under which he is permitted to exist. To see the picture and denounce the villain is a satisfying emotional experience. Only misguided persons would care to jar our inner comfort by asking whether such a picture ever existed or could exist.

Let us, however, commit the solecism and try to put some meaning into the "power" concept. A monopolist has power over supply and hence over price — he is able to decide that he will sell (or buy) only that amount which results in the maximum advantage to him. (It may or may not be the maximum profit in the usual short-run sense.) The fewer the available substitutes, the wider are the limits on his freedom of action and the greater is his power. At the other extreme, the seller under pure competition has no power at all — he accounts for so small a part of the total that whether he puts more on the market or holds back makes no perceptible difference in supply or price.

For a concern with any significant degree of monopoly power, price discrimination may serve to increase profits. If it is possible to separate buyers according to the prices they are willing to pay, and keep the favored from reselling to the disfavored, the combined total profit on sales to all of them exceeds the maximum possible at a single price to all buyers — that is, the average revenue exceeds the simple monopoly price. (A buyer who can separate sellers can discriminate among them with the same effect.)

Trading items

Without any control over supply and price, there can be no price discrimination. A seller who is a very small part of the market can and does sell everything at the market price. He is unable to charge anyone more, and he has no reason to charge anyone less. The firm with no bargaining power is invulnerable to the pressures of buyers seeking discriminatory low prices.

Thus, the presumption of "tribute" exacted from a host of "small firms without bargaining power" quickly disappears. Indeed, the presumption is all the other way. Unless we can show some special conditions under which the small suppliers could not dispose of their output at the market price, we must assume that there was no discrimination. But such examples, which do exist and will be discussed, must be highly atypical. Otherwise it would imply that small suppliers typically have monopoly power!

Matters are not changed if we assume the existence of one or a few large buyers, with considerable power over the price. These single or collective monopsonists will presumably restrict their demand in order to drive the price down to lower levels than would prevail under more competitive conditions. And they might well discriminate as buyers in paying lower prices to some than to others. Hence seller A may receive a lower price than does seller B if he has no alternative except to sell to buyer X, who pays him just enough to keep him in business. But if there are any buyers other than X, there is no reason for A to discriminate by selling them part of his output at a higher price and the rest to X at a lower price. He sells all of his output to others at the higher price. The only way out of this conclusion is to assume that *seller A occupies so large a portion of the market* that he can only dispose of his total output either by lowering his price to all or by selling the excess to the monopsonist at a discriminatory low price. This is precisely the point: we are very far from a small seller with no "bargaining power."

This theoretical conclusion agrees with the record. A & P's advertising agency once suggested that the cost of advertising mats for certain A & P private label goods be borne by the suppliers, who "would gladly defray the cost of such mats . . . [which] would bring increased sales and of course increased orders."[5] Parr, who knew the industry structure intimately, noted:

This may not be possible on an article like Iona tomatoes, for instance, where we spread the business among a great many small canners, but it does seem to be a reasonable request where we buy all or a very large part of our requirements of some private label items from one or two concerns.[6]

Obviously, a canner who was one of "a great many small canners" sold at what price he could get, and was not interested in an advertising allowance or any other form of price concession. It was the oligopolists, the "one or two concerns" supplying "all or a very large part" of the market, who were sensitive to this pressure.

We may also consider Zoller's description of a large part of his purchases:

[5] Memorandum, Paris & Peart to the merchandising committee, May 1, 1940, attached to GX 1068.
[6] Parr to Vogt, May 9, 1940, GX 1068.

These goods were all bought on a quality and underselling price basis. . . . While our canners naturally want to get as much for their products as they can, they are in a position to undersell because their factories are largely personally owned and personally managed. [They were also better located than most of their competitors.] While we are open to draw supplies from practically all canners in this territory, we have found it advisable to confine the bulk of our purchases to a selected list, approximately 200. These canners know their business, have a high sense of contract obligations and recognize the true great value of our outlet.[7]

Obviously, A & P was concentrating its buying with more efficient canners and these canners were accepting a price lower than other buyers were paying other sellers at the same time. But if we interpret this passage as indicating price discrimination in favor of A & P, we cannot explain why these canners discriminated. It matters little that they could *afford* to; they did not need to. Even as a group, they were only a small minority of all canners, as the letter indicates; had any one of them (or even all of them) turned from the A & P outlet to food brokers or through his own sales force to the Baltimore market generally, he could have secured the current market price. He would not have depressed the price by increasing the supply because he was too small a part of total supply and because A & P would have had to make up its purchases by buying elsewhere. In the face of such common-sense objections, and without any evidence to support it, the hypothesis of price discrimination cannot possibly stand.

This does not mean, however, that A & P did not buy more cheaply than did competitors. It did, through the saving of distribution costs by canners who could sell to an assured market ("the true great value of our outlet"). This is another way of saying that there was a distinct economy of integration by contract, some of which went to A & P, some to the canners. A & P's share of the savings must have been much larger than the costs of operating the Baltimore office and paying the salaries of Zoller and his staff.

We have emphasized throughout the immense variety and changeability of the markets in manufactured foods. Certain food products are so costly to ship that there are many local markets

[7] Zoller to Churchill (Atlantic Division purchasing director), May 8, 1939, GX 855.

small enough for sellers to be few. Most products are sold either nationally or in the large regional centers, where A & P field buying offices operate. A & P's share of a national market around 1940 would be in the neighborhood of 10 per cent; where the market was regional (i.e., the product was not a regional specialty shipped all over the country, but was both produced and consumed regionally) its share might go as high as 15 or 20 per cent.

Were the goods fed into the market at a constant rate, one could dismiss offhand the notion that A & P had at any moment any power even to influence the price, let alone induce discrimination in its favor. But this is not the case. In any given week, or on any given day, A & P may constitute much less or much more than the average 10 per cent. It cannot swing its buying in and out of the market simply to manipulate the price; for that would sabotage the steady deliveries which it must assure to the warehouses. But it is able to hold off at the market peaks for short periods if the warehouses have enough to tide them over; and it can absorb large amounts of bargains at market troughs because it has such a large channel in which to dispose of them. This probably means that it pays a lower average price over time than does the average buyer. Nevertheless, we still have not detected any way in which it can pay *discriminatory* low prices.

The possibility exists, however, of a momentary condition of relatively few suppliers, so that a firm with a relatively small market share finds itself suddenly and for the moment one of a very few sellers. These few try to obtain as high a price as they can obtain. A & P will normally be one of the first to leave the market as prices rise because, as just explained, it has more alternatives. It can call on other and more distant buyers, or can fall back on warehouse stocks, etc. Under these circumstances a processor may find it possible and profitable to charge it a lower price and the rest of the market a higher price. Such occasions probably will not be many; it is in the interests of all the buyers and all but a few of the sellers to avoid them. And as theory would predict, there are no examples of this in the record.

However, let us now introduce stronger imperfections in the shape of a manufacturer who sells a large part of his output to A & P. Is it possible for A & P to demand and receive a lower *net* price than what others are paying? It surely can happen in the short run. For, although there are many other buyers, the cost of changing sales methods in a short time and of making contact with the market may, for a given type of product, be so great that the seller would be penalized even more than by granting the discriminatory low price (see Appendix III). But surely it can happen only once, unless the manufacturer is so gullible that he probably cannot survive anyway. Again, there are no examples of this in the record.

Thus, general reasoning would predict that we would find but few examples in the A & P record of trading items, sold by many firms, subject to price discrimination. In point of fact, *we do not find any.* Nor do we find that standard item of folklore, the small processor who comes to rely wholly upon the chains and is then confronted with a sudden demand for lower prices — or else.

This absence becomes doubly impressive when we recall that the record is no random or representative sample of A & P transactions. It was chosen to discredit a defendant; and few things are more damning in the current state of public opinion than abusing small businessmen. The prosecution did explicitly assert that trading items were subject to widespread discrimination (and its party line has been repeated by some whose professional training deprives them of any excuse) :

A & P obtained a host of varying types of preferential rebates and price concessions from suppliers on "trading items." *In some cases* . . . A & P's net price was . . . substantially *less than those at which any wholesaler* could buy (Tr. 2851, Tr. 2862, Tr. 2880). A & P's suppliers were the recipients of a storm of protest from A & P's competitors when a few of the concessions which A & P had obtained were publicly disclosed before a congressional committee (GX 495, Tr. 2001–3). Illustrative examples of this type of discriminatory preference are cited elsewhere.[8]

This paragraph merits very close examination. The reader will note, first, that only *"in some cases"* is the net price to A & P said to be lower than to wholesalers. Since A & P is a wholesaler, this amounts to saying at the outset that there will only "in some cases" be any discrimination — except, as usual, Robinson-Patman

---

[8] GB(AC), p. 36 (italics added, parenthetical material in original). The "elsewhere" is stated on pp. 160–164 of the brief.

"discrimination." The "some cases" actually cited come to just three. All three were purchases from the nationally known firm of Ball Brothers, and they were all list-price items. (The actual amount of discrimination is discussed in Appendix III.) Let us now turn to the other "illustrative examples" promised in the last sentence quoted. There the brief says that, although there were "numerous" such concessions on trading items, "only a few examples" will be offered. They repeat the transcript citations which refer to Ball Brothers, perhaps reckoning that the reader will not bother to crosscheck across 125-odd pages. Their next reference turns out, upon examining the transcript, to be the following vague statement, by a discharged A & P employee, who testified *in full* on this topic as follows:

Q. Do you recall whether or not you received any [discounts] from the local milk companies?
A. *Well, I don't*, but it was received from the local milk companies.
Q. Were these paid as discounts or merchandise received?
A. Special discounts, it had always been the custom of the trade.[9]

There follows a reference, not to milk at all, but to two Los Angeles baking companies and one Dallas baker who allegedly gave rebates to the A & P unit there. Bread and milk were sold largely under localized oligopoly. Moreover, they were sold from price lists. In neither sense were they trading items.

Next, the brief cites a comparison of a Utica (N.Y.) retailer's buying prices with those of the A & P unit there.[10] The comparison is between prices charged by a jobber to a retailer for *store delivery* with purchase in bulk for delivery to *an A & P warehouse*. The government brief never mentions this fact. It would be wrong to call them deceitful; they honestly assume, as usual, that A & P *should* by rights pay the prices of other retailers, even though it acts as a wholesaler. But let us now consider the "trading items" in question: if we examine the actual document cited, it is clear that all seven items are well known brands.[11]

[9] Crocker, Tr. 10786 (italics added).
[10] GB(AC), pp. 160–162.
[11] Ludlum to Schincke, December 7, 1939, GX 858, listing Mueller's macaroni, Campbell's soup, Borden's evaporated milk, Karo (Corn Products Refining Company), Beech Nut baby foods, Maxwell House coffee, and Crisco.

The government brief then refers to Parr's list, which will be discussed shortly; then to Zoller's letter about numerous efficient small canners (cited above), which furnishes neither an example of price discrimination nor any basis for supposing any. The next item refers to canned meats, sold by price lists, but which are often departed from because of raw material price fluctuations (see Appendix IV, Armour). Finally, there is a reference to Wisconsin Honey Farm, which, far from selling trading items, shipped a trade-marked item as far as a thousand miles distant (see Appendix IV).

So far, the "numerous examples" have shrunk to precisely zero. We have not even one instance of a small firm with an undifferentiated product and small market share making a discriminatory price concession to A & P.

The list submitted to the House Committee

Let us turn now to the list submitted by A & P to the Congressional committee. The statement in the brief that the list contained only "a few of the concessions which A & P had obtained" is false. A member of Congress questioned as follows:

> *Mr. LUCAS.* Does that [list] include every kind and character of rebate or every advantage that A & P receives through the contracts, of any kind?
> *Mr. GUNDREY.* Yes sir.[12]

Had the list not been complete, A & P would have been in contempt of Congress! At any rate, the government ignores Parr's explicit statement that most of the products on the list were nationally (let alone locally) advertised brands; [13] and it cites not even *one* product as an example of a trading item.

The list itself is worth some brief analysis. The number of manufacturers included was 295, of whom 98, or just over one third, were listed in *Moody's Industrials*. In 1935 the total num-

---

[12] *Hearings Before the Special Committee on Investigation of the American Retail Federation*, H. R., 74 Cong., 1 sess., revised printing, p. 461 (Washington, 1936), hereafter cited as ARF; see also p. 445. The list is in the A & P record as GX 11.

[13] Parr, Tr. 227.

ber of food manufacturing corporations (excluding such nonfood goods as soap, and excluding unincorporated manufacturers) was 10,645.[14] The 1935 *Moody's* listed only 170 food manufacturers,[15] or 1.7 per cent of the industry member. Thus the firms granting allowances to A & P contained about twenty times as large a representation of "big" (publicly listed) firms as did the food industry generally.[16] No matter how we measure it, big firms are much more frequently found among those granting allowances than among the whole population of manufacturers.[17]

But size of firm is of course only one aspect of the problem. Of the 310 commodities listed (a firm might sell more than one), 44 are listed by brand name, and 125 others can readily be identified as branded products — a total of 169. The remaining 141 cannot be identified by the author one way or the other. Not one of them can be identified as a trading item. Moreover, of the total of 362 agreements (a product might be covered by more than one agreement), 252 were for advertising allowances and hence must have involved branded goods, an additional 49 can be identified as branded products — a total of at least 301, or a minimum of five sixths of the total. The list submitted to Congress was overwhelmingly composed of list price items, and there is no evidence of even a single trading item.

The "storm of protest" aroused by the list is itself worth examining more closely. There are two documents in the record.

Mr. John . . . inquired as to whether or not I had any comments from any of the manufacturers whose names were in the list. . . .

I told him I had heard from just one, and that was the R. B. Davis Company [Cocomalt, Cutrite wax paper] who lately called up to find out what it was all about.

Since then I have also heard from Mr. McCabe of the Scott Paper Company, and he said that the publication of their arrangement was going to cause them a lot of trouble, because it was so much more than they allowed anyone else.

[14] Treasury Department, *Statistics of Income for 1935* (Washington, 1937).

[15] Excluding sugar refining; also soap and other nonfood products.

[16] Headquarters dealt in 1940 with about one thousand firms, while the lower echelons dealt with many more (Tr. 24,414).

[17] Obviously, the discounts to A & P were a mixture of discriminatory and nondiscriminatory elements. Unfortunately, there is no way of analyzing the list in order to separate them.

Mr. Jay Gould of Best Foods also telephoned and was quite perturbed as he had heard from his principal competitor, Kraft, who accused them of doublecrossing them. . . . He said things would not have been so bad had he had an opportunity to think over what sort of an explanation he was going to make. . . .

The Hecker H-O Company advises that several of their customers had already called them and wanted to see them because of the publication of our arrangement with them . . . they feel they have some tall explaining to do in trying to pacify their other customers because of giving us so much. . . .

I just received the attached letter from the Alabama-Georgia Syrup Company, Montgomery, Alabama, with whom we have an arrangement on canned syrup under their brand. With it they enclosed a copy of a letter from Mr. J. H. McLaurin, President of the United States Wholesale Grocers' Association, in which he expresses his point of view in no uncertain terms, and before replying to these people I should like to get your thoughts.[18]

We may digress for a moment to note this Mr. J. H. McLaurin. Years earlier, when president of the Southern Wholesale Grocers Association, he had been convicted and fined for criminal contempt of a court decree under the Sherman Act forbidding collusive price fixing.[19] But Mr. McLaurin was about to receive a final vindication. For in 1936 he was president of the United States Wholesale Grocers Association, whose lawyer wrote the law [20] which Mr. Patman introduced and Congress enacted.

Five days later Morrow supplemented this memorandum with one to Parr, where he noted "two more complaints, if you can call them such." They concerned Southern Molasses Company (B & O Molasses) and Seminole Paper Company (toilet tissue), both of which sold branded goods over large areas and could not be classed as trading items.[21]

There is no other evidence of trade or public reaction. Perhaps this constitutes "a storm of protest"; in any case, no trading items

[18] *Memorandum*, Morrow to R. B. Smith, July 17, 1935, GX 495.
[19] U.S. v. Southern Wholesale Grocers Association, 207 F. 434, 444 (N. D. Alabama 1913).
[20] We have this on the authority of Mr. Patman. See the *Hearings Before the Committee on the Judiciary on H.R. 8442* . . . , House of Representatives, 74 Cong., 1 sess. (1935), p. 7.
[21] Morrow to Parr, July 22, 1935, GX 496.

were involved. The names mentioned were mostly of large manufacturers, and even the smaller ones named sold list price items.

We may conclude as follows: the government attempted to prove an important part of its case — that trading items were subject to very widespread discrimination. Its methods of proof were ingenious — the transmutation of one list price item (Ball Brothers) into three transcript references, insinuated as trading items, was surely the most ingenious. It came up with not a single example from the whole record. In view of this showing, which confirms our theoretical reasoning, it is clear that the small firm with a small part of its market, devoid of any power or influence over supply, could not be and in fact was not "coerced" or "bludgeoned" or "threatened" into discriminating in favor of A & P.

We turn now to the examples of genuine discrimination in the A & P record, which are digested in Appendix IV. These fall into several well-marked categories.

Local markets. Examples are in bread (Mrs. Baird's, Langendorf's) and the outrageous incident in fluid milk, William Weckerle. There are also local distributors of a nationally sold product (L. D. McKinzie, Coca-Cola Bottling of New York). In all these cases the market was so small that the supplier was a large part of it and was able to maintain a high price to some buyers while charging a lower price to chains, including A & P. In the writer's opinion there was more price discrimination in bread and other local bakery products than appears in the record. For not only would excess capacity and heavy distribution costs exert pressure on the seller; A & P did its own baking, and to the extent that it could freely choose, would be very reluctant to pay more for a purchased loaf than it would cost it to procure from its own bakery. (Cost would include the appropriate return on investment.)

Where considerable brand preference existed, A & P was not free to choose, and could not insist on discriminatory preferences. But otherwise there must have been much price discrimination that went undetected. Nevertheless, this is only the writer's conjecture.

Maintained prices. Wisconsin Honey Farm produced under its own brand name, and its product was shipped as far away as Boston. The A & P record on it is rather tantalizingly incomplete,

but the essence is there. At the price current in 1940, demand fell
short of supply. There may well have been a collusive agreement
among honey producers, but more likely there was simply a fixed
determination not to cut prices unless forced to do so. The obvious
course was to make some special sales at discriminatory low prices.
Unfortunately for Wisconsin, its first such customer resold at a
lower price, which was observed by A & P, which then became
the second buyer to get a bargain. Throughout this period, Wisconsin was quoting higher prices through brokers. The discriminatory price concessions were incidents in the competitive breakdown of a price structure maintained (probably) by an unspoken
convention.

The correspondence is full of the usual tearful avowals that the
low price was below cost or at least afforded no "legitimate profit,"
etc., and the prosecution swallows it all and regurgitates with
italics.[22]

Highly advertised and branded products. This group overlaps
with the class of large sellers. But the two are definitely not the
same. Thus we find Loudon, a small firm just launching a new
product, imposing resale price maintenance and brushing off
A & P; Olney & Carpenter paying for only as much advertising as
it thought it was actually receiving from A & P; Capital City
charging A & P a higher price than that paid by other wholesale
buyers. The soap companies discriminated against A & P, and
their allowances were from 12 to 15 per cent of all headquarters
and local allowances in 1940–1941.

The most highly advertised products are those of greatest bargaining power. The extremes meet: next to the many small sellers
under near-pure competition, this group makes the fewest concessions to A & P.

But this holds only at the extremes, and as reinforced by the
Robinson-Patman Act. As we noted earlier, there is an inherent
vulnerability about the position of the advertisers. In the first
place, a large firm might maintain a single price or even have
hidden discrimination against A & P on its branded goods and
yet grant equality or discriminatory preferences on goods sold
unbranded. In fact, these are among the most striking examples

[22] GB(AC), Appendix, pp. 20–23.

of discrimination in the record: Quaker Oats (probably oligopoly in the unbranded product), Ralston Purina, and (probably) California Packing Company. The Ralston case is very interesting because it was a fairly good example of bilateral oligopoly. There were only three firms selling corn flakes for private label. There was a somewhat larger number of buyers; but A & P took 60 per cent of the output. Doubtless any other seller could have entered the manufacturing business; for capital requirements were low. But only to A & P were the possible savings so large as to make such a step worth while; for only A & P could count on a ready-made market, and only A & P had a manufacturing organization ready to take over. Thus the potential economies of vertical integration, essentially the avoidance of "the high cost of persuasion," [23] led, in an industry of three sellers, to price discrimination. The Ralston arrangement was a contract governing all sales of the product. In contrast, the Calpack discriminations were sporadic, and covered only individual transactions. It is not clear to which class the Quaker Oats discriminations belong. As for Olney & Carpenter, it was a permanent arrangement, though barely on the margin of discrimination; since its saving on selling costs more than equaled the discount granted. (We take no account of the spurious "savings" of overhead.)

Secondly, the "strength" of a brand varies, and at some point the manufacturer becomes sufficiently hungry for additional volume to make a discriminatory bargain, accept additional short-run profits, and hope that his long-run position will not suffer unduly. Thus we have the simplest case — the brand conferring a limited degree of monopoly, which is exploited by discrimination. The difference between this case and the strong-brands case is that demand for the strong brand may be almost equally inelastic in all segments because of few suppliers or consumer demand, so that the large buyers like A & P have no alternative.

It is difficult to say how permanent or transitory was the weak-brand discrimination. During 1936–1942 Brillo's preference was almost certainly permanent. Cranberry Canners, Glaser Crandell Company, Larsen, and Walker's Austex Chile were probably in this group. So were the two Minnesota canning companies, except

[23] The phrase is that of Richard B. Heflebower.

that one cannot be sure that there was *any* net discrimination; for, if we were able to take account of brokerage, as we are unable to do in this instance, it might account for all or even more than the whole discount.

On the other hand, Ball Brothers discriminated in fairly sporadic fashion to meet the lower prices of competitors; Crosse & Blackwell may have desired a permanent arrangement, but certainly did not have one; Hills Brothers were not slow to withhold an advertising allowance when they felt A & P had not earned it, and they discriminated only on one specific sale of citrus juices.

Conclusion

Small firms with only a small share of their respective markets and with no "bargaining power" could not and did not discriminate in price in favor of A & P. At the other extreme, sellers of the most highly differentiated products "dumped" only occasionally. A & P could and did secure discriminatory price reductions under local or national oligopoly, or from sellers who were less successful in differentiating their product. These concessions might be permanent or transitory.

XI

THE EXTENT AND SIGNIFI-
CANCE OF DISCRIMINATION
IN FAVOR OF A & P

As we have emphasized throughout, A & P bought goods in a bewildering variety of markets. On any given day it might be paying discriminatory low prices, excessively high prices, and non-discriminatory prices. In order to see what the effect might have been upon the food trade, we ought to know the amount of discrimination for and against them, in order to see the net effect, and whether it was substantial or trifling.

However, for reasons largely stated in the last chapter, the data do not exist to show the extent of discrimination against A & P, both by law and by the private action of suppliers. Thus all that our calculations can do is show the gross figure of discrimination in their favor — a procedure analogous to showing assets without liabilities.

Furthermore, even the calculation of discrimination in their favor is exaggerated, because no allowance has been made for cost savings in manufacturing or distribution. In this chapter, an additional bias will be introduced — the profits of field buying offices (often called brokerage operation) will be reckoned as all discriminatory gains. The reason is that whatever discrimination was received was embodied in the earnings of the field buying offices. Since we are unable to make any division, we include the whole item, and at least know the direction if not the magnitude of the bias.

MEASUREMENT OF DISCRIMINATION IN FAVOR OF A & P

In seeking to determine the aggregate of discriminatory payments to A & P, we start with three series: the headquarters allowances (Account 702), the profits of the field buying offices (brokerage offices), and the local allowances. This covers only processed goods, including meat. The buying of fresh fruits and vegetables by Acco will be considered later.

The 702 Account, according to the testimony of the prosecution accountant, included quantity discounts and cost savings agreements discounts, some minor allowances, and advertising allowances.[1] Advertising which was not specifically required in a contract with a supplier was *not* deducted from the entry in 702. That is, a contract might specify performance in general terms; A & P would, in the course of the year, do enough advertising to satisfy the supplier; but the cost of this advertising would not ordinarily be deducted. The rationale of this accounting procedure is that A & P had to do a certain amount of advertising anyway, whether it was reimbursed or not. Thus the outlay on advertising was, up to a certain point, a fixed cost. Allowances by suppliers would thus be considered as clear gain, except to the extent that an allowance necessitated a *specific* increment of cost. The cost of specific services rendered pursuant to specific agreements, however, was debited to the Specific Advertising Account which included advertising outlays in general.[2] Only the surplus went into 702. This rule also held for local allowances.[3]

The 702 Account was clearly a catch-basin for any and all types of allowance. As we previously saw, "rebates" and "confidential allowances," which became "advertising allowances" in the late 1920's (above, Chapter VII), were included. It was essentially the gains A & P realized through headquarters buying.

[1] Nelson Perry, Special Agent, F.B.I., Tr. 13,370–71, 373.

[2] Memorandum, sales department, Southern Division, to all unit heads (buyers, and office managers) Dec. 1, 1941, GX 1114.

[3] The Southern director of sales wrote a unit sales head as follows: "Of course, you can only get credit in your advertising account for the amount actually spent but if there is a substantial additional amount it goes into the advertising allowance which is profit for the Company right on and should in most cases be realized." Carlton to Cash, October 10, 1941, GX 1110.

As for the field buying offices, after June, 1936, receipt of brokerage was illegal, and the term disappeared from the accounting records. It is known that some quantity discount and cost savings agreements were negotiated as a substitute for the old brokerage, and were folded into the 702 Account. It seems proper, therefore, to add the totals of 702, the local allowances, and the brokerage earnings, as a first approximation to discriminations received by A & P. Our next step is to determine to what extent this total tends to understate or overstate the elements of discrimination.

Possible understatements

The first possibility to be considered is that our total includes only *discounts* from invoice prices, and not simple price reductions, which might also be discriminatory, but never enter 702.

Certain items of evidence suggest such a possibility at first glance. Thus, the first plan worked out with Sylmar Packing Corporation provided for

a 10% quantity discount off *their most recent list*. . . . No quantity has been agreed on at this time. However, the 10% will be deducted directly from the face of the invoice so that there will be no bookkeeping necessary at the end of the year.[4]

The significance of direct deduction from the face of the invoice is simply that instead of accumulating the discount on the books until such time as A & P reached some specified volume, the discount became effective immediately. The discount was deducted *from* the invoice price, not deducted to make a *lower* invoice price. The detailed bookkeeping was avoided, and the amount went into 702 as a single amount — purchases multiplied by ten per cent. The real significance of this passage is that it shows the volume requirement to be altogether perfunctory; A & P said it would buy a large amount in the course of the year, and that was enough to secure a 10 per cent discount immediately.

This interpretation is strengthened by another incident. In 1941, Armour & Co. offered an advertising allowance

[4] Beckmann to Parr, February 24, 1939, GX 1462 (italics added).

in return for one newspaper ad each month. This allowance is not deductible from invoices but must be covered by a contract and will be paid on submission of proof of advertising.[5]

In this case, proof of performance *was* required, and the allowance was only paid upon receipt of the proof. In contrast is the deduction from the face of the invoice; i.e., automatically whenever an order is filled and the A & P unit is billed for it. Thus, the phrase "deduction from the face of the invoice" does not signify an unrecorded price reduction at all; it has no connection with the possibility.

These are the only two agreements which even suggest the possibility of price reductions, discriminatory or otherwise, coming as simple price reductions rather than discounts. There is, therefore, no evidence in the record of flat price reductions not involving discounts. It would be surprising to find many. Thus in the Sylmar agreement, the bargain was not simply a given *price*, but a given *differential* from the "most recent list" price. This was not a matter of taste, but a necessity in a market where price changed frequently, or could change without much notice. In general, unless purchases were strictly spot, a price reduction needed to be in terms of a discount from price, and would enter the accounting records that way.

The question now arises, how important were the spot purchases where there was no continuity of relationship, and where a differential might have come as a flat price reduction, with nothing added to 702? Discriminatory gains on such transactions through the field buying offices would increase their profits by that amount, and we have already agreed to count *all* their profits as discriminatory. However, after the Robinson-Patman Act, there must have been many transactions where brokerage equivalent was allowed in the form of a lower invoice price. We assume that A & P was as successful in obtaining this type of differential as in obtaining 702 differentials, and hence Table 10 estimates a total of disguised brokerage profits after 1936. This involves much double counting, for where A & P was successful in converting a brokerage into a

---

[5] Memorandum, J. W. Fraser (National Meat Department), February 18, 1941, GX 1287.

TABLE 10. Gross Allowances to A & P, 1927–1941
(millions of dollars)

Year	Headquarters allowances (702 Account)	Profits of field buying offices (brokerage offices)	Local allowances	Total allowances
	(1)	(2)	(3)	(4)
1927	4.70	0.73	0.8 [a]	6.23
1928	6.39	1.10	1.1 [a]	8.89
1929	7.81	1.61	1.3 [a]	10.72
1930	7.51	1.78	1.3 [a]	10.59
1931	8.42	2.10	1.4 [a]	11.92
1932	8.57	2.10	1.4	12.07
1933	7.79	2.20	1.8	11.79
1934	6.59	1.33	1.2	9.12
1935	7.90	1.72	1.6	11.22
1936	4.75	0.88	1.1	6.73
1937	3.12	0.58 [b]	1.0	4.70
1938	2.88	0.53 [b]	0.9	4.31
1939	4.72	0.87 [b]	1.2	6.79
1940	5.26	1.97 [b]	1.4	7.63
1941	6.40	1.19 [b]	1.4	8.99

Source. *Annual Binder*, respective years.

[a] Not available in 1927–1931. During 1932–1941, average annual headquarters allowances were on the average six times average local allowances, and it is assumed that the same ratio held in 1927–1931.

[b] Item no longer recorded after 1936. Estimated by assuming changes after 1936 to be proportional to changes in the total of the 702 account. This involves double counting, because some field buying office discounts were converted to discounts going into the 702 account.

quantity or other discount, the latter went into 702. We count it there, and again in column (2).

We may conclude that the total of brokerage plus local and headquarters allowances omits no significant amounts of price discrimination in favor of A & P. We now turn to the problem of whether the total includes any nondiscriminatory elements, and whether it is possible to make specific adjustments for them.

Subtractions

Brokerage. Some large element of the brokerage net earnings — probably the great bulk of them — are obviously nondiscriminatory, and represent simply a payment for services rendered. Unfortunately, there is no way of knowing how large this nondiscriminatory element may be. All we can say is that the brokerage earnings are a very large overstatement of the actual discrimination received by the field buying offices. This overstatement is in addition to the double counting after 1936.

Advertising allowances pose several problems. To the extent that an advertising allowance is merely a reimbursement for A & P costs actually incurred, it is not a price reduction to A & P at all, discriminatory or nondiscriminatory. The supplier has merely purchased advertising space from A & P rather than from a newspaper, etc. Hence, if we charged against each allowance the full outlay on all advertising done to support the supplier's product, the limit of possible discrimination would be lowered by that amount. But A & P did not follow this procedure. The rationale of the 702 Account was marginal cost: advertising outlays over and above those *specifically required* by certain contracts were considered clear gain; because those other expenditures would have been made anyway. A completely analogous situation would be where A & P rented a garage under a long-term lease and was able to sublet space to other business concerns. Since the rent was a fixed cost, the payments from sublessees involved no additional cost, and could be considered as clear gain. But the approach favored by most of the accounting profession would be to say that subleasing was only possible because the rental was being paid, and that a portion of the rental should properly be charged as a cost against the revenues from the sublease. If we were to follow it, the deductions from 702 would be considerably larger than under marginal cost accounting, and net discrimination much less.

The writer would use marginal cost. In the first place, there is a presumption in favor of using A & P's own accounting concepts where not clearly erroneous or inappropriate. Second, it enables us to bypass the vexing joint cost problem of advertising allowances fully re-expended, which were a joint benefit to A & P as well as to the suppliers, and hence were a consideration which lowered the net price paid by A & P for their goods. To the extent that others did not receive such benefits, A & P's benefit was discriminatory. The use of 702 amounts narrows this joint-benefit element down to: (1) the re-expended portion of (2) specific advertising done pursuant to a contract, and (3) not also given to other buyers. These are three restrictive conditions, and little if anything gets past them. Furthermore, the most important of these specific performance contracts were undoubtedly the deals with the soap companies, which, about 1940, were running around a million dollars a year.[6] These were discriminatory against A & P.[7] Hence this joint-benefit element must have been very small or negative, and it was offset by certain others now to be considered.

In order to follow the marginal cost approach consistently, one must recognize that advertising was not a wholly fixed factor. For example, a 1942 meeting of the Merchandising Committee [8] stated its "belief that the available wall space in stores is too valuable to the products of the Company's own subsidiaries to permit manufacturers to post their advertising." This reasoning applies more generally. Granted that A & P advertising had to feature specific commodities, and granted that advertising was largely though not wholly a fixed expense, yet every mention of a purchased commodity was at the expense of a commodity manufactured at home, on which the profit was greater. Within this range, advertising was a variable, not a fixed, cost; for the sake of advertising its purchased goods, A & P incurred the opportunity cost of not advertising its own goods. Therefore, even on the strict marginal-cost theory, the 702 Account is an overstatement of net price reductions. On the marginal-cost theory, not the total but some *fraction* of the advertising expenditure was a sacrifice of advertising which might have featured their own product.

Whichever adjustment we choose, full cost or marginal cost, it is substantial. As Table 11 shows, advertising other than national (which is presumed not to feature commodities) was remarkably stable both in absolute amount and as a per cent of sales. The ratio of goods procured from A & P sources to all goods stayed fairly steadily around 20 per cent including Acco, around 15 per cent excluding Acco. This is a substantial percentage, indicating

[6] See Appendix IV, section on Colgate-Palmolive-Peet et al.
[7] See Appendix IV.
[8] February 10, 1942, DX 237.

TABLE 11. A & P Advertising, By Type, Related to Sources of Supply
(amounts in thousands of dollars)

Year	Signs and circulars	Newspaper advertising	Column (1) plus column (2)	Column (3) as per cent of sales	National and other advertising	Total purchases from subsidiaries as per cent of total Purchases	Column (3) times column (6)
	(1)	(2)	(3)	(4)	(5)	(6)	(7)
1927						15.8	
1928	1,370	4,056	5,426	0.6	715	15.5	841.0
1929	1,177	4,752	5,929	0.6	862	16.3	966.4
1930	1,049	4,736	5,785	0.6	937	16.3	942.0
1931	1,059	4,824	5,883	0.6	1,268	16.2	953.0
1932	995	4,273	5,268	0.6	1,211	17.4	916.6
1933	978	3,947	4,925	0.6	1,038	18.2	896.4
1934	853	4,294	5,147	0.6	703	21.1	1,086.0
1935	1,014	3,954	4,968	0.6	703	20.2	1,003.5
1936						21.5	
1937	1,155	3,417	4,572	0.5	580	21.6	987.6
1938	1,193	2,897	4,090	0.5	1,199	21.3	871.2
1939	1,420	3,536	4,966	0.5	1,005	20.5	1,018.0
1940	1,280	3,881	5,161	0.5	502	20.2	1,042.5
1941	1,005	3,893	4,898	0.4	331	21.3	1,043.3

Sources. Columns 1, 2, 4, 5, from *Annual Binder*, respective years. (Column 6, from Appendix Table 21.)

that goods made at home were large enough to be worth promoting. We do not know what per cent of A & P advertising promoted A & P products, but an additional 20 per cent could easily have been devoted to A & P products at any time without running into seriously diminishing returns. Therefore, even if we consider A & P product advertising as a fixed expense necessary to keep its name before the local buying public, one must recognize the variable component, of which our best estimate — subject, of course, to a considerable margin for error — is in column 7 of Table 11. Thus, in 1941 about $1 million of advertising allowances represented a real opportunity cost, and should be deducted to obtain the net gain from the 702 Account. Again, we attempt no detailed numerical adjustment, for the precision would be deceptive; but the overstatement must be kept in mind.

Cost savings. It is universally agreed that some percentage of the discounts and allowances in 702 represented cost savings. Even the prosecution might nod to the principle, although they invariably disregarded it in practice:

While a part of these "savings" or profits may include valid discounts incident to the volume purchased, or a legitimate cost saving, the greater part of them is accrued directly as a result of discriminatory rebates and concessions available to no other competitors on substantially equal terms.[9]

Thus, according to the government, "a greater part," i.e., something in excess of 50 per cent of the discounts and allowances, constituted discrimination. Out of the thousands of pages of briefs and records, not even a few more lines could be found to clarify such a basic matter, or to indicate how far over 50 per cent.

Unfortunately, there is no way of adjusting for such savings. Some of them crop up even in the government's sample, tabulated in Appendix IV, where there was probable or definite cost savings for eleven suppliers and twenty-seven transactions (including brokerage savings). Again, we must simply keep in mind that our failure to make the adjustment gives the figure an important upward bias.

Comparison with discounts given others

We now attempt to discover what part of the allowances granted A & P was also given to other firms.

The FTC chain store investigation tabulated prices paid by chain stores and independents in four cities during 1929–1931,[10] as shown in Table 12.

The net buying prices of the nonchains were generally about 1½ per cent above the prices paid by the chains. On the assortment of goods bought by chains, their advantage ranged between 0.2 and 2.5 per cent; on the assortment bought by nonchains, from *minus* 0.1 per cent to 3.5 per cent.

The difference between the results using chain weights and independent weights is usually substantial; in the case of Mem-

[9] GB(AC), p. 365.
[10] Table 12 is based on the underlying studies of the FTC investigation, and *not* on the Final Report. The less said about the summary in that document, the better.

TABLE 12. Comparisons of Chain and Independent Selling Prices, Buying Prices, and Gross Margins, 1929–1931

	Washington, 1929			Cincinnati, 1929			Memphis, 1930[b]			Detroit, 1931		
Independent price or margin as per cent of chain price or margin	Chain weights	Independent weights	Geometric mean	Chain weights	Independent weights	Geometric mean	Chain weights	Independent weights	Geometric mean	Chain weights	Independent weights	Geometric mean
Selling prices	107.1[a]	105.7		108.5	109.2		109.1	107.5		112.2	108.8	
Net buying prices	101.8[a]	101.6[a]	101.7	100.2[a]	99.9[a]	100.02	102.3[a]	103.5[a]	102.9	102.5[a]	102.1[a]	102.3
Gross margin	129.7	124.7		149.1	150.9		132.0	121.6		153.4	135.4	
Difference in weighted aggregate buying price: as per cent of difference in weighted aggregate selling price;	20.5	23.6		1.55	−1.0		19.2	35.8		16.6	19.2	
As per cent of gross margin of chain	7.7	7.6		0.77	−0.5		7.6	11.9		10.7	8.4	
Per cent of sales included in sample:												
chains	19.0	17.7		17.0	18.8		22.9	22.3		20.1	19.0	
independents	23.0	20.9		23.3	25.3		27.7	25.2		25.0	25.9	

Sources. Federal Trade Commission, *Chain Stores* (72–74 Cong., 1930–1934), *Prices and Margins of Chains and Independent Distributors* (respective volumes for), *Washington*, appendix tables 6–7; *Cincinnati*, appendix tables 9A and 10A (data relating to two large chains); *Memphis*, appendix tables 6 and 7; *Detroit*, appendix tables 6 and 7. All computations from unrounded data. Geometric mean in original data.

[a] No special discounts reported on "direct" items, supplied directly to individual stores of chains or independents, or on "semidirect," supplied to chain warehouses but directly to independent stores.

[b] A & P did not operate in Memphis.

phis, the differential is almost twice as large on the basis of independent weights. Chain stores and nonchain stores obviously sold different assortments of goods. On the goods sold by the chains, some 15 to 20 per cent of the difference in selling prices was accounted for by differences in buying prices. On the bill of goods sold by the nonchains, the range is so great — from less than zero in Cincinnati to 36 per cent in Memphis — that the average of 19.4 has very little meaning. The samples for both chains and nonchains are large, but the method of selection is not explained, and the wide variations are a warning of haphazard selection and bias.

In Table 13, we compare the unadjusted A & P discount and allowance data with the FTC data just presented.

It will be seen that our computations from the A & P accounting records check fairly well with the FTC data for the four cities (except Cincinnati) so far as percentages of gross margin are concerned. But where a given error of estimate is applied to a much smaller quantity, the resulting percentage of error may become so large as to rob the average of meaning. This seems to be the case with the FTC estimates of chains' price advantage over independents, which varies within the space of one year from 1.7 to 2.9. This is so erratic that it can only be said to confirm the general order of magnitude of our calculations from the A & P record.

Perhaps the FTC results are best considered as four subsamples; if so, their average is much more meaningful than any single observation. The unweighted mean of the four cities is 1.73 per cent, as compared with 1.58, the average in column 1.

We turn now to the FTC estimates of special prices and allowances granted by manufacturers to various classes of buyers in 1929 and 1930. Here the apparent discrepancy is larger, as shown by Table 14.

The reason for the apparent discrepancy appears in interviews conducted by the FTC with 76 manufacturers, who were about one sixth of the total sample, and one third of the number granting discounts (see Table 15). A sixth (13 of 76) of this group granted special lower prices to chain stores. Some were in recognition of larger quantity or larger volume; others were "arrived at by

TABLE 13. Comparison of A & P Data and FTC Store Data, 1929–1931

	A & P discounts			Chains' advantage over nonchains (FTC)				
Year	As per cent of purchases	As per cent of gross margin		As per cent of purchases	As per cent of gross margin		As per cent of purchases	As per cent of gross margin
	(1)	(2)		(3)	(4)		(5)	(6)
1929	1.49	7.7	Washington:	1.7	7.7	Cincinnati:	0.02	0.27
1930	1.48	7.5	Memphis:	2.9	9.7		..	..
1931	1.78	8.5	Detroit:	2.3	10.0		..	..

Source. Tables 10 and 12, and Appendix Table 21.

trading to the best advantage"; others were "based on competitive conditions. . . . Other manufacturers grant chain stores *the same prices as wholesalers.*" [11] The italicized words show that the FTC

TABLE 14. FTC Reports and A & P Accounts — Special Discounts and Allowances as Per Cent of Purchases from All Manufacturers Reporting

| | 1929 | | 1930 | |
	A & P accounts	FTC	A & P accounts	FTC
	(1)	(2)	(3)	(4)
A & P	1.49	2.37	1.48	2.42
Next largest three chains	. .	1.29	. .	1.43
All other chains	. .	1.41	. .	1.72
All chains	. .	1.89	. .	2.02
Wholesalers	. .	0.87	. .	0.91
Cooperatives	. .	1.00	. .	1.04

Source of columns 2 and 4. 73 Cong., 2d sess., Senate Document No. 89, *Report of the Federal Trade Commission on Chain Stores. Special Discounts and Allowances . . .* , table 1 and appendix.

regarded an equal price to a wholesale warehouse and an A & P warehouse as a special lower price. But as a matter of economics, it is of course nondiscriminatory.

Sixty-three per cent (48 of 76) granted so-called "promotional allowances," which include advertising allowances and other sales effort. According to the Commission:

Frequently money advanced for advertising was not used for that purpose at all but used for the purpose of reducing the price to the consumer.

TABLE 15. FTC Report — Types of Allowances Granted

| Type of distributor Allowances receiving | Per cent of total amounts disbursed as allowances for | | | | | | | |
| | Volume | | Advertising | | Miscellaneous | | Total | |
	1929	1930	1929	1930	1929	1930	1929	1930
Grocery chains	44.0	42.3	38.4	43.0	17.5	14.8	100	100
Grocery wholesalers	64.4	52.1	13.9	19.7	21.7	28.2	100	100
Grocery cooperatives	48.5	36.2	33.9	44.0	17.6	19.8	100	100
Total	45.4	42.6	36.8	41.7	17.8	15.7	100	100

Source. See Table 14.

[11] *Final Report*, p. 61.

Some manufacturers, however, keep a complete check or audit on all newspaper advertising done by customers and pay the customer line for line for such service. A similar check is also made, in some instances, on the counter and window display service and other types of featuring [but not on] . . . sales effort or clerk promotion.[12]

Here is another conceptual difference, in that the Commission included the gross advertising allowance, while the A & P 702 Account included only the net amount over and above the incremental cost of fulfilling the contract. (The amount over and above the full cost of fulfilling the contract would be even smaller.) Also, "frequently" is a weaker word than "usually" or "generally," and it seems to imply that the greater part of these allowances were re-expended. Unless the language of the *Final Report* is extremely loose, a large or major portion of the allowances were thus not retained by any recipient. Again, the FTC made no attempt to arrive at the net payments; compounding the neglect, they did not try to see who received the payments and who did not.

Forty per cent (31 of 76) of the manufacturers granted larger discounts to chains than to wholesalers or other retailers. Thus, chains might receive 10 and 3, wholesalers 10, and retailers from 2 to 5. This would not in itself produce any discrepancy between the A & P accounts and the FTC estimates.

One third (24 of 76) of the manufacturers granted brokerage or an allowance therefor to chain store buyers. Since the "brokerage" item in the A & P tables on sources of profits is *net earnings* by buying offices rather than *gross brokerage* paid, the A & P figures must be about one third less than the manufacturers' gross allowances.

It is clear that the FTC estimate has large elements of upward bias as compared with the A & P accounting record: it includes advertising allowances actually re-expended, the expenses of maintaining field buying offices (brokerage offices), and "lower" prices made to A & P as a wholesaler — which it was.

. Furthermore, we must consider the nature of the two samples. The A & P record is of course a complete count for fourteen years. The FTC covered $158.9 million and $150.4 million of A & P

---

[12] *Final Report*, p. 61 (italics added).

purchases for 1929 and 1930, respectively 22 per cent and 21 per cent of all processed goods purchased in those years. We do not know how representative the FTC's sample may be, for there is no explanation or listing. Since they were looking for price preferences of various kinds, they would naturally address themselves not to manufacturers in general but to manufacturers who, they had reason to believe, were granting them. This is another way of saying that the sample would be biased in the direction of overstating preferences. Further doubts about the representativeness of the FTC sample are aroused by some of the details. Table 14 shows allowances to A & P, as a per cent of purchase, to be much more than to the next three largest chains; but these three actually received *less* than "all other" chains, including many small ones.

In summary: the FTC estimates of *chain store price preferences*, technically very deficient, agree fairly well with ours. The FTC estimates of *suppliers' differentials* contain large elements of upward bias which the A & P accounts do not, and which ought to be excluded from any estimate of price discrimination. The unwanted elements could easily account for all of the difference or even more. The FTC estimates are also a minor sample selected in an unrevealed and probably biased way. We shall therefore continue to use the A & P accounting record as the first approximation to a measurement of price discrimination.

Discounts also granted to others

Our next problem is to take account of discounts which were also given to other concerns (not merely "made available"). Obviously, if several concerns each receive the same discount, there is no discrimination among them. According to the theory of the prosecution, a discrimination would be measured by the difference between the price paid by A & P and the price paid by unintegrated retailers; but this nonsense need not be pursued here. Our comparison must be with wholesalers and with other chains performing the wholesale function. As Table 14 shows, during 1929 and 1930 wholesalers received concessions at the rate of 0.87 and 0.91 per cent of their purchase prices. These rates of allowance are respectively 36.8 per cent and 37.6 per cent of the rates granted to A & P, average 37.2 per cent; hence 62.8 per cent of the allowances were not made to others. This is of course a comparison with wholesalers who relied on brokers and salesmen to come to their door; it implicitly treats the gross discount of the field buying offices as wholly discriminatory. Nevertheless, we are unable to make any correction, and must use these factors as they stand.

Our tabulation in Appendix IV of deals with suppliers during the period 1936–1942 suggested that about 60 per cent of concessions to A & P were also given to others. (The median per cent of net differential as per cent of gross was 39.9.) The FTC data and the trial record are separated by half a decade and by the Robinson-Patman Act. An estimate that *before* the Act around 60 per cent of A & P's special concessions were not made to others while *after* the Act about 40 per cent were not, can only be criticized as being implausibly low for 1937–1941.

This leaves us with the intervening years, which covered the worst of the Great Depression. In our judgment, it would be a mistake to apply either set of factors. Allowances as a per cent of purchases increased substantially during those years, but in such an economic earthquake the uniformity of nature largely disappears. Lacking any detailed evidence, it seems best not to attempt any adjustments. The discriminatory content may have increased substantially, but we cannot say.

Table 16 carries us about as far as statistics can go. But it has a large upward bias, as may be seen by considering certain components during the year 1941. The estimated brokerage profits (around a million dollars) are exaggerated in amount through double counting, and contain little or no discriminatory element. As for Account 702 items, the allowances from the soap companies came to about a million dollars, and were if anything discriminatory against A & P. Another million dollars would represent the opportunity cost of running advertising which could have been used for A & P products. These items alone account for over a third of all allowances for the year 1941, suggesting a corrected percentage of 0.24 rather than 0.36 per cent. No account has been taken of phantom brokerage or other discriminations against

TABLE 16. Maximum Estimate of Gross Price Discrimination in Favor of A & P, 1929–1941 (as per cent of purchases of processed goods)

Year	Unadjusted total	Adjusted for discounts also given to wholesalers
1929	1.49	0.94 [a]
1930	1.48	0.92 [b]
1931	1.78	[c]
1932	2.17	[c]
1933	2.26	[c]
1934	1.73	[c]
1935	1.99	[c]
1936	1.17	[c]
1937	0.83	0.33 [d]
1938	0.77	0.31 [d]
1939	1.05	0.42 [d]
1940	1.02	0.41 [d]
1941	0.91	0.36 [d], 0.24 [e]

[a] Factor 0.632. Source: Table 14, and Appendix I, Table 18.
[b] Factor 0.624. Source: Table 14, and Appendix I, Table 18.
[c] No estimate possible. See text discussion.
[d] Factor 0.399. See Appendix IV.
[e] Subtracting brokerage earnings, soap allowance, opportunity cost of advertising allowances; factor 0.399. See text discussion.

A & P under the Robinson-Patman Act, nor of any cost savings. According to the economist in charge of the FTC investigation, quantity discounts "have relatively seldom represented the full amount of the savings in selling and delivery costs that were involved. . . ."[13] He does not explain, however, whether he refers only to quantity or also to volume discounts, which are often miscalled "quantity."

Were we able to quantify these adjustments, we could subtract them from Table 16 to arrive at a best estimate or most probable estimate of discriminatory discounts to A & P. Since we cannot do so, Table 16 remains as an estimate of the *upper limit* of possible discrimination. We can only state that an unbiased estimate of price discrimination for 1929 would be something substantially less than 0.94 per cent of purchase price; for 1941 something substantially less than 0.36 per cent, or even substantially less than 0.24 per cent.

[13] W. H. S. Stevens, "An Interpretation of the Robinson-Patman Act," *Journal of Marketing*, 2:44 (July 1937).

SIGNIFICANCE OF DISCRIMINATION IN FAVOR OF A & P

Buying prices and resale prices. So far, the discussion has been confined to price reductions as a percentage of purchase price. This is obviously significant as indicating the degree of control or power over the suppliers. If we slough off those differentials which corresponded to differences in function, as this chapter has done to some extent, it becomes clear that the discriminatory residual was very small. Dominance over *manufacturers*, then, was of almost negligible importance. This merely confirms the conclusion reached earlier, when discussing market structures.

Discrimination as per cent of purchases is also of interest as indicating the power conferred on A & P to cut its retail prices. A very approximate calculation is made on page 239 — any claim to precision would be deceptive. If short-run elasticity of demand in 1941 is around 2 (as calculated in Appendix II), prices would be cut by 0.21 per cent, and the increase in sales would be less than half of 1 per cent. Over the longer run, assuming a demand elasticity around 15, one would expect a sales increase of about 3 per cent.

Thus, if 1929–1931 conditions persisted over the long run, we would have expected A & P sales to increase by 8 to 12 per cent of the sales that would be made without the discrimination, other things being equal. If in some community A & P without discrimination would have made (say) 20 per cent of sales, discrimination would have enabled them to make around 22 or 23 per cent. In 1941, discrimination would have enabled them to increase their market share from 20 per cent to less than 21 per cent. (We assume no change in unit costs.)

This conclusion runs so contrary to fixed opinion, especially in the trade, that there is not the slightest hope that it will ever be dislodged. But as Table 15 shows, the FTC data point almost as strongly to the same result. It is of course a conclusion not about any specific commodity but about grocery service — the whole line of goods. Let us also recall that during the time of greatest price concessions, as Table 16 shows, the company acted like a short-run monopolist and actually increased its relative prices; contrariwise, it was when concessions were smallest that they were passed on to the consumer.

Gross and net margins

Another useful comparison is between price difference and gross margin. Applying this to the A & P data, in 1929–1930 aggregate price discrimination did not exceed 5 per cent of gross margin;

A & P: Possible reduced selling price and increased volume through discrimination

A. Reduced selling prices

		Discriminatory reduction in:	
		Selling price	
Time period	Buying price	If gross margin is 0.20	If gross margin is 0.12
1929–1931:			
Maximum estimate	0.93	0.74	—
More probable estimate	0.67	0.54	—
1941:			
Maximum estimate	0.36	—	0.32
More probable estimate	0.24	—	0.21

B. Per cent increase in sales volume, assuming selling prices reduced by full amount of discriminatory reductions

	1929–1931		1941	
	0.074 per cent	0.54 per cent	0.32 per cent	0.21 per cent
Selling prices reduced by:				
Elasticity assumed 2:	1.5	1	less than 1 per cent	
Elasticity assumed 15:	11	8	5	3

on the eve of World War II it was around 4 per cent. The decline in discrimination relative to gross margin is not nearly so great as it is relative to purchase price. The reason is obviously the supermarket revolution, which cut the gross margin so drastically between 1937 and 1941. Nor was this an arithmetical accident; it reflected a structural economic change. The size of the grocery retailing operation, as measured by the dollars of labor and capital necessary to encompass it, had shrunk relative to the extractive and manufacturing operations. Hence a given discrimination in price was greater relative to gross margin.

Granted, however, that the comparison with gross margin is appropriate, whose gross margin? The question is especially pointed for the 1937–1941 period. Let us suppose that A & P was the only concern to go supermarket, and that the rest of the food trade stayed with the old methods. To say that a given discrimination was more important to A & P because they had reduced their expense of handling goods would be to count that expense reduction twice. The discriminations received would acquire greater importance only to the extent that the food trade generally, or at least the competitors of A & P, adopted supermarkets and shortened their margin.

As an approximation to the gross margin of "the industry" one may perhaps use the margins of the corporate chains, as recorded in Appendix Table 19. As a per cent of its closest competitors' gross margin, A & P discriminations on the eve of World War II were about 3 per cent.

Instead of gross margin, one may wish to consider the expense rate, and a reduction in the purchase price is best appraised by considering it a reduction in the cost of doing business. The results would not greatly differ from those reached with gross margin.

Another comparison would be with net profit. At one extreme, we might assume the firm to retain none of these gains, but to pass all of them on to consumers. The effect then depends on the reduction in selling price and the elasticity of demand, which brings us back again to discrimination as a per cent of purchase and sales price. We have already seen that neither in the short nor the long run were even the 1929–1931 discriminations of any substantial significance.

At the other extreme we might suppose that the firm retains all of its discriminatory gains as increased profits. If the profits are paid as dividends, there is no effect on the food trade. If the profits are reinvested, their importance is measured relative to gross margin or expense rate. That is, if discriminatory gains were 5 per cent of the gross margin, which is the cost of food distribution, they would in any given year provide the funds for a 5 per cent expansion of operations. But this expansion would not be undertaken unless it promised to increase net profits more than the investment of the money in some other use. The financial history of A & P is conclusive on this point. Their greatest discriminatory gains, and their greatest net profits, did not give rise to larger investment in retailing or other operations. The management preferred short-term government securities at a return of around 2 per cent. We must not forget that the favored concern could only expand into the retail food trade through direct price competition or by otherwise giving the consumer more utility per dollar expended. This would bring us back to discrimination as per cent of net sales. We cannot count the same amount twice.

We come closer to understanding the significance of discrimination by recalling the comparison of A & P and its most efficient competitors' operating costs.[14] It will be convenient to express the difference in terms of dollars per $100 of sales receipts. In 1939–1941, the difference was $6.77. The gross discriminatory gains could have been no higher than 36 cents, and probably nearer 24 cents. Thus the total cost advantage to A & P might have been as high as $7.13, of which 36 cents, or 5 per cent, was the gross discriminatory advantage; it was more probably in the neighborhood of $7.01, of which 24 cents, or under 4 per cent, was gross discriminatory advantage. In other words, from 94 to 96 per cent of the competitive problem consists of the lower operating costs of A & P; only popular mythology supports the idea that A & P and the rest of the chain stores grew to greatness because of price discrimination.

This conclusion is reinforced by the statistics of the Federal Trade Commission report. As Table 12 showed, only 15 per cent of the higher selling prices of the independent retailer could be explained by the higher buying prices; the other 85 per cent could only be explained by his higher operating expenses and higher unit profit margins. That 15 per cent, as we have demonstrated, was very far from being all discriminatory; but even disregarding our evidence, the 85–15 ratio is decisive for the structure of the food trade. The widespread impression that the growth of chains was "based largely on special price concessions from manufacturers"[15] is legend.

So far, then, it appears that price discrimination can be dis-

---

[14] Above, Chapter IV, and Appendix Table 19.
[15] FTC, *Chain Stores: Final Report*, p. 90.

carded as an explanation for price, output, and the sharing of the market as among A & P, other chains, and the rest of the market. What happened to A & P and the rest of the food trade generally would have happened anyway, discrimination or not. In the short run, the discriminatory advantage would be too small, and demand elasticity too low, to make even a slight difference. Buying price would have no appreciable effect on resale price, the impact being on the profits of the firm's owners. In the indefinitely long run the effects of discrimination would be very small and swamped by the lower operating costs of the favored firms, which would enforce the same result anyhow, and much sooner.

But in view of Part I of this book, we must enter certain reservations. We saw that A & P's great problem in the 1930's was the inability to cut prices and increase sales and profit. The pressure impinging upon them was loss of existing profits. But as their market position deteriorated, coincidentally their bargaining power increased. As price structures gradually buckled in the depression, A & P, like General Forrest, must have been "fust with the most." Preferences increased in absolute amount, and probably also in discriminatory content. In 1929–1930, allowances in round numbers were nine million dollars, gross discrimination six to seven million, and this represented 15 to 20 per cent of net profit. In 1932, allowances were nearly eleven million, the gross discriminatory content perhaps eight to nine million, or nearly a third of net profit; in 1935, allowances were nearly ten million, gross discrimination perhaps seven million, or well over a third of net profit. These calculations are of the very roughest, of course. Yet surely they sustain the conclusion that as A & P lost its grip, their loss of profits was partly offset and disguised by the increase of discriminatory gains. The pressure on the pocketbook nerve, which should have shaken A & P out of its lethargy, was dulled; the company was anesthetized by the concessions made to it. Hence their realization was delayed for years, and our impression is again confirmed that the Robinson-Patman Act was a blessing in disguise; the loss of profits, and the shock of being discriminated against, was the best kind of cure for the lethargy that ailed them.

If competition be defined as a set of pressures on businessmen — the hope of gain and the fear of loss — toward the most efficient use of resources, then price discrimination in favor of A & P was anticompetitive in effect. Not for the popular reasons but for precisely the contrary reasons. Discrimination in favor of A & P did not result in lower prices but in higher prices; discrimination did not result in A & P driving out competitors but in losing a share of its market. By supporting A & P profits, it blurred the company's vision for the main chance and the big gain.

Hence, if our criterion for public policy is the promotion of competition to increase output and lower prices, then our public policy should largely condemn the discriminations in favor of A & P. Conversely, if our public policy is to be directed toward the "competition" which means having many happy competitors, then discrimination in favor of A & P was desirable because it kept the company from realizing its need and its opportunity, kept it at the old high-price-low-volume position, and allowed competitors to expand their share of the market.

REPORT OF THE RESTRICTIVE TRADE PRACTICES COMMISSION OF CANADA

After this chapter was completed, the Restrictive Trade Practices Commission of Canada issued a report on pricing practices in the grocery trade.[16] It is a careful study worth close reading, but our only interest in it at this point is in comparing its results with those of this chapter.

A questionnaire was sent to 78 manufacturers, of whom 68 returned usable replies. Fifteen firms reported giving no discounts to anyone; most of them sold only to large buyers.[17] Firms selling only to large buyers, considered as a group, i.e., chains and whole-

---

[16] Restrictive Trade Practices Commission. *Report Transmitting a Study of Certain Discriminatory Pricing Practices in the Grocery Trade made by the Director of Investigation and Research.* Department of Justice: Ottawa, 1958. The study was the work of L. A. Skeoch, now of the Department of Economics at Queen's University.

[17] *Report,* p. 95.

salers, and not to single-outlet retail stores, reported few discounts, rather irregularly granted.[18] Firms selling to all classes of dealers, but with minimum shipment requirement, charged less to chains and wholesalers than to others, and chains could "ordinarily . . . get such prices by taking delivery in sufficient quantity." But sometimes wholesalers received lower prices in any case, while sometimes chains received allowances which wholesalers did not. For example, a wholesaler would receive 12 per cent off, and a chain 8 per cent plus 5½ per cent advertising allowance. Which buyer was better off, net, cannot of course be said without knowing what expense the chain undertook. But "in general wholesalers and chains received the same prices."[19]

Firms selling to all classes of dealer, with no minimum shipment requirement, sold largely perishable goods and, unlike the others, had rather complex discount schedules. "The most common practice, however, was the treatment of chains in the same manner as wholesale customers."[20] Quantity discounts were important, e.g. for a carload, or for 100 cases, and were available on the same terms to all: the presumption that these involved lower costs is strengthened by the "risk of deterioration if stored for long periods."[21] Cumulative (volume) discounts were the chief basis for differentiation of price among buyers. Chains sometimes did better than wholesalers, and sometimes less well but "there was no general tendency to place either of these groups in a preferred position."[22]

The Report next considered special discounts and allowances, often but not necessarily for advertising and promotion, granted to thirteen large chains and thirteen large wholesalers. It was very difficult to compile information in a consistent manner, and certain inconsistencies could not be eliminated from the data.[23] Bearing these limitations in mind, "it is clear that there is no regular progression from a high discount rate accruing to chains with the largest purchases to lower discount rates obtained by

[18] *Report*, pp. 98–100.
[19] *Report*, pp. 100–103.
[20] *Report*, p. 104.
[21] *Report*, p. 105.
[22] *Report*, p. 105, summarizing pp. 95–105.
[23] *Report*, pp. 113–125.

chains with smaller purchases"[24] and "there is even less support for this [tendency] in the case of wholesalers than in the case of chains."[25] There is a very weak tendency (which this writer would call not significant statistically) for chains to patronize small suppliers and others, large suppliers.[26] As between discounts granted by "small" or "large" suppliers to "small" or "large" buyers, "it is difficult to trace any consistent pattern in these data."[27] According to returns from about 300 suppliers who gave information in a special questionnaire and whose reported sales were less than half of chain store purchases, discounts to chains as a group averaged 2.10 per cent of sales; to all others, only 0.78 per cent, and to wholesalers, only 0.90 per cent.[28] But the chains, on their total purchases, reported only 0.74 per cent.[29] The discrepancy could not be explained.

Variation in the sales mix (above, p. 230) was explored in a special study of discounts granted to chain stores and wholesalers in the Metropolitan Toronto area, for three fixed assortments of goods. Discounts as per cent of net invoice price were as follows:[30]

Buyers	Every item purchased by every buyer		Not every item purchased by every buyer
	43 items	103 items	221 items
Chains:			
A (second largest)	2.88	1.69	1.67
B	2.21	1.45	1.49
C (largest)	2.55	1.76	1.80
D	2.05	1.06	0.95
E	1.21	—	0.89
Wholesalers:			
AA (smallest)	1.91	1.18	1.67
BB (largest)	2.22	1.33	1.33
CC (middle)	1.85	—	1.27

The order of magnitude of the discounts and allowances, as a

[24] *Report*, p. 125.
[25] *Report*, p. 130.
[26] *Report*, pp. 136–137.
[27] *Report*, p. 138.
[28] *Report*, tables 5–3 through 5–5.
[29] *Report*, table 5–3.
[30] *Report*, pp. 155–159.

per cent of purchases, come quite close to those of the FTC and the record discussed in this and the preceding chapters.

But although one can only admire the research of the report, one must regret one conclusion:

The fact that certain buyers were disadvantaged by the differential treatment would not necessarily mean that it would be criticized from the economic point of view [since] in certain circumstances discriminatory buying terms could be the means of improving economic performance.[31]

It may well be true that in some circumstances discrimination might heighten the competitive tone of a market, and improve its performance; but the evidence of the Report simply does not permit us to reach that question. For it is impossible to say of its data, any more than of much of ours, that they indicate discrimination in the economic sense, i.e., any price differentials over and above cost differentials. The differentials in special allowances permit only two alternative hypotheses: first, that they did no more than make an allowance for lower costs, or for additional services rendered; second, that they had a significant discriminatory element. The second hypothesis can only be supported by an analysis of cost differentials, but the Report contains none. The second hypothesis is also hard to reconcile with the lack of differentials in invoice prices, which serve as an experimental control on other prices. For if there were any market forces making for substantial discrimination, it is difficult to see why they avoided invoice prices, though it is not impossible. Also, if there were discrimination, one would expect to see a relationship of some kind between size and the amount of differential, since the larger buyer will, in general, have the widest alternatives and therefore the most price-responsive demand. But there is no such relation.

Indeed, on the next page the Report considers "the possibility of encouraging price competition through price discrimination that accords closely with costs. . . ."[32] This as much as says it has been considering only differentials, not discrimination in the economic sense. The Report does not clearly consider that differentials according with costs are not merely "justified" or

[31] *Report*, p. 194.
[32] *Report*, p. 155.

"proper" or "fair," or whatever value judgment one wishes to make about them — they are different facts, reflecting a different set of market forces at work, nondiscriminatory rather than discriminatory prices.

About all we can say on this purely factual point is that on a given assortment of goods, the gross advantage of the chains over wholesalers is somewhere in the following area:

	Differential (per cent) on:		
	Every item purchased by every buyer:		
Differential between:	43 items	103 items	All 221 items
Largest chain and largest wholesaler	0.33	0.43	0.47
Average of chains and average of wholesalers	0.19	0.24	minus 0.06

These differentials are of about the same order of magnitude as those which we considered the maximum discrimination in favor of A & P; but as in that case, we cannot say whether, if we could establish cost differentials, there would on balance be any net discrimination. My own conjecture is that there would be.

What emerges clearly from the Report is the immense variety and complexity of the price structures to be found in the food trade. There is no slightest trace here of the know-it-all simplicity of the A & P prosecution and its defenders:

On the whole — if one may judge from the replies received in this survey — the discount structures of many of the major suppliers of grocery products in Canada have been the product of intuitive adjustment at some stage over a period of years rather than of systematic calculation based on profit or cost considerations. This might have been expected, and it does not follow, of course, that they are therefore *necessarily* any the less well adapted to their function. Price-making is not a precision process. At the same time, there is a danger that discount structures will become "traditional" and will continue in force long after the conditions that called them into existence have disappeared. . . . It may be that a careful review of discount structures in the light of changing distribution patterns would be in the best interests not only of a healthy distribution system but, equally to the point, of the supplier, himself.[33]

[33] *Report,* p. 107 (italics in original).

XII

INTEGRATION OF MANUFAC-
TURING WITH WHOLESALING
AND RETAILING

Throughout its recent history A & P has not only bought processed foods, but has manufactured in its own plants a substantial proportion of its requirements. In this chapter we shall look at the manufacturing operation more closely: its investment and profit, the pricing of goods transferred from the plants to the warehouses, the management control of integration, and the effect on buying policy.

Appendix Table 21 is, despite its size, deficient in some important items. What we would most like to know is the percentage of columns (4) and (6), A & P factory output and bakery output, to total purchases of comparable goods. This would exclude meat, flour, dairy products (including eggs), nonfood items, and any other lines where A & P manufacturing was not done or contemplated; and perhaps exclude coffee, where purchased lines were always minor compared with A & P's own. Furthermore, the percentages are of total purchases, not of sales; they cannot be used to estimate percentages of total sales attributable to own-manufacturing because the markups vary so widely. Finally, the table shows on its face the kinds of assumptions used in its calculation; and some and perhaps all may be wrong. Had the trial proceeded in quest of knowledge rather than the reverse, the record might have a few sensible answers to simple questions.

A & P has processed tea since 1859, coffee since 1862, and miscellaneous products since 1885.[1] Large-scale manufacturing prob-

---

[1] U. S. v. A. & P. Civil Action No. 52–139 (S.D.N.Y. 1950), *Answer*, p. 28.

ably dates from 1920, the year when the A & P Products Corporation was formed.[2] (The name was changed to Quaker Maid Company in 1929). But this earlier history is absent from the record. We know nothing about the discussions that must have preceded the new activity, which might be as informative as the discussions about field buying.

By 1925, when the detailed record begins, manufacturing was already one of the major concerns of top management. Before examining the discussions, it may be well to set out briefly their rationale. In principle, the desirability of manufacturing is gauged by observing three rules. First, the goods must be transferred at the current market price, or some defensible approximation to it. For the goods transferred are "worth" what it would cost to obtain them elsewhere, or what could be got for them elsewhere. Second, the profits computed by using this market price must be compared with that of other manufacturers as a test of relative efficiency and the economies of integration. Third, the profits must also be compared with the expected rate of return which could be earned in other activities available to the company. Or, what comes to the same thing, the cost of obtaining the goods through manufacture at home must include the profit that could be obtained from an alternative use of the money, making due allowance for any differences in risk.

In the absence of monopoly power, these three conditions express not only the maximum profit for the integrated concern — the greatest private economy — but also the greatest social economy in the use of resources. As we shall see, the elements of monopoly were not few and unimportant; but they were external to A & P, whose action tended to reduce them.

Transfer prices

As the writer understands the evidence, goods were transferred at market price. This was denied by A & P at the trial, at least for the period before 1934. In that year, corporations were prohibited from filing consolidated income-tax returns. In order to

[2] See the Stipulation, GX 1.

show accurately the income earned by subsidiaries, it was required that prices for intrafirm transactions be equivalent to the result of "arm's-length bargaining," i.e., market price.[3] The contention of A & P that this was a new policy is impossible to accept. First, had the markup over manufacturing cost previously been a mere "arbitrary up-charge," to use one of the defense's favorite expressions, there would have been no point in calculating profits and rates of return, and making close comparisons with other manufacturers and other branches of the company — as was actually done. By setting the price at some arbitrary figure, manufacturing profits can be made to equal any amount whatever, positive or negative; and further study of such "profits" is a waste of time. It is difficult to conceive of intelligent management paying close attention to data which they can change at will. Profits attributable to manufacturing were not merely the company's love of unnecessary arithmetic.

The second reason for rejecting the defense contention is that no documents were produced which authorized any change in practice, and informed responsible A & P personnel of it. It would have been a rather important change. Third, an examination of Table 17 shows no abrupt increase in manufacturing sales or profits as between 1933 and 1934. It is impossible to reconcile this with the company's contention that prior to 1934 billings were at approximate cost.[4] Finally, there is direct evidence in the record itself of billings at market or estimated market prices prior to 1934.[5]

The billing practices of Quaker Maid were orthodox. The usual practice was very well described by the Quaker Maid treasurer, who also pointed to unit freedom of choice as the essential condition:

In establishing our prices, we were guided by what other manufacturers were charging. In other words, if our price on an article was 60 cents per dozen, and we knew that a competitive manufacturer would sell an article

[3] T. E. Ryan, treasurer of Quaker Maid, Tr. 17,338; John D. Ehrgott, controller of A & P, Tr. 1687.

[4] Tr. 17,337–8.

[5] See the *Annual Binder*, vol. 4, pp. 118 and 118-A, DX 489, which refers to May 23, 1929; and the divisional purchasing directors' meeting, October 16, 1929, GX 401.

of comparable quality to ours to our warehouses at 50 cents a dozen, we had no alternative but to bring our price down to that 50 cents a dozen.[6]

For example, canned salmon was sold at the price charged by other canners for comparable products, and was therefore set without regard for the production cost of A & P's subsidiary:

Your cost might be entirely out of proportion to the market at which you could sell it, in which case you would be forced to sell it below cost or you would not sell it.[7]

There is more detailed information on canned milk. In 1929 the standing practice was to maintain a differential of 48 cents per case (wholesale) under standard advertised brands. At a later date, warehouses were sold at a price reckoned with reference to the retail price, which was to be 15 cents per case under the advertised brands, which was the same price as was paid to outside suppliers of unadvertised brands.[8] As prices fluctuated in raw-material and final-goods markets, there might be substantial short-run profits and occasional losses.[9] This was conspicuously true of White House Milk in 1927–1934.[10]

Occasionally Quaker Maid would reduce its prices to a warehouse in order to permit it to sell at the usual retail price for A & P products without violating a state sales-below-cost law. This was a purely formal arrangement, however, because the warehouse receiving this price reduction would have it deducted from the allocation of subsidiary profits.[11]

The ascertainment of an outside price for Quaker Maid to meet involved occasional problems. For example, the Boston unit purchased and forwarded a sample of competitive peanut butter which was being retailed by competitors at a very low price. Quaker Maid asked for a firm quotation by the manufacturer, upon the receipt of which it "would take it under immediate consideration." [12] Apparently this was a typical instance. Ryan testified

[6] Ryan, Tr. 1710.
[7] Ryan, Tr. 1712.
[8] Ryan, Tr. 1708, 1716, 17,341.
[9] Central Western meeting, October 14, 1932, GX 457.
[10] See the reports in the *Annual Binder* for the respective years.
[11] Ryan, Tr. 17,328-9.
[12] J. A. Cunningham to W. A. W. Holcomb, February 20, 1940, GX 478.

If a manufacturer quoted them a price which was lower than the price at which we were billing them for a product of comparable quality, we would meet that price if possible, or in some instances, we would make a reduction in our price, which might or might not be as low as the competitive manufacturer's price.[13]

It is clear that information on competitive prices was not only welcomed but deliberately sought out by Quaker Maid.[14] Yet it is not clear that it automatically and completely met competitive prices. Perhaps, since price fluctuations were frequent and frequently substantial, there was no point in making a change today that would be undone tomorrow; the units could set retail prices on the basis of some expected normal, and the advantages or disadvantages would cancel out. There was also a rule against selling Quaker Maid products at less than manufacturing cost: it is summed up in a penciled memorandum from the treasurer to the assistant treasurer:

We agree with you that Libby is an advertised brand and that our usual practice is to sell at a differential under an advertised brand. But we do not agree that we should follow this practice in this instance because the stores are retailing our Juice at less than our production cost. Retail price $1.92. Production cost $2.01. Our billing price $1.67.[15]

Subsequently the price was raised to equal cost.[16] We cannot say with confidence whether this was a kind of informal averaging, or the usual superstitious prejudice that prices must not be below full cost at any moment; or whether it resulted from the beginning of the Department of Justice investigation which eventually culminated in the trial.[17]

There are only five instances in the record of Quaker Maid products being sold below cost, allegedly in order to meet the prices of competitors.[18] Since the prosecution was avidly in search of such instances, we may safely conclude that if they could not

[13] Ryan, Tr. 17,333–4.
[14] See the penciled comment, Kennard to Miles, on the memorandum, Ryan to Miles, April 8, 1940, GX 34.
[15] Miles to Ryan, January 15, 1941, GX 336.
[16] Ryan, Tr. 17,324.
[17] Miles to Kling, April 1940, GX 339.
[18] In 1937, see GX 332; in 1939, see GX's 364, 3299; in 1941, see GX's 346, 347, 348, 335, 336.

produce any more, there surely were no more. Furthermore, the 1939 sale below cost was on a commodity whose production was being discontinued.

With negligible qualifications, therefore, it can be said that transfer was at market price. When market price went below full cost, there was a definite reluctance to follow it all the way, but it usually was followed.

Investment, profit, rate of return

Table 17 gives the investment, profit, and rate of return for most of the period under consideration. The unadjusted profit of the bakeries includes the retailing profit as well as the manufacturing profit. As an approximation to retail profit, we have multiplied retail sales of bakery goods by the current A & P retail net profit rate for all goods. This has been subtracted from the unadjusted profit to yield an estimate of bakery profits attributable to the manufacturing operation only. There is a possibility that the investment base is too large because it may include part of the warehouses and retail stores as well, but this cannot be checked. In general, the investment is the total of assets committed to manufacturing; it is not a prorated share of company assets or net worth.

Table 18 is in effect a yardstick for Table 17. The difference is impressive. In 1938, the last year of complete data, A & P manufacturing (including baking) earned a profit of $9.0 million on an investment of only $11.6 million. Of course, one year's results can be misleading, but the rate of return of the factories during the depressed 1930's was usually between 40 and 50 per cent per annum; even the adjusted data for the bakeries show them to be considerably higher; profit for 1938 is one and a half times the total investment. Putting aside such years as unrepresentative, and making some allowances for errors and inconsistencies, there is no escaping the conclusion that A & P manufacturing is far more profitable than food manufacturing generally. The A & P management was aware of this as far back as 1925 when Table 19 on the comparison of profitability was compiled by them.

How can the great profitability of the operation be explained?

TABLE 17. Manufacturing Sales, Investment, and Profit, 1924–1941 (amounts in thousands of dollars; rates in per cent)

| | Factories | | | | Bakeries | | | | | |
| | | | | | | | Unadjusted | | Adjusted | |
Year	Invest-ment	Sales	Profit	Rate of return	Invest-ment	Retail Sales	Profit	Rate of return	Profit	Rate of return[a]
1924	3,920	15,200	936	23.89	2,569	9,162	440	17.1	120	4.5
1925	4,662	18,829	1,374	29.48	3,086	15,174	407	13.1	−53	−1.7
1926	4,881	21,840	1,558	31.93	3,288	21,913	1,998	60.8	1,384	42.2
1927	6,174	28,913	1,442	23.36	3,668	29,646	2,585	70.5	1,840	55.8
1928	6,024	35,298	2,158	35.83	4,268	34,627	3,540	82.9	2,539	59.3
1929	7,889	35,011	1,227	15.55	4,698	36,451	3,855	82.0	2,796	59.2
1930	7,681	38,172	1,712	22.30	4,871	38,752	5,464	112.2	4,224	86.8
1931	6,903	41,950	2,779	40.25	4,951	37,824	4,621	93.3	3,391	68.4
1932	6,446	37,577	1,528	23.71	4,859	32,413	3,885	80.0	3,303	67.9
1933	6,346	39,624	2,631	41.47	4,373	34,391	2,942	67.3	1,703	39.1
1934	7,391	45,100	2,997	40.55	4,014	38,126	3,176	79.1	1,956	48.6
1935	7,245	47,757	3,440	47.49	3,681	41,027	3,156	85.7	2,374	64.6
1936	7,530	50,148	3,832	50.88	3,461	42,183	2,784	80.4	1,898	55.0
1937	9,724	46,508	3,199	32.84	3,313	41,793	2,956	89.2	2,538	76.7
1938	8,532	48,617	4,119	48.28	3,035	40,853	5,191	171.1	4,333	142.9
1939	n.a.	56,200	4,668	..	3,315	43,262	n.a.	..		
1940	n.a.	63,546	4,928	..	n.a.	46,975	n.a.	..		
1941	n.a.	88,720	5,863	..	n.a.	55,077	n.a.	..		

Source. DX's 486, 487, 489–495, 500; GX 314 (all *Annual Binders*).

[a] Adjusted bakery profits estimated as follows: bakery sales are multiplied by the retail net profit rate for the year, yielding the estimated retail profit on bakery goods. This is subtracted from the unadjusted profit, and a rate of return calculated on the same investment base.

TABLE 18. Investment and Rate of Return, Nine Food Groups, 1939

Group	Number of companies	Total business investment (millions of dollars)		Rate of return, (per cent)	
		1938	1939	1938	1939
Biscuits and crackers	4	165.3	165.7	11.44	11.47
Bread and bakery products	7	..	140.5	..	8.88
Cereal preparations	8	..	75.0	..	21.78
Confectionery	11	..	117.8	..	23.83
Corn products	5	..	99.4	..	15.15
Food specialties [a]	4	..	155.4	..	19.65
Soap, cottonseed products, cooking fats	10	..	263.5	..	18.42
Soap	5	..	n.a.	..	23.28
Other	5	..	n.a.	..	1.45
Milk and milk products	12	..	361.7	..	10.70
Fruit and vegetable canning	10	..	183.6	..	16.31

Source. Federal Trade Commission, *Industrial Corporation Reports* (1940–1941).

[a] Gelatin, baking powder, tea, coffee, chocolate, salad dressing, frozen foods, etc.

There were no striking technical economies of scale. There is no mention of patented processes; nor of any trade secrets or anything else not available to other competitors, many of them much larger than A & P.

The more important sources of economy must be found on the demand side. The A & P plants run steadily at the most economic level of operations, as near to the equating of marginal revenue

TABLE 19. Comparison of Profitability, 1924

Manufacturer	Average capital tie-up [a] (thousands of dollars)	Per cent rate of return
Average independent [b, c]	2,770	8.1
Beech Nut [c]	10,623	20.6
A & P	2,661	30.7

Source. Computed from tables presented to DPM, February 3, 1926, DX 213.

[a] Total equity plus long and short-term debt, minus intangible assets.

[b] Number of firms not stated.

[c] Weighted by relative importance of product in A & P manufacturing.

and cost as a manufacturing business can come in practice. They sell all their output at the current market price. Goods move steadily into consumption, and there are no inventories (except for those physically necessary) to spoil or be marked down. Above all, there are no selling or advertising costs. A comparison with Chapter 7, Table 9, shows how great an advantage this is. In bakery products, which are the local oligopoly situation par excellence, combined selling-advertising costs were nearly five times the net profit; in cereal preparations, biscuits and crackers, and fruit and vegetable canning, selling-advertising costs at least exceeded net profit. This suffices to explain the showing of the A & P facilities: they avoided much of the cost of transfer between manufacturing and distribution. In part it was a saving on making contact, which is a cost even under pure (but imperfect) competition; in part the profit was the return from A & P advertising, which built up the A & P brands and enabled the retail stores to charge prices nearer or even equivalent to the advertised brands. As we noted earlier, advertising is a fixed expense to a retailer. A & P manufacturing received advertising service, and it received the profits of sales promotion, at no *additional* expense. And to the extent that advertising costs increased the sales prices of purchased goods, A & P manufacturing had an umbrella held over its head.

This kind of saving is an economy of vertical integration in the strictest sense. As such, it cannot be attributed to the manufacturing plants alone. For, had the wholesaling-retailing part of the enterprise disappeared, the cost savings and high manufacturing profits would have disappeared with them. The economies are joint economies; absent either side, they could not exist.

The A & P calculations of manufacturing profits, brought together in Table 17, were calculations of the *incremental* profit, investment, and rate of return. It would have been equally logical to compute the wholesale-retail investment in warehouses and stores, and compute the distributing profit inclusive of savings in distribution costs. A & P management never did so; they could take it for granted that they were in the retailing business. But as we shall see now, they were extremely sensitive to the comparison of additional revenue on additional manufacturing investment versus additional revenue on additional retailing investment.

The comments on Table 17 apply also to Appendix Table 22: manufacturing (and Acco) profits are a marginal not an average return. They measure the increment to total A & P profit from the increment to investment in factories, other things being equal, i.e., taking for granted the wholesale-retail organization, the assured market, advertising, etc. This means that distribution costs are estimated at nearly zero; in other words, the economies of integration are imputed altogether to manufacturing.

The fullest discussion is in the divisional presidents' meeting of June 1925, and it is worth quoting at length:

Mr. Hartford . . . explained the capital tie-up in stores, warehouses, bakeries, factories, etc., and the effect which the outside activities had on the return on the investment.

Charts were displayed showing just how the tie-up in these outside activities affected the return on the investment. It was the consensus of opinion of all present that we should not build warehouses or bakeries in the future unless it was absolutely necessary to do so; the feeling was that we should get outside parties interested in building for us, which would allow us to use our capital in opening up new stores, which would show a greater return and keep our assets in a more liquid form.

It was also the spirit of the Meeting that we should not make further investments in factories or extend our line of products at this time, but to continue with the more important products which we have, [possibly] eliminating some of the minor articles later. In this way the investment per store would continue to be reduced from year to year with the further development of stores.

Mr. Kling, Superintendent of the Brockport Factory, was brought into the Meeting and Mr. Hartford explained to him that the business was growing very rapidly, and it was necessary for us to determine at this time whether or not factories were a good thing for the business and just what effect they would have on the return on the invested capital, in the business. While we are not worrying about the present we must consider conditions five years from now. . . .

Considering all conditions his judgment was that in normal years the Brockport factory would have a return of between 30 and 50% on the investment. This is made possible by the large production and quick turnover. . . .

The opinion of all was that we should continue to establish new Bakeries where conditions warranted the same as Bakeries were of considerable advantage to the business, inasmuch as they gave the opportunity to undersell competition and give the public quality bread. . . .[19]

Later in the year, as already noted in Table 19, the 1924 rate of return of the individual A & P plants was compared with those of independent manufacturers of comparable products, to the advantage of the A & P plants.

Policy on making or buying

Despite the profits on manufacturing as a whole, many particular branches were regarded, in the late 1920's, as not paying their way. Mere apparent profitability was not the criterion. As the 1925 meeting stated it, an additional investment in manufacturing was advisable only if it could earn a *higher* rate of return than in retailing.

Throughout 1925 the constant preoccupation was to stay liquid and reduce the ratio of fixed total assets; for 1926, fixed assets were not to exceed 50 per cent of the additional investment, and A & P was "not to make any further investment in Factory Activities." The factories were considered "a little too aggressive in . . . trying to force the units to take their extra production, regardless of whether or not they wanted it." But, apart from the aggressiveness, there was insufficient contact between the factories and the units.[20] In mid-1926 Kling's recommendation to close down the cocoa and chocolate plant was approved; and he was directed to meet with the sales directors to decide on other goods to be discontinued. The same meeting discussed the buying and operation of A & P's own trucks in typical fashion: "Charts [tables] were displayed showing the returns on our own equipment, the estimated returns if we invested in our own equipment where we now hire trucks, and the returns on the investment of the U. S. Trucking Corporation." In the end, discretion was given to the divisions.[21] Space forbids our doing more than mentioning four other examples of this sharp-penciled calculation: printing

[19] DPM, June 25, 1925, GX 103.
[20] DPM, October 27, 1925, GX 104.
[21] DPM, June 30, 1926, DX 486.

work,[22] advertising,[23] engineering work,[24] and butter procurement.[25]

We may also mention planning of factory locations. Even in January 1927, when the company was de-emphasizing manufacturing, Kling made a comparison of freight saved by proposed new plants in any one of five midwestern locations with overhead saved by increasing output in the old plants.[26] The question was held in abeyance for eighteen months. Then it was decided that since the return on investment (including freight savings) near Chicago was 38 per cent, and the corresponding return in an Eastern extension 35 per cent, the choice was for Chicago.[27]

The manufacturing plants could also be used as a bargaining lever. Curiously enough, the company did not itself see this advantage in making deals with manufacturers, until one of them thrust it upon its attention. Late in 1925, Campbell Soup Company offered to buy the A & P bean and spaghetti plants. John Hartford considered this "most interesting and encouraging, as it gives us a new thought as to the value of the factories." He seemed rather disposed to sell. Others were concerned lest Campbell buy the plants and then raise its prices to A & P, but Hartford seemed to think it might be induced to sign a five-year contract protecting the company. Bofinger and Byrnes were concerned for secrecy on "our policy discontinuing manufacturing," since this would hamper A & P in making favorable deals with manufacturers. But Hartford felt that company manufacturing also had an unfavorable effect: "We could not convince any manufacturer that we would give him our wholehearted support when we were manufactuirng and selling a competing article." The meeting decided to negotiate further, but there is no record of any sale.[28]

Late in 1926 there was a discussion about the "advisability of keeping quiet about our policy regarding discontinuing manu-

[22] DPM, October 27, 1925, GX 104; DPM, January 27, 1927, GX 108.
[23] DPM, October 22, 1920, GX 106.
[24] Memorandum, Van Inwegen to Hartford, DPM, June 30, 1926, GX 249.
[25] DPM, January 27, 1927, GX 108.
[26] DPM, January 27, 1927, GX 108.
[27] DPM, August 16, 1928, GX 114.
[28] DPM, October 27, 1925, GX 104.

facturing." In some cases this would be a help to negotiations with manufacturers; in others, it might weaken the Company's hand.[29]

A little later, Hartford suggested that the A & P gelatin plant might be turned over to the Postum Company, and a larger profit earned by special concessions for support of its product than could be had by private manufacture.[30] Chocolate making had just been discontinued, pursuant to a very good deal with Hershey. The decision was "to discontinue or push the sale of our private brands in order to assist the Purchasing Directors in making our relations with the manufacturers satisfactory to the Company as a whole." [31] A month later, losses in the baked-bean department led to further discussion of the Campbell deal, which was still a live possibility.[32] However, it never came off, and the idea of trading manufacturing for bargains disappeared. As we have already noted, A & P was annoyed by demands for resale price maintenance around this time, and even considered the "very radical" step of manufacturing and selling to the trade generally.

References to bargaining always concern large manufacturers of branded goods. But the discussion died out of the record after 1925–1927.[33] True, the manufacturing plants seem to have become a little more profitable in the early 1930's than the late 1920's, but retailing profits were also at a peak. Yet in 1931 and 1932, years when one would suppose relations with manufacturers to be at their most "satisfactory," there is record of pleasure over increases in sales of Quaker Maid products, at the expense of outside purchases; and mention of "a definite program of supporting the entire Quaker Maid line to [its] fullest extent." [34]

---

[29] DPM, October 21, 1926, GX 106. The language is ambiguous. It could hardly have meant actual liquidation of manufacturing; for at the same meeting Kling received $183,000 for replacement and improvements, and was complimented for his work.

[30] Meeting of divisional sales directors, December 27, 1926, GX 107.

[31] Meeting of divisional purchasing directors, December 27, 1926, GX 438.

[32] DPM, January 26, 1927, GX 108.

[33] At the end of 1928 an A & P rice packing plant was considered and rejected. DPM, December 26, 1928, GX 400.

[34] DPM, June 25, 1931, GX 131; and Central Western meeting of September 15, 1932, GX 387.

As might be expected, the markup provisions of the NRA codes gave some impetus to procuring through Quaker Maid.[35] But the great divide was marked by the Robinson-Patman Act in 1936. We have already seen (above, Chapter IX) how the company responded by deciding to stress private brands, including — but not limited to — own-manufactured. The conversion to super-markets had to take precedence as an immediate task, but in November 1938 the merchandising committee was formed at head-quarters, largely to promote private brands. Its first meeting was held jointly with the divisional sales directors, and the discussion was very important. The chairman (apparently Bofinger) indi-cated its purpose when he pointed out that

because of such recent legislation as the Robinson-Patman Law, costs to us on advertised brands were the same or, very often, higher than to others, amounting to discriminations against us, which is a vastly different picture than that of ten years ago.[36]

This again confirms our impression that the makers of heavily advertised items were the chief beneficiaries of the Robinson-Patman Act. Bofinger had already commented that the shift to supermarkets was concentrating the company's sales in ever fewer stores, and "the greater the concentration . . . the greater the vulnerability of the business." But this only sharpened the real problem:

Price competition on brands which are available to our competitors has levelled off. It is difficult for A & P's supermarkets to meet many of the prices competitors establish on nationally-known brands, and it is always possible for a competitor to undersell A & P on those products. . . .

We must find a way to maintain and increase our sales volume *at a profit*. . . . The answer seems to be found in the active, intensive and vigorous promotion of the brands which A & P controls.

The advantages of such planned promotion are obvious. A & P products are exclusive to A & P stores. Other food retailers cannot sell them at all. Of consequence, they cannot sell them at lower prices than A & P. . . . And, finally, A & P products are the largest single source of profits which A & P has. To increase these profits is our one aim.[37]

[35] Middle Western meeting, May 8, 1934, GX 388.
[36] Joint meeting of merchandising committee and divisional sales directors, November 7, 1938, GX 317.
[37] November 7, 1938, GX 317 (italics in original).

The subsequent discussion included advertising and other promotional means, although "sound and attractive retail prices" were regarded as "a foundation stone." To this end, B. F. Friele of the merchandising committee "would vary manufacturing profits with market and competitive conditions so that the spread be kept as great as possible between ours and outside brands. . . . The Chairman urged cooperation between the organization and the Committee [on] this important matter of subsidiary price structure." [38] This policy was maintained in the last years before the war.[39] A meeting of the same committee, two years later, reviewed the program and urged the divisions to concentrate upon home-manufactured goods.[40] A month later, there was a joint meeting of the New England, Eastern, and Atlantic Divisions, where a Quaker Maid official pointed out:

Generally speaking, every 10 per cent increase in volume [of home manufactures] results in a 20 per cent increase in profit. [This may be observed] either in additional profit distribution, additional funds for advertising, demonstrations, or possible lower prices to the consumer, etc.[41]

The same note was struck in April, both at a meeting of the merchandising committee,[42] and at a Middle Western meeting which Bofinger attended.[43] Bofinger's remark, later in the year, sums up:

We are vitally interested in cutting corners wherever possible . . . and if we thought for a moment it would be advantageous for us to manufacture, we [headquarters] would be the first to advocate entering the field.[44]

The total of sales of the factories and bakeries expanded considerably during the last prewar years. However, they did not expand more than sales in general. The writer finds it hard to believe that the discussion was just so much talk. Most likely the expansion had to be a careful and measured one, because it in-

[38] GX 317.
[39] See DPM, March 27, 1940, GX 218; June 25, 1950, GX 8.
[40] Merchandising committee meeting, December 23, 1940, GX 324.
[41] Joint meeting, New England, Eastern, and Atlantic Divisions, January 29, 1941, GX 327.
[42] April 15, 1941, GX 233.
[43] April 22, 1941, GX 394.
[44] Bofinger to Toolin, August 27, 1941, GX 1370.

volved large fixed investment and basic policy. But the swift increase in national income after 1938, and in the price level of foods during 1941, was unexpected, and hence sales kept pace with the expansion of home produced goods. Furthermore, there was a striking increase in the sale of meat, which A & P has never processed.

What one misses, however, is a rounded discussion of alternative price-making policies. On the one hand, A & P could sell its own brands as close as possible to the prices of the advertised brands, and take the maximum profit per unit sold. Or as Friele urged, it could price lower in the hope of an increase in volume sufficient to return a larger total profit. This kind of policy involved choices in several dimensions over several time periods. Thus, higher prices close to advertised brands necessitated some additional advertising outlay. The other policy, of minimum prices and maximum differentials per unit, had little appeal in the short run, for A & P factories were not burdened with excess capacity; but if the market was sufficiently responsive, there might be large profits in expanding capacity at existing plants or building new ones.

A & P top management, as already seen, was sensitive to these problems, and one would wish for further discussion of them. Unfortunately, this is not to be found after 1941; the record thins out, and in any event A & P has not known a normal year since then. The war came right afterward. In the absence of a lawsuit, manufacturing would have been expected to expand swiftly after World War II. But the Sherman Act prosecution was undertaken in 1944, and the District Court decision came late in 1946. Discussion had already commenced in the Antitrust Division of an equity suit to divorce the manufacturing plants from the warehouses and stores. The decision of the Court of Appeals was rendered in February 1949, and the equity suit duly arrived in September, and was not settled until 1954. It would have been folly to undertake a sizable investment in own-manufacturing before then. And even since then, A & P has had to walk cautiously.[45] What one would expect to find after the war would be

[45] "Tethered Titan: A & P's Manners Turn Mild After Epic Tangle With The Trustbusters," *Wall Street Journal*, December 22, 1958, p. 1.

increasing use of private brands, purchased as well as own-manu-factured, for the discriminations against A & P on list-price items must have worsened after the District Court decision. But there is no information.

Influence on the market

So far we have treated A & P integration as largely a matter of cost comparison and decision: when it was cheaper to make than to buy. We now inquire whether by virtue of its manu-facturing A & P exercised any influence over prices in any market. This inquiry divides naturally into two parts: whether A & P manufacturing was large enough in any market to have any effect on the price there; and whether manufacturing or the threat of manufacturing lowered prices in any buying market.

Share of the market. At the trial, the defense presented some estimates, whose accuracy was not disputed but which cannot be precisely checked, of A & P products as percentages of total national sales in 1937. One group of products, accounting for $8.8 million or 18.9 per cent of manufacturing sales, ranged from fractions of 1 per cent to 11.7 per cent. The following frequency distribution condenses their exhibit (see Table 20).

TABLE 20. Share of National Market, Various A & P Products, 1937

A & P sales as per cent of census sales	Per cent of products included [a]
Less than 1 per cent	6.6
1–4.99 per cent	49.2
5–9.99 per cent	40.8
10 or more per cent (average 11.7 per cent)	3.4

Source. Computed from DX 479, which is based on the *Census of Manufactures,* 1937.
[a] Per cent of the $8.8 million sales accounted for, weighted by sales size.

In salad dressing and related products A & P had a larger per cent of the market; the six types classified ranged from 2.6 to 17.7, with a median figure of 10.3. A & P production of canned salmon was estimated at around 5 or 6 per cent of the Alaskan pack.[46] White House (evaporated) milk in 1932 amounted to 14 per cent of national consumption, but by 1936 it was down to around 10 per cent.[47] However, even this smaller percentage made A & P third among national producers, exceeded only by Carnation and Pet milk.

As for bakery products, the comparison in Table 21 is adapted from one the company thought of great interest.

TABLE 21. Sales by Four National Bread Companies and by A & P, 1935–1941
(millions of dollars)

Bread company	1935	1936	1937	1938	1939	1940	1941
Continental	51.0	58.2	69.5	66.7	63.7	64.2	69.4
General	39.2	42.3	43.2	41.9	39.0	39.3	42.1
Purity	31.5	35.1	39.0	36.5	36.2	37.3	41.4
Ward	32.6	35.6	38.4	34.5	32.2	33.4	36.7
Subtotal	154.3	171.2	190.1	179.6	171.1	174.2	189.6
A & P sales, estimated wholesale value	33.0	34.1	34.0	33.4	36.0	40.1	47.5

Source. Same as preceding table. Wholesale value of A & P baked-goods sales calculated by assigning the current gross profit rate to its retail sales of those goods. There are some objections to using this method, since it tends to inflate the wholesale value when mark-ups are falling. But the alternative would be far worse: comparing competitors' wholesale with A & P's retail sales.

Although A & P's gains were not spectacular, they exceeded those of the national bread companies. Its gains after 1939 were striking. By 1941 it was second among them, and expected eventually to be first.[48]

As for coffee, which has always been a best beloved offspring in A & P, its share of the national market expanded steadily, from 3.8 per cent in 1917 to 16.3 per cent in 1932. Thence it leveled off, fluctuating around 14 and 15 per cent through 1941.[49]

We catch a brief and inadequate glimpse of A & P manufacturing in 1947–1948 in the Answer filed in the civil suit. On a variety of food specialties, Quaker Maid's percentage of total

[46] Ryan, Tr. 17,345.
[47] Annual Binder (1941), p. 67, GX 314.
[48] DPM, April 8, 1941, GX 93.
[49] Annual Binder (1941), GX 314.

industry production ranged from 2.7 per cent to 10.0 per cent, with the median 5.0 per cent (the list is not comparable with the 1937 list). White House Milk was far down, to 5.6 per cent, salmon and coffee were about the same as in 1941.[50]

All of the foregoing except bakery products are sold in national markets, and A & P's share of and influence on the price were too small to be mentioned or discussed in its records, or at the trial. It would be an exaggeration to say that A & P could not affect the price if it tried to do so. Were it to cease purchases of coffee, for example, there is no question that the spot price would immediately decline. But this would serve no purpose except to help its competitors fill their shelves with lower-priced coffee. The power of A & P over buying price is too small to be manipulated in such a way as to give it a lower buying price and a higher selling price for a greater total profit, as in the classic analysis of a buying-selling monopoly.[51] What general reasoning would predict is confirmed by the absence from A & P records of any indication that the company could, or ever tried to, manipulate wholesale coffee prices for its profit. Since coffee was the item where A & P had the largest share of the market, and which it advertised and promoted the most, this conclusion follows *a fortiori* for its other products.

So far, however, we have dealt only with products sold in national markets. But bakery products, especially bread, are sold in local markets. Competitors are few, capacity is often in excess of demand at current prices, the bread is extravagantly "sold," and price-fixing agreements, especially with labor union help, are easily made.[52] Since markets are often intrastate, and

[50] U. S. v. A & P, Civil Action No. 52–139 (S.D.N.Y. 1950), *Answer*, p. 27.

[51] Joan Robinson, *Economics of Imperfect Competition* (London, 1933); William H. Nicholls, *Imperfect Competition within Agricultural Industries* (Ames, 1941), pp. 58–63.

[52] FTC, *Bakery Combines and Profits* (1927), pp. 7, 10, 19, 94; *Competition and Profits in Bread and Flour* (1928), p. 19; *Distribution Methods and Costs*, part I (1944), chapters II and III, especially pp. 25, 30, 36, 45.

Distribution costs were 35 per cent of net sales of biscuits and crackers, 24 per cent of bread sales (of wholesale bakers). See also, for a good study of a Canadian local market, *Bread and Other Bakery Products*, Report of Commissioner, Combines Investigation Act (Department of Justice, Ottawa, 1952). This was the predecessor agency to the present Restrictive Trade Practices Commission, whose study of price structure was discussed in Chapter XI.

there is less of the glare of publicity that plays upon large business concerns, overt or tacit collusion is easier to practice. The result is a large gap, not only between price and incremental cost, but between price and total manufacturing cost, and (when agreements flourish) between price and total cost. The situation is made to order for A & P or any other integrated firm or contractual arrangement. Either they can meet the local price level, staying only a little lower, and earn a very high profit per unit; or they can set some low markup over manufacturing cost, drastically underselling the local bakers and hoping to earn a larger total profit on a higher volume. This problem of choice is found wherever the cost-price gap exists; and A & P's case is further complicated by the possibility of securing lower discriminatory prices from the bakers.

Since the problem is so important, it is unfortunate that little evidence is in the record to shed light on it. There is no discussion anywhere, so far as the writer knows, of any general price policy on baked goods, particularly bread. There are two examples of discriminatory low prices secured from local bakers (see Appendix IV), but they do not suffice to prove anything.

As a *manufacturer,* then, A & P acted like a small processor of trading items, paying no attention to any minute influence it might have on the price. But it was also a *retailer* of those products. Within each market, for each type of product, A & P faced the typical problems of a differentiated seller. The price of its private label goods, both purchased and own-manufactured, was set with reference to the advertised goods. For any given set of prices on advertised items, A & P faced the problem of deciding how much lower to price on private labels in order to maximize its profits on them. There existed the further problem of promoting and advertising its own labels in order to narrow that differential. The process is one of piecemeal adjustments, and in the nature of the industry it never ceases. But the Robinson-Patman Act gave the sellers of advertised and branded goods so great an advantage that some major changes in policy needed to be considered.

Bargaining as influenced by own-manufacturing. In general one would expect that A & P would be unwilling to pay a price higher than the sum of its own manufacturing cost plus return obtainable elsewhere on the necessary investment. Hence the possession of its own manufacturing plants would be expected to have some influence on the prices it paid. Judged by the quantity and quality of evidence in the A & P record, this influence is real but not important. We have already seen how possession of factories influenced bargaining with large manufacturers in the 1920's; but that line of evidence dies out after 1927. The Robinson-Patman Act stimulated interest into own-manufacturing because of the disadvantage in dealing with large producers of advertised brands. Yet we know of no attempt to threaten manufacturing or private-label procurement in dealing with the large canners. If attempted, it certainly was a flat failure as far as Stokely, Libby, and Del Monte were concerned; and there is no record of success elsewhere.

When the company was attempting to promote direct selling (by-passing of brokers), one obstacle which it encountered was the fear of some canners of adopting a method of distribution and then being compelled to revert to that old one, with all the costs and dangers involved.

In January 1940, Sumner S. Kittelle, the company's attorney, and Anthony W. Vogt, its Midwestern buyer, interviewed a large number of processors in Vogt's territory, desiring to find out their attitudes toward selling exclusively direct (above, Chapter IX). One packer, who had formerly been an official of Standard Brands, and whose opinion Kittelle obviously respected,

said the greatest fears of most packers in going over to a strictly direct-selling basis [are] that they will put all their eggs in A & P's basket and then A & P will set up its own manufacturing plants. . . . A & P should come out with a definite statement of policy . . . that if it decides to open its own plants, it will give packers a reasonable time to adjust themselves.[53]

If we may turn the proposition around: A & P's bargaining power toward such manufacturers consisted in the cost of changing distribution outlets. Over the long run, this cost approached zero; in the short run it was significant.

There is only one instance in the record of the threat of manu-

[53] Kittelle to Bofinger, January 27, 1940, GX 1623.

facture actually bringing A & P a lower price; and there is another instance where the hope of a lower price might at least be said to have had some influence in having a product manufactured for it. Both instances are worth a brief glance.

Ralston-Purina. We have already seen how A & P bought the advertised products of this firm without any discount, discriminatory or not. However, the Ralston manufacture of corn flakes was 90 per cent for private label, and upwards of 60 per cent to A & P alone.[54] During the late 1930's there were only three manufacturers of corn flakes for private label; and probably no more than about a dozen customers,[55] so that the market was one of tight bilateral oligopoly. The private label corn flakes were always sold at a differential under the advertised brands.[56] Unquestionably General Foods and Kellogg's considered the private brands a nuisance or worse to their advertised brands. At the beginning of 1938 they reduced prices and Ralston followed immediately on the unbranded goods, wiring the A & P buyer:

Now it is up to distributors to fight harder than ever to hold business. Otherwise you will play into other fellow's hands, *who will get you out of picture and then quietly raise price.* . . .

Now instead of futile arguing between ourselves, let's push together and lick this threat to private label.[57]

Whether Kellogg's and General Foods ever actually engaged in such predatory conduct, we do not know. But by 1945 each of them had bought up one of the two other private label corn-flake plants, thus putting an end to the annoyance.[58]

This takes us ahead of the story, however. The Ralston private label corn-flake plant was a consistent money-maker, even when other divisions of Ralston were not.[59] In other words, they were much like the A & P plants; their savings on advertising and selling costs more than compensated for the lower price they had

[54] C. A. Renard of Ralston-Purina, Tr. 570.

[55] Renard, Tr. 5798; 5701–2; 5802. Renard mentioned National Tea, First National, Red & White, and said that there were others.

[56] Renard, Tr. 5806, 5806–8, 5828.

[57] Telegram, D. A. Danforth to Frank H. Tully (Milwaukee buying office), January, 1938, DX 34 (italics added).

[58] Renard, Tr. 2798–99.

[59] Renard, Tr. 2802.

to accept for their unbranded goods. In 1937 plant capacity was approximately tripled.[60] The move drew the attention of J. F. Tully, of A & P's Milwaukee buying staff, who thought the business was well worth entering. Assuming a midyear investment of about $900 thousand, and a full twelve-month profit of $196 thousand, this would indicate a slightly better than 20 per cent return to Ralston. Under the circumstances, the discount to A & P was considered insufficient; it was hardly any larger than that granted to customers who took not one fifth of A & P volume. Tully went on to revive the suggestion made by John Hartford a decade earlier: to manufacture and sell corn flakes under some name other than A & P, or Quaker Maid, "so that it would not indicate the Tea Company is the manufacturer of merchandise offered for resale to others." [61]

While negotiations were beginning, Quaker Maid undertook a study of the cost of manufacturing corn flakes in an annex to an existing plant at Terre Haute, Indiana. The report was finished at the end of April 1938, and its conclusions were striking. A & P could fill its requirements by an investment of $175 thousand; and, if it charged the warehouses the price paid to Ralston, the annual manufacturing profit would be 68 per cent on the investment. Moreover, if the saving in general plant overhead spread over the new facilities were to be reckoned, then the return (marginal revenue) on the new investment would be 73 per cent.[62]

Ralston seemed to be vulnerable; loss of the A & P account might have meant a loss on the Battle Creek plant; in fact, it might have been necessary to change over to some other products.[63] Yet it was fully twenty-one months later, when Tully rather belatedly offered to let Ralston look at the cost accounting estimates, that it agreed even in principle. During the next seven months the negotiations were largely about the form of the contract. A & P wished to have a "cost savings" agreement, with the

---

[60] Renard, Tr. 5725, gives the following value for the plant and equipment account of the Battle Creek plant (in thousands): 1936, 440.2; 1937, 1491.2. The increase is 239 per cent.

[61] Tully to Parr, October 6, 1937, GX 1626.

[62] C. W. Westrup to J. F. Gismond (Quaker Maid headquarters), April 28, 1938, DX 705. The report itself is an enclosure, marked as DX 706.

[63] Renard, Tr. 5727.

usual statements about the manufacturers' savings on selling to A & P, and the availability of similar discounts to other customers. Ralston would have preferred to have the contract state, among other things:

WHEREAS, the Purchaser . . . , indicating that it could advantageously manufacture its own flakes, . . . has declared its intention to do so unless it is adequately compensated for its forbearance; . . .[64]

The final agreement provided for a discount to A & P of 17½ cents per case, which came to about 9½ per cent;[65] A & P had originally demanded 21 cents, or about 11½ per cent.[66]

The contract was signed in January 1940. Two years later Ralston cancelled it. "This action is taken with sincere regret, but is necessary in view of today's costs."[67] However, a recent price increase by Kellogg and General Foods probably had more to do with it[68] — not to mention the impossibility of A & P's building a plant during the war. But the company had the last laugh. The Office of Price Administration ruled that the price of the flakes was net of discount, whose cancelation would amount to an increase illegal under the General Maximum Price Regulation. The discount therefore continued throughout the war.[69]

Shortening. The other case which is in the record of bargaining through A & P manufacture or private label was much less successful for the company. In mid-1939 the decision was reached to have shortening made for A & P, to sell for 5 cents a pound (about 25 to 30 per cent) under Procter & Gamble's Crisco and Lever Brothers' Spry, which were price-fixed by the manufacturers.[70] In August Mylott of A & P attempted to obtain a larger discount for carload orders, and was turned down by both of them, although a carload discount appears to reflect an obvious cost difference. Mylott was not too chagrined, writing to Mac-Keachie of the New England buying staff:

[64] Draft of contract prepared by Ralston, GX 1632. The A & P draft is GX 1635 and 1635-A.
[65] GX 1639 and GX 1640-A.
[66] Renard, Tr. 5733.
[67] Letter dated January 30, 1942, GX 1646.
[68] Renard, Tr. 5809.
[69] Renard, Tr. 5792.
[70] Mylott to Churchill, July 13, 1939, GX 2531.

Bear in mind that . . . when we go into the private brand shortening business, we believe that our retail will be very attractive when compared with the price on Crisco or Spry, and for that reason we think we shall be able to secure many more concessions than we can under our present set-up. Therefore . . . do not . . . push them too hard at this time.[71]

By the end of October an arrangement had been completed for Durkee's Famous Foods to manufacture "Dexo" on a cost-plus basis.[72] Unfortunately, the price of cottonseed crude oil promptly rose, and Dexo had to compete with branded products whose prices reflected the previous crude prices, for the National Meat Department of A & P was not permitted to run a loss on it. With the retail price differential thus narrowed, Dexo was off to a rather poor start. At the end of January, 1940, P & G and Lever reduced their prices. "Of course it is quite obvious the reason," an A & P official said. A & P was unable to follow, although the differential was still fairly good. By July the retail stores were sent photographs showing them how to feature Dexo with other shortenings in such a way as to emphasize the price difference;

[71] Mylott to MacKeachie, August 23, 1939, GX 2532.
[72] T. E. Skaggs of the A & P National Meat Department to Durkee, October 25, 1939, GX 2533. The following account is based on the GX's cited in this footnote. It would be impracticable to cite each of them in place. They are all letters originating in, or addressed to, the National Meat Department.

GX	Date
2534–2537	December 7, 1939; January 8, 30, 1940; February 2, 1940
2542-A	July 15, 1940
2543–2545	August 12, 21 and 21, 1940
2548-A	Chart, November, 1939, to October, 1940
2549–2551	January 20, 22, 1941; March 11, 1941
2557	March 12, 1941
2568	July 2, 1941
2581	August 1, 1941
2583	August 7, 1941
2585	August 7, 1941
2587–2588	August 15, 17, 1941
2596–2597	October 9, 1941
2604	October 27, 1941
2605	November 21, 1941
2606	October 14, 1941

In the correspondence the product is always spelled *dexo*. It seems less confusing to spell it *Dexo*.

they were also warned that where they ran Spry or Crisco advertising in accordance with an agreement for allowances, they were to avoid brightly colored language.

Late in August crude oil prices fell sharply, and it was hoped to give Dexo some intensive promotion. But then the prices of Crisco and Spry were again cut. By the end of October, a year of operations was summed up in a chart which showed that despite bargain offers by Lever and P & G, Dexo had gained ground and was now A & P's leading brand. It had absorbed the increase in shortening sales as a whole, and had to some extent displaced Crisco and Spry. By January 1941, when the branded shortenings were raised in price, a modest profit had been accumulated on Dexo. By early March of 1941, the relative prices were fairly well established, but they were not nearly as favorable as had been hoped. The price of Dexo to the warehouse was 9.6 per cent lower on one-pound cans, and 14.1 per cent lower on three-pound cans. However, this was after the addition of one per cent which the National Meat Department has accumulated as a "kitty" for future price wars. By midyear, Dexo was again caught in the squeeze of rising crude prices and rigid branded prices, and the "kitty" had been turned into a deficit. "The manufacturers are obviously willing to use this temporary situation to embarrass and possibly eliminate such private label shortenings as Dexo." Not only was the price held but in August Crisco and Spry were offered at large allowances under very generous terms as to performance, and Dexo was actually being undersold! "It is difficult for us to understand how Procter & Gamble and Lever Brothers can come out with price deals of this kind."

By October the hoped-for price rise in Spry and Crisco was still like the hoped-for breeze in summer. Accordingly, Durkee was approached "to contribute something toward meeting this situation. . . . In view of the fact that we are getting Dexo exclusively from Durkee, it was as much their affair as it was ours." It was strangely difficult to locate the appropriate Durkee official: in New York he was always to be found in Chicago, and vice versa. But by the end of the month there was a reduction of approximately 10 per cent to A & P warehouses. And there, at the end of 1941, we are forced to let the matter rest.

Conclusion

Integration into manufacturing was highly profitable for A & P.[73] The management of the company seems to have been at all times in complete control of the operation, as they were not in control of sales policy during 1929–1937. Their approach to it was a model of economic — that is, profit-maximizing — conduct, subject to constraints of capital budgeting, liquidity, and growth of the retailing end of the business which at times promised a larger if indefinite return in the longer run.

The profits of the company were earned by eliminating many costs of transfer from manufacturing to distribution, i.e., they were a saving of integration, not to be imputed to distribution alone or to manufacturing alone, any more than the child can be imputed to the father or mother alone. Since these economies of integration were not offset by diseconomies elsewhere, they were a social as well as a private gain. The war and the antitrust litigation probably kept manufacturing at a lower level than business (and social) advantage would dictate.

The possibility of entry into manufacturing allowed A & P an additional alternative to buying from food processors; and the company was able to exploit this threat several times during the 1920's, and once during the 1930's, so far as the facts show. Manufacturing, as well as purchase, of private-label goods, was a natural response of avoidance of the discrimination imposed against A & P by the Robinson-Patman Act.

[73] The notion that the validity of the high profit figures is suspect because A & P manufacturing did not expand is theoretically wrong, and in addition it cannot be reconciled with the facts of record. The profit figures were compiled for comparison with outside firms and alternative opportunities, and were repeatedly used and discussed. Meaningless profit figures cannot be reconciled with the intelligence of A & P management, and the careful consideration they gave the data. The high rates of incremental return on the existing investment do not indicate that additional investment would have drawn an equal rate; still less, that the rate would have been equal to that available in retailing. Finally, the war prevented expansion, and the legal status of own-manufacturing has never been clear.

XIII

THE ATLANTIC COMMISSION
COMPANY (ACCO)

The markets

THE Atlantic Commission Company (Acco), incorporated by
A & P in 1926, operated as the buyer of fresh fruits and vegetables
for A & P warehouses and (until April 1949) as a broker selling to
the trade. The markets in which Acco operated were very similar
to those in which the field buying offices bought trading items;
indeed, there was some slight overlapping of functions. But
produce (which we will use as a one-word equivalent for "fresh
fruits and vegetables") is a special kind of trading item. Competition is very keen, and more nearly approaches purity in the
sense that no buyer or seller has any large share of the market.
Acco purchases were 8 per cent to 10 per cent of the national total
during 1939–1942, and had probably changed little in the preceding decade.[1] In the great terminal markets at the consuming
centers, Acco's share would normally be expected (since there
is much reshipment to surrounding or even distant areas) to be
somewhat lower than A & P's share of the *local* consumption of
produce, which would be of the order of magnitude of 10 to 15
per cent.[2] However, for reasons to be explored later, the various
terminal markets are fed by overlapping tributary areas, so that
the apparent precision of market share would be misleading, and

[1] See DX 557-A, a compilation from official data, principally "Agricultural
Statistics." Acco shipments ranged between 8.2 per cent and 9.7 per cent, the
median being 9.2 per cent. Its share fell to 7.0 per cent in 1943, but this was a
wartime distortion.

[2] See Appendix Table 15 for the respective market shares by divisions and
units.

also exaggerated. Another way to analyze the market is by principal products. During the year ending February 29, 1936, Acco's share of the national output of ten important fruits and vegetables varied between 3.01 per cent and 7.46 per cent; the median was 5.24 per cent.[3]

But if competition is close to being pure in the produce markets, the market itself is very imperfect, because of the extreme perishability of the product. At any given instant, for any particular transaction, the alternatives of any particular buyer or seller may be limited. True, there is nobody and nothing to stop him from looking over the whole market for the best bargain — except that long before he has seen even a large fraction of all possible bargains, the produce has all been sold and he must be off at other tasks.

Over time, however, the buyer or seller does have freedom to range over the market and find the consistently better sources or outlets. This is a process of statistical averaging of better and worse bargains; of arbitrage bringing the higher and lower prices closer together. Once we speak of statistical averaging, the law of large numbers is involved, and the advantage to the large operator starts to become apparent; arbitrage, as we saw earlier, is A & P's forte.

Let us look first at the terminal markets in the large consuming centers where prices are actually determined and reflected back to the field. Much the largest and most important is the one contained in twelve blocks along the narrow canyon of Washington Street, on the lower west side of Manhattan in New York. The market and most of the present buildings were operating long before the Civil War.[4] Forty and more years ago, they were viewed as gravely inadequate, and in 1953, the Legislature of the State of New York held hearings to establish the same unsurprising fact.[5]

[3] FTC, *Report on Agricultural Income Inquiry,* Part III (Washington, 1938), p. 149.
[4] The Faneuil Market in Boston is over two hundred years old.
[5] See "High Produce Prices Here Linked to Outmoded Washington Market," *New York Times,* August 4, 1953, p. 23; and State of New York, Legislative Document No. 24 (1954). . . . *Report on . . . Washington St. Produce Market . . .*—hereafter cited as New York State *Report.*

The New York market is important to growers far and wide, not only because of the volume of their products that is actually handled but also because of its influence on price elsewhere. It has often been called the price-making market of the country.[6]

Produce pours into this market from a number of unloading points widely separated not by miles but by cost: the trucking effort and money expenditure needed to breast the swirling tides of Manhattan traffic and endure the choking congestion of the narrow streets.[7] There is little in a 1919 FTC study which need be changed today, except to change the word "wagons" to "trucks" and to use even stronger language of amazement, disgust, and despair.

This scatter of sources makes it all the more necessary to have some central location for which the shipments are all bound; but a buyer is always torn between the desire to "visit these many places to learn the comparative quality and prices of offerings" [8] before they come into the center, or to stay at the center and be sure of retaining some general view of available alternatives. By going nearer the source, the buyer may get the better bargains, but he may also miss out altogether.

With increasing emphasis on quality and appearance, which depend mainly on freshness, more and more buyers have come into the market and must spend more time at the central location.[9] Buyers large and small must physically go to market. Only small percentages of sales are made by telephone or by any method except that of personal inspection. There is so much variability, both in the products themselves and in the supply, that daily comparison of quality and determination of price are essential.[10]

[6] U. S. Department of Agriculture, *The Wholesale Fruit and Vegetable Markets of New York City* (Washington, 1940), p. 1. This excellent study is, unfortunately, still up to date, as the New York State *Report* indicates. See also the U.S.D.A. Marketing Research Report No. 201, *Wholesale Food Distribution Facilities for Philadelphia* (Washington, 1958).

[7] See above, note 6, particularly the first-named publication, pp. 19, 48, 56. See also FTC, *Report on the Wholesale Marketing of Food* (Washington, 1919), pp. 145–149.

[8] U.S.D.A., *The Wholesale Fruit and Vegetable Markets of New York City*, p. 19.

[9] *The Wholesale Fruit and Vegetable Markets of New York City*, p. 21.

[10] *The Wholesale Fruit and Vegetable Markets of New York City*, p. 32.

The very small buyers, to be sure, do not go to Washington Street, but purchase from secondary distributors closer to home. But in 1938–1939, no fewer than 60 per cent of a representative sample of New York City retailers purchased at least part of their supplies directly from that source:

There he can find the greatest variety of daily offerings — not only variety of products, but for any one product a great variation in size, quality, and condition, with corresponding price differentials. It is not enough that a market have a full line of products to offer — buyers also wish to have a selection of these other factors.[11]

Furthermore, supplies do not arrive at the same rate that they move into consumption. Hence inventories must willy-nilly come into existence and influence prices according to their perishability and according to expectations of future arrivals and their effects upon price. But this kind of information, for reasons already explained, is difficult to gather and evaluate. Hence there must be wide differences of opinion:

Lack of complete and accurate information results in wide price variations and fluctuations. . . . If sellers and buyers have incomplete or inaccurate knowledge regarding supply and demand, they are hampered in arriving at a price that will hold throughout the sale period.

It is difficult for either sellers or buyers to gain definite information regarding the quantity and quality of perishables available in these several locations. . . . There also exists a similar lack of information regarding the combined needs, desires, and activities of all buyers, which represents the other side of the supply-demand equation. . . . This lack of market information, due in large part to the scattering of supplies and demand . . . results in wide variations in price during a single trading period, leading to difficulties and dissatisfaction for shippers, dealers, and buyers.[12]

This dissatisfaction is tempered, as the Federal Trade Commission noted 40 years ago, by the realization that "all are laboring under the same general expenses and lack of facilities . . . [and] such additional costs, as well as losses and wastes which are proportionally equal, are passed on to the retailers and by them to the consumers, in the cost of the goods. They know that

[11] *The Wholesale Fruit and Vegetable Markets of New York City*, p. 36.
[12] *The Wholesale Fruit and Vegetable Markets of New York City*, pp. 51–52; see also the New York State *Report*, pp. 29–30.

all other dealers are under similar handicaps." They have no alternative but to stay and endure it. To leave the district "would indeed be business suicide in most cases."[13]

The picture is complete of distributive wastes reflected in high margins, and prices. But the higher the costs, the greater the incentive to reduce or avoid them. Within the market, a large firm employing many buyers must in any case spot them throughout the market. At no additional cost, the firm resolves the dilemma between going to the sources and staying at the center, for it is in both places. Furthermore, Acco also has a large force in the field, near growing centers, thus redoubling the advantage. Frank J. Boyce, Acco vice-president for the New York area, testified

We base our prices upon what market conditions are, what the shipments have been, what the track holdings are in the principal markets, what the weather conditions are in shipping points and competitive shipping points, and also the same information relative to competitive items, competitive commodities.[14]

Much information, to be sure, is publicly available through the local offices of the Department of Agriculture. But helpful as it is, it falls far short of what the buyer needs. As the Department's own study indicates, only the general contour of the market is known to all. Mr. Boyce's information, as none seem to disagree, is better, faster, and more detailed. For example, the Acco office at Chicago, the largest railroad center, issues a "rolling broadcast" every morning; they call 15 to 20 distributors, find out what they have for sale, and notify all other offices by teletype.[15] As mentioned earlier, it is the differential advantage in which business men are interested. A busy and harassed buyer or seller trying at the same time to examine produce, get his trucks through the snarled traffic, and balance in his head the information on price and supply, can hardly be expected to do as well over time as the Acco organization.

Another source of superior knowledge is on the demand side. Acco's forecasts are based on all the A & P stores in the territory, for which it makes estimates three weeks in advance.[16] Again the

[13] FTC, *Report on the Wholesale Marketing of Food*, p. 147.
[14] Tr. 18,026.
[15] Doherty, Chicago manager, Tr. 18,035.
[16] Baum, Tr. 19,420.

law of large numbers comes into play, as errors are mutually offset, and an overstocked store or warehouse can call on an understocked one. Furthermore, at any particular terminal market, a price higher than elsewhere serves as a flag to attract produce which is rolling eastward and can be diverted. A buyer who keeps only a one-day supply on hand for his retail store(s) may be forced to pay the higher price if he anticipates no relief within 24 hours; but if he has the information which Boyce listed, and can act upon it, he may not have his hand forced, and will be able to buy later at a lower price when the additional shipments come in.

This ability to ride even a little better than average on price swings is of very great importance. The USDA report mentions the very wide price fluctuations. During 1941, for example, average wholesale value per Acco carload was about $720.[17] Yet a large Chicago produce dealer testified that the fluctuation in a particular commodity *on a given day* in a given market might be as much as $300 per carload! [18]

Thus, even staying within the terminal market organization and its tributaries in the field, a large buyer can in the course of a day pay a lower daily average price for its goods even if it is at any given moment paying as much as, or even more than, its neighbor.

An additional economy of scale is available to buyers whose needs over a very short period are at least as great as the minimum unit of shipment — a carload or truckload. They can by-pass the terminal market by taking direct shipment from the field to an outlying distribution point or even directly to a warehouse. Table 22 gives some indication of the cost structure and the possible economies. The savings are remarkable, although the writer would urge great reserve in accepting them as precise. For one thing, Acco is not a disinterested source of information. Second, the saving is of the order of 75 per cent; a rough estimate based on the USDA study is of the order of only 50 per cent.[19] Never-

[17] See Table 23. In 1941, Acco handled 142,372 cars, and its sales were $103,503,000. (*Annual Binder*, 1941, GX 314).

[18] L. F. Gillarde, Tr. 8003.

[19] *The Wholesale Fruit and Vegetable Markets of New York City*, table 11, p. 46.

TABLE 22. Terminal Costs of Fresh Fruit and Vegetables, New York City, 1938–1939 (dollars per carload)

Expense	Total movement May 1938–April 1939		California oranges to Jersey City, N.J.			
			Wholesale channels		Acco	
Margins	73.10[a]		58.00[b]		24.00	
Cartage and porterage at terminal	35.80		20.00		none	
Total terminal costs		108.90		78.00		24.00
Cartage to retail outlets	54.25		32.00		15.48	
Margins	40.40		75.00		8.40	
Total costs		203.55		185.00		48.08
Total margins	113.50		133.00			32.40

Sources. Column 1 computed from tables 10 and 15 in U.S.D.A., *The Wholesale Fruit and Vegetable Markets of New York City* (Washington, 1940). (We have excluded costs borne by railroads, and costs imputed to inadequate facilities and lost time.) The total number of carloads handled was 154,367. Columns 2 and 3 computed from GX 2319.

[a] Brokerage and auction charge.
[b] Includes O.C. charge, mostly a racket surcharge.

theless, even the smaller figure is very impressive, and explains why A & P's example has been widely imitated since the end of World War II.[20]

Also impressive are the large distributors' margins both at the terminal and at secondary distribution points. This is of course painfully familiar, but the writer has no intention of swelling the chorus about "superfluous middlemen." The middlemen are not superfluous. So long as markets function in their present form, physical movement is slow and expensive, and the making of contact even slower and more expensive. The "contactual function" is a genuine cost of marketing, and as this fragment confirms, the largest single element in the total marketing cost.[21]

Tables 23 and 24 compare the gross margins of a sample of wholesale distributors with that of Acco for the year 1941. As might be expected, the latter's margin is much lower. But one

[20] New York State *Report,* pp. 40ff.
[21] Edmund McGarry, "The Contactual Function in Marketing," *Journal of Business of the University of Chicago,* 24:99 (1951).

TABLE 23. Acco Sales, Expenses, and Margins, 1941

	In thousands of dollars	Per cent
Sales	103,503.2	100.00
Cost of goods sold	99,609.9	96.25
Gross margin	3,893.3	3.75
Other income (brokerage to trade)	411.1	0.40
Total gross income	4,304.4	4.16
Expenses	2,440.7	2.36
Net profit	1,863.7	1.80

Source. GX 3597. Detail does not always add to total, because of rounding.

cannot make a simple comparison of margins as a test of relative efficiency. The most nearly comparable group are perhaps the "primary receivers," who buy in large amounts; but Acco's functions include that of all three groups. The larger the volume of sales, the more do large-bulk transactions predominate, and the smaller the gross margin. The fourteen firms in the largest size-group, whose sales averaged $3.0 million, had a margin of 6.5 per cent; Acco, with sales of $103.5 million, worked on a margin of 3.8 or 4.2 per cent, depending on the inclusion or exclusion of brokerage income. There can be little doubt that the unit warehouses absorbed some of Acco's jobber functions. When some allowance is made for this, the margin is still impressively small. Also important is that a larger proportion of Acco's gross was retained as net profit. Its superior efficiency is scarcely in dispute.[22]

The organization

The key figure is the manager at the terminal market — for example, Boyce at New York. He buys about 20 to 25 per cent of his requirements directly by spot purchase or auction purchase in the terminal city; the rest comes from field buyers, who report to him.[23] His position is strategic because he must ascertain the

[22] See A. C. Hoffman, *Large Scale Organization in the Food Industries*, TNEC Monograph No. 35 (Washington, 1941), p. 68.
[23] Boyce, Tr. 18,026–7.

TABLE 24. Fresh Fruit and Vegetable Wholesale Distributors: Gross Margin by Size of Firm, 1941

Size of business (sales in thousands of dollars)	Primary receivers [a]			Secondary jobbers [b]			Full service wholesalers [c]		
	Number of companies	Average sales (thousands of dollars)	Gross margin	Number of cos.	Average sales (thousands of dollars)	Gross margin	Number of cos.	Average sales (thousands of dollars)	Gross margin
Less than 250	12	133	10.6	58	122	12.1	19	178	12.6
250–499	16	338	9.9	25	344	12.2	33	358	12.8
500–999	19	751	9.7	25	720	9.5	35	746	13.5
1,000–1,999	21	1,415	6.9	} 6	} 1,715	} 11.1	27	1,453	12.3
2,000 and over	14	3,040	6.5				10	3,470	7.5
Total	82	1,138	7.4	114	394	10.8	124	939	11.2

Sales Volume, Gross Margin, and Net Profit, 31 Companies, 1941, 1943, 1944

Distributor	Number of companies	Sales (millions of dollars)			Gross margin			Profits (incl. salaries)		
		1941	1943	1944	1941	1943	1944	1941	1943	1944
Primary receivers [a]	9	13.3	24.9	25.4	7.1	7.9	7.3	2.0	4.1	3.2
Secondary jobbers [b]	5	3.8	6.4	5.7	8.9	7.3	8.1	2.5	2.5	2.6
Full service wholesalers [c]	17	15.9	30.2	30.2	13.4	12.2	12.3	2.5	4.5	3.9
Total	31	33.0	61.5	61.3	10.3	10.0	9.8	2.2	4.1	3.5

Source. OPA Economic Data Series No. 12, *Survey of Fresh Fruit and Vegetable Wholesale Distributors* (Washington, May 1947), tables 4, 5, 6, 7.

[a] Less than 50 per cent of sales to retailers.
[b] More than 50 per cent of sales to retailers, less than 50 per cent of purchases in carlots.
[c] More than 50 per cent of sales to retailers, more than 50 per cent of purchases in carlots.

needs of the retail stores, judge all the buying markets, and decide what, how, and when to buy. For reasons already stated, there is greater safety in buying at the terminal markets: the products are highly perishable, must travel long distances to market, and price fluctuations may turn profits into large losses. Yet on a long-run basis, the risk is more than compensated, and Acco's advantage is greatest, if it buys at shipping points, and especially in the unstable commodities.[24] This was explicitly recognized in 1939 by accounting reforms designed to relieve the terminal manager of some of the responsibility of running a paper "loss," and thus make him more aggressive.[25] This weakened him somewhat as against subordinates in the field, who could thereby make paper profits; they did not benefit personally, but it made their performance look better. Thus, on purchases of lettuce in 1940:

Some of the boys insist upon chiseling. The latest case is one where they presumably buy, when the market looks good [i.e., likely to rise] f.o.b. shipping point . . . and take advantage of the market advance and make two to three hundred dollars on the car and sell it to the Tea Co.[26]

But the letter also makes it clear that such instances were relatively few. This was also the opinion of Harvey A. Baum, Acco general manager.[27] We may conclude that Acco was not seriously afflicted with what was called "localitis" in the U.S. armed forces in World War II.

As already stated, the field offices (not to be confused with field buying offices for processed goods) do about three fourths of the buying. In August 1939, Acco had about a hundred buying offices in the East, South, and Mid-West;[28] presumably they had about half as many in the Pacific Coast area. At harvest time,

[24] Henry A. Wehman, Acco vice-president, Tr. 18,499–500; and circular letter, Baum to Boyce (New York), Waddington (Philadelphia), et al., May 24, 1939, GX 3757.

[25] GX 3757.

[26] P. A. Egan, Acco vice-president, to Baum, April 27, 1940, GX 2153.

[27] Baum to Egan, November 15, 1939, GX 2155. This letter referred to intra-Acco chiseling, rather than to sales from Acco to A & P, but the important thing is Baum's opinion that it had been greatly overemphasized and needed no central action from him to correct.

[28] August 13, 1939, DX 44.

they are "set up at the producing area. These field buyers canvass the different producing areas, packing houses, and all cooperative organizations and growers, and report back to the sales office." [29] They may examine the crop before it is harvested, and make estimates of its quality. Below the field buyer is the "solicitor," generally a local man who visits growers and shippers, discusses market conditions with them before harvesting, and gets merchandise assembled where it can be loaded onto trucks or railway cars. The solicitor is a buyers' representative, and is known as such. Acco employed both full-time and part-time field buyers and solicitors.[30]

In the field, operations shift from place to place as harvests arrive and are completed; the discussions of shippers and buyers refer not to a smooth flow of goods through time, but to a single "deal," completed within a relatively short period of time, after harvesting:

Where the merchandise grows and is harvested, graded, and packed, that is the deal.
Q. It contemplates the movement of a crop when it is harvested at the production point?
A. That is right — harvested for movement out.[31]

Field buying, reselling and "demoralization"

Field buying. Buyers who are first on the scene can spot the better offers and fill their needs more cheaply than can their competitors. But in addition, if they are able to take everything that is available, confident that they can dispose of it all, whether to their own organization or elsewhere, their profit on the transaction is greater, and is achieved with no additional investment other than the financing of inventory. From the very beginning, Acco bought for resale as well as for the A & P stores, and they earned both profits and resentment. For if the thousand-eyed buying office found a lot appreciably cheaper than most of the market,

[29] Testimony of Henry J. Williams, Acco vice-president in charge of field operations in all states east of the Mississippi, and three west of it. Tr. 17,797-17,800.
[30] Tr. 17,497–17,800.
[31] Williams, Tr. 17,797.

and not needed for A & P retail stores, they might forthwith place it on sale and gain an arbitrage profit. But there were other repercussions which must be examined in more detail, for it was alleged in the trade that Acco resale could depress the general price level in a market.

The process is eloquently described by a shipper.[32] It was bad enough that Acco tried to institute a system of competitive bidding by those offering the product. This could obviously transfer income from lower-cost shippers to Acco. The same effect would follow if Acco spotted the bargains, and hence bought more cheaply than the average. But at least that affected only the price on their own purchases. There was a much greater outrage in Acco's buying for resale, for then "a cheap price today . . . [for Acco] becomes the price tomorrow for everybody."

Such sales to Acco might be made by large shippers or small; admittedly they might in themselves be profitable, but:

While the grower made a profit on that particular sale on that particular day, the result is that tomorrow the market will react . . . to that price . . . and again down goes your market.

. . . . This vicious circle goes on until we find ourselves having to meet through our brokerage connections the same price at which the Atlantic Commission Company has placed that car in the hands of the first jobber.[33]

Moreover, A & P allegedly featured the cheap goods at retail prices lower than their competitors', who were moved to stop buying unless they too could obtain a cheaper price, though not necessarily as low as A & P's. The result was still lower prices as the repercussions spread back to the field.[34]

Mr. Hebert mentioned the apple and cherry "deals" as examples of sellers being "forced to meet" Acco's resale price. The same process was at work elsewhere. The head of a California orange cooperative spoke to the next year's Yakima meeting:

You are familiar with the fact that one or two tramp cars of fruit rolling around the United States can do more to reduce the price than any

[32] *Minutes of the Atlantic Commission meeting with Growers and Shippers* . . . , August 25, 1940, GX 2319.
[33] GX 2319, pp. 4–5.
[34] GX 2319, pp. 5–6.

other factor. We find one fly-by-night quoting oranges all over the United States has the same effect as 1,000 cars all over the United States.[35]

At the same meeting, a Mr. Kelley, described how:

If one fellow can sell a potato at a dime below the other fellow, they all want them a dime cheaper, . . . and the next week you would be selling your box at another ninety cents less until it comes down to where the grower is nickeled down to operating costs.[36]

There were also complaints that Acco undersold dealers on North Carolina potatoes.[37]

Again, in September 1939, the Florida Citrus Producers Trade Association passed a resolution censuring Acco for "seriously weakening the established distribution system." Once more, it was the Acco field offices which they disliked most:

The practice of the Atlantic Commission Company in purchasing only the smallest possible portion of its supplies . . . at terminal markets . . . results in the lowering of general price levels for all Florida citrus fruits.

That Acco limited its purchases to a few sizes and to U.S. No. 1, they alleged, tended to depress prices on all other grades. Furthermore, price reductions by retail stores "force its competitors to demand similar reductions." Worse yet, other chains and independents were meeting A & P competition by copying A & P practices. As a result, prices "in most cases, already are far below the cost of production." [38]

These complaints are worth some analysis. Undoubtedly Acco did better than the average field buyer both because of its complete local coverage and its knowledge of the terminal markets:

Unintelligent shippers [according to the Federal Trade Commission] may forward all shipments to one market. . . . Intelligent shippers continuously collect data . . . and allot quotas of shipments . . . in such a manner as not to burden any market with an over-supply and as to obtain the maximum total proceeds for the entire supply to be marketed.[39]

[35] GX 2319.
[36] GX 2319, p. 110.
[37] GX 3582.
[38] The resolution was passed September 25, 1939, and is in the record as GX 4480.
[39] FTC, *Report on Agricultural Income Inquiry*, Part II (Washington, 1937), p. 163.

However, this does not mean any decline in the average price realized by growers.

Nor was there any allegation, except in Northwest apples (and wrongly there) that Acco had a large enough share of the market to depress or manipulate prices by means of their purchases. Acco's share of the market was simply too small to influence the price level. The Florida citrus growers, for example, were under no compulsion to sell to A & P, whether in the field or in the terminal markets. Nine tenths of their crop went to other buyers, and Acco could not have repeatedly thrown even its small weight around, and stayed out of the market at strategic times, for that would have sabotaged the flow of produce to the stores. Nor is there any evidence of such manipulation.[40]

A careful reading shows that the various complaints were not of a lower net price received by *growers* but by *distributors*, through upsetting "the established distribution system." To the extent that the growers were organized, and had integrated into distribution, their interests as distributors did clash with Acco's. Rural public opinion may be shaped by the former as much as by the latter.

This was sometimes explicitly recognized by the growers. Thus, at the Yakima meeting already discussed, a Mr. Finnegan said of his firm:

We are shippers and packers. We are not a marketing organization. We have no wire connections in the east. We are not interested in any brokers. . . . Our main object is to get as much money as possible back to our growers. Since 1931, we have been shipping most of our fruit through [Acco]. Some of it is sold to other . . . marketing organizations. We are in a position to know the practices of both of them. . . . We have never found that they [Acco] have tried to buy that fruit from us for any less than any other buyer in the district.[41]

Even stronger evidence is in the continuing good relations with Acco's sources of supply. About 60 per cent of all Acco supplies

---

[40] A & P officials denied that they speculated thus. Testimony of Earl French and Henry J. Williams, Tr. 18,215 and 17,811, respectively. Baum claimed at certain meetings with growers that Acco purchases were actually *more* consistent than average in apples, oranges, and lettuce; but it has not been possible to confirm or disprove this.

[41] GX 2310.

were purchased from cooperatives, and it was stated without contradiction that none of them had ceased to do business with Acco.[42]

In any case, how could "upsetting the established distribution system" possibly depress the market price? How could "one or two" carloads in the whole United States have the same effect as one thousand? Where the price in a market represents a balance of supply and demand, an insignificant increment to supply can have only an insignificant effect on price. Hence it must be that the complaints assumed not a balance but an imbalance; specifically, that supply *exceeded* demand at the current price, *and that the cooperatives and other large sellers were trying to keep a price above the supply-demand equilibrium.*

Aside from some farm products whose sale is highly concentrated,[43] how can artificially high prices exist in so competitive a set of markets? We must bear in mind the "deal," that is, a large block of produce moving out of a producing area in a relatively short time. The first prices quoted by the sellers could well be above the equilibrium price. Chance alone would do this half the time, and cupidity the rest. Under these circumstances, a lower price quoted here and there *would* serve as a signal that the artificially (or mistakenly) high price could not be maintained, and the other sellers must follow suit. Hence Acco, as a reseller, was the bearer of bad tidings, and actually profited by conveying the information. The shippers' complaints make it clear that *what they resent is the price being driven down to equilibrium.* For if it were already there — that is, if price equated supply and demand — there would be neither motive nor opportunity for Acco to affect it.

The sellers are of course indignant at the loss of prospective profits, and it is perfectly natural for them to use the accusation of "monopoly" against a firm which is helping to disrupt an informal price agreement. This "monopoly" is merely the ritual invective of business, and expresses the deep human desire

[42] Baum, Tr. 18,543.

[43] Before World War II, the California Fruit Growers' Exchange ("Sunkist") sold 72 per cent of the oranges, 67 per cent of the grapefruit, and 89 per cent of the lemons produced in California and Arizona. See USDA Circular C-121 (Washington, June 1940).

for a personal, tangible, scapegoat instead of indifferent market forces.

Another kind of Acco practice must have also reduced the profits of distributors (and of growers where they were integrated). Baum wrote to a subordinate:

Our organization is giving entirely too much thought to brands instead of the contents in the crates. I have just recently returned from a southern trip, visiting a number of the southern units, and from personal observation I note that there are many shippers who do not have these crack brands yet who have very satisfactory merchandise that is selling considerably less than the differential on the peak terminal markets like New York and Chicago.[44]

If this advice was acted upon, the result would be some weakening in the differential.

Retail pricing. There was also resentment against low retail prices in A & P stores. In 1939, there were complaints by farm organizations concerning low A & P retail prices, and there was obvious anxiety to avoid "the fire and criticism of these influential people."[45]

In March of 1940, a grape juice cooperative complained to Gordon C. Corbaley, president of the American Institute of Food Distribution.[46] McAuliffe, A & P (not Acco) field buyer in Rochester, did not think it worth bothering about. But French of Acco warned Parr that "since the Co-ops are associated with the National Cooperative Council, who have considerable influence in legislation, it might we well to maintain a friendly attitude toward them." Because of low A & P retails, the cooperatives had allegedly found some of their contracts canceled, including one with Kroger. Parr, in drawing this to Bofinger's attention, added that raising prices would be "good business" anyway, since the juice was moving too quickly at the low price, and stocks might be gone inside of three months.[47] Accordingly, prices were raised.[48]

Maine potatoes are another example of attempted retail price

[44] Baum to Egan, November 13, 1939, GX 2155.
[45] Merchandising committee, December 18, 1939, GX 2348.
[46] Corbaley, Tr. 6307-9.
[47] Parr to Bofinger, March [no date] 1940, GX 1737.
[48] Bofinger to Parr, March 7, 1940, GX 1738.

maintenance in farm products. There is record of ill-feeling against the A & P in Aroostook County, late in 1931. Boycott petitions were circulated and "business has been cut very drastically as a result." The alleged offense was selling Maine potatoes very cheaply as a leader, and selling Long Island potatoes at higher prices.[49] In January of 1940, an advertising firm retained by the State of Maine received word of drastic price cuts by A & P and a rival chain in Cleveland. At first, they believed that A & P were not the "guilty parties,"[50] but soon claimed to have "conclusive proof" that they were.[51] French, to whom they imparted the accusation, considered it "an extremely serious matter and one which must . . . be cleared up as quickly as possible," i.e., one must prove that A & P had not *begun* the price reductions, only met them.[52] The grievance of the Maine advertising counsel was:

This very low price was the equivalent of carlot wholesale price in Cleveland, and the wholesalers out there were threatening to turn to Michigan or Western New York or Pennsylvania potatoes . . . as they could not get the trade to buy Maine potatoes to meet the price in the Cleveland district.[53]

The low prices were no temporary flurry, but continued throughout the year. This makes it difficult to believe either that the retail price was equal to carlot wholesale, *or* that wholesalers were actually boycotting Maine potatoes. Only in December 1940 did Dorrance prevail upon French and Baum to raise the price a little, but "not as much as [he] had hoped for."[54]

The matter was considered important enough to call for a special report to John Hartford from Baum. He denied selling at wholesale price, but claimed to have sold Maine potatoes "close" in order to obtain for the growers "a considerably wider distribution," which was needed for price stability and disposition of the entire crop. To increase prices at the urging of others was both

[49] New England meeting, December 23, 1931, GX 2347.
[50] Report by Sturges Dorrance, February 5, 1940, GX 1805.
[51] Dorrance to French, February 12, 1940, GX 1810.
[52] French to Baum, February 13, 1940, GX 1806.
[53] Dorrance, Tr. 6581.
[54] Dorrance, Tr. 6598–6600. The writer doubts that this actually happened; it was not in the interests of the defense to question it.

bad merchandising and a possible violation of the Sherman Act.[55] Hartford agreed.[56] Dorrance did not let the matter rest. Over a year later, in April 1942, he again wrote French asking for a price increase; [57] the reply took three months in coming, and was not only a flat refusal but a request not to discuss prices any more.[58] Dorrance replied, hinting at action by Maine Representatives and Senators,[59] but there is no evidence of any further action.

The Maine incident was heavily stressed at the trial — which reveals more about the trial than about the price of potatoes. Certainly A & P did not sell below the sum of delivered cost plus a markup. In the first place, there is no evidence except the self-serving statement of interested parties. Second, Dorrance himself privately admitted that Acco's cost of moving Maine potatoes (at least to East Coast markets) was so low that they could make a profit at prices which other sellers could not meet.[60] Third, the lower price was not temporary but continuous for two and a half years. Hence it was no attempt to discourage rivals by below-cost selling for a limited time, after which prices could be raised to monopoly levels and the losses of the campaign recouped. Fourth, it is impossible to put rivals out of business merely by underselling them on one commodity, accounting for an insignificant proportion of their total sales.

In 1940, the Atlantic Division was warned that its advertisements had stressed low prices too heavily, which had "led grower and producer groups to believe that A & P is depressing retail markets." [61] But belief does not make it so.

In September 1940, a Trade Relations Committee of Tokay grape growers wired Baum and Hartford:

Please advise who [is] selling [at a] nickel [a] pound [in] Middle West markets. Absolutely imperative for welfare of industry you hold retail .06 pound Tokays and not be influenced by possible minor competition as

[55] Baum to Hartford, January 2, 1941, GX 1826.
[56] Hartford to Baum, January 5, 1941, GX 1827.
[57] Dorrance to French, April 14, 1942, GX 1824.
[58] French to Dorrance, July 14, 1942, DX 40.
[59] Dorrance to French, July 21, 1942, GX 1823.
[60] Dorrance to Charles F. Adams, May 22, 1940, DX 38.
[61] Bulletin to all units, from sales manager, Atlantic Division, May 10, 1940, GX 2356.

you know industry here endeavoring to do everything to have orderly marketing program in order to make fair return to grower. . . . We do not feel that the Great Atlantic and Pacific Tea Company would intentionally wish to do otherwise than cooperate with this . . . program. . . . The [Acco personnel] in California have apparently done everything possible to manipulate and depress prices *by working with small shippers to break down the price structure when major portion of industry is trying [to] cooperate.*[62]

The appeal was apparently not successful. Baum subsequently defended himself in a letter by arguing that:

Analysis of our sales last year in relation to retail prices in a number of offices revealed that the volume of Tokays increased from 75 to over 200 per cent as the price was reduced from 6 cents to 5 cents a pound. . . . Maintaining an arbitrary retail price level out of line with cost price . . . is an unsound [principle] of marketing. . . . Strong competition [exists] from seedless grapes which were sold in a great many places at 5 cents a pound. Many consumers [buy] these interchangeably.[63]

In general, the writer is inclined to agree with Geoffrey Shepherd and with A. C. Hoffman, who wrote:

[There is] a notion that price reductions by a strong chain system will compel other retailers to bid lower for their supplies in order to meet competition, and in this way the wholesale and ultimately the farm prices will be brought down. Price-making is a complex phenomenon, and may at times be influenced by considerations of this sort. But it should also be remembered that the most effective way to induce consumers to buy more is to reduce the price.[64]

Williams' testimony is worth citing:

The demand in the terminals reflects the demand in the market. In other words, if your terminals are clogged up and buying is slow, it backs up into the producing areas.
Q. And vice versa?
A. That is right.[65]

[62] Telegram, Langford to Hartford (copy to Baum), September 8, 1940, GX 1701 (italics added).
[63] Baum to Langford, September 16, 1940, GX 1707.
[64] A. C. Hoffman, *Retail Sales Campaigns for Agricultural Products* (Washington: U.S. Department of Agriculture, December 1938), p. 14. See also the general discussion in Shepherd, *Marketing Farm Products*, appendix C.
[65] Williams, Tr. 17,825. See also the Stillwell Report on grape prices, GX 1709.

Appraisal of the evidence

Acco's role in the wholesale markets for produce, both in the field and at the terminals, is clear. Because they were large and everywhere, they could and did buy at the cheapest range of a widely fluctuating market, thus owning their goods at a lower average price than paid by other sellers. One reason for their success was their sales to the trade, for this enabled them to take any favorable offer even if it was much larger than was needed by the retail stores, since they knew they could resell at no loss to themselves. Reselling in markets of this type meant large-scale arbitrage, and a tendency to undermine the scattered, transitory monopoly of some sellers who might otherwise garner a fleeting rent. There seems no reason to doubt that this arbitrage meant, on the average, a net decrease of the margin to rival distributors. But there is equally little reason to suppose that it lowered the net price to growers.

The prosecution theory of Acco influence on retail-wholesale prices is, when clearly stated, a gem of purest ray serene:

Being the largest food handler in America, the A & P group may push supplier prices in particular produce and food items up and down by the simple device of raising or lowering its own retail prices on the same items, in approximately the same way that the Federal Reserve Banking System affects the primary cost of commercial credit by raising and lowering its own rediscount rate on commercial paper.[66]

But for the most part, the prosecution uses the resounding word "demoralization," which is so vague as to defy analysis. A shadowy picture is created of A & P driving down prices to farmers and hurting people, though it is not clear how they are able to do any such thing, or why they would want to do it. Of course, the prosecution merely echoes the agitation for the Robinson-Patman Act and even uses the same language. In the hearings on the Robinson-Patman bill, the secretary of the National League of Wholesale Fresh Fruit and Vegetable Distributors testified:

Mr. HERR. [Acco's] representative testified under oath before the N.R.A. . . . that 60 per cent . . . was bought for and sold to the A & P. So that they were in 60 per cent of their business, by their own admission,

[66] GB(DC), pp. 518–519.

performing a buying service for their parent company, yet they were charging the producer and the shipper the full brokerage. . . . Now that has
thoroughly demoralized this fresh-fruit industry and vegetable industry,
and [the proposed legislation] . . . will do exactly what we tried to do in
N.R.A. code. . . .

The CHAIRMAN. *How can they get control unless they pay a higher
price?*

Mr. HERR. Oh, they do have behind them the volume, . . . and by the
duress of their buying power they can persuade me to go along on that
sort of situation. [What sort of situation, was never explained.]

The CHAIRMAN. . . . *They control such a high percentage of the outlet* that the independent commission man does not have enough clients to
whom to sell?

Mr. HERR. That, in part, is true.

The CHAIRMAN. *Is that your contention?*

Mr. HERR. But here is a ramification of the thing that I had not intended
to go into. . . . They get control of a large tonnage of perishable commodities . . . ; they go . . . into the New York market, which domi-
nates pretty much the entire country, . . . and they can throw four or
five cars of any commodity on that market at any time and break that
market and immediately depress — immediately, Mr. Chairman, within
24 hours, depress that product in the wholesale price in the New York
market, which is reflected in the buying district. That inevitably happens.

The CHAIRMAN. You mean they break the market at the distributing
end and *use that depressed market to buy at a lower price at the producing
end?*

Mr. HERR. Exactly. And it has happened in your State time and time
again.

The CHAIRMAN. *Now, how do you know that?*

Mr. HERR. We know that from every-day experience. . . . They [Acco]
buy the stuff for the A & P and then, instead of throwing it to the A & P
outlets, they throw it back on the market and break the market. . . .
[Furthermore] the chain stores buy a couple of cars . . . — it does not
make any difference what they pay for them — at the beginning of the
season, and put them out as leaders, or loss leaders. . . . The effect is,
that reduction is reflected right back to the grower. . . .

Mr. LLOYD. *Where does the chain make any money out of that?* If
they depress the price to the grower, that price is reflected in the next purchase, it it not?

Mr. HERR. That is true.

Mr. LLOYD. Then *where do they make any money* by depressing the price to the grower? . . . You said the first day out they depressed the price and then that price is the price to everybody.

Mr. HERR. That is right.

Mr. LLOYD. Then *where does the chain make any money out of it?*

Mr. HERR. The chain does not necessarily make any money out of the transaction that breaks the market.

Mr. LLOYD. What is the purpose?

Mr. HERR. *I do not know what the purpose is, sir* . . . .[67]

Thus the wholesalers' representative finally had to postulate a kind of aimless malice on Acco's part; it profited them nothing to demoralize markets, but like the inhabitants of Dogpatch, "they just natcherly likes to be mean." And the incident is also characteristic of the Robinson-Patman catechism and the A & P prosecution in the way that every argument is supplied with grappling-hooks to another. The common-sense question as to *how* one gets control without paying a higher price is parried by "volume" and "buying power." When this leads logically enough to a question about *shares* of the market, we are off to "breaking the market" which "inevitably" happens. "We know that from every-day experience." Before it becomes apparent that this "demoralization" is nonsense, there is a shift to loss-leaders, and we are off again.

[67] *Hearings Before the Committee on the Judiciary, on H.R. 8422* . . . , 74 Cong., 1 sess., to amend the Clayton Act (Washington, 1935), pp. 71–74 (italics added). There is no evidence of loss leaders.

XIV

THE IMPACT OF ROBINSON-PATMAN ON ACCO; CL-LCL TRANSACTIONS

THE impact of the Robinson-Patman Act on the produce markets is relatively easy to understand, since there are so few elements of permanent market control. Before the Act, Acco bought and sold as one among many, with too small a share of the total market to influence the price. By offering frequent savings to sellers and buyers in the incessant and expensive making and remaking of contact, they frequently bought at lower prices while affording sellers a net return at least equal to that obtained elsewhere. When Section 2(c) required shippers to collect phantom brokerage from Acco, this resulted in extra profits to the shippers. *Only in the extreme limiting case of complete evasion of the Robinson-Patman Act could there have been nondiscrimination.* Acco was therefore discriminated against, but we cannot say to what extent.

The amount of discriminatory superprofit secured from Acco changed constantly with every shift in supply and demand. It gave Acco a bargaining power to get price reductions which removed all or part of the legal discrimination against them. This bargaining power rested on the fact that every shipper knew that there were plenty of others who wanted the superprofitable Acco business and would be willing to give up some of the phantom brokerage in order to get or keep the rest. The seller made the concessions because he was still ahead even after making them.

It was a typical black-market situation, since it was to the interest of both buyer and seller to break the law.

Adaptation to the Robinson-Patman Act

As may be seen in Appendix Table 7, the Acco profit held fairly steady after 1928, at a little under one million dollars. In 1936, there was a bulge to $1.4 million, which fell off by 45 per cent the following year. But by 1938, the recovery seems complete; there was slow growth up to 1941, and then a spectacular leap upward of nearly 50 per cent. Apparently Acco was able to continue much less hampered by the law after 1936 than were the buyers of manufactured goods, because of the more competitive market structure in which it operated.

As soon as the Robinson-Patman Act came into operation, Acco was ready with both "net" price agreements and with quantity discounts, of which there were more than 600 by 1939.[1] But they were not always granted. California Packing Corporation, whose obstinacy we have already noted in the case of its Del Monte branded products, was no more cooperative on fresh vegetables.

On asparagus that you job [resell to the trade] we allow you the same commission that we allow other brokers, and on asparagus turned over by [Acco] to [A & P] we cannot, by law, allow commission or anything in lieu thereof. We are not in position to accept Mr. Baum's proposal that he shall pay us *the same net return* on grass [asparagus] delivered to your stores as we receive on similar grass shipped to our brokers.[2]

The long and unedifying story can be reduced to this: that many shippers *were* in a position to accept "the same net return," and could be induced to do so.

The order of the Federal Trade Commission against the parent company, upheld by the Circuit Court of Appeals,[3] made new expedients necessary. Late in 1939 and early the next year, there were some attempts to use more quantity discount and cost savings agreements. But by the end of January 1940, the decision had already been made to abandon them both in favor of a differential on cash purchases. The ostensible theory was that since a cash buyer assumed responsibility for the merchandise at the shipping

[1] They are listed in the record as GX 1828.
[2] California Packing Corp. to Beckmann, February 24, 1939, GX 1829–A (italics added).
[3] See above, Chapter IX.

point, he was assuming a risk for which he ought to be reimbursed. Hence Acco could ask a lower price on grounds unrelated to the forbidden brokerage.[4]

The cash-differential system. In the Spring of 1940, Acco was informed by Baum that it must abide strictly by the terms of the FTC order. He added that purchases should so far as possible be on the basis of cash and carry at shipping point, and pointed out how to comply with the law and yet pay lower prices:

> Fluctuations of market conditions intermittently during the trading hours, or else the differential in prices owing to standards according to quality of merely hair-breadth U.S. #1 or U.S. #1 plus fancy or extra fancy will likewise justify differentials in prices. Also any savings to the shipper in the form of telephone and telegraphic communications, less sales personnel in their sales staff, clerical help, credit risk, collection charges on drafts; in fact any and all savings exclusive of brokerage or commissions.[5]

In "a considerable number of instances" soon afterward, the buying organization continued to use the expression "net" with references to purchases, and Baum was very anxious to have this cease.[6] Although Baum did not say so, he knew that in the words of a memorandum by the A & P lawyers:

> It is pretty generally conceded that no cash discount is justifiable on the basis of saving in cost. It can hardly cost a manufacturer, for example, 2 per cent more to get his money in 31 days than to get it in 30 days.[7]

The savings in communications expenses, credit risks, etc., were nothing new, and most of them had been claimed four years earlier as justifications for quantity discounts.[8] It is not easy to distinguish them from brokerage. The only really novel feature in the cash buying arrangement was the assumption of in-transit risk on the part of Acco. We shall see that they attempted to shed it as soon as possible. At any rate, the cash buying scheme was in full operation by April 1941.[9]

[4] Baum to R. B. Smith, January 14, 1940, GXX 1870; Wehman to Feldman, January 19, 1940, GX 1872; Feldman to Bofinger, January 22, 1940, GX 1874.

[5] Stencil (circular letter) No. 326, April 11, 1940, GX 1883.

[6] Minutes of the Acco merchandising meeting, May 4, 1940, GX 1895.

[7] Feldman & Kittelle to Baum, August 19, 1940, GX 1915.

[8] Stencil No. 628, August 12, 1936, GX 1769.

[9] This may be inferred from a memorandum from an Acco vice-president, which reveals that "the change in the method of purchase . . . resulting from

Those who like exercises in casuistry can revel in the argument of whether or not the savings on cash buying were the old brokerage in a new form, or whether the word "net" can be spelled in many more letters than three. The important thing, so far as we are concerned, is that Acco and the shippers now had a new occasion or justification for setting price differentials which the shippers found it worth while to grant. We would gladly trade all the voluminous evidence on verbal hair-splitting for only a little more material on the extent to which the new system replaced the old. We know that after March 1940, some 75 per cent of Acco purchases were on the cash shipping point basis,[10] and it seems only reasonable to assume that Acco would have paid cash only where it received some consideration therefor. The presumption is strengthened by the accounting record already cited. On the other hand, there is no doubt that some shippers took advantage of the brisk demand in 1940 and 1941 to refuse differentials for cash. In December 1940, California lettuce growers did so, and Washington apple growers the following March.[11] We shall now explore to what extent the new buying system permitted net prices to go below Robinson-Patman levels.

In-transit risk. The assumption of in-transit responsibility was a genuine increase in Acco cost, for it meant either a larger inspection force in the field, or more rejected produce at the terminal.[12] Had the shippers' price concessions merely reflected the additional saving, Acco would have been no better off. Their object was to use a genuine saving as a cloak for a price concession larger than the saving, though still not discriminating in favor of Acco when all terms were considered. Hence Acco attempted so to construe terms of sale that the shipper guaranteed quality

the Patman Law decision . . . meant purchasing for cash at shipping point a large part of our requirements." Hence there had been an increase in inventories and in accounts payable. Acco both took the goods and assumed the liability for payment at shipping time. Wehman to Smith, April 15, 1941, GX 1930.

[10] Testimony of Wehman, Tr. 18,493; and Baum, Tr. 18,523. Unfortunately, they do not distinguish between purchases in the field and at the terminals.

[11] See, respectively, P. A. Egan to Wehman, December 23, 1940, GX 1917; and Hayes to Baum, March 20, 1941, GX 1923.

[12] Florida citrus is one example. See W. R. Ward (Acco district manager) to Baum, September 25, 1940, GX 1914. Miscellaneous vegetables in Virginia and the Carolinas are another. Ward to Baum, April 23, 1940, GX 1887.

upon, arrival despite the fact that the sale was supposed to be final at the shipping point. In a circular letter, late in April 1940, Baum amended previous instructions.

In the absence of personal inspection merchandise is to be bought for acceptance as to grade and quality upon destination arrival.

We are somewhat doubtful that this would constitute a cash purchase, hence . . . we have a selected list of shippers . . . [who] will protect this merchandise (although we have paid for same) as equivalent to U.S. #1 upon arrival at destination, and should there be any losses sustained owing to not being up to grade and quality . . . they will assume any losses suffered by us in making adjustments or resale of this merchandise.[13]

A month later, there were 127 such sources.[14] But again we are unable to say how much of Acco's purchases were covered in this manner.

Price arrival and sales arrival. The shifting of in-transit responsibility was also the keynote of Acco's method on merchandise which it did not buy for f.o.b. cash. Prices of some highly perishable products, which were also hauled long distances, were so unstable that to book an order at a firm price was to risk a substantial devaluation by the time it arrived at the terminal.[15] Therefore such commodities were bought "price arrival"; produce was shipped with price subject to agreement at the terminal, after inspection. As might be expected, the price was not always easy to determine; there was no single definite price in the market which both parties could take as a standard, but rather a daily spread of fluctuating prices; the results of "isolated exchange," of which this was a very mild case, are notoriously indeterminate.

Baum, to be sure, considered that what he called "the prevailing average market . . . is a rather definite price from day to day . . . the going price of the larger operators." [16] But Baum stated at the trial that there could be a number of such going prices in the course of a single day, and that there could be as much as 20 per cent difference in the space of six hours; the going

[13] Stencil No. 372, April 25, 1940, GX 1891 (italics added).
[14] Stencil No. 514, May 24, 1940, GX 1899.
[15] Baum to Boyce (New York), to Waddington (Philadelphia), and to other terminal managers, May 24, 1939, GX 3757.
[16] Baum to M. G. Mann, of the Farmers' Cooperative Exchange, March 28, 1939, GX 1946.

price was not necessarily the average of such momentary market prices.[17]

Hence there is no surprise at the complaints lodged with Acco (or any other buyer or broker) by shippers. They might allege that the terminal office used the lowest price quoted during the day, instead of the average; or a price quoted while the shipment was in transit, rather than the one prevailing when it arrived.[18] Some disputes over the pricing of potatoes shipped into the Philadelphia market prompted Baum to write the terminal manager there that

it will be necessary for your shippers to accept the price we place on this merchandise at the time of arrival and discontinue this bartering over 5¢ differential and if . . . this procedure is not in accordance with their ideas . . . then of course it is their privilege to discontinue.[19]

Since Baum saw fit to circulate his letter among other terminal managers, the problem must have been widespread and important. Baum's rather high-handed tone reflected his bargaining position: accept our terms or lose your phantom brokerage. But this was complicated by general uncertainty as to price.

By the middle of 1940, six months after the Supreme Court decision, there was a definite shift from "price arrival" to "sales arrival." Apparently it was precipitated by a shipment of melons into Philadelphia on a price arrival basis.[20] The growers had expected a premium for quality, and at least one of them "was very much upset" about the Acco offers. Baum then decided that Acco terminal managers were "at liberty to withdraw [an] offer after a reasonable time for acceptance by the shipper and if you so wish not to make a revised offer for a future date." Or, as an Acco vice-president put it: "If they don't want the price we offer them when the merchandise arrives they are at liberty to go elsewhere with it." [21] By December of 1940, the term "price arrival" was entirely discontinued in favor of "sales arrival," which freed

[17] Baum, Tr. 19,267–8.

[18] Egan to Boyce, July 24, 1939, GX 2150.

[19] Baum to Waddington (copies to Ward in Macon and Bennett in Washington), June 14, 1939.

[20] The incident is easily reconstructed from two letters, Baum to Waddington, June 4, 1940, GX 1902, and Egan to Waddington, June 6, 1940, GX 2357.

[21] GX 2357.

Acco of any obligation to take the goods.[22] But there were "times when a firm positive commitment is made:" the choice of terms was itself a matter of bargaining.[23]

As early as 1939, Acco was forced to discontinue price arrival on lettuce, "as it is out of the question at this time with those shippers having six orders for every car of good merchandise they load." [24] In California Tokay grapes, such sales had practically died out years before 1945.[25]

"Sales arrival" price or S.A.P., did nothing of itself to narrow the uncertainty about the appropriate price. There is an Acco interoffice communication from a shipping point to Baltimore which lists some abuses at the terminals which the field men wanted stopped:

(1) Poor handling; (2) Unfair pricing; (3) Falsifying the going market; (4) Setting a price, and then notifying the shipper so late that he had no possibility of sending it elsewhere; (5) Falsifying quality: "If the fruit . . . was as bad as indicated in your reports, you made a mistake in selling the fruit to the Teaco." Then a general reminder:

The shipper puts this fruit in your hands and to do so he must have confidence in our ability and willingness to protect his interests at all times.[26]

Two months later, the same office voiced similar complaints. They cited an offer of $1.40 per box of oranges. The shipper refused it, and diverted the car to Pittsburgh, where he was able to sell it at $2.00.[27] A short time later, there were similar complaints about Florida potatoes.[28] Too many such instances would cost Acco the resale business it desired, they warned.

This brief survey of the cash differential shipping system leaves small room for doubt that it constituted little more than a means of partially evading the brokerage clause, and cutting down on the amount of phantom brokerage paid.

[22] Williams, Tr. 17,851.
[23] Williams, Tr. 17,854.
[24] Salinas to New York (personal to Boyce), August 24, 1939, GX 2150.
[25] Sanguinetti, Tr. 6172.
[26] Plant City, Florida, to Baltimore, November 20, 1940, GX 2359.
[27] Plant City, Florida, to Baltimore, January 17, 1941, GX 2363.
[28] Plant City, Florida, to Baltimore, April 18, 1941, GX 2368.

Resale business and "conflict of interests." About 75 per cent of the produce handled by Acco was purchased for A & P retail stores, about 5 per cent was purchased for resale, and about 20 per cent was sold by Acco as broker for the shippers.[29] We have already indicated why resale transactions must have been profitable. Our presumption is supported by more direct evidence that Acco personnel were urged to obtain this sort of business. As Baum said in 1939:

a child can sell . . . good quality, but it takes salesmanship to sell merchandise of poor quality to regular trade outlets, and, of course, a shipper needs this service under adverse conditions and our organization in order to be able to develop and *maintain constant consignment tonnage under all conditions* needs to exert effort in selling poor merchandise that has to go thru some channel at times.[30]

There is also the anxious reassurance of the Acco manager at Houston to his chief in Denver that he was "after these fellows [shippers and jobbers] every day for business." [31] In July 1940, Baum urged his organization not "to let up in your discretionary efforts in effecting regular trade sales." [32]

The final bit of evidence in this regard is a letter written in June 1941, where a regional manager apologized to Baum for a decline in trade sales during the first quarter of the year. Despite "all efforts [humanly] possible," produce was becoming so scarce that they could barely manage to fill A & P warehouse needs.[33]

Much of the consignment business went through auctions, where Acco could usually do an effective job for the seller:

We are usually able to realize auction average prices for any of our offerings in this [Cincinnati] market, due to the fact that so many of the auction buyers do business with us on other commodities and in this way we are able to ask them for support on any of our auction cars.[34]

On consignment sales, it was ordinarily in Acco's interest to realize the highest possible price for the consignor. But if the

[29] Baum, Tr. 18,631-2.
[30] Stencil No. 221, May 8, 1939, GX 2149 (italics added).
[31] Houston to Denver, July 31, 1937, GX 2276.
[32] Stencil No. 779, July 17, 1940, GX 2175.
[33] F. C. Kniesner to Baum, June 16, 1941, GX 2148.
[34] Interoffice communication, Cincinnati to Plant City, Fla., September 25, 1939, GX 2355.

merchandise ultimately went to A & P, there might be a conflict of interests, since it was possible for Acco to sell to A & P at fictitiously low prices, cheating the seller for the benefit of the parent company. There is no evidence whatever of this kind of dishonesty, which is hardly surprising. The word would have gone around. Furthermore, under the Perishable Agricultural Commodities Act, Acco had to maintain a record of every transaction, on pain of losing its license, and the Department of Agriculture could have investigated any complaint or rumor. Acco would have lost its license and the resale business they found so profitable. Offenders might even have gone to jail. Hence the "conflict of interests" seems tenuous at best, and is supported by no facts. Actually, shipper complaints of poor service were forwarded and supported by an Acco office. Here, too, long-run considerations would be expected to enforce honesty.

However, in February 1940, the attention of the Federal Trade Commission moved Baum to renounce brokerage from the seller on any part of carlot which was bought by Acco at auction for A & P warehouses.[35] Somewhat later in the year, as will shortly be seen, when the system of splitting carlots was changed, brokerage was also waived on merchandise sold to A & P outside of auctions.[36]

The net effect was to overcompensate produce shippers for any possible downward pressure on that small part of their merchandise which was consigned to Acco and eventually resold to A & P. Presumably no abstract justice moved Acco. To the writer it seems like a desirable solution to a very minor problem; the Robinson-Patman Act and the Federal Trade Commission deserve all due credit.

Carlot sale and LCL repurchase. At the terminal markets, the A & P retail stores needed much produce in LCL quantities. In fact, it would be a strange coincidence if their requirements of any product happen to add up to an integral number of carloads. Acco did not find it expedient to do the job of breaking up carlots and selling LCL lots to the trade. Instead, they sold carloads to jobbers, and repurchased part from them. It can easily be seen that

---

[35] Stencil No. 129, February 9, 1940, GX 2282.
[36] Form letter to heads of Acco divisional offices, May 1, 1940, GX 2166.

jobbers were willing or anxious to buy a carload from Acco if offered a guarantee or reasonable assurance that they could without additional effort dispose immediately, at the going price, of as much of the carload as could not be conveniently sold elsewhere. Acco was in effect selling produce *plus* insurance against failure to find buyers immediately, or insurance against incurring any cost of making contact. This kind of service was and is in very high demand in markets like Washington Street. In a free market, produce plus insurance must fetch a higher price than produce alone. But this purchase of LCL produce, which was an additional service to the jobber and was reflected in better prices or better availability, was a business necessity for Acco as for any other retailer. Hence an agreement to split a carload was an advantage both to Acco and to the jobber. Both parties were better off: the eagerness with which jobbers sought Acco business, which will be illustrated below, is proof enough; for they were under no compulsion to stay with Acco.

Up to May 1940, Acco made definite prior agreements with jobbers to buy back stated amounts of the carlots they sold them. Usually the brokerage allowed Acco was canceled by the jobber's markup in reselling to Acco. The net result was simply that Acco and the jobber each had an LCL shipment at CL prices. However, the January 1940 decision of the Supreme Court, and the renewed interest of the Federal Trade Commission, caused Acco to substitute two alternative methods of splitting carlots:

(1) Acco sold the jobber CL and agreed to buy back a definite LCL quantity at the same price. There was neither Acco brokerage nor jobbers' markup. This had been the usual result under the old arrangement, but was now specified in the bargain.

(2) Acco sold the jobber CL without making any definite repurchase agreement, but merely promised that the jobber would be given preference on LCL purchases provided his price and quality were at least as good as anybody else's. On the sales, Acco collected brokerage; if it repurchased from the jobber, it paid his usual fee.[37] Again, the results were the same as under the old system except that Acco had more freedom of action; it was not tied down to any jobber. Doubtless both the company and the

---

[37] Baum, Tr. 18,587–18,591.

Commission were gratified by this reform. The jobbers' opinion was not ascertained.

Sales promotion: double brokerage. Evidence has been cited that Acco was very desirous of resale business, and that jobbers found dealings with them especially profitable. *Within the limits of the additional profit to the jobber,* Acco had great bargaining power, since jobbers were relatively many, while Acco's service was almost unique both on the buying and selling side. Hence Acco could and doubtless did demand as much as possible of the economies, up to the point where the jobber found no inducement to deal with them rather than with the market at large. Since Acco needed an assurance of client firms, it would of course be foolish to attempt to take all the gain. But the line between reasonable and excessive was a vague and shifting one. Hence the occasional complaint that:

> we, in endeavoring to sell merchandise to trade customers, have threatened to boycott them by not purchasing any of their merchandise for Teaco requirements unless they bought their fresh fruit and vegetable requirements through us . . . [and] that we have overloaded trade buyers.[38]

For example, there was pressure on a shipper to make his Washington, D. C., sales through Acco, in view of the large amount of purchases they were making from him.[39] This might be dismissed as an isolated instance were it not for the comment of the Acco district manager that he wanted to be kept informed "so that we can follow up these cases and possibly impress upon shippers the fact that we know what is going on and expect the proper treatment."[40] Again, there was dissatisfaction with some Texas produce jobbers who were enjoying substantial sales to A & P warehouses, but bought without using Acco: "Since these customers are serving our stores . . . we are due a big part of their business. Let's do all we can to *break up this working direct.*"[41] Again, in December 1940, a Florida citrus shipper expressed his regret at

[38] Stencil No. 779, July 17, 1940, GX 2175.
[39] Interoffice communication, Miami to Plant City, February 24, 1940, GX 2284.
[40] W. R. Ward to Miami office, February 27, 1940, GX 2285.
[41] Interoffice communication, Houston to San Francisco, May 28, 1936, GX 2275 (italics added).

having sold a carload of tangerines in New York without using Acco, and promised them exclusive handling of any fruit shipped into New York.[42]

Moreover, some jobbers bought carlots through brokers, and then rebought them through Acco, paying brokerage to both. In the record, there are six such sales in 1940, forty-five in 1941, and two in 1942.[43] Total Acco sales were around 180,000 carloads annually, so that double brokerage was not negligible but infinitesimal. Nevertheless, the reasons given by the jobbers are of some interest.

Q. Can you tell the Court why this was done?
A. No reason at all. I have no reason to give. . . . Well, I will tell you, Judge. I just wanted to give some business to the Atlantic Commission Company, that is all.
Q. Why?
A. Oh, just as an appreciation. I was getting some of their business, they were giving me a lot of information in their teletype. . . .

Another testified:

Well, they wired to Chicago and got me a quotation . . . and then I had the further — not a guarantee — I had the further feeling that I might be able to make a few sales. That is the service that I consider.

A third had been approached by the local Acco representative, who "thought he was entitled" to some business; he complied because he expected it to promote his LCL sales. Another was also approached by a local Acco man, and had "felt that our turning brokerages to the Atlantic Commission Company might influence that less than carload business."

The jobber witnesses made a bad impression. They were evasive and sometimes impertinent, one had been "kicked out" by his old partner;[44] another had been convicted of giving false information about the contents of a car.[45] However, their testi-

---

[42] Interoffice communication, Plant City to New York, December 11, 1940, GX 2297. See also the two preceding exhibits.

[43] The testimony of a dozen jobbers is strung through the Transcript, pp. 7888–8582, and is the source of this and the following paragraphs, except as otherwise noted.

[44] Tr. 8329, 8349.

[45] Tr. 8481–82.

mony is consistent with our knowledge of the produce market. Double brokerage may arouse our indignation, but the service Acco offered was perfectly genuine. The reasonable assurance of a buyer for their LCL produce meant that much less fruitless search for customers, less spoilage, and fewer distress sales. Jobbers were willing to pay hard cash for such assurance. Such payments are a measure of what it is worth to save the cost of contact in produce marketing. The jobbers would never have paid unless they expected to save more through Acco patronage than they paid for it. Everything else being equal, this would mean a larger return for these client firms. Because they were numerous, and Acco could pick and choose among them, they could be induced to hand over much or most of these gains to Acco, by way of lower prices, or quicker accommodation, or better quality, or double brokerage. But Acco was only a small part of the alternatives open to the jobbers. Both parties had a competitive market to deal with, and both gained.

Quality and availability. We have already seen that one of the strongest reasons for Acco's resale business was that it could dispose of more merchandise than A & P needed, and cull it for better quality. But the search for quality started in the field.

Up to 1939, Acco required that its Florida citrus be all U.S. #1. After a protest by the citrus trade association, they required proportions of 60 and 40 for #1 and #2 respectively; the government standard was 40 and 60.[46]

Late in 1940, the scarcity of California lettuce prompted the grocers to refuse any cash differentials. Yet they were still willing to allow Acco something:

At the present time the only advantage we have is the selection of merchandise and the fact we can get it when it is scarce and high.[47]

By March of 1941, a field buyer was reporting:

We shall find it hard trying to buy celery, selecting the "cream" . . . insisting on a net cash price as low or lower than that price which other cash buyers pay, and also asking the shipper to guarantee a certain grade on arrival. . . . Shipments [are] none too heavy, quality mostly good,

---

[46] Baum, Tr. 19,276–19,281.
[47] Egan to Wehman, December 23, 1940, GX 1917.

f.o.b. and delivered markets strong, and cash buyers active. It would probably be easy to get shippers to listen to guarantees if these conditions were on the reverse. . . . [At present they feel that] they are doing their part by us . . . by selecting the best quality, lots, and brands.[48]

When merchandise was difficult to obtain, first choice of Acco produce always went to A & P warehouses.[49] By May of 1941, the Acco Detroit office had very little jobbing business, but they found it worth while to sell produce on consignment, paying the customer jobber the exact fee the shipper allowed to Acco. "Oftentimes we have first disposed of good packages to the Tea Co., the remainder of the car being jobbed." [50] Despite the absence of money profit, the better quality was worth getting.

The larger the Acco sales, the easier to get the right quantities of the right produce at lower prices. This was one reason for the frequent Acco sponsorship of special promotional drives on commodities which were plentiful, and could be bought and featured at low prices. They are tabulated as follows: [51]

Year	1936	1937	1938	1939	1940	1941 (first 9 months)
Sales	16	23	23	29	29	23

The circular letters which Baum sent to divisional sales directors ask for "a big play," "special merchandising assistance," and the like; they are obviously based not on conditions already current, but expected within a few days or a week. Our evidence all relates to 1939, 1940, and 1941, but A. C. Hoffman's comments of December 1938 seem entirely applicable:

In general, the chain systems accompanied their sales-promotion efforts with some reduction in prices to consumers. . . . In the opinion of the

---

[48] C. H. Taylor to W. R. Ward, March 22, 1941, GX 1926.

[49] Baum to Egan, January 21, 1941, GX 2146; and F. C. Kniesner to Baum, June 16, 1941, GX 2148.

[50] Letters to divisional sales directors — on potatoes: June 8, 1939, GX 3754; June 10, 1940, GX 3755; May 23, 1941, GX 3753; on tomatoes: June 9, 1939, GX 3759; on cantaloups: July 11, 1940, GX 3760.

[51] Baum to W. R. Watkins, September 10, 1941, GX 3764. Baum once stated to a meeting of Northwest apple shippers that he did not need the consent of the retail organization in order to run a special promotional campaign. "We tell them to do it and we go ahead and buy." Minutes dated August 25, 1940, in record as GX 2319.

writer the resultant narrowing of margins was one of the best features of their efforts.[52]

The drives were essentially commodity speculation in the better sense. To profit itself, Acco was inducing larger consumer expenditures, geared to the inflow of lower priced goods.

[52] Hoffman, *Retail Sales Campaign for Agricultural Products*, p. 14.

XV

CONTACT WITH GROWERS AND SHIPPERS: FINAL APPRAISAL OF ACCO BUYING

Dᴏᴍɪɴᴀɴᴄᴇ of distributors over growers and shippers is commonplace in the produce markets. It usually is based on the advancing of funds to finance the crop.

The sum [involved] is undoubtedly large, as the practice is extensive and reaches from all the principal terminal markets into practically every production area.[1]

As late as September 1941, and in a highly prosperous area, an Acco vice-president could state:

I find, as far as California shippers are concerned, that you can have an organization of shippers that will represent the control of 85 per cent of the shipments but the individual shippers actually haven't got control of their own shipments due to the fact that a large proportion of their shipments are controlled by Eastern operators on account of advances.[2]

Acco seems generally to have avoided any such arrangement. For example, the grape grower-shipper Sanguinetti had sold Acco his entire output for some years prior to 1939, but there was a disagreement in that year, and they received only half.[3] In 1940, however, Baum arranged a loan for Sanguinetti with some New York commission merchants, who were repaid out of the proceeds

[1] FTC, *Report on Agricultural Income Inquiry*, Part II (Washington, 1937), p. 483.
[2] Egan to Baum, September 16, 1941, GX 1722.
[3] Sanguinetti, Tr. 6208–6211.

of that year's crop, despite the fact that Acco handled it, not they.[4]

But if the relations between Acco and its suppliers were not based on financial accommodation, upon what were they based? The contact was far more than a meeting of minds over specific transactions. For example, in 1941, Sanguinetti had his subordinates spread the (erroneous) word that he had the inside track with Acco. Obviously it was worth something to him to be known as an Acco man. Whether it strengthened his own buying hand (for Sanguinetti was a shipper as well as a grower), or whether it was a means of demonstrating his loyalty and cementing his connection with Acco, is hard to say. For what it may be worth, his testimony indicates that over time, prompt disposal to Acco even at a somewhat lower price realized greater proceeds than uncertain disposal at a somewhat higher price.[5] Where there was a saving in cost, there was room for both buyer and seller to gain. This seems also to be the meaning of an incredibly lengthy and tangled sentence in a letter which Baum addressed: "To All Growers and Shippers."

You fully appreciate that sales effected to our organization even under the Cost Savings Agreement should net back to your farm or packing houses a greater amount on merchandise supplied to us than through brokerage outlets and of course in conformance with our policy this is our desire, however, at the same time we wish the benefits that we accrue to you in the savings in the selling costs as outlined above and we wish you to make known to us these savings on a per package basis according to commodity or commodities that you handle. . . . [The same sentence runs for several lines more.] [6]

It might be paraphrased: although you grant us a discount, whereby we gain, you receive more from us net than from any other buyer, whereby you gain; please state your savings.

Of course, Baum's statement does not make it so. There is practically no good evidence that growers were better off with Acco — or would have done better without them.[7] We noted earlier that 60 per cent of all Acco suppliers were obtained from coopera-

[4] Sanguinetti, Tr. 6250, 6262.
[5] Sanguinetti, Tr. 6254.
[6] January 6, 1940, GX 1870–A.
[7] But see note 13, below.

tives, none of whom had ever ceased to do business with Acco. But let us review the facts on the way that grower and shipper organizations would "build in" with Acco, and perhaps the benefits to each party, if any, will be seen.

Grape shippers afford us good examples of the kind of organization Acco did *not* like. Some of them came together at Bakersfield in 1939 "to regulate f.o.b. prices. However most of them willing to make confidential cuts. . . . Look for much lower prices. Suggest . . . hold off for commitments until market adjusts itself." [8] This reaction of an Acco executive gives us a glimpse of the Commission Company's power to shift markets and break up sellers' cartels, but not to make itself beloved of sellers. A year later there was proposed an organization to include both buyers and sellers. Baum woud have none of it, and his reasons are interesting:

It involved a concentration of sales which, in our opinion, could be construed as contrary to the Anti-Sherman Law [sic]. Furthermore, we would lose our identity. . . . Prices would be pooled instead of the individual results to the respective grower and shipper organizations that we have been doing business with over several years and shown better competitive results.[9]

The second reason is especially important, because it underlies Acco's program of separate contact committees to arrange special promotional drives. Where they simply joined those sponsored by the Department of Agriculture, they lost their separate identity and the chance to make the best possible bargain for themselves. Seven such committees are mentioned in the record, promoted and largely financed by Acco.

Contact committees — purposes

Baum once described the purposes of these committees in a memorandum. They were to represent all growers of importance, and be organized on an industry rather than on a strict commodity basis. They would frequently "advise with" Acco on long-run and short-run objectives. In the first group might be included lower

[8] Egan to Baum, wire on or about July 17, 1939, GX 1716.
[9] Baum to Ralph W. Burger, June 14, 1940, GX 1724.

distribution costs, better grading and packing, plans for orderly marketing which would smooth out price fluctuations, etc.

The "season-to-season phase" of the program was concerned largely with ascertaining the right moment for a special A & P promotional drive when shipments were at their peak, and insuring that it was efficiently run from both ends. But the committee would also encourage use of Acco's teletype system to acquaint them with market conditions. The network would also be a means of coordinating crop movements and drives originating in different parts of the country.[10]

On their face, these proposals pose no new problems. Shippers would make use of Acco facilities, and depend on it for a ready market. These benefits, which represented little or no incremental cost to Acco, the growers would doubtless be willing to consider when setting prices; the end result would be lower prices, better quality, or greater availability for Acco in buying. Again, some of Acco's overhead would be shared by shippers, and Acco would obtain part of the resulting economy.

"Building in" with shippers. In our few examples of "building in" of shippers with Acco, this picture seems to be fairly well borne out. We may consider Mutual Orange Distributors (M.O.D.), who represented 3,000 growers and 28 packers, and was the second largest citrus cooperative in California. From 1936 onward, Acco was their exclusive representative at most terminal markets, and their fruit was shipped on a price arrival basis. In areas covered by auctions, the auction price became M.O.D.'s price; elsewhere it was negotiated, and was supposed to approximate the "average prevailing market" for comparable citrus fruit. It is worth noting that this is an average, not a "going" price. During 1936–1939, Acco also received a quantity discount.[11] It is difficult to see any particular inequality of bargaining power in this arrangement.

Nor is it possible to say that M.O.D.'s prices were any lower than they would have been had they sold to other buyers. Such

---

[10] Baum, "Outline of a tentative program and objectives of the Eastern Shore advisory committee," GX 1868–A.

[11] The foregoing paragraph is based on the testimony of Baum, Tr. 18,650–3, and of J. A. Steward, general manager of M.O.D., Tr. 8683–4.

fragmentary evidence as we have points rather the other way. A study made by the Federal Trade Commission, which covered several markets in the late fall of 1936, showed that the average growers' return on California navel oranges sold to chains was 19 per cent higher than to independents; for Valencia oranges, 13 per cent higher.[12] Moreover, nearly three fourths of all California oranges were sold through the California Fruit Growers' Exchange and bore their "Sunkist" brand.[13] Therefore the great bulk of oranges sold to independents must have borne a deduction for advertising, of which M.O.D. did very little.[14] Hence the differential between the net return from chains and from independents was even greater than the FTC data suggest. We cannot push the comparison too far, for many of the sales to chains were made by Sunkist; furthermore, average quality of chain purchases may have been higher. But the available data make one suspect that M.O.D. members were doing at least as well as or better than their brethren in C.F.G.E., although Acco was doing better than the average buyer.

A letter from Egan to Baum reinforces the impressions. For it suggests a deal with two large apple shippers in Washington, "something along the lines we have with the M.O.D. . . . We could do this quietly and without any hubbub, and an arrangement of this kind would make it possible to reduce our personnel up there."[15] The saving of expense in such a deal is obvious; so is the fear of hostility from the shippers. Acco was not, in this case, looking for sellers with weak bargaining power, but for large shippers; the implication seems warranted that in the M.O.D. arrangement, which they considered a model, the basic consideration was simply a saving in the cost of operation.

Relations with Florida citrus producers were much less harmonious. Late in 1939, Baum wrote to a large shipper, complaining that Acco's suppliers were frequently squabbling among themselves for larger shares of the Commission Company's business. This scarcely suggests lower returns from Acco. Baum suggested

[12] FTC, *Report . . . on Distribution Methods and Costs*, Part I (Washington, 1944), pp. 137–140.
[13] Geoffrey S. Shepherd, *Marketing Farm Products* (Ames, 1946), p. 325.
[14] Steward, Tr. 8684.
[15] Egan to Baum, July 5, 1939, GX 2311.

that his correspondent's cooperative set up "centralized packing houses," and estimated that by concentrating the Acco business there, about 25 cents could be saved per box, which he was willing "to reflect directly back to the grower." [16] There is no record of an answer. But Baum's action may well have been prompted by the censure of the Florida Citrus Producers Trade Association three months previously, which had been sent with a covering letter to John Hartford.[17] One of the Association members was the Florida Citrus Exchange, with whom Acco had done a good deal of business, and whom Acco's southeastern manager asked to withdraw from the parent organization at once.[18] This they refused to do, and Baum indicated his displeasure: "You can rest assured that we are not going to give preference to any organizations that do not appreciate our business." [19]

In mid-1941, a small cooperative which was a member of the Florida Citrus Exchange attempted to sell directly to Acco, without paying a fee to the Exchange, but was rebuffed, and then withdrew anyway.[20] Baum assured the Exchange that he would permit no such by-passing; nevertheless, in 1942, the former member of Florida Citrus Exchange sold Acco about half as many cars as in 1941.[21] Presumably Acco was not simply disregarding its word, but found it difficult to procure enough citrus in 1942.

In both cases, M.O.D. and Florida Citrus Exchange, there is no reason to suppose that the members were abused. The apparent friendliness of the officers with Baum, willingness to help in setting up contact committees, and in reassuring growers and shippers who complained of Acco tactics, were a help to Acco. But the committee members knew the returns they and their neighbors were getting. There is no evidence that they were done

[16] Baum to Kramer of Lake Wales, Fla., December 20, 1939, GX 4479.
[17] Florida Citrus Producers to Hartford, November 22, 1939, GX 4479.
[18] C. C. Commander, general manager Florida Citrus Exchange, to Baum, December 2, 1939, GX 4461.
[19] Baum to Commander, December 5, 1939, GX 4462.
[20] Commander to Baum, May 28, 1941, GX 4466; Baum to Ward, June 1, 1941, GX 4464.
[21] Baum to Commander, note attached to GX 4464; testimony of Lester F. Collier, Tr. 7722, 7726-7.

out of anything. The statistics suggest that they realized better than average return.

Relations with the Farmers Cooperative Exchange of North Carolina are more difficult to assess. M. G. Mann, its general manager, knew little about produce marketing,[22] but made a deal with Baum in 1939 whereby Acco took the entire Farmers Cooperative Exchange potato crop of about 700 cars. The price to A & P warehouses was "prevailing average market," which in this case was construed as "the going price of the larger operators." There was a quantity discount; but Acco was to place A & P sales so as to minimize the freight charges, which would have been a saving to the Cooperative. Sales outside A & P were on a brokerage basis; ungraded potatoes were to be shipped on consignment to large Eastern markets.[23]

There seems to be nothing oppressive in the contract itself. But the voluminous correspondence between Mann and Baum is sufficient indication that if Acco had the desire and the opportunity to interpret the contract in the way most favorable to them, they could have done so, at least over the one season. The tone of the letters is fairly rendered by what Mann wrote Baum after one trip at Acco's expense:

Well, we are back home and I do want to thank you for a wonderful trip and the opportunity which you gave to me to attend the conference and the most wonderful opportunity that I think I have ever had — to meet Mr. George and Mr. John Hartford. Frankly, I shall think of this as I travel along life's pathway as one of the very high spots in my life.[24]

Hence there is no surprise in seeing that when the Farmers Cooperative Exchange sales manager, who had himself been suggested by Baum, complained about pricing of the Exchange's carlots,[25] Mann took Baum's hint and decided he ought to be let go.[26]

The liabilities of building in with Acco are well shown by a

[22] Mann to Baum, December 28, 1937, GX 3575.
[23] Baum to S. E. Bennett of Acco, March 4, 1939, GX 3723; and Baum to Mann, March 28, 1939, GX 1946.
[24] Mann to Baum, August 16, 1940.
[25] Robinson to Baum, July 17, 1940, GX 3736; Robinson to the Norfolk office of Acco, same date, GX 3737.
[26] Mann to Baum, November 21, 1940, GX 3738.

letter from the Exchange's marketing section manager to Mann. On a heavy sweet potato crop, of good quality:

> We are in need of some support. . . . Because of our support to the Acco, the outside trade is not supporting us as they might otherwise. In lining up with the Acco as we are and then they do not give us any support, we are going to be in a bad way. . . . We need help and need it quick.[27]

The crop years 1939, 1940, and 1941 were poor. All the Exchange could show for the three-year deal with Acco was $650 which Acco had paid as salary to the sales director they had suggested as a replacement.[28] There is no evidence that the Acco connection was responsible for the poor showing, and no attempt was made at the trial to prove it. A previous Sherman Act indictment of Acco had resulted in a directed verdict or not guilty.[29] Nevertheless, one cannot help feeling some doubt that the Farmers Cooperative Exchange could have done no better without Acco.

Another example of a cooperative official paid by Acco is the secretary of a watermelon group in Georgia. Apparently the membership considered it worth while because it saved them the expense of paying him a salary.[30] According to his own testimony, he suggested that in-transit risk be assumed by his cooperative, but did not suggest that the differential for cash be reduced or eliminated.[31] Perhaps the cooperative members would have found a salary less expensive in the not-so-long run.

No general statement is justified about the effects of relations with shipper organizations. Acco found them worth while. But this does not mean that the shippers lost out. Voluminous evidence about social contacts tells very little of what a few price data might tell. But the law, like the Almighty, has its own purposes.

"Super Coop." Baum explained on the witness stand that he

---

[27] J. J. Hilton to Mann, December 7, 1940, GX 1983.

[28] Mann to Baum, July 11, 1941, GX 3583.

[29] U.S. v. Atlantic Commission Co., Criminal 1710, indictment brought on December 8, 1941, in the Eastern District of North Carolina. At the close of the government evidence, the court ruled that it could not support the allegations of the indictment.

[30] Testimony of J. J. Parrish, Tr. 18,431.

[31] Parrish, Tr. 18,432.

was "a firm believer in farm organizations" because they gave the farmer-members "better trading power than they have as individuals." [32] However that may be, he was certainly interested in promoting cooperation with Acco. Early in 1938, he conferred with Hartford and other company officials, Carl Byoir, the publicity man, and Bruce Holsomback, a Texas shipper who handled most of Vice-President Garner's private business affairs. Baum's idea was, in fact, political as well as economic:

A national distributive institute of fresh fruit and vegetable shippers would be an excellent organization for the benefit of shippers, this institute to furnish these shippers with information and statistics as well [as] combat various detrimental factors in the business such as dealer financing; support for the more economical distributors . . . promotional work for these shippers . . . etc.[33]

Nothing came of these early discussions. A year later, Baum suggested that the proposed organization make Acco "distributors for the total or at least the bulk of the merchandise" they shipped, in return for which Acco would turn back 50 per cent of its profits to them. Growers would also benefit by the assured market. Nor was this philanthropy on Baum's part, for there would be solid gains to Acco:

(1) . . . Our tonnage would increase by approximately one-third within a short time, which if realized would pare operating expenses by at least $6 a car. [This would have been a reduction of 29 to 35 per cent.[34]]

(2) It would insure a greater availability of supplies for the A & P . . . particularly for the extra demand created through special sales efforts, features, drives, etc.; also would allow a somewhat wider selection of merchandise which at times would permit the filling of orders more closely in keeping with actual store needs and specifications.

(3) . . . Through . . . intimate contact and close working arrangements . . . facilities would be provided for quickly setting into motion organized agricultural opposition to punitive and discriminatory legislation.[35]

[32] Baum, Tr. 18,539.
[33] Executive meeting, Acco, March 15, 1938, GX 2019.
[34] Income statement of Acco for 1938, as included in the 1941 *Annual Binder*, GX 314.
[35] There was nothing secret about the statement; in fact, it was intended to serve as the basis of a press release. Dated June 29, 1939, in the record as GX 2022-A.

The statement is worth quoting as an example of Acco's purposes in general, as well as in sponsoring the new organization. Most striking is the first paragraph: despite its large volume of business, even Acco was still working well below the optimum, and incremental costs were well below average costs. Market information was a large indivisible factor, largely responsible.

The history of the Cooperative Fruit and Vegetable Association, usually referred to as "Super Coop," launched the following year and abandoned by Acco early in 1942, is summarized in the District Court's opinion.[36] The purposes have been made plain enough. As for the potential effects on competition, this would have depended on the share of the market which Acco might have gained.

Appraisal of Acco buying

In general, the remarks on buying of trading items hold for produce as well. Acco was a large buyer who operated in many imperfectly connected markets. Because of its size and resources, its superior information, and its ability to shift from market to market, it was able to buy at lower net prices than paid by its rivals. It was able to merge or eliminate overlapping functions between its sellers and itself, particularly the function of assuming risk in holding the merchandise while seeking a buyer.

By spreading lower prices throughout the system as soon as they appeared anywhere and, conversely, by spreading its bidding farther afield as soon as scarcities appeared Acco increased the perfection of the market, and the speed with which it registered changes in supply and demand. Its arbitrage profit must have been substantial.

The policy of a buying monopolist, or of a combination of buyers who take note of each others' actions, will be "nonaggressive." Bidding for goods will be pushed only so far as that amount which maximizes the buyer's profits. To bid further would raise the price not only for the additional goods but for all previous goods. Hence the increment to cost attributable to the increment of goods purchased would be so high as to be unprofitable. There-

---

[36] 67 F. Supp. 656–659.

fore a single or group monopoly results in lower purchases at lower prices.[37] There is no hint of this behavior in Acco's operations; on the contrary, their policy seems to have been always directed toward buying more.

The advantage to A & P is partly expressed in Acco's high profits, which reflect highly efficient operation; partly in quality and availability, which conferred money benefits not usually traceable. Or, what comes to the same thing, A & P bought more cheaply through Acco than it would have by merely having agents in Washington Street and other terminal markets. Since Acco as seller to the trade was able to undersell, wholesalers and retailers other than A & P were able to buy produce a little cheaper. There is no evidence of any offsetting diseconomies; hence one must conclude that Acco's savings were not only private but social as well, and that there was a net saving of labor and capital because of its activities. By introducing a superior way of doing business, i.e., the integration of produce buying and selling, A & P was able to draw business away from its rivals. The reader may call this competition or anticompetition, depending on his taste in words and economic systems.

Growers have received at least as high a price from chains as from independents. To the extent that farmers had become, through their cooperatives, middlemen as well as producers, their incomes may have suffered. But it is also possible that even their losses as distributors were wholly or partly offset by the larger demand for farm products. Over the longer run, as consumers become more familiar with fresh fruits and vegetables and more insistent on them in the daily diet, the benefit to farmers seems clear.

Absence of price discrimination. In discussing the purchase of manufactured foods, we isolated and analyzed in much detail the elements of discrimination in favor of A & P. It existed where and only where sellers had some appreciable amount of market control. This might be based either on a large share of a market or on a differentiated product which had not been pushed through

---

[37] The problem has been analyzed, as definitively as is possible in this field of economics, in Nicholls, *Imperfect Competition within Agricultural Industries* (Ames, 1941), chapters 3 and 7.

the "sonic barrier" into the region where consumer demand would force distributors to buy all at the same price.

Neither condition for price discrimination existed in Acco markets. There were no sellers with enough market control to discriminate. And, with the possible exception of two purchases of bananas,[38] which are almost monopolized by United Fruit Co., there is literally no evidence in the record of a single discriminatory sale.

What we do find is a large-scale evasion of 2(c), the brokerage clause of the Robinson-Patman Act. The basis for evasion is already familiar from Chapter VIII. The most that Acco could achieve through evasion was equality of treatment. They could not do better, because sellers had plenty of alternative outlets — some nine tenths of the market, in fact. Acco's object, and its principal obstacle, are summed up beautifully in the letter from Del Monte.

Acco *tried* to persuade shippers to give it equal treatment, and to accept the same net return from Acco as from their buyers. Not that Acco would have had the slightest objection to paying a lower price! But the economics of the produce markets and Acco's small share of those markets prevented any such discrimination. But that same market structure gave them many opportunities to escape the discrimination against direct buyers that Section 2(c) prescribes. Del Monte, as their letter makes clear, knew that they were a large corporation, visible, and hence liable to prosecution. The great bulk of sellers were under no such handicap. They knew that Acco was forbidden to accept brokerage or the equivalent, but that plenty of other sellers were willing to give away most of the phantom brokerage in order to get or keep some. Furthermore, there were definite marketing costs to be saved at the terminal markets. Even if nothing was left of the latter, they were still no worse off than in selling to other buyers. And Acco was a good customer; steady sales to them saved the expense of maintaining the contact function, and resulted in a net saving, and a higher net return to the seller, even when the price net of brokerage was the same.

---

[38] Gallagher (vice-president, Southern Division) to sales manager, March 30, 1935, GX 1762; Wehman to Eckert, January 10, 1941, GX 875.

Of course, Acco took some and perhaps most of these cost savings; likewise the economies of splitting carloads at the terminal markets. In general, A & P did have a buying advantage over the average of its rivals, and did own its goods at a smaller outlay. But this resulted from economies of scale in the produce markets, not from price discrimination. Many of these economies came into existence as arbitrage profits, serving to make the markets a little less imperfect, and narrowing somewhat the very wide limits between the high and low ranges of price fluctuations in any given time period.

PART III

ECONOMIC THEORY
AND PUBLIC POLICY

XVI

THE A & P LITIGATION: THE ECONOMIC THEORY AND POLICY OF THE PROSECUTION

The sneaking arts of underling tradesmen are thus erected into political maxims for the conduct of a great empire. . . .

ADAM SMITH

In this and the next chapter we examine the history of the A & P litigation and analyze the economic theory, public policy, and legal doctrine underlying the prosecution and the judicial decisions. Our aim is to discover by economic and legal analysis what was said by "judge and company," [1] for the two are members of one another. We are not concerned with "why" they said it, or whether they "really" intended to say something else. To paraphrase Holmes: we do not inquire what the prosecutors and judges meant; we ask only what the briefs and decisions mean.[2] For reasons explained in the Introduction, this chapter must be very long. The extraordinary confusion and evanescence of the government case makes it necessary to go over the whole ground and sometimes to retrace it. The following brief survey, it is hoped, will ease the task.

---

[1] Jeremy Bentham: "The law is not made by judge alone, but by judge and company." Quoted in Paul Freund, *On Understanding the Supreme Court* (Boston, 1950), p. 78.

[2] "We do not inquire what the legislature meant; we ask only what the statute means." Oliver Wendell Holmes, *Collected Legal Papers* (New York, 1920), p. 207.

We first review briefly the history of the litigation, from the original indictments through the trial and appeal of the criminal case; the civil suit; and the final consent decree. Turning to the government case, we first analyze that part dealing with general sales and price policy, as distinct from any local practices. Next is integration in manufacturing and distribution. Buying policy is considered under two aspects: the pseudo-discrimination (in the economic sense) of arbitrage or "demoralization," brokerage in general and as a fiduciary abuse, and resale by buying offices. We then consider true price discrimination, both as it existed and as only assumed for the sake of the argument, in order to explore the logical implications of the prosecution argument. This includes the important government theory of recoupment, the effect of discrimination upon the market process, and finally the role of advertising allowances.

We then have a reconsideration of selling and buying policy as a whole — the impact upon competitors of the real and fancied "competitive advantages" of A & P as seller and buyer. We first indicate the likelihood of predatory competition by A & P in its many markets, then review the voluminous evidence offered to show "sales below cost in selected areas" — the allocation of subsidiary profits, operations in particular areas, prices lowered to meet competition and then raised, the record of actual "red ink stores," and local predatory actions. The method of analysis used in this chapter (and the others) has been ardently attacked as "unfair"; and this is discussed in Appendix V.

The Legal History of the Prosecution

In June 1939, as noted in Chapter IV, when conversion to supermarkets and low prices was in full swing but already a proved success, the divisional presidents' meeting noted that the National Association of Retail Grocers had petitioned for an investigation of A & P. During 1940 and 1941 the Department of Justice conducted an investigation of the food trade and examined suppliers' files. In October 1941, an official of the Antitrust Division explained "what was then a new program in antitrust activities" to the United States Wholesale Grocers' Association, Inc.[3] Perhaps J. H. MacLaurin (see Chapter X, p. 216) was in the audience and able to rejoice.

In November 1942, a grand jury was convened and an indictment was secured at Dallas, charging a conspiracy to restrain and to monopolize the trade in food, in violation of Sections 1 and 2 of the Sherman Act. A & P's demurrer was sustained by the District Court, but reversed by the Court of Appeals, and the Supreme Court denied certiorari.[4] Upon remand, the District Court ordered the prosecution to strike out some of the charges and to file a bill of particulars,[5] and the case was set for trial early in 1944. But on February 26, 1944, the Antitrust Division dropped the case in Dallas,[6] and on the same day filed a criminal information in the District Court at Danville, Illinois.[7] The defendants waived a jury, and trial commenced in April 1945. The transcript of record accumulated about 30,000 pages, and 5,600 exhibits were filed. If we include also the various briefs and appendices filed by both sides, the total volume was around 50,000 pages, perhaps exceeded only by the incredible 100,000 pages in the *Second Cement* case.[8] The trial ended in April 1946, and in September the Hon. Walter C. Lindley, District Judge, filed an opinion which found nearly all the defendants guilty of violating both Sections.[9]

As a study in advocacy and procedure, the trial deserves more study than the writer has time or training to give it. The defense perhaps made their first mistake in waiving trial by jury, for although a prolonged trial would have aroused the anger of the

[3] Address on A & P Decision . . . , published by United States Wholesale Grocers' Association, Inc., Washington 5, D. C., October 1946 (mineographed), p. 1.

[4] United States v. Great Atlantic & Pacific Tea Co., 137 F.2d 459 (5th Cir. 1943), *cert. den.*, 320 U. S. 783 (1943).

[5] U. S. v. the New York Great Atlantic & Pacific Tea Co., 52 F. Supp. 681 (N.D., Tex. 1943).

[6] More precisely, they filed a nolle prosequi without prejudice in the Dallas court (54 F. Supp. 257). The defense objection was overruled.

[7] A criminal information differs from an indictment in that it is filed by a prosecuting officer on his information and belief, rather than returned by a grand jury after its own investigation.

[8] Federal Trade Commission v. Cement Institute et al., 333 U.S. 683 (1948).

[9] U. S. v. the New York Great Atlantic & Pacific Tea Company et al., 67 F. Supp. 626 (E.D. Ill. 1946). Hereafter referred to as 67 F. Supp., with appropriate page number.

jurors, it needed only one of them turning his ire against the government to insure no conviction. This first error was not the last. The defendants thought it expedient to keep their experienced lawyers on the sidelines, and permitted the trial to be conducted largely by local attorneys. This was perhaps a deeply considered stroke of "shrewd" psychology, an "adroit" catering to the prejudices of the local populace, etc. If so, it met the fate it deserved. The defense attorneys were often bumbling and sometimes arrogant; above all, they had no inkling of any general strategy. It is perhaps unjust to criticize from hindsight; but from hindsight it is clear that in law as in politics one can't beat something with nothing. The government did have a coherent theory or "vision" of the case, and the best the defense could do was say: whatever it is, we didn't do it. The defense realized that they were fighting a Robinson-Patman case in disguise, but they tried to fight it in detail, offering Robinson-Patman defenses, such as not knowing of price preferences. They did not grasp the government strategy, which was brilliant and productive of new law: a linking up a number of Robinson-Patman violations with vague but dramatic insinuations of coercive and predatory behavior, to compose a pattern or at the least to constitute enough smoke to imply fire.

Moreover, the government attorneys knew how to try an antitrust case. The volume of evidence was huge; the court was inundated and completely unable to keep it in focus. Little or nothing could be retained from this traumatic experience except the spicy phrases noted earlier: "Two price levels"; "They would not care how much money you lost"; "It would take half the population of the United States to police this sort of thing," and so on. All in all, the A & P case contributed its share to the store of "immortal antitrust prose."[10] Perhaps none of the literary gems of the case are equal in quality to the best in, say, *Socony-Vacuum*[11] or *Hartford-Empire*.[12] There is something prosaic about the food trade. The French have a feeling for words, and when they consider someone as the last word in everyday dull-

---

[10] The phrase is that of Jerrold G. Van Cise of the New York Bar.
[11] Socony-Vacuum Oil Co. et al. v. U. S., 310 U. S. 150 (1940).
[12] Hartford-Empire Co. v. U. S., 323 U. S. 386, 431 (1945).

ness, they call him *épicier,* a grocer. But in quantity of colorful phrases, the A & P case does not suffer by comparison.

The company took an appeal late in 1946 to the Seventh Circuit Court of Appeals in Chicago, and it was argued in January 1949. In sharp contrast to the trial, the defense presentation was now of high quality. But their task was hopeless; appeals are supposed to be directed to matters of law, not of fact, but the new law was embodied in the "facts" as the District Court had seen them. In February 1949, the conviction was affirmed.[13] Shortly thereafter company announced that it would not appeal further, and it paid the fines, totalling $175,000.

In September 1949, the long-awaited civil suit was filed in New York, asking that A & P be dismembered by divorcing the manufacturing plants, dissolving Acco, and dividing the retail establishments into seven parts corresponding to the seven divisions.[14] The offenses charged in this complaint were stated to be "substantially identical with the conduct" of which they had been convicted in the criminal trial.[15]

Suits of this kind are usually launched with a flurry of statements by prosecution and defense, descanting on the respective wickedness and uprightness of the defendants. Thereupon both sides fall silent and settle down to the work of preparing and trying a case. In this case the precedent was to be broken. Before a week had passed, A & P launched a nation-wide advertising campaign attacking the suit. The contempt of many a public-relations expert for the intelligence of the human race was clearly audible in the tom-tom repetition of the "the antitrust lawyers . . . the antitrust lawyers . . . the antitrust lawyers" allegedly persecuting A & P. Doubtless the company was not committing any contempt of court in the legal sense. It is difficult to call the campaign anything but contempt of the judicial process (see also below, Chapter XVII). Moreover, like the other brilliant stroke

[13] New York Great Atlantic & Pacific Tea Co. v. U. S., 173 F.2d 79 (7th Cir. 1949). Hereafter cited as 173 F.2d, with appropriate page number.
[14] In the United States District Court for the Southern District of New York, U. S. v. the New York Great Atlantic & Pacific Tea Co. et al., Civil Action No. 52–139, filed September 15, 1949.
[15] Civil Action No. 52–139, para. 23, p. 22, of the original mineographed complaint. There seems to have been an error in the numbering scheme.

of using local attorneys, the huckster tactic turned out to be ill-advised from the company's own point of view. For the Complaint virtually admitted that there would not be much new evidence available at the civil suit.[16] Hence, there were grounds for hoping that the government would eventually be willing to accept a more or less innocuous consent decree in lieu of the drastic relief asked — since a careful second consideration of the evidence, with no advantage of surprise to the prosecution, would have exposed its lack of content. But the publicity campaign made it impossible for the Antitrust Division to back down.

Both sides thereupon began the legal war by long-range bombing preparation. The missiles were huge interrogatories propounded by plaintiff to defendant and vice versa, to answer which fully would have consumed several times the available man hours of both adversaries. Throughout the years 1950–1953, the work of preparation continued, although the outside world cannot know whether it was continuous or desultory. In April 1953, it became publicly known that A & P had offered a proposed consent judgment to the government.[17]

To press or not to press the suit was, of course, a difficult question for the Attorney General. An innocuous judgment might antagonize many voters; and, even if a public-opinion poll were to show a majority in favor of such a settlement, the reaction of the unfavorable minority might be more important. For they might have much stronger feelings on the subject, and as local men of affairs be in a much better position to register them with Congress. As Smith wrote to Adams back in 1940:

A ruthless politician can cause us a lot of grief with a small amount of support from the independent retailers, disgruntled manufacturers, and agricultural groups. . . . Mr. and Mrs. Public think a lot of us as long as we serve them well, but when we get into trouble they are not much help.[18]

Aside from the political repercussions, the legal merits could not easily be appraised. The prosecution started with a great advantage: the courts had ruled that A & P had violated the

[16] Civil Action No. 52–139, para. 23; and part V, paras. 3, 6.
[17] *New York Times*, April 7, 1953, p. 21.
[18] R. M. Smith to O. C. Adams, July 16, 1940, GX 217B.

Sherman Act. Since this violation had been established "beyond a reasonable doubt" at a criminal trial, and upheld on appeal, it sufficed a fortiori at a civil trial. Hence the question of liability was already decided, needing only a reaffirmation which a District Court could not refuse.[19] One could therefore proceed directly to the question of relief.

So far, so good, but the question would then arise as to what relief was appropriate to the violation. Perhaps the fine and its implied warning might be considered sufficient. In order to dispose of this question, one would need to consider not the ultimate conclusion of the District Court, but the detailed findings, as to buying, selling, Acco, etc. Unfortunately, the District Court never made any formal findings of fact, and its long memorandum opinion actually contains very few. We shall urge at a later point that these many doubts and ambiguities really do credit to the Court, but they did make it very difficult to point to many definite conditions and say: *these* are offensive to the law, and, because of their nature, they can be ended only by dissolution.

Matters were much better, from the prosecution point of view, with the Circuit Court opinion, which in effect made a number of findings of fact. But were these to be considered findings in the sense of *res adjudicata*? In general, an appeals court exists to consider questions of law, not of fact. Furthermore, the Circuit Court opinion stated at the outset that it was considering only such evidence as was favorable to the District Court's opinion.[20] Of course, there was nothing biased or improper about this; its function was obviously not to retry the case but to see whether there was "substantial evidence" for the District Court opinion, even though, on perusal of everything in the record, it might not have agreed with that opinion. But if the Court of Appeals considered only evidence favorable to the District Court opinion, it is not obvious that its statements of fact had the status of findings of fact binding on later courts, since these statements were not made on the basis of the record as a whole.

Enough has been said to show that the civil suit, had it been tried, might well have been decided on purely legal or procedural

---

[19] U. S. v. National City Lines, 118 F. Supp. 465 (N.D. Ill. 1953).
[20] 173 F.2d 79.

grounds having little relation to economics. In any event, on January 19, 1954, eleven years after the beginning of the criminal action, and more than four years after the filing of the civil suit, a consent decree was entered into by the Department of Justice and the company.[21] Its terms, which will be discussed in more detail later, imposed certain minor disadvantages on the purchasing operations of A & P. Aside from these, the consent decree was a sweeping victory for the defense, and the position of the company was much better than it had been at the end of the criminal trial, though not as good as before the trial.

The Government Case

A. Sales and price policy in general

The essence of the case can be put in terms of a simple diagram. As Figure 2 [22] indicates, and both parties would agree: within limits the lower the gross margin, the larger the sales; and the larger the sales, the lower the expense rate. At sales of OA,

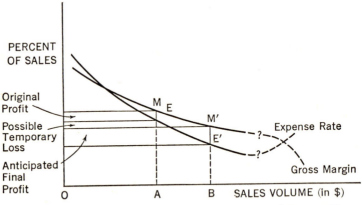

FIGURE 2. Hypothetical Relation of Gross Margin and Expense Rate to Sales

[21] In the United States District Court for the Southern District of New York, U. S. v. the New York Great Atlantic & Pacific Tea Co., et al., Civil Action No. 52–139, Final Judgment, January 19, 1954.

[22] The slopes should be disregarded; only the general shape is of interest.

expenses per unit sold would be AE, gross margin would be AM, profit per unit would be EM, and total profit would be the rectangle labeled "original profit." Now, if the company, in pursuit of greater volume, lowered the gross margin to BM', sales would increase to OB, the expense rate would fall to BE', and, as indicated by the rectangle, final profit would be much greater than the original profit. But, as Part I has shown in detail, there was a risk. The actual slope of the demand curve was unknown and could only be found by trial and error. If consumers for a time did not respond, sales would be no larger, the expense rate no lower, and the profit might be turned into a loss, as represented by the rectangle labeled "temporary loss."

According to traditional economic analysis, unrestrained competition for additional business will drive firms in just this manner to reduce prices and costs, thereby passing on to society the benefits of more efficient operation. The basic criticism of effective monopoly is that the firm or firms seek greater profit by restricting output short of the least-cost point and hence keeping prices up.

But the case against A & P is precisely the contrary: it attacks the company's attempt to move in the direction of greater output at lower cost. By lowering the gross profit rate in order to induce greater volume, A & P was selling below cost and unfairly burdening competition. In the words of the government brief:

In speaking of how meat business . . . had increased from $200 to $1,200 per store, he [John Hartford] pointed out: "This was accomplished by reducing the gross profit rate until the volume was built up to a point where the expense rate was low enough to permit the store to operate at a profit." *We know of no more clear and concise words with which to express the Government's charge. . . .*

Hartford then attempted to advance what amounted to a plea in confession and avoidance: "Well, I knew that just as soon as we could get on a proper operating basis, we would have every reason to believe, from our experience, we would get the volume that would take care of it." . . . The evil, however, which is inherent in this pattern lies in the selection of an arbitrary gross profit rate chosen without regard to the expense rate and fixed at a figure which defendants believe will produce the chosen figure of desired volume.[23]

[23] GB(DC), pp. 110 and 837 (italics added).

. . . Gross profit rates in selected areas have been set below the expense rates in such areas. [It is incorrect to] argue merely that *eventually* such a practice will result in a profitable operation since the increased volume produced by setting the gross profit rate below the expense rate will *eventually* reduce the expense rates to a point where *ultimately* a profit will be earned.[24]

Of course, the lowering of gross profit rates may *ultimately* result in increased sales and hence in increased profits. But [this] ignores the restraining effect upon A & P's retail competition during the interval required for increased sales to reduce the expense rate.[25]

In what sense is this "selling below cost?" Suppose — and this is what actually happened — that consumers are so quick to see, compare, and decide that A & P receives the increased business immediately, and overnight moves from one profitable position to an even more profitable one. In that case, there is never any loss and never any selling below cost. But of course this may not happen. Consumers may or may not respond; costs may fall with higher output, or they may rise. As Figure 2 shows, the instant result of a price reduction may be a (proportionately) much larger profit reduction or an actual loss. A businessman trained in economics has well said that "it takes courage as well as sagacity to gamble on a rate of demand that will bring forth the volume needed for lower costs." [26] Part I has elaborately demonstrated this fact. Competitive price cuts of any magnitude (1) typically involve the risk or expectation of "selling below cost" until and unless the market responds; and (2) invariably aim at larger profits (or smaller losses) through larger volume. If A & P's price cutting is illegal, then most price competition, where profit margins are narrow, is illegal.

A & P, in order to serve its own interests, absorbed progressively fewer resources per dollar or per ton of the goods it handled and passed along to consumers a large part of the savings. Obviously, A & P sold "below the cost" which it *might* have incurred if it had preferred to stay at the old inefficient level. The

---

[24] GB(AC), p. 373 (italics in original).

[25] GB(AC), p. 384 (italics in original). The second sentence is a really grand misstatement, since prices were the same during and after "the interval."

[26] Oswald W. Knauth, "Monopoly Reconsidered," *Political Science Quarterly*, December 1945, p. 566.

government insists that it *should* have stayed there. An "honest retailer" would attempt to "price his merchandise in the traditional American way, that is, cost, plus expenses, plus a profit." [27]

In fact, even if there is no temporary loss suffered — as there was none in the A & P case — the defendants were still considered as selling below cost. Thus:

With premeditation the divisional office of the Southern Division told the Dallas Unit that since the program was an absolute one, emanating from Headquarters, no one had any choice in the matter. The only hope of staying out of large red figures was that sales would respond to the low gross profit program and the additional business might decrease the expense rate. *Thus the cart was placed before the horse.* If the defendants were not operating their business with a design to injure competitors, they could *fix their gross profit rate in accordance with their expense rate* and in proportion to the amount of increase of business they would do *operating on an orthodox basis,* rather than deliberately taking planned losses for the purpose of increasing volume.[28]

This is clear. The only lawful way to do business is to price on an "orthodox" basis, by cost plus an expense rate assuming only the past or present sales volume. The illegality consists in assuming, or aiming at, a higher sales volume at lower prices.

We shall later be forced to return to "selling below cost," in connection with horizontal and vertical integration. But it must be carefully noted that integration is an offense additional to and separate from "selling below cost" by means of "reducing the gross profit rate until the volume was built up to the point where the expense rate was low enough to permit the store to operate at a profit."

For it was of this statement, *standing alone,* that the prosecution said: "We know of no more clear and concise words with which to express the Government's charge." There is no reference here to "subsidies" from other branches of the business, or to elimination of competition, or to anything else but the single fact that A & P estimated in advance what markup would be most profitable, set that markup, and adhered to it.

---

[27] GB(DC), p. 405.
[28] GB(DC), p. 842 (italics added).

B. *Integration in manufacturing and distribution*

In a sense, every other issue of the A & P case reduces ultimately to integration. But we shall find it more expedient to divide it into three parts: in manufacturing, in wholesaling-retailing, and in buying. The government brief in the District Court stated the issue as follows:

> The profits from the non-retail end of the business . . . subsidized the retail business, so that the latter could operate at an uneconomic profit rate, *a privilege not possible to A & P's competitors.* This, the Government contends, is an inherent abuse of the vertical integration of A & P's System.[29]

> Profits from all operations of the System are siphoned into its retail stores in order to offset uneconomic retail profit rates. The effect on competition of this unreasonable subsidization of retail operations is apparent in the relationship of profits from retail sales to the subsidies from non-retail sources.[30]

> As non-retail profits increased, Headquarters reduced the amount of profits from retail operations in order to place its stores in a position of price supremacy over competitors. By 1942, the crediting of non-retail profits to retail operations enabled A & P to operate its stores with inconsequential profits on retail sales.[31]

> The profits from A & P's non-retail operations are credited to their retail operations. . . . These direct subsidies make it difficult, if not impossible, for less strongly integrated, or for non-integrated competitors engaged only in retailing, to compete or survive.[32]

"Nonretail profits" consist of three parts: manufacturing profit, 702 allowances, and Acco profits.[33]

[29] GB(DC), p. 86 (italics added).
[30] GB(DC), p. 87.
[31] GB(DC), p. 94.
[32] GB(DC), p. 1075.
[33] I omit the discussion of gains by short-weight cheating of retail customers. It was trivial. Also, the FTC chain store investigation showed it was more prevalent in non-chain than in chain stores. See FTC, *Chain Stores, Final Report*, 74th Cong., 1 sess., Document No. 4 (1934), p. 48. Moreover, the District Court considered this as irrelevant to any issue of monopoly. 67 F. Supp. 643.

Acco profits are really a mixture of two types. One is alleged discriminatory gains, which will be discussed later. Otherwise, Acco may be considered as a profit-making subsidiary, such as a manufacturing subsidiary would be; to that extent, the following comments on manufacturing apply to it as well.

In what sense are the manufacturing or trading profits of A & P a "subsidy" to its nonmanufacturing operations? As we saw in Chapter XII, goods were transferred from the manufacturing to the selling department at market prices, and profits or losses were calculated for the A & P factories. The purpose of the company's accounting system was to picture its manufacturing and retailing separately, as if each one sold or bought in the open market rather than to and from each other.

These "profits" are an accounting device to indicate the economy or diseconomy of manufacturing at home instead of buying from other concerns. The mere existence of *some* accounting profit is no indication of economy. In the middle 1920's A & P was on the point of giving up some of its profitable manufacturing facilities because the capital employed there could apparently draw a higher return in retailing. Had this continued to be the case, A & P would have been worse off than a retailer who had devoted an equal capital exclusively to retailing. Their "subsidized" retail stores would have been at a disadvantage in competing with the "unsubsidized."

Any integrated company whatever — in steel, automobiles, meat-packing, textiles, distribution — can, and many do, keep books in the same way as A & P simply by setting a market price on goods transferred from one department to another.[34] So long as the earlier stages of any integrated company could be said to earn anything, however little, these fictitious "earnings" could be "siphoned" to abuse competition in the later stages. And this would be the case even when possession of the earlier stages was a burden on the integrated company because they were earning too small a rate of return!

[34] See D. H. Wallace, *Market Control in the Aluminum Industry* (Cambridge, 1937), ch. VIII, where the technological advantages of integration are analyzed. Every such advantage is expressed for the business firm in costs lower than suppliers' prices. Hence there arises a "profit" on making the goods at home.

The only way to reconcile the legality of integration with the illegality of "subsidizing" — for they are simply two names for the same thing — would be to throw the whole burden of blame on the accounting system. Either any and all integration is illegal, or else a rational form of accounting is illegal, or both. This is the only possible implication of the government case.

But there is also another error which goes to the root of the whole "siphoning" and "subsidy" argument. As we saw in Chapter XII, the accounting of subsidiary profits was strictly in terms of *incremental* profits, investment, and rate of return. This accounting device merely reflects the fact that the large profits of Quaker Maid are attributable to an assured market, steady operations, and lack of any selling or advertising costs. Geoffrey Shepherd has referred to the often "stupendous" cost of ownership transfer from one stage of distribution to the next; [35] and these costs are what A & P has been able to eliminate. Were there no warehouses and stores to which they could transfer goods so cheaply, their profits would never be so large. Therefore the "nonretail" manufacturing profits are just as properly imputed to the retail stores as to the factories and bakeries. These economies of integration are a joint product, attributable to two productive agents together and to neither of them individually.

These physical and social economies are to be called illegal because they are "a privilege not possible to A & P's competitors," and because they make it "difficult, if not impossible, for less-strongly integrated, or for non-integrated competitors engaged only in retailing, to compete or survive." Read "economies of integration" for "direct subsidies" and this becomes perfectly clear. It *is* difficult for less efficient firms to compete with more efficient firms — unless they have the Antitrust Division as their avenging angel.

During the oral argument before the Circuit Court, government counsel conceded that profits of manufacturing subsidiaries were really all right but were "commingled" with illegal profits made through price "discrimination," whereupon both were used for the illegal attack upon competitors; and he then quickly slid over to another subject.

[35] Geoffrey Shepherd, *Marketing Farm Products* (Ames, 1946), p. 391.

C. Buying policy

Pseudo-discrimination. (1) *"Demoralization."* An imperfect market, containing not a single price but a spread of prices (net of transfer costs), can be exploited by a large buyer who can be "all over the place" at any given moment and take the better offers. The effect of such a buyer is to narrow the range of prices, lower their average, and make for a single price in the market.

Evidence both in and out of the record indicates that sellers have a dislike for such buying offices, a dislike which is out of proportion to the size of their operations.[36] Letting the big buyer inside the market is considered very bad because concessions granted to him have such an unfortunate tendency to spread. Sellers who might otherwise receive higher prices because of their customers' ignorance of lower prices elsewhere in the market are forced to meet these lower prices. The large buyer may undercut them directly by reselling some bargain offers which he cannot use. Or he may set off vigorous price competition at a later stage in the productive or distributive process. As we saw above, A & P did both. It is not difficult to understand sellers' and competitors' resentment at such "demoralization."

This being everywhere at once was a genuine economy of size, not only for A & P but for the whole economy. What the prosecution means by "demoralization" is simply arbitrage. As with manufacturing integration and with a rational cost-price policy, this is an economy of large size, not available to smaller competitors. Therein lies the offense. This economy of size, incidentally, has nothing to do with monopsony power, which A & P lacked.

(2) *Brokerage.* An enormous volume of evidence, digested in earlier chapters, proved that much brokerage or its equivalent was being collected by the field buying offices, and by Acco.

There was no attempt by the prosecution to show that these allowances were in excess of actual cost savings to those granting

---

[36] See above, Chapters V–VII and XIII–XV *passim*; also Charles F. Roos, *NRA Economic Planning* (Bloomington, 1937), pp. 277–279, 293–304, 408, 503, 505; Charles Albert Pearce, *NRA Trade Practice Programs* (New York, 1938), p. 78.

them. (Such excesses would, of course, constitute price discrimination.) The mere collection of brokerage equivalent was urged as a sufficient offense. This is pure Robinson-Patman. Under Section 2(c) of that Act, there is no cost defense, and no pretense of examining any facts. *Equality of net return to the seller and equality of net price to all buyers is illegal per se.* Price discrimination is not only permitted but prescribed. The only way to stay within the law is to use "a sales system which constantly results in his [the seller's] getting more money for like goods from some customers than he does from others." [37] The Supreme Court's definition of price discrimination fits 2(c) — and the A & P case — perfectly.

Let us consider two buyers at one location. One of them buys goods delivered by the seller; the other buys f.o.b. and does his own transport. If both pay the seller the same price, it is obvious that the second is suffering discrimination. He is paying for a service he himself performs, and the seller is getting a higher net return from him than from the other. The middleman or broker function is entirely analogous to the transport function. Where A & P paid the same prices as those who bought through brokers, the net return to sellers would be greater on sales to A & P. As we saw in the earlier chapters, this was indeed the case and explains most of the record after 1936.

The legal doctrine urged here by the government amounts to this: the violation of 2(c) of the Robinson-Patman Act is a per se violation of the Sherman Act — an inherently unfair practice like price fixing. Section 2(c) of Robinson-Patman is now to be part of our "charter of industrial freedom." Undoubtedly the government intended this result.

But this argument is also an economic analysis and prescription. If we were to assume that A & P buying offices needed no personnel, premises, or equipment, and cost the company nothing to operate, then there might be sense in speaking of brokerage payments *in the gross* as a "rebate" or "a preferential buying advantage." [38] But only under such an assumption would this conclusion be warranted.

---

[37] Federal Trade Commission v. Cement Institute, 333 U.S. 683, 725 (1948).
[38] GB(DC), p. 225.

Of all the economic fallacies perpetrated by the Department of Justice, this is probably the most crude. For A & P's buying office had the same investment to make and the same costs to meet as anyone else's office. The Antitrust Division betrayed no understanding of the difference between a gross and net saving. The famous quotation about the "two price levels" (above, pp. 187–8) is treated as evidence of "discrimination," although it clearly describes a price difference corresponding to a cost difference. On this logic, there is discrimination when a primary steel mill pays "only" the cost of raw materials, while a fabricator or warehouse pays the market price of steel. The fallacy consists here in reckoning at zero the costs of operation of the steel mill. The government reckons at zero the costs of operation of the buying offices. Hence the whole revenue of the buying offices becomes an "advantage."

The government is quite clear on this point. It is not only the earning of profits through brokerage that is at fault: even if the brokerage offices only broke even, and earned no profit, that would still be an advantage and an illegality! [39]

(3) *Brokerage as a fiduciary abuse.* Brokerage "discrimination" is given the additional color of an abuse of fiduciary obligation. Thus:

The ordinary broker's primary allegiance in negotiating sales is to the seller who pays for his services. But when A & P bought from a seller, it became, as to that transaction, a party of opposing interest to such seller. In this situation, the strange role of the so-called "A & P broker" required that he . . . pass the seller's fee over to A & P. . . . By means of this thinly disguised rebate A & P secured a preferential buying advantage over competing retailers.[40]

Acco undertook to act as the agent of sellers and at the same time to act as the produce buyer for the A & P Group. Thus, it was obligated to obtain as high a price as possible for its seller-principal, and as low a price as possible for its purchasing agent. Acco consistently honored the second obligation and disregarded the first. In so acting through Acco, appellants patently violated the most elementary fiduciary obligations.[41]

Of course, brokers can represent buyers or sellers; and tradi-

[39] GB(AC Supplemental Brief), p. 31.
[40] GB(AC), p. 29.
[41] GB(AC), p. 356.

tionally they have done both. Furthermore, the statement is completely false as to field buying of processed foods, and is literally about 99 per cent false as to Acco buying. Both the brokerage offices and the Acco offices bought outright. They did not represent to sellers that they would secure the best possible prices from third-party buyers; they were themselves the buyers, and known as such. The seller had the alternative of selling either directly to them, or selling to others, or selling through brokers. He made the choice most profitable to himself. There was no fiduciary obligation by the field buying office or by Acco since nothing was entrusted to them: there was simply a process of offers, counteroffers, and final sales between the principals in face-to-face bargaining. Of Acco's total gross income in 1941, only 9.6 per cent was brokerage; 90.4 per cent was a margin between sale and outright purchase (see Table 23).

On that 10 per cent where Acco did assume an obligation to sell to others, there was no conflict of interest because the higher the price that Acco secured for the shipper, the higher its commission and the better its prospects of getting repeat business from the shipper and from others.

The "conflict of interests" reduces to the share, probably around 10 per cent,[42] of that 10 per cent which was first consigned to Acco and was eventually sold to A & P: the best estimate is therefore one per cent of Acco sales. As to it, there were and are well-established legal safeguards against cheating the supplier in the Perishable Agricultural Commodities Act (PACA), administered by a branch of the Department of Agriculture, which had the power to follow up any lead, rumor, or complaint; for whom the record of every single transaction had to be retained; and which could not only investigate but also take the drastic action of withdrawing Acco's license and putting it out of business.[43] Not a single instance of a doubtful transaction is recorded. The prosecution statement that "many of the dis-

[42] Since A & P accounted for about 10 per cent of food sales, it would be expected to buy roughly that per cent of consigned products. Since much of the produce was sold to others because it was below A & P quality, even this is probably an overestimate.

[43] See Shepherd, *Marketing Farm Products*, pp. 429–32, for a description of the PACA.

criminatory preferences which appellants obtained in the purchase of produce arose directly from Acco's breach of trust," [44] is not only contradicted by evidence; it is also inherently improbable because of the government safeguards thrown around these transactions.[45] And yet the fiction of fiduciary abuse was repeated innumerable times, and strongly influenced the courts.

Had the government made no more of the brokerage argument than that it was a practice forbidden by the Robinson-Patman Act, to violate which might also offend a much more loosely worded act,[46] the issue would have been one of statutory interpretation in the strict sense. But the real importance, and the brilliant ingenuity of the Department of Justice, was this: by confusing "discrimination" in law with discrimination in economics, they conveyed the impression that there was a great deal of economic discrimination involved in brokerage. It seems too obvious to the layman that discrimination involves the power, unrelated to efficiency, to obtain what others cannot get, and also the threat to increase that power by excluding competitors. Since there was a record replete with bargaining, wherein A & P often seemed to get its way, it seemed to follow that A & P had a great deal of market power. And this would have a good deal to do with a Sherman Act offense. (It is not obvious — but happens to be true — that real discrimination favoring or disfavoring A & P indicated market control *by sellers*.)

The only way in which the defense could have met this charge would have been by going to the fundamental point that the Robinson-Patman Act required discrimination, and that A & P's partial evasion of that Act was simply competition breaking through a discriminatory price structure and removing some of the additional payments which A & P had to make. The defense could not do so because they were themselves so completely en-

---

[44] GB(AC), p. 357.

[45] Within limits, however, there would be at least a *presumption* that such shippers would run the *risk* of receiving a price somewhat less than the market. The obvious remedy would seem to be some kind of compensation device. As we saw earlier (Chapter XIV), Acco waived the collection of brokerage on such sales.

[46] Turner, "Trouble Begins in the 'New Sherman Act': the Perplexing Story of the A & P Case," *Yale Law Journal*, 58:969 (1949), p. 981.

meshed in Robinson-Patman theory that they could not distinguish between economic discrimination and legal "discrimination." Furthermore, such a frank admission of evasion would have seemed very bad trial tactics. Perhaps they should have known that evasion was going to be established anyway, and that they might as well grasp the nettle and prove that the Acts conflicted. However, they would not run the risk. Instead, they pointed out repeatedly how, upon the receipt of discounts from suppliers, A & P purchases increased sharply — which was just what the prosecution wanted them to say.[47]

(4) *Resale profits of buying offices.* After completely neglecting the expenses of buying operations and speaking only of gross brokerage or commission as a "rebate," the government turned around to say that competition was also "abused" *over and above* this advantage by the net profits of the buying offices! This was not a charge that a given act violated two laws. It was simply counting the same thing twice. About three fourths of these "profits" were on resales to the A & P and are, therefore, as purely formal and meaningless as the manufacturing "profits" discussed earlier. But in addition, the company profited by Acco's reselling of goods to competitors, thus in effect drawing a "subsidy" from the very firms with which they were competing.

This is an important and general doctrine because it makes superfluous any inquiry into the possible monopoly power of the integrated seller, i.e., the possible dependence of competition on him as a customer or source of supply. There is not the slightest reference to Acco's or A & P's market share, or to any other fact which would bear on its control of supply and price. Such an inquiry would have quickly revealed a very small market share and other indications of lack of monopoly power. There is nothing to constitute the offense except the bare fact that A & P made profitable sales to competitors. Since there is no other *differentium specificum* of these sales, and no hint of any peculiarity that made them illegal, the only conclusion is that profitable sales — or, the prosecution urged, even unprofitable sales [48] — are illegal per se. (A & P ceased, in the spring of 1949,

[47] GB(AC), pp. 366–69.
[48] GB(AC Supplemental Brief), p. 31.

to make sales to the trade. They gave up a profitable business, taking the unpleasant medicine because on this point the government case was so clearly upheld by the courts that the law left them no other choice.)

The analytic confusion is fairly obvious. Had A & P withdrawn its personnel and investment from buying and devoted them instead to some other profitable occupation — say, the opening of new retail stores — competitors would have had to pay no less for produce, and possibly more, while A & P would have been as much strengthened against them. The profits of new supermarkets would have "subsidized" the other stores just as effectively. But why stop there? Under penalty of contradicting itself, the Department of Justice must insist that at any moment of time half the stores are "subsidizing" the other half; or rather that every individual store is "subsidizing" every other. Nor need we confine ourselves to the food industry, or to big business. The repair department of an automobile dealer gives rise to profits which "subsidize" and give an unfair advantage to his sales department in its rivalry with dealers who have no repair shops and so proceed ad infinitum.

To sum up the new doctrine: it asserts illegal restraint of competition to exist in any business firm which (1) can be set up as more than one accounting and profit-making unit, or (2) directly or indirectly sells anything to a competitor. We shall seek a long time, I fear, before finding any firm which is not breaking the law. This suggests a synthesis of the two criteria. They are both logical consequences of the notion that business profit is somehow a subsidy or gift; it follows that the return on every separate transaction is a subsidy to every other, making each one a separate act in restraint of trade.

Price discrimination. Economic discrimination was so confused by the prosecution with "discrimination" à la Robinson-Patman that one can never be sure which is in question. In order to demonstrate the logic of this part of the case we will assume, except as otherwise noted, in this section that they are the same, and that "discrimination" as the prosecution calls it is discrimination in the economic sense.

Why should the receipt of price discrimination be considered as a violation of the Sherman Act? It may have unfortunate consequences, such as forestalling entry or possible competition, enabling the larger but no more efficient to survive, etc. There was no attempt in the A & P case to demonstrate any consequences, actual or probable.

The prosecution argument before the District Court was "that the defendants' use of their massed buying power to secure price preferences over competitors constitutes an unreasonable restraint of trade in violation of Section 1 of the Sherman Act. This is made abundantly clear by decisions involving the motion picture industry."[49] In these decisions the courts had found that the movie exhibitors, who were local monopsonists, had secured lower prices than their rivals, or had forced the producer-distributors to impose unfavorable terms upon competitors. As the Supreme Court said of one of these cases:

There was ample evidence that the combination used its buying power for the purpose either of restricting the ability of its competitors to license films or of eliminating competition by acquiring the competitor's property or otherwise.[50]

Were the A & P prosecution to proceed on the same tack, it would need to show, first, monopsony power by A & P, which as we saw earlier did not exist. It would also need to show "ample evidence" of competitors being eliminated, or intimidated, and so on. What we must pause to examine and admire is the way that the prosecution was able completely to dodge the need of *any* evidence. After making the comparison with the movie cases, it again referred to Acco and the fanciful "abuse of fiduciary duty," then back to the movie cases, and then to other cases involving genuine monopoly power, and then it happily concluded that it had proved its case of "unreasonable restraints upon the sellers."[51] It had, of course, proved no restraints either on buyers or sellers; the essential point of A & P power was never made except by endless repetition.

The utter absence of any such evidence began to be a little more evident during the proceedings before the Circuit Court.

[49] GB(DC), p. 1078.
[50] U. S. v. Crescent Amusement Company, 323 U.S. 173, 181 (1944).
[51] GB(DC), p. 1084.

Here the government was careful in its discussion of buying policy to avoid any allegation that any rivals had been eliminated. They urged merely that A & P had "set up a two-price structure for the food industry, the lower prices being made available to A & P, the higher prices being available to competitors of A & P." [52]

As an example, they offered the direct buying campaign:

By virtue of its national network of warehouses and its centralized buying policies, A & P was in a position to buy directly from suppliers. Most of its retail competitors were not so equipped. To these retail competitors it was, therefore, a business necessity that middleman channels remain available. Under the conditions imposed by A & P's anti-broker campaign, competing retailers who by reason of size and location must buy through brokers were disadvantaged in two ways. First, they were restrained from purchasing at all from any of the numerous suppliers who had agreed with A & P to become exclusively direct sellers, and second, they were forced to turn for food products to another group of suppliers who sold at a price level higher than that of the group from which they had been excluded as purchasers. [53]

This rich specimen merits detailed examination. We may note, first, that in it there is nothing whatever about price discrimination. It does allege that A & P induced suppliers to go exclusively direct, and that this was a burden on competing retailers. There is no statement as to how many suppliers were induced to go direct, and how large a part of the market they constituted. Nor is there any recognition of the fact that if A & P bought exclusively from direct suppliers, they bought that much less from other suppliers, and left as much available for their rivals as before. In fact, there is no explanation of how the trade of any rivals could have been affected in even the slightest degree. There is only the unsupported and meaningless statement that rivals were "forced" to turn to more expensive suppliers. But how on earth could A & P tie up the more economic suppliers and prevent them from selling to others? What was the source of its power? Its share of buying markets was quite small, as we saw earlier. And if competing retailers were to pay higher prices, surely they might as well pay them to the old suppliers and so prevent them

[52] GB(AC), p. 205.
[53] GB(AC), p. 206.

from going exclusively direct in the first place. Why did they not try to do so? The only possible answer is that the "two-price structure" is simply a reflection of a cost difference. The direct sellers would sell to anyone who took the same bundle of goods and services as did A & P at the same price as that charged A & P. The supposed "exclusion" from these more economical suppliers is a piece of fiction, explained by no logic and supported by no evidence. Or rather it is a demand that A & P rivals be charged the same price even when it costs more to serve them. The argument is a protest against the recognition of cost differences which resulted in a lower (nondiscriminatory) price being quoted to A & P. It is a demand for Robinson-Patman discriminatory price equality.

Let us proceed:

> On the supplier level, other restraints were effected. The suppliers who resisted A & P's demands either lost patronage or were denied the opportunity of competing for A & P's patronage on an equal basis with those suppliers who acceded to A & P's demands.[54]

Let us assume what occasionally happened — that suppliers who refused to go direct were not patronized. Similarly, suppliers who could not supply the right quality or quantity or time of delivery or price might also not be patronized. What is noncompetitive or illegal about this? The government has a ready answer:

> Indeed, it would be enough to render appellants' scheme unlawful that it eliminated a class of distributors — the brokers who "died" so hard.[55]

Of course, there was no such elimination, and no evidence of even *one* broker's being eliminated. There was a comment that brokers were "dying hard," i.e., threatening action against A & P. The meaning of the colloquialism is well enough known. And that is *all* the evidence for a conclusion of fact which sets off a spate of reference to cases — the law is invoked as though the pertinent facts had just been proved.

Finally, we get to the issue of price discrimination:

[54] GB(AC), p. 206.
[55] GB(AC), p. 207.

The competitive restraints emerging from appellants' insistence upon preferential quantity discounts, rebates, and concessions hardly need spelling out. Other retailers who bought higher had to sell higher and thereby were forced to surrender the important weapon of price appeal as a means of attracting retail patronage.[56]

And since the facts "hardly need spelling out," they are not spelled out.

By the early stages of the civil suit, the essence of the prosecution theory, and its intellectual and legal origins, was plainly revealed:

[The Antitrust Division] has not attempted to measure . . . the extent of the injury sustained by individual buyers. . . . [They] claim instead that price or quality preferences necessarily impose a self-evident injury against those who do not receive them. The United States Supreme Court has made much the same point, in Trade Commission v. Morton Salt Co., wherein it held:

It would greatly handicap enforcement of the [Robinson-Patman] Act to require testimony to show that which we believe to be self-evident, namely, that there is a reasonable possibility that competition may be adversely affected by [price differences]. . . .[57]

What we know at last is that the Department of Justice never "attempted to measure" the injury *even to any individual competitor* — to say nothing of injury to competition. Price "discrimination" as defined in Robinson-Patman was to be a per se offense under the Sherman Act. It should disabuse the reader once and for all of the idea that the prosecution made the slightest attempt to find out the impact of alleged discrimination upon the market in food.

(1) *The theory of recoupment.* The gap between "discrimination" and its consequences was filled, however, by a famous economic theory, which, like the rest of the A & P case, was straight out of Robinson-Patman.[58] This is the theory which might be

---

[56] GB(AC), p. 208.

[57] In the U. S. District Court for the Southern District of New York, U. S. v. the New York Great Atlantic & Pacific Tea Co., et al., Civil Action No. 52–139, Plaintiffs' Answers to Interrogatories Propounded by Defendants, filed November 16, 1951, p. 39, para. 18(l) and (m). The decision cited is FTC v. Morton Salt Co., 334 U.S. 37, 49–50 (1948).

[58] Compare the following paragraphs with the frequently quoted statement of Representative Utterback, *Congressional Record*, 80:9416 (1936).

called "inevitable recoupment": if sales are made to one buyer at a price lower than that charged others, price to the others is *necessarily* increased in order to offset the loss or the smaller profit on the sale of the first buyer. Or, what comes to the same thing, price concessions to some buyers can never lower the average gross revenue of any seller. This is true at all times and under all circumstances with no qualifications whatever: Thus,

A & P not only benefits by the discriminatory lower purchase price, but the supplier giving the preference must charge A & P's retail competitor a price sufficiently higher than would otherwise be the case to absorb the loss or reduction in profit incident to his sales to A & P. . . .

The price differential between A & P and its retail competitors was enhanced further because of the necessity that suppliers increase the price to competitors of A & P over and above the price differential in order to recoup losses incurred in sales to A & P.[59]

Every competing retailer pays a part of A & P's cost of doing business and contributes to the low prices available to customers trading in A & P stores by paying for his groceries at prices which are surcharged with the losses his suppliers have been forced to absorb in sales of the same products to A & P.[60]

The burden of lower prices is borne not by suppliers (strange that they have always made such a fuss about it!) but by other retailers and ultimately by the consuming public. This is extraordinary stuff and nonsense, and it is also of extraordinary importance. For this theory was so important that it went into the Legal Argument, the climax of the brief, before both District and Circuit Courts; it is the most important single economic theory in the whole case. Furthermore, the same fable was repeated in the announcement of the civil suit,[61] and on more other occasions than I could begin to discuss here.[62]

It is important to specify precisely what this theory says. It does not say that a seller conceivably *might* or under some conditions (probability not specified) *could* recoup himself. It does

[59] GB(DC), pp. 1075, 1078.

[60] GB(DC), p. 1104. See also GB(AC), p. 390.

[61] Press Release, Department of Justice, September 15, 1949.

[62] See, for example, the remarks of Senator Kefauver, *Congressional Record* (March 18, 1953), pp. 2125–26.

say that this must "always," "inevitably," and "necessarily" happen.

It is necessary, but also delightful, to explore the Land of Oz conjured up by the theory of inevitable recoupment. Let us apply it to the market for legal services. Suppose that Client A tells Lawyer X: "Either I reduce the retainer I pay you, or I'll have to get a new lawyer." Lawyer X consents to this cheerfully, for it does not cost him a cent. He immediately calls Client B and tells him: "Client A has just cut his retainer, so I *must* increase yours. Sorry. And why not make that retroactive to the first of the year?" There is no reason why Lawyer X should ever have a cent less income than he now enjoys; and as becomes clear after a moment's reflection, since he has the power to increase his retainers whenever he feels that he *must*, there is no reason why he should not keep increasing them until he becomes as rich as Croesus. Nor is there any reason why everybody else cannot do so too, and make us all infinitely wealthy overnight. Small wonder that the theory of inevitable recoupment has a deep psychic attraction, for within it are vistas of Utopia, of the escape from all material cares and from the dismal forces of supply and demand.

Let us come back to the real world. What actually does happen when a business firm sells to a number of markets, and the price in one market goes down? Obviously, the seller, whether monopolist or competitor, will channel as much as is advantageous to the higher priced markets, thereby increasing the supply there and lowering the price, "in sympathy" with the first market. This is the way price movements diffuse throughout the economy.

Recoupment is theoretically conceivable under certain special conditions: (1) A supplier selling in markets A and B might previously have been able to raise a price in market A, but failed to do so because of sheer inertia, out of which he was jolted by the price decrease in market B. This might be called the trivial solution. Inertia can explain anything whatever — or its contrary. (2) The seller might have been holding down the price in market A for the sake of some longer run advantage.[63] (a) If he had

---

[63] The seller may be considered as maximizing "utility" or present value of assets, rather than profits. See also Joe S. Bain, "Pricing in Monopoly and Oligopoly," *American Economic Review*, 38:65–82 (1948).

been trying to discourage entry into market A, or increase his share of that market, or deliberately not taking advantage of a temporary and reversible upsurge in demand, the loss of revenue in B would not make any difference. For if there was a good business reason not to raise prices in A before they were lowered in B, then there would still be no reason afterward. (b) The seller might have been trying to discourage entry, etc., into both A and B as a unit, by keeping the combined profit down to a predetermined level. If that profit was now lowered, he could raise it back to the old level by raising the price of A. But the difficulty with such an explanation is that if markets A and B are so separable that opposing price movements can occur, entry into each market must usually be separable from entry into the other. Hence, if the low price was good strategy before the fall in the price of B, it would still make sense after it. Therefore we are reduced to the more special case (c) where the markets are separable on the demand side, but employ the same or overlapping facilities on the supply side; the chemical industries might furnish some examples. (d) The price decline in B might so strip the firm of cash that it would be forced to increase prices in A, and sacrifice its longer run interests for the sake of maintaining short-run liquidity.

(3) The elasticity of demand of some buyers may be much reduced as an indirect repercussion of lower prices made to others. In brief, a buyer favored by discrimination may win away the more price-responsive customers of a nonfavored buyer. The latter's derived demand curve is now less elastic, so that a higher price can be exacted from him.[64]

(4) "Recoupment" may also be viewed as a misleading version of traditional theory. As noted earlier, if a seller with market control is able to separate buyers and discriminate in price, he

[64] See Rashi Fein, "Price Discrimination and the A & P Case," *Quarterly Journal of Economics*, 65:271–279 (1950); and my own comment immediately following. Fein's reasoning contained a logical error which could be corrected while leaving his conclusion unimpaired. But the conditions implied by him are so special as to make the case a curiosity of no importance for the A & P situation. In justice to Fein, it should be stressed that his argument has no logical relation with the crude fallacies of the A & P prosecution. Moreover, he has avoided the oversophisticated booby trap of supposing that recoupment is absurd only upon the assumption of short-run profit-maximizing behavior.

will *only* do so in the case where it increases profit. (There are cases where it would not.) Total receipts under discrimination must therefore exceed those under nondiscrimination, or else the seller will not discriminate. For this to happen, the excess over simple monopoly price paid by disfavored buyers must exceed the allowance made to favored buyers. In technical language, the buyers composing the less elastic section of the demand curve lose some — in the limiting case, all — of their consumers' surplus. This is the seller's reward for being able to separate his markets, as well as for his power over price. But if the more price-responsive buyer, who can and will stop buying if he is charged more than the discriminatory low price, now has additional alternatives and gets a lower price, the higher-paying buyers are no worse off. Conversely, if the higher-paying buyers find some additional alternatives and can demand a lower price, the favored buyer is no worse off. But in both instances the seller is worse off.

This premium on separability of markets accrues even when a nonmonopolist seller is practicing what we called "passive" discrimination (above, p. 158). For example, let us suppose that a chain store earns higher profits in Philadelphia, where competition is not so keen as in New York. Were the markets to be merged into one, the price to all customers would need to be lowered to the lower New York level, for otherwise the chain would lose so much volume as to decrease profits. Thus the chain is better off by reason of its Philadelphia operations, by meeting local competition as it finds it, rather than by selling in only one market. In general: the profits of price discrimination are the gain from immobility of factors or buyers, whether that immobility is contrived by a (monopolist) firm, or exists independently of the efforts of the firm.

All but (1) of these possibilities require substantial market power by the sellers, and to a greater or lesser degree involve some attention to longer run strategy. A manufacturer with market power who cut the price to A & P and then proceeded to use his price-raising power against A & P's competitors would be weakening them in the competitive race, and channeling sales in the direction of A & P, the customer from whom he netted less. As longer run strategy, this hardly makes business sense. One would expect the contrary action: that manufacturers would attempt, if possible, to discriminate against A & P even at the expense of short-run profits in the hope of strengthening their rivals. And this was the actual case, as shown by the soap and shortening allowances, and the history of drop shipments.[65]

To sum up: the general case is that a price decline in one or more markets must, in the presence of rational behavior — including but not limited to profit maximization — generate price declines in all other markets where the seller operates. This tendency is reinforced by quasi-economic power considerations. It can be confirmed by any price history of any industry, and also by manufacturers' frequent support of resale price maintenance because of their fear of retail price decreases spreading and generating pressure on their prices. Recoupment is theoretically conceivable in some special cases — aside from the government nonsense. It would at most be a slight offset to the predominant effect — if an example of it were ever found. None ever has, in or out of the A & P record.

The theory of recoupment — price reductions in one market exerting an upward push elsewhere — belongs with certain more familiar paradoxes. We know that under some circumstances a fall in the price of a product may reduce its sales, since it may be an "inferior good" in the technical economic sense.[66] Again, the demand for platinum is said to have decreased when its price fell, because it lost snob appeal; and so on. A few examples of such perverse effects can actually be found; yet no economist has ever tried to propound the theory that an increase in income or a decrease in price will "inevitably," "always," and "necessarily" reduce the demand for a commodity. This is just the blithe kind of theorizing which the Antitrust Division perpetrated, except that it regards it not as "theory" but as obvious common sense.

[65] Above, Chapters VII and IX, and Appendix IV.

[66] For example, in a very low-income community, where potatoes may form a large part of consumer budgets, a fall in the price of potatoes may release to consumers so much additional income that they are able to afford some additional foods in place of potatoes. Hence, the decline in potato prices leads to smaller potato consumption.

(2) *The market process.* This is perhaps the more interesting and important aspect of price discrimination. In many imperfect markets an integral part of the process of price reduction is unsystematic, buyer-enforced price discrimination. To forbid this kind of discrimination is simply to subvert competition. In the A & P record itself the emphasis on secrecy, and the dislike of buying in the field, is sufficient evidence of sellers' well-justified fear of general reductions if the news gets out. Looking more widely, the long history of many trade associations, their opposition to price discrimination, and their unwearying attempts to stamp it out should speak for themselves.

It should be clear by this time that price discrimination is not one phenomenon but two. Precise, systematic, permanent discrimination can exist only in the presence of strong monopoly elements; competition must break it down. But unsystematic discrimination is a powerful force for competition in many industrial markets. Economists have drawn attention to this fact for many years.[67] As one puts it:

The existence of price discrimination and secret rebates is often a very needed safeguard to the consumer against collusive price agreements, as well as against the price rigidity which commonly results from . . . price leadership. When one group of distributors receives discriminatory discounts as against another, the result is often a general reduction of actual prices all along the line.[68]

Nelson spoke from his extensive experience with price data as assembled by the Bureau of Labor Statistics. His statement is much less eloquent than is a pamphlet issued some years earlier by the National Association of Manufacturers.[69] This remarkable publication anticipated both the theories of secular economic stagnation and of monopolistic competition, but we are concerned only with the latter, and then only as it relates to price discrimination. It praised efforts to end discrimination:

[67] J. M. Clark, *Economics of Overhead Costs* (Chicago, 1923), pp. 416–33; Arthur R. Burns, "The Anti-Trust Laws and the Regulation of Price Competition," *Law and Contemporary Problems*, 4:317–19 (1937).

[68] Saul Nelson, "Trade Practice Conference Rules and the Consumer," *George Washington Law Review*, 8:457 (1940). See also by the same author, "Discussion," *American Economic Review Supplement*, 30:217 (1940).

[69] National Association of Manufacturers, *Profits Versus Price Cutting* (New York, 1930).

In this way it is possible that one of the great curses of the depressed price level [of 1929], namely price cutting in individual sporadic instances, can be practically eliminated. . . . It might appear that this ruling has no effect on price cutting in the form of a general price reduction policy. . . . On careful analysis it is evident, however, that strict and uniform adherence to a predetermined price schedule . . . would make evident to each manufacturer, to a degree never before possible, the indisputable fact that *profitable* price cutting, or *profitable* general price reduction, is an illusion. . . .

Once the illusion is destroyed, that greater profits can accrue from an increase in volume built on price cutting, the root of the depressed price level problem [of 1929] is solved.[70]

The government objects to this kind of discrimination, but as already seen, it blesses — indeed, it requires — precisely those systematic, ordered patterns of discrimination which collusive oligopolies have traditionally used to keep price cutting out in the open and, therefore, at bay.

(3) *Advertising allowances.* Concessions to A & P frequently were in the form of payments or allowances in return for including and featuring the supplier's product in A & P advertising. Much was simply re-expended in the purchase of advertising space. Some was a net gain, for one or both of two reasons: A & P might take payment for advertising that would have been carried out anyway, and which required no additional expense. Or A & P would be able to buy advertising space at much cheaper rates than its suppliers, and in effect resell space to them at a profit. In either case the effect was to reduce, by a somewhat smaller amount, the net price which the company paid for its goods.

In the first case, advertising which was an overhead expense to the company (since A & P advertising nearly always had to feature some specific commodities) could also be made to serve, and did serve, its suppliers. Had the company sublet parking space in their garages to their suppliers' trucks, and been paid a fee for this, the economic effect would have been no different from an advertising allowance. In either case an existing facility would be exploited jointly by more than one party; all would share in the expense, and all would be better off because they would be able

---

[70] *Profits Versus Price Cutting*, pp. 13–14 (italics in original).

to save space — advertising space or garage space. Since joint advertising was a more economical way of doing business, it made things uncomfortable for competitors.

Where A & P, like any retailer, was able to buy advertising cheap and sell it dear, the cost to suppliers of such advertising was less than by alternative methods; otherwise they would not have bought it. Again, both parties could benefit by reducing their combined advertising bill and sharing the saving. (The monopoly element was created by the newspapers and benefited also the retailers, including A & P.)

As we saw earlier, the discriminatory element in advertising allowance payments — money not re-expended, and in excess of payments to other retailers — must have been small. In accordance with our procedure of making the maximum the most probable estimate, we classified advertising allowance payments as entirely discriminatory because it was impossible to measure the respective components.

In any event, A & P had no control over the supply or price of the commodity it bought. Its advantage lay in a lower cost method of operation. The seller, instead of buying more advertising, in effect cut his net price for the sake of A & P patronage. To him, a cut in price and an advertising expenditure stood on the same footing — each was a temporary sacrifice for the sake of a future gain, and the choice between them depended on which promised a greater return for a smaller sacrifice. But a saving of advertising expenditure, with the volume of goods distributed unchanged, is a net social gain.

Thus the collection of "excessive" allowances meant lower prices to A & P. If one assumes the post-1937 price policy, there were also lower prices to the consuming public, which encouraged or forced other retailers to seek and pass along the same economies. But to the government, A & P was forcing its suppliers to pay for its advertising. It might equally well have claimed that by exacting lower prices in some other form, A & P was forcing its suppliers to meet its payroll or its bill for electric power. But doubtless many competitors and suppliers of A & P would agree with the Department of Justice that there was something "foul, strange, and unnatural" in cutting prices to increase sales.

D. Buying and selling policy considered as a whole

Let us now return to selling policy. Since we have been forced to depart from it a very long way, it is well to recall briefly: first, lowering the gross profit rate in order to induce greater volume was a complete and sufficient offense. Second, economies of integration — "subsidies" — are also illegal per se because unintegrated competitors are at a disadvantage. Third, the receipt of what the government calls price "preferences" which may be "discriminatory" in Robinson-Patman terms is also a complete and sufficient offense. It is illegal per se under the Sherman Act, whether or not the "preferences" are discriminatory in the economic sense, whether or not any kind of consequences can be shown to follow. Fourth, also illegal per se is the making of sales to a competitor, at a profit or even not at a profit.

But there is a further charge which ties all the threads together, and is best stated in the Appeals Brief:

It is at the retail level that the conspiracy reached full fruition. It was there that the full impact of appellants' abuse of their massed buying power was directed against A & P's retail competitors through their practice of selling at retail in selected areas at prices lower than elsewhere, thus engrossing desired percentages of selected retail markets, and using income from other areas, and from operations of the business other than retail, to offset losses or reductions incident to such price cutting. . . .

[Furthermore] A & P deliberately sold merchandise in selected retail areas below their cost of doing business at retail, for the purpose of eliminating retail competition, and recouped such losses in other areas or from operations of the business other than retail. This double-barrelled attack, each part of which is illegal standing alone, is even more illegal when the two parts are considered as an integral whole. The end result has been that under the force of these dual classes of unlawful restraints A & P has been able, at will, to occupy any retail area or any desired percentage of a particular retail market.[71]

---

[71] GB(AC), pp. 362, 363. The following is also worth noting: "If appellants had bought more cheaply than their competitors because they were better businessmen or because they were more efficient, and this enabled them to sell more cheaply, the Government would not have brought this case, even though substantial retail competition had been eliminated thereby. The Sherman Act holds no umbrella over inefficient businesses." GB(AC). p. 362. The government has no use for Tweedledum; it does demand Tweedledee.

It is necessary to examine this resounding passage, step by step. A & P allegedly sold, first, cheaper in some areas than in others; second, below the cost of doing business in some areas; third, "for the purpose of eliminating retail competition," and with that effect; last, the end result was that it could occupy any desired percentage of any retail market.

The last allegation may best be disposed of first. It is supported by no evidence, and also is contradicted by practically everything in Part I, including Appendix Tables 15 and 16. Putting this fact aside, we may ask of the other three: how could A & P have done any of them?

"Massed buying power" at best merely repeats the presumption that a "discriminatory" price (à la Robinson-Patman) must burden competition; it adds nothing new to the argument. What facts were brought forth to support it?

Under the title "Elimination of Competition by Sales in Selected Areas below Cost of Doing Business" the Government Brief in the District Court devotes about three hundred and fifty pages to "price wars" in the respective divisions, units, and stores.[72] No reference to these price wars was made in Part I of this book, which is a work of fact rather than fiction. As we shall see in a moment, if we did agree to accept the government's fiction as though it were fact, then the whole discussion of local price and sales policy in divisions or lesser units would become entirely superfluous. Furthermore, whatever we think of the definition of "cost" and "below cost," it may categorically be stated at this point that no evidence of "elimination of competition" was ever presented.

But before we examine the detailed evidence, we need to ask: What is the probability that cutthroat competition can exist in the food industry? In language more congenial to the lawyer, would a "reasonable and prudent" business management, ardently desirous of securing a monopoly and restrained by no moral considerations — Holmes' famous model of the bad man — attempt to practice cutthroat competition in the food trade? If an A & P conspiracy to monopolize was proved by other evidence — say documents or oral testimony — the apparent foolish-

---

[72] GB(DC), pp. 628–986; the corresponding pages in GB(AC) are 76–119.

ness of the conspirators would not excuse them. But the question here is whether there was or was not a conspiracy. In weighing the evidence, it is relevant to ask whether and how the alleged conspirators would benefit by the conspiracy. *Likelihood of cutthroat competition.* If we were to array all industries in the order of probability of cutthroat competition being practiced, the food trade would rank near the bottom. Let us be perfectly clear that by "cutthroat competition" we do not mean price competition, or vigorous competition. We do mean the deliberate incurring of losses by business firms in order to injure competitors. This kind of conduct can have only two possible objectives. The first is to kill off the rivals. The second is to show them who is master, in order that they may follow the price or other business policy desired by the dominant firm.

(1) *Ease of entry.* But cutthroat competition is an expensive pastime. If the cutthroat competitor is bent on serving his own interest, he kills or abuses his rivals in order to increase his long-run profits — either by being the sole survivor, or by being able to enforce a policy which is most advantageous for him. Therefore, if this tactic is to be successful, entry into the market must be difficult. For if it is easy, an attempt to reap the fruits of the monopoly or dominance can never succeed. As soon as prices increase, and the prospect of profit improves, before the monopolist has even begun to recoup some of his losses, he is faced with additional competition all over again.

As Wilcox put it:

Even if all of the larger trading corporations were to combine, it may be doubted that they could obtain or hold a position of monopoly. There is no obstacle to entrance to the field. Capital requirements, particularly in the retail trade are low. Quarters may be rented cheaply or obtained without expenditure. . . . The necessary equipment is inexpensive and can be bought at second hand. Stocks of goods are abundant; sources of supply are numerous and widely scattered; credit is readily available. Labor may be provided by unskilled workers hired at low wages, by the retailer himself, and by members of his family. The processes of distribution are simple. Technical training and managerial experience are not required. . . . New types of distributive agencies are constantly springing into life; the field is in a constant state of flux.[73]

[73] Clair Wilcox, *Competition and Monopoly in American Industry*, TNEC Monograph No. 21 (Washington, 1940), p. 57.

It will be noted that Wilcox speaks of the retail trade in general; every statement applies to the food trade more strongly than elsewhere.[74] Even on these general grounds, therefore, it seems impossible that there should be a campaign of extermination. Let us now examine the more particular circumstances.

(2) *Profitability of permanent low prices.* As we saw earlier, the expense rate for A & P, by the end of the 1930's, was roughly a fourth lower than their closest rivals'. (This, of course, does not necessarily indicate economies of scale as such.) Furthermore, the evidence is overwhelming that A & P top management believed that consumers would respond to low prices by larger purchases, making the profits larger at lower than at higher prices. Would A & P be expected to waste time and their subordinates' energy in encouraging or condoning cutthroat competition, or would they try to keep lowering prices until the volume and profits arrived? Local predatory tactics and below-cost selling would be a nuisance and a distraction to the larger design which their low expense rate permitted: simply to keep lowering prices. The repeated resolutions against below-cost selling, and the refusals to use loss leaders, had the strongest of business reasons — they interfered with higher profits.

(3) *Political considerations.* There was another reason why cutthroat competition was inconceivable: A & P's political vulnerability. In this connection, the relation of A & P with retail food associations and their price-fixing activities is of considerable interest.[75] We have seen earlier that the company was opposed to selling below cost, and there is evidence that it took action to inform manufacturers when competitors sold below cost.[76] But compliance with state sales-below-cost laws, usually enforced by trade associations, was another matter.[77]

[74] Ralph M. Cassaday and Ewald T. Grether, "Local Price Differentials in the Western Grocery Trade," *Harvard Business Review*, 31:190, 205–206 (Winter 1943).

[75] The government alleged and the District Court seemed to agree, that A & P had participated to a sufficient extent to violate the Sherman Act. See next chapter.

[76] Divisional memorandum, Southern Division, February 28, 1938, GX 4071.

[77] For a thorough discussion, see Richard H. Lovell, "Sales-Below-Cost Laws," *Yale Law Journal*, 57:391 (1948). Lovell suggests at p. 425 that these

A & P counsel prepared a memorandum [78] for discussion at a divisional presidents' meeting in December 1940. Information was requested on the effect of these laws on A & P pricing, any abuses or illegalities committed, who in the community favored or opposed those laws, and "the effect in your Divisions from a trade-relations or public-relations standpoint if the Company took a public position either for or against any of these laws."

Counsel repeatedly warned management, what they knew from long experience, that price fixing was no thing apart for these associations, but, rather, their whole existence:

The Company's experience has been that these "enforcement agencies" often start out with a bona fide intention of seeing that the state sales-below-cost law is complied with. Almost invariably, however, they gradually extend their activities until they reach the point where they are flagrantly violating the anti-trust laws.[79]

Sometimes A & P was in direct conflict with the associations. On at least five occasions, local units were sued for noncompliance by local associations; in Minnesota, California, Wisconsin, Illinois, and Ohio.[80] None of these suits was successful. On the other hand, there was evidence of A & P participation in illegal or at least doubtful activities in Maryland [81] and Pennsylvania.[82] On several occasions, state or local retail associations or groups of retailers were named in indictments charging price fixing, and A & P was not included; but local A & P units were involved in others, and had pleaded nolo contendere in some of them.[83] Nothing very definite can be said about activities in Iowa.[84] In Minnesota there was some reluctant cooperation, the extent of which is not clear.[85]

---

laws ought to be challenged in the federal courts as being in conflict with the antitrust laws of the United States.

[78] Feldman to Hartford, December 3, 1940, DX 870.

[79] Memorandum to all divisions, February 15, 1941, GX 3988. See also DPM, December 17, 1940, GX 98; DPM, April 8, 1941, GX 93; Merchandising Committee, May 27, 1941, GX 4069 (relating to resale price maintenance.)

[80] George J. Feldman, of A & P counsel, testifying at Tr. 19,961 ff.

[81] Tr. 13,190 ff, and documents cited.

[82] Tr. 13,380–13,750; 16,390–16,475, and documents cited.

[83] Feldman, Tr. 19,981 ff.

[84] Middle Western correspondence, DX 563, 564, and 565.

[85] Middle Western correspondence, GX 3381.

Some interesting light is shed by a letter from the assistant superintendent of the Chattanooga unit to a divisional vice-president. Referring to a withdrawal from a local association, he said:

I regret [this action] very much. . . . As the condition stands now, it has been said and continues to be repeated that we have no desire to cooperate with local leading competitive merchants.[86]

After some discussion in mid-1940, the New England purchasing director wrote to A & P counsel thanking him for approval of continuing membership in the various State Food Councils:

I appreciate very much your taking this up with Mr. Hartford and his permission to continue.

I understand the dangerous possibilities in the activities of these Councils, and I believe it will be possible for us over a period to cut down our participation in such a way that the reaction will not be unfavorable to the food trade as a whole.[87]

Later in the year, in response to the questionnaire from headquarters, the divisional purchasing director wrote:

We have, as you know, cooperated fully with the Councils who are policing the laws, and this has been one of the reasons why the quarrel between the independent and wholesale grocers and the chains has not been very evident in New England. The attitude of New England representatives of these grocery groups in national affairs has been proof of this. Furthermore, in order to carry on these policing activities funds are needed, and the chain stores have been the backbone of this financial structure, it being very difficult to collect from the independent grocer even though the use of the money is entirely in his favor.[88]

Unfortunately, the political blackmail apparently came at too high a price, as revealed by a letter from the general counsel of A & P to John Hartford three months later:

I have always been afraid of these Associations and Councils, however well intended. . . . The Government has recently been investigating the [New England Food] Council. . . . I was worried like hell over the mere fact of an indictment, whether we are guilty or not. . . .

[86] Robertson to Vinson, June 22, 1939, GX 3818.
[87] MacKeachie to Feldman, July 5, 1940, GX 4483.
[88] MacKeachie to J. J. Byrnes, December 13, 1940, GX 4498.

If indicted, I would hate like hell to plead guilty, but on the facts stated to me I have not as yet been able to figure out a defense. . . . We have done exactly the thing for which . . . others were fined $45,000 in Colorado.[89]

This hesitant policy is unique in the A & P record. Why the voluminous correspondence between headquarters and divisions on whether things might not be going too far; why visits by company lawyers to the divisions; why John A. Hartford's opinion that "this was a matter which should be left to the discretion of the local people?"[90] This does not sound like the highly centralized A & P.

How easy it would have been, and how logical, to avoid all this unpleasantness by a simple rule forbidding membership in these associations. Some explanation is clearly needed for this uncharacteristic conduct, and it is clearly evident: fear of the ill opinion and of the political influence of other retailers. Since A & P management were so sensitive to political risks, how likely was it that they would engage in a cutthroat campaign which was not good business anyway, even from narrowest self-serving point of view?

(4) *Conclusion.* There are three reasons why A & P would not have engaged in cutthroat competition. First, it was useless and would not pay. Second, it was politically impossible. Third, a contrary policy would pay. Any single one of these three would be sufficient; taken together, they are overwhelming. What contrary facts can be presented to show that A & P sold below cost in selected areas for the purpose or with the effect of destroying competition?

Evidence offered to show sales below cost in selected areas. (1) *Allocation of subsidiary profits and allowances.* Since these were considered as nonretail profits, the prosecution thought they should be deducted from the retail accounts. On this basis, many of the divisions, units, and stores were considered as operating at a loss; hence, "selling below cost."

In essence, the prosecution worked out a rule whereby the profit for any individual store would have deducted from it at

---

[89] Carothers Ewing to John Hartford, March 11, 1941, GX 4488.
[90] Quoted in Ewing to George, November 18, 1938.

least 90 per cent as being "nonretail." So drastic a reduction of the offsetting profit could and did easily throw whole units or divisions into the red, often for years at a time.

This deduction was not derived from anything in the records or operations of divisions, units, or stores. It was the result of a calculation with company-wide figures only, as shown in Table 25. It will be seen that "retail" profit, on the government reckon-

TABLE 25. Calculation of "Retail" Profit, A & P, 1941 (in thousands of dollars)

Item	Interim (statistical) amount	Final (accounting) amount
Headquarters allowances and discounts	6,400	6,400
Manufacturing	5,626	6,359
Acco	1,767	1,864
Coffee operations	2,945	3,274
Bakeries	943	943
Miscellaneous subsidiaries	–	955
Local allowances and discounts	–	1,420
Inventory gains (gross)	–	1,953
Subtotal	–	23,168
Other items (residual)	8,344	5,476
Total profit	26,025	28,644
less final (accounting) deductions	23,168	
"Retail" profit, government definition	2,857	

Sources. Interim and final profits, *Annual Binder* (1941), GX 314, Calculation of " 'retail' profit, government definition," condensed from GX 3670.

ing, was a trifle over 10 per cent of the total company profit in 1941. In other years, it was around 6 per cent. But the precise figures are not particularly important; the method is, however.

As we saw earlier, in noting the McCarthy–Thomas report in 1940 and some current correspondence, there was serious dissatisfaction with the interim or "statistical" profit indicators, and some reform in their calculation. However, the company itself maintained an annual calculation from which column one is taken. It will be observed that the subsidiary profits are less on the interim reckoning than on the final, because of the exclusion of minor items which it was more convenient to take up at the year's end, after the interim figure was available. Accordingly, the total interim profit is invariably and substantially lower than the total final profit.

In column two we see how the government improved upon A & P's system. They took the final manufacturing profit figures, as well as headquarters allowances. To this they added local allowances and discounts, though the "nonretail" character is never explained. Also added were inventory *gains*, but inventory *losses* were not deducted or offset against gains. The theory was that inventory losses were simply operating expenses, but that inventory gains could result only from cheating the customers by short-weighting, etc. Leaving the merits of this theory to one side, the "nonretail" character of this alleged cheating is not explained either. The deductions come to $23,168 thousand by the final accounting calculation. But all these final (accounting) amounts are subtracted *not from the final accounting profit, but from the interim statistical profit,* thus causing about half of the "truly retail" profit, even on their own definition, to disappear under the rug.

For any given division, unit, or store, in any given year, the evidence of "losses" amounts to nothing more than Table 25, or its counterpart for any other year. The geographical breakdown may be minute, the repetition overwhelming, and the blending of atmosphere masterful, but the actual "losses" are nothing more than the subtraction of 90 per cent (or more, as the case might be), of the profits of the money-making stores, then subtracting the losses of the losing stores.

As noted earlier, the earnings of the company's manufacturing subsidiaries are as much attributable to the distributing function as to the manufacturing. As for deducting the savings of the buying offices and the Headquarters 702 Account: why and how purchasing has become a "nonretail function" — how to sell without first buying — is unfortunately not explained. Advertising and other allowances which were given directly to local units are also excluded, although their "nonretail" character is not explained either. So are inventory gains allegedly arising from short-weighting of customers which, proper or improper, the District Court considered irrelevant to the case, and which are, in any event, a "strictly retail" method of cheating. And of course the neatest trick of all is the manipulation of subtotals to beat down a residual, as shown in Table 25. By these various methods, some nine tenths of A & P profits were declared "nonretail" and subtracted from profit. Under this method of accounting, many divisions and smaller divisions and units could be portrayed as operating at a loss for years on end. This is "selling below cost."

The government insists that the "nonretail" savings secured through headquarters must be added to retail costs in order to get the true figure of retail costs. Curiously enough, the expenses of operating the headquarters which has procured those savings are not to be deducted from unit or store expenses — apparently these are genuine "retail" outlays. If headquarters and divisional expenses are deducted, however, the red ink usually disappears.

Clearly, the offenses both of integration ("subsidies") and of purchasing ("preferences") are headquarters offenses. If we decide that headquarters allocations cannot lawfully be made, headquarters stands condemned and that is the end of the matter. To say first that it improperly credited stores with certain savings and then to go to the divisions and stores to point out the improper crediting is not only saying the same thing twice, but is taking an unconscionably long time to say it. One might as well say first that the sales of A & P were two billion dollars, and then count, dollar by dollar, to two billion.

Thus we are reduced to two alternatives: (1) if we cannot accept the government case that integration is illegal per se and subsidiary earnings are "direct subsidies" and therefore also illegal; that one can sell without first buying; and that one must under penalty of law price by cost-plus, then the "price wars" are a figment of the imagination. (2) But if we do accept the government case, its repetition in a thousand parts is superfluous.

(2) *"Selling below cost" begins and ends at headquarters.* Assuming for the sake of argument that the government theory of profits is sound, it means that the operations of A & P as a whole were simply one big selling-below-cost, and hence illegal. But it has yet to be seen what connection there is with "elimination of competition . . . in selected areas."

The accounting records of A & P treated these "profits" as reductions in the cost of procuring goods — as, of course, they were. Hence, in computing the profits of any division, unit, or store at the end of the year, they deducted from "cost of goods sold" a pro rata share of the subsidiary profits.

What we would expect to find, in the case of cutthroat competition, would be disproportionately large allocations to particular areas, made to reimburse those areas for predatory losses, or to equip them for future predatory losses. There is no such example. The deduction was mechanical and uniform. The sales of the division, unit, or store were multiplied by a factor which was the same everywhere. These "profits" could not be known, of course, until the year's end; and they could not even be estimated until the quarter's end. Hence in the day-to-day operation of the stores, units, and divisions, calculations were always made with "operating profit," i.e., with no allowance for later allocation of subsidiary profit. But these current "operating profits" *did* include as a cost the allocated expense of running the units, divisions, headquarters, the buying offices, and so on. Hence the operating expenses and the interim operating profits were useful and used *only for comparisons in time and among stores.* An "operating profit" which reflects the expenses of administration but not its benefits, and which excludes profits that could not exist without the stores — such a "profit" has no other meaning or use.

But it has a different type of use. For what the prosecution was able to do was to show not only the losses of the true red-ink stores, but a great many others. For page after page, in unit after unit and division after division, it paraded the "losing" stores. What should have been a single issue of fact and law became a flood of print and an army of "losing" stores. So the genuine losses, their time pattern forgotten, plus the spurious losses, plus the phrases like "turn on the heat," began to form a pattern all the more menacing because so vague.

But there was something more. When the A & P top management was trying to get store prices down, they repeatedly urged and finally commanded that gross margins be brought and held down to some predetermined level, regardless of immediate consequences. Certain that lower margins and prices would bring more business and larger profits, they were willing to run the risk of being wrong in the aggregate, and hence losing money. And they were of course not bothered by the certain knowledge that with some stores they would be wrong and end up with genuine losses. The answer was easy: close the store.

This strenuous campaign, as Part I shows, was a success. The lower prices brought more volume and higher profits. There is no doubt that they hurt A & P's competitors, and it seems like an actuarial certainty that some must have gone out of business. Vigorous competition always hurts somebody. But there is in this no suspicion of temporary price cuts made to put competitors out of business. Margins were to be kept permanently low.

And now we come to our essential ambiguity. It is possible to interpret the government case as sheer economic illiteracy. To say the same thing more kindly, they, the prosecution, had not the analytic equipment to distinguish the losses of the red-ink stores from the "losses" obtained by subtracting "nonretail" profits; to distinguish temporary price cuts to kill off rivals from permanently lowered prices, etc.; just as they had not understood the difference between price discrimination as an economic fact and price "discrimination" in Robinson-Patman terms.

But there is another way of looking at the matter. If our purpose is to understand the workings of competition or to promote competition, or both, then these distinctions are important, even vital. But if our purpose is to protect competitors from competition, then these distinctions have almost no meaning and certainly no importance. The "nonretail" profits are merely a measurement of the economies of integration. The policy of low margins and prices was the result of greater efficiency. But a competitor can be put out of business just as quickly by the superior efficiency of his rivals as through their predatory conduct. Hence if our concern is with injury to the competitor rather than with injury to competition, it is no matter that "predatory competition" is being given a radically different meaning. What we are concerned with now is not mistakes in the analysis of economic facts. We are concerned with a change in the law, under which vigorous price competition is to be considered as illegal per se.

(3) *Operations in particular areas — the prosecution version.* The nearest A & P ever came to planning a loss for any area was

set out above, in Chapter IV. This contemplated a very slight "operating loss," i.e., *before* crediting of subsidiary profits, for the year 1939, for the New England and Eastern Divisions. If these divisions are credited with even the subsidiary profits, then even if we follow the curious practice of loading them with headquarters' expenses while not counting headquarters' contribution to lower buying prices — there is no "loss." And this is the extreme example. There is no other instance in the record of even an "operating loss" being planned, whether for a division, a unit, or a store. A careful examination of the government briefs show that they never alleged any such action. *Their argument invariably came back to allocation of subsidiary profits; this was the only "planned" action to which they could point.*

Even if we were to accept the government novelties in accounting, it would be necessary to seek out the specific areas in which losses, even if unplanned, did result, and to see whether there was any logical connection between the "losses" and what happened to the retail food trade in the area. Again, there was no attempt to show any coincidence or correlation between "losses" and increases of business. Instead, there is endless repetition of a single statement, only the particular names and amounts being varied:

The Boston Unit operated in the red [government style] from 1934 to 1941; sales increased from $44,496,176 in 1932 to $45,709,106 in 1941.[91]

The reader will note that a sales policy apparently beginning in 1934 is tested by comparing with results starting two years earlier, in 1932, at the bottom of the Great Depression. Even so, if we allow for price increases, the Boston unit obviously sold substantially *less* in 1941 than even in 1932. And since the volume of retail food sales increased materially during these years, A & P's share of the Boston market *fell* materially. And, of course, there is no evidence of any plan at any time to drive competitors out of Boston.

(4) *Prices lowered to abuse competition, and then raised.* In any cutthroat campaign, the lowering of price is temporary, to kill or intimidate rivals. The *raison d'être* of these temporary

[91] GB(DC), p. 661.

decreases is that they will become eventual increases. There is not a single instance in the record of the sequence: lower prices — fewer competitors — higher prices again.

But although the prosecution never directly alleged any such sequence, they insinuated one as follows:

Eventually such a practice will result in a profitable operation since the increased volume produced by setting the gross profit rates below the expense rates will *eventually* reduce the expense rates to a point where *ultimately* a profit will be earned.

[But first,] since the savings secured from preferential buying were secured illegally, the mere allocation of such "savings" to retail operations . . . does [not] change their essentially illegal character.

Second, . . . a substantial part of appellants' retail sales were made at *net* losses, that is, the operations were loss operations even after the allocation. . . . It is no defense to argue . . . that ultimately such below-cost sales will increase their volume sufficiently to convert the losing operations into profitable operations since such an argument utterly ignores the effect of the illegal restraints imposed upon competitors during the entire period of *net-loss* operations. [This is] no more than a confession that [A & P] deliberately undertook campaigns in selected areas which contemplated immediate net losses but with the expectation that ultimately they would gain sufficient volume and market control to realize a profit.[92]

As usual, the confusion must be unraveled strand by strand. First, the words "eventually" and "ultimately." What A & P did plan and intend was that a low gross profit rate, set and *permanently maintained,* would in and of itself bring higher volume and profits. There was no question of the later increase of gross profits rate; on the contrary, the strongest pressure not only to lower the rates, but, after the company was profitable again, to keep them down. By using and stressing the words "ultimately" and "eventually" the government skillfully insinuates that after the "interim period" prices will be raised again, after "market control" — that is, monopoly power — has been gained. In this way, an impression is created precisely the contrary of the truth, which is that while "net losses" were being suffered, it was A & P which was losing business because its prices were *too high.*

Second, the reader will note that the alleged discrimination

[92] GB(AC), pp. 373–74 (some italics have been omitted, none added).

does not only double but triple duty; first, as a per se illegality; then as part of the general plan of illegal "allocation"; then as part of the plan to undersell in particular areas — to which it is, of course, wholly irrelevant.

After enumerating many units and divisions in a confusing tangle of figures, the brief continues:

These consistent net losses constitute convincing proof, not only of the fact that appellants actually planned programs which contemplated net losses, but also the charge that [A & P] sold merchandise in selected areas lower than in non-selected areas, and partially offset losses incurred in selected areas by profits made in non-selected areas.[93]

Thus, the fact of "losses" is "convincing proof" that those "losses" must have been planned. People never lose money unless they plan to! If profits were lower or negative in some areas, prices must have been lower. How could it be otherwise? The higher one's prices, the higher one's profits, and vice versa.

With this cause-effect foundation laid, the brief is able to make a considerable display of statistics — and for once they are in the form of a table — about losing stores. Then they return to the same argument:

Of course, the lowering of gross profit rates may *ultimately* result in increased sales and hence in increased profits. But appellants' argument here wholly ignores the restraining effect upon A & P's retail competition during the interval required for increased sales to reduce the expense rate. Such an interval may encompass several years. That several years were required is indicated by . . . the period 1932–1941, inclusive.[94]

And there the argument ends. The "interval," aside from its being grandly or infinitely overstated (for its usual time span was zero), is meaningless because prices are the same during it and after it. No evidence of any kind has yet been presented of deliberate losses to kill or intimidate competitors in particular or competition in general. There is nothing but the monotonous repetition on page after page, of division after division and unit after unit stating their net profit, deducting the "nonretail" component, and stating the "losses." There is not a single attempt to connect up *any* of these losses with *any* particular competitors, or

[93] GB(AC), p. 376.
[94] GB(AC), p. 384.

any share of the market — only the same misleading comparison of 1932 with 1941. And the incidence of the losses, as will be shown later, at page 408 and Appendix Table 18, is a further and sufficient disproof of any predatory action.

(5) *Actual losses — the red-ink stores.* Although there is no instance of an actual net loss being planned at any time, there were, of course, at any given time, many stores actually losing money. The subject was covered in some detail in Chapters II and V, and Appendix Table 4. The reader may recall the distress over the "red-ink" stores, which were recognized throughout as the result of charging *too high* prices, and were a serious drain on company profits and morale. As the mistaken policy of high prices persisted in the early 1930's, the number and losses of the red-ink stores *increased,* and the company's market shares *decreased.* As A & P management regained control of operations after 1937, they regained enough assurance to close down the red-ink stores where their prices could not be brought down. Thus the facts of the red-ink stores, far from recording an actual or attempted predatory campaign, are a sufficient refutation of it.

When A & P was again prosperous, its attitude is well summarized in some correspondence of which the government quotes this ambiguous tidbit:

Mr. Toolin remarked . . . he would prefer the store losing money by going after sales rather than lose it on a high expense rate due to low sales.[95]

The complete picture, in Toolin's own words, is not ambiguous:

I am compelled to remind you that the decision was if we were unsuccessful in building the sales of this store up to a minimum of $2,500 [weekly], it would be closed. . . .

I find it impossible to understand your line of reasoning when you anticipate that operating it on a higher price structure will solve your problem in Dyersburg. It seems to me, and certainly this has been our experience, that boosting the prices is not going to help the business any . . . quite the reverse . . . and if you are unable to get your share of the business in Dyersburg on the lowest price structure in town, how in the world do you expect to hold your business by putting your prices on a higher scale?

[95] Alldridge to Greene, July 8, 1940, GX 224 (omission in original).

I will go along for one more quarter, and that is all, with the understanding that if this store has not shown a satisfactory improvement in sales by the close of our fiscal year [within four months], it will be closed without any further discussion.[96]

(6) *Local predatory actions*. The period covered by the trial was from 1925 through 1943. The average number of stores was in excess of twelve thousand. Thus, there were well over 200,000 store-years, and assuming two to three competitors for each store, in round numbers about half a million opportunities to commit predatory or destructive acts. The significant question is whether there were enough such acts to indicate a position of market power capable of abuse; the legal question is whether there were enough such acts to justify a prosecution under Section 1 of the Sherman Act, and whether they indicated a power which might violate the higher standard of Section 2. The reader is invited to set his own standards: a 10 per cent predatory rate (50,000), a one per cent rate (5,000), or one tenth of one per cent (500), etc.

It is possible to present herewith a complete record of *all* such alleged acts.

First, a discharged former employee of A & P testified that there had been a wager that a certain competitor would be closed by Christmas of 1933, although he could not recall who had bet whom on which side, or why it was going to close, and he did not think the store had in fact closed by Christmas, or at any other time. This witness had apparently told the Grand Jury in Dallas a rather different story. We do not know what this other story was, but the government attorney was obviously vexed at the discrepancy between the two versions.[97]

Second, in May 1939, a new store was opened by a local Pittsburgh food chain which was known as a keen competitor who allegedly sold a number of items below cost.[98] In May, 1939, John A. Hartford received a letter from the attorneys of this local chain, reporting that King, the head of the A & P Pittsburgh unit, had visited some of the executives and threatened to ruin

---

[96] Toolin to J. B. DeJarnatt, November 20, 1940, DX 151. The store was closed. Toolin, Tr. 15,539.

[97] Tr. 11,036–040.

[98] Lynch to Hodgson, April 1, 1938, DX 304; this was over a month before the incident to be related in the text.

them.[99] Hartford replied by return mail, promising an investigation and a stop to the practice if found as they described.[100] At the same time he sent Brooks, the president of the Central Division, a copy of this correspondence, indicating his deep concern over it and his intention to discuss the matter with Caruthers Ewing, A & P's general counsel.[101] The Margiotti firm sent Ewing a long and detailed letter.[102] By the time Ewing read it, he had already been out to Pittsburgh, and on his return to New York, he wrote Brooks as follows:

Accusations have been made time and time again that this illegal and inexcusable conduct had been indulged in by A & P in the past, and it has been stoutly denied by us. The accusations have been general and without support in evidence, as related to any specific case. Here was a specific case, supported by evidence brought to our attention by a reputable law firm, which did not write in a hostile spirit.

If Mr. ——— said and did that which it was claimed he said and did, and that became matter of public record by action or proven allegations, I think it would result in Patman again becoming in the ascendant, and could easily be followed by the passage of laws which would put the company out of business.[103]

John Hartford, he said, had discussed the matter both with him and George Hartford, and the brothers had decided that on the evidence the Pittsburgh attorneys' statements were accurate. Ewing hoped the employee would not be discharged, since

if he were retained he would never repeat the offense. I think the company could better afford the loss of $500,000,000 in sales than to let the Streamline story be made public, and a recurrence of such a thing would simply be ruinous beyond measure.[104]

At the same time, Ewing wrote to the Margiotti firm, conveying "the deepest disapproval" of, and regret for, what King had done, and stating that any prices cut had already been restored.[105] Ac-

[99] Margiotti, Pugliese, Evans & Buckley, Attorneys, to Hartford, May 16, 1939, GX 3308.

[100] Hartford to Margiotti et al., May 18, 1939, DX 1016.

[101] Hartford to Brooks, May 18, 1939, GX 3309.

[102] Margiotti et al. to Ewing, May 24, 1939, GX 3311. Certain enclosures are GX's 3312–3314.

[103] Ewing to Brooks, May 25, 1939, GX 3314.

[104] GX 3314.

[105] Ewing to Margiotti et al., May 25, 1939, GX 3317.

cording to Hartford's testimony at the trial, he forced King to resign, but Ewing interceded, whereupon Hartford changed his mind, but warned King: "Don't you ever go into another competitor's store, not even to look at a piece of equipment." Shortly thereafter, he received a letter of thanks from the Margiotti firm.[106] Apparently the incident was closed.

The last incident lends an agreeable touch of scandal — *cherchez la femme* — to a sober tale. In April 1939, a grocer, formerly an A & P employee, wrote John Hartford that personal differences between himself and an A & P official had caused the latter to reduce prices in the A & P store in his town in order to destroy him.[107] Hartford immediately wrote for a report, which was a denial of the allegation.[108] Apparently Hartford wanted more details, and the inquiry, which obviously did not concern him nearly as much as the Pittsburgh affair, dragged on into June.[109] By early June, Hartford apparently had made up his mind that "you [used collectively] made a very grave mistake, and I wish you would take every precaution to guard against similar cases developing in your division in the future." [110] The reply was that the action had indeed been a mistake, already rescinded. Two subordinates had called on the aggrieved grocer, who actually seemed quite friendly toward A & P:

His whole concern seemed to be the attitude of the Assistant Superintendent. There seemed to be a personal issue between [them] with reference to one of the girl clerks in the store, and it looks as though [the A & P official] was very friendly with this girl and that was true of [the grocer] and evidently [the former] was in no way friendly with [the latter].[111]

That appeared to end the matter.

Thus we come to the end of the great A & P campaign to eliminate competitors. There is no evidence of even one elimination, or

[106] Hartford, Tr. 20,453.

[107] April 16, 1939, DX 287.

[108] Hartford to Meier, April 19, 1939, DX 286; Meier to Hartford, April 26, 1939. Further correspondence consists of DX's 288, 290, 292, 296, 297.

[109] The correspondence is in the record as GX 3322 and 3323.

[110] Hartford to Brooks, June 7, 1939, DX 298.

[111] Brooks to Hartford, June 15, 1939, DX 299. The final correspondence, indicating general satisfaction, is in the record as DX's 300–302.

even one attempt to eliminate. There are precisely two threats of this kind of action, neither of them carried out, and both of them obviously a source of embarrassed and even fearful concern to top management. This completely blank page is precisely what economic analysis of A & P and of the market would predict. It is, therefore, an altogether logical response for those interested in the higher ethics of "fair competition" to reject a search for the facts in favor of consulting the Delphic oracle known as "the opinion in the trade"; and to reject the economic theory of the firm as a rational and profit-seeking mechanism.[112]

There is a remarkably close parallel between the story of A & P's "elimination of competition" and Ko-Ko's "elimination" of Nanki-Pooh in *The Mikado*. Ko-Ko argued that since the Emperor was all-powerful, when he gave an order to execute somebody, the latter was as good as dead. "Practically speaking, he *is* dead. Then why not say so?" The logic is above reproach. But then there is no need for the elaborate story of how Ko-Ko bared his "big right arm," Pitti-Sing cheered the prisoner's last moment, and Pooh-Bah received the homage of his detached head. The government's logic is also sound. But just as one may, looking at the alive and grinning Nanki-Pooh, decline to accept the definition of "execution," so one may for similar reasons reject the government's definitions of cost and "elimination." In that case, the hundreds of pages in the District Court brief, sprinkled thickly with figures and references, dwelling lovingly on every phrase like "turn on the heat" or "crack down" — these become, like the elaborate description of Nanki-Pooh's execution, "merely corroborative detail employed to give an air of verisimilitude to an otherwise bald and unconvincing narrative."

[112] See Appendix V, and John S. McGee, Book Review, in *American Economic Review*, 45:452 (1955).

XVII

THE A & P LITIGATION:
THE ECONOMIC THEORY
AND POLICY
OF THE DECISIONS

The District Court

"Say nothing but good of the dead" is a motto no honest historian (or economist) ought to adopt. It is not, therefore, the death of Judge Walter C. Lindley [1] which impels us to write that among all those participating in the A & P litigation, his was the most creditable role. Nobody acquainted with the transcript could accuse him of prejudice. He struggled manfully, with no assistance, to understand a mass of evidence. He failed, but the manner of the attempt did him credit, and his effort was by no means in vain. His doubts and confusion are stated plainly in his opinion,[2] and anyone willing to read carefully will learn much from it.

Judge Lindley begins by noting the two counts in the information: a conspiracy to restrain trade, and a conspiracy to "monopolize a substantial part of [food] products." [3] Not that there was "any expressed undertaking" to do either; the charge was rather that "all of the actions of defendants . . . in the end amount inevitably to illegal restraint of trade . . . and to an attempt to

---

[1] See the obituary in the *New York Times*, January 4, 1958, p. 15.
[2] U. S. v. New York Great Atlantic & Pacific Tea Co., 67 F. Supp. 626 (E.D. Ill. 1946). Hereafter cited as 67 F. Supp., with appropriate page number.
[3] 67 F. Supp. 629.

create a partial monopoly. . . ."[4] Neither restraint of trade nor conspiracy to monopolize are further discussed. Nor does the Court explain what is meant by "a partial monopoly." One possible meaning would be: substantial power to influence supply and price, while falling short of complete control. This, needless to say, was not substantiated in the record, but perhaps the judge thought so; one cannot say. The other, more likely, meaning is the exclusion of other competitors from a substantial section of the food market. Any company, by its mere existence, excludes all others from selling that part of the supply which it furnishes, from that part of the market which it occupies. If, then, pure exclusion from a substantial amount of sales, without more, is the offense, substantial size per se is the offense. The attempt to maintain and increase sales amounts to a "partial monopoly." If size alone is not the offense, one must ask what is. Unfortunately, the Court did not ask or answer the question. In his haste to plunge into details, Judge Lindley even committed a glaring oversight in both logic and law.[5]

What Judge Lindley did was essentially to summarize the government argument, and then — very briefly — the defense reply. He did not try to analyze these arguments for logical consistency, and on the facts his long opinion is very hard to follow or check because it is so cryptic on dates and time sequence. There are practically no exhibit or transcript citations, and great caution is needed in using it.[6]

[4] 67 F. Supp. 631.

[5] The issue . . . [is] whether the evidence points inevitably, beyond all reasonable doubt, to guilt, or whether it discloses such facts as are consistent only with innocence" (67 F. Supp. 631). The judge overlooked the middle ground, that the evidence could be consistent with either guilt or innocence, or was at least not clear beyond all reasonable doubt, in which case an acquittal would be necessary.

[6] For example, at 67 F. Supp. 668, Judge Lindley quoted in succession two brief extracts from two separate letters, on two different subjects, to two different people, two months apart (Hodgson to Bristow, November 2, 1938, GX 3209; and Hodgson to Perrin, January 10, 1939, GX 3263). He did indicate that there were two separate sentences, and it is at least possible to read them as concerning two different subjects. But it took a university economist to run Lindley's two extracts together as a single sentence, and drop qualifying language from one extract; so that the two letters become "a statement" showing a policy of "preventing competition." See Robert F. Lanzillotti, "Pricing Objectives in Large Companies," *American Economic Review*, 48:935 (December

On general sales and price policy, Judge Lindley apparently accepted the "profit" definitions of the prosecution, and the errors flowing from them, though he would not call them "subsidies." What inspires respect not only for the judge's integrity but also for native shrewdness is that while he was much impressed by the government's version of the facts, and set it forth at great length, nowhere will he come out with the flat statement: *this is how it was.* His conclusion on size, selling policy, and integration is therefore inconclusive: "The charge . . . means that in their integrated industrial effort, defendants must have overstepped the line by injecting into their competitive methods and into their integrated competitive power, illegal factors of such importance as *to taint the entire operation.*" [7] And a moment later the same note: ". . . whether A & P's methods, even though they look to a legitimate end, have in them an inherent factor of such legal malevolence as to taint the operation." [8] But at this point, the "taint" had not yet appeared, and some vague general speculation as to how it might was never followed up. There was eventually to be little doubt as to where the "taint" originated.

The opinion, after dismissing "stock gains" (*anglice,* cheating) as a factor of any interest or importance,[9] turned to purchasing of processed food products, and here the tone hardens, as the Court dwells on the evasive adaptation to the Robinson-Patman Act, particularly the brokerage clause. Judge Lindley never understood that this clause provided sellers with super-profits on sales to an integrated buyer like A & P, which they were willing to give up in part in order to assure the rest. Hence he probably (one cannot be altogether sure) neglected A & P's buying costs and agreed that for A & P to pay the same prices

---

1958). The article summarizes a book by A. D. H. Kaplan, Joel B. Dirlam, and Lanzillotti, *Pricing in Big Business* (Washington, 1958). This is not the place to discuss the book. So far as the references to A & P are concerned, a sample of the method of research has just been given; the resemblance to reality is usually faint and often nil. Thus at page 287: "Only an A & P could afford to absorb large losses in some sales areas in the process of penetrating or maintaining to [sic] a target minimum market share, because it had the resources to sustain the campaign." No supporting evidence is offered.

[7] 67 F. Supp. 642 (italics added).

[8] 67 F. Supp. 642.

[9] 67 F. Supp. 643.

as competitors who used brokers gave them a purchasing advantage.

As a conscientious judge, the custodian of the law, he could not help being outraged by persistent evasion of the Robinson-Patman Act. One need not be a judge to feel the same way. A decent respect for law — any law — is a much more important part of the fabric of civilized society than is a larger and better distributed national income — or any other object of the antitrust laws the reader happens to place at the head of the list.

But indignation, even justified, is no substitute for analysis, nor for a statement of the grounds for decision. In fact, the Robinson-Patman Act prescribes constant discrimination in price against buyers like A & P. An actively competitive market beats constantly against fixed patterns of discrimination. The strong temptation for both buyers and sellers to violate the law is simply evidence of competitive markets in the food trade. And if the Sherman Act is concerned with control of supply and price, with power to exclude competing supply, the whole sorry record of Robinson-Patman evasion is simply evidence of strong competition. On the other hand, if as a matter of law Robinson-Patman evasion is to be a per se violation of the Sherman Act, one should say so.

Turning then to quantity and related discounts, the opinion reviews dealings with a number of suppliers, and concludes:

I have not been greatly interested in what either defendants or their suppliers said in this respect. I am essentially interested in what they did, and . . . it seems to me that though defendants have been careful to secure from their vendors avowals of compliance with the Robinson-Patman Act, they have been far from meticulous in acceptance of preferences which . . . they knew or should have known other purchasers did not receive and that they so acted as to procure preferential discounts either under that term or other terms resulting in an unfair competitive advantage.[10]

On general advertising allowances: "Defendants admit that there is voluminous evidence that many suppliers violated the law in granting A & P buying preferences but they say that they had no knowledge of such preferences."[11] But the judge cites

[10] 67 F. Supp. 649.
[11] 67 F. Supp. 649.

some evidence to show that "advertising allowances frequently performed the same function as allowances in lieu of brokerage, rebates or discounts and were . . . frequently infractions of the Robinson-Patman Act. It is difficult to attribute good faith. . . ."[12]

This language is of great importance, and conveys not only the "feel" of the opinion, but a glimpse of the law as it comes into being. The defendants have evaded the Robinson-Patman Act, which is supposedly part of the family of "the antitrust laws" under which the defendants have been tried, and so their evasion brings them at least into the shadow of Sherman Act violation. Moreover, it suggests as a fact that the defendants somehow were able to buy at lower net prices than charged to rivals — which, if true, would be of real importance. The judge assumes this to be obviously true, and so a new rule of law has come into existence, at least tentatively — violation of Robinson-Patman is per se violation of Sherman. (Or, to put it bluntly, active competition is a violation.) It is a fascinating, if depressing, instance of the organic growth of the law. Of lesser importance, it shows the mistaken tactics of the defense attorneys, who offered the lame Robinson-Patman defense of not knowing about the price differentials.

Judge Lindley turned next to the Atlantic Commission Company. Here, it was at once evident, like a theme sounded in the strings and later enlarged in the brasses, came the "taint" for "the entire operation" for which he had earlier called:

The Atlantic Commission Company, a subsidiary incorporated in 1926, ostensibly to purchase produce for A & P, from the beginning acted with the full approval of headquarters, as purchasing agent for A & P and as sales agent for certain suppliers. [Eventually] it bought outright for cash for A & P and sold to others as brokers on regular terms. Its practices over the years leave a bad odor. It exploited its inconsistent positions; it collected brokerage from others for A & P's coffers; its position and its practices created a sharp differential between A & P's purchases of produce and those of its competitors. It persistently selected the highest quality of produce for A & P and the less desirable for its outside buyers, thus securing for A & P not only a buying price differential but also a preference in quality. Obviously the larger the volume Acco handled for

[12] 67 F. Supp. 650.

customers other than A & P the larger were A & P's subsidiary earnings, inevitably reducing A & P's costs and increasing its annual income. This in turn served to give to A & P's retail units a preferential position in competition with other retailers, at the expense of the latter, who indirectly at least contributed brokerage and other earnings to Acco which in the end came to A & P. *Restraint of competition, it seems to me must follow conclusively* from the multiple irreconcilable, inconsistent functions of Acco, including its obligation as an agent for sellers to sell high and its obligation as buying agent for A & P to buy as cheaply as possible. Any attempt to perform these and other inconsistent functions, I think it is *obvious*, must have *inevitably* resulted in illegal restraint of competition, *when we keep in mind that Acco was the arm of A & P and that all its profits redounded to the credit of A & P.*[13]

Many pages later, after having skipped over the highlights of Chapters XIII–XV above, the opinion concludes:

In the end, by the use of its integrated power and control, defendants purchased merchandise at prices that they would not otherwise have obtained, at prices less than those of competitors, *with a resulting handicap to competitors. But even this, again, might not, standing alone, have constituted violation of the law.* There is the further fact that Acco, in its predominating position in the produce industry, acting as a buyers' broker, a sales broker, a direct buyer for A & P, through its intimate relationship, was realizing *profits for A & P* as a result of *its inconsistent legal positions.* Acco owed one employer a duty to buy merchandise from the seller as cheaply as possible, with choice of quality. Add to this the undisputed fact that the earnings and *profits of Acco* received as buyer broker or as seller broker or otherwise eventually became a part of the *profit of A & P* and eventually a substantial help to the local stores to supplement their [net earnings]. Competing retailers were confronted with sales prices and profit rates added to, supplemented and increased by the *profits of A & P* upon merchandise sold to those competing retailers. *The resulting restraint of competition and commerce seems to me obvious.*[14]

It is clear that Judge Lindley was deeply offended by Acco's operations, and his opinion deserves detailed analysis.

1. It is stated in the opinion at least sixteen times that Acco was earning profits which went to A & P. It is hardly too much to say that the Court is obsessed with profits. But how do profits constitute evidence of discrimination, or of market control, or of restriction of competition? As a matter of law, perhaps the earn-

[13] 67 F. Supp. 655 (italics added).
[14] 67 F. Supp. 663–64 (italics added).

ing of profits by sales to a competitor is per se illegal. Or perhaps Section 2(c) of the Robinson-Patman Act has been read into the Sherman Act, and the collection of brokerage by direct buyers is also per se illegal. But these are matters of law, not of fact. And the fact was that nobody had to sell to A & P in the field or at the terminal markets; and therefore nobody had to pay it brokerage except for necessary services actually rendered, which would have cost at least as much to get from others. No reason is given by the Court why the collection of brokerage and the earning of profits, without more, constitutes evidence of monopoly power or discrimination.

2. The next theme overlaps considerably with the profits issue. Acco is said to have occupied and exploited "inconsistent positions," since it represented both buyer and seller in a single transaction, and had to favor one or the other. But as we saw in the previous chapter, this will not bear close examination. About 90 per cent of Acco dealings were straight purchases, on which there could not possibly be any conflict of interest. Of the remaining 10 per cent, most — probably about nine tenths — was sold to parties other than A & P, and Acco could have only one interest — to get the highest possible price. Perhaps about 10 per cent of the 10 per cent, i.e., 1 per cent of Acco total sales, went to A & P after being consigned to Acco as a broker. But even as to this insignificant scrap: collusion between Acco and A & P to cheat the seller would have been a crude and obvious illegality, quite apart from the antitrust laws. There is no record of complaints by injured sellers or any investigation by the Department of Agriculture under the P.A.C.A. This was no matter of *noblesse oblige*. Acco wanted the profitable trade business, and sharp practice would have lost it because shippers had plentiful alternatives to dealing with them. After 1940, Acco waived brokerage altogether on that part of consigned supplies which eventually went to A & P. As advance compensation for all possible downward bias in the price, making assurance doubly sure, it was a desirable action, and it cost Acco little enough.

The "inconsistent functions" of Acco never existed. The apparent evidence is spurious, and thus confirms that the structure of the market did not permit such inconsistency; Acco would have been penalized by loss of business, and by the P.A.C.A.

3. Much the same comment applies to the culling of produce. Acco was able to take a large lot at any favorable moment, despite its knowledge that much of the lot was not acceptable for A & P. Thus it paid a lower price for the acceptable and the unacceptable, taken together, than it would otherwise have paid. Had it not been engaged in the resale business, however, it would have had to search out buyers to dispose of much of the purchase. But since its channels of trade were well established, it could sell off the balance of the purchase with no additional effort. This is another facet of the economies of large transactions in the produce markets. Acco, therefore, did own its goods at a lower net cost because its procurement mechanism was more efficient. The Court preferred another (and correct) way of stating this same fact: it increased the profits of Acco. More efficient methods do generally mean higher profits.

But all this does not begin to constitute evidence of market control. The mere selection of better produce for A & P is meaningless unless Acco resold the lower grade produce *at higher grade prices*. This, too, is a simple and crude offense that needs no antitrust laws for its chastisement; and of this too there is no evidence whatever, either in the record or in the actions of the Department of Agriculture. Nor would we expect to find any because cheated customers would never have bought from them again and would have spread the word. Nor is there any "preference" or discrimination in buying a mixed quality first and separating by quality.

4. The same comment applies to the splitting of carlots. Just as Acco economized by being able to take diverse quality when it was most advantageous to do so, it saved by taking whole carloads. The Court is essentially correct in saying that this practice "permitted A & P to acquire LCL produce without any jobber markup, whereas, when others bought from the same brokers in LCL quantities, they paid the higher prices." The comment is exaggerated because those who bought from brokers at higher prices had made no investment and had taken no risk in handling produce. But there was a genuine economy of large scale and of joint operation with the jobber; it was shared between them. Acco had no means of control over jobbers. Had terms ever been

offered to a jobber which involved net costs to him higher than that which was available in a market of virtually pure competition, he would never have joined with Acco again. That Acco had less than 10 per cent of the market is wearisome to repeat, but fatal to overlook.

Furthermore, the Court does not explain why Acco's profits through split carloads "burdened" A & P's competitors. Acco's economies certainly were a competitive advantage to A & P. But the notion that competitors were abused because they were "contributing to Acco's earnings" or that competitors paid higher prices because of Acco's operations is completely wrong. The jobbers who resold to A & P's competitors enjoyed lower costs because of their cooperation with A & P — otherwise they would not have cooperated. If we accept the Court's premise that higher or lower costs to jobbers are necessarily reflected in higher or lower prices charged to retailers, then these retailer-competitors of A & P paid *lower* prices because of Acco's operations. Had Acco never existed, jobbers and retailers would have paid no less for their produce, and probably more.

5. The Court's conclusion of widespread acceptance of brokerage under a variety of names is well supported by the evidence. Whether or not this evasion of legal discrimination, by violating 2(c) of the Robinson-Patman Act, is to be considered a per se violation of the Sherman Act need not be discussed here. But this evasion constitutes not price discrimination in favor of Acco but the partial removal of the price discrimination *against* them. There is nothing in the District Court's opinion which is inconsistent with the view that on balance, taking all transactions after 1940 as a whole, Acco was discriminated *against*. (This was not necessarily true, as we saw earlier, of manufactured foods.)

6. The "demoralization" of produce markets adduced by the Court has nothing whatever to do with Acco's buying operations.[15]

7. No evidence was presented that any of the contact committees with growers resulted in lower prices received from Acco than from any other buyer. If there were any evidence in the record of Acco *apparently* receiving "discriminatory differentials," it would need to be very carefully examined because there was no

[15] See above, Chapter XIII; and 67 F. Supp. 659.

reason for any seller to discriminate in favor of A & P. It would be particularly necessary to separate out allowances for brokerage savings. But the important part about the Court's opinion is its clear revelation that no such evidence was ever presented:

The Government does not claim that there was anything evil *per se* in such actions, but it does contend that . . . [they] helped *inevitably* in the end to bring about discriminatory preferentials. . . . I think that such was the *inevitable result*. . . . Growers and shippers relied more and more on Acco's facilities and advice, all of which served to increase Acco's advantageous preferential relationship, its business as selling broker and as buying broker and its resultant profits at the expense of A & P's retail competitors, all of which went into A & P's treasury and eventually into competition with other retailers.[16]

There is no reference in the opinion to actual evidence of price discrimination. It is simply assumed as "the inevitable result of continuing relations with shippers." The Court never asks *why* shippers built in with Acco over the years when they could have sold in the other 90 per cent of the market, unless they enjoyed a net return *higher,* if anything, than realized elsewhere. The question is never asked because of the Court's obsession with Acco profits, and the competitive advantage to A & P. The fallacy is of course compounded by also making it a higher price to A & P's competitors.

The lengthy discussion of relations with cooperatives and the abortive formation of Super-Coop is left hanging in air. As usual, the Court is a bad theorist, but an honest observer. Acco's motives were clearly and correctly stated: a large increase in business would directly and indirectly reduce operating expenses; and it would have political advantages. There is no mention here of market control or price discrimination. When the Court relates this evidence to the general problem of monopoly, competition, and discrimination, there is simply no bridge or connection.

The difficulties of an honest man wrestling with a problem of economic analysis which he is not equipped to handle are never better brought out than in the last paragraph dealing with Acco, which was quoted above, p. 385. It epitomizes the whole discussion of buying, even the whole opinion, and it is worth rereading

[16] 67 F. Supp. 659 (italics added).

several times. The judge concedes that the relationship between Acco and shippers might in itself indicate nothing about competition. But the relationship did result in Acco's paying lower prices "with a resulting handicap to competitors." If this statement means price discrimination, it is supported by nothing in the record or the opinion; if it means simply lower operating expenses, it is supported by both. We are never told which. But then at last the gap is bridged by "inconsistent positions" again, and profits, profits, profits — mentioned four times in the last two sentences.[17]

The Court's whole lengthy discussion boils down to one basic fact and to one assumption. The fact is that Acco enjoyed economies which were reflected in its profits. The assumption is that these profits *in and of themselves* are a violation of law. But even if one were to accept that conclusion, it remains literally true that in all of the Court's lengthy discourse there is not a hint of price discrimination in the economic sense, nor of even a slight degree of market control.

From Acco, Judge Lindley turned to the so-called price wars, which were discussed very much like sales and price policy in general. The opinion summarizes the government contentions, with practically no comment or overt conclusion. Judge Lindley clearly swallowed the fallacies about nonretail profits, and hence about units or divisions running at a loss or on very small profits. But after stating the government case, "that at times, prices were so lowered as to bring events into accepted definitions of price wars,"[18] he never tried to indicate what "accepted definitions" are, and whether or not there were any price wars.

Nor did Judge Lindley find that *any* competitors had been eliminated, either by A & P discriminatory prices in its stores, or by any other method, or that there was any "intent," by that or any other name, to eliminate competitors.

Judge Lindley then turned to the charge of resale price maintenance in collusion with suppliers, and of price fixing in collusion with other distributors. Almost nothing is said on the first point.

---

[17] Incidentally, Acco profits in 1941, its best year, were $1,863,700, of which about one fourth must have been on trade sales, or, in round numbers, about $465,000 (see Chapter XIII, Table 23). This was not much more than one per cent of A & P profits for that year (see Appendix Table 12).

[18] 67 F. Supp. 664.

On the second, the court said, accurately summing up the record:

On the whole, it must be agreed that headquarters' policy was against price fixing. . . . [But] there can be no doubt that some of A & P's agents' activities went beyond what could legally be done. . . . Apparently A & P's counsel were at all times desirous of preventing activities from over-reaching the law but just as apparently their advice was not always followed.[19]

Judge Lindley also gave only brief and passing attention [20] to one of the most unappetizing parts of the record — the creation of apparently independent consumer and business groups, sponsored, financed, and operated by A & P's public relations counsel to oppose chain store legislation and other actions unfavorable to the company. It clearly contributed to his guilty verdict in the A & P case, for the public relations firm was named and convicted along with the individual and corporate defendants. Some years later, the activities of this firm on behalf of certain railroads resulted in a treble damage suit against their clients.[21] The opinion noted that the public relations firm had made a presentation to prospective clients which "laid great stress on the success of that firm . . . particularly . . . in connection with A & P activities." [22] Of these activities, and the ones on behalf of the later clients, the judge said that they "show a studied, consistent and contemptuous attitude toward the antitrust laws of the United States, and [a] willingness to flout them at will if the price was right." [23] And in awarding damages, the Court specified that 20 per cent was to be paid by the public relations firm, and not reimbursed by their clients.[24] The Court's opinion was pretty obviously that not only the antitrust laws had been flouted, but common decency as well.

Judge Lindley's final comments are noteworthy. Profit margins are small in the food trade, so that even a small "unfair advan-

[19] 67 F. Supp. 673.
[20] 67 F. Supp. 673–74.
[21] Noerr Motor Freight, Inc., et al. v. Eastern Railroad Presidents Conference et al., 155 F. Supp. 708 (E.D. Penna. 1957).
[22] 155 F. Supp. 778.
[23] 155 F. Supp. 817.
[24] 155 F. Supp. 833, 836. The Court later rescinded this provision for technical reasons (see 166 F. Supp. 170); but it is an index of the judge's reaction.

tage" or "illegal factor" can be decisive. And thus casually (and quite wrongly) did the judge assume the structure and functioning of the food industry, and the slightness of any possibility of such a monopoly as A & P was charged with conspiring to attain. That "illegal factor" was Acco:

> The conscious, knowing adoption by all defendants of a plan of action by Acco affecting every department of A & P and every retail store. . . . With the flaw of Acco's tainted record permeating all the operations of A & P's integrated system, the activities of A & P other than those directly involving Acco take on a polluted colored light. Manipulation of gross profit rates, at times sufficiently to do away entirely with retail profit, in competition, procurement and enjoyment of buying preferences heretofore discussed, whether in the form of discriminatory discounts, advertising allowances or otherwise, supplementing retail earnings or overcoming deficits with earnings of manufacturing subsidiaries, the coffee department and Acco, and other actions heretofore mentioned, even though some one or all of them standing alone might not amount to a violation of the law, when coupled and inextricably interwoven with the activities of Acco, reflect inevitably the misuse of defendants' power in competition with others to such an extent as to create undue interference with commerce, — undue restraint of trade, — of such character as to result in monopoly.[25]

The Circuit Court of Appeals decision [26]

The Circuit Court decision is a much more smooth and readable job than the District Court opinion. The Court of Appeals was far enough from the brute facts to be untroubled by Judge Lindley's doubts, and they wrote an opinion much more favorable to the government. Since the ground they covered is already familiar, we need review the opinion only very briefly.

Unlike Lindley, they explicitly rather than implicitly adopted and repeated the crude fallacy that the expenses of an integrated buyer may be disregarded in comparing the prices he pays with those paid by an unintegrated buyer. Having noted that A & P buying offices bought at prices which were the same as those charged to brokers, and therefore lower than those charged by

---

[25] 67 F. Supp. 678.
[26] U. S. v. New York Great A & P Tea Co., 173 F.2d 79 (7th Cir. 1949). For a fuller discussion, see the writer's "Integration and Anti-trust Policy," *Harvard Law Review*, vol. 63:56 (1949).

brokers to their customers, the Court declared that A & P was therefore buying more cheaply than its retailer competitors.[27]

In fact, the court managed to compound the fallacy with the one about culling of produce and with sheer double counting:

Suppose an item was selling in the market at 100. Acco could buy it for A & P and have its choice of the quality at 95. The balance of the trade could buy at 100 and pay Acco a 5% brokerage. Thus, the price to A & P was 95 and to A & P's competitors 105. . . . Acco collected brokerage from the trade, which increased the price to A & P's competitors, and the brokerage went into A & P's coffers to increase its competitive advantage.[28]

In justice to the Court of Appeals, it should be noted that it did not explicitly call the receipt of brokerage or other discounts a violation of the Sherman Act. It did, as the preceding passage indicates, consider buying integration as an inherent competitive advantage, and as at least contributing to illegality. The basic fallacy is in not understanding the connection between price differentials and integration. Only after a lengthy discussion of buying-price differentials does the Court move to vertical integration by name; they obviously did not realize that they had been discussing it all along.

We saw in Chapter XVI that the prosecution wished to call illegal per se the fact that the manufacturing departments of A & P were earning a profit, i.e., were efficiently organized by market standards. It does not appear that the court agreed, but it is difficult to make out what it did say.

The food-processing subsidiaries of A & P

were satellites of the A & P system. Their products were sold only to A & P stores and were invoiced at a markup above the cost of production. These corporations were tools in the hands of A & P, used and useful in maintaining the two-price level to enable it to maintain its position of dominance in the retail food business.[29]

Phrases like "satellites" and "tools" imply a right-and-left-hand conspiracy, but perhaps they were not so intended. The "two-price level" originally referred to the spread between products sold di-

[27] 173 F.2d 82.
[28] 173 F.2d 85.
[29] 173 F.2d 86.

rectly and through brokers; in using it here the Court again confuses a gross saving with a net.

The court correctly remarked that manufacturing profits represented simply a lower cost of procuring goods for sale and, taken together with discounts and allowances, which are even more obviously reductions in the cost of goods, a large proportion of the profit of A & P.[30] And in this inconclusive fashion, the discussion of vertical integration ended in the paragraph where it began; savings from all sources were considered together in order to discuss horizontal integration and sales policy in the divisions.

The Court says the following of sales practices (numbers have been supplied for more convenient reference):

[1] If Area X is having a tough experience competition-wise or the area looks prospective [sic] in which to increase the volume of business, the gross profit percentage in this area is lowered. This lowers the price at which goods may be sold and the volume increases at the expense of somebody. Sometimes the gross profit rate is fixed so low that [2] the store runs below the cost of operation, even with all the advantage derived by the store in reduction of the cost of its merchandise occasioned by the headquarters' allocation of its predatory profits and accumulations. [3] When the gross profit rate is reduced in Area X, it is an almost irresistible conclusion that A & P had the power to compensate for any possible decline in net profits by raising the gross profit rate and retail prices in Area Y, where it was in a competitive position to do so. [4] The record is replete with instances of deliberate reductions of gross profit rates in selected areas. Thus Area Y, at the desire of the policy makers of A & P, can be brought to aid in the struggle in Area X, [5] which in numerous instances, as the record shows sustained heavy net losses for periods extending over a substantial number of consecutive years. [6] There must inevitably be a compensation somewhere in the system for a loss somewhere else, as the over-all policy of the company is to earn $7 per share per annum on its stock.[31]

Comments 1 and 4 are basically correct. Since the profit variability they represent is universal in the business world, the requirements of even-handed justice can only be served by forthwith declaring every horizontally or vertically integrated firm illegal. The margin (price) variation among A & P units has in actual fact been remarkably small.[32] Moreover, markets were

[30] The reference is to GX 3670 (see above, Table 25 and text discussion).
[31] 173 F.2d 87.
[32] From 1936 to 1941, when A & P tactics were successful in regaining a

gained and regained by keeping gross margins uniformly low.

Comment 2 is also correct, but the losses to which it refers are not the same as those mentioned in 5, which result from the government's unique accounting method (discussed earlier). If the reader is unwilling to accept these novelties in accounting, he must reject 5.

The losses mentioned in 2 are genuine enough, but to speak of them as a deliberate competitive tactic is a great joke on A & P — though they may not laugh as readily as the rest of us. For the losing stores were always recognized by the A & P management as a drain on the company; inability to mend them or end them was a symptom of near-collapse in the 1930's, and their elimination in later years was an indication of A & P's recovery.

As for the "irresistible" conclusion of 3, it meets the immovable question, "Why?" If it is alleged only that prices and profits differed from one location to another, it says no more than Comment 1. But if it implies that upon reducing prices in X, prices in Y were forthwith increased, it says something for which there is no evidence, and which is inherently absurd.

It is noteworthy that Judge Lindley avoided the recoupment theory, but that the Court of Appeals accepted it. But it must be said to the credit of both of them, and also — surprisingly enough — of the prosecution, that they never tried to prove the recoupment theory by pointing to periodic meetings or other division actions which revised some gross margins upward while others were being revised downward. As a matter of bureaucratic routine, this was the only way to handle any necessary changes. Chance, correction of errors, and constant cost-demand changes suffice to explain the continual revisions. But of course it did not follow, because the X margin was being cut at the same time that the Y

---

large share of its lost markets, the Central Western Division appeared to be one of the most successful, and the New England Division was undoubtedly the least. The *maximum* variations in gross profit margins between the highest and lowest units of the Central Western Division during this period ranged from 2.40 per cent in 1936 to 0.70 per cent in 1938, five out of six years being less than 2.0 per cent. In the New England Division, the spread was from 0.60 per cent in 1936 to 1.64 per cent in 1940. The greatest spread occurred between the highest unit in the New England Division and the lowest in the Central Western Division, ranging from 3.25 per cent in 1936 to 1.47 per cent in 1941. See Appendix Table 17 and Chapter XVIII.

margin was being raised, that either was the cause of the other —
cum hoc ergo propter hoc.

As for 6, if there is something wrongful in meeting competition
or, much more important, in setting off local competition at the
expense of profit margins, then the only alternative is a rigidly
uniform profit margin on all products and in all localities, and no
attempts to risk temporary losses for eventual profits by means of
price reductions. One must also note the interesting suggestion,
akin to the recoupment theory, that there "must inevitably" be a
compensating profit because there is a *policy* of making a profit.

Turning to standards for competition: there are exactly four
references to competitive effects. First, in discussing the "direct
buying" program, "This clearly affected the business of brokers.
. . ." [33] Again, in the passage already quoted: "The volume [of
A & P sales] increases *at the expense of somebody*." [34]

Third, "There is evidence in this record of how some local
grocers were quickly eliminated." [35] This is completely untrue;
there is no such evidence, no such claim by the prosecution; and
no such finding by the Court below. Yet undoubtedly the Court believed there was. In part, it is the power of suggestion; in part,
Ko-Ko's reason — since it is must "inevitably" happen, it must
have happened.

So far, the court is at least consistent in its concern for competitors and its disregard for competition. But the final reference is to
the latter:

The inevitable consequence of this whole business pattern is to create a
chain reaction of ever-increasing selling volume and ever-increasing requirements and hence purchasing power for A & P, and for its competitors
hardships not produced by competitive forces, and, conceivably, ultimate
extinction.[36]

"If true, it were a grievous fault." It is no criticism of the Court
of Appeals to say that as a statement of fact the passage is wildly
inaccurate. There is no "inevitable consequence" and no "chain
reaction." Neither in the national market nor in local markets did

[33] 173 F.2d 83.
[34] 173 F.2d 87 (italics added).
[35] 173 F.2d 88.
[36] 173 F.2d 88.

A & P improve its position after the early 1930's, and in the middle years of the decade it lost as much ground as it later regained.[37] To have obscured this simple fact is a major achievement. One is left with a kind of reluctant admiration for a judicial process that could, upon a record of 50,000 pages, manage to ignore the history of the defendant, the economic conditions which make even local monopoly in the food trade so improbable,[38] and the gross and obvious fact that if A & P and the other chains have done anything it is to bring active and beneficial competition into the retail food trade.

The civil suit and consent decree

By April 1949, two months after the Court of Appeals affirmed the District Court decision, A & P had made two easy if unpleasant decisions. One was not to appeal to the Supreme Court. The other was to stop making sales to the trade, and announce it publicly. In view of the District Court's many strictures against making profits on sales to competitors, and the Appeals Court's remarks, they could be sure that this practice was illegal. There simply was no other way to interpret the decisions. What other changes took place in buying we cannot say. The writer had at this time an interview with the executive of a large supplier who was actually hilarious over the timidity of A & P buyers to take even the most routine and thrice-approved discounts; other informants concurred. But these remarks were not for identification, and cannot be considered as evidence.

The expectation and then the fact of a civil suit seeking dismemberment of A & P placed the company in a difficult position, since almost every feature of its operation had been declared illegal per se, and the only prudent thing to do was take no chances.

After more than four years of preparation and negotiation, however, both parties framed a consent judgment which became effective in January of 1954. It is a brief document.[39] Very little of the potential threat was ever realized.

[37] Above, Part I.
[38] Above, Chapter XVI.
[39] In the United States District Court for the Southern District of New

Acco was ordered dissolved (IV). There was nothing to stop A & P from continuing to buy produce, but it was forbidden to purchase any food products for the outside trade, or to act as agent or broker (V-A, V-B, V-C) in any area where it was selling at retail (V-A, V-B, V-C). If A & P was to resell to the trade in any other area, the Department of Justice "shall have the right to move this Court for such further orders as . . . necessary to [prevent] . . . defendants' obtaining unlawful competitive advantages. . ." (V). Profits on resale to the trade are obviously the most sensitive point. Sales to the trade had of course stopped everywhere for the previous five years.

The company was barred from: "Dictating systematically to . . . suppliers . . . (1) to refrain from [using] . . . brokers, (2) . . . offering of premium deals, (3) [increasing] the prices charged to the outside trade for store delivered . . . food products" (V-D). Since the company was not under the illusion that it could even unsystematically dictate to suppliers, or otherwise induce them to do any of these things, even to remove discrimination against A & P (see Chapters VI–XI), these provisions were not hard to take. Neither was the next provision, against "dictating systematically . . . the prices or other terms or conditions of sale, upon which such suppliers shall sell or distribute . . . food products to the outside trade" (V-E). Indeed, the company was expressly permitted to continue "advising such suppliers as to the marketing or pricing of their products so long as such advice is general. . . ."

Not all of the buying provisions were meaningless, or made compulsory what had already been done. A & P was not to receive any label or container allowance greater than allowed to others "even though the cost to [A & P] of the labels or containers may be in excess of the amount of such allowance" (V-F). The supplier had to make a phantom label or container charge even when he supplied neither. In other words, A & P was forbidden to supply its own labels or containers unless everybody else also did so. Thus the systematic Robinson-Patman discrimination against A & P

York, U. S. v. The New York Great A & P Tea Co., et al., Civil Action No. 52–139, *Final Judgment* (January 1954). References are to the sections as numbered there.

was carried a little farther, but the amount thus affected was very small.

No discounts or allowances might be based upon quantities purchased by more than one A & P unit (V-G, V-H) except that carload and truckload discounts might be taken and shared. So could "savings in the cost of labels or containers growing out of purchases by more than one unit" (thus partially modifying V-F). In brief, annual volume discounts, based on total company purchases, may no longer be claimed, even if they merely correspond to lower costs. This too extends somewhat the discrimination against A & P, though again we cannot tell by how much. Furthermore, no payments could be made to field buying offices or to headquarters (VIII). However, there was no prohibition of negotiations carried on through buying offices or headquarters. A & P could no longer prepare any contract forms for any kind of discounts; the suppliers had to do so (VI-I). This seems meaningless. Both VI-I and VIII are largely padding; but to some extent they reflect a touching faith in the *form* of the transaction.

Unlike the buying operations of A & P, manufacturing and sales policy are completely untouched by the decree. Even the sale of manufactured foods to the trade (never of even minor importance) is expressly permitted (V-B). But such sales must be "at prices no higher and on terms of sale no less favorable than those . . . upon which such products are sold to defendants" (VI). Aside from its unimportance, this provision is literally preposterous, putting the cart before the horse. Prices to outsiders are the market reality; prices to one's own subsidiary are either a mere reflection of market prices or else a purely formal bookkeeping entry. If the company were a monopolist of the products it manufactured, and sold them to the trade at exorbitant prices, it would not be hampered one jot by the need to "charge" its warehouses the same high prices.

One subsection is of real, if slight, importance. Processed foods were not to be sold "at less than regular billing prices for the purposes of circumventing State Minimum Mark-up Laws" (VI-B). Thus the decree acts to protect a set of crude price-fixing conspiracies (see Chapter XII above).

As for sales policy, nothing is said about the "traditional American" or "orthodox" method of cost-plus pricing. The company is prohibited from assigning any predetermined gross profit if this "will result in the operation of any such Division at a loss, for the purpose of or with the intent of destroying or eliminating competition in the retail purchase, sale or distribution of food or food products" (VII). No divisions were ever planned to run at a loss. Moreover, since "the purpose" is an obvious illegality, and always has been, this is no more than an agreement not to do anything illegal. What is really significant is that there is no whisper of any "operating profit" net of "nonretail profits," i.e., after deduction of manufacturing profits and of discounts. Furthermore, "The purpose or intent . . . shall not be presumed merely by reason of the operation of a Division at a loss" (VII).

Thus the deadly display of "red-ink stores," and "planned losses" to "eliminate competitors" by "price wars," which occupied three hundred pages of the District Court Brief, and was taken so seriously by the courts and some writers, disappears into thin air. By the criterion of the consent decree, there were never any divisional losses planned or incurred; still less any "purpose or intent" to destroy or eliminate competition. And this accords with economic theory and common sense. Only the vague theorizing about "inevitable tendencies" had created the illusion of destroying competition.

The consent decree was therefore a sweeping victory for the A & P Company. Their sales policy and manufacturing integration were almost untouched. Their buying operations were restricted only in one significant way: they, and the cooperating jobbers, could no longer enjoy the economies of bulk transactions and resale in produce. This was an obvious restriction on competition and a social waste.

The decree clearly marked the limits of government intervention. So long as these had not been indicated, the vagueness of the decisions meant that A & P was forced, in common prudence, to stay well back from them. The decree gave them, in effect, a license to do most of what they had been doing — above all in their sales policy and their manufacturing. The continuing discrimination against them under the Robinson-Patman Act could at least in part be offset by buying for private label from specialized manufacturers, or by expanding their own manufacture. On this subject, however, there is no trustworthy information. It is easy to believe, however, that the atmosphere of A & P operations has been affected significantly; and that many acts and policies which are legal under the decree are still considered doubtful or impossible.[40]

One aspect of the judgment deserves only praise. A decree providing for minute supervision of the details of the company's business practices would have been not only irksome to them but a social waste and a drag on their competitive potential. The decree is not of this type. The compliance can be put into a set of very simple rules which buying personnel can learn once and for all. To be sure, the larger result of the lawsuit was that the A & P must comply strictly with the Robinson-Patman Act, which is of course a statutory detailed regulation of buying; but the decree can hardly be blamed for that. It is always tempting to both sides to use detailed regulation as a bargaining counter in writing a consent decree; and here both sides did well to avoid it.

[40] "Tethered Titan: A & P's Manners Turn Mild After Epic Tangle With The Trustbusters," *Wall Street Journal*, December 22, 1958, p. 1.

XVIII

THE A & P CASE
AND PUBLIC POLICY

Standards for antitrust policy

The reader may be receptive to the suggestion that no more should be written on this general subject than is absolutely necessary for proper consideration of the A & P case. We ignore all but economic standards. It may surely be, first, that there are other and higher ends to be served. The manufacturers, wholesalers, and retailers who are enabled by such decisions as these to charge somewhat higher prices and lead a somewhat more quiet life may be more worthy in the sight of higher authority than A & P itself and the consuming public, both of whom benefited by the company's operations. Furthermore, there may be no justification for giving the consumer what he wants because he has been indoctrinated with the wrong set of values, and *ought* to prefer something else to mere price and quality. These social-political or other aspects are not considered here.

The economic theory of competition can be briefly sketched. The existence of alternatives to buyers and sellers prevents the existence of, or limits the amount of, control which any firm can exercise over supply and price. Without this power, there must, over time, be a constant erosion of profit margins toward bare subsistence — the minimum return to capital and enterprise needed to prevent the cessation of output. The firm can escape this fate only by greater efficiency than its fellows', or by introducing new methods or products. This is how a private-enterprise society makes the most of its scarce resources. Since imitation and the development of rival methods or products takes time, the innovating firm enjoys profits higher than normal. These competitive advantages are a kind of limited and temporary monopoly.

Aside from the minor and perhaps decreasing class of "natural monopolies," the supposed conflict between competition and efficiency is an illusion. Competition is a selective agent, permitting only the most efficient to survive; it is both cause and effect of industrial progress.

All business conduct might well be termed a perpetual flight from the ultimate competitive no-profit position. Borrowing from the language of the tax laws, we may say that business firms must always attempt either to "avoid" or "evade" competition: the first by superior efficiency or innovation; the second by blocking or at least greatly slowing down the competitive process. This latter requires substantial control over supply and price.

If the flight from competition is prevented from going through the "evasion" channel, businessmen will only be able to proceed, and will try all the more to go, through the "avoidance" channel. Put differently, if the law makes it difficult or impossible for businessmen to acquire control or *power over supply,* they will work all the harder for the *power to enjoy lower costs or to innovate.* Any discussion of corporate "power" which fails to distinguish between these two concepts is quite without meaning.[1] As will be seen in a moment, however, the law does not always draw this distinction, and there are compelling reasons (whether we like them or not) for this myopia.

The meaning of economic "power." But setting the law aside and speaking strictly in terms of understanding the market, the amount and incidence of power over supply is the hypothesis to be tested. Edward S. Mason has pointed out that the tests fall broadly into two types: that of market structure: for example, number and concentration of sellers, absence or presence of collusion — and that of market performance: price-cost-profit behavior, etc.[2] Despite a plain warning that these tests must be

[1] Cf. George W. Stocking, "Comment," in *Business Concentration and Price Policy,* National Bureau of Economic Research (Princeton, 1955), pp. 331–352.
[2] Edward S. Mason, "The Current Status of the Monopoly Problem,"

used to complement rather than to exclude one another, the distinction quickly became hackneyed and exaggerated, and all good men were (and still are) called to come to the aid of one side or another. In point of fact, it is simply impossible to use tests of either structure or performance (or behavior) alone. One cannot do so elementary a task as counting the sellers in the market until one defines the market. And this definition is the end, not the beginning, of a process of examination of cost-price behavior, to see where in fact the boundaries should be drawn, at what lines (or in what zones) substitution becomes negligibly weak. That, after all, was almost the only issue of fact in the *Cellophane* case.[3]

The operations of the A & P Company are relatively easy to understand and judge, once we have cleared away the immense encumbrance of the government's "unfacts." Competition in the retail food trade vibrates at each location between the opposing forces of spatial monopoly on the one side and easy entry on the other. It has not been necessary to judge their respective strengths in various locations and arrive at a properly weighted result because we have been able to use the sensitive registering instrument of A & P management, its view of the situation, and, what is even more important, the testing of its view by the market.

The company was able to innovate, and profited greatly thereby, until its innovation was imitated. By the early 1930's the demand for its services had become fairly elastic; the differential advantage was largely gone. Some in the company, notably John Hartford, could see this; most could not. And the market punished A & P for its corporate inability to read the signals and act upon them. It had no substantial market control, and no power to control the supply or the demand of any commodity, and hence the price. All it has is, like any retailer, the chance of some of the spatial monopoly which is widespread in distribution, which may be in any place substantial, but may also be undermined.[4]

Harvard Law Review, vol. 63 (1949), reprinted in Mason, *Economic Concentration and the Monopoly Problem* (Cambridge, 1957).

[3] U. S. v. E. I. Du Pont de Nemours & Co., 351 U. S. 377 (1956).

[4] See Margaret Hall, *Distributive Trading* (London: n.d.), and Richard H.

But A & P had at all times the "power" to attain lower costs than some, at least, of its competitors. As a buyer, by virtue of its size and ubiquity, it certainly enjoyed the power to seek out the best alternatives in time and space. Where suppliers discriminated against A & P, for their own reasons or to comply with the Robinson-Patman Act, or both, the company's size and access to many sellers often gave it "power" to evade the discrimination. Whatever one may think of the propriety of this conduct, it had nothing to do with monopoly power, and everything to do with economies of scale.

As an integrated manufacturer-wholesaler-retailer, A & P had other cost advantages. The "rebates," "subsidies," etc., were perfectly real economies. True, there is no magic in integration, and it is not necessarily more efficient and profitable. Somebody must make an investment in factories, warehouses, trucks, and stores; certain physical movements of goods must be made, and certain pieces of paper must circulate to keep the movements under control. There is some reason to suspect that A & P warehousing is unusually efficient, but this cannot be checked.[5]

If there are restrictions on competition, even of the most informal lawful type — but which tend to maintain prices; or if for any other reason, such as the minimizing of inventory, sales personnel, or advertising, the expense of using the customary transfer apparatus grows larger than necessary — this supplies a supernormal profit margin for an integrated concern which can reduce the transfer of goods to a purely physical task. What Richard B. Heflebower has called "the high cost of persuasion" can be saved where the job can be done without persuasion; as Chapter XII showed, the savings can be large. Many customers want a familiar brand. But some, at least, will be satisfied with an A & P (or other retailer's) brand, which means that for at least part of its supply A & P wants the bare physical product, devoid

---

Holton, "Marketing Structure and Economic Development," *Quarterly Journal of Economics*, 67:344-361 (1953).

[5] An executive in a large supplying concern told me that A & P warehouses incurred only 5 per cent of the average demurrage by all warehouse customers. "You mean 5 per cent *less* than the average?" I asked. "No, 95 per cent less. When the car comes in, they are ready for it, unload it right away, and it starts back." But this was one man's opinion on one line of goods.

of the "utility" conferred upon it by the manufacturer's advertising.

The manufacturing is not only profitable in itself; but, by supplying an additional alternative to A & P, it is an additional source of competition to its suppliers. Supplier X may be "coerced" to come to terms because of the better offer of Supplier Y; read "own-manufacture" for "Supplier Y," and the result is the same. The "coercion" and "compulsion" are nothing but highly colored words for "competition."

A & P as a diversified enterprise. Of these three kinds of "power" (buying; manufacturing; selling) to enjoy lower-cost operations, the selling advantage is perhaps the least obvious. As a seller, A & P was large enough to take a risk and gamble on the common sense and rationality of the consumer. And it had another advantage of size — that of diversification. If its sales policies were basically correct, local circumstances might distort the results upward or downward in any particular location; but the aggregate result would be profitable. An individual store operator, following the same policies in only one location, could yet go bankrupt because he had misread some particular sign, such as a change in local income and buying habits; under the same circumstances A & P would close the store and salvage its basic assets (trained manpower) for use elsewhere.

The chain store does not depend for its existence on profits at any particular location; it can run short-term losses there and yet not go out of business. (Obviously, a concern which does not operate in many locations but sells many different products is in the same position, though not necessarily to the same or any significant extent.)

This independence of profit from the single location or single product has evoked a notable bitterness, particularly in Congressional hearings. Yet the protest cannot be said to be a clear one. If this independence of local profitability has some kind of inherent vice, then the chain store as such should not be suffered to continue to exist; for it is inherently the most extreme form of diversification. But if the vice is not inherent, it must depend on particular circumstances, whose nature has not been made clear.

The economics of diversification are an interesting subject, but need no more than a brief discussion here. A firm which draws profits from at least two wholly or partly independent sources (if there is no independence, there is no diversification) has a measure of self-insurance against certain kinds of business risk, chiefly the loss of liquidity. The greater the number of profit centers, the greater the insurance. But even an infinite number of profit centers would do nothing to raise the *average* profit over any appreciable time period; all this kind of insurance does is protect against crippling loss in any one short time period. If insurance is a real economy of scale (and the matter is not wholly clear), it of course makes life that much more difficult for those not able to acquire it; it is "a privilege not possible to A & P's competitors."

The advantages of this insurance are not nearly proportional to size or to the number of stores. The situation is analogous to diversification of an investment portfolio. A holding of stock in ten companies in ten different major industries is far more diversified than a holding of one company's stock. To add another ten companies in another ten industries does not add nearly as much diversification. Even going from ten to one hundred does not add as much diversification as going from one to ten, because it would be difficult to find ninety major industries independent of the first ten major industries.

To return to A & P, if diversification is an economy of size, a chain store is an example par excellence, but the economies are largely exhausted by the time the chain is even a small fraction of the size of A & P.

In the Congressional hearings, as in the A & P case, there is often an artistic identification of diversification with predatory competition. But independence from local profitability is not a necessary condition for predatory action; a plentiful line of credit will suffice; and a local concern can as easily practice cut-throat competition, or even more easily than a large one, since it is politically less vulnerable. The truly necessary condition is local oligopoly and difficult entry. If the market is easy to enter by many firms in a short time, it is no use killing off the rivals; as soon as prices are raised to reap the ill-gotten harvest, numerous competitors will be in the field to benefit by them. If it were a question of one or two concerns, they might indeed be scared or killed permanently. But, particularly in the retail food trade, where entry is easy, both in the same location and from the fringes, predatory tactics make no sense, and Chapter XVI showed the notion to be not only nonsupported but actually refuted by the detailed evidence. But there is a short crucial experiment which also disproves it.

Appendix Table 18 permits us to make a statistical test of the probability that units were run at a loss by deliberate design in order to eliminate or browbeat competitors. The profitability of such a policy should be about the same from one part of the country to another; no one has (yet) suggested the contrary. Hence, the pattern we should expect to see is of A & P's cutting prices, running a loss in one place for a year or two at a time, accomplishing its purpose, then raising prices back to the old, or a higher, level, and then going on to repeat the whole game elsewhere. In short, the distribution of the "unit-loss-years" (a unit running a loss for one year) should be approximately random. On the other hand, if losses were due largely to inefficiency or misfortune of location, etc., we should expect them to be localized to a disproportionate extent in certain units and divisions.

As Appendix Table 18 shows, there were 468 unit-years (a unit operating one year) for which we have information. There were 54 unit-loss-years, a rate of 11.54 per cent. On the predatory hypothesis, this percentage should be approximately uniform among divisions. For example, we should expect the New England Division, with 64 unit-years, to have 7.0 unit-loss-years, and the Central Division, with 70 unit-years, to have 7.7. In fact, New England had not 7.0 but 14 unit-loss-years; Central had not 7.7 but 1. The well-known chi-square test permits us to measure the probability that the divergence of the actual from the expected pattern is due to chance. Appendix Table 18 performs the test for the various divisions. There are about 17 chances in ten thousand (i.e., seventeen hundredths of one chance in one hundred) that such a divergence of actual from expected values would occur by chance.

Let us, however, suppose that the New England and Eastern

Divisions, which together accounted for well over half of all unit-loss-years, although for much less than a third of all unit-years, had been designated for the predatory work. Then we should have most of their units running losses at one time or another. But this is not true either. Two units (out of six) accounted for ten of the fourteen unit-loss-years in New England. Of the seventeen unit-loss-years in the Eastern Division, two units (out of eight) accounted for fifteen. The Southern Division does show a relatively diffuse loss pattern, but then the great majority of its units had no losses at all at any time. In Central Western, two out of six units accounted for all unit-loss-years; in Middle Western, two out of five units accounted for all unit-loss-years.

Thus the data on unit-loss-years provide independent, additional confirmation of the conclusion that losses were the unplanned result of poor management or other local situations which could not easily or quickly be cured.

The only model that makes any sense in analyzing business conduct in the economic-political environment of a company like A & P is what the lawyers call the "reasonable and prudent" man and what economists call rational or maximizing behavior. The chain store, or the otherwise diversified business concern, has the "power" to live with a losing store or branch, and even to cut its prices below cost, without going out of business. But such action is utterly improbable if it would not pay. It is the assumption of rationality which permits economists to make sensible statements about economic life. And the peculiar bitterness, also among some economists, against economic theory as applied in antitrust [6] is not its uselessness and inapplicability — quite the contrary. It is its relevance and its determinateness. Without the assumption that firms will seek the greater profit and shun the lesser, fancy and art are free to roam and to suggest; to slide, with an ease of which the A & P case is a classic example, from the fact of diversification to competitive advantage, to the "inevitable" elimination of competitors, or at least the inevitable "intent" to eliminate. It is economic theory which keeps us out

---

[6] For a striking example, see Myron W. Watkins, Book Review, *American Economic Review*, 47:747–753. (1957).

of these green pastures, "cabin'd, cribb'd, confin'd" in the one resting place that facts and logic will allow. The nature of the market makes predatory behavior unprofitable; the political power of the retailers — as shown by the chain-store taxes, state minimum markup laws, Robinson-Patman Act, and fair-trade acts — makes it suicidal. Therefore, one must predict that there will be no predatory behavior. And the exhaustive search of the Justice Department only verifies the hypothesis. Stronger proof is rarely found in economic life.

Nor will either theory or fact support the notion that A & P practiced, if not predatory tactics, then at least preclusive ones of the sort followed by the United Shoe Machinery Corporation. This company, although it did not try to kill off competition, set its lease terms to yield widely varying rates of return on the applicable investment. "In the face of competition, and with the purpose of meeting or defeating that competition, and retaining or expanding its own share of the market," United Shoe lowered prices or improved quality to "reach only that area of the shoe machinery industry which [was] being assailed by a competitor." [7] A highly sophisticated District Court recognized that this kind of price discrimination might be a manifestation of competition under certain conditions, which were not present in the particular case.

The contrast between A & P and United Shoe could not be clearer. First, United's share of the market was overwhelming.[8] The differentials were substantial and permanent. Thus the evidence of market share and discrimination constituted two independent confirmations of the hypothesis that United had monopoly in the sense of control of supply. In the case of A & P, market shares were generally small (see Appendix Tables 15 and 16), variations in gross and net profit were irregular and due to variations in efficiency, as just seen. There is no positive correlation between either gross or net profit rate, on the one side, and share of available business, on the other. Finally, where United, as a "reasonable and prudent" management or as a profit-seeking

[7] United States v. United Shoe Machinery Corp., 110 F. Supp. 295, 326-29, 340 (D. Mass. 1953), *affirmed*, 347 U.S. 521 (1954).

[8] 110 F. Supp. 303-307. See also Carl Kaysen, *United States v. United Shoe Machinery Corporation* (Cambridge, 1956).

firm, had much to gain by cutting prices as far as needed to discourage entry — which was difficult and infrequent — A & P had nothing to gain and much to lose.

The United Shoe pattern is sometimes generalized by asserting a "tendency" for large firms to diversify by producing new lines and selling at prices which do not cover "full costs." If the cost of doing the additional business is less for the diversifying firm than for an individual firm producing the single product line (i.e., long-run incremental cost below full cost), there must be genuine economies of integration, such that resources are saved by doing the two jobs in conjunction. Then the complaint of the excluded single-product firm about "unfair" conduct and "strategic" advantages is simply a protest against more economic methods.

If there are no such economies, then the supposed tendency does not exist. Of course, a diversified firm may be, as was A & P, "passively" discriminating [9] by doing the best it can in several markets of unequal competitive intensity, in none of which it has any substantial monopoly power. But the large diversified firm is no more and no less willing than any other firm to take permanently thin or zero margins over cost. Like any other firm, it may do so in the hope that demand will revive and prices improve; or it may be stuck with an operation out of which it will try to take as much of the investment as it can, and then get out. There is no rhyme or reason in such behavior as a permanent matter except by a monopolist who is able but unwilling to switch from the lower profit to the higher profit market because he would flood the latter, bring down the price, and reduce his total profit. This is not even a caricature of A & P selling activities.

Thus the slogans about "power," and "strategic advantage," and "unfair competition" can again be analyzed, at Stocking's suggestion,[10] either as economies of size-plus-integration or as monopoly power. If monopoly power is in fact absent, then the protest is against more economic ways of doing business; and the slogans are merely a way of hiding that fact.

[9] See above, p. 158.
[10] See above, note 1.

We mentioned earlier that, aside from natural monopolies, there was no conflict between competition and efficiency, the former being a means to the latter. The various advantages of A & P in buying manufacturing, and selling were all quite real, but limited. Had they been great, they would preclude the existence of smaller firms; the grocery trade would be, like much manufacturing industry, occupied mostly by a few large firms. This is obviously not the case.

Conclusions on "economic power." It is not even a consistent value judgment to object to "economic power" in general, no matter what its source — power to compete through lower costs, or power to control supply — no matter, power is itself odious. It is sheer logical error. For the two kinds of power are not merely distinct, but contradictory in the strict logical sense. The power of some buyers to range over the market or to integrate, the power of some sellers to carry on a low-price policy, limit the power of other sellers to raise prices. The more there is of the first kind of power, the less there is of the second. One may choose or reject either kind of power, but not both, not "power" in general, or "countervailing power" in general. It is as useless as a choice in favor of "freedom." There is no such thing; there are only a large number of particular freedoms, half of which contradict the other half. Freedom from fear of physical violence can only be had by abolishing the freedom to wreak it; freedom of speech can only exist by forcing private or public bodies to respect it. To be in favor of "freedom" or opposed to "power" — these are equally empty slogans. A consistent set of value judgments must justify some kinds of "freedom" or "power" for some stated end.

One such purpose would be the best use of resources. If this is to be our criterion, there were clearly two possible faults in A & P operations. The first is inseparable from the large chain store and the large diversified firm. The enterprise as a whole had to stand a market test, and speedily; but this was not true of any particular unit or store. There is no doubt that units like Los Angeles, Seattle, or Boston would have had for some years little reason for existence, and some of them little chance of it, had every tub stood on its own bottom. Similarly, it was possible that, at least in the early or mid-1920's, some of the manufacturing facilities might better have been cut loose. The firm was interposed between the correctives of the market and the particular activity. Wherever this happens, integration can be objectionable and wasteful. The writer doubts that a public policy can be built on this possibility, but there is no reason to forget it as a factor in weighing any particular situation. Second, permanent systematic discrimination favoring (or disfavoring) A & P distorts the selective process, permitting inefficiency to thrive (above, p. 242).

The last word on the operations of A & P was probably had by that much misunderstood philosopher, Sir John Falstaff. "I am not only witty in myself," he said, "but the cause that wit is in other men." So it was with A & P; sharply limited by competition, yet managing to thrive under it, the company was also the cause that others felt it.

Conspiracy in law and theory in economics

One particular aspect of the A & P case is of much interest for the way it shows the interrelation of legal and economic analysis. The A & P information alleged not the accomplishment of monopoly, but a "conspiracy" and "attempt" to monopolize. Judge Lindley noted at the outset (see Chapter XVII) that there was no question of specific intent, which could be proved by documents and testimony, to accomplish the forbidden end, but rather that the acts of the A & P Company "in the end amount . . . to an attempt to create a partial monopoly." If this language means anything, it means that the conspiracy was inferred from actions which were considered to have a substantial probability of resulting in a monopoly (perhaps because there was a "clear and present danger" of such a result, to borrow language from the field of civil liberties). Such a concept is by no means new in antitrust law; as long ago as 1904 Justice Holmes noted that the Sherman Act, "like many others, and like the common law in some respects, directs itself against that dangerous probability [monopoly] as well as against the completed result." [11]

Moreover, the Clayton Act is specifically directed against cer-

[11] Swift & Co. v. U. S., 196 U. S. 375, 396 (1904).

tain kinds of acts or practices "where the result may be substantially to lessen competition or tend to create a monopoly," and this language is generally used to denote a substantial probability of such a result occurring.[12] Hence, the A & P case is a useful example — even if a reverse one — of how to evaluate evidence bearing on an alleged tendency or probability.

The consequences of any conduct flow from the interaction between that conduct and its environment, and without understanding that environment one cannot make any respectable judgment of probable results. Hence, if conspiracy to monopolize was the issue, Judge Lindley was sadly mistaken in excluding evidence on the economics of the food industry, such as the Federal Trade Commission's *Report on Distribution Methods and Costs* (1944), on the grounds that this would not help him decide whether the defendant had violated the Sherman Act. On the contrary, unless he knew enough of the industry to know what kinds of results were likely to follow, he was unable to understand what significance to attach to any actions of the defendants. A motorist driving at thirty miles per hour through a crowded residential area at school closing time is driving recklessly fast; the same speed on a limited-access highway is dangerously slow. In neither case does the fact of the speed alone entitle one to estimate the probability of danger to life; it is the speed in the particular environment, plus a theory of what is likely to happen under such conditions.

Thus an alleged tendency or an alleged conspiracy cannot but thrust any trier of facts into economic research and theory, admitted or not. This has nothing whatever to do with exculpation on the grounds that everybody else is doing it, or that the attempt to monopolize was really in the public interest, etc. We do not reach that question, and premature reaching of it is responsible for endless confusion. The point is rather that some systematic economic appraisal is necessary above all in cases of alleged conspiracy or "probable tendency." Not that volumes need to be written on the subject. On the contrary, the virtue of systematic analysis is that it frequently spots the one or few relevant points

---

[12] *Report of the Attorney General's Committee to Study the Antitrust Laws* (Washington, 1955), p. 118.

of fact and permits their complete coverage at the expense of irrelevancies, or shows what kinds of results are too improbable for judicial consideration or findings. Viewing the A & P trial — and many others — where days drag by in the accumulation of the tag ends of irrelevancies, in complex documents monotonously read through sleepy afternoons, one is thankful .for results no worse.

One salient point of economic theory which has been much used in this book is nothing but the counterpart of the reasonable and prudent man in the law. If a man is proved to have conspired unlawfully to bring some profit to himself, it may be only a feeble excuse, or none, to point out that there was little chance of his actually profiting thereby; that he is so foolish as to be harmless. But if the question is still to be answered, whether *in fact* he did conspire, and if he is intelligent and informed, then the improbability of his ever benefiting through a conspiracy becomes important evidence in helping to decide whether or not he conspired in the first place. This would be important even where there was some evidence, in itself inconclusive, of specific intent. But where the latter is admittedly absent, and the conspiracy, monopoly, or tendency is altogether a matter of inference from conduct — in that event, the findings of the case reduce to nothing but an economic analysis of the market.

It would be wrong to say that in the A & P case, as in others like it, there was no economic theory to give life to details of fact. Quite the contrary — there was a plenitude of theories: recoupment of lower prices, "inevitable elimination" of competition, price discrimination, etc., etc. These theories were duly admitted and taken with the utmost seriousness by judge and company — they entered in disguise, were never considered as theories, but as "obvious" common sense. The facts never had a chance.[13]

Nowhere is economic theory more severely criticized than among professional economists, which is as it should be. But, accepting all of its alleged limitations, the little it can teach us about the real world is yet essential. If nothing else, it can detect sheer logical error, and can save us from excessive —

---

[13] Cf. Morris R. Cohen, *Law and the Social Order* (New York, 1933), p. 13.

implicit — theorizing. Only by deliberately examining our premises can we avoid assuming conclusions, mixing up facts with supposed rights and wrongs, and arriving at a result which may be nonsense in economics, or a miscarriage of justice in law.

The legal significance of the A & P case

To the business firm "the law" consists of whatever the state will do if any particular action is taken, or fails to be taken. Those things which can be done (or omitted to be done) without fear of penalty are legal. Not that every possible action is examined for its legality or illegality; this would be impossibly time-consuming. Very much as with purely economic behavior, the firm does a vast amount of constant learning and absorbs thousands of patterns which are followed by rote, economizing on the scarce time and energy needed for conscious decisions. But the limits and bounds of action are there, just as with profit-conserving or profit-maximizing behavior. These learned patterns may be reinforced by purely moral sanctions. One refrains from cheating ultimately because there will be fines or imprisonment; proximately, because it would be a dishonorable act; and routinely, because it just is not done. Indeed, if behavior were governed only by the ultimate sanctions of legal penalties, enforcement would break down for lack of manpower; nine tenths of the population would be needed to police the remaining tenth. But this does not alter the fact that the outer boundaries of permitted action are where it will collide with the sanctions imposed by the state.

But the possible actions of business concerns, with permutations and combinations, run to astronomical numbers. The laws which govern them are relatively few. The lawyer, the client, and the judge are all involved in a syllogistic process — discerning the general principle, understanding the particular actions in question, and then seeing whether the acts fall into the class set up by the law. Hence, the great importance of precedent, not merely because of the rule of *stare decisis,* but because the very meaning of any general proposition, such as a law, lies in the deductions that may be drawn from it; and the meaning of a statute or common-law rule lies in the behavior situations which courts will hold to lie within the rule.

As courts go about their business of settling particular controversies by reference to "the law," therefore, they themselves cannot help making some new law. Unless the new fact situation is a perfect repetition of an old one, the judge must in deciding extend and enrich the meaning of the general commandment. And occasionally the situation is so new, and the gap in "the law" so substantial, that when the court fills it, there has been a substantial if "interstitial" legislative act, to use Holmes's phrase. Clearly, this judicial legislation has the most intimate kind of connection with the process of fact ascertainment by which the court has decided what situation needs the new interpretation.

Nor do courts legislate only by filling in gaps. As social and economic conditions change, new situations arise, and new principles are discerned and invoked to cover them. In the absence of some definite command from the legislature or other sovereign, the accretion of decisions may slowly evolve a wholly net set of commandments. The growth is evolutionary, but now and then there are real mutations of policy. These are sometimes difficult to see. As Holmes pointed out:

The principles of substantive law which have been established by the courts . . . have been somewhat obscured by having presented themselves oftenest in the form of rulings upon the sufficiency of evidence.[14]

To understand the change in the law, therefore, one must analyze the changed kinds of data which are admitted into evidence, and the significance which is given to them, in order to predict what the courts will do under similar circumstances.

But analysis is not the same as prediction. To state the logical implications of a decision is not to predict that the court will abide by those implications in the future. Our reference to "mutations of policy" is somewhat literally meant. Most biological mutations are born into an unreceptive environment and quickly perish. In the realm of law, a new decision may conflict with others. Even with no conflict, an isolated decision has not the

[14] Oliver Wendell Holmes, *The Common Law* (Boston, 1881), p. 120.

force of a line of precedents. A court will unknowingly or half-knowingly invoke a new general principle in order to settle a particular controversy. As the implications are understood, the decision may be strengthened and rounded out by later ones; and the new principle becomes "the law." But if unacceptable to the dominant sentiment of the community, the case is distinguished or ignored, and the undesired stream of doctrine is lost in the sands of hostility or neglect.

The tendency of a principle to expand itself to the limit of its logic may be counteracted by the tendency to confine it within the limits of its history.[15]

The true legal significance of the A & P decisions cannot, therefore, be briefly stated; in the nature of things, perhaps it cannot be stated at all. In the preceding chapters, we have analyzed what the courts declared to be "facts," unearthing the economic theories of bench and bar, and their research techniques. It is clear that the prosecution "facts" embodied an attack on price competition per se, and on vertical and horizontal integration when they economized resources and hence were a "competitive advantage." But we cannot say how much of this was sheer economic ignorance and incompetence and how much was policy. Plainly, both elements were there. It is also clear that the courts rejected none of the government's economic or legal theories. Hence, all of them could be persuasive in the future; and probably some would be. But it is harder to be more definite. How much of the prosecution case would be acceptable to a court which was better advised by opposing counsel? Will the mutations of policy visible in the A & P decisions be found acceptable by the courts? The answers to those questions can only be guessed at, but are worth some discussion.

The A & P case and "exclusion" in antitrust law. In the ten years since the A & P decisions were rendered, they have been little cited by the courts. There would be some warrant for supposing them to be a judicial sport, born of nothing more than ignorance, were it not for their connection with an important part of the antitrust tradition.

[15] Benjamin Nathan Cardozo, *The Nature of the Judicial Process* (New Haven, 1921), p. 51.

The well-known article by Edward S. Mason on "Monopoly in Law and Economics" [16] reads better today than when it appeared twenty years ago because so much has been verified by the developments since then. Before and after the Sherman Act, the law had always been concerned with restraints on the freedom of action of some business concerns imposed by the action of other concerns; and the most extreme form of restraint was of course total exclusion from the market, sometimes called monopolization. These acts of restraint also had economic content and could be analyzed accordingly. But although the concept of restraint-exclusion might overlap and frequently coincide with the economic concept of control over prices and output, they were by no means the same thing; neither necessarily implied the other.

Restriction of competition is the legal content of monopoly; control of the market is its economic substance. And these realities are by no means equivalent.[17]

There is in fact a basic ambiguity in the concept of exclusion. Concerns are excluded from the market every day for lack of efficiency, and this is the heart of the competitive process in economizing scarce resources. Or concerns may be excluded, although they are no less efficient, because of restrictive arrangements or predatory warfare. Thus, a prohibition of restraint of trade and of exclusion (or monopolizing), such as the Sherman Act, must in practice, as actually applied to market situations, show an ebb and flow of its basic emphasis. The concept opposed to monopoly was freedom [18] — but for whom, to do what, was never defined in economic terms during the legislative history of the Act,[19] or (as will be seen in a moment) during its judicial history. The Senators who wrote the Act, and who thought they were incorporating the common law of the several states and the British jurisdictions, certainly accepted the presence of big business; the

---

[16] *Yale Law Journal*, vol. 42 (1937); most recently reprinted in Edward S. Mason, *Economic Concentration and the Monopoly Problem* (Cambridge, 1957).

[17] Mason, p. 334.

[18] Mason, p. 334.

[19] These remarks summarize the writer's review of Hans B. Thorelli, *The Federal Antitrust Policy* (Baltimore, 1955), in *American Economic Review*, 46:481–487 (1956).

notion that these conservative gentlemen wrote a trust-busting instrument is altogether mistaken.

Senator George F. Hoar defined monopoly as "the sole engrossing to a man's self by means which prevent other men from engaging in fair competition with him." And the Senator's concept of "fair competition" is clearly revealed in his opinion in 1891 that a group of sellers could lawfully agree on a common price and a pooling of profits — complete cartelization — if this was "a contract, though in partial restraint of trade, which is reasonable and . . . which has for its object merely saving the parties from destructive competition with each other." Obviously, if there is anything at all in the economic theory sketched earlier in this chapter, it is well that "fair competition" has not been the guiding beacon for judges interpreting the Sherman Act. But neither has it disappeared. The desire for what would today be called workable or effective competition, as opposed to merely protecting businessmen who felt threatened by the trusts, had always been present in some degree; judicial decisions brought competition toward the center of the stage from out of the wings. It has stayed there ever since, along with the older purpose; the two are often in harmony and often not.[20]

The development of the Act away from "fair competition" and toward effective competition has been most marked and clear-cut in the interpretation of Section 1, against "restraint of trade," which today approaches a total prohibition on communication among competitors as to price or price-affecting terms of the bargain. The public forums are still left open for general discussion, and probably always must be — freedom of speech must be given a higher priority than competition — but private communications on this subject are very nearly equated to conspiracy. The tendency may even have gone a little too far and have covered some situations which involve no market power.

Section 2 of the Act, covering the single firm accused of "monopolizing," has not had any such intelligible history. This is, of course, no place to undertake a survey of it. It may be said, however, that until the landmark *Alcoa* decision in 1945, there

[20] Cf. Edward H. Levi, "A Two-Level Anti-Monopoly Law," *Northwestern University Law Review*, 47:507 (1952).

could be no violation of Section 2 unless there were some kind of flagrant predatory tactics.[21] The *Alcoa* decision needs a brief glance, on two points. The first is the interrelation between fact and law, so lengthily pursued in this work. Judge Hand found Alcoa to be a monopolist in having control over supply; but he found also that Alcoa had consciously and deliberately "monopolized" because of constant building ahead of demand, "embracing each new opportunity," and in general acting like an alert and aggressive competitor. The model of good behavior, by implication, was the enterprise which made room for its rivals, let them live, disturbed nobody, and was the very model of a modern cartel gentleman. The later decision on relief, which for convenience may be called *Second Alcoa*,[22] softened the impact; but not until the *Shoe Machinery* case of 1953 [23] did the door appear to close on the suggestion that lower costs and rivalrous conduct were ingredients of the offense. With surpassing skill, Judge Wyzanski stayed within the confines of the *Alcoa* decision while completely recasting it to provide that the defendant who was a monopolist in the sense of control of the market could escape if he proved that his position was due solely to superior skill, better products, "low margins of profit maintained permanently and without discrimination" — which is of course a perfect fit to A & P policies, among others — or economies of scale.[24]

The intensely controversial, not to say unfortunate, aspect of Judge Hand's original decision was altogether unnecessary, or would have been if the antitrust process had been able to do a proper job of fact finding. But in *Alcoa* as in *A & P* — though surely not with the same squalid results — the facts were never found. In the year in which the Alcoa case opened, there appeared Donald H. Wallace's classic study [25] which demonstrated that, far from anticipating growth, the company had acted like a sen-

[21] U. S. v. Aluminum Co., 148 F.2d 416 (2d Cir. 1945). See, however, the brilliant decision, also by Judge Learned Hand, of twenty-nine years earlier: U. S. v. Corn Products Refining Co., 234 Fed. 964 (S.D.N.Y. 1916).

[22] U. S. v. Aluminum Company, 91 F. Supp. 333 (S.D.N.Y. 1950).

[23] U. S. v. United Shoe Machinery Corporation, 110 F. Supp. 295, 344–46 (D. Mass. 1953).

[24] 110 F. Supp. 342–46; the quotation is from 342.

[25] Donald H. Wallace, *Market Control in the Aluminum Industry* (Cambridge, 1937).

sible monopolist and had dragged its feet, expanding at a slower rate than a group of competitors would have done.

The other noteworthy aspect of the decision comes in a well-known paragraph:

possession of unchallenged economic power deadens initiative, discourages thrift and depresses energy; . . . immunity from competition is a narcotic, and rivalry is a stimulant, to industrial progress; . . . the spur of constant stress is necessary to counteract an inevitable disposition to let well enough alone.

This is an excellent statement of competition as the economic goal of the law. But it is followed immediately by this:

It is possible, because of its indirect social or moral effect, to prefer a system of small producers, each dependent for his success upon his own skill and character, to one in which the great mass of those engaged must accept the direction of a few.[26]

These two criteria cannot be reconciled. If the "indirect social or moral effect" is worth its cost (the writer's opinion to the contrary notwithstanding), this means that it is worth the loss of the competition which would destroy many "small producers" where they are less efficient.

By and large, but with many turns and lapses, the antitrust law has developed to follow the economic criterion. In the late 1940's, following *Alcoa* and *A & P*, it was a fair question whether the road was not taking a sharp turn. Indeed, the 1947 *Yellow Cab* case clearly implied the rule, beautiful in its simplicity, that vertical integration was illegal per se.[27] But when the Supreme Court was confronted with the rule a year later, it distinguished cases.[28] With *Alcoa* absorbed and reinterpreted by *United Shoe Machinery,* and with *A & P* apparently a dead letter, it is now clear that the turn did not take place. Nevertheless, the *A & P* case is still of considerable importance from a purely legal point of view. First, it shows that if the circumstances are favorable, the Robinson-Patman Act can be incorporated into the Sherman Act, in approximately the same way that the Trojan Horse was

[26] U. S. v. Aluminum Company, 148 F.2d 416, 427 (2d Cir. 1945).
[27] U. S. v. Yellow Cab Co., 332 U. S. 218 (1947).
[28] U. S. v. Columbia Steel Co., 314 U. S. 495 (1948).

incorporated into Troy. The existence of a precedent makes it all the more likely.

Second, there is the amended Section 7 of the Clayton Act, forbidding mergers where they may lessen competition or tend toward monopoly. By the end of 1957, thirty-three complaints had been filed, of which no less than twenty-four allege that the acquisition will give the merging companies "a substantial competitive advantage," or some other euphemism for economies of scale or of integration. Economies of vertical integration can again be transmuted into "subsidies," "rebates," etc., when they are "a privilege not available to . . . competitors." Furthermore, where uneven vertical integration leads to a concern's making sales, presumably at a profit, to competitors, that can become yet another "subsidy." The primitive misconception that a payment by a buyer to a seller is somehow a gift or a net advantage to the seller was, we may recall, even embodied in the Final Judgment. And it needed not even an allegation that A & P had any monopoly power or control in the markets where it sold to other business concerns; profits made on sales to them were a complete and sufficient offense.

Furthermore, the hearings on the amendment to Section 7 contain virulent attacks on "conglomerate," i.e., diversified, concerns. A & P is of course the extreme case of the conglomerate firm, and shows how such attacks may be clothed in the appearance of maintaining competition, and become part of the law.

Third, it is so obvious as to be easily overlooked that the A & P case involved marketing. In this area the impact of economical methods upon some "small producers" may be quite obvious and painful. Here is where the doctrines of protectionism are most likely to be acceptable to the courts. Moreover, marketing is the area in which the Congress is most obviously concerned, and most obviously protectionist. The Robinson-Patman Act and the Miller-Tydings Act (validating state fair-trade laws) were in part depression products. But in the late 1950's the popularity of the two is still overwhelming; fair trade was re-enacted quickly when the Supreme Court destroyed a vital part of its machinery. In the past few years, lengthy and well-publicized investigations of bigness and "oligopoly" in automobile manufacturing have led to laws, passed by overwhelming majorities against the opposition of the antitrust agencies, not to lessen that oligopoly but to strengthen the local monopoly position of the retailer.

A subcommittee of the United States Senate has induced a group of suppliers to institute together a system of "fair trade" (resale price maintenance) in the marketing of gasoline.[29] As this book is written, the Federal Trade Commission is conducting a study of the food industry, conspicuously including the chain stores. Those who wondered about the object of the inquiry were advised to pay attention to a forthcoming speech by a Senator well known as the most vocal champion of "fair trade," and to be delivered to the National Food Brokers Association.[30] The entry of a new small firm through lower prices and distribution through chain stores, to the discomfiture of large and small established firms alike, is "incipient monopoly." The case has been "tried" before a Senate subcommittee, and the culprit declared guilty of violating the Sherman Act, and perhaps others as well.[31] The "defendant" may feel no immediate pain; but appropriate legislation will in time be attempted.

Although competition as a goal of social policy is irreconcilable with protectionism, or "fair competition," the writer's best guess is that, like some other irreconcilables, they will continue to co-

[29] The essence of any collusive agreement is that the firms agreeing will continue to stick together. "Esso Standard Oil Co. . . . reinstituted fair trading in New Jersey last week. But the action's effectiveness depends on whether other majors . . . follow along. . . . Happier retailers and quieter gasoline markets could have a great effect on the industry. Fewer government investigations would be one result. . . . One of the more active agencies in oil industry probes, however, the Senate Small Business Committee, has called the Esso fair-trade decision a 'laudable effort to end ruinous price wars.' Sen. Hubert Humphrey (D., Minn.), chairman of the distribution subcommittee, says that it will 'keep a very close watch on the reactions of other major gasoline marketers in New Jersey to the olive branch offered by Esso.'" (*Petroleum Week*, May 11, 1956, pp. 38–40.) The subcommittee had held lengthy and well publicized hearings to bring about this result. See *Gasoline Price Wars in New Jersey*, Report of the Select Committee on Small Business, U. S. Senate, 84 Cong., 2 sess. (Washington, 1956).

[30] "Food Men Await Inquiry by FTC," *New York Times*, November 16, 1958, Financial Section, p. 1.

[31] *Case Study of Incipient Monopoly*. Report of the Subcommittee on Antitrust and Monopoly of the Committee on the Judiciary. 85 Cong., 2 sess. (Washington, 1958), particularly pp. 46–50.

exist more or less nonpeacefully. A healthy society can afford a
few neuroses of policy and, like most of the individuals in it,
carry in its bosom the conflicting ideals so eloquently stated by
Judge Hand. But if the A & P case should, in the perspective of
hindsight, really turn out to have been a major step, it would be
a curious reversal of trends as between this country and Western
Europe. The Common Market treaty of the six nations will, if
successful, greatly widen the market and thereby *exclude* inefficient business concerns which are today sheltered from competition; their resources will be put to better use. It would be a
choice in favor of "industrial progress" and the "power" to lower
costs; against the "system of small producers" and the power to
maintain prices. The example of contemporary France throws
light on the supposed benefits of that system. It would be curious
if this country were now adopting the policies discredited in, and
now apparently discarded by, the nations of Western Europe.

APPENDIXES

APPENDIX I
STATISTICAL TABLES

APPENDIX TABLE 1. Personal Consumption Expenditures for Food Purchased for Off-Premise Consumption, 1919–1957 (billions of dollars)

Year	Amount	Year	Amount
1919	13.3	1939	14.2
1920	14.9	1940	15.0
1921	11.9	1941	17.1
1922	11.2	1942	20.3
1923	11.9	1943	22.6
1924	12.7	1944	24.5
1925	13.5	1945	26.7
1926	14.4	1946	33.3
1927	14.1	1947	38.7
1928	13.9	1948	40.3
1929	14.8	1949	39.2
1930	13.5	1950	40.4
1931	10.8	1951	44.6
1932	8.2	1952	46.9
1933	8.6	1953	47.8
1934	10.8	1954	49.1
1935	12.2	1955	50.6
1936	12.9	1956	53.3
1937	14.8	1957	57.1
1938	14.1		

Sources. For 1929–1947: *Survey of Current Business*, Supplement, "National Income" (1954 edition), table 30, line I-1. The 1929 estimate found there has been extrapolated back by the use of ratios derived from Simon Kuznets, *Commodity Flow and Capital Formation* (New York: National Bureau of Economic Research, 1938), table V-4, line 3, of the first group, p. 288. For 1948–1957: U.S. Income and Output, A Supplement to the *Survey of Current Business* (November 1958), table II-4, line I-1.

APPENDIX TABLE 2. Sales by Food Stores in the United States, 1929–1957 (millions of dollars)

(1)	All food stores			Chain food stores						A & P Company				
	(2)	(3)	(4)	(5) Grocery & combination	(6)	(7) Other	(8)	(9) Total	(10)	(11)	(12)	(13)	(14)	(15)
	Grocery & combi-										As per cent of			
Year	nation	Other	Total	Amt.	% of Col.2	Amt.	% of Col.3	Amt.	% of Col.4	Amt.	Col.2	Col.3	Col.5	Col.9
1929	7,353	3,614	10,967	2,833	38.5	642	18.2	3,475	31.7	1,054	14.4	9.6	38.3	30.4
1933	5,004	1,772	6,776	2,909	58.1	385	21.7	3,294	48.6	820	16.4	12.1	28.2	24.9
1935	6,423	2,018	8,441	2,508	39.0	450	22.2	2,958	35.0	872	13.6	10.3	34.7	29.4
1936	6,959	2,227	9,186	2,630	37.8	497	22.3	3,127	34.0	907	13.0	9.9	34.4	29.0
1937	7,239	2,431	9,670	2,619	36.2	522	21.4	3,141	32.4	882	12.1	9.1	33.6	28.0
1938	7,293	2,326	9,619	2,630	36.1	490	21.0	3,120	32.4	879	12.1	9.1	33.4	28.1
1939	7,806	2,475	10,281	2,901	37.2	708	28.6	3,609	35.1	990	12.7	9.6	39.1	27.4
1940	8,450	2,614	11,064	3,162	37.4	537	20.5	3,699	33.4	1,116	13.2	10.1	35.2	30.1
1941	10,018	3,069	13,087	3,949	39.4	626	20.3	4,575	34.9	1,378	13.8	10.5	34.8	30.1
1942	12,412	3,704	16,126	4,533	36.5	750	20.2	5,283	32.7	1,471	11.8	9.1	32.4	27.8
1943	13,373	4,229	17,602	4,368	32.7	843	19.9	5,211	29.6	1,311	9.8	7.4	30.0	25.1
1944	14,638	4,521	19,160	4,712	32.1	891	19.7	5,603	29.2	1,402	9.5	7.3	29.7	25.0
1945	15,847	5,011	20,859	4,947	31.2	970	19.3	5,917	28.3	1,435	9.0	6.8	29.0	24.2
1946	19,154	5,640	24,794	6,647	34.7	1,081	19.1	7,728	31.1	1,909	9.9	7.7	28.7	24.7
1947	22,868	6,083	28,951	8,703	38.0	1,173	19.2	9,876	34.1	2,546	11.1	8.8	29.2	25.7
1948	24,073	6,381	30,454	9,529	39.5	1,210	18.9	10,739	35.2	2,837	11.8	9.3	29.7	26.4
1949	24,800	6,165	30,965	9,553	38.5	1,175	19.2	10,728	34.6	2,905	11.7	9.4	30.4	27.1
1950	26,412	6,356	32,768	10,489	39.7	1,204	19.1	11,693	35.7	3,180	12.0	9.7	30.3	27.2
1951	29,816	7,124	36,940	11,569	38.8	1,352	19.0	12,921	35.0	3,393	11.4	9.2	29.3	26.3

New series

1951	30,346	..	37,626	10,718	35.3	..	11,705	31.1	3,393	11.2	9.0	31.7	29.0
1952	32,238	..	39,771	11,606	36.0	..	12,554	31.6	3,756	11.7	9.4	32.4	29.9
1953	33,623	..	40,777	12,404	36.9	..	13,392	32.8	3,989	11.9	9.8	32.2	29.8
1954	34,993	..	40,100	13,359	38.2	..	14,345	35.8	4,140	11.8	10.3	31.0	28.9
1955	36,900	..	42,000	14,223	38.6	..	15,250	36.3	4,305	11.7	10.3	30.3	28.2
1956	39,200	..	44,200	15,894	40.5	..	16,636	37.6	4,482	11.4	10.1	28.2	26.9
1957	42,444	..	47,800	17,377	40.9	..	18,221	38.1	4,769	11.2	10.0	27.4	26.2

Sources. In all cases, U. S. Department of Commerce and, except as noted, *Survey of Current Business*. Cols. 2, 3, 4: 1929–1941, November 1943, p. 6; 1942–1945, September 1948, p. 22; 1946–1948, October 1949, p. 22; 1949–1950, February 1952, p. 22; 1951 (old series), September 1952, p. 17; 1951 (new series), 1953, February 1955, p. 25. Col. 2: 1954, February 1955, p. 25; 1955, February 1956, p. 28; 1956, February 1957, p. 29; 1957, Bureau of the Census, *Annual Retail Trade Report* (Washington, 1958), p. 5. Col. 2: 1954–1957, February 1958, p. 23. Cols. 5, 7, 9: for 1929–1938, February 1944, p. 12; 1939–1947, January 1949, p. 10; 1948–1950, February 1951, p. 22; 1951 (old series), September 1952, p. 17; 1951–1952 (new series), September 1953, p. 8; 1953–1957, Bureau of the Census, *Annual Retail Trade Report* (Washington, 1958), p. 5. Col. 11: Appendix Table 5.

APPENDIX TABLE 3. A & P Retail Sales, Quarterly, 1919–1941 (in dollars)

Years	Quarters				Total [a] (dollars)
	First	Second	Third	Fourth	
1919	$42,653	$45,610	$49,164	$55,379	$192,806
1920	65,571	62,954	55,959	49,936	234,421
1921	49,925	43,868	51,923	56,280	201,997
1922	59,012	57,588	61,870	67,494	245,965
1923 [b]	72,467	69,725	76,047	78,223	296,461
1924	82,089	81,525	91,212	97,204	352,030
1925	100,464	102,041	113,863	123,645	440,014
1926	138,026	133,697	145,682	156,676	574,080
1927	178,758	178,541	196,064	207,874	761,237
1928 [b]	234,846	218,539	234,775	271,698	959,859
1929	252,346	245,527	264,965	277,641	1,040,478
1930	274,848	258,019	257,798	261,313	1,051,978
1931	270,828	250,799	244,842	230,141	996,609
1932	233,735	213,434	209,168	197,964	854,301
1933	197,536	203,342	201,922	204,478	807,279
1934 [b]	207,093	199,557	198,158	224,818	829,626
1935	216,544	204,763	213,338	226,080	860,724
1936	226,408	222,216	219,332	224,968	892,924
1937	228,965	207,671	215,801	216,828	869,264
1938	219,356	206,676	216,536	228,944	871,511
1939	237,852	232,004	251,906	259,632	981,394
1940 [b]	267,467	258,862	266,280	311,771	1,104,442
1941	312,001	321,602	339,731	380,642	1,354,018

Source. *Annual Binder*, respective years.

[a] Slight arithmetical errors are evident. These have been reproduced as found in the series.

[b] The period covered is 53 weeks.

APPENDIX TABLE 4. A & P Sales (dollars) and Net Profit (as per cent of sales), by Size of Store, 1927–1935

1927		1929		1934		1935	
Weekly sales	Net profit	Weekly sales	Net profit	Weekly sales	Net profit	Weekly sales	Net profit
Groceries only							
356	−10.9	450	−5.0	445	−1.3	440	−1.4
462	−3.0	630	0.0	570	1.1	610	1.5
618	0.5	800	1.7	720	2.7	795	3.0
800	2.6	1000	2.7	880	3.7	990	4.0
993	4.1	1200	3.5	1035	4.1	1185	4.3
1194	5.0	1450	4.1	1260	4.7	1450	4.0
1450	5.9	1850	4.8	1550	5.1	1860	5.0
1834	7.1	2280	4.9	1920	5.1	2260	5.3
2263	7.4	2920	4.9	2470	6.4	2840	6.0
2839	8.3	..	..	..	..	..	..
Combination stores							
638	−10.1	1000	−6.3	710	−4.4	630	−7.0
817	−5.1	1220	−2.2	890	−1.9	830	−3.8
964	−3.3	1510	0.2	1050	0.0	1010	−0.1
1206	−0.2	1910	1.7	1200	1.2	1210	1.0
1498	2.0	2280	2.8	1450	1.9	1500	1.9
1891	3.4	2730	3.4	1760	2.6	1890	2.8
2276	4.6	3240	3.4	2120	3.5	2280	3.5
2719	4.8	4350	4.2	2540	4.2	2730	4.0
3223	5.9	..	..	3000	4.4	3200	4.2
4163	5.4	..	..	4000	4.1	4700	3.6

Source. *Annual Binder*, respective years.

APPENDIX TABLE 5. A & P Stores, Employees, and Sales, 1919–1957

| | End of fiscal year | | Employees,[a] full-time | Gross sales [b] | Physical volume |
Year	All stores	Super- markets	equivalents (thousands)	(millions of dollars)	of sales, tons per store
1919	4,200		n.a.	194.6	3.14
1920	4,600		n.a.	235.3	3.11
1921	5,200		n.a.	202.4	3.60
1922	7,300		n.a.	246.9	3.37
1923	9,300		n.a.	302.9	2.90
1924	11,400		n.a.	352.1	2.83
1925	14,000		n.a.	440.1	2.73
1926	14,800		n.a.	574.1	3.27
1927	15,600		n.a.	761.4	4.26
1928	15,100		n.a.	972.8	5.32
1929	15,400		n.a.	1,053.7	6.04
1930	15,700		n.a.	1,065.8	6.28
1931	15,600		n.a.	1,008.3	6.74
1932	15,400		n.a.	864.0	6.61
1933	15,100		62.8	819.6	6.36
1934	15,000		70.8	842.0	6.06
1935	14,900		71.2	877.2	6.14
1936	14,700	20	70.3	907.4	6.48
1937	13,300	282	69.1	881.7	6.40
1938	10,800	775	63.4	879.0	n.a.
1939	9,100	1,127	62.3	990.4	12.92 [c]
1940	7,100	1,413	66.0	1,115.8	17.82 [c]
1941	6,200	1,594	75.1	1,378.7	23.76 [c]
1942	5,900	1,667	n.a.	1,471.2	n.a.
1943	5,900	1,666	60.8	1,310.8	n.a.
1944	5,800	n.a.	n.a.	1,401.6	n.a.
1945	5,600	n.a.	n.a.	1,434.8	n.a.
1946	5,200	n.a.	n.a.	1,909.0	n.a.
1947	5,100	n.a.	n.a.	2,545.6	n.a.
1948	5,000	n.a.	97.0	2,837.3	n.a.
1949	4,700	n.a.	n.a.	2,904.6	n.a.
1950	4,500	n.a.	n.a.	3,179.8	n.a.
1951	4,400	n.a.	n.a.	3,893.5	n.a.
1952	4,400	n.a.	n.a.	3,755.7	n.a.
1953	4,200	n.a.	n.a.	3,989.1	n.a.
1954	4,200	n.a.	n.a.	4,140.0	n.a.

Appendix Table 5 (*continued*)

End of fiscal year		Employee,[a] full-time equivalents (thousands)	Gross sales[b] (millions of dollars)	Physical volume of sales, tons per store
Year	All stores	Super-markets			
1955	4,200	n.a.	n.a.	4,305.0	n.a.
1956	4,100	3,000	110.0	4,481.8	n.a.
1957	n.a.	n.a.	n.a.	4,769.2	n.a.

Sources. Stores and supermarkets, *Annual Binder* (1941), GX 314. For 1942 and 1943, from the respective fourth-quarter *Store Profit Summary*, DX's 712 and 713. For 1944–1950, Standard & Poor, *Industry Surveys: Retail Trade*, vol. 119, no. 16, sec. 2, "Basic Analysis," April 19, 1951. For 1951–1956, Standard & Poor, *Industry Surveys: Retail Trade*, sec. 2, PR63, "Basic Analysis," November 14, 1957. Estimated supermarkets are only a guess.

[a] "Employees" is the total company payroll divided by the average fulltime wage (from GX 314). The figures for 1933–1939 are as of March 10, 1940; 1941, mid-November; 1943, mid-October. For 1948 and 1957, the figures are only a rough estimate, based on the increase in sales, adjusted for price changes and productivity.

[b] For 1919–1926, this refers to "retail sales," to which it was apparently equal. For 1919–1941, from GX 314; later years from *Moody's*.

[c] GX 314. The 1939–1941 figures refer to the last quarter.

APPENDIX TABLE 6. Prices and Costs, 1919-1943

Fiscal year	Indexes (1929 = 100)		At current prices [c]		At 1929 prices [d]		Indexes (1929 = 100)	
	Urban retail food costs (BLS) [a]	A & P retail prices [b]	Expense (% of sales)	Gross profit (% of sales)	Expense (% of sales)	Gross profit (% of sales)	Expense outlay per physical unit	Margin per physical unit
1919	113.0	134.7	12.52	16.00	16.86	21.55	108.7	117.4
1920	127.4	146.0	14.14	16.19	20.64	23.63	133.0	128.6
1921	96.8	103.2	15.27	19.55	15.76	20.18	101.6	109.9
1922	90.5	99.8	16.02	20.12	15.99	20.08	103.0	109.4
1923	93.6	107.5	17.18	21.01	18.47	22.58	119.0	123.0
1924	92.8	105.9	18.10	21.67	19.17	22.95	123.6	125.0
1925	101.7	109.7	18.32	21.50	20.10	23.58	118.2	128.6
1926	102.6	106.6	17.37	20.15	18.52	21.48	119.3	117.0
1927	99.2	102.1	15.89	18.67	16.22	19.06	104.6	103.8
1928	98.4	101.4	15.32	18.09	15.43	18.34	99.5	99.9
1929	100.00	100.0	15.52	18.36	15.52	18.36	100.0	100.0
1930	92.3	94.3	16.43	19.58	15.49	18.46	99.9	100.5
1931	75.6	82.8	17.61	20.79	14.58	17.21	94.0	93.7
1932	63.4	73.2	19.08	21.90	13.97	16.03	90.0	87.3
1933	64.9	73.3	18.59	22.25	13.63	16.31	87.8	88.4
1934	71.6	78.5	18.73	20.86	14.70	16.38	94.8	89.2
1935	76.0	82.4	17.56	19.50	14.47	16.07	93.3	87.6
1936	76.2	81.8	17.26	19.23	14.12	15.81	91.0	86.2
1937	78.8	84.4	17.63	18.67	14.88	15.76	95.9	85.4
1938	73.4	77.4	16.25	18.28	12.58	14.15	81.1	77.0
1939	71.9	73.4	14.66	16.84	10.76	12.36	69.3	67.4
1940	73.1	72.8	13.5	15.61	9.8	11.4	64.1	58.2
1941	82.0	84.2	11.8	13.71	9.9	11.6	65.4	61.5

Year						
1942	95.6	n.a.	11.43	12.99	n.a.	n.a.
1943	104.1	n.a.	12.43	14.20	n.a.	n.a.

[a] Bureau of Labor Statistics index shifted from a 1935–1939 base to a fiscal 1929 base (March 1929–February 1930), except for years prior to 1924.

[b] A & P retail prices from DX 498, GX 214, and GX 314.

[c] Expense and gross profit rates at current prices are A & P's own figures, from GX 314, DX 712, and DX 713.

[d] Rates at 1929 prices are the current rates multiplied by the current index of A & P prices. They are algebraically equivalent to a series derived by deflating the sales figure to obtain sales in constant dollars, and then expressing the undeflated margin as a percentage of the deflated sales:

$$\text{Expense rate} = \frac{\text{Expense outlay}}{\text{Sales}};$$

$$\text{Constant dollar sales} = \frac{\text{Sales}}{\text{Price index}};$$

$$\frac{\text{Expense outlay}}{\text{Constant dollar sales}} = \frac{\text{Expense outlay}}{\text{Sales/Price index}} = \text{Expense rate} \times \text{Price index}.$$

Therefore the rates at constant prices can be regarded as measures respectively of the money cost or money cost plus profit of distributing a constant quantity of goods. These have been expressed in index form in the last two columns. They would need to be deflated by a composite index of hourly wage rates, rentals per square foot, etc., in order to obtain an index of real not money cost of distribution. As a rough approximation, we may use the implicit price deflator for the gross national product (National Income Supplement to the *Survey of Current Business*, 1951, p. 146, table B). This index number declined by 9.3 per cent from 1929 to 1937, and rose by 6.8 per cent to 1941. This would indicate that the A & P expense rate in "real" terms rose by about 5 per cent from 1929 to 1937 and then fell about 36 per cent to 1941.

APPENDIX TABLE 7. A & P Investment and Profit, 1919–1957
(dollars in millions; rates in per cent)

		Profit		Rate of return		
Year	Equity invest- ment [a]	Before taxes	After taxes	Before taxes	After taxes	Equity investment turnover [a][b]
1919	20.7	6.7	4.4	31.46	21.41	9.41
1920	24.5	4.8	3.9	18.78	13.90	9.62
1921	28.2	8.4	7.1	30.80	25.10	7.18
1922	32.7	8.8	6.6	25.75	20.26	7.55
1923	40.0	11.2	8.7	28.20	21.68	7.58
1924	49.6	13.2	11.6	25.78	23.31	7.10
1925	58.0	13.8	12.0	23.79	20.66	7.59
1926	66.9	16.2	14.0	24.18	20.91	8.58
1927	77.7	21.3	18.4	27.39	23.69	9.80
1928	92.6	27.5	24.2	29.07	26.16	10.11
1929	110.9	29.5	26.2	26.61	23.65	9.38
1930	125.9	35.0	30.7	27.75	24.41	8.35
1931	144.0	34.0	29.8	23.62	20.69	6.92
1932	157.4	26.5	22.7	17.15	14.69	5.52
1933	159.1	23.9	20.5	15.00	12.87	5.08
1934	161.9	19.3	16.7	11.90	10.32	5.12
1935	161.3	19.2	16.6	11.92	10.29	5.34
1936	161.0	20.4	17.1	12.66	10.61	5.55
1937	158.2	11.0	9.1	6.92	5.76	5.50
1938	158.9	19.4	15.8	12.21	9.96	5.48
1939	161.7	23.0	18.7	14.20	11.54	6.07
1940	163.0	25.4	18.3	15.60	11.25	6.77
1941	163.7	28.6	16.7	17.49	10.23	8.42
1942	164.9	23.4	11.5	14.17	6.98	8.94
1943	166.3	24.3	12.6	14.66	7.58	7.88
1944	167.7	25.9	13.2	15.45	7.88	8.37
1945	167.9	28.8	12.3	17.16	7.33	8.55
1946	188.1	50.1	30.2	26.61	16.04	10.13
1947	211.5	66.5	39.8	31.44	18.82	12.04
1948	234.0	64.2	38.7	27.44	16.54	12.13
1949	249.1	57.3	33.4	23.00	13.41	11.66
1950	266.6	60.6	32.9	22.73	12.34	11.93
1951	277.8	60.5	27.2	21.78	9.79	12.21
1952	240.9	67.1	29.2	23.07	10.04	12.91
1953	305.6	69.7	30.4	22.81	9.95	13.05
1954	321.8	69.3	32.3	21.54	10.01	12.87

Appendix Table 7 (*continued*)

Year	Equity invest- ment[a]	Profit		Rate of return		Equity investment turnover[a][b]
		Before taxes	After taxes	Before taxes	After taxes	
1955	341.1	77.2	35.4	22.63	10.38	12.62
1956	367.6	90.4	41.9	24.59	11.40	12.19
1957	389.9	110.7	50.7	28.39	13.00	12.23

Source. For 1919–1941, *Annual Binder*, GX 314; for later years, *Moody's*.

[a] Equity investment is estimated by adding capital stock, surplus, and minor items. As a check, the estimate was computed back for ten years, and compared with A & P's own record. The average discrepancy is a little more than one tenth of one per cent, and in no year is it as much as one half of one per cent. Some of the company's adjustments to its investment account are unwarranted, in my opinion; but the amounts in question are never as large as one per cent.

[b] Sales divided by equity investment.

440

APPENDIX TABLE 8. The Asset Structure of A & P, 1919-1957

Year (1)	Sales (2)	Total assets [a] (3)	Inventories (4)	(5) [b]	Fixed assets (6)	(7) [b]	Other assets [a] (8)	(9) [b]	Cash and govt. bonds (10)	(11) [b]	Columns (5) plus (11) (12) [b]
1919	$194.6										
1920	235.3	$31.2	$14.9	47.8	$5.9	18.9	$1.7	5.4	$8.7	27.9	75.7
1921	202.4	37.3	18.4	49.3	5.8	15.5	0.8	2.1	12.3	33.0	82.3
1922	246.9	44.1	27.3	61.9	7.9	17.9	0.5	1.1	8.4	19.0	80.9
1923	302.9	51.5	29.9	58.0	10.0	19.4	1.7	3.3	9.9	19.2	77.2
1924	352.1	63.0	36.6	58.1	12.5	19.8	1.4	2.2	12.5	19.8	77.9
1925	440. [c]	78.0	45.7	58.5	14.0	17.9	2.6	3.3	15.7	20.1	78.6
1926	574. [c]	92.4	50.3	54.4	13.5	14.6	5.2	5.6	23.4 [d]	25.3	79.7
1927	761.4	113.3	62.2	54.9	15.9	14.0	4.1	3.6	31.1	27.4	82.3
1928	972.8	132.7	71.1	53.6	21.0	15.8	8.7	6.6	31.9	24.0	77.6
1929	1,053.7	147.4	69.3	47.0	29.5	20.0	7.8	5.3	40.8	27.7	74.7
1930	1,065.8	170.5	60.0	35.2	31.8	18.6	5.3	3.1	73.4	43.0	78.2
1931	1,008.3	183.0	53.1	29.0	31.4	17.2	7.9	4.3	90.6	49.5	78.5
1932	864.0	188.7	50.9	27.0	29.4	15.6	9.3	4.9	99.1	52.5	79.5
1933	819.6	193.8	62.9	32.4	25.7	13.3	8.7	4.5	96.5	49.8	82.2
1934	842.0	189.2	72.4	38.3	23.6	12.5	10.2	5.4	83.0	43.9	82.2
1935	872.2	190.5	72.5	38.1	21.7	11.4	7.7	4.0	88.6	46.5	84.6
1936	907.4	191.3	82.8	43.3	21.1	11.0	7.1	3.7	80.3	42.0	85.3
1937	881.7	184.6	70.0	37.9	20.9	11.3	8.2	4.4	85.5	46.3	84.2
1938	879.0	190.3	68.3	35.9	21.4	11.2	1.9	1.0	98.7	51.9	87.8
1939	990.4	195.7	74.2	37.9	23.4	12.0	11.4	5.8	88.6	45.3	83.2
1940	1,115.8	204.3	80.6	39.4	26.5	13.0	9.3	4.6	87.9	43.0	82.4
1941	1,378.7	221.9	106.6	48.0	30.7	13.8	9.3	4.2	75.3	33.9	81.9
1942	1,471.2	218.1	119.1	54.6	31.7	14.5	8.6	3.9	58.7	26.9	81.5
1943	1,310.8	228.1	134.5	60.0	26.7	11.7	11.1	4.9	55.8	24.5	84.5

1944	1,401.6	223.0	107.3	48.1	24.1	10.8	9.5	4.3	82.1	36.8	84.9
1945	1,434.8	231.1	128.3	55.5	22.9	9.9	9.6	4.2	70.3	30.4	85.9
1946	1,909.0	307.9	174.5	56.7	30.4	9.9	13.8	4.5	89.2	29.0	85.7
1947	2,545.6	322.8	186.3	57.7	46.1	14.3	15.0	4.6	75.5	23.4	81.1
1948	2,837.3	358.7	180.9	50.4	70.2	19.6	15.2	4.2	92.3	25.7	76.1
1949	2,904.6	368.0	182.9	49.7	89.0	24.2	14.6	4.0	81.4	22.1	71.8
1950	3,179.8	416.2	210.9	50.7	110.6	26.6	16.4	3.9	78.3	18.8	69.5
1951	3,392.5	419.8	197.1	47.0	103.0	26.3	15.9	3.8	96.5	23.0	70.0
1952	3,755.7	447.2	198.3	44.3	109.1	24.4	16.5	3.7	123.3	27.6	71.9
1953	3,989.1	470.4	213.3	45.3	111.0	23.6	17.7	3.8	128.4	27.3	72.6
1954	4,140.0	491.7	209.9	42.7	116.4	23.7	18.3	3.7	147.1	29.9	72.6
1955	4,305.0	509.9	221.9	43.5	124.9	24.5	18.5	3.6	144.6	28.4	71.9
1956	4,481.9	545.3	238.1	43.7	137.2	25.2	20.2	3.7	149.8	27.5	71.2
1957	4,769.2	596.2	252.7	42.4	151.3	25.4	21.1	3.5	171.1	28.7	71.1

Source. *Moody's* and *Poor's* before 1928; *Moody's* to date.
a Deducting goodwill.
b In per cent of total assets (percentages do not add because of rounding).
c Estimated from Company records, GX 314.
d "Cash and marketable securities" identical during the two following years with "Cash and government securities," as the account is subsequently called.

APPENDIX TABLE 9. Sources and Uses of Funds, A & P Company, 1919–1956
(thousands of dollars)

1920–1925

Sources of funds		Uses of funds	
[Total earnings after taxes, 49,900]		Increase in:	
Retained earnings [a]	41,242	Fixed assets	9,477
Increased reserves	1,759	Inventories	21,833
Increased short-term credit	1,267	Cash	8,665
Employees' stock subscrip-		Misc. assets [b]	1,435
tions and increased		Total assets increase	41,410
subsidiaries' stock	1,092	Funded debt paid off	3,950
Total sources	45,360	Total uses	45,360

1925–1931

Sources of funds		Uses of funds	
[Total earnings after taxes, 143,372]		Increase in:	
Retained earnings	79,180	Equipment and fixtures	19,560
Stock issues [c]	9,922	Cash and govt. bonds	76,585
Increase in:		Inventories	7,396
Accounts and notes payable	14,534	Accounts receivable	3,212
Reserves	3,019	Deferred charges, etc.	1,062
Decrease in:			
Land and buildings	1,160		
Total sources	107,815	Total uses	107,815

1931–1937

Sources of funds		Uses of funds	
[Total earnings after taxes, 102,717]		Increase in:	
Retained earnings	7,006	Inventories [d]	16,952
Liquidation of:		Accounts receivable	625
Land and buildings	706	Misc. assets	642
Equipment and fixtures	10,819	Redemption of stock	84
Decrease in cash and		Decrease in:	
govt. bonds	5,087	Notes and accounts payable	2,932
		Reserves	2,383
Total sources	23,618	Total uses	23,618

Appendix Table 9 (*continued*)

1937–1946

Sources of funds		Uses of funds	
[Total earnings after taxes, 149,297]		Increase in:	
Retained earnings	29,303	Equipment and fixtures	9,583
Liquidation of land		Cash and govt. bonds	3,733
and buildings	133	Inventories	104,502
Increase in:		Accounts receivable	628
Short-term loans	31,927	Misc. assets	4,938
Accounts payable	42,633	Redemption of stock	110
Reserves	19,498		
Total sources	123,494	Total uses	123,494

1946–1950 [e]

Sources of funds		Uses of funds	
[Total earnings after taxes, 144,753]		Increase in:	
Retained earnings	77,424	Accounts receivable	1,353
Increase in:		Inventories	36,369
Accounts payable	33,579	Land and buildings	572
Federal tax reserve	7,527	Equipment and fixtures	79,686
Insurance reserve	1,084	Deferred charges	2,418
Other reserves	738	Decrease in:	
Decrease in:		Short-term loans	12,000
Cash	10,844		
Govt. securities	10		
Other securities	1,192		
Total sources	132,398	Total uses	132,398

1950–1956 [f]

Sources of funds		Uses of funds	
[Total earnings after taxes, 196,274]		Increase in:	
Retained earnings	98,289	Accounts receivable	736
Increase in:		Inventories	27,184
Accounts payable	37,617	Equipment and fixtures	27,689
Federal tax reserve	11,324	Deferred charges	3,162
Insurance reserve and		Cash	71,422
Other reserves	1,791	Decrease in:	
Decrease in:		Short-term loans	20,000
Govt. securities	12		
Other securities	9		
Land and buildings	1,151		
Total sources	150,193	Total uses	150,193

Appendix Table 9 (continued)

Sources. *Poor's* for 1923, 1925, 1926–1929; *Moody's* for 1929 and later years.

(The financial manuals do not give the A & P income statement for 1922; we have substituted from the company's own records in its annual statistical binders. The two sources are consistent for years where both are available.)

ᵃ Retained earnings are equal to (a) total earnings less dividends paid during the period covered by the statement; which should in turn be equal to (b) the change in the surplus account, after adjustment for write-ups and write-downs. In this case, the discrepancy is insignificant, and we have used (b) in order to maintain consistency with the balance sheet.

ᵇ Miscellaneous assets (the sum of receivables, securities, etc.) were actually $263 thousand less in 1925, but since goodwill of $1,697 thousand had been written off, there was actually an increase of $1,435 thousand. The goodwill item was also added back to "retained earnings."

ᶜ The 1926 data pertain to the reorganized A & P Tea Company of America, the Maryland corporation which took over the New York corporation. More than three fourths of the New York company's surplus was transferred into preferred and common stock of the new company, but since there was no actual absorption of funds, this portion of the increase in stock is not shown as a source of funds.

Although A & P made no public sales of securities during this time, it did permit employees to subscribe for shares. The entire increase in outstanding stock is here attributed to such sales, for the following reasons.

The following tabulation is self-explanatory (all items in thousands of dollars):

Year	1925	1926	1927	1928	1929	1930	1931
Increase in capital stock outstanding	..	2,176	3,061	658	3,553	578	o
Employees subscriptions for stock	1,658	2,592	o	2,993	o	o	o
Due from employees on account of stock subscriptions	552	2,193	o	865	o	o	o

(The total increase is somewhat greater than the entry in the main table, since the latter is net of retired subsidiaries' stock.)

It seems likely that when an employee signed a stock subscription, the total amount was immediately entered as a company liability; and the portion paid in would increase cash, and the unpaid balance would be a debt owed the company, hence an asset. Subsequently, as shares of stock were fully paid for, they would be transferred from the "subscription" to the "capital stock" account.

We should then expect that there would be a rough positive relationship between (a) stock increases, (b) subscription accounts for the preceding year, and (c) "due from employees" for the preceding year, and that (a) > (b) > (c). The table bears this out. Hence our procedure seems plausible, although it has certainly not been proved correct.

ᵈ This was a gradual trend, rather than a part of the 1937 inventory boom. In fact, end-of-1937 inventories were lower than a year previously.

ᵉ Period *from* Feb. 28, 1947, *to* Feb. 28, 1951 (*Moody's*).

ᶠ Period *from* Feb. 28, 1951, *to* Feb. 28, 1957 (*Moody's*).

APPENDIX TABLE 10. Computation of Superfluous Cash, A & P, 1921–1957
(dollars in millions)

Year	Payments [a] (1)	Average cash & govt. securities (2)	Ratio of column (2) to column (1) (per cent) (3)	Transaction cash: $r \times$ column (1) (4)	Superfluous cash: column (2) — column (4) (5)
1921	198.8	10.5	5.281	6.6	3.9
1922	250.8	10.35	4.127	8.34	2.01
1923	301.4	9.15	3.036	10.02	—.87
1924	349.5	11.2	3.204	11.62	—.42
1925	436.8	14.1	3.228	14.52	—.42
1926	566.3	19.55	3.452	18.82	.73
1927	753.7	27.25	3.615	25.05	2.20
1928	972.0	31.5	3.240	32.31	.81
1929	1,044.8	36.35	3.479	34.73	1.62
1930	1,033.2	57.1	5.526	34.34	22.76
1931	991.1	82.0	8.273	32.94	49.06
1932	855.0	99.85	11.678	28.42	71.43
1933	822.2	97.8	11.895	27.32	70.48
1934	855.5	89.75	10.491	28.44	61.31
1935	866.6	85.8	9.901	28.80	57.00
1936	915.7	84.45	9.222	30.43	54.02
1937	876.5	82.9	9.458	29.13	53.77
1938	865.8	92.1	10.638	28.78	63.32
1939	1,000.5	93.15	9.310	33.26	59.89
1940	1,116.5	88.25	7.904	37.11	51.14
1941	1,390.7	81.6	5.868	46.23	35.37
1942	1,487.8	67.0	4.503	49.45	17.55
1943	1,313.7	57.25	4.358	43.67	13.58
1944	1,375.3	68.95	5.013	45.71	23.24
1945	1,446.6	76.2	5.267	48.08	28.12
1946	1,890.1	79.75	4.219	62.83	16.92
1947	2,559.3	82.35	3.218	85.07	—2.72
1948	2,820.5	83.90	2.975	93.75	—9.85
1949	2,915.5	86.85	2.979	96.91	—10.06
1950	3,182.9	79.89	2.510	105.79	—25.90
1951	3,374.4	87.40	2.590	109.33	—21.93
1952	3,728.9	109.88	2.947	120.82	—10.94
1953	3,984.0	125.86	3.159	129.08	3.22
1954	4,121.3	137.78	3.343	133.53	—4.25
1955	4,307.6	145.85	3.386	139.57	—6.28
1956	4,476.7	147.16	3.287	145.05	—2.11
1957	4,747.3	160.73	3.386	153.81	—6.92

Source. Appendix Table 8.
Method. Sales are conceived as an inflow of cash, which may be spent on operating expenses, purchase of new assets, taxes, or dividends. Whatever is

Appendix Table 10 (*continued*)

left — the net inflow of cash — indicates the portion of receipts not used for payments. Obviously, then, total sales less the net inflow of cash equals total payments.

The ratio of cash to payments will, for any given class of business, fluctuate around some "norm." For lack of anything better, the norm, r, is defined here as the average ratio for 1920–1928, a period of rapid company growth; r is equal to 0.00324. If r be multiplied by the total payments in any given year, the product is an approximation to the amount of cash needed to carry on that volume of payments. The balance is cash not so needed. Of course, the table gives no hint as to *why* cash accumulates or dwindles.

It seems clear that during the post World War II period, the normal ratio r was moderately lower than it had been twenty years before, probably around 3.0 per cent. During 1948–1952 a moderate cash shortage was covered by short-term borrowing.

[a] Equals sales *less* cash increment or *plus* decrement.

APPENDIX TABLE 11. A & P Supermarket Expense Rates, by Division and Size of Store, September–November 1939

Sales class	No. of stores	Per cent of all stores	Average weekly sales (dollars)	Clerks' salary	Gen'l. branch	Adver-tising	Handlg. & de-livery	Rent &[a] write-offs	Mgrs' salary	Super-vision & adm.	Total expense
Less than $4,000											
New England	5	4.3	3,687	4.29	2.61	1.14	1.00	3.21	2.62	2.77	16.52
Eastern	:	:	:	:	:	:	:	:	:	:	:
Atlantic	1	.8	3,326	3.49	2.77	1.33	1.14	3.20	3.30	1.47	16.67
Southern	5	8.1	3,647	4.19	2.76	0.70	1.08	2.37	2.46	1.41	14.97
Central	5	2.6	3,773	3.53	2.27	1.10	0.93	2.63	2.66	1.59	14.71
Middle Western	1	.7	3,850	4.22	2.06	0.93	0.70	3.21	2.48	1.67	15.27
Central Western	3	2.3	3,161	3.69	2.53	1.92	0.82	3.97	2.93	1.61	17.47
Total	20	2.2	3,610	3.94	2.53	1.14	0.97	2.97	2.66	1.56	15.77
$4,000–4,999											
New England	17	14.8	4,549	3.76	2.20	1.19	1.01	2.33	2.08	1.46	14.03
Eastern	:	:	:	:	:	:	:	:	:	:	:
Atlantic	8	6.8	4,624	3.76	2.27	1.19	0.95	2.67	2.18	1.44	14.46
Southern	7	11.3	4,568	4.20	2.70	1.21	1.23	2.62	2.06	1.33	15.35
Central	15	7.9	4,559	3.47	2.04	0.96	0.97	2.98	2.16	1.38	13.50
Middle Western	4	2.7	4,509	4.35	2.18	0.86	0.76	2.88	2.52	1.31	14.86
Central Western	1	.8	4,027	3.62	2.07	1.66	0.75	2.78	2.68	1.40	14.96
Total	52	5.6	4,553	3.78	2.23	1.11	0.99	2.54	2.16	1.41	14.22
$5,000–7,499											
New England	57	49.6	6,325	3.54	2.04	1.08	1.06	1.82	1.56	1.29	12.39

Appendix Table 11 (continued)

Sales class	No. of stores	Per cent of all stores	Average weekly sales (dollars)	Per cent of sales							
				Clerks' salary	Gen'l. branch	Adver-tising	Handlg. & delivery	Rent & write-offs [a]	Mgrs' salary	Super-vision & adm.	Total expense
Eastern	22	14.0	6,887	4.30	2.17	0.58	0.74	1.47	1.53	1.09	11.88
Atlantic	52	44.1	6,220	3.53	1.89	0.95	1.16	1.72	1.60	1.31	12.16
Southern	31	50.0	6,279	3.70	2.19	0.74	1.06	1.72	1.52	1.20	12.13
Central	78	41.0	6,209	3.38	1.86	0.78	1.03	1.85	1.65	1.21	11.76
Middle Western	80	54.1	6,264	3.53	1.83	0.77	1.01	1.70	1.73	1.19	11.76
Central Western	31	23.3	6,498	3.23	1.96	0.78	1.06	1.50	1.55	1.27	11.36
Total	351	38.0	6,316	3.54	1.95	0.84	1.03	1.73	1.62	1.24	11.95
$7,500–9,999											
New England	32	27.8	8,646	3.33	1.77	1.13	1.29	1.39	1.20	1.12	11.23
Eastern	63	40.1	8,791	4.17	1.94	0.55	0.86	1.20	1.29	1.02	11.03
Atlantic	44	37.3	8,423	3.88	1.92	0.91	1.17	1.53	1.25	1.14	11.80
Southern	11	17.7	8,769	3.78	2.20	0.94	1.25	1.35	1.16	1.11	11.79
Central	52	27.4	8,655	3.28	1.76	0.64	1.17	1.55	1.27	1.03	10.70
Middle Western	41	27.7	8,614	3.49	1.71	0.73	1.16	1.34	1.31	1.05	10.79
Central Western	41	30.8	8,718	3.29	1.95	0.67	1.09	1.43	1.24	1.11	10.78
Total	284	30.8	8,656	3.64	1.87	0.74	1.11	1.39	1.26	1.07	11.08
$10,000–14,999											
New England	4	3.5	11,764	3.26	1.71	0.99	0.95	1.14	0.97	0.86	9.88
Eastern	61	38.9	11,460	4.25	1.87	0.61	0.94	1.11	1.02	1.02	10.82
Atlantic	11	9.3	12,042	4.00	1.73	0.90	1.09	1.58	1.00	1.00	11.30

449

Southern	6	9.7	11,811	3.67	2.00	0.67	1.35	1.16	0.82	0.99	10.66
Central	29	15.3	11,524	3.32	1.66	0.65	1.10	1.45	0.99	0.94	10.11
Middle Western	20	13.5	11,241	3.58	1.65	0.70	1.05	1.18	1.08	0.99	10.23
Central Western	45	33.8	11,933	3.30	1.83	0.61	0.92	1.16	1.02	1.03	9.88
Total	176	19.1	11,622	3.72	1.79	0.66	0.99	1.21	1.02	1.00	10.39
Over $15,000											
New England											
Eastern	11	7.0	16,384	4.36	1.83	0.58	1.11	0.92	0.78	0.96	10.54
Atlantic	2	1.7	17,503	4.37	2.17	0.78	0.79	1.89	0.69	0.99	11.68
Southern	2	3.2	18,094	3.44	1.71	0.52	1.11	0.94	0.57	0.98	9.28
Central	11	5.8	18,516	3.12	1.46	0.64	1.15	1.11	0.66	0.78	8.92
Middle Western	2	1.3	21,191	3.66	1.89	0.65	0.90	0.97	0.63	0.96	9.66
Central Western	12	9.0	17,692	3.36	1.82	0.58	0.99	0.95	0.79	0.91	9.40
Total	40	4.3	17,744	3.62	1.74	0.70	1.08	1.07	0.72	0.91	9.84

Source. *Annual Binder*, vol. 15 (1939), DX 500.
[a] Rent & write-offs are equal to the sum of rent, deferred opening expenses, and depreciation of equipment.

APPENDIX TABLE 12. A & P Stores Losing Money, 1919–1942

Year	All stores (thousands)	Stores losing money (thousands) Total	Open three years or more: Total	Losing money for at least 2 yrs.	3 yrs.	4 yrs.	Closed	Losing stores open 3 yrs or more as per cent of all losing stores	Losing stores closed as per cent of all losing stores	Total losses (thousands of dollars)	Total losses as per cent of annual profit (before taxes)
1919	4.2										27.64
1920	4.6										21.91
1921	5.2										15.67
1922	7.3										11.19
1923	9.3										
1924	11.4										
1925	14.0	4.8	1.1					23		3,815	7.22
1926	14.8	4.3	1.4					32		3,549	7.79
1927	15.6	3.6	1.1					31		3,337	7.93
1928	15.1	2.3	0.8					35		3,078	11.80
1929	15.4	2.1	0.8	0.3	0.2	0.1	0.44	38	21	2,129	12.49
1930	15.7	2.1	1.1	0.5	0.2	0.1	0.36	52	17	2,725	19.49
1931	15.6	2.5	1.6	0.6	0.3	0.2	0.40	64	16	2,697	18.57
1932	15.4	3.3	2.6	1.0	0.3	0.2	0.43	79	13	3,127	14.35
1933	15.1	3.1	2.6	1.4	0.5	0.3	0.39	84	13	2,985	
1934	15.0	3.9	3.4	1.5	0.7	0.4	0.25	87	7	3,761	
1935	14.9	3.7	3.2	2.1	1.0	0.5	0.25	86	7	3,565	
1936	14.7	3.5	3.1	2.0	1.1	0.6	0.33	89	10	2,928	

1937	13.3	4.4	4.0	1.7	1.1	0.7	1.46	91	33	4,040	36.73
1938	10.8	2.4					2.70		110ᵃ	2,156	11.11
1939	9.1	1.6					1.79		110ᵃ	1,574	6.84
1940	7.1	0.9					1.71		190ᵃ	1,314	5.17
1941	6.2	0.6					0.96		160ᵃ	933	3.26
1942	5.9	0.8					0.24		30	1,328	5.68
1943	5.9	1.1					0.08		8	1,562	6.43

Sources. *Annual Binders*, 1925–1941, DX's 486–500, and GX 314; *Store Profit Summaries*, 1942 and 1943, DX's 712, 713.

Detail does not always add to total, because of rounding.

ᵃ Losing stores closed during entire fiscal year exceeded number of losing stores during fourth quarter.

APPENDIX TABLE 13. A & P Rent Paid on Stores Closed During Quarters, 1935–1941

Year	Quarter	Rent Paid (thousands of dollars)
1935	4	14.4
1936	1	17.7
	2	12.2
	3	10.9
	4	13.3
1937	1	22.1
	2	29.0
	3	24.3
	4	45.8
1938	1	52.4
	2	85.6
	3	72.8
	4	58.6
1939	1	48.0
	2	44.1
	3	50.4
	4	49.5
1940	1	38.3
	2	32.6
	3	33.2
	4	47.3
1941	1	14.1
	2	12.2
	3	22.7
	4	21.4

Source. *Annual Binder* (1941), GX 314.

APPENDIX TABLE 14. A & P Conversion to Supermarkets, 1937–1943

	Stores			Net sales (millions of dollars)			(In per cent of net sales)			
							Expense rate		Net profit rate	
	Super-markets	All stores	(1) as per cent of (2)	Super-markets	All stores	(4) as per cent of (5)	Super-markets	All stores	Super-markets	All stores
	(1)	(2)	(3)	(4)	(5)	(6)	(7)	(8)	(9)	(10)
1937	280	13,058	2.14	53.1	864.4	6.14	n.a.	17.63	n.a.	1.04
1938	771	10,671	7.23	220.4	868.4	25.37	11.86	16.25	2.76	2.03
1939	1,119	9,021	12.40	401.4	975.8	41.03	11.58	14.66	2.67	2.16
1940	1,396	7,073	19.74	593.5	1,098.7	54.02	11.46	13.48	2.31	2.13
1941	1,552	6,042	25.69	864.4	1,348.1	64.12	10.51	11.78	1.96	1.93
1942	1,633	5,821	28.06	934.0	1,435.2	65.08	10.51	11.43	1.50	1.56
1943	1,646	5,751	28.62	760.8	1,258.6	60.45	11.84	12.43	1.81	1.77

	Profits (millions of dollars)			Regular stores			
						(In per cent of sales)	
	Super-markets	All stores	(11) as per cent of (12)	Sales (millions of dollars)	Stores	Expense rate	Net profit rate
	(11)	(12)	(13)				
1937	n.a.	9.0	n.a.	811.3	12,778	n.a.	n.a.
1938	6.1	17.6	34.66	648.0	9,900	17.74	1.78
1939	10.7	21.1	50.71	574.4	7,902	16.81	1.80
1940	13.7	23.4	58.55	505.2	5,677	15.85	1.92
1941	16.9	26.0	65.00	483.7	4,490	14.05	1.88
1942	14.0	22.4	62.50	501.2	4,188	13.18	1.67
1943	13.8	22.3	61.88	497.8	4,105	13.33	1.71

Source. *Annual Binders*, 1937–1943.

APPENDIX TABLE 15. A & P Per Cent of Available Business, By Divisions and Units, 1925, 1932–1941

Territory	1925	1932	1933	1934	1935	1936	1937	1938	1939	1940	1941[b]
Albany	9.70	12.92	11.15	11.76	11.51	10.84	9.75	10.36	11.00	11.70	12.55
Boston	11.99	11.94	10.71	9.41	9.11	8.72	7.85	7.60	7.13	7.15	8.04
New Haven	10.01	14.76	13.04	12.12	11.24	10.19	9.07	9.12	8.40	8.17	
Portland	9.30	13.73	12.26	11.86	12.51	11.93	10.92	12.20	12.91	12.93	12.56
Providence	11.37	13.80	12.92	11.91	11.54	10.30	9.10	9.28	8.77	8.76	11.36
Springfield	14.01	11.80	10.67	10.63	11.14	10.54	9.24	9.08	8.77	8.86	8.13
Montreal		3.02	2.66	2.37	2.64	2.71	2.17	2.13			
Toronto		6.02	5.08	4.15	3.60	3.23	2.95	3.15			
NEW ENGLAND DIVISION	11.13[a]	10.47	9.29	8.46	8.43	7.99	7.09	7.13	8.40[a]	9.00[a]	9.57[a]
Westchester	8.65	19.31	17.42	17.17	17.63	16.18	15.29	15.93			
Bronx		8.26	8.03	8.06	7.39	6.77	6.20	6.82	9.94	10.00	10.66
Newark	14.90	13.84	12.00	12.10	11.04	11.90	10.90	12.15	12.26	12.85	14.04
Paterson	17.14	16.32	14.33	13.98	12.82	13.14	12.14	13.35	12.96	14.12	13.24
Brooklyn	12.33	8.17	7.27	6.79	6.20	6.51	5.56	6.41	7.93	9.26	10.67
Garden City		19.05	16.26	14.46	13.15	13.29	12.43	14.16	15.56	18.27	19.85
EASTERN DIVISION	11.91	11.66	10.46	10.24	9.43	9.40	8.57	9.52	10.66	11.52	12.46
Baltimore	10.60	10.93	10.29	10.61	10.28	10.54	9.97	9.95	8.54	8.40	8.72
Philadelphia	9.83	10.29	9.49	9.97	9.39	9.36	8.16	7.85	7.79	7.21	7.84
Richmond	6.78	8.75	8.31	8.82	8.25	8.25	7.55	7.64	8.34	8.88	7.54
Scranton	9.77	15.78	15.28	17.91	18.41	17.19	16.00	16.21	16.55	16.74	17.10
Washington	8.93	14.78	14.65	12.38	12.40	12.38	11.03	9.89			
ATLANTIC DIVISION							9.91	9.69	9.39	9.20	9.27
Jacksonville	14.94	10.79	10.51	11.56	10.68	10.33	10.21	11.11[c]	11.02	11.63	10.46
New Orleans	1.46	3.01	3.09	3.81	4.06	4.32	4.37[c]	4.21[c]	3.92[c]	4.14[c]	4.44[c]
Houston		5.55	4.82	5.50	5.26	5.30					
Birmingham		5.15	5.32	7.55	8.14	7.60	7.37	8.30	10.81	11.88	11.88
Atlanta	3.59	7.51	7.44	8.78	8.83	8.76	8.43	9.35	9.68	9.95	8.17
Charlotte	4.13	8.02	8.49	10.02	9.43	9.43	8.78	9.30	10.22	11.00	11.02
Dallas	0.38	6.41	5.93	7.43	6.97	6.61	6.60	6.32	5.76	6.61	7.49
SOUTHERN DIVISION	5.89	9.11	8.72	9.74	9.53	9.26	7.35	7.75	7.89	8.45	8.24

	(1)	(2)	(3)	(4)	(5)	(6)	(7)	(8)	(9)	(10)	(11)
Pittsburgh	11.53	12.92	13.30	17.71	17.60	17.90	18.72	20.51	19.67	19.52	19.81
Columbus	4.00	6.94	6.32	8.57	8.94	8.55	8.29	9.17	10.27	10.02	10.97
Altoona		13.24	13.58	19.30	19.52	18.48	17.38	18.00	18.07	17.62	19.46
Youngstown	9.92	10.83	10.01	14.30	14.95	13.44	13.48	14.48	14.83	16.78	19.14
Cleveland	12.55	10.57	9.93	10.93	11.36	10.81	10.34	11.14	11.03	11.69	11.59
Buffalo	7.09	10.71	10.37	12.53	12.19	11.02	10.06	10.31	9.43	9.73	8.91
Syracuse		10.31	10.59	14.85	14.72	13.52	13.34	13.97	13.75	13.70	13.84
CENTRAL DIVISION	9.20	10.68	10.46	13.57	13.67	13.16	12.98	13.92	13.77	13.99	14.20
Chicago (Combined)	7.71	10.72	9.08	10.54	10.33	10.60	9.91	11.01	12.60	14.05	15.00
St. Louis	4.77	4.43	5.06	6.10	6.52	6.21	6.20	7.10	7.68	8.38	8.47
Milwaukee		7.82	6.89	6.96	6.78	6.78	6.86	8.38	8.89	10.33	11.60
Des Moines	0.57	4.39	4.24	4.08	3.86	3.80	3.37	3.90	4.19	4.37	4.71
Kansas City		4.70	3.24	4.33	4.31	5.13	5.36	5.04	5.13	5.53	5.21
Minneapolis		3.36	3.28								
Oklahoma		1.76									
MIDDLE WESTERN DIVISION	n.a.	6.84	6.17	7.06	6.98	6.96	6.71	7.56	8.37	9.22	9.73
Detroit	10.45	10.22	10.12	13.21	12.77	11.26	11.03	12.58	13.25	15.08	13.40
Toledo	8.56	9.03	9.51	13.00	12.43	10.99	9.81	10.91	11.23	12.32	14.44
Indianapolis	2.84	8.03	8.56	8.93	8.94	8.93	6.97	7.21	7.58	8.37	8.49
Cincinnati	5.67	5.45	5.20	5.56	5.73	6.03					
Louisville	4.20	8.62	8.20	8.94	9.84	9.87	9.61	10.30	9.19	9.79	9.30
Grand Rapids		13.17	14.05	16.07	16.33	15.42	14.48	15.42	15.74	17.08	18.28
CENTRAL WESTERN DIVISION	n.a.	9.00	9.09	10.76	10.78	10.21	9.72	10.57	10.75	11.87	11.80
Los Angeles		2.85	2.11	2.51	2.77	2.56	2.20	2.31	1.63	1.51	1.46
Seattle					1.22	1.58	1.68	2.12	2.38	3.46	4.17
TOTAL, A & P TERRITORY	7.44	9.22	8.60	9.35	9.17	8.93	8.37	8.90	9.46	9.96	10.15
TOTAL, UNITED STATES	6.62	n.a.	n.a.	8.46	8.28	8.00	7.47	7.95	8.20	8.63	8.83

Source. *Annual Binder*, respective years. Data not available for other years.

a Excluding Canada.
b Third quarter.
c Includes Houston.

APPENDIX TABLE 16. A & P Percent of Available Business by Size of City, 1939

Size of city (thousands)	Number of cities	A & P (per cent)
Over 1,000	7	8.5
750–1,000	4	8.0
500–750	3	12.9
300–500	10	8.8
200–300	13	11.8
100–200	43	11.0
75–100	22	13.7
50– 75	67	11.0
25– 50	157	12.8
10– 25	505	15.5
Less than 10, with supermarkets	n.a.	23.5
Less than 10, without supermarkets	n.a.	8.2
Total		10.4

Source. *Annual Binder,* 1940, pp. 11–21.

N.B. City includes only corporate limits, not rest of metropolitan area. The average ratio of the former to the latter in 1940 was about 2:3. See Warren S. Thompson, *The Growth of Metropolitan Districts in the United States: 1900–1940* (Washington, Bureau of Census, 1947), p. 6.

APPENDIX TABLE 17. A & P Gross Profit Rate (G) and Expense Rate (E) by Divisions and Units, 1931-1944
(as per cent of sales; parentheses indicate losses)

Year	Division G	E	Albany G	E	Boston G	E	Portland G	E	Providence G	E	New Haven G	E	Springfield G	E
							A. New England Division							
1931	21.29	17.90	20.98	16.57	21.35	18.10	21.90	16.11	21.90	17.27	21.56	18.25	21.33	18.33
1932	22.66	19.71	22.36	18.20	22.89	20.05	22.31	17.32	23.10	19.23	23.03	19.51	22.60	20.91
1933	23.12	21.01	22.81	19.39	23.12	21.27	23.01	18.58	23.52	20.28	23.46	21.29	(22.62)	22.87)
1934	21.37	20.86	20.89	19.15	(21.20)	21.70)	21.52	17.89	22.01	20.28	22.12	21.06	(21.77)	22.33)
1935	19.12	19.08	19.18	17.42	(18.87)	20.00)	19.20	16.04	19.90	19.16	(18.94)	19.22)	(19.20)	19.23)
1936	19.91	18.55	19.71	16.81	19.73	19.40	20.31	15.49	20.18	18.71	20.13	19.21	20.31	18.97
1937	19.37	19.24	19.88	18.20	(19.43)	20.17)	19.60	16.38	(19.06)	19.69)	(19.55)	19.49)	(19.22)	20.08)
1938	19.00	18.05	19.48	17.42	(19.48)	19.51)	19.38	15.71	18.44	17.65	(18.54)	18.74)	(18.57)	18.56)
1939	17.15	15.88	17.47	15.06	(17.41)	17.83)	17.72	14.49	16.80	15.68	17.90	16.24	17.14	16.21
1940	15.50	14.09	15.09	14.04	15.61	15.26	16.95	13.96	15.31	13.97	combined with		15.74	15.01
1941	13.39	11.71	13.61	12.06	13.60	12.30	14.52	12.32	13.30	11.33	Springfield		13.31	12.26

Appendix Table 17 (continued)

B. Eastern Division

Year	Division G	Division E	Brooklyn G	Brooklyn E	Garden City G	Garden City E	Newark G	Newark E
1931	21.39	16.75	20.88	17.16	21.33	16.69	21.36	16.89
1932	22.34	17.98	21.59	18.12	22.83	18.18	22.19	18.26
1933	22.49	19.20	22.02	19.60	22.33	19.43	22.50	19.51
1934	21.30	19.12	20.91	20.12	20.47	19.21	21.31	19.04
1935	20.72	18.71	20.46	19.75	19.95	19.04	20.68	18.53
1936	20.74	18.67	20.21	19.87	20.05	19.07	21.04	18.35
1937	20.38	19.28	(19.57	21.12)	(18.41	19.28)	20.71	18.82
1938	19.56	17.04	17.59	16.40	17.92	15.99	20.36	17.48
1939	17.63	15.18	15.71	13.59	15.73	13.33	18.62	16.12
1940	15.90	13.64	14.60	12.31	14.48	11.86	16.80	14.34
1941	13.48	11.75	12.75	11.00	12.91	10.65	14.16	12.28

B. Eastern Division (continued)

Year	Paterson G	Paterson E	Seattle G	Seattle E	Los Angeles G	Los Angeles E	Bronx G	Bronx E
1931	20.61	16.54	not available		(19.94	21.14)	22.11	16.50
1932	21.39	17.94	not available		(20.46	22.21)	23.08	17.63
1933	21.61	18.95	not available		(22.36	27.12)	23.13	18.78
1934	20.72	18.91	(20.47	23.05)	(20.77	24.08)	22.02	18.69
1935	20.07	18.51	(17.99	20.32)	(19.41	21.14)	21.39	18.24
1936	20.15	18.47	(17.30	17.63)	(19.35	20.83)	21.28	18.17
1937	20.03	19.15	(17.32	17.46)	(19.47	20.28)	21.16	18.74
1938	19.18	16.99	(15.94	15.99)	(18.38	20.15)	20.81	17.50
1939	17.45	15.16	15.54	14.52	(17.36	18.80)	19.06	16.35
1940	15.99	13.66	14.49	14.20	(17.41	17.73)	16.89	14.99
1941	13.49	11.84	12.95	11.98	15.85	14.92	13.85	12.51

B. Eastern Division (concluded)

Year	Westchester G	Westchester E
1931	21.80	16.25
1932	23.06	17.29
1933	23.44	18.28
1934	22.14	17.94
1935	21.62	17.61
1936	21.69	17.58
1937	21.29	18.31
1938	20.77	17.49
1939	combined	
1940	with	
1941	Bronx	

Appendix Table 17 (*continued*)

	C. Atlantic Division (part of Southern Division until 1938)					
	Division		Baltimore		Philadelphia	
Year	G	E	G	E	G	E
1938	18.70	17.75	19.66	17.60	(18.05	18.31)
1939	17.16	16.51	17.67	16.51	16.13	15.70
1940	15.56	14.23	16.23	14.02	(14.32	14.70)
1941	13.88	12.13	14.54	12.23	13.11	12.11

	C. Atlantic Division (*concluded*)					
	Richmond		Scranton		Washington	
Year	G	E	G	E	G	E
1938	19.48	17.96	19.25	16.69	(18.34	18.73)
1939	18.13	16.42	17.58	14.99	combined	
1940	16.87	15.38	15.78	13.29	with	
1941	14.58	12.91	13.93	11.67	Baltimore	

	D. Southern Division							
	Division		Dallas		Houston		New Orleans	
Year	G	E	G	E	G	E	G	E
1931	20.66	17.37	21.03	18.17	19.53	17.98	(20.68	20.95)
1932	22.05	18.69	22.08	19.80	20.53	19.26	22.09	21.79
1933	22.28	18.41	22.33	19.40	21.76	19.52	22.00	20.58
1934	21.07	18.14	21.22	18.82	20.01	18.09	21.61	19.33
1935	19.87	17.68	19.89	18.71	18.81	17.85	20.58	18.14
1936	19.85	17.95	20.30	19.52	19.67	19.19	19.86	18.00
1937	19.11	18.39	(18.72	20.60)	(18.05	18.99)	19.30	18.46
1938	19.13	16.88	(17.60	17.76)	20.36	17.98	20.67	16.72
1939	18.54	15.96	17.35	16.71	combined		19.08	16.42
1940	17.29	15.08	16.38	15.73	with		18.71	15.49
1941	15.18	13.34	14.61	13.27	New Orleans		16.70	13.73

Appendix Table 17 (*continued*)

D. Southern Division (*continued*)

Year	Birmingham G	Birmingham E	Atlanta G	Atlanta E	Jacksonville G	Jacksonville E	Charlotte G	Charlotte E
1931	20.67	17.69	20.86	17.14	21.27	16.98	19.78	17.47
1932	21.22	19.33	21.85	18.41	21.90	17.04	21.76	18.67
1933	21.80	19.71	22.22	18.16	22.78	17.13	21.65	18.21
1934	20.21	18.71	21.77	17.49	21.62	16.51	20.47	18.20
1935	19.44	17.71	19.85	16.73	21.63	19.56	19.96	17.90
1936	20.12	18.07	19.47	16.20	20.96	17.54	19.54	17.39
1937	19.96	18.08	18.98	16.83	20.41	17.68	18.95	17.66
1938	18.33	16.32	18.09	16.14	21.26	17.37	18.82	16.58
1939	17.37	14.88	17.58	15.47	20.80	16.37	17.77	15.49
1940	15.82	13.82	16.59	14.79	19.38	16.12	16.39	14.36
1941	13.81	12.08	14.34	13.34	16.55	14.40	14.82	12.94

D. Southern Division (*continued*)

Year	Richmond G	Richmond E	Washington G	Washington E	Baltimore G	Baltimore E	Philadelphia G	Philadelphia E
1931	20.57	17.62	20.82	17.22	20.85	16.20	21.13	18.38
1932	22.46	18.96	22.19	17.54	21.94	17.48	22.96	20.48
1933	22.89	19.06	22.02	18.20	22.32	17.66	22.58	20.06
1934	21.70	18.42	21.33	17.78	21.49	18.07	20.89	20.01
1935	21.51	18.14	19.86	17.42	20.46	18.00	19.27	18.16
1936	20.46	17.54	19.72	18.55	20.40	17.88	19.52	18.27
1937	19.26	18.02	(18.93	19.37)	19.49	18.10	(18.86	19.70)
1938	Atlantic		Atlantic		Atlantic		Atlantic	
1939	Division		Division		Division		Division	
1940								
1941								

D. Southern Division (*concluded*)

Year	Scranton G	Scranton E
1931	19.94	15.43
1932	21.20	16.61
1933	22.05	15.80
1934	20.70	15.95
1935	19.31	15.34
1936	19.31	15.77
1937	18.68	17.15
1938	Atlantic	
1939	Division	
1940		
1941		

Appendix Table 17 (*continued*)

	E. Central Division						
	Division		Pittsburgh		Altoona		Buffalo	
Year	G	E	G	E	G	E	G	E
1932	20.61	19.03	20.93	18.50	21.72	20.50	20.30	18.51
1933	21.11	18.12	20.49	16.99	22.10	18.45	20.71	18.03
1934	19.88	16.98	19.29	16.09	20.47	16.51	19.86	16.88
1935	18.55	15.47	17.44	14.74	19.43	15.61	18.39	15.56
1936	17.46	14.78	15.97	13.14	18.36	14.82	17.62	15.93
1937	17.25	15.31	15.69	13.73	18.83	15.90	17.95	17.13
1938	17.13	14.64	16.23	13.59	18.33	15.14	17.51	16.03
1939	15.81	13.37	15.31	12.70	16.81	13.77	15.89	13.98
1940	15.11	12.60	14.71	12.26	16.14	13.16	15.31	12.79
1941	13.38	11.14	13.41	11.13	13.86	11.80	13.44	11.17

	E. Central Division (*concluded*)						
	Cleveland		Columbus		Syracuse		Youngstown	
Year	G	E	G	E	G	E	G	E
1932	(20.29 | 20.58)	20.42	18.88	20.02	17.73	20.64	19.37
1933	21.67	20.13	21.65	18.91	20.83	16.94	21.80	18.79
1934	19.94	19.24	20.34	17.51	20.40	15.98	20.14	17.59
1935	19.32	17.17	18.69	15.31	19.33	14.89	19.51	15.62
1936	19.13	17.69	17.70	14.59	17.83	14.05	18.67	15.51
1937	19.07	17.74	17.27	15.00	17.43	14.39	17.89	15.94
1938	18.14	16.27	17.03	14.30	17.11	14.17	17.66	14.78
1939	16.35	14.38	15.99	13.53	15.88	13.35	15.48	13.01
1940	15.33	12.95	15.31	13.15	15.52	12.79	14.42	11.69
1941	13.31	11.00	13.31	11.35	13.43	11.26	12.88	10.39

	F. Central Western Division						
	Division		Detroit		Cincinnati		Indianapolis	
Year	G	E	G	E	G	E	G	E
1932	21.17	20.15	21.12	20.28	(20.88 | 21.00)	22.00	20.23
1933	21.91	20.63	22.61	21.45	(21.17 | 21.33)	21.68	19.95
1934	21.01	19.21	21.12	19.38	(20.33 | 21.25)	21.54	20.24
1935	19.40	17.27	19.28	17.59	19.23	18.83	20.29	18.37
1936	18.54	16.67	18.86	17.57	18.63	17.95	19.08	17.13
1937	18.07	16.95	18.74	17.84	(18.11 | 18.39)	18.42	17.63
1938	17.32	15.01	17.06	14.71	combined with Indianapolis		17.76	16.43
1939	15.82	13.03	15.28	11.98			16.14	14.23
1940	14.97	12.11	14.23	10.98			15.35	13.31
1941	13.57	11.02	13.05	10.13			13.86	12.03

Appendix Table 17 *(continued)*

F. Central Western Division *(concluded)*

Year	Grand Rapids G	Grand Rapids E	Louisville G	Louisville E	Toledo G	Toledo E
1932	21.09	18.70	20.68	19.20	(21.29	21.96)
1933	22.03	19.51	21.15	19.34	(21.54	21.57)
1934	21.24	17.51	20.34	18.34	21.11	19.36
1935	19.37	16.03	18.67	15.10	19.89	18.43
1936	18.38	15.34	17.06	14.67	19.46	17.75
1937	17.95	15.37	16.76	15.23	18.23	17.89
1938	17.38	13.91	17.30	14.68	17.14	15.26
1939	15.92	12.50	16.28	13.63	15.90	13.65
1940	15.25	11.60	15.59	13.24	15.10	12.28
1941	13.76	10.54	14.38	12.26	13.39	11.01

G. Middle Western Division

Year	Division G	Division E	Chicago G	Chicago E	St. Louis G	St. Louis E	Kansas City G	Kansas City E
1931	20.93	17.72	20.50	16.75	21.91	19.70	21.75	20.21
1932	22.22	19.56	22.15	18.19	22.23	21.79	(21.72	22.06)
1933	22.66	20.97	23.32	20.89	21.89	20.70	22.00	21.75
1934	20.40	18.20	20.74	17.87	19.79	17.90	20.39	18.74
1935	18.94	16.71	19.25	16.33	18.18	16.12	19.02	17.77
1936	18.36	16.10	18.89	16.67	18.06	15.54	17.81	16.01
1937	17.67	16.25	18.41	16.92	16.65	14.83	17.05	16.89
1938	17.41	14.87	17.82	15.21	16.85	13.80	17.18	16.05
1939	16.36	13.94	16.56	14.05	15.79	13.07	16.42	16.25
1940	15.35	13.20	15.59	12.99	14.90	12.68	(14.93	15.79)
1941	13.54	11.75	13.66	11.58	13.22	11.50	(13.27	13.74)
1942	12.63	11.38	12.65	11.09	12.33	11.06	(12.30	12.68)
1943	13.80	12.68	14.03	12.41	13.53	12.42	13.28	13.12
1944	14.24	12.73	14.30	12.50	14.10	12.48	14.29	13.11

Appendix Table 17 (*continued*)

G. Middle Western Division (*concluded*)

Year	Des Moines G	Des Moines E	Milwaukee G	Milwaukee E
1931	21.73	18.84	20.92	17.40
1932	22.71	21.49	22.33	19.98
1933	21.88	21.06	22.11	21.01
1934	20.28	18.46	19.98	19.11
1935	19.34	18.52	18.32	16.54
1936	18.02	15.77	17.69	15.32
1937	17.56	16.69	17.06	15.06
1938	17.32	15.50	17.02	14.04
1939	16.51	14.76	16.19	13.02
1940	15.55	14.68	15.05	12.30
1941	13.92	13.00	13.37	10.99
1942	(12.85	12.95)	12.80	11.00
1943	(13.62	14.51)	13.79	12.23
1944	(14.72	14.08)	14.29	11.97

Sources. Most recent divisional executive committee meetings.

APPENDIX TABLE 18. Test of Randomness of Unit Loss-Years,
A & P Divisions

Division	Unit Years [a]	Unit Loss-Years [b] O	E	O−E	(O−E)^2	(O−E)^2/E
New England	64	14	7.24	6.76	45.70	6.31
Eastern	82	17	9.28	7.72	59.60	6.42
Southern [c]	74	4	8.37	4.37	19.09	2.28
Atlantic [c]	52	4	5.89	1.89	3.57	0.60
Central	70	1	7.93	6.93	48.02	6.00
Central Western	56	6	6.35	0.35	0.12	0.02
Middle Western	70	7	7.93	0.93	0.86	0.10
Total	468	53	52.99	..		$\chi^2 = 21.79$

Source. Appendix Table 17.
Note. Unit loss-years are 11.32 per cent of unit years; degrees of freedom, 6;
P = 0.0017, estimated by linear interpolation between P = 0.010 and P = 0.001.
[a] One unit operating one year.
[b] One unit operating at a loss for one year. O = observed; E = expected. Detail of "estimated" does not add to total because of rounding.
[c] Atlantic units included as Atlantic for all years, even when included in the Southern Division in earlier years. See Appendix Table 17.

APPENDIX TABLE 19. Average Sales, Gross Profit Rate, and Expense Rate in Chain Groceries, By Size of Chain, 1939–1946

(size group by annual net sales, in millions of dollars)

Year	I. Under 1 million			II. 1–5 million			III. 5–10 million			IV. 10–25 million		
	Average sales	Expense rate	Gross profit	Average sales	Expense rate	Gross profit	Average sales	Expense rate	Gross profit	Average sales	Expense rate	Gross profit
1939	0.728	17.23	20.34	2.017	18.13	19.61	3.901	18.48	19.87	7.373	19.27	21.14
1940	.615	18.69	21.69	1.670	18.62	19.64	4.343	17.96	19.28	8.028	18.91	21.30
1941	.570	16.98	17.95	1.848	17.64	20.18	5.251	17.32	19.46	9.453	18.32	21.03
1942	.619	16.87	19.56	2.046	16.22	19.02	6.619	16.08	19.53	12.090	16.68	20.26
1943	.732	15.51	18.42	2.302	15.64	18.33	7.307	16.16	19.48	12.854	16.64	19.85
1944	.766	15.17	17.91	2.249	15.81	18.41	7.760	16.72	19.96	13.901	16.96	20.07
1945	.774	14.89	17.53	2.268	16.27	18.99	8.098	16.84	20.22	14.857	17.53	20.77
1946 [a]	.843	14.86	17.72	2.419	15.57	19.31	8.771	16.05	19.94	16.265	15.82	20.49

Year	V. 25-100 million			VI. Over 100 million (excluding A & P)			VII. A & P			VIII. Over 100 million (including A & P)		
	Average sales	Expense rate	Gross profit	Average sales	Expense rate	Gross profit	Average sales	Expense rate	Gross profit	Average sales	Expense rate	Gross profit
1939	25.748	21.90	23.69	243.2	18.33	19.89	975.8	14.66	16.84	426.356	16.23	18.14
1940	28.922	21.34	23.32	254.1	17.99	18.98	1098.7	13.48	15.61	465.292	15.33	16.99
1941	39.476	19.58	22.26	301.0	17.09	18.55	1348.1	11.78	13.71	564.298	13.87	15.61
1942	49.852	17.89	20.54	394.1	14.93	16.58	1435.2	11.43	12.99	654.401	13.01	14.61
1943	51.300	17.85	20.19	400.8	16.81	17.86	1258.6	12.43	14.20	615.252	14.26	15.99
1944	55.385	17.67	20.52	398.7[b]			1401.6[c]			649.455	14.23	16.25
1945	60.991	17.83	21.03	400.6[b]			1434.9[c]			659.167	14.67	16.81
1946[a]	72.259	16.78	21.03							762.450	14.23	17.02

Source. For all groups but VI and VII, OPA Economic Data Series No. 26, "Survey of Retail Chain Grocery Stores and Wholesale Grocers" (Washington, 1947), pp. 2–9; Group VI represents Group VIII *less* Group VII (A & P). In Appendix Table 20, it is proved that Group VIII includes A & P. For Group VII, see Appendix Table 6.

[a] First half of 1946.

[b] Gross sales.

[c] Gross sales.

APPENDIX TABLE 20. Supporting Data for Table 19 — Sales of Retail Grocery Chains, Annual Sales Over $100 Million, Excluding A & P, 1939–1945

(dollar amounts in millions)

Year	A & P [a] (1)	Safeway [b] (2)	Kroger [b] (3)	American stores [b] (4)	Columns 1+2+3+4 (5)	OPA "4 chains" (6)	First National [c] (7)	Discrepancy (col. 5 − col. 6) [d] (8)	Discrepancy corrected (9)	Discrepancy as per cent of col. (5) (10)
1939	975.8	385.9	243.4	114.8	1719.9	1705.4	124.2	+ 14.5	− 2.0	0.1
1940	1098.7	399.3	258.1	124.8	1880.9	1861.2	131.0	+ 19.7	−11.2	0.6
1941	1348.1	475.1	302.8	157.7	2283.7	2257.2	142.7	+ 26.5	−15.6	0.7
1942	1435.2	611.1	388.8	209.1	2644.2	2617.6	174.4	+ 26.6	n.a.	n.a.
1943	1258.6	588.8	422.4	212.1	2481.9	2461.0	187.8	+ 20.9	n.a.	n.a.
1944	1401.6	656.6	448.4	227.6	2734.2	2597.8	164.9	+136.4	n.a.	n.a.
1945	1434.9	664.8	457.3	233.5	2790.5	2636.7	170.2	+153.8	n.a.	n.a.

Sources. Columns 1–4, *Moody's*; column 6, Appendix Table 19.

[a] Fiscal year ending Feb. 28 for respective years. Figures for 1944 and 1945 are gross sales.

[b] Fiscal year ending Dec. 31 for respective years.

[c] Fiscal year ending Mar. 30 for respective years.

[d] Column (8) is overstated by the amount of the upward bias in the A & P series for net sales (column 1), because the A & P fiscal year includes two calendar months which are not included in the comparable fiscal years of the other companies in this sample, and because the A & P series increases over time.

Step 1. To correct for this bias, A & P net sales can be totaled by quarters to obtain a closer fit (data from Appendix Table 3, not available for years after 1941):

	1939	1940	1941
4th qtr. (Dec. Jan. Feb.)	229	260	311
1st qtr. (Mar. Apr. May)	238	267	312
2nd qtr. (June, July, Aug.)	232	259	322
3rd qtr. (Sept. Oct. Nov.)	252	266	340
Adjusted A & P sales	951	1052	1285
Col. (1) fiscal year A & P sales	975.8	1098.7	1348.1
Correction to col. (8)	−24.8	−46.7	−63.1

Step 2. An overcorrection for the A & P two month upward bias has been made in Step 1. The A & P sales totaled by quarters have a *one month* downward bias, owing to the inclusion in each year of the December of the previous year. To eliminate this downward bias, we assume that the downward revision of A & P sales for each year is linear over the three months involved in the adjustment. Hence the total downward revision divided by 3 represents a close approximation of the necessary correction for the overcompensated result in Step 1. Hence:

$$1939 \quad \frac{-24.8}{-3} = +8.3; \qquad 1940 \quad \frac{-46.7}{-3} = +15.8; \qquad 1941 \quad \frac{-63.1}{-3} = +21.0$$

Summarizing the corrections for column (8):

	(8)	Step 1	Step 2	Corrected
1939	+14.5	−24.8	+8.3	−2.0
1940	+19.7	−46.7	+15.8	−11.2
1941	+26.5	−63.1	+21.0	−15.6

Conclusion. The companies listed in cols. (1), (2), (3), and (4) must be those which comprised the sample taken in OPA Economic Data Series No. 26, "Survey of Retail Chain Grocery Stores and Wholesale Grocers" (Washington, 1947), p. 4. The greatest error resulting by comparing cols. (5) and (6) is 0.7 per cent for the years corrected for the bias in the A & P series. The data for First National, the next largest chain, are provided only as a check.

APPENDIX TABLE 21 (first half)

A & P Purchases from Subsidiaries and Outside Processors, 1919–1941

Year	Gross sales (millions of dollars)	Gross profit as per cent of column (1)	Total purchases: Col. (1) – [col. (1) × col. (2)]	Factory sales (millions of dollars)	Bakery sales, retail value (millions of dollars)	Bakery sales, wholesale value Col. (5) – [col. (5) × col. (2)]	Coffee sales (millions of pounds)	Wholesale coffee price in cents per pound [a]	Coffee sales, wholesale value (millions of dollars) [b]	Total Acco sales (millions of dollars)
	(1)	(2)	(3)	(4)	(5)	(6)	(7)	(8)	(9)	(10)
1919	194.6	16.00	163.5				36.4	24.8	12.5	
1920	235.3	16.19	197.2				38.5	19.0	10.2	
1921	202.4	19.55	162.8				38.3	10.4	5.5	
1922	246.9	20.12	197.2				48.8	14.3	9.7	
1923	302.9	21.01	239.3				53.6	14.8	11.0	
1924	352.1	21.67	275.8	15.2	9.2	7.2	56.2	21.3	16.6	
1925	440.0	21.50	345.4	18.8	15.2	11.9	60.9	24.5	20.7	
1926	574.1	20.15	458.4	21.9	21.9	17.5	80.9	22.3	25.1	
1927	761.4	18.67	618.6	28.9	29.6	24.1	114.9	18.7	29.9	21.7
1928	972.8	18.09	796.8	35.3	34.6	28.3	130.9	23.2	42.2	25.2
1929	1,053.7	18.36	860.2	35.0	36.5	29.8	145.6	22.1	44.7	43.8
1930	1,065.8	19.58	857.1	38.2	38.8	31.2	175.9	13.2	32.3	53.2
1931	1,008.3	20.79	798.7	42.0	37.8	29.9	198.8	08.7	24.0	46.2
1932	864.0	21.90	674.8	37.6	32.4	25.3	205.1	10.7	30.5	33.0
1933	819.6	22.25	637.2	39.6	34.4	26.7	195.3	09.3	25.2	34.4
1934	842.0	20.86	666.4	45.1	38.1	30.2	186.8	11.2	29.1	49.6
1935	877.2	19.50	706.1	47.8	41.0	33.0	208.8	08.9	25.8	50.1
1936	907.4	19.23	732.9	50.1	42.2	34.1	214.1	09.5	28.3	65.1
1937	881.7	18.67	717.1	46.4	41.8	34.0	209.0	11.1	33.2	59.0
1938	879.0	18.28	718.3	48.6	40.9	33.4	231.3	07.8	25.1	63.6 [b]
1939	990.4	16.84	823.6	56.2	43.3	36.0	254.4	07.5	27.2	68.3
1940	1,115.8	15.61	941.6	63.5	47.5	40.1	270.7	07.2	26.6	79.3
1941	1,378.7	13.71	1,189.7	88.7	55.1	47.5	270.5	11.4	37.7	103.5

Sources. Cols. (1), (2), (4), (5), (7): *Annual Binder*, respective years.
Col. (8): U.S. Dept. Labor, Bureau of Labor Statistics, Bulletins 493, 521, 543, 572 (see footnote [a]).
Col. (9): entries for 1939, 1940, 1941, are from GX's 3595, 3596, 3597; for prior years see footnotes [b] and [c].
Col. (10): Atlantic Commission Company, Comparative Income Profit & Loss Statement, from GX's 3595, 3596, 3597; and *Annual Binder* for earlier years.
Cols. (11), (12): DX 576A.
Cols. (13), (14): for years prior to 1932, see footnote [e].

APPENDIX TABLE 21 (concluded)

A & P Purchases from Subsidiaries and Outside Processors, 1919–1941

Total Acco sales (1,000 carlots)	Acco sales to trade (1,000 carlots)	Percentage of total Acco carlot sales to A & P	Percentage of total Acco carlot sales to trade c	Acco sales to A & P, col. (10) × col. (13) (millions of dollars)	Total purchases from subsidiaries, wholesale values (sum of cols. (4), (6), (9), (15)) (millions of dollars)	Total purchases from outside processors, col. (3) − col. (16) (millions of dollars)	Processed goods supplied by subsidiaries, sum of cols. (4), (6), (9) (millions of dollars)	Processed goods supplied by all sources col. (3) − col. (15)	Col. (18) as per cent of col. (19)	Year
(11)	(12)	(13)	(14)	(15)	(16)	(17)	(18)	(19)	(20)	
										1919
										1920
										1921
										1922
										1923
										1924
		69.0	31.0							1925
		69.0	31.0							1926
		69.0	31.0	15.0	97.9	520.7	82.9	603.6	13.7	1927
		69.9	30.1	17.6	123.4	673.4	105.8	779.2	13.6	1928
		70.8	29.2	31.0	140.5	719.7	109.5	829.2	13.2	1929
		71.7	28.3	38.1	139.8	717.3	101.7	819.0	12.4	1930
		72.6	27.4	33.5	129.4	669.3	95.9	765.2	12.5	1931
89.3	23.6	73.6	26.4	24.3	117.7	557.1	93.4	650.5	14.4	1932
85.1	24.6	71.1	28.9	24.5	116.0	521.2	91.5	612.7	14.9	1933
89.9	24.5	72.7	27.3	36.1	140.5	525.9	104.4	630.3	16.6	1934
90.8	25.4	72.0	28.0	36.1	142.7	563.4	106.6	670.0	15.9	1935
96.0	29.8	69.0	31.0	44.9	157.4	575.5	112.5	688.0	16.4	1936
92.4	27.8	69.9	30.1	41.2	154.8	562.3	113.6	675.0	16.8	1937
94.2	26.7	71.7	28.3	45.6	152.7	565.6	107.1	672.7	15.9	1938
104.2	28.9	72.3	27.7	49.4	168.8	654.8	119.4	774.2	14.2	1939
115.6	28.8	75.1	24.9	59.6	189.8	751.8	130.2	882.0	14.8	1940
129.4	30.2	76.8	23.2	79.5	253.4	936.3	173.9	1,110.2	15.7	1941

a "Wholesale coffee price per pound" represents the annual average price for Santos #4, at dockside New York. "The use of Santos 4's as a basis of calculation reflects the fact that such coffee is by far the major factor in the retail competitive situation at the present time." (Statement taken from the results of an industry-wide study of coffee costs in 1934 by the NRA, published in "Utilization of Farm Crops," Senate Committee on Agriculture and Forestry, Hearings before a Subcommittee; Washington, 1950; pt. 3, pp. 1310 ff.)

Appendix Table 21 *(continued)*

[b] For 1939–1941, coffee sales are from the company records. For years prior to 1939, column 9 equals column 7 times column 8 times a factor of 1.39 which represents the markup attributable to roasting and distributing operations between the dockside and the warehouse. This was computed by applying the ratio of total coffee sales (by the A & P subsidiaries to A & P warehouses) to the product of columns 7 and 8 for the years 1939 and 1940. The factor thus computed has been applied for years back through 1919.

Method:

Year	Column 7		Column 8		Coffee sales (dockside value)	Coffee sales (actual)
1939	254.4	×	.075	=	19.08	27.2
1940	270.7	×	.072	=	19.49	26.6
Total					38.57	53.8

Therefore factor $= \dfrac{53.8}{38.6} = 1.39$

Data for 1941 were not utilized in the above computation, for the following reasons: The Wholesale coffee price (Column 8) refers solely to New York dockside prices of green coffee. Dockside coffee prices rose sharply following the Inter-American Coffee Agreement in November, 1940. Hence, green coffee purchases in 1941 were not representative of years prior to 1939 when prices changed more gradually. In general, American Coffee Corporation purchases of green coffee in the Brazil market take place earlier than transactions at dockside New York. In a year of constant or gradually changing prices, the two markets are nearly equivalent, if allowance be made for transport costs. But in a period of rapidly changing prices, the dockside New York price does not accurately represent the cost of purchasing coffee in the Santos market. (For an excellent statement of the relationship between these two markets, see the testimony of Francis M. Kurtz, President of the American Coffee Corporation (A & P) in "Utilization of Farm Crops," Senate Committee on Agriculture and Forestry, Hearings before a Subcommittee; Washington, 1950; Pt. 3, pp. 1275–1309.)

An alternative method of estimating A & P coffee sales was attempted using the results of an industry-wide study of coffee costs in 1934 by the NRA. (See the Hearings, pp. 1309–1310.) However, this method resulted in wide margins of error when checked against actual data for the years 1939, 1940, and 1941.

[c] For the years 1925–1931 the percentage distribution of ACCO carlot sales was estimated from the following data: "The records indicate that of the total business done through the Atlantic Commission Company, the Tea Company purchased 69% and the Atlantic Commission Company sold 31% to outsiders." (Minutes of the Divisional Purchasing Directors' meeting in February 1928, GX 423, p. 9.) No specific time reference is made, and therefore this is considered an estimate for all of the period of Acco's existence, i.e., the years 1925, 1926, and 1927. The difference of 4.6 percentage points between 1927 and 1932 was allocated evenly to intervening years. According to the statement of Nichols at Tr. 14,981, Acco trade sales were 25 per cent for the period from 1932 to 1942. In point of fact, Acco trade sales for this period averaged 26.9 per cent.

APPENDIX TABLE 22. A & P SOURCES OF PROFITS, 1927–1941

(millions of dollars)

Year	Advertising allowances, etc.	Manufacturing			American coffee	Acco	Buying offices	All other	Total
		Factories	Bakeries	Total					
1927	4.70	1.55	2.58	4.14	1.31	0.46	0.73	9.93	21.28
1928	6.39	2.25	3.54	5.79	1.29	0.40	1.10	12.57	27.53
1929	7.81	1.38	3.85	5.23	1.40	0.90	1.61	12.54	29.50
1930	7.51	1.71	5.46	7.18	1.25	0.80	1.78	16.43	34.95
1931	8.42	2.78	4.62	7.40	0.64	0.96	2.10	14.50	34.01
1932	8.57	1.53	3.89	5.41	0.37	0.88	2.10	9.21	26.54
1933	7.79	2.63	2.94	5.57	0.14	0.94	2.20	7.22	23.86
1934	6.59	3.00	3.18	6.17	−0.30	0.92	1.33	4.28	19.26
1935	7.90	3.44	3.16	6.60	0.67	0.92	1.72	1.42	19.22
1936	4.75	3.83	2.78	6.62	0.54	1.36	0.88	6.23	20.38
1937	3.12	3.20	2.96	6.16	−0.03	0.74	..	0.96	10.95
1938	2.88	4.12	5.19	9.31	1.22	0.99	..	5.01	19.41
(figures below this line not always comparable with those above)									
1937	3.12	3.03	..	..	0.93	0.74	..	1.23	9.06
1938	2.88	3.96	0.85	..	2.58	0.99	..	6.24	17.51
1939	4.72	4.52	1.10	..	3.38	1.05	..	6.45	21.31
1940	5.26	4.75	1.00	..	4.07	1.19	..	7.14	23.41
1941	6.40	5.63	0.94	..	2.94	1.77	..	8.34	26.03

Sources. From tables in the *Annual Binders* DX's 490, 492, 494, 498, 499; and GX 314.

Note. Detail does not always add to totals, because of rounding.

APPENDIX II

Two Calculations of Implied Elasticity of Demand

The A & P meeting of divisional presidents of August 31, 1937,[1] decided on the following program. Every store would mark down shelf goods to a total of not more than $100, and feature them as aggressively as possible without special advertising. Furthermore, this would be the first step in a more general campaign to reduce the gross profit rate by one per cent during the third quarter of 1937. It was expected that sales per store would increase by $100 to $150.

It is possible to calculate two kinds of elasticities which the meeting contemplated: of *price* and of *margins*; the relation of one to the other, and their respective time periods, seem of some interest.

Average sales per store in the second quarter of 1937 were almost precisely $1100.[2] Let us call "price" one dollar; then the quantity sold is 1100 times the amount that could be bought at the unit price, or 1100 units. With the $100 reduction in effect, it would be possible to buy the same quantity for only $1000. "Price" would therefore have been reduced by 9.1 cents. How would quantity be affected? Consider for a moment the more conservative estimate. If weekly sales at the new price rose to $1200, the quantity, valued at the old prices, would be 1200×1.1 or 1320 units. The increase is 220 units. If sales rose to $1250, the new quantity would be $1250 \times 1.1 = 1375$, and the increase would be 275.

Accordingly, we calculate the elasticity of demand with respect to price: [3]

$$-e = \frac{dq}{q_0 + q_1} \div \frac{dp}{p_0 + p_1} = \frac{220}{1100 + 1320} \div \frac{0.091}{1 + 0.909} = 1.91,$$

on the more conservative assumption, and

$$-e = \frac{dq}{q_0 + q_1} \div \frac{dp}{p_0 + p_1} = \frac{275}{1100 + 1375} \div \frac{0.091}{1 + 0.909} = 2.33,$$

on the more optimistic assumption.

The price of grocery service is the gross margin, and elasticity of demand with respect to it can be measured in the same way. The gross margin, during the second quarter of 1937, was 0.1844, and the proposed reduction was to 0.1744. Then $p_0 = 0.1844$, $p_1 = 0.1744$, $dp = -.01$; $q_0 = 1100$, and q_1 is equal to $1200 \times \dfrac{0.1844}{0.1744}$, which equals 1269, or, alternatively, to $1250 \times \dfrac{0.1844}{0.1744}$, which equals 1322; and dq equals either 169 or 222.

[1] GX 189.

[2] GX 189, table (called "chart") 20.

[3] The method is from R. G. D. Allen, "The Concept of Arc Elasticity of Demand," *Review of Economic Studies*, 1:228 (1934), formula 5.

Therefore:

$$-e = \frac{169}{1100 + 1269} \div \frac{0.01}{0.1844 + 0.1744} = 2.56,$$

on the more conservative assumption, and

$$-e = \frac{222}{1100 + 1322} \div \frac{0.01}{0.1844 + 0.1744} = 3.29,$$

on the more optimistic assumption.

On the face of it, these two pairs of estimates are inconsistent. They almost seem like a simple arithmetical error. For if gross margin were reduced from 0.1844 to 0.1744, by one percentage point, an assortment of goods formerly selling at $1100 could be reduced by only one per cent, or $11; our "price" as defined above would be reduced from one dollar to 99 cents. An expected increase in sales of $100 to $150 would imply price elasticity coefficients calculated as follows (dollar sign omitted):

$p_0 = 1.00$; $q_0 = 1100$;

$p_1 = .99$; $q_1 = 1200 \times \dfrac{100}{99} = 1212$; or $q_1 = 1250 \times \dfrac{100}{99} = 1263$.

$$-e = \frac{dq}{q_0 + q_1} \div \frac{dp}{p_0 + p_1} = \frac{112}{2312} \div \frac{1}{199} = 9.65,$$

on the more conservative assumption, and

$$-e = \frac{163}{2363} \div \frac{1}{199} = 13.80 \text{ on the more optimistic assumption.}$$

The explanation is hinted at in the minutes, and seems fairly obvious in the light of the decisions of the meeting. The $100 reduction was only temporary; the cut from 0.1844 was permanent. What the one would achieve in the short run, the other would in the long. Differently stated, the short-run price cut was the means of advertising or spearheading the long-run gross margin cut. That is, the first pair of coefficients approximates the short-run elasticity of demand with respect to price; the third pair represents the long-run elasticity.

No great precision can be claimed for any of these coefficients. They are subjective rather than objective; furthermore, it is possible that if the persons who implicitly assumed these elasticities had been confronted with them, they would have revised them. But nobody at the meeting questioned the reasonableness of the plans. The general magnitudes of the coefficients are interesting, and most important of all is the wide difference between short and long run.

Of course, these elasticities cannot be assumed to hold throughout the whole range of A & P demand curves. At higher prices, the elasticities would increase considerably, that is, A & P would lose — and had lost — considerable business.

APPENDIX III

Opinions of Fifteen Suppliers on Going Exclusively Direct

During most of January 1940, Sumner S. Kittelle and Anthony W. Vogt, who were respectively counsel for the company and its midwestern buyer, were engaged in holding interviews with what Vogt called "a representative cross-section of the suppliers in his area." Their immediate purpose was to determine how many of the suppliers could be induced to sell exclusively direct, and thus eliminate brokers. Kittelle wrote a 30-page report on 15 suppliers (attached to a letter, Kittelle to Bofinger, January 27, 1940, GX 1623), from which we have drawn up the following summary.

Type of operation	Size	Sales method	Willingness to eliminate brokers	Remarks
(1) Meat packer	"Large"	Through brokers	Interested in this as a "long run proposition."	An efficient and low-cost operator. Important in the Indiana Republican Committee.
(2) Canner	"Medium"	Through brokers	"He is probably afraid he cannot get enough sure business from direct buyers alone."	May change his mind when voluntary chains are restricted by the FTC. His capacity is 200,000 cases, but he packed only 74,000 last year, "for which he blames the New Deal."
(3) Canner	"Large"	Through own sales force to small buyers; direct to A & P; in outside territories, through brokers, at high prices.	Volume in "outside territories" worth having, but too small to warrant the expense of a sales force.	None
(4) Two cherry packers	Not stated	Through a common sales company	Not stated	Possible to have one firm sell exclusively direct, the other through brokers. Any "surplus" could be "sold" to the other firm.

Type of operation	Size	Sales method	Willingness to eliminate brokers	Remarks
(5) Packing of apple butter and related items	Not stated: probably medium to large	In some territories, through brokers. In the remaining ones, A & P takes 95 per cent of his output	Same as (3)	Could easily show large savings in "handling, labeling, billing, shipping, and selling" costs on sales to A & P.
(6) Packing of apple butter and preserves	Not stated	Sells about 70 to 80 per cent through brokers	Not for a long time.	None
(7) Packing of pickles, potato salad, etc.	Not stated: probably medium to large	Sells almost exclusively through his own sales force, and delivers in his own trucks	Willing	Low prices; a good source of supply. A former Standard Brands official, very well informed. He suggests: (a) avoidance of "small and irresponsible packers"; (b) that A & P reassure suppliers on operating its own plants.
(8) Canning of vegetables	"Fairly large"; operates three plants	Sells almost exclusively direct	Willing	None

(9) Not stated	Not stated; probably large	Sells partly through brokers	Little prospect of early elimination, but he would like to comply with A & P policy by selling or leasing plants to legally "separate" companies.	Recently reorganized, but seems now to be operating at a profit.
(10) Packing Chinese foods	Not stated	Sells partly through brokers	Same as (3)	None
(11) Canner	Not stated	Sells through brokers, but directly to A & P and Kroger	"Not a chance." Same as (3)	Cannot afford a sales force of his own.
(12) Sales company for three separate canneries	Not stated	Sells partly or wholly through brokers	Same as (3)	None
(13) Canner	Not stated	Same as (12)	Same as (3)	None
(14) Stokely-Van Camp	National	"Rely very heavily on brokers."	Not willing	Has sold very little to A & P recently, and can see no savings in selling them direct
(15) California Packing Corporation (Del Monte)	National	Through various methods, but at the same price to everyone, on Del Monte items	Not "under any circumstances."	Sells A & P some trading items, "whenever the market is right."

APPENDIX IV

Analysis of One Hundred and Forty-two Agreements with Forty-six Suppliers

APPENDIX TABLE 23. Summary of 142 Agreements with 46 Suppliers

Gross and Net Differentials Granted A & P, 1936–1942

(each year treated as one item wherever known)

Supplier and date of agreement	Gross discount or differential	Net differential	Net differential as per cent of gross differential
Albany Packing Co., 1937–41	2¢ per lb.	*minus* 1¢	less than zero (5 years)
Armour & Co., 1938 ᵈ	5%	none	zero
Armour & Co., 1940	3%	no information	presumed 100%
Ball Brothers, 1939	6.5%	4.5%	69%
Ball Brothers, 1940	7%	5%	71%
Ball Brothers, 1941	7%	5%	71%
Boston Sausage & Provision Co.	none	none	..
Brillo Mfg. Co., 1938–42	10%	4%	40% (5 years)
California Packing Corp.ᵃ,ᶜ,ᶠ			
May 1939 deal	15–20%	12–17%	80–85%
September 1939 deal	10–22.5%	7–19.5%	70–87%
1940 deal	5%	2%	40%
Capital City Products Co.	1¢ lb.	*minus* 1¢	less than zero
Coca-Cola Bottling Co. of			
N.Y., 1940	5¢ per case	none	zero
N.Y., 1941	8.6¢ per case	3.5¢ per case	40%

	miscellaneous	less than zero	less than zero; number of agreements not ascertainable, assumed seven (with 3 companies, total 21)
Colgate-Palmolive-Peet } Lever Bros. } Procter & Gamble }			
Comet Rice Mills	5%	probably none	probably zero
Consolidated Biscuit Co.[a] 1936–1944	5%	Cf. IGA, 2% / Cf. IGA, 1% (1937) / [Cf. brokers, less than zero]	40% (6 years) / 20% (1937)
Cranberry Canners 1937-38	3%	2%	66⅔%
Cranberry Canners 1938-39	4%	3%	75%
Cranberry Canners 1939-40	4%	3%	75%
Cranberry Canners 1940-41	2%	1%	50%
Crosse & Blackwell,[c] 1941	10%	3%	30%
Dailey Pickle & Canning Co.[d]	unknown	unknown	presumed 100%
Doughnut Corp. of America, 1939-40	8.5%	8.5%	100% (1 year)
1940-41	6.3%	6.3%	100% (1 year)
Glaser, Crandell Co., 1938-1941	5%	existence certain, extent unknown	presumed 100% (4 years)
Hills Bros., 1936-1941	5%	probably zero	probably zero (6 years)
Hills Bros., 1941	2%	2%	100%
Hills Bros., 1942	3%	minus 1.5% to minus 3%	less than zero
Hunter Packing Co.,[e] 1941-43	10%	10%	100% (3 years)
I. J. Grass Noodle Co.,[a] 1940-42	5.2%	[cf. brokers, zero / cf. other chains, 3.8%	zero]
Illinois Meat Co.,[a,d] 1941	5.5%	[cf. brokers, none / cf. others, unknown]	73% (3 years) / zero]
Langendorf Bread Co., 1937	10%	10%	presumed 100%
Larsen Co., 1938	7%	3%	43%

APPENDIX TABLE 23. Summary of 142 Agreements with 46 Suppliers (*continued*)
Gross and Net Differentials Granted A & P, 1936–1942
(each year treated as one item wherever possible)

Supplier and date of agreement	Gross discount or differential	Net differential	Net differential as per cent of gross differential
Larsen Co., 1939	$8.0 thousand	$3.8 thousand	47%
Larsen Co., 1940	4.7%	0.7%	14%
Larsen Co., 1941	5.0%	1.0%	20%
Larsen Co., 1942	5.0%	1.0%	20%
Loudon Packing Co., 1938–39	none	less than zero	less than zero
Minnesota Consolidated Canneries [b]			
1939–40	5.6¢ per case	4.2¢ per case	75%
1940–41	7.0¢ per case	5.1¢ per case	73%
1941–42	6.0¢ per case	4.5¢ per case	75%
Minnesota Valley Canning Co. [b]			
1939	15.2¢ per case	4.9¢ per case	32%
1940	15.0¢ per case	6.1¢ per case	41%
1941	15.6¢ per case	8.2¢ per case	53%
Mrs. Baird's Bread Co., 1936–41	5%	5%	100% (6 years)
Olney & Carpenter, 1938–39 [c]	varied from 4.2 to 4.5 weighted average	varied	100% (4 years)
Olney & Carpenter, 1939–40 [c]			
Olney & Carpenter, 1940–41			
Olney & Carpenter, 1941–42			
Phillips Packing Co., 1936	4%	1%	25%
D. W. Putnam Co.	Sold nearly all output to A & P (see text)		..
Quaker Oats Co.			100%
R. J. Peacock Canning Co.	$1400	less than zero (phantom brokerage)	less than zero

Ralston Purina, 1937–39	7.5¢ per case	2.5¢ per case	33.3% (3 years)
Ralston Purina, 1940–41	17.5¢ per case	12.5¢ per case	71.4% (2 years)
Salmon Packers	6.75%	sold all output to A & P	..
Southern Rice Sales Co.	10.4%	0.4%	4%
Southern States Foods, Inc.	$300–$600 per year	unknown — insufficient data	..
Stahl-Meyer, Inc., 1940	5%	unknown — insufficient data	..
Sunsweet Prunes,[e] 1936	7.5%	4.5%	60%
Sylmar Packing Corp., 1939–40	10%	zero	zero
Sylmar Packing Corp., 1940–41	5%	less than zero	less than zero
Sylmar Packing Corp., 1941–42	3%	less than zero	less than zero
Virginia Dare Extract Co., 1940	Jobbers' and wholesale grocer's price	zero or less	zero or less
Virginia Dare Extract Co., 1941	none	zero or less	zero or less
Virginia Dare extract, L. D. McKinzie Co., 1941	5%	5%	100%
Walker's Austex Chile Co.,[b] 1936–43	7.5%	2.5%	33⅓% (8 years)
Wheatley Mayonnaise Co., 1939–42	5%	none	zero (4 years)
Wm. Weckerle & Sons, 1938–43	5%	5%	100% (6 years)
Wisconsin Honey Farm,[e] 1939–42	5%	5%	100% (4 years)
Wisconsin Honey Farm, 1940	8.9%	4.9%	55%
Wisconsin Honey Farm, 1941	5.6%	0.6%	11%

[a] Brokerage excluded from net differential.
[b] Brokerage included in net differential because it was impossible to separate.
[c] Definite cost savings reckoned at zero to insure consistency.
[d] Probable cost savings reckoned at zero to insure consistency.
[e] Agreement only discussed, never entered into, but included in Summary Appendix Table 24.
[f] Probably for unbranded goods, in which case net differential would be much less.

APPENDIX TABLE 24. Summary: Frequency Distribution of Net Differentials as Per Cent of Gross Differentials

Range of per cent	Agreement-years
Less than zero	32
Zero	16
0–9.9	1
10–19.9	2
20–29.9	4
30–39.9	13
40–49.9	16
50–59.9	3
60–69.9	3
70–79.9	13
80–89.9	1
90–99.9	0
100	33
Total	137
Median per cent	39.9
Agreements without differentials, or differentials not ascertained	5
Total analyzed	142

Source. Appendix Table 23.

Albany Packing Co. sold A & P at 2¢ a pound off list in 1925–26, at 1¢ off in 1928–29, and at 3¢ off from 1932 or 1933 to 1936. This 3¢ was and continued to be the discount quoted to wholesalers but to no other retailer (W. C. Codling, vice-president, Tr. 2392–94, 2447–48, 2477–79). After the Robinson-Patman Act, several large customers, including A & P, were given 1¢ off list (Tr. 2451–53). This arrangement apparently was in force throughout 1937–1941.

During 1937–1941, Albany had an advertising allowance contract for another 1¢ a pound or equivalent, for which the performance was usually (but not always) to their satisfaction. How much of the extra 1¢ was thus re-expended by A & P is not known (Tr. 2406). From time to time, some other such agreements were made with other dealers, but none was continuous as was the one with A & P (2407–8, 2461–2). During March–August 1938, Albany bought wall signs in seven A & P stores, but resisted pressure to buy some more (Tr. 2410), and then let the existing ones lapse. When the contract expired in July 1941, Albany agreed to take 2¢ off the invoice rather than 1¢ off and 1¢ later in a check (Tr. 2423–25). This arrangement ended in March 1942, when A & P ceased to get the additional 1¢.

Albany's salesmen, by A & P request, did not call at any A & P store (Tr. 2491–93).

Appraisal. As compared with wholesalers, A & P was discriminated against, for A & P received at most 2¢ to their 3, and performed the additional function of advertising, which cost them some unspecified amount. We arbitrarily reckon at zero the cost savings because of no sales effort. A & P achieved equality with wholesalers by 1932, but lost it with the Robinson-Patman Act.

Armour & Company. A quantity discount, to be kept secret from most Armour personnel was discussed in 1935 (Connors to Bofinger, May 31, 1935, GX 1195), but nothing more is heard about it. The biggest bone of contention was Armour's reluctance to grant any discount on fresh meats.

In November 1938, a special arrangement for 5 per cent on certain canned meats netted A & P $2,400 (Fraser to Gundrey, November 23, 1938, GX 1196) so that the transaction involved $48,000. There is no hint of discrimination; the prosecution did not allege it.

In February 1941, Armour offered an advertising allowance, payable "on submission of proof of advertising" rather than "deductible from invoices." The offer was made to retailers "in position to render newspaper advertising service." The National Meat Department was "not particularly enthusiastic" and it is not known whether the offer was accepted (unaddressed memorandum from Fraser, February 18, 1941, GX 1287).

After prolonged negotiations between November 1938 and March 1940, a contract was made up which provided for a discount of 3 per cent on canned meats provided that A & P purchased at least $1.5 million annually (correspondence among Fraser, Gundrey, and Connors, GX 1196–1200, 1278–79, 534–7). The letter recording the agreement alleged that "this large purchase will result in a saving to us [Armour] of at least 3 per cent in the cost of manufacture, sale, and delivery," but no explanation of the source of the saving. Similar contracts were made with Swift and Cudahy (Connors to Gundrey, Dec. 19, 1939, GX 1279). It is not known whether any other customers had similar or equal agreements. There is correspondence about "price concession" at the local level, in Pittsburgh, Jacksonville, Philadelphia, and Boston, but they are not clearly explained (GX's 1270–76 and 1286, all during February–April and August, 1940).

Appraisal. By comparison with wholesalers and brokers, A & P was probably discriminated against, except perhaps on the 3 per cent discount agreement. This was approved by the Armour legal department as not in violation of the Robinson-Patman Act; hence it must be presumed that Armour (and Swift and Cudahy) thought they could "justify" a 3 per cent discount independently of the brokerage saving by showing savings in manufacturing, sales, etc. We arbitrarily reckon any such cost savings at zero for the purposes of the Appendix.

Ball Brothers is the well-known manufacturer of fruit jars used in home preserving. They sold to jobbers on consignment, receiving payment only as the goods were sold off to retailers. A & P, Kroger, and two or three others, however, bought outright and received a 5 per cent discount (a 2 per cent discount for cash was available to any customer) [Frank E. Burt, Sales Manager, Tr. 2834–36]. Their sales manager testified that competition in the trade was "strong"; there had been six important rivals all along, and eight to ten new small entrants in recent years (Tr. 2872). As to whether or not Ball would respond to price reductions,

That would depend, I think altogether on the market conditions and the particular territory in which these lower prices were quoted by competitors. We did not meet all competition [Tr. 2875, 2876].

Q. Didn't you frequently lower your prices to all customers to meet competition?

A. Not frequently but sometimes.

Q. In other words, if your competition quoted lower prices to the trade generally, you met those prices?

A. Yes, sir.

Q. But when competition quoted a lower price just to the A & P, you met it only on that particular matter?

A. If we chose to meet it we did, yes.

Changes in the discount structure during 1939–1942 were numerous and difficult to follow, especially because not only jars but several types of caps were involved. Moreover, the prosecution challenged the reliability of certain tabulations presented by the defense, although the court denied a motion to strike (Tr. 19,501). However, it seems to be agreed that in 1939 an *additional* discount of 4.5 per cent was allowed A & P, and 2.5 per cent to Kroger, both made to meet competitive offers (Burt, Tr. 2848–51). A & P was buying caps (though apparently not jars) more cheaply than any jobber customer. In 1940, Ball declined to meet other competitive offers (telegram, Ball to Morrow, June 10, 1940, DX 650). According to a tabulation disputed by the government, A & P in 1938 actually paid more for some items than did other customers in Arkansas, Georgia, and Tennessee, because of the policy of meeting competition (Ball Brothers, Carload Discounts and Allowances for Meeting Competition for the Year 1938; Fruit Jars, P.L. Caps, Vacu-seal fittings [3 tables], DX 778). Since that policy is well substantiated, this haphazard result is about what one would expect, and does not negate the impression that A & P was *generally* buying more cheaply.

During 1940, the small group of outright purchasers were allowed an additional 5 per cent off (Morrow to MacKeachie, June 24, 1940, DX 777).

In 1941, according to one tabulation which is happily acceptable to all concerned, A & P bought caps at $1.63 less 2 per cent, or $1.60 net cash discount, or a sample of fifteen wholesaler purchasers paid prices ranging from $1.63 to $1.79 per gross. The median price was $1.72, twelve cents or 7 per cent higher than the price to A & P (C. C. Smith, Tr. 19,482–84). This accords fairly well with the other evidence.

Appraisal. The discounts to A & P seem to have been discriminatory. In the first place, many were avowedly special price cut to meet specific competitive offers, not in respect of cost savings. (The furious government opposition to the "meeting-competition" argument is revealing, for this is a Robinson-Patman defense.) The 2 per cent discount to outright purchasers was available to all and was presumably a reasonable allowance for lower costs of doing business, including credit risk (Tr. 2866–2872). But no such reason was offered for the additional 4.5 per cent in 1930, or the additional 5 per cent in 1940.

Hence we estimate the discriminatory element as 4.5/6.5, 5/7, and 5/7 for 1939, 1940, and 1941, respectively. The 1938 tabulations show that A & P sometimes paid more than others; hence our percentage estimates are probably too high. Furthermore, we have taken no account of tabulaations protested by the government but admitted by the court, which would considerably increase the A & P price, and decrease the gross and net differential. The true ratio of net to gross must be lower than our estimate, and it may be very considerably lower. The repeated prosecution emphasis that A & P paid less than *wholesalers'* prices, usually italicized, as though mere equality with wholesalers were a discrimination, and this super-added, is very revealing.

The Boston Sausage and Provision Co. makes sausages and other pork products. Since 1928, they have sold a large part of their output for the A & P label, and during 1938–1942 between 80 and 90 per cent, practically all to the New England Division (Harold I. Horwitz, vice-president, Tr. 4339–40, 4350, 4358–9, 4362).

During 1928–1936, Boston Sausage allowed A & P brokerage (Tr. 4359). During 1938–1942, they made 129 floor space rental agreements with New England units (tabulated as GX 1251). *Total* advertising outlay during 1939–1942 was $7.1 thousands as compared with $12.3 million in sales: hardly over 1/20 of 1 per cent.

Appraisal. The amounts involved appear to be miniscule, and there is no evidence that they were discriminatory. Where one customer takes so large a proportion of total output, there can scarcely be discrimination anyway. It is possible that because of the Robinson-Patman Act, Horwitz found it necessary to become practically an exclusively direct seller.

Brillo Manufacturing Co. produces steel wool and other cleansing pads. Advertising allowances have been paid since 1927 (Milton B. Loeb, vice-president, Tr. 4483). During 1938–1942, they paid A & P a 10 per cent advertising allowance (the agreement is in the record as GX 1262). In 1940, a Brillo letter complained that "we are obliged to make special appropriations in order to be assured of the advertising, which for the substantial percentage we are outlaying, should be received automatically" (Loeb to Morrow, March 4, 1940, GX 1264). Morrow replied with some heat; after citing some advertising, he said:

Don't ever let me hear you again tell us that we do not support Brillo. It is quite evident that you do not even attempt to see whether or not we advertise, or perhaps you do not read the newspapers. Knowing you as we do, your criticism of the setup will doubtless be that we did not have you on the front page of all these newspapers [Morrow to Loeb, March 19, 1940, DX 22].

There was similar correspondence, but milder in tone, in 1941 (February 28, 1941, DX 23; December 4, 1941, GX 1263). To the writer, A & P seemed to have the better of the argument, since they were able to cite specific details of performance which Brillo did not deny. Be this as it may, the crucial problem is A & P's surplus over outlay as compared with its competitors'. Morrow of A & P testified he had been told by Loeb of Brillo that nobody outside of A & P received over six per cent (Tr. 19,022), and this is confirmed by a letter (Loeb to Morrow, April 30, 1940, GX 1261) which specifies 2 per cent, respectively, for a circular feature, a poster and window display, or newspaper or other advertising. However, Loeb testified that Brillo's contracts actually included allowances between 2 and 10 per cent, depending on services rendered (Tr. 4489). He was not challenged to give any example, and the testimony of Morrow, who knew him best at A & P, is revealing:

A. After he wrote that letter telling us his maximum discount. — I think it ran from two to six per cent, which incidentally, I doubted.

Q. Yes.

A. I got him over at the office and we discussed the pros and cons and again I tried to nail him down to something, and I asked him why he was paying us ten percent when he said in his letter that the maximum discount was six. *He stated to me that his contract with me had been reviewed by the Federal Trade Commission.* I said, you are a lawyer — you ought to know what you are doing better than the average layman, and I said to him, was our contract reviewed by the Federal Trade and he said it was. *I said, how do you account for the fact that you pay us more than six percent.* He said he was paying for services rendered. That he considered the services we gave him worth that and I gathered also that he had allowances beyond six percent.

Q. What do you mean when you say you gathered that?

A. I mean from the fact that he was willing to pay us more than he was paying to others. [Tr. 19024–25, italics added].

Appraisal. Judge Lindley stated that the discriminatory portion of the differential was that between 10 per cent and 6 per cent, or 40 per cent (67 F. Supp. 626). And this is probably as good a guess as can be made.

California Packing Corporation sells under the familiar Del Monte label, although it will occasionally sell trading items for private labels. Before the Robinson-Patman Act, they had a firm commitment from A & P (almost unknown in the company) to buy 2.5 million cases of Del Monte label goods annually at the price quoted in July of each year (Charles W. Parr, Tr. 312–13). A & P received a 5 per cent discount, and did some advertising or other "support" (Parr, Tr. 418). The net accruing to A & P is unknown. After the Robinson-Patman Act, this stopped and was never renewed. A & P was strongly resentful, discontinued any sales promotion work, and aimed to buy Del Monte only to the extent that they were demanded by the public anyway (Parr to Beckmann, Oct. 21, 1936, GX 579; Bofinger to all sales and purchasing directors, December 10, 1936, GX 581).

In May 1939, Cal Pack offered 105,000 cases of various sizes of canned pineapple juice at 15–20 per cent off list (bulletin, Churchill to all buyers, quoting letter from San Francisco field buying office, GX 856). In September, there was an offer of 100,000 cases, at 10 to $22\frac{1}{2}$ per cent off. Both offers (presumably accepted) were to be kept strictly confidential (telegram, Beckmann to Meehan, Sept. 21, 1939, GX 857). If they were revealed, other packers would "undoubtedly" meet them, and A & P would lose the advantage (Beckmann to Headquarters, as quoted in a letter from W. Churchill, Jr. to Atlantic Division buyers, May 22, 1939, GX 856).

In 1940 four packers, including Cal Pack, offered A & P a 5 per cent allowance to promote the sale of pineapple juice (Beckmann to Parr, March 13, 1940, GX 1105). This is not to be confused with the secret deals on juice of a year earlier.

Appraisal. The 1939 deals are perhaps the clearest example *both* of discrimination *and* of A & P performing's the broker's function as probably no broker could have done. In each case, one must subtract the appropriate brokerage fee for this type of commodity, from the gross allowance. Brokerage on canned fruits and vegetables varied from $2\frac{1}{2}$ to 5 per cent (Parr to E. H. Green [Sullivan & Cromwell], April 6, 1933, GX 493). Hence 3 per cent seems a minimum estimate.

The median allowances are $17\frac{1}{2}$ per cent and $16\frac{1}{4}$ per cent in 1939, and 5 per cent in 1940; the net as per cent of gross is $14\frac{1}{2}/17\frac{1}{2}$, $13\frac{1}{4}/16\frac{1}{4}$, and 2/5, or 83, 82, and 40 per cent respectively.

It is probable that the juice was sold under A & P private labels rather than under the Del Monte brand. Otherwise it would seem impossible to keep so large a deal secret. If so, the unbranded item should not (even under Robinson-Patman logic) be charged with advertising, and not with all selling costs. If we reckon advertising alone at around $4\frac{1}{2}$ per cent of the sales price (see Chapter VII, Table 9), the net allowance as a per cent of gross would be $10/17\frac{1}{2}$, $8\frac{3}{4}/16\frac{1}{4}$, and $2\frac{1}{2}/5$, or 52, 54, and less than zero, respectively. There is no reason to think that the lower price did not simply approximate the unbranded price for comparable quality. However, it is not definitely known that the pineapple juice went for private label; so, in accordance with our usual rule of presuming discrimination where not disproved, we use the maximum rather than the most probable estimate.

Capital City Products Company of Columbus, Ohio, manufactured shortening and Dixie brand margarine. In 1936–39, its price for the latter stayed unchanged at 17¢ to retailers, 16½¢ to chains, and 14½¢ to distributors (testimony of Wade E. Utley, of Capital City Products Co., Tr. 2588). A & P was allowed a 1¢ volume discount, for a net price of 15½¢. The president testified that he considered selling to chains cheaper, "although there is no definite figures [sic]. . . . You could make one call for a hundred sales. . . . After the initial distribution your trucks calling on the chains was more or less of a service proposition, where in calling on the retailers it was a continuous selling job" (Tr. 2620). Furthermore: "We had found that if we sold chains in a territory, it was easier for us to get and maintain distribution with retail stores" (Tr. 2609). The half-cent differential was dropped in 1940, except where delivery was made to the chain warehouse (F. R. Hearn, later president, Tr. 2641).

In mid-1938, Capital City noted that margarine sales to A & P were off about 30 per cent. After consulting their attorneys, they decided that they were not "justified" in continuing the 1¢ per pound quantity discount. The president wrote in their vein to A & P, who he thought could with a little effort sell much more Dixie brand margarine, especially if they would permit it to be stocked in certain additional units (Wade E. Utley, president of Capital City, to J. J. Mylott, June 29, 1938, GX 738).

A & P replied that they had been all set to push Dixie, except to the extent of hindering sales of their own brand; and they added the rather meaningless suggestion that Capital City pay a 1¢ advertising allowance, if they preferred that to a quantity discount. Or they could pay ½¢ on account of each. The total, in either case, would be unchanged at 1¢ per pound, and appropriate contracts were enclosed (Mylott to Utley, July 1, 1938, GX 739). Capital City ignored the overture; A & P wrote again, repeating its suggestion (Mylott to Utley, July 22, 1938, GX 740); whereupon Capital City made a counteroffer of a ½¢ advertising allowance (Utley to Mylott, July 25, 1938, GX 741). A & P refused, and told Capital City that it would be unable to sign any contracts with local units (Mylott to Utley, July 27, 1938, GX 742); its product would be barred from company warehouses, that is, unless local demand had to be satisfied.

This was not a complete boycott, however, and the old contract was still in force. Both parties were "sort of jockeying for position, trading a little," as Utley put it (Tr. 2604). A & P made the next move, inviting him to visit Bofinger in New York before A & P made "several contemplated changes in our merchandising policy surrounding the sale of margarine" (Mylott to Utley, August 9, 1938, GX 746). At the meeting in A & P Headquarters, Bofinger again proposed the 1¢ advertising allowance and Utley again refused. In that case, said Bofinger, he was not anxious to do business with Utley, and walked out of the room.

Mr. Mylott then said that I probably should not have talked the way I did, that I had made Mr. Bofinger a little mad, possibly, but that he, Mylott, would again talk to Mr. Bofinger and see if he couldn't straighten things out, and I would hear from him later [Utley's testimony, Tr. 2604–2605].

Utley did, but the terms were the same, 1¢ per pound advertising allowance. This time he signed, and the contract remained in force through February 1944 (Tr. 2630). As soon as the agreement was made, a circular letter was sent to all purchasing and sales directors, urging them to push the sale of Dixie margarine because the company could earn "a substantial sum of money" thereby (letter dated September 16, 1938, DX 9).

Appraisal. Since the A & P warehouse is a wholesale outlet, the additional 2¢ per pound is discrimination against it. A & P succeeded during 1936–44 in removing half the discrimination, but was still 1¢ removed from equal treatment. Actually, since some promotional expense was involved in the contract, the discrimination against them was somewhat greater than 1¢.

Coca-Cola Bottling Co. of New York sells in most of New York State and over the whole metropolitan area of New York City (Rudolph G. Nagel, Assistant Treasurer, Tr. 2512). Up to 1941, they charged all distributors 80¢ a case, less 5¢, or 6¼ per cent, advertising allowance (circular letter to Purchasing Director, February 3, 1941, GX 732).

For 1941, Coca-Cola discontinued the allowance, replacing it with a quantity discount schedule (GX 732). The result was estimated by Coca-Cola Bottling as follows:

| Quarter of 1941 | A & P | | | All others |
	Cases bought (in $000s)	Allowance (in $000s)	Allowance per case (in cents)	Allowance per case (in cents)
I	29.5	2.2	7½	5 – 6½
II	62.1	6.2	10	5 – 7½
III	62.3	6.2	10	5½–10
IV	35.7	2.7	7½	5 – 7½
Year	189.6	17.3	8.6	5.1 – 7.9

Source. GX's 710, 711, 712, 713.

If we assume that all other customers received the low of the range, or 5.1¢, the net difference per case was 3.5¢ or 40 per cent of the gross difference. This is of course a considerable overestimate, and it neglects any possible cost savings by Coca-Cola Bottling.

Appraisal. The 1940 advertising allowance contract was possibly slightly discriminatory against A & P. The 1941 contract was definitely discriminatory in their favor. The ratio of net to gross differential was zero or less than zero in 1940, and 40 per cent in 1941, at a maximum.

Colgate-Palmolive-Peet Co., *Lever Bros.*, and *Procter & Gamble* are the well-known soap and shortening manufacturers. They maintain identical advertising-allowance contracts (in the record as DX's 632–36, 746–47) paying on a per-case basis for specified services. Usually, A & P did not sign the agreements, which they did not like, but they performed the service anyway and collected. The advertising allowances were available to all, both in theory and practice, and the prosecution did not even allege that they were discriminatory.

A & P complained that "we are being discriminated against by their present contracts which make us do so much more than some of our competitors in order to qualify for the allowance" (Leach to Southern buyers, January 19, 1938, GX 2418). A Divisional Purchasing Directors' meeting also noted that they were "urging soap dealers to modify their plans in such a way as to equalize our positions with those of the jobbers and independents" (April 22, 1938, GX 315). Later, Bofinger wrote that "some of these manufacturers are going to the Units and insisting upon very definite performance, yet we know of other customers of those soap companies who are giving them very little mention and are being paid equally as much as in the case of the Tea Company" (Bofinger to Meehan, March 24, 1939, GX 1063).

The allowances were very large in relation to performance, however. Thus, the Southern Division in 1938 collected $20,000 from one manufacturer and spent only $5,000; in 1939, it collected $100,000 and spent only $12,000 (GX 1063, and Meehan to Mylott, March 21, 1939, GX 1062). The difference was not clear gain. As Bofinger pointed out, there were a lot of additional hidden costs — "a tremendous burden on the organization . . . a lot of other incidental effort . . . which costs the Company money," as well as the necessity of lowering prices — while the sales were on (Bofinger to Meehan, March 24, 1939, GX 1063). But even when allowance is made for the hidden costs, they could scarcely have raised total costs to, say, more than a third of total receipts, which were large. For the period April 1940–March 1941, Lever paid over $300,000; for the first nine months of 1941, they paid over $260,000, and P & G paid $350,000. This was considered a representative year (Gundrey, Tr. 161; Arthur F. Burchard, former Lever vice-president, Tr. 18,679; Mark Upson, a P & G employee, Tr. 19,123). Hence total receipts from the soap companies were running around a million dollars a year in 1940 and 1941. This is between 12 and 15 per cent of all Headquarters and local allowances for those years.

It is clear that the soap companies intended to give customers large net rebates. They amounted to limited, temporary reductions in price, much easier to initiate and to revoke than straight price cuts.

It is an interesting question why A & P had to suffer discrimination and could not obtain equal treatment. One would expect them to propose to one soap company that A & P receive a larger allowance, in return for which A & P would promote one branch of soap to the exclusion of the others. But this never happened. One or both of two reasons seem plausible: first, consumer brand loyalty might have been so intense that A & P would simply lose sales if they shunted one or two brands aside; second, it would be easy for the three soap companies to have a tacit understanding that the promotional allowances were to be the same for all customers, with no additional payments for additional services rendered. No overt collusive action would be necessary to establish such a policy, which would obviously be in the interests of all.

Appraisal. Discrimination against A & P; amount unknown, but large.

Comet Rice Mills, in early 1940, had an agreement for a 5 per cent advertising allowance to A & P. In March of that year, Parr told the New Orleans field buying office to cancel the contract and refer Comet to A & P headquarters if Comet "is granting the [same] . . . to all purchasers" (Parr to Wilson, March 1, 1940, DX 555).

The old contract was cancelled, indicating that Comet *had* been granting five per cent to all customers. But the new contract also provided for 5 per cent (Mylott to Comet Rice Mills, April 10, 1940, GX 798). It is clear that A & P did not take its advertising responsibility very seriously (Mylott to Director of Purchasing, April 24, 1940, GX 4455).

Appraisal. It seems likely that Headquarters tried to get a larger allowance than others were receiving, failed to do so, and took the old one for lack of anything better.

Consolidated Biscuit Co. sold soda crackers and graham crackers from plants in Louisville, Chicago, and Boston. Shipments were to wholesalers or warehouses and to a few supermarkets buying in large enough quantities (E. F. Chambless, vice-president, Tr. 2742–51). With a number of customers they had a cooperative merchandising plan under which allowances were made: 3 per cent to IGA without reference to the amount purchased (Tr. 2783), and 4.76 per cent to Hi-Lo Food Stores (Tr. 2816). With A & P, and no other customer, they had, from 1936 through 1944, a quantity-discount schedule with a maximum of 5 per cent (Tr. 2786), which A & P received every year except 1937, when they qualified for only 4 per cent (Tr. 2809). The "quantity" discount was actually a volume discount, all shipments to A & P warehouses being aggregated for that purpose. Chambless, the Consolidated vice-president, thought there were economies in selling to A & P, but he did not specify them (Tr. 2798–2800).

Consolidated sold through brokers and also through its own sales force. Brokerage on first-grade crackers, and A & P purchases were 98 per cent first grade (Tr. 2810), was 5 per cent. Terms to wholesalers are not indicated.

Appraisal. The discounts to A & P, IGA, and Hi-Lo were obviously disguised brokerage. Since they did not always get the brokers' 5 per cent, did buy larger quantities, and did give a rather good advance assurance of volume, clearly A & P suffered some small discrimination as compared with brokers. But as compared with other purchasers buying under similar conditions, they did receive a net differential: 40 per cent of the gross differential under IGA (2 of 5), 5 per cent of the gross differential under Hi-Lo (0.24 of 5.0). Since most of the Consolidated output went either to wholesale channels or to such large chains (larger than Hi-Lo) as American Stores, First National, and Kroger, the net differential toward buyers other than brokers could scarcely have been greater than 20 per cent, and was probably less.

Cranberry Canners, Inc., during the fiscal year 1937–38 (September–August), sold to various customers under a "quantity"-discount plan whereby purchasers of over 50,000 cases received 2 per cent off, and purchasers of over 75,000 cases received 3 per cent. However, A & P were the only ones to qualify for 3 per cent. For fiscal 1938, the schedule was revised to begin with one per cent on the first 25,000 cases, and up to 4 per cent for over 100,000 cases. A & P was presumably the only recipient of the 4 per cent rebate (MacKeachie to Mylott, March 31, 1938, GX 651; and MacKeachie to Cranberry Canners, April 6, 1938, GX 652; M. L. Urann to Mylott, Oct. 3, 1938, DX 758). Urann suggested that they buy more than 200,000 cans in 1938–39, and offered discounts up to 6 per cent (Urann to MacKeachie, Sept. 9, 1938, DX 754; see also GX 649, fourth paragraph).

In September 1939, A & P submitted a cost-savings agreement, and the ensuing correspondence is worth quoting at some length:

Government men have been down here a number of times and seem to be chasing around to see just what we are doing with you people. For this reason it seems that we should be very careful to do nothing that we cannot justify.

Your first paragraph says that you normally buy in large volume for delivery in large shipments. It seems that a carload is the breaking point where economy starts in. There is a saving in shipments in carloads.

Increased volume unless it should materially increase our pack would not justify an additional discount. For instance, we are now packing rising a million cases, and unless you should take say 250,000 or 300,000 cases it would not reflect a saving in our packing cost.

Now, there are other people of course buying in carloads, and buying almost as much as you do, so it would seem as if our attempt to stand on your first paragraph would on analysis and presented for hearing land us both in an uncomfortable position.

We cannot based on these orders show a manufacturing economy, and therefore it seems to me very unwise to claim it, for if we should fail to substantiate our claim at a hearing we again would be in a very uncomfortable position.

I am inclined to believe that we had better come right out openly and give you a quantity discount as we did last year; 1% on 25,000 cases, 2% on 50,000, 3% on 75,000, and 4% on 100,000 and over. It would make the case still stronger if you took 1% on the first 25,000, 2% on the second 25,000, 3% on the third 25,000, and 4% on the fourth 25,000 and everything above. That you will observe cuts the amount of your discount.

That is really the basis on which we are working with others, and we have no one else who is getting more than 2%.

We pass this along for your consideration, but we really think we would weaken our case with this agreement as you sent it. Under the arrangement last year we were not binding ourselves to prove a particular thing, same as you do in this agreement as to increased volume and economy because of it. We simply give you the discount and when the time comes to prove that it is justified then we are not handicapped in any way, but will just meet the situation when and if it arises with whatever conditions at that time will prove the most effective [Urann to MacKeachie Sept. 27, 1939, GX 649].

The A & P lawyers commented:

There is probably some truth in the statement made in the enclosed letter that the seller has no savings in delivery costs in selling to A & P since savings disappear rapidly after the carload quantity has been reached. It is also probably true that this seller experiences very litle savings in his manufacturing costs, as the savings due to the increased production arising from a large order must be distributed among all buyers and cannot be credited entirely to the one buyer submitting the large order.

These are the very reasons, however, that we decided to use the new cost savings agreement form instead of the old one which provided for a sliding scale of discounts based on the quantity purchased. The new contract recognizes that most of the savings are due to the A & P's method of purchasing and are not dependent entirely on the quantities purchased. The volume discounts based on a sliding scale, which this seller wishes to use, give too much emphasis to quantity, the importance of which the seller himself questions. I suggest you point out to him the savings in selling costs realized on sales to A & P. He apparently has not taken these into consideration along with the delivery and manufacturing costs. Since these savings are present regardless of the amount purchased, you might be able to convince him that the flat percentage is the safer system. Some, if not all, of the savings in selling expenses brought out in the Federal Trade Commission case probably exist in this case, for example, salesman's salaries and expenses, communication expenses, market information, advice on packing, lower credit risk, billing and collection expenses, etc.

The writer of the letter is troubled by one other point. He hesitates to sign the contract since it states the bases upon which the discount is made. He would prefer not to state the source of the savings until called upon to do so. There is no advantage in this. In the first place the "whereas" clauses in the contract are broad enough to cover any savings which might possibly be relied on later. Furthermore, he is not estopped from showing the savings which actually exist regardless of what appears in the contract. The purpose of this part of the contract is to indicate that the discount is justifiable on the basis of savings which are allowable under the cost proviso. It does not in any manner restrict the savings which may be relied on. While the volume discounts suggested in the letter are probably justifiable, I think a flat percentage discount would be safer from the standpoint of both buyer and seller as the Commission in the *Brill* case indicated its disapproval of volume discounts [Feldman to MacKeachie, October 20, 1939, GX 648].

With no clear decisions reached, the earlier contract was renewed (DX 757), and apparently A & P again received 4 per cent off (Mylott, Tr. 19,148).

For 1940–41, Cranberry Canners paid only 2 per cent to all purchasers taking more than 50,000 cases, including A & P (Urann to Mylott, Oct. 22, 1940, DX 762). For the period September–December 1941, Cranberry Canners offered a merchandising allowance of 2 per cent to buyers who gave rather specific performance (announcement, Oct. 1, 1941, DX 755). A & P accepted the offer and received an additional 2 per cent.

Appraisal. During 1937–38, A & P received a 2 per cent advantage compared with the lowest-bracket purchasers, who received 1 per cent, so that the net differential was two thirds of the gross. During 1938–39 and 1939–40, A & P had a net advantage of 3 per cent. For 1940–41, the net allowance was 1 per cent. All these estimates disregard any possible cost savings, and hence are on the high side. Nothing is known about brokerage.

Crosse & Blackwell evidence is difficult to evaluate. For 1935, they had an "advertising agreement" (GX 773) under which they paid A & P $12.8 thousand. This was 3.5 per cent of A & P purchases (Sidney Thornton, vice-president, Tr. 2689, 2692). For 1936, they had a 5 per cent discount, which was cancelled after the passage of the Robinson-Patman Act (Tr. 2691). It is impossible to tell the importance of these arrangements or the extent to which either one was discriminatory.

Crosse & Blackwell made store-door delivery, and stores tended to get loaded up with their slow-moving items, much to the annoyance of headquarters (Merchandising Committee, June 21, 1940, DX 232; Mylott to Meehan [So. Div.], December 19, 1940, GX 776; Mylott to Meehan, February 24, 1941, GX 779). During 1940, negotiations were opened with a view to handling merchandise exclusively through the warehouses, with A & P receiving an allowance to reflect the cost saving in eliminating store-door. Crosse & Blackwell were willing to ship only through warehouses, and to allow a 5.14 per cent discount, but only if shipments were to be in 500-case lots (Mylott to George, April 4, 1941, GX 782), and warehouses which could not dispose of such large amounts were to consider the advisability of discontinuing the C & B line altogether. During 1941, then, A & P was the only customer to rate a 5.14 per cent allowance because they were the only ones to take warehouse delivery (Thornton, Tr. 2693, 2696).

However, the arrangement did not work out, for the volume of sales in 1941 was less than half of 1935 (Thornton, Tr. 2692). We may presume that for most warehouses, the 500-case minimum was more than they wanted, especially because the size of all cases was arbitrarily doubled during the year, so that the true threshold was 1,000 cases on a comparable basis. Crosse and Blackwell cancelled the arrangement in October 1941 (Thornton, Tr. 2697–98).

Crosse and Blackwell had no system of "functional" discounts, all classes of buyers paying the same price. Up to May 5, 1941, they had sold on a scale of quantity discounts which were put in the form of decreasing net prices, ranging up to 6.1 per cent (Thornton, Tr. 2691, 2693–95). After that date, they sold at quantity discounts ranging from 3 per cent for six cases to 7 per cent on 500 or more cases (Tr. 2691, 2693–95). Since A & P warehouses were obliged, under the 1941 agreement, to take 500 or more cases and receive only 5.14 per cent, it is plausible that this 5.14 per cent must have been over and above the scheduled 7 per cent. We assume that the discount was indeed in excess. It actually came to 3.09 per cent (Thornton, Tr. 2697–98).

Appraisal. There is too little evidence for any appraisal of the 1935 and 1936 discounts. The 1941 arrangement must be considered discriminatory, since the savings attendant on quantity would presumably be reflected in the quantity-discount schedule, and since Crosse & Blackwell cancelled the contract because sufficient additional volume was not forthcoming. Since a 500-minimum buyer would receive 7 per cent, and A & P received 3.09 per cent in addition, for a total of 10.09 per cent, it follows that 30 per cent of their gross differential must have been discriminatory. As usual, we disregard the savings on warehouse delivery.

Dailey Pickle & Canning Co. originally sold pickles to the wholesale trade. However, starting in 1938, it has been selling A & P 50–60 per cent of its output (W. E. Dailey, vice-president, Tr. 4909), and National Tea has since 1940 taken most of the remainder (Tr. 4914–15). Tabulations presented by the government (GX 1376–85) show prices lower to A & P than to wholesalers, but it is impossible to measure even the gross differential.

Dailey testified that there were definite cost savings in selling to A & P, mentioning the packaging, the movement from the production room straight to the truck or railroad car, carload lots, and less bookkeeping expense (Tr. 4897–8, 4906–09). No formal cost study was ever made, however; and it probably would not pay in view of the small size of this supplier. In 1939, Dailey employed about 60 men and had sales of about $265,000 (Tr. 4888, 4896), and he had no cost-accounting departments (4916).

Dailey did not hold strictly to its list prices (Tr. 4902–5), and there are some instances of A & P paying higher prices than National Tea (Tr. 4901). Up to April 1940, they sold some of their output through brokers (Tr. 4857, 4873, 4912), but at that time they went exclusively direct (Vogt to Parr, May 4, 1940, GX 1387).

Dailey gave advertising allowances, but they were negligible.

Appraisal. The tabulation shows price differences which appear discriminatory; but the switch to National Tea seems to indicate that the apparently lower prices to the chains were more remunerative than the higher prices to the wholesaler. However, in accordance with our rule, we disregard cost savings. Since all customers were wholesalers, the differences are considered wholly discriminatory.

Doughnut Corporation of America sold to A & P both in the United States and Canada. Because of the Canadian tariff, rapid changes in the raw-material markets, and a profit-sharing arrangement of the D.C.A. with its Canadian manager, there was prolonged haggling over prices and terms from 1935 to 1941. In 1939, a refund of $1,000 was made to A & P Canadian units, which was the equivalent of 1¢ per pound, or 8.5 per cent, apparently because of competitive offers by Joe Lowe & Co. (MacKeachie to Bird, April 6, 1939, GX 1346; Bird to MacKeachie, April 13, 1939, GX 1347; testimony of B. C. Black, vice-president, Tr. 4773, 4813). The discount was to ¾¢ on March 1, 1940, and discontinued on July 1, 1941 (Gundrey to MacKeachie, July 7, 1941, GX 1362).

Appraisal. Although the record is far from clear, the price reduction seems to have been wholly discriminatory, made in order to keep A & P business from Joe Lowe.

Glaser, Crandell Co. manufacture pickles, preserves, jelly, mustard, and sauces. Their line is sold under their own brand and is "more or less in competition with our own [A & P] factories" (Parr to Vogt, January 25, 1938, GX 891). They granted A & P a volume discount during 1938–1941, with highly pleasing results, for their sales nearly quintupled from 1937 to 1938 (Lee S. Glaser to Vogt, April 7, 1939, DX 666). A & P was uneasy about the legal status of the "quantity" (actually, volume) discount, but Glaser wrote them that his lawyers, "upon examination of actual cost accounting analysis," had assured him it was legal (Glaser to Vogt, January 9, 1940, DX 669). Subsequently, he explained that he had identical agreements with several other large purchasers (Glaser to Vogt, November 8, 1940, DX 673). A & P still did not like the agreement because of their well-founded distrust of volume discounts, and in 1941 they suggested a cost-savings agreement, with their second choice a flat discount of 4 or 5 per cent (Parr to Vogt, January 9, 1941, GX 892; Vogt to Glaser, Crandell, January 16, 1941, GX 892). Glaser was unwilling to comply because other customers used the agreement; and he liked it because it tempted customers into the higher-volume, higher-discount brackets (Vogt to Parr, January 27, 1941, DX 673A). The agreement was therefore renewed for 1940 and again for 1941 (Glaser to Vogt, October 10, 1941, DX 676).

Appraisal. Glaser's reasons (DX 673A) suggest that his discount structure was discriminatory. He was offering lower prices for additional orders. There may have been some genuine cost savings involved which by our rule are presumed zero. Nothing more can even be guessed at.

Hills Brothers sell a varied line under the well-known Dromedary label. From 1934 through 1941, they had a regular agreement with A & P, as with other suppliers, providing a maximum 5 per cent advertising allowance. In 1940, they had a dispute with A & P over performance, Hills claiming that A & P had only earned 3 per cent and A & P disputing this "very strongly" (W. F. Redfield, president, at Tr. 4624–26). Hills paid only 3 per cent that year, but agreed that if A & P performed acceptably the next year, in 1941, they would get the "carry-back" two per cent "so that at the end of the two years they would average five per cent, the same as anybody else" (Tr. 4627). (In Appendix Table 23, we include only the years 1936–1941; we are not attempting to tabulate earlier years, since the data are much too scanty.)

For the fiscal year Nov. 1, 1941–Oct. 31, 1942, Hills granted A & P a "quantity" discount of 2 per cent on citrus products in return for A & P's purchasing 60,000 cases. This was their response to loss of business from A & P; nobody else was offered such a deal, and "nobody else purchased that quantity or anywhere near it" (Tr. 4608, 4612, 4654). Hills Brothers labeled their canned juices, but they could not disregard competition on price. As their president put it:

This business, which is standard canned goods, is highly competitive. . . . Any large buyer can usually buy and nearly always buys at a lower price than our list price [which] is usually slightly higher than the average. We try to pack something a little better than the average [Tr. 4608].
We had for very many years enjoyed a very good business with A & P on citrus products. . . . We began losing that business to lower prices, in one form or another. . . . Many canners need a large buyer as their backlog. . . . [They] take that contract to the bank and get enough money to operate on, so that any large buyer could get a price lower than our list price.
As we began to lose this business — which we liked very much, it was good business under our own brand — we cast around for the reasons and saw that it was a matter of pricing in one form or another, a flat price, or just a plain lower price, or a discount, and we endeavored to meet it [Tr. 4640–4641].

Hills Brothers' action was characteristic. They offered A & P a 2 per cent discount if they would purchase 60,000 cases of citrus juices during 1941–42. At no time did they offer such discounts to the trade generally; it was simply that "where our business was threatened . . . we met competitive price" (Tr. 4607; GX 1305; quotation from Tr. 4640). In a word, they were meeting competitors' offers which A & P had been able to elicit (Tr. 4608). "Nobody else purchases that quantity or anything near it"; furthermore, shipments to A & P were "almost invariably" in carload lots (Tr. 4612).

During 1941, Hills Brothers also attempted to step up sales on cake and frosting mixes and fruit breads, all of which were widely advertised and more definitely branded products (Tr. 4643). They offered premiums for purchases greater than a "very small" minimum made between May 15 and July 1, 1941 (Tr. 4620). A & P, as always, was opposed to premiums, and they were finally able to obtain a 3 per cent discount on the purchases of these products during the stated period. Redfield considered that A & P's refusal "worked out very badly" for them; but the company's opinion was not on record (Tr. 4617–4620; 4649). They probably regarded the principle of opposition to premiums as more important than the gain on any particular deal.

In the spring of 1941, Hills Brothers also offered premiums (furniture, hosiery, etc.) to the trade for increased purchases. A & P, in accordance with its policy, refused the premiums, and was allowed 3 per cent instead. This was much lower than the 4.5 per cent to 6 per cent cost of the premiums, as Redfield estimated them (Tr. 4614–4619). Nobody else received this cash option, however.

Appraisal. The 1934–1941 deals were nondiscriminatory; and much or most of the allowances were re-expended. The 1940 dispute over performance is significant in showing the supplier's control of the advertising allowance deal, and since A & P was being held to its performance, discrimination must have been little or nothing. The 1941–42 arrangement was largely discriminatory, although there were undoubted savings on account of carload shipments; following our rule, we disregard the savings, and reckon the allowance as wholly discriminatory. The 1942 arrangements were, if the witness be trusted, discriminatory against A & P. Their rigid no-premium rule was apparently worth that to them. We consider the two premium deals as one.

Hunter Packing Co. is an integrated full-line meat packer in East St. Louis, selling throughout the metropolitan area largely through its own sales force, who visited or called customers and transmitted their orders to the plant, whence delivery was made by truck the next morning. (Frank A. Hunter, Jr., president, Tr. 5552, 5526).

In January 1941 Hunter entered into a cost-savings agreement with A & P providing for a 5 per cent allowance (GX 1589). For 1942 and 1943, the allowance was changed from 5 per cent to 1¢ per pound, since the price of meat had risen and a percentage allowance would have risen proportionately (Tr. 5524–25). This means that the new allowance, as a per-cent deduction, was less than the old.

Thirty-seven invoices (in the record as GX's 1594–1609) were placed in the record, comparing prices on identical items, all fancy meats, to A & P and to others. The median price difference between A & P and others was about 5 per cent. These 37 invoices covered three days, during which time between 3,000 and 4,500 invoices had been issued, so that they represent about a one per cent sample (Tr. 5573), and subject to bias because of the short time period covered. Nevertheless, there was no complaint that the sample was biased unfavorably to the prosecution. Furthermore, the price list to A & P was different from, and lower than, the regular price list (Tr. 5510-11, and correspondence referred to there). A & P paid strictly according to its price list, while salesmen were permitted to shade prices on other accounts, and this would be reflected in the invoice prices (Tr. 5512).

The evidence as to cost savings by Hunter is impressive. (The fact that he signed a cost savings agreement, as did very few suppliers, indicates a confidence that he could prove them to an unfriendly inquiry.) The average size of sausage orders delivered to an A & P store was greater than $60, and to all other stores only $8 (Tr. 5563-4). Furthermore, A & P bought a fixed "basket" of goods, and there was no process of negotiating or choosing as with other accounts (Tr. 5568-69). Hunter salesmen were rather well-paid employees, their salaries averaging from $60 to $70 weekly (the equivalent of perhaps twice that in 1959) [Tr. 5585]. Delivery, accounting, and production savings would be in addition.

Appraisal. The gross differential to A & P was around 10 per cent. Cost savings probably more than accounted for it. Setting aside cost savings, however, as we do for the sake of consistency, the net differential is the same as the gross, for there is no evidence that other customers received any allowances.

I. J. Grass Noodle Co. of Chicago manufactured noodles and dried-soup mix. They sold under their own label through brokers at a 5 per cent commission, directly to about a dozen large customers, including A & P, and the larger part through truck distributors who made store-door delivery (Irving J. Grass, Tr. 4365-71).

For 1939-1942, the Grass Company had a 5 per cent advertising-allowance agreement with the A & P Chicago unit. They received newspaper mention and store display in the spring and fall (Tr. 4382-87). No such agreement was made with any other customer, but advertising allowances were also given to other chains, as shown in the table on p. 500 (dollars in thousands):

Year	Total sales to all customers	Total sales to A & P	Chicago Unit, A & P Purchases	Per cent allowance	Chicago Unit, National Tea Purchases	Per cent allowance	Chicago Unit, Jewel Food Stores Purchases	Per cent allowance	Chicago Unit, Kroger Purchases	Per cent allowance
1940	896.3	44.7	37.0	5.8	24.1	5.1	10.3	..	5.4	..
1941	1,484.6	103.6	56.1	5.0	27.9	3.5	16.4	2.4	8.0	0.6
1942	1,780.5	138.8	54.2	4.9	43.3	0.9	23.8	1.3	7.8	..
Totals			147.3	5.2	95.3	2.7	50.5	1.4	21.2	..

Sources. DX 77, GX 4221.

Appraisal. Equating the value of the advertising to zero, the payments by the Grass Company seem to be disguised brokerage. Grass sold to A & P through brokers in some towns (Tr. 4370), and he doubtless considered himself better off getting the same net return on a larger volume of sales, with advertising thrown in. But as compared with National in 1942, and Jewel in 1941–42, the allowance was discriminatory, although it is difficult to say how much. At a rough guess, one might compare their 5.2 per cent with the lowest (Jewel 1.4 per cent), setting the net discrimination at 3.8 per cent. This is of course a considerable overstatement of the preference over National Tea, which would be only 2.5 per cent. We may set the ratio of net to gross differential at 3.8/5.2, or 73 per cent.

Illinois Meat Company sells a full or nearly full line of fresh, canned, and smoked meats, through brokers and through its own sales force, to wholesalers and chains (Charles E. Martin, general sales manager, Tr. 3365–66).

Before 1941, Illinois had a sliding-scale-volume discount with A & P, which Martin thought "was offered to everyone" (Tr. 3429), but on which there is no further information. For 1941, A & P agreed to buy not less than $790 thousand of canned meat, receiving a 3 per cent discount, and a very similar arrangement was made for 1942, in carload lots, except that the minimum volume was one million dollars (GX's 997,998). No other buyer had such an agreement (Tr. 3425–26).

The Illinois general manager claimed that the quantity discount was advantageous in promoting sales to A & P, which was undoubtedly true but does not disprove discrimination. He also claimed cost savings, but did not present evidence of them (Tr. 3425–26). It is true that the guaranteed volume was large, but it covered a wide variety of products. Admittedly, *if* Illinois was sure of a stable product mix or *if* the basic ingredients did not vary much, it could embark on large purchases and long runs and save money; unfortunately, we do not know the stability of the mix or of the ingredients.

Illinois also gave a 2.5 per cent discount for carload or equivalent lots (Tr. 3371–72).

Appraisal. The carload discount was not questioned and may therefore be assumed nondiscriminatory. The 3 per cent "quantity" discount was largely disguised brokerage, also nondiscriminatory. Hence there was no net differential. There were probably also some manufacturing and delivery savings, uncertain in amount. Following our rule, we will equate manufacturing and delivery economies to zero.

Langendorf Bread Co. is a local baker, supplying the Los Angeles Unit. Our only knowledge of them is in the following letter:

The allowance we received from Langendorf Bread Company represents 10%

of our bread purchases. This allowance has always been paid to about three of the large chains previous to the Robinson-Patman Bill and was paid in cash. Their reason for paying us in cash and requesting us to make entries as "John Doe", is that *they are afraid that either someone in their office or ours might leave and go with a competitor and the information would become known.* When Mr. George Feldman was here — checking Mr. Beckmann's Office, I discussed this matter with him, and he advised that as far as he could see it was perfectly legitimate. I feel we are above any criticism in accepting this money and you may rest assured I will never intentionally embarrass the Company" [Gibbon to Charlton, June 10, 1937, GX 895; italics added].

A secret rebate is always suspicious. Langendorf's expressed reason was to keep competition from finding out that he was underselling. Presumably he sold to customers other than the three large chains at a higher price.

However, the very obviousness of the discrimination makes one puzzled why A & P's attorney should consider it "perfectly legitimate." Our best explanation is that the commerce was wholly intrastate, and the discrimination therefore beyond the reach of federal law.

Appraisal. Wholly discriminatory.

The Larsen Company is a packer of vegetable specialties, sold under its own brand names of Veg-All and Layer-Pak. Before and after the Robinson-Patman Act, Larsen sold through brokers, whom it paid 4 per cent, and treated A & P's Milwaukee office as it would any other broker (R. E. Lambeau, an executive not further identified, Tr. 3219–3221). Following the Robinson-Patman Act, Larsen sold A & P "net" according to the system which was finally declared illegal in January 1940 (Tr. 3222). At the same time, he paid 4 per cent brokerage, and was still doing so at the time of trial, to the Independent Grocers' Alliance (Tr. 3260–62). Payment of brokerage to IGA was declared illegal in March 1952 (FTC Complaint Docket 5533; 203 F.2d 941 (7th Cir. 1953).

At about the same time that "net" buying was being declared illegal by the FTC, Larsen made a cost savings agreement with A & P for 1939, and $4.2 thousand was remitted on that account during 1939 (Tr. 3226–27, and GX's 957–959), but it is not possible to make out just what the arrangement meant; presumably it continued the brokerage under a new name.

During 1937–42, Larsen had cooperative advertising arrangements with A & P. In 1939–42, there was some negotiation about performance, which occasionally seemed to threaten a breakdown of negotiations (Vogt to Mylott, Nov. 1, 1940, GX 978; Nov. 26, 1940, GX 982).

It is impossible to calculate the gross and net differentials for 1937. During 1938, total payments (including both "net" and advertising) to A & P were 7 per cent of purchases (Mylott to Vogt, November 17, 1939, GX 963). During 1939, in addition to the $4.2 thousand already mentioned, A & P received $3.8 thousand, total $8.0 thousand. For 1940, the deal was for a $10 thousand rebate on estimated purchases of $150 thousand, or 6.7 per cent, but as it turned out, purchases were actually $255 thousand and the rebate 4.7 per cent. For 1941, they projected $250,000 of purchases and $12,500 as a rebate, or 5 per cent (GX's 978 and 984). For 1942, $17,500 was paid (GX 988), and it was expected to be 5 per cent on a volume of $400 thousand (Parr to Vogt, Oct. 27, 1941, GX 987). The prosecution made certain tabulations to show that A & P received much larger rebates per case than did all other customers, on the average. But they did not include brokerage allowances made to others than A & P, and hence the amounts are simply noncomparable. Were the prosecution tables in the form of *percentages* of the sales price or sales receipts, one could make an adjustment and a comparison inclusive of brokerage or net of it. Unfortunately the tables are in cents per case.

Appraisal. The payments which were disguised brokerage (4 per cent) merely put A & P on an equal footing with all other buyers. Following our general rule, everything in excess of the 4 per cent will be considered discriminatory, as follows: 1938, 3 per cent; 1939, $3.8 out of $8.0 thousand; 1940, 0.7 per cent; 1941 and 1942, 1.0 per cent. The ratio of net to gross differential is: 1938, .43; 1939, .47; 1940, .14; 1941 and 1942, .20.

Life Savers Corporation up to December 1941 allowed chain stores, including A & P, a 10 per cent savings allowance. In that month, it withdrew the allowance (Churchill to Atlantic Division buyers, December 16, 1941).

Appraisal. Evidence too scarce.

Loudon Packing Co. is discussed elsewhere at length. The heart of the disagreement was their refusal to make any allowance for warehouse delivery during 1938 (Stewart Rose, Jr., vice-president, Tr. 4673–5, 4720–32, 4679; Vogt to Mylott, May 27, 1939, GX 1316), although in 1939 they were willing to allow A & P a 15 per cent distributor discount (Vogt to Mylott, July 3, 1939, GX 1321), but not anything more, while the regular distributor also received additional discounts (Rose, Tr. 4739–40).

Appraisal. There was some discrimination against A & P, but its amount is impossible to determine.

Minnesota Consolidated Canneries, Inc. are canners of vegetables under the Butter Kernel trade name. They sell through brokers at 3 per cent; also direct to A & P and a few others (Robert L. B. Wilson, secretary, Tr. 3770–73). Before the Robinson-Patman Act, they allowed A & P the same brokerage as others (Tr. 3974). A & P is their largest customer, but the price (aside from allowances shortly to be discussed) is identical to all customers (Tr. 3799). M.C.C.'s secretary claimed that he had always required, received, and checked up on performance of advertising agreements. But negotiations were on the basis of value to M.C.C., not cost to the customer (Tr. 3800–01). The tabulation on p. 504 is based on a government presentation.

PURCHASES IN THOUSANDS OF CASES, ADVERTISING IN CENTS PER CASE

Year Aug. 1– July 31	A & P		American Stores		Safeway		All customers		All customers (Excl. A & P)		All nonchain customers		Excess of A & P allowance over all other customers (cents per case)	Excess of A & P allowance over all nonchain customers (cents per case)
	Purchases	Advertising payment	Purchases	Advertising payment	Purchases	Advertising payment	Purchases	Advertising payment	Purchases	Advertising payment	Purchases	Advertising payment		
1939–40	197.4	5.6	59.5	9.5	36.4	3.0	389.3	4.9	191.9	3.7	96.0	1.4	1.9	4.2
1940–41	361.7	7.0	61.9	8.1	31.8	4.4	498.5	5.6	236.8	4.0	143.1	1.9	3.0	5.1
1941–42	357.4	6.0	69.3	7.0	46.7	3.0	711.7	4.4	354.3	2.6	238.3	1.5	3.4	4.5

Source. GX 4220.

In each year, A & P bought the most, but received a per-case allowance between American and Safeway. This might indicate that American did more in the way of promotional activity, except that their increase in sales is both absolutely and relatively very small compared to the A & P increase; in fact, Safeway did as well as American absolutely and better relatively.

Appraisal. The three largest buyers were discriminated against, since they all had to pay phantom brokerage. However, we are unable to calculate the percentage of this item, since sales data are on a case, not a dollar, basis. As among the three large buyers, there is no evidence of discrimination, despite the fact that sales to A & P were two to three times the sales to the other two combined. Whether the three largest buyers as a group were favored or disfavored cannot be ascertained. One needs to know whether their net gain from advertising allowances, minus that of other customers and minus the 3 per cent phantom brokerage, was greater than zero. The apparent nondiscrimination within the group, and the dependence of allowances on promotional activity, make it more likely that the large buyers were disfavored. However, in accordance with our rule of presuming discrimination where not clearly disproved, and reckoning it as against the most disfavored class (actually disfavored or only apparently), we estimate the ratio of net to gross differential as follows:

$$1939\text{–}40 - 4.2/5.6, \text{ or } 75 \text{ per cent}$$
$$1940\text{–}41 - 5.1/7.0, \text{ or } 73 \text{ per cent}$$
$$1941\text{–}42 - 4.5/6.0, \text{ or } 75 \text{ per cent}$$

Minnesota Valley Canning Company sells the familiar Green Giant peas, corn, and asparagus. It sells through brokers, with all paying the same price. A & P is the only direct customer. "They pay the same price [as all others] but we do not pay any brokerage to them" (Ward H. Patton, vice-president, Tr. 3897, 3974–75). A & P are a very large part of their market: in 1939–41, their share fluctuated around one third of the total (Tr. 3974–77).

Minnesota has used cooperative advertising since 1928 (Tr. 3976), and was paying A & P an allowance in 1934 (GX 11) but did not do so in 1936–37 (Vogt to Parr, July 30, 1940, GX 1178). The situation for later years is shown as follows (purchases in thousands of cases, allowances in cents per case):

Customers	Purchases	Allowances	Purchases	Allowances	Purchases	Allowances	Purchases	Allowances
A & P	590.0[a]	16.7[b]	822.6	15.2	1,000.9	15.0	1,120.9	15.6
Kroger			55.2	16.2	72.0	13.8	106.7	9.6
Safeway			146.9	3.4	212.8	1.6	276.1	1.8

Customers	Purchases	Allowances	Purchases	Allowances	Purchases	Allowances	Purchases	Allowances
American Stores			61.6	13.8	87.8	9.4	100.0	13.0
First National			28.4	11.6	31.2	9.8	32.5	10.1
N.R.O.G.			146.1	15.5	168.7	13.8	187.4	10.7
All other customers advertising							..	11.0
All other, incl. advertising and nonadvertising			1,249	10.3	1,414.5	8.9	1,628.9	7.4
All customers			2,509.9	12.05	2,988.0	10.8	3,452.5	10.4

Source. GX 1171, except: [a] Vogt to Parr, April 24, 1940, GX 1175, and [b] Approximate, Vogt to Parr, July 30, 1940, GX 1178.

Obviously there is no significant relation between size and advertising allowance per case: Kroger, buying less than one tenth of A & P's purchases in 1939, actually received a larger allowance. The reason given, and doubtless truly, was that they gave more service than A & P (Robert McDonald, advertising manager, Tr. 4021). There probably was also some large element of chance and lack of control. Vogt reported in 1940 that "they [Minnesota] were a little concerned because in working it [advertising allowances] back to a case basis, there are extreme variations in what they were paying their different customers. Nevertheless . . . with some of their larger distributors operating like our own organization their plan of operation has been to pay for specific performance, consequently it would be inconsistent to endeavor to tie it up to a flat case basis" (Vogt to Parr, July 30, 1940, GX 1178).

Minnesota was a close trader. In September 1936 they wanted simply to reimburse distributors for actual advertising outlays, permitting no net gain to their customers ("W.F.F." to Vogt, September 17, 1936, GX 1172). This extreme position was untenable, and at the trial a Minnesota vice-president testified that he expected customers to make some profit in advertising, particularly because they paid local rates which were about half the national rate (Tr. 3394).

Correspondence in the spring of 1940 indicates that A & P was worried that Minnesota was favoring small buyers, by making store-door delivery at the same list price as to an A & P warehouse, by giving advertising allowances to wholesale grocers who did no advertising, and in some other ways. They tried to get definite information, but were apparently not successful (Parr to Vogt, April 2, 1940, GX 1774; Vogt to Parr, April 24, 1940, GX 1175; Parr to Vogt, May 8, 1940, GX 1176).

Appraisal. A & P and the others doing cooperative advertising received not only reimbursement for their expenses but a net rebate, most of it consisting of the evasion of a discriminatory schedule of advertising rates set by newspapers. Unfortunately, we have no way of knowing what part of the "cents per case" is reimbursement and how much is rebate. Furthermore, even if we had the rebate, we would need to compare it with phantom brokerage in order to arrive at a net figure. As among those getting advertising allowances, there is no evidence of any discrimination, and this would support the view that there was no discrimination in general.

Minnesota, its hand strengthened by the Robinson-Patman Act, paid less brokerage to some customers than to brokers, and in addition it received advertising service from them. A & P was discriminated against. Following our rule, however, we reckon as discriminatory the excess of A & P's allowance over the most disfavored class of nonchain customers. The ratio of net to gross differential would be as follows:

$$1939 — 4.9/15.2, \text{ or } 32 \text{ per cent}$$
$$1940 — 6.1/15.0, \text{ or } 41 \text{ per cent}$$
$$1941 — 8.2/15.6, \text{ or } 53 \text{ per cent}$$

Mrs. Baird's Bread Company operates bakeries in Dallas, Fort Worth, and Houston. Bread was a highly competitive, "sensitive" commodity, and there were many price wars in Dallas during 1935–41, during which the bread company allegedly sold "below cost" (Roland W. Baird, Tr. 12,162; 12,178; 12,187).

From 1935 to 1939, Baird's paid a "confidential discount" of 5 per cent to the superintendant of the Dallas unit (Tr. 12,162–63), and to other chains as well (Tr. 12,167–70, 12,191–93). After the Robinson-Patman Act, it was paid not by check but in cash (Tr. 10,787–94). From 1939 to 1941, Baird's president testified, it continued to pay the discount; the Dallas unit head during these years entered what Judge Lindley apparently considered a denial which did not deny.

Appraisal. As among A & P, Safeway, and two local chains, there was probably no discrimination; as against other buyers, there probably was, to the amount of 5 per cent of the purchase paid. Following our rule of comparison with the most disfavored class, we consider this entirely discriminatory.

Olney & Carpenter process canned and frozen foods. After discussions with McAuliffe and MacKeachie, with whom he was personally friendly, H. A. Carpenter started the manufacture of potato sticks. As noted in the text, the novelty was in the packaging and in extensive advertising. Hence the efficiency of advertising media and advertising allowances was very important, but also very hard to determine in advance. "Sometimes we were stuck badly and sometimes it made us even more money than we had invested" (testimony of Frank E. Burt, Tr. 2870).

Despite their friendly relations, there was frequent wrangling over the performance of A & P units in advertising the product (testimony of H. A. Carpenter, president of Olney & Carpenter, Tr. 5314, 5320). In 1940, A & P tried to forestall Carpenter by asking for lower prices, but this was refused, and better advertising service became a counterdemand; they finally renewed as the contract stood, because the product was considered of somewhat better quality (See GX's 1477–1485). But then Carpenter went so far as to have an advertising firm evaluate the A & P promotional support, and paid only the sum they estimated as its value or cost (testimony of H. A. Carpenter, Tr. 5325).

Almost everyone selling the product had advertising allowances at one time or another: Economy Stores had 7.5 per cent at one time, First National a 5 per cent quantity discount (Tr. 5309–5310). At one time, National Retail Owned Grocers (N.R.O.G.) was able to buy for their private label at 8 to 10 per cent under the price of the branded goods (Tr. 5349–5350).

Olney & Carpenter granted A & P a quantity discount during and after 1939, which is discussed in the text. It must be mentioned here, however, because it strengthened Carpenter's hand in negotiating for payments over and above the discount. Moreover, there were other considerations, which could not be reckoned in money, but were considered important. As the Rochester field buyer wrote:

We would naturally like to continue with Olney & Carpenter if their price is anywhere near in line, inasmuch as you probably know, they are one of the direct sellers we have on canned vegetables and have worked very closely with us for a number of years [M. L. McAuliffe to G. F. Morrow, July 18, 1940, GX 1498].

As a matter of fact, A & P was dealing with Olney & Carpenter despite the fact that competitors could offer better prices on potato sticks (A. W. Holcombe to M. L. McAuliffe, August 23, 1940, GX 1499). Then, at the end of October, Carpenter voided the advertising allowances altogether, claiming that he received no benefit. But the quantity discount arrangement kept A & P in line. Headquarters, in reporting the action to Rochester, explained:

We doubt very much . . . that you can throw the O & C brand entirely out and if we are going to have a quantity discount arrangement again with Olney & Carpenter, we will need all the business in order to reach the maximum discount. It cannot be divided; it simply has to be Schuler's or Olney & Carpenter [Morrow to McAuliffe, October 11, 1940, GX 1506].

Headquarters made some attempts to reinstate the advertising allowance, but in March 1941, Carpenter wrote that the plant was on three shifts, building an addition, and adding new equipment (Carpenter to McAuliffe, March 15, 1941, GX 1511). A & P recognized the logic; but "after they have had an opportunity to catch up on their production, it is quite possible we might interest them at a later date" (McAuliffe to Morrow, April 16, 1941, transmitting the letter from Carpenter, GX 1512).

But later dates saw only the intensified war boom. Late in 1943, Olney & Carpenter's cost accountant reported to them, and they were "surprised and not pleased" to find that they could no longer "justify" the quantity discount. Since production was limited, and demand higher than ever, there was less and less reason to make concessions (Carpenter to Parr, October 6, 1943, DX 26).

Appraisal. The "lower cost" arising from spreading the overhead over a large volume (see text) is of course arbitrary and not assignable to the A & P purchase. The saving of sales expense, however, was a genuine economy, and was always more than equal to the discount granted A & P. However, for the sake of consistency, we must follow the rule of disregarding cost savings, which makes the Olney & Carpenter quantity discount wholly discriminatory. On the advertising allowance, however, they received almost complete performance, and were quick to reduce payment or even cancel. Unfortunately we cannot estimate its importance.

Phillips Packing Company, Cambridge, Md., is first noticed in 1932, as a large canner, especially important in tomatoes. Phillips was the central firm to about 50 smaller canneries, whom it supplied, and whose output it controlled. Phillips cooperated closely in those days with A & P, recognizing their right to special prices for large quantities. Zoller, in thus describing them, added: "They need us badly as an outlet and they are valuable to us as a source of supply." (Zoller to Parr, April 4, 1932, GX 48. In the record, the date is given as 1943; but from the context, this is certainly incorrect. Not only are the relations with Phillips characteristic of 1932, and earlier than 1935 [to which later documents refer]; but the discussion about lining up friendly canners to testify in an inquiry by the Federal Trade Commission is also dated 1932.) Phillips were somewhat "peeved" over lack of A & P support on some lines which they were promoting in order to maintain plant operations in winter, which competed with A & P products, and which other chains were promoting. But any unfriendliness would be dissipated, Zoller expected, when they needed to dispose of staples (trading items).

In September 1935, we catch a glimpse of prolonged negotiations over a new contract, and A & P's position, although strong, is now less so. A company memorandum (unsigned memorandum, September 4, 1935, GX 499) noted that Phillips was becoming "nationally established and some of our warehouses *require*" his branded goods (my emphasis). "As packer goes more and more into [advertised] products, he is worth less and less to us on staples." The suggested terms were: (1) A & P was to receive the lowest price at all times; (2) Phillips' local stocks were to be available to A & P stores at all points; (3) Special local drives should include

A & P, with prices lowered sufficiently to stay in accordance with (1), and with guarantees of warehouse stocks against price declines; (4) 5 per cent brokerage and 5 per cent additional advertising allowance.

As finally agreed, A & P received the lowest-price assurance and treatment equivalent to the most favored customer on protection against price decline, the 5 per cent brokerage, but only 2.5 per cent advertising allowance. Phillips was reported thus amenable because he was "anxious" for more sales to Divisions which had hitherto been closed to him, or had given his products very little support (Zoller to Parr, September 5, 1935, GX 500; see also the pencilled memorandum which is in the record as GX 503). A circular letter soon called for support in all Divisions (circular letter, September 13, 1935, GX 501). But a few months later the Boston office of the New England Division drew attention to a contract, more advantageous than the national one, which Phillips had previously signed with them and not formally voided. A letter from Headquarters to the New England purchasing director approved his action. "You might even go a step further and get 10 per cent [advertising allowance] from him instead of 5 per cent, and more power to you" (unsigned letter to D. C. MacKeachie, April 16, 1936, GX 502). But the attempt did not succeed, and the New England contract was finally dropped (undated memorandum, GX 507).

But relations did not settle down, because Phillips spared no efforts trying to break out of trading items and into branded goods. In April 1936, Zoller wrote (Zoller to Parr, April 28, 1936, GX 506): "Phillips still has the price control idea in mind . . . We doubt if he can maintain his volume except as a cut price seller." Zoller like the low-priced Phillips staples, but saw no reason to make concessions on his branded goods.

The next day, Zoller wrote Parr (Zoller to Parr, April 29, 1936, GX 507), and he was thoroughly aroused. A Congressional investigating committee had revealed that Phillips, despite the contract, had also allowed 5 per cent to First National, Safeway, Kroger, and others. "We have a claim against Phillips for this 5 per cent." Phillips, he added, had sold himself to Headquarters, "but we never looked upon him as anything but an operator who would put it over on you if he could. . . . His line should be considered a trading line. He certainly has no prices, changes from day to day and from hour to hour." As for his brands, Phillips was secretly contemplating a price increase. Moreover, he thought he was getting insufficient local support, and "wants his retail prices maintained." A & P had of course no enthusiasm for price maintenance.

In July 1936 Phillips withdrew the advertising allowances, and neglected to pay the "net" prices which now served to screen brokerage from Robinson-Patman actions (Zoller to Parr, July 18, 1936, GX 546). Renewed negotiations led to a compromise which was not too favorable to A & P; Phillips agreed only to a 4 per cent differential in lieu of brokerage, as compared with the previous 7.5 per cent. Nevertheless, the news came as an obvious relief to Zoller, who wrote Parr (Zoller to Parr, August 1, 1936, GX 647):

Thank you for getting the Colonel [Phillips] to work according to what we consider right.

We believe fact that we cut him out entirely on everything except Phillips Delicious had something to do with his change of position. There is nothing brings the manufacturer around like putting him on the bench.

There is no further record of dealings with Phillips.

Appraisal. The Phillips case is on both sides of, and even right on, the borderline between trading items and list-price goods. On trading items, they were useful to A & P, but on branded goods sold at higher prices, A & P was useful to them. The 7.5 per cent they received up to 1936 was a mixture of discriminatory and nondiscriminatory elements; the 4 per cent of 1936 probably represented 3 per cent disguised brokerage and one per cent discrimination. Since only arrangements after the Robinson-Patman Act are considered here, we have the single bargain with net differential 25 per cent of the gross.

D. W. Putnam Co. Sometime in 1928, Deyo Putnam, a grape commission merchant of upper New York State, found himself with a surplus of grapes which he could not sell.

There happened to be a press in this building we owned in Hammondsport, so I pressed the grapes and made it into juice. I got a beer capper and a rubber hose, and filled some bottles [as samples] and I had a truck, and I started out and tried to sell it to stores. You can call it peddling. I didn't have very much success. Then I heard about the Tea Company. I saw Mr. McAuliffe who said he never heard of grapes being put in barrels, and asked me how much I wanted for it. I told him whatever the market was. He did not have to buy it all. He informed me that I didn't know very much about the grape juice business, and asked me if I had any idea how much the Tea Company could use in a year [condensed from Putnam's testimony, Tr. 6392–6394].

Within a few years, Putnam was devoting himself largely to the production of grape juice, which he sold either in bulk to Quaker Maid (the A & P manufacturing subsidiary) for further processing, or in bottles to the A & P warehouses; about 95 per cent of his production was sold to the company (Tr. 6395). As might be excepted, Putnam also tried to build up a market for the juice under his own label, but by 1939 he gave up the idea (Tr. 6396). He had attempted to charge a higher price on his own brand; why he did so when it was unknown and unwanted is not explained (apparently he took the higher price for granted; see Tr. 6397). Costs on it were of course higher than on production for sale to A & P, because of shorter bottling runs, selling expenses, and credit risks (Tr. 6403–6408). Prices to A & P were lower by 60¢ per case (GX 1732, Tr. 6323; and Tr. 6327); costs on sales to them, Putnam stated, were lower by about 60¢ to 70¢ (Tr. 6408). The cost differential fits the price dif-

ferential like a well-made dress, with an adequate hem. However, in view
of the negligible sales to outsiders, possible discrimination is of no importance.

Putnam purchased grapes not only for his own but also for the company's account. He must have been useful to them during the incessant
playing for position as the economic and legal winds shifted. For example, in January 1940, the Supreme Court declined to hear the A & P
appeal in the FTC suit (Great Atlantic & Pacific Tea Co. v. Federal Trade
Commission, 106 F.2d 667 [AC-3]; *cert. den.*, 308 US 625). The secretary of the Concord Grape Juice Institute promptly circularized the
membership, informing them of the decision, and recommending "that
no special concessions be made to this company in spite of the fact that
they are one of the largest users of grape juice" (GX 1734-A). Putnam,
himself a member of the Institute (Tr. 6402), was disgusted with them:
"There wasn't a damn one of them who had any sense of loyalty." But he
had a plan for insuring adequate supplies to A & P at a proper price —
and expected the collaboration of three of the Institute's nine directors
(Putnam to McAuliffe, January 6, 1940, GX 1734). Whatever the reason,
by March 1940, "the company has been enjoying a favorably low purchase price on grape juice bought through our Rochester office" (Bofinger to the Central Division, March 7, 1940, GX 1738). By August,
Putnam could write McAuliffe,

There is no question but what is left of the Concord Grape Institute is drawing up their lines and looking for blood and scalps. . . . They can do only
one thing and that is accuse us of robbing the grower. . . . It is a lot of fun
to carry the flag you have to keep your rear flanks protected with this gang
shooting at you [Putnam to McAuliffe, August 22, 1940, GX 1741].

By this time, Putnam had apparently resigned from the Institute (Tr.
6402).

Putnam's loyalty was reasonable enough. He was in financial difficulties,
and had borrowed "all that I could borrow" from the Farmers & Mechanics Trust Company at Bath, N. Y., of which he was a director (Tr.
6423-6424). He was able to borrow $25,000 from the Chase National
Bank during 1940, "through the good influence of the A & P," who
agreed in June that they would advance him the sum around the end of
the year in order to pay it off. In a profusely thankful letter, written on
December 2, 1940, Putnam told McAuliffe this would not be necessary
(Putnam to McAuliffe, December 2, 1940, GX 1742; other examples of
Putnam's attitude are GX's 1739, 1742, 1750, and 1758).

In 1941, Putnam was still on the firing line, and a short crop (the
price of grapes per ton, in 1939, 1940, 1941: $35, $30, $50) was keeping
him busy. Warned by Bofinger "not to let any grapes get away from us"
(Putnam to McAuliffe, August 15, 1941, GX 1749), Putnam mentions
some obstacles:

If M. Kaplan comes in the market for $50 per ton with a few extras and on top of that advertises the fact we are certainly going to have a hell of a time buying grapes at $40 per ton. We don't know what his game is but if you want our honest opinion it stinks, as . . . a 20–30 per cent increase over last year's price would be satisfactory to the growers [Putnam to McAuliffe, September 2, 1941, GX 1749].

Putnam's contracts with A & P for 1940 and 1941 provided that his prices could not be any higher than the lowest offer of any other processor (the contracts are respectively GX's 1732 and 1745). The amount was flexible: a single telephone call was enough to assure a 66 2/3 per cent increase over the original order (Putnam to Bofinger, June 26, 1940, GX 1739). In January 1941, Putnam undertook to supply a larger amount than in 1940, and assumed that the 1941 price was therefore settled. He was disabused of this notion at the end of the month: "it was felt to be too early to determine what the price of this year's juice would be" (Parr to Putnam, January 28, 1941, GX 1744). In August, Putnam wrote that because of the rising price of grapes, juice would be raised as well; he was then informed that there was "a firm contract" in operation, and no price change to be considered (McAuliffe to Putnam, August 29, 1941, GX 1748). Putnam was "disappointed at the attitude taken by Headquarters. . . . Common sense shows" that the price of grapes had something to do with the price of juice (Tr. 6391). Since the 1941 price of grapes was two thirds higher than the 1940 price, it is easily understood why Putnam did not let the matter rest (Putnam to McAuliffe, September 2, 1941, GX 1749). The company buyers requested (Putnam to Bofinger, October 20, 1941, GX 1750) and received (Tr. 6418) a cost analysis by a certified public accountant; whereupon they promptly sent an A & P accountant to examine his books; Putnam was not permitted to see this auditor's report (Putnam to McAuliffe, December 3, 1941, GX 1755). However, the result was an increase in the price of bottled juice, and a smaller increase in bulk juice. Almost immediately thereafter, he was told to supply more bulk juice and less bottled. As Parr wrote to McAuliffe, "Putnam will no doubt object strongly to this." The "squawk" thus anticipated (Parr to McAuliffe, December 2, 1941, GX 1754) was duly received (McAuliffe to Parr, December 4, 1941, GX 1756), and ignored (Tr. 6419). No further action on price is mentioned. Again Putnam wrote in protest, offering to go on a cost-plus basis (Putnam to McAuliffe, December 15, 1941, GX 1758). Receiving no answer, he wrote again three days later: "Every time the telephone rings we do not know whether it is the sheriff or some other demon and the result is we are very unhappy. Can't you arrange to help us out?" (Putnam to McAuliffe, December 18, 1941, GX 1759.) But the sheriff's call, if it ever came (Putnam, Tr. 6426: "I thought maybe that would hurry some more orders to us"), must have been a social one, for in mid-1945, when he testified, Putnam was still very much in business and no less devoted to A & P. He testified that the company wanted him to make a profit (Tr. 6418). Moreover,

One year we bought them [grapes] $5. a ton lower than I anticipated and I went down to Headquarters and saw Mr. Bofinger and told him . . . and his reply was I ought to do pretty well that season.
Q. . . . You didn't give any money back?
A. No. [Tr. 6422].

Defense counsel then asked the question three more times, and received the same answer each time. It is doubtful that Judge Lindley was quadruply impressed.
Appraisal. No appraisal possible for purposes of the Appendix.

The Quaker Oats Company sold three types of goods: bulk rolled oats, a trading item (George B. Whitfield, comptroller, Quaker Oats Company, Tr. 14,876), packaged goods for seven different private brands "all of which are identical as to quality and packaging" (Tr. 14,892), and the familiar branded Quaker items. The last-named accounted for over 90 per cent of sales and were sold at the same price to everyone; A & P received no concessions (Tr. 14,920). Packaged goods were sold at a delivered price identical at all points east of the Rockies, at a 10 per cent discount (Tr. 14,906-7). As for the bulk oats, at the government's request, Quaker Oats listed all prices received by them from all purchasers in the State of Michigan during the period from July 1, 1943 to January 1, 1944. The defense did not object that the period and area were not representative. The price comparison shown there was considered by Quaker Oats as representative of the entire United States because prices were uniform f.o.b. (GX 4443). The following tabulation is based on that list. Prices refer to five-pound bags (the original list and the government presentation are on a pre-bale basis; bales are not of uniform content, and the whole discussion is rather confusing; the original list is GX 4443):

Price in cents per bag	21–21.9	22–22.9	23–23.9	24–24.9	27–27.9	28–28.9	29–29.9	30–30.9	31–31.9	32–32.9	33–33.9
A & P	1	9	9	5							
Others					15	13	4	11	8	1	1

Appraisal. The discounts on bulk oats were made to meet competition, and must be considered as wholly net differentials. Nothing is known about quantities or the possibility of cost savings, or of possible price fluctuations during the six-month period.

R. J. Peacock Canning Co. is believed to be the largest sardine canner in Maine. Before the Robinson-Patman Act, Peacock sold through brokers, merchandise brokers (who bought for their own account and resold), and the A & P Rochester buying office, allowing the same rate to all. After the Robinson-Patman Act, they did the same thing by selling on a "net" basis (Milroy Warren, president, Tr. 5594–96, 5630–32).

In November 1940, an FTC complaint was issued against several canners, including the Peacock Co., and a cease-and-desist order was entered by consent in February 1941 (Tr. 5630–41). Since Peacock had been selling about 35 per cent of their output to A & P and about the same proportion to merchandise brokers, both of whom were forbidden to receive brokerage (Tr. 5599, 5630, 5655), they naturally chose to go exclusively direct, charging everyone the old price less 5 per cent.

The Peacock Co. might well have moved even without the FTC order, for in January of 1940, following the Supreme Court decision, A & P announced its direct buying policy and cut down severely (about 80 per cent) on its purchases from Peacock (Tr. 5598–9, 5633). A & P paid phantom brokerage on these remaining purchases. In the fall of 1940, they came back as heavy volume purchasers (Tr. 5649–50). For October–November, Peacock sold A & P a special pack of sardines, and under an advertising agreement, A & P ran at least 100 lines of advertising on two occasions in 28 newspapers, along with some features, and received $1400 (the agreement in GX 1610).

Appraisal. The advertising allowance is the typical situation of brokerage being reduced in amount and also calling for advertising performance. The discrimination against A & P is perhaps as clear as in any other case in the record. However, it lasted for only a few months, until Peacock went exclusively direct.

Ralston-Purina Co. are the well-known manufacturers of cereal and related products. On their advertised branded products, A & P received no discounts (C. A. Renard, legal staff, Tr. 5802). Cornflakes sales, both for the Ralston label and for others, ran about eight tenths of one per cent during the years around 1940 (Tr. 5799). Up to 1937 a small per cent of the cornflakes sales for private label were at list price; other buyers received 5 cents per case (about 2.7 per cent) discount; and A & P 7½ cents (a little over 4 per cent) [Tr. 5702; and J. F. Tully to Parr, October 6, 1937, GX 1626 and DX 702]. The difference at this time corresponded to a difference in label costs, since A & P's larger volume permitted this saving (Tr. 5702, 5742, 5830–32). After the negotiations described at some length in the text, the discount to A & P was raised to 17½ per cent.

Appraisal. Since cost savings are disregarded by rule, we consider the net differential as 2½/7½ in 1937–39, and 12½/17½ in 1940–44, or 33 1/3 per cent and 71.4 per cent, respectively.

Small Salmon Packers in Alaska. A & P's canning subsidiary, Nakat Packing Corp., bought the entire pack. The price was set as the lowest for unbranded salmon of equal quality, at delivery time. The regular discounts were ¼ per cent for spoilage ("swells"), 1½ per cent cash, and 5 per cent unspecified. The canners were able to exchange and absorb surplus fish by arrangement with Nakat's own plants. This privilege is apparently not regarded as very important by the company's field buyer, but it "may appear to be a benefit . . . justifying the various discounts" (H. B. Friele to Parr, May 2, 1940, GX 460).

The table shows that in 1942 the selling costs of a sample of Alaska salmon packers ranged from 4.4 to 6.0 per cent; since Red was by far the most popular type, we may take 5.3 as an approximate average. If we assume that the fall in selling costs for Alaska salmon canners was of about the same magnitude as for tuna canners, the salmon canners in 1940 must have been spending about 6.2 per cent of sales receipts on selling. This would exceed the unspecified discount granted to Nakat, and suffice to explain them, as a saving in selling costs when the whole pack is sold to a single buyer.

A. Selling and Advertising Costs of Tuna and Tuna-Like Fish Canners

	Cost as per cent of net sales		
Year	Selling	Advertising	Total selling and advertising
1937	5.0	1.9	6.9
1938	4.5	1.8	6.3
1939	4.5	1.9	6.4
1940	4.6	1.9	6.5
1941	4.7	1.0	5.7
1942	3.9	0.9	4.8
1943	3.5	0.8	4.3

B. Selling Expense of Alaska Salmon Canners
(dollars per case)

Salmon type	Year	Operative margin	Price	Selling expense (cents per case)	Selling expense as per cent of price
Pink	1942	0.90	7.64	43	5.6
	1944	−0.29	7.92	30	3.8
Red	1942	4.73	14.40	76	5.3
	1944	2.18	14.64	49	3.3
Chum	1942	1.60	7.26	44	6.0
	1944	.19	7.54	29	3.8
Coho	1942	3.42	11.34	53	4.7
	1944	2.50	11.37	44	3.9
King	1942	2.36	13.49	60	4.4
	1944	1.72	13.68	54	3.9

Source. Office of Price Administration, OPA Economic Data Series No. 23, *Survey of Fish Processors* (Washington, 1947), tables 1 and 13.

Appraisal. The discount went into the 702 account, and was non-discriminatory, but it cannot be included in our tabulation because sales were made to only one buyer.

Southern Rice Sales Co. sells through its salesmen and also through brokers (Fred Soyka, assistant to vice-president, Tr. 17,457; 17,473).

During 1938–1943 Southern had a "quantity"-discount agreement with A & P providing for 20¢ per case up to 50,000 cases, and 25¢ per case on the next 10,000. As will be seen shortly, 20¢ was the equivalent of 10 per cent, and 25¢ in the next 10 thousand would bring the average up to 10.4 per cent. Higher discounts on larger amounts never became effective (the agreement is DX 557, 536, 551–54; see also Wilson-Parr correspondence, GX's 22–24).

A & P did not know what arrangements Southern had with competitors (Parr to Wilson, Nov. 4, 1940, GX 29). They were informed that Southern's next largest customer received 10¢ per case less than A & P (Wilson to Parr, December 14, 1940, GX 32). This was literally true but actually false. Southern had three methods of billing, all of which came to exactly the same result. The customer bought "net" (probably a disguised brokerage allowance), or took one free case with every ten, or took a 20¢ quantity discount (Soyka, Tr. 17,494; 17,478–79; and a series of orders and confirmations in the record as DX's 537–48). Thus A & P's only net advantage was the additional 5¢ per case on the amount over 50,000. Assuming that they reached 60,000, which they actually did not (Tr. 17,484), they would be better off by only 0.4 per cent net out of 10.4 per cent gross. Since the rest of the trade had an additional 1 per cent discount on certain tonnages per shipment, and for a time a 2 per cent carload discount (Tr. 17,562–63), A & P probably was more often behind the game than ahead of it.

There were also advertising allowances of 10¢ per 30-lb. case and 15¢ per 50-lb. case, which were apparently nondiscriminatory (Tr. 17,458–59).

Appraisal. At most, the net differential (0.4) was four per cent of the gross (10.4). More likely, there was no discrimination in favor of A & P; possibly some slightly against it.

Southern States Foods, Inc., sold oleomargarine, salad dressing, and miscellaneous related products. They had a quantity discount, asserted without contradiction to be nondiscriminatory, a 10 per cent discount on salad dressing, and a cash discount on other products (H. S. Smith, vice-president). They gave advertising allowances on margarine to the Dallas unit during 1938–42 (GX's 1567–1581, 1524–1558; Tr. 5467–68), which was 11 per cent of all cooperative advertising in 1940, 9 per cent in 1941, and 8 per cent in 1942 (computed from GX's 1524–1558). There is no evidence of any discrimination, nor any indication of the proportion of the payments to the total A & P purchases.

Appraisal. Insufficient data.

Stahl-Meyer, Inc. sells frankfurters in metropolitan New York. In 1940, they had a cost savings agreement with A & P, providing for a 5 per cent discount. For 1941, they renewed it, but offered only 3 per cent (Parr to Fraser, February 25, 1941, GX 943). This was accepted (March 3, 1941, GX 945).

Appraisal. Insufficient data.

Sunsweet Prunes are the well-known California packers. In July 1936, just after the passage of the Robinson-Patman Act, Sunsweet proposed to grant A & P a 7½ per cent discount if they would buy 10 million pounds. Headquarters thought the sales figure to be impossibly large, and was willing to take the discount only if Sunsweet would be willing to overlook the ten million pounds. The letter ends: "Please destroy this letter" (Mylott to Beckmann, June 30, 1936, GX 1390). Apparently Sunsweet was willing to do this provided A & P "did not go over to other labels" (Beckmann to Mylott, July 11, 1936, GX 1391). This was acceptable to Mylott:

However, we wish to caution you not to ask Mr. Thayer if he has a similar arrangement with any other firm. Our reason for making this request is because as you undoubtedly know, legally the burden of proof is entirely up to the manufacturer.
Therefore, if we do not ask for such information, we have no way of knowing of any other arrangements should anything arise in that respect.
We suggest that you draw up contract on the basis of 10,000,000 pounds, to be paid at the end of the year regardless of how much we purchase. . . .
Please let us have the full particulars after final arrangements have been completed. Also, please be sure to destroy this letter as soon as you have finished reading it [Mylott to Beckmann, July 17, 1936, GX 514].

The contract was never actually entered into, but there is no explanation why not (Tr. 19,127–28).

Appraisal. The arrangement was probably disguised brokerage, and reckoned as 60 per cent discriminatory. One would wish to know why it was never made.

Sylmar Packing Corporation are packers and sellers of ripe olives. For the fiscal year 1938–39 they agreed to allow A & P a 10 per cent "quantity" discount, on the tacit understanding that A & P would buy at least $75 thousand worth. Apparently, there was no firm commitment by A & P (Beckmann to Parr, Feb. 24, 1939, GX 1462; Parr to Beckmann, February 28, 1939, GX 1463). For 1939–40, there was a cost-savings agreement (in the record as GX 1466) which mentioned only "large volume" rather than any amount, but again provided for 10 per cent. The Sylmar president testified that a large wholesaler, Francis H. Liggett of New York, also received 10 per cent in 1939–40 and 1940–41 (Tr. 5110–11). Later he said that Liggett and one other wholesaler received 10 per cent (Tr. 5163).

In 1940–41, Sylmar sold through a paper subsidiary, Los Angeles Olive Growers' Association (LAOGA), although the very same people packed, shipped, billed, etc. LAOGA isued its own price list, 5 per cent under Sylmar's, and sold to A & P, its sole customer, at that price without discount. Sylmar charged a price 5 per cent higher than LAOGA, but allowed discounts, and various customers took 2½ or 3½ per cent. Liggett received 10 per cent (Tr. 5110, 5129–32, 5137, 5150–53), as well as another 2 per cent "in the form of interest" on cash advanced to Sylmar (Tr. 5144–45). Moreover, one other wholesaler (Steele-Wedeles) got 8 or 10 per cent (Tr. 5164).

After December 1941, all customers buying over $10 thousand of olives per year, including A & P, received 3 per cent off. But even in 1941–42, Liggett received 10 per cent off (Tr. 5110–11).

Appraisal. For 1938–39, we know nothing about other buyers. For 1939–40, Liggett and A & P both received 10 per cent off; and there was no discrimination between them, nor is there evidence of discrimination against anyone else.

For 1940–41, A & P was 3 to 5 per cent behind Liggett and Steele-Wedeles, although A & P bought more than either; considered as a wholesaler A & P was discriminated against.

The basic assumptions of the prosecution are strikingly revealed in this passage:

> It seems a strained and tortuous justification of A & P's discriminatory buying prices as a *retailer* to point . . . to the fact that two *wholesalers* bought in 1941 at greater discounts, especially when the discount of one wholesaler was uncertain, and when the discount of the other wholesaler was part and parcel of a bargain under which that wholesaler had advanced $50,000 to keep Sylmar solvent [Government Brief (Circuit Court), p. 17; italics in original].

To the government, status (as a wholesaler) confers the right to receive a lower price, and departures from this rule are "discriminatory"! The words following "especially when," etc. are highly misleading. The "uncertainty" was between 8 and 10. Even 8 is greater than 5, which A & P received. The 10 per cent discount to Liggett, far from being "part and parcel" of the special bargain to advance cash, had been received the two years previous. The *extra* service of advancing credit was paid by the *extra* allowance of 2 per cent. What it all indicated is that A & P was discriminated against to the extent of at least 3 per cent and possibly 5 per cent; and that the government was indignant that the discrimination was not greater.

Virginia Dare Extract Co. sells a beverage concentrate. In 1940 they sold it at the following prices, in cents per dozen: distributors, 36; jobbers, 37½; wholesalers, 38; nonfood chains, 39; supermarkets, 45 (Walter Jarmon, executive, Tr. 3319). A & P wanted the distributor price, but Virginia Dare refused, alleging that distributors performed certain services which A & P did not, and which really amounted to the sort of features embodied in a promotional advertising contract. But a distributor might pay 36¢ on a fifty-case order while A & P would pay 37½¢ on a carload (Jarmon, Tr. 3349). They finally compromised on the jobbers' price, which was equalized to wholesale grocers (Wallace to Schincke, May 7, 1940, GX 994). Next year, A & P closed buying, except for purchases at 45¢ less 5 per cent (41.75¢) in the Central Division (Middle Western Purchasing Director to all buyers, May 9, 1941, GX 992; Jarmon, Tr. 3332–36).

Appraisal. Discrimination against A & P.

L. D. McKinzie Co., a distributor of Virginia Dare extract, made an advertising agreement with the Central Western Division providing for a 5 per cent discount from the 45¢ price (41.75¢ net) for A & P supermarkets (in the record as GX 995); no other grocery stores in the four towns covered (Veedensburg and Attica, Indiana; Paris and Charleston, Ill.) received the discount (L. D. McKinzie, Tr. 3357–59).

Appraisal. Since delivery was apparently made directly to supermarkets, there was no service absorbed by A & P to explain the discount, nor did others receive it. Hence A & P received a discount wholly discriminatory as compared with other supermarkets. As compared with other types of distributors, A & P was discriminated against. Following our rule, we consider this as wholly discriminatory.

Walker's Austex Chile Co., Austin, Texas, sells chile con carne, tamales, and other "Mexican type" dishes under it own brand name. Before the Robinson-Patman Act, they allowed A & P 5 per cent brokerage. Shortly after it was passed, a 5 per cent quantity discount (except for one brand on which it was 2.5 per cent) was established which, as the New Orleans field buyer put it, "will naturally take the place of the brokerage which we have previously enjoyed" (Wilson to Gundrey, Aug. 14, 1936, GX 919). Nobody else had any such agreement (Fred W. Catterall, Jr., vice-president, Tr. 3037). It provided for a sliding scale beginning with 1 per cent at $10,000, and running up to 6 per cent on $75,000 or over. A & P qualified for the 6 per cent (Wilson to Gundrey, Jan. 4, 1941, DX 45). The top bracket was reduced to 5 per cent in 1941, and remained unchanged through 1942 and 1943 (the agreements are in the record as GX's 914, 915, and 916).

There were also advertising allowances, approximately 2.5 per cent, during 1936–43 (in the record as GX's 903–908). Walker's usual advertising allowance rate was 5 per cent, however, and they had it with "thousands" of others, some continuously, some intermittently (Tr. 3112–13). There may have been closer checkup on the others than on A & P (Tr. 3112–13; and Tr. 3080). There were also some special promotions with A & P and others (Tr. 3087–89).

Walker's general system of distribution was complex. They rented space in about forty public bonded warehouses, whence they made delivery, charging the customer the transportation cost from there. (Tr. 3035–36). They used brokers and also their own sales force (Tr. 3077). Walker's salesmen operated out of its bonded warehouse calling on the wholesaler's warehouse and on the retailers who would give orders, which the salesmen turned over to the wholesalers, who filled the orders (Tr. 3077–78). In contrast, the only contact with A & P was at the A & P warehouse (Tr. 3077–78), so that they functioned, and were treated, as a wholesaler. No other retail customer was offered the arrangement. A & P bought about 14 per cent of Walker output; Kroger, the next largest, bought 5 per cent; Safeway, 3 per cent (Tr. 3076–77).

We shall assume, first, and probably contrary to fact, that A & P had never any claim to brokerage, although Walker did use broker service; second, that Safeway et al. could not take delivery on a wholesale basis; third, that the 2.5 per cent differential against A & P in respect of advertising allowance was not discriminatory, but was accounted for by differences in performance. It would follow that there was no discrimination as among A & P, the wholesalers, and all others. If A & P took on the same terms as brokers, they would be discriminated against; if Safeway and Kroger could have taken on the same terms as A & P, and were not permitted to, they were discriminated against.

Appraisal. A & P's gross discount, for any year, would be 12.5 per cent, the sum of the 5 per cent ordinary trade discount, the 2.5 per cent advertising allowance, and the 5 per cent "quantity" discount. The first two are nondiscriminatory. As for the third, which was possibly discriminatory in one direction but certainly not discriminatory in another, we shall assume it as half-discriminatory. Thus we would have a discriminatory element of 2.5 per cent in a gross differential of 12.5 per cent, or 20 per cent discrimination. We shall further assume, however, that the 5 per cent trade discount was never credited to 702 (see Chapter XI), so that we arrive at a 2.5 net differential out of a gross of 7.5, of 33 1/3 per cent discrimination.

Interestingly enough, the government for once made a very cursory guess at gross and net differential, arriving at the same final result as ourselves (Appendix to the Government Brief [Circuit Court], p. 10).

Wheatley Mayonnaise Co. makes mayonnaise, potato salad, salad dressing, etc., under the Lady Betty brand name. It has factories in Louisville, Jacksonville, and Terrell, Texas. When it made a 5 per cent advertising allowance with A & P in 1938, it referred to this as "your brokerage" (Richard Wheatley, president, to Carey of the A & P Detroit office, July 7, 1939, GX 1024). The writer of the letter explained that this was a typographical error: "brokerage" should have been "advertising" (Wheatley, Tr. 3516). In 1942, an A & P invoice for this "advertising" (in the record as GX 1035) was marked as chargeable to Wheatley's account 623, brokerage. Wheatley explained that this too was a mistake; it should have been to account 624, advertising (Tr. 3491–92). The 5 per cent, whatever it represented, was allowed from 1939 through 1942.

Wheatley told the Department of Justice in 1945 that "when putting a new item on the market, he would offer some incentive to the dealer." "Large chains" were offered 5 per cent. "When there is a broker connected with the sale, it is usually split brokerage, allowing the broker 2 per cent and the chain organization 3 per cent, or vice versa" (Wheatley to the Anti-trust Division, U.S. Dept. of Justice, March 14, 1945, GX 1030). In a word, the chain was getting 2 or 3 per cent disguised brokerage, and only paying 3 or 2 per cent phantom brokerage, instead of paying 5 per cent phantom brokerage as required by law. But Wheatley later explained that what he *really* meant was that the broker might on his own initiative pass on some of his 5 per cent for the sake of advertising Wheatley's products (Tr. 3474–75).

Wheatley also had advertising allowance contracts with other distributors (Tr. 3530–31, 3538–39) — in 1941, between 100 and 300 (Tr. 3531–33). These varied — one even ran up as high as 25 per cent — but most of them appear to have kept to 3 per cent or 5 per cent (GX 1028 and DX 692 refer to 1941; Wheatley's testimony at Tr. 3538 refers to 5 per cent as the general target).

Furthermore, between May 1941 and February 1942, three less-than-truckload shipments were made to A & P at the truckload price (Vogt to Wheatley, December 14, 1944, GX 1031, and Wheatley at Tr. 3484–85). The average reduction was 3.6 per cent.

Appraisal. The 5 per cent disguised brokerage was not discriminatory, since it was only equivalent to the usual broker's fee, and Wheatley also received some advertising out of it. The 3.6 price reduction for less-than-truckload lots were probably discriminatory; but three shipments constitute too small a set of transactions to include in the table, since one year's sales are considered as an observation.

William Weckerle & Sons is a dairy in Buffalo, N. Y. The following letters from Headquarters to the Central Division Purchasing Director are worth quoting at length:

As you no doubt are aware, we have a public relations man working with a great many firms with whom we do business in the State of New York with the idea of promoting as much good will for our organization as possible, in view of the chain store tax legislation about to be enacted in this state.

In this regard, the Dairymen's League is a very powerful political organization in New York which would undoubtedly be able to give us some help.

At the same time, they, being quite conscious of what they can do for us, are naturally horse traders, and they have asked us to give them support in the Buffalo market, where they own and control the second largest dairy in the city, William Weckerle & Sons. The largest dairy in that city, we understand, is Dodd's.

They are very eager to secure our milk business which consists of approximately 140 stores and which is now being given to Pierce who has his milk bottled by a firm named Jones. The Dairymen's League tried to buy out Pierce but apparently negotiations have fallen through. Pierce, it seems, owes the Dairymen's League somewhere in the vicinity of $25,000.00 and they feel that it is only a question of time when he will be unable to carry on because of his very poor financial structure. We have been informed that we are Pierce's only large customer.

Now this is the point — the Dairymen's League wants us to consider giving Weckerle the business which we are now giving to Pierce. We, naturally, are in a dilemma because we do not know the local situation. If we remember correctly, you told us sometime ago that Pierce owed us some money and we are wondering what our present status is in this regard. What would happen if we should take this business away from Pierce who rates about fifth in the city of Buffalo as far as size and general conditions are concerned?

We should like to have you check the situation and let us have your views concerning the possibility of making such a change.

The whole thing will have to be handled tactfully and confidentially as we do not want Pierce to get wind of the activities of the Dairymen's League.

Please destroy when you have finished with this [Mylott to Schincke, December 13, 1937, GX 1419].

The reply was as follows:

We have made arrangements to have William Weckerle & Sons, the Buffalo dairy of the Dairymen's League, supply our stores with fresh milk and cream effective January 1.

Confidentially, our arrangements with the League call for their paying us a discount of 5% on all of our purchases made from Weckerle, but since they do not want Weckerle to know of this agreement, payments will be made by the League to this office and it will be necessary for us to devise some method for passing this allowance on to the Buffalo stores. We suggest that you do not notify our Buffalo buyer about this discount until you have an opportunity to tell him personally as it is important that we keep the matter strictly confidential.

Accordingly, we have notified the Dairymen's League that effective the first of the year, we shall turn over to Weckerle the business which we are now giving to Pierce. From the correspondence which we have had with you on this subject, we assume that these arrangements will be entirely in order as far as you and the Buffalo unit are concerned [Mylott to Schincke, December 24, 1937, GX 1420].

The 5 per cent was paid to Headquarters, but credited to the Buffalo Unit, during 1938–43 (Mylott, Tr. 20,282). All chains received the discount, but practically no independents (Herdlein, Weckerle sales manager, at Tr. 5010–18).

Appraisal. This is another example of A & P receiving a discrimination as compared with some customers but not others. Following our rule, all the discrimination will be counted as net.

The "squeeze play" on Pierce was outrageous. The commerce involved seems to have been entirely intrastate, and therefore beyond the reach of the Sherman Act. Had A & P's coconspirator been a large corporation, rather than the Dairymen's League, there would surely have been great emphasis on this episode in the A & P record. The incident is also revealing of A & P's political vulnerability.

Wisconsin Honey Farm processes honey at Oconomowoc, and sells its own brand through brokers, at 5 per cent, to wholesalers, jobbers, and large chains (C. W. Aeppler, Tr. 3630, 3633, 3563). Before the Robinson-Patman Act, they allowed A & P brokerage (Tr. 3564); after passage of the act, they ceased to do so. During 1936–40 they did not sell much to A & P, but in the spring of 1940 they were selling to the Milwaukee and Chicago units, and to the Boston unit through a broker (Tr. 3564–66).

In the spring of 1940, Wisconsin was quoting (through brokers) at $4.50 per dozen of five-pound pails, l.c.l., and made a special sale to a distributor (not A & P) at a special price. The distributor resold at a low price, drawing the attention of A & P. Under the Wisconsin Fair Trade Act, the distributor's margin over $4.50 was illegally small, indicating that the price to him must have been lower than $4.50 (Vogt to Aeppler, May 17, 1940, GX 1047). A & P suspected the price was perhaps even lower than the $4.25 which Wisconsin Honey Farm admitted (Aeppler to Vogt, May 21, 1940, GX 1048; Vogt to Aeppler, May 22, 1940, GX 1049). At any rate, when Wisconsin offered at $4.25 less 5 per cent "advertising allowance," or $4.03 net, Vogt counteroffered $4.00, implying he could get it elsewhere at that price (GX 1048–49). In fact, honey was being offered at $3.90 by a competitor (Aeppler, Tr. 3626–8). Wisconsin replied distressfully that they would never have sold the lot cheaply if they had known it was going to be resold so cheaply, and reduced the asking price to $4.10, "a ridiculously low figure." A & P accepted (Aeppler to Vogt, May 24, 1940, GX 1050; B. Vogt [not Anthony Vogt] to Aeppler, May 27, 1940, GX 1051).

It is very interesting that A & P preferred a price of $4.10 to $4.25 less advertising allowance. Vogt feared that it would look like disguised brokerage and a possible violation of the Wisconsin Fair Trade law (GX 1049); while Aeppler thought that "we will get a little benefit [from the advertising]. It might help us to move a little additional honey" (GX 1050).

During the time that Wisconsin was selling at a special low carload price and then at $4.10 l.c.l., they never told their brokers that they were willing to sell at less than $4.50 l.c.l. (Tr. 3029), and they presumably made sales at $4.50.

During the summer of 1940, Wisconsin sold to the Chicago unit at $4.25 l.c.l. and to the Boston unit at $4.10 l.c.l. (Tr. 3589).

During 1939–1942, Wisconsin paid A & P a 5 per cent advertising allowance. (It did not apply to the transactions just discussed. The agreements are in the record as GX's 1057, 1058, 1059.) The Wisconsin proprietor testified that he paid it because he had a lot of honey to move, and

A & P "seemed to be the only outlet through which it could be done." Hence he did not offer it to anyone else (Tr. 3613).

There were definite cost savings on sales to A & P, since they took delivery directly from Oconomowoc, and the price was f.o.b. Other buyers were supplied from warehouse stocks in Boston, Philadelphia, Birmingham, and Cleveland, with Wisconsin absorbing both freight and storage. We cannot say how much these cost savings amounted to.

Appraisal. The special deals of $4.10 and $4.25 were reductions of 8.9 per cent and 5.6 per cent, respectively; making allowance for 5 per cent phantom brokerage, they were discriminatory by 4.9 and 0.6 per cent, ratio of net to gross differentials, .55 and .11, respectively. The advertising allowance was merely a special low price to "move" excess goods; neglecting A & P's outlay, it was entirely discriminatory. We disregard the cost savings on sales to A & P.

APPENDIX V. DIRLAM AND KAHN ON THE A&P CASE

The foregoing interpretation of the government's case has been attacked as incorrect and "unfair" (not to mention stronger language) by Joel B. Dirlam and Alfred E. Kahn.[1] They assert that the government case was correct in its economics, and not merely correct by accident [2] — which is to say that the government theories were correct. But one searches their writings in vain for any systematic explanation or even statement of any of the government theories of the case. As for the critics of those theories, Dirlam and Kahn have been extremely cursory — to put it mildly — in reading them.[3]

Dirlam and Kahn also claim to have examined the A & P record, and to base their analysis upon a knowledge of it. The claim will not bear examination.[4] The reader interested in full details must consult the index and the text. At this point we need examine briefly only the differences of general method.

"The opinion in the trade" is a major source for Dirlam and Kahn, cited repeatedly. There is no indication of either printed source material for "the opinion in the trade," or of the number or type of interviews, the questions asked, or the answers. Nor is there a hint that "the" opinion in the trade may not be unanimous or monolithic.[5] This "source" bears a heavy weight of important conclusions. Thus, "all of [A & P] discounts were generally regarded in the trade as discriminatory." [6] (Would rivals

[1] "Antitrust Law and the Big Buyer: Another Look at the A & P Case," *Journal of Political Economy*, 60:118–132 (1952), "Integration and Dissolution of the A & P Company," *Indiana Law Journal*, 39:1–27 (1953).

[2] "Antitrust Law and the Big Buyer," p. 119; see also pp. 126, 130, 132.

[3] M. A. Adelman, "Dirlam and Kahn on the A & P Case," *Journal of Political Economy*, 61:436 (1953), especially p. 436.

[4] Adelman, pp. 436–441; and "A Reply," *Indiana Law Journal*, 39:367–370 (1953).

[5] "*Wall Street Journal* men have been questioning men all around the country who come into constant close contact with the chain, and the answers differ almost as much as those of the blind men who felt the tusks and tail of an elephant and gave different descriptions of the beast." "Tethered Titan: A & P's Manners Turn Mild After Epic Tangle With The Trustbusters," *Wall Street Journal*, December 22, 1958, p. 1. No honest and competent journalist could report otherwise. The documents in the record are an assembly and appraisal of often conflicting evidence by men whose business it was to act on their knowledge; and by critical examination one can see where lay the truth.

[6] "Antitrust Law and the Big Buyer," p. 130.

say anything else?) And henceforth they are discriminatory. As alternative sources of data, we may cite Chapters VI–VII, X–XI, Appendix IV.

Closely allied to the problem of discrimination is that of net buying costs. Economic theory suggests that in decentralized and imperfect markets with fluctuating prices, a larger buyer may realize substantial economies. Chapters V–VII and Chapter XIII above explored and confirmed this hypothesis, using data both in and out of the record. Citing and discussing neither source, Dirlam and Kahn present their sole and sufficient evidence: "Discussions with food marketers . . . indicate a general opinion that A & P's size and huge requirements discourage the quest for bargains." [7] Again, proof by folklore suffices.

Furthermore, A & P is repeatedly called a monopsonist, though monopsony is logically irrelevant to price discrimination in *selling*. The conclusion is also contrary to the record, as explained above, and contrary to the examples offered by Dirlam and Kahn themselves.[8]

The basing of major conclusions upon assertion and "general opinion" is not a novel method. When in 1689 the Irish Parliament passed the famous Act of Attainder, forfeiting the lives and property of those listed, the bill was reported favorably with the explanation: "Many of the persons here attainted have been proved traitors by such evidence as satisfies us. For the rest, we have followed common fame." [9] Some more recent examples come to mind, but need not be pursued.

Two further points of method are connected with "the opinion in the trade." (1) In 1948 an indictment was brought in Chicago against certain dairy companies, alleging that they had discriminated in price in favor of certain buyers, including A & P. The indictment came to trial and was dismissed for lack of proof.[10] Promptly the Department of Justice reformulated some of its allegations into a civil complaint, which did not mention A & P at all.[11] An indictment is an accusation, and an accusation is not evidence. But the 1948 indictment, which no longer existed even as an accusation, was nevertheless cited in 1952 to prove discrimination in favor of A & P.[12]

(2) We indicated above why the A & P prosecution case (which was upheld on this point by the courts) could only be interpreted as prohibiting resale to competitors. This was another "unfair" interpretation.[13]

[7] "Antitrust Law and the Big Buyer," p. 126.

[8] "Antitrust Law and the Big Buyer," pp. 126–127; cf. "Dirlam and Kahn on the A & P Case," p. 438.

[9] Thomas Babington Macaulay, *History of England from the Accession of James II* (New York: G. P. Putnam's Sons, n.d.), 5, 255.

[10] Commerce Clearing House, *Trade Regulation Reporter: Court Decisions*, Par. 61, 351 (1951).

[11] Civil Action No. 51-C-947, U. S. v. the Bowman Dairy Co. et al., filed June 18, 1951.

[12] "Antitrust Law and the Big Buyer," p. 128.

[13] "Antitrust Law and the Big Buyer," p. 130.

But shortly after the Circuit Court decision in April 1949, A & P announced that it would no longer make any resales to the trade. This might indicate that our theory, however "unfair," had perhaps been correct. But three years afterward, Dirlam and Kahn did not mention the stopping of resales.

On both the dismissed indictment cited as evidence and the stoppage of trade sales, it is surprising that despite their intensive cultivation of "the opinion in the trade" through interviews "with food marketers from independent wholesalers to giant chains," [14] etc., yet both these overt facts, noted in the trade press and available to any ordinarily curious person, somehow failed to come to our authors' attention. (The alternative explanation is that they *had* heard of these facts, but chose not to inform their readers.)

In Chapter XVI, some attention was paid to the prosecution theory of "recoupment." Dirlam and Kahn accept this theory, on the general theory that business men do not try to maximize profits.[15] On this infinitely convenient assumption, any kind of business behavior at all is as likely as any other. At another point, they profess to find evidence of recoupment in A & P's own actions on gross profit rates.[16] This amounts precisely to that *cum hoc ergo propter hoc* fallacy which as we saw was too crude for even the prosecution and the courts to accept.

The last point of method may be the most important. Our authors lay much stress on "intent" as the crucial element in violation of the Sherman Act.[17] We shall not presume to explain what is meant by this "intent." The meaning of a generalization lies in the deductions that may be drawn from it, and the meaning of "intent" is understood by examining a case squarely in point. The authors regard the A & P case as such a one. In their peroration (and their italics) the main issue in the case is the *"intention . . . to eliminate competitors by discriminatory sharpshooting in selling."* [18]

When there is a lot of sharpshooting, over a long time, a lot of people are bound to get shot. With thousands of stores, over more than a 20-year period, even a limited, temporary, ineffective campaign of predatory sharpshooting would give us hundreds or thousands of victims. Where are they? Despite allegedly "numerous instances" of threats or attempts to "put specific rivals out of business," Dirlam and Kahn are unable to say "how typical these tactics were or how many rivals actually were bankrupted" because the government's examples "are not convincing on this score." [19] (The government offered no examples.) So for years on

[14] "Antitrust Law and the Big Buyer," p. 126.

[15] *Fair Competition* (Ithaca, 1954), p. 208.

[16] "Rejoinder," *Journal of Political Economy*, 61:443n.10 (1953).

[17] "Integration and Dissolution of the A & P Company," p. 21. *Fair Competition* (Ithaca, 1954), Chs. 3, 4.

[18] "Integration and Dissolution of the A & P Company," p. 21.

[19] "Integration and Dissolution of the A & P Company," p. 19.

end there was this decisive *intent* "to eliminate competitors," yet not a single eliminated competitor to cite, nor any evidence that the (supposed) examples were genuine. To paraphrase Sir Winston Churchill: some elimination, some intent!

We are now able to understand our authors' "intent" as it has been revealed in use. They do not need actual attempts (successful or not) to destroy competitors by local discrimination. Nor do they need letters or documents expressing a desire or expectation or plan to destroy. For no such documents exist in the record, and none were ever cited, either by the government or by Dirlam and Kahn. They expressly reject any consideration of the economic background which would make predatory acts more or less probable.[20] By elimination, therefore, we are left with a perfectly clear concept of this "intent," namely, dangerous thoughts.[21]

The method of Dirlam and Kahn is apparently not based on mere prejudice against big business. For Kahn wrote a sweepingly pro-big business article [22] at about the same time he wrote the other articles, and there is no indication anywhere in his *Fortune* essay that he is stating any but his own opinions.[23]

A reviewer of the Dirlam-Kahn book has pointed out that: "Although they profess little confidence in economics, the authors deal with problems that require it . . . . [Their] errors . . . betray an inadequate understanding of the economic tools the authors condemn." [24] But merely to demonstrate this conclusion in detail is not an adequate reason for this Appendix.

This book will have served some purpose if it helps make clear the essential unity of scientific method. The opposition between "deductive" and "empirical" work does not exist; the two are necessary to each other. The week-end gardener who lays out a circular flower bed and finds the

[20] "Antitrust Law and the Big Buyer," p. 119.

[21] Not long ago (see the Boston *Herald*, May 15, 1956) in Washington, D. C., a woman entered a man's apartment and shot him dead. According to her statement, the man had neither used nor threatened violence to her; nor had he suggested that she comply with any carnal wishes. Yet she claimed her action had been in self-defense because "he was psychologically aggressive toward me." Clearly, one of the great virtues of "intent" is that it serves equally well the ends of public and private justice.

[22] A. D. H. Kaplan and Alfred E. Kahn, "Big Business in a Competitive Society," supplement to *Fortune*, February 1953; with a foreword by Alfred P. Sloan, Jr.

[23] However, he also subscribed to an equally sweeping anti-big business dissent to the *Report of the Attorney-General's Committee to Study the Antitrust Laws* (Washington, 1955). See *Antitrust Bulletin* 1:15 (1955). See also Official Report of Proceedings before the Federal Power Commission, in the Matter of Champlin Oil & Refining Co., *et al.*, Docket Nos. G-9277, Vol. 40-LC, March 30, 1959, p. 5461–5462 (testimony of Alfred E. Kahn), which should be compared with the *Fortune* article.

[24] John S. McGee, Book Review, *American Economic Review*, 45:452 (1955).

circumference is apparently twice the diameter will readily conclude either that the shape is not a circle, or that he has made some mistake in measuring it. Thus geometric theory picks out errors of fact. Matters are no different in economics. The method used, however haltingly, in this study, is the only way to observe the social as well as the physical world. It is compatible with many and various public policies or legal standards (since these depend also on certain preferences), but the method is totally irreconcilable — has nothing in common — with the warm assurance of those who *know* monopoly or competition on sight, *know* what needs to be done, and regard economic theory and statistical analysis not as imperfect tools but as barriers to results they *know* are right. Out of abundance of certainty comes a distaste for the concepts of economic theory, a preference for "power," "strategic advantage," "intent," and the like, to be verified by referring to an infallible source known as "the opinion in the trade."

INDEX

1 Dougeal App 1
Torgeh on me syumos
130 RPM 1

Eschenly Paus

38 · Galei
Ra T
v Rn S

Nr P389